Ralf Reussner • Michael Goedicke •
Wilhelm Hasselbring • Birgit Vogel-Heuser •
Jan Keim • Lukas Märtin
Editors

Managed Software Evolution

Editors
Ralf Reussner
Institute for Program Structures and Data Organization
Karlsruhe Institute of Technology (KIT)
Karlsruhe, Germany

Michael Goedicke
paluno
Universität Duisburg-Essen
Essen, Germany

Wilhelm Hasselbring
Software Engineering Group Dept. Computer Science
Kiel University
Kiel, Germany

Birgit Vogel-Heuser
Institute of Automation and Information Systems
Technische Universität München
Garching, Germany

Jan Keim
Institute for Program Structures and Data Organization
Karlsruhe Institute of Technology (KIT)
Karlsruhe, Germany

Lukas Märtin
Institute for Programming and Reactive Systems
Technische Universität Braunschweig
Braunschweig, Germany

https://doi.org/10.1007/978-3-030-13499-0

This book is an open access publication.

Foreword

Modern society completely relies on software: it could not operate without it. Software constitutes both the brain and the nervous system that give life to society. It evolves continuously as society evolves. Understanding and supporting software evolution is thus vital for society. The decision of the German Research Foundation (DFG) in 2012 to launch the Priority Programme SPP 1593/1 "Design for Future - Managed Software Evolution" has recognised the crucial role of software evolution as a research challenge and as a societal priority.

I had the privilege of being involved in the initial review of the research proposals submitted for funding and the initial bootstrapping phase of the coordinated research efforts that were selected, by participating in lively workshops in Munich (Fall 2013) and in Herrsching am Ammersee (Spring 2014). What impressed me most at the time was not only the top quality of researchers engaged in the various coordinated projects and the scientific value of each individual project but also the overall coherence of the entire research proposal and the enthusiastic adherence of all members to a common research agenda.

The results of the Priority Programme even exceeded my high expectations. The programme has delivered an incredible number of outstanding research outputs, published in top conferences and journals. Contributions span different aspects of software evolution and lay the foundations for engineering it in a systematic and predictable manner. In a way, this has not been a real surprise: excellent scientific publications can be expected as an outcome of a coordinated research programme, given the highly qualified set of top researchers who participate in the various projects. What especially struck me was the coherence, cohesion, and maturity of the approach developed in the programme and its potential impact on further research, on education, and on the practice of software evolution. This book makes this impact very clear.

The book is based on three main conceptual assumptions. First, to support software evolution, knowledge about the system and its design should be made accessible. Second, evolution has to be guided by suitable methods and processes. Third, software and its infrastructure must be designed to support a continuous, dynamic evolution. After an introduction to the nature of software evolution and its challenges in Part I, the three main conceptual assumptions are elaborated and substantiated by research results in Part II. Part III focuses on how the results of research can be applied and further developed. To strengthen the cohesion of all contributions, two case studies are used consistently throughout the book: CoCoME and PPU/xPPU. CoCoME is an example of a modern business application, while PPU/xPPU represent a laboratory plant for automated production systems. The two case studies are examples of two main classes of systems evolution: information systems, in the case of CoCoME, and machine and plant automation, in the case of PPU/xPPU.

This book has three main target audiences: software engineering researchers, practitioners, and students. It provides a definitive view of software evolution in today's world, from which all three audiences may greatly benefit. A previous—visionary—systematic treatment of software evolution goes back to the work of Belady and Lehmann in the late 1970s, which resulted in the book "Program evolution: processes of software change" (Academic Press, 1985). However, the 1970s can be considered as pre-history in software engineering. At the time, software did not completely permeate the societal fabric as it does today. Software had well-defined boundaries, and its use and evolution were under the responsibility of a single authority. Today, software is a heterogeneous conglomerate of interconnected subsystems, which results in systems of systems, involving multiple parties and responsibilities. Evolution was only an offline activity, while today it occurs while systems are up and running and providing critical functionalities. Software was mainly supporting business or scientific activities, while today it interconnects the entire human society with the physical world. Evolution has scaled to unprecedented levels, which demanded for the new approaches discussed in this book.

This book has associated artefacts, mostly described in Part III, which make it unique. The two realistic and extensive case studies developed through coordinated effort not only served as living lab-size test beds in the development of the various research efforts but are also offered as potential community case studies for use by other researchers. They can also be used as support tools in teaching software evolution to set up hands-on learning activities. This is a laudable initiative that further amplifies the potential outreach of this research effort to further research, practice, and education. Bringing research results to a mature stage, where others can readily pick them up and develop further, is an increasingly relevant social responsibility of researchers. It enables faster advances in science, a better selection of research targets, and a timely adoption of the most promising results. This research programme establishes best practices in the area of reusable and reproducible software engineering research.

Politecnico di Milano Carlo Ghezzi
DEIB - Dipartimento di Elettronica Informazione e Bioingegneria
Milano, Italy

Contents

Contributors

Sven Apel Chair of Software Engineering I, Department of Informatics and Mathematics, University of Passau, Passau, Germany

Bernhard Beckert Institute of Theoretical Informatics, Karlsruhe Institute of Technology (KIT), Karlsruhe, Germany

Safa Bougouffa Technische Universität München, Lehrstuhl für Automatisierung und Informationssysteme, Garching, Germany

Bernd Bruegge Technische Universität München, Institut für Informatik I1, Garching, Germany

Johannes Bürdek Technische Universität Darmstadt, Fachbereich Elektrotechnik und Informationstechnik, Darmstadt, Germany

Jens Bürger University of Koblenz-Landau, Institute for Computer Science, Koblenz, Germany

Kiana Busch Institute for Program Structures and Data Organization, Karlsruhe Institute of Technology (KIT), Karlsruhe, Germany

Suhyun Cha Technische Universität München, Lehrstuhl für Automatisierung und Informationssysteme, Garching, Germany

Abhishek Chakraborty Helmut-Schmidt-Universität, Fakultät für Maschinenbau, Professur für Automatisierungstechnik, Hamburg, Germany

Mina Fahimipirehgalin Technische Universität München, Lehrstuhl für Automatisierung und Informationssysteme, Garching, Germany

Alexander Fay Helmut-Schmidt-Universität, Fakultät für Maschinenbau, Professur für Automatisierungstechnik, Hamburg, Germany

Sinem Getir Institut für Informatik, Humboldt-Universität zu Berlin, Johann-von-Neumann-Haus, Berlin, Germany

Michael Goedicke paluno – The Ruhr Institute for Software Technology, Specification of Software Systems, Universität Duisburg-Essen, Essen, Germany

Lars Grunske Institut für Informatik, Humboldt-Universität zu Berlin, Johann-von-Neumann-Haus, Berlin, Germany

Wilhelm Hasselbring Software Engineering Group, Department of Computer Science, Kiel University, Kiel, Germany

Christopher Haubeck Universität Hamburg, MIN-Fakultät, Fachbereich Informatik, Hamburg, Germany

Robert Heinrich Institute for Program Structures and Data Organization, Karlsruhe Institute of Technology (KIT), Karlsruhe, Germany

Jan Ole Johanssen Technische Universität München, Institut für Informatik I1, Garching, Germany

Reiner Jung Software Engineering Group, Department of Computer Science, Kiel University, Kiel, Germany

Jan Jürjens University of Koblenz-Landau, Institute for Computer Science, Koblenz, Germany

Timo Kehrer Institut für Informatik, Humboldt-Universität zu Berlin, Berlin, Germany

Jan Keim Institute for Program Structures and Data Organization, Karlsruhe Institute of Technology (KIT), Karlsruhe, Germany

Udo Kelter Praktische Informatik/Softwaretechnik Siegen, Fachbereich Elektrotechnik und Informatik, Universität - GH - Siegen, Siegen, Germany

Anja Kleebaum Universität Heidelberg, Mathematikon - Institut für Informatik, Heidelberg, Germany

Sandro Koch Institute for Program Structures and Data Organization, Karlsruhe Institute of Technology (KIT), Karlsruhe, Germany

Stefan Kögel Institut für Softwaretechnik und Programmiersprachen, Universität Ulm, Ulm, Germany

Marco Konersmann Institute for Software Technology, Research Group Software Engineering, Universität, Koblenz-Landau, Koblenz, Germany

Matthias Kowal Institute for Software Engineering and Automotive Informatics, TU Braunschweig, Brunswick, Germany

Jan Ladiges Helmut-Schmidt-Universität, Fakultät für Maschinenbau, Professur für Automatisierungstechnik, Hamburg, Germany

Winfried Lamersdorf Universität Hamburg, MIN-Fakultät, Fachbereich Informatik, Hamburg, Germany

Michael Langhammer Institute for Program Structures and Data Organization, Karlsruhe Institute of Technology (KIT), Karlsruhe, Germany

Sascha Lity Institut für Softwaretechnik und Fahrzeuginformatik, Technische Universität Braunschweig, Informatikzentrum, Braunschweig, Germany

Malte Lochau Technische Universität Darmstadt, Fachbereich Elektrotechnik und Informationstechnik, Darmstadt, Germany

Lukas Märtin Institute for Programming and Reactive Systems, Technische Universität Braunschweig, Braunschweig, Germany

Jakob Mund Institute of Informatics L4, Technical University of Munich, Garching, Germany

Praktische Informatik/Softwaretechnik, Fachbereich Elektrotechnik und Informatik, Universität - GH - Siegen, Siegen, Germany

Felix Ocker Technische Universität München, Lehrstuhl für Automatisierung und Informationssysteme, Garching, Germany

Barbara Paech Universität Heidelberg, Mathematikon - Institut für Informatik, Heidelberg, Germany

Dennis Reuling Praktische Informatik/Softwaretechnik, Fachbereich Elektrotechnik und Informatik, Universität - GH - Siegen, Siegen, Germany

Ralf Reussner Institute for Program Structures and Data Organization, Karlsruhe Institute of Technology (KIT), Karlsruhe, Germany

Ina Schaefer Institute for Software Engineering and Automotive Informatics, TU Braunschweig, Brunswick, Germany

Kurt Schneider Leibniz Universität Hannover, Fachgebiet Software Engineering, Hannover, Germany

Andy Schürr Technische Universität Darmstadt, Fachbereich Elektrotechnik und Informationstechnik, Darmstadt, Germany

Stephan Seifermann Institute for Program Structures and Data Organization, Karlsruhe Institute of Technology (KIT), Karlsruhe, Germany

Daniel Strüber University of Koblenz-Landau, Institute for Computer Science, Koblenz, Germany

Gabriele Taentzer Philipps-Universität Marburg, Fachbereich Mathematik und Informatik, Marburg, Germany

Emre Taşpolatoğlu Software Engineering, FZI Forschungszentrum Informatik, Karlsruhe, Germany

Thomas Thüm Institute for Software Engineering and Automotive Informatics, TU Braunschweig, Brunswick, Germany

Matthias Tichy Institut für Softwaretechnik und Programmiersprachen, Universität Ulm, Ulm, Germany

Mattias Ulbrich Institute of Theoretical Informatics, Karlsruhe Institute of Technology (KIT), Karlsruhe, Germany

André van Hoorn Institute of Software Technology, University of Stuttgart, Stuttgart, Germany

Cyntia Vargas Technische Universität München, Lehrstuhl für Automatisierung und Informationssysteme, Garching, Germany

Fabien Patrick Viertel Leibniz Universität Hannover, Fachgebiet Software Engineering, Hannover, Germany

Birgit Vogel-Heuser Technische Universität München, Institute of Automation and Information Systems, Garching, Germany

Jürgen Walter Chair of Computer Science II, Universität Würzburg, Würzburg, Germany

Alexander Weigl Institute of Theoretical Informatics, Karlsruhe Institute of Technology (KIT), Karlsruhe, Germany

International Board of Reviewers

Antonia Bertolino, ISTI Pisa, Italy
Ivica Crnkovic, Chalmers University, Sweden
João M. Fernandes,[1] Universidade do Minho, Portugal
Anthony Finkelstein,[2] University College London, United Kingdom
Harald C. Gall,[1] University of Zurich, Switzerland
Carlo Ghezzi,[2] Politecnico di Milano, Italy
Peter Göhner,[2] University of Stuttgart, Germany
Paola Inverardi, University of L'Aquila, Italy
Gerti Kappel, Technical University Wien, Austria
Raffaela Mirandola, Politecnico di Milano, Italy
Bashar Nuseibeh,[2] The Open University, Milton Keynes, United Kingdom
Hans van Vliet,[2] Vrije Universiteit Amsterdam, Netherlands
Martin Wirsing,[2] Ludwigs-Maximilians-University Munich, Germany

[1]Only in second funding period.

[2]Only in first funding period.

Acronyms

ACC	Accuracy
ADL	Architecture description language
AES	Advanced Encryption Standard
AM3D	Architectural Modelling with Design Decision Documentation
APM	Application performance management
aPS	Automated Production Systems
BSPs	Basic security predicates
CFA	Control-flow automata
CoCoME	Common Component Modeling Example
ConDec	Continuous Management of Design Decisions
CPPS	Cyber Physical Production Systems
CSE	Continuous Software Engineering
CTMC	Continuous Time Markov Chain
DDM	Decision Documentation Model
DES	Data Encryption Standard
DK	Decision Knowledge
DTMC	Discrete Time Markov Chain
ESR	Essential Security Requirement
FNR	False negative rate
FPR	False positive rate
IAL	Intermediate Architecture Language
IDE	Integrated Development Environment
IS	Information Systems
ITS	Issue Tracking System
JEE	Java Enterprise Edition
k-NN	k-Nearest neighbors algorithm
KAMP	Karlsruhe Architectural Maintainability Prediction
KAMP4aPS	Karlsruhe Architectural Maintainability Prediction for automated Production Systems
LCS	Lowest common subsume
LQN	Layered Queueing Network

MIC	Model Integration Concept
MUC	Misuse case
NLP	Natural Language Processing
PAAD	Performance-annotated activity diagram
PCM	Palladio Component Model
PPU	Pick-and-Place Unit
RAC	Runtime Architecture Correspondence Model
SCK	Security Context Knowledge
SEURAT	Software Engineering Using Rationale
SI	Security incident
SIF	Secure Information Flow
SLA	Service level agreement
SMM	Security Maintenance Model
SMR	Security Maintenance Rule
SPE	Software performance engineering
SPL	Software product line
SPLE	Software product line engineering
SVM	Support Vector Machine
UC	Use case
UML	Unified Modeling Language
VCS	Version Control System
WP	Workpieces
xPPU	Extended Pick and Place Unit
XSS	Cross site scripting

Part I
Introduction

Chapter 1
Introducing Managed Software Evolution

Ralf Reussner, Michael Goedicke, Wilhelm Hasselbring, Birgit Vogel-Heuser, Jan Keim, and Lukas Märtin

"Software eats the world!" Although this famous statement by the entrepreneur Marc Andreesen targets the disruptive change of business models enabled through software, it also describes a process ongoing over decades. Software already invaded basically all parts of our daily lives, at work as well as in private affairs. As a consequence, there is software in daily use to support critical processes in enterprises, machines, or production systems, which was initially developed decades ago. And still this software needs to be maintained and adopted to newly required functionality or modern information technology (IT) platforms. Estimations exist that assume that more than half of software budgets are spent in software maintenance [Gla01]. Sommerville states that the costs for running, maintaining, and evolution exceed

R. Reussner (✉) · J. Keim
Institute for Program Structures and Data Organization, Karlsruhe Institute of Technology (KIT), Karlsruhe, Germany
e-mail: reussner@kit.edu; jan.keim@kit.edu

M. Goedicke
paluno – The Ruhr Institute for Software Technology, Specification of Software Systems, Universität Duisburg-Essen, Essen, Germany
e-mail: michael.goedicke@s3.uni-due.de

W. Hasselbring
Software Engineering Group, Department of Computer Science, Kiel University, Kiel, Germany
e-mail: hasselbring@email.uni-kiel.de

B. Vogel-Heuser
Technische Universität München, Institute of Automation and Information Systems, Garching, Germany
e-mail: vogel-heuser@tum.de

L. Märtin
Institute for Programming and Reactive Systems, Technische Universität at Braunschweig, Braunschweig, Germany
e-mail: l.maertin@tu-braunschweig.de

R. Reussner et al. (eds.), *Managed Software Evolution*,
https://doi.org/10.1007/978-3-030-13499-0_1

the development costs by a factor of at least two up to 100 [Som10]. Empirical studies from the industry support these numbers [Erl00, PA98, PM97]. However, it is actually even not clear how to interpret such figures. Are they bad signs, showing efficiency problems in maintenance, or are they good signs, showing that software is sufficiently good and valuable, that its maintenance is justified, as opposed to just throwing the software away and writing a new solution from scratch. Anyhow, the effects of software deterioration through long-running maintenance are well documented [Par94, VB02].

In the past, there were plenty of examples where software maintenance was challenging at least. The *Year 2000 problem*, also known as *Millenium bug*, struck many systems. Planning for long-living software did not factor in the turn of the millennium, causing a wide range of different problems. In 2009, customers of T-Mobile had no voice services or short message services (SMSs) available for several hours. Although the case was not a maintenance problem, at least the lack of knowledge about structural and architectural dependencies delayed the fix considerably. Flawed software on security chips of EC and credit cards caused a problem in 2010 because the card readers could not process the year properly. In 2016, the update of the operating system iOS for iPhones to version 10 caused alarm clocks to not go off any more because the new "bedtime alarm mode" interfered with the functionality of the existing alarm clock.

All these examples have in common the belief that problems could be related to lack of knowledge about the already existing system. From a bird's-eye view of software engineering, it is clear that knowledge is created during the process of developing software, but most of the time this type of knowledge is not documented. This leads to loss of knowledge about these systems, which can lead to problems in following development cycles and during maintenance. The results are much higher mean time to repair and much longer cycles until a new version of a system can be released. Additionally, lack of knowledge can also lead to more bugs, thus leading to a lower mean time to failure. In some cases, updates even introduce problems that were previously known and solved. For example, in 2017 an update for macOS accidentally reintroduced the critical "root bug".[1] Already in 1994 Parnas described the concept of hidden and lost knowledge [Par94]. Because of size and complexity, along with the interconnectedness of software systems, this problem gets worse.

Up to now, the focus in research and practice is mainly on developing new systems. New methods and tools are developed and existing ones refined to create optimal results for the initial operation of software systems. However, the long-term operation phase, along with the necessary adjustments and further development of software, is of paramount importance. This problem gains more weight when factoring in higher costs for maintenance and evolution in comparison with initial developments. Even in the research field of software evolution, the aspect of different evolutionary cycles for software and its execution and operating environment is yet not properly dealt with. The different life cycles of software and

[1] https://www.wired.com/story/macos-update-undoes-apple-root-bug-patch/.

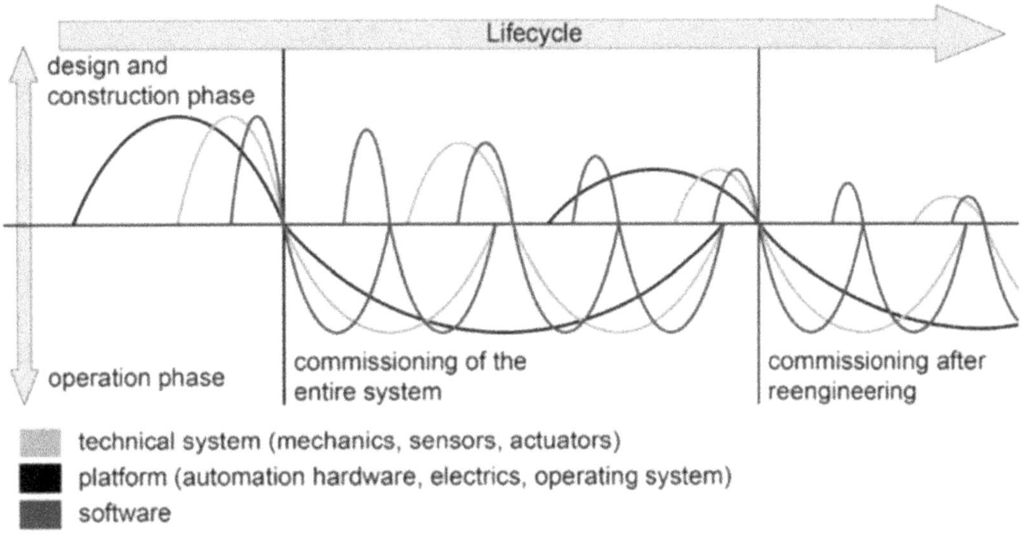

Fig. 1.1 Integration of the development and operation of hardware/software systems [Li+12]

its platform, as well as the technical systems, are shown in Fig. 1.1. There you can see the life cycles of software in grey, platforms in black, and technical systems in light grey. Vertical amplitudes show in which phase the software, platform, or technical system is. Life cycles of platforms are much longer, starting with longer design phases, and have much longer operation phases. In contrast, software is pretty short-lived and new versions replace older software rather fast. These differences need to be addressed. Some techniques used to simplify the creation of new software systems like Software-as-a-Service can lead to problems in combination with these varying life cycles. Although the potential exchange of services is seen as a benefit on evolution, published service interfaces are even harder to change than internal interfaces; hence, services lead to frozen interfaces hindering evolution. In addition, the required complex technology stack creates many—often undocumented—dependencies, which makes evolution to new platforms even harder, as the knowledge to decouple business functionality and platforms is lost rather soon after the initial development.

This leads us to problem areas for long-living software systems, which are explained in the following. Firstly, lacking understanding and knowledge about functionality, structure, dependencies, and other properties of software systems impedes a proper evolution of these systems, which are in agreement with the originally stated requirements. This leads to a deficit in those systems. Secondly, functional correctness and conformity with the architecture can often not be guaranteed because of misunderstood methods and techniques for software evolution. Finally, the complexity of development from the functional point of view on one side and the development of platforms and technologies on the other side obstruct each other regularly and are hindering the evolution of applications and application systems.

This shows that there is the necessity to make systems adaptable to changing requirements and environments and to make knowledge about systems accessible. Additionally, instead of separating the development, adaptation, and evolution of software and their platforms, as well as operation, monitoring, and maintenance, all these should be integrated into the process. This new paradigm should be developed and elaborated. For this we created three major guiding themes that are explained below.

Following this line of motivation, the German Research Council ("Deutsche Forschungsgemeinschaft (DFG)") initiated in 2012 the Priority Programme "Design for Future – Managed Software Evolution", to develop fundamentally new approaches in software engineering with a determined focus on long-living software systems. Over its funding periods, 59 proposals were evaluated by a board of scientifically outstanding international reviewers from the fields of software engineering and automation technology (see Board of reviewers section). The accepted 14 projects for each funding period included in total over 50 researchers and 31 principal investigators. As an anchor for these projects, three guiding themes were put into foreground, namely:

"Knowledge carrying software"
: This is the overarching theme of the whole Priority Programme. The principle of this guiding theme is that knowledge contained in software or its underlying design needs to be integrated and made accessible, both for functional and for quality properties. To realise this, sophisticated meta-models need to be developed for defining and managing suitable models.

"Methods and processes"
: They have to ensure that knowledge is preserved and integrated into the design and evolution of software. Therefore, a new model for the life cycle of software or software/hardware systems needs to be developed. This model needs to allow and consider different evolution cycles on different levels of the software, platform, and hardware stacks.

"Platforms and environments for evolution"
: One goal is to develop suitable middleware and robust runtime environments for monitoring and updating during operation to provide infrastructure for the evolution of software and software/hardware systems. It is an important principle for this guiding theme that design and runtime information need to be made accessible wherever needed during the operation of systems.

In Fig. 1.2 the three guiding themes are set in relation to relevant fields of research for today's software engineering [Gol+15]. The guiding themes are embedded into various areas of software engineering like requirements management, software architecture design, artefact management, and operation and infrastructure. All these areas play an influential role for the Priority Programme.

As a second means for project integration, the Priority Programme established two community case studies: the Common Component Modelling Example (CoCoME) for business-oriented software systems and the Pick-and-Place Unit

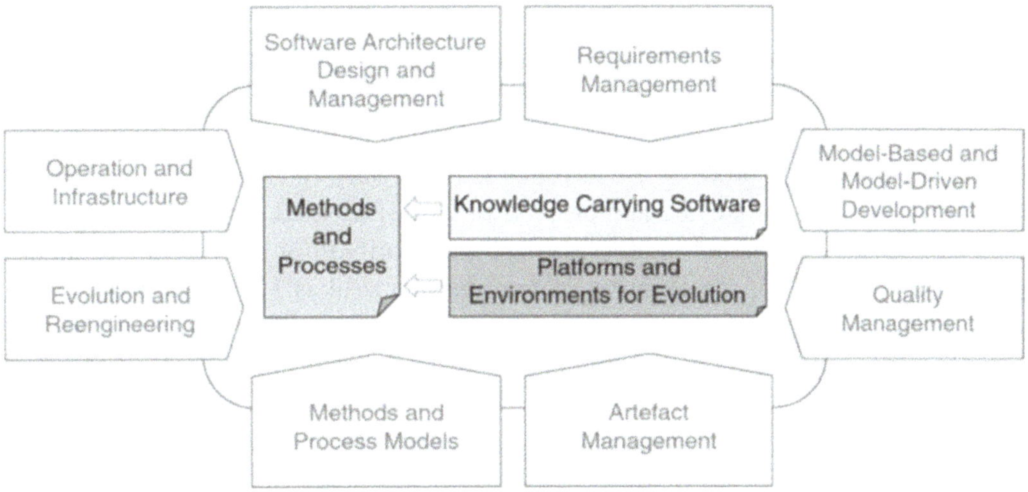

Fig. 1.2 Guiding themes related to current research in software engineering [Gol+15]

(PPU) as an exemplary automated production system. Each of the projects contributed to at least one of these studies.

Although or even because several hundred internationally high-ranked scientific publications were created during the course of the Priority Programme, the principal investigators see the need for a more integrated way to present the results to the scientific community and to academically trained practitioners in the field. Therefore, we wrote this book, with all the projects contributing in an integrated way. Hence, the following chapter overview describes the overarching results of the Priority Programme.

Overall the book is split into three major parts. The first part of the book deals with introductions into the topics. In Chap. 2, an introduction to the nature of software evolution is given, followed by the challenges that occur in Chap. 3. Lastly in this part, an introduction to the case studies we used is given in Chap. 4. In the second part of the book, there are the main chapters about knowledge-carrying software, starting with Chap. 5 on tacit knowledge in software evolution. Next, continuous design decision support will be covered in Chap. 6. Chapter 7 covers SPL round-trip engineering, followed by performance analysis strategies in Chap. 8. Maintaining security in software evolution is tackled in Chap. 9, before the topic about learning from evolution for evolution, which is tackled in Chap. 10. This second part in the book is completed with Chap. 11 on formal verification of evolutionary changes. Finally, the last part of the book presents results and spin-offs. There, Chap. 12 describes the case studies for the community, along with their benefits and deliverables. The lessons learned are collected in Chap. 13. We close the book in Chap. 14 with an overview of future research topics.

Chapters without author names are written by the editors of the book, while other chapters refer to the scientists who contributed as authors. A complete author list can be found at the end of the book. The editors would like to thank all the authors for their considerable effort in writing a cohesive book on the results of the Priority Programme. Additionally, we would like to thank all the authors who peer reviewed the chapters, which helped improve the quality of this book. We also would like to thank the office of the DFG, in particular Dr. Gerrit Sonntag and Dr. Andreas Raabe and their teams, for all their administrative support and for organising the review process. We also like to thank very cordially our international reviewers, who not only evaluated projects but also provided us with very valuable feedback during the whole funding period of the Priority Programme. Special thanks go to the managers of the Priority Programme, Dr. Lukas Märtin und Jan Keim, who served and organised the whole programme in an excellent manner and also managed the writing process of this book extremely well. We also want to thank Prof. Dr. Wilhelm Schäfer, who supported us invaluably as a programme director before his health condition unfortunately disallowed further contributions. We are also deeply indebted to Prof. Dr. Ursula Goltz, the first speaker of the coordination board. She successfully brought the programme through the review and application process and set it up in 2012, leading the programme during its first phase. Her unfortunate and sudden health problems made it impossible for her to carry on with this responsibility. We wish her good luck and furthermore a good recovery.

Chapter 2
The Nature of Software Evolution

Gabriele Taentzer, Michael Goedicke, Barbara Paech, Kurt Schneider, Andy Schürr, and Birgit Vogel-Heuser

In this chapter, we consider the nature of software evolution: What kinds of software systems are evolved? Which quality aspects of software systems play a role throughout evolution? What kinds of software changes exist, and which evolution processes are considered? What is the impact of these changes? The purpose of this chapter is to clarify the fundamental aspects of software evolution, which are being taken up again in the following chapters. Hence, this chapter shall explain the basic terminology used in this book. To a small extent, it shall also provide a domain analysis of the area of software evolution. And finally, for more details,

G. Taentzer (✉)
Philipps-Universität Marburg, Fachbereich Mathematik und Informatik, Marburg, Germany
e-mail: taentzer@informatik.uni-marburg.de

M. Goedicke
paluno – The Ruhr Institute for Software Technology, Specification of Software Systems, Universität Duisburg-Essen, Essen, Germany
e-mail: michael.goedicke@s3.uni-due.de

B. Paech
Universität Heidelberg, Mathematikon - Institut für Informatik, Heidelberg, Germany
e-mail: paech@informatik.uni-heidelberg.de

K. Schneider
Leibniz Universität Hannover, Fachgebiet Software Engineering, Hannover, Germany
e-mail: kurt.schneider@inf.uni-hannover.de

A. Schürr
Technische Universität Darmstadt, Fachbereich Elektrotechnik und Informationstechnik, Darmstadt, Germany
e-mail: andy.schuerr@es.tu-darmstadt.de

B. Vogel-Heuser
Technische Universität München, Lehrstuhl für Automatisierung und Informationssysteme, Garching, Germany
e-mail: vogel-heuser@tum.de

R. Reussner et al. (eds.), *Managed Software Evolution*,
https://doi.org/10.1007/978-3-030-13499-0_2

further scenarios, and examples of the fundamental aspects of software evolution, the reader can find references to follow-up chapters. In this way, this chapter helps to identify how the contributions of subsequent chapters fit into the big picture of software evolution.

2.1 Introduction

The main purpose of this chapter is to present a conceptual basis for the core aspects of software evolution. Evolution is a natural phenomenon in the life cycle of software systems according to diverse reasons for change. Software evolution occurs in incremental development where large systems are achieved in small steps and as a reaction to changes in the environment, purpose, or use of the considered software system. We clarify the core aspects of evolution processes. Changes of a software system may have an impact on its quality, referring to aspects such as correctness, consistency, usability, and maintainability. Evolving software shall preserve or even improve its quality (defined in the ISO standard 25000 on software product quality [Sta14b]) throughout software changes. Our considerations of the nature of software evolution are largely independent of application domains for software systems. Throughout the book, however, two application domains are focused on, namely business information systems [Hei+15b] and product automation [LFV13].

2.2 Software Systems

As a conceptual basis, we consider fundamental aspects of software systems. *Application domains* and *system scopes* set the environments of software systems; *artefacts* and potential software *variants* refer to the ingredients of software systems or even software product lines (SPLs) [CN02].

2.2.1 Application Domains

An application domain for software systems is a problem field being characterised by common requirements, terminology, processes, and functionality for software systems. Throughout this book, various application domains for software systems are considered. They are mostly considered from a rather technical point of view. In particular, two domains—business and product automation—occur very prominently in the subsequent chapters due to our case studies Common Component Modeling Example (CoCoME) and extended Pick and Place Unit (xPPU). They are introduced in Chap. 4.

2.2.2 *Scopes and Environments of Software Systems*

A *software system* is a set of coherent components that provide services (or features) to users. A software system needs a *platform* to run, consisting of hardware and further software components such as operating systems, libraries, and special software components provided by the environment. The hardware comprises not only computers of any kind but also networks of computers (especially the Internet). Depending on the domain, additional hardware may come into play, such as mechanical and electrical components. The *scope of a software system* defines a range of items that can be shaped and designed when developing software systems [Int18]. Besides the code for the system itself, it comprises, for example, the system requirement specification, any kinds of system documentation, models, data sets, and test suites.

The *environment* of a system contains not only the platform for running the system but also any other part relevant to the software system and its scope, such as users on which the system has an impact and regulations that should be obeyed. An explicit consideration of the environment is important when it comes to evolution since various kinds of environment changes can occur, such as new versions of the underlying operating system or programming language, related software components, external regulations that shall be obeyed by the software, and many more.

Two interesting examples of software systems are the following: In Chaps. 5 and 6, the authors investigate the evolution of *socio-technical systems* where developers and/or users are explicitly considered within the system scope. The interrelation of social and technical aspects and their joint optimisation are of special relevance here. A very different form of system are mechatronic systems such as automated Production Systems (aPS), which consider the interplay of mechanics, electronics, and software (in Chaps. 10 and 8).

2.2.3 *Software Artefacts*

Software development and software changes usually involve a number of *software artefacts*. Even the kinds of software artefacts are manifold: Analysts elicit requirements and write requirement specifications that may comprise analysis models. Software architects take these specifications into account to develop the design of a software system, often by constructing design models. Software engineers and programmers develop models and write codes that are structured in various files and directories. Moreover, they write test cases and documentations organised in additional file structures. Once a software system is deployed, it may produce even further artefacts for reporting about continuously running processes, for example. The system behaviour at runtime and its ad hoc changes, for example, are considered in Chap. 10. To summarise, there are usually a vast number of artefacts of various kinds within the scope of a software system.

Software artefacts are usually not isolated but inter-related. Hence, we have to take care of consistency relationships between them and we have to maintain them throughout software evolution. For example, the evolution of requirement specifications, design decisions (comprising design knowledge about problems, solution, context, and rationale), and architecture specification models is in the focus of Chap. 6.

In software engineering, there are quite a number of languages used to create software artefacts. Besides programming languages such as Java and C, there are various modelling languages such as the Unified Modeling Language (UML) and Matlab/Simulink. Documentations are usually semi-structured natural text, often written in HTML, LaTeX, or Word. Moreover, there are domain-specific languages, especially for specific modelling purposes, such as AutoFocus [Leg+14, RTV15, TH15] for embedded system development presented in Chap. 11 and variability-modelling languages like decision models [SRG11], orthogonal variability models [PBL05a], and feature models [Kan+90b], as considered in Chaps. 7 and 8. Furthermore, there exist specific languages to describe the syntax and semantics of modelling languages, for example EMF [Ecl18], and to specify differences resp. transformations between models to formally express their evolution, for example Henshin [Are+10]. They are used in Chap. 10 to understand historical evolutions between different versions of models, as well as to recommend future evolutions based on these historic evolutions.

2.2.4 *Software Variants*

Most modern software systems A collection of software variants that share common artefacts that are commonly processed is called a *software product line*. A software variant is called *product* in this context. Variants of a software system can occur independently of any time periods, while chronologically changed software is usually called a *version*. Version management is specifically considered in Sect. 2.4.

In Chap. 7, statechart models are presented that are able to integrate all product-variant behaviour into one model. A feature model serves as configuration specification; the product line is implemented by preprocessor-based C-code. Similarly, in Chap. 8, software variants are explicitly considered for evaluation of performance. In particular, strategies for performance evolution are discussed for variants co-existing at the same time and versions that are the result of software evolution.

2.3 Software Quality

Preserving and improving software quality are often the main drivers of software evolution, such as improving the performance of a software solution. The ISO 25000 standard [Sta14b] defines software quality based on a number of aspects covering functional and non-functional ones. *Functional software quality* refers to the extent the software conforms to a given functional requirement specification. Aspects of functional software quality are, for example, correctness, consistency, dependability, and usability. *Non-functional software quality* tells us how well a software system meets non-functional requirements concerning, for example, performance (cf. Chaps. 8 and 10), maintainability, and security aspects (cf. Chap. 9). In the following, we recall the main quality aspects of software systems and point out examples.

2.3.1 Consistency

As there may be various artefacts within the scope of a software system, an immediate question is: *Are the various software artefacts within the scope of a software system consistent with each other?* Artefact relations may be purely *syntactical*, such as models conforming to their meta-models. Software artefacts may also be related w.r.t. behaviour. The most prominent shape of behaviour consistency is *behavioural equivalence* (also known as bi-simulation). Weaker notions of behavioural equivalence like conditional and relational equivalence are introduced as consistency notions in Chap. 11. Besides this *outer consistency* being established in between several artefacts, there is also an *inner consistency* considering the content of just one artefact. Here, consistency means that *an artefact does not contradict itself* [EN96]. Inner consistency comprises, for example, the internal consistency of requirements within one requirement specification or the declaration of a variable before its use in a program.

Even if artefacts are consistent on creation, changes to one software artefact may not necessarily be reflected immediately in all related artefacts that are affected by the same modification. This means that the quality aspect of consistency is endangered by changes. If changes are made in one place, consistency may call for changes in several other artefacts. There is the resulting challenge of keeping systems consistent over time. As consistency cannot be always (re)established easily; there is also the general need for *inconsistency management*. Intermediate inconsistency gives developers the flexibility and the freedom to postpone the re-establishing of consistency for increasing productivity. If explicit relationships between artefacts, that is traces, are considered, a form of traceability link management is needed here [Fel+16]. Traceability is explicitly considered in the context of identifying and extracting tacit knowledge in software evolution (Chaps. 5 and 10) and continuous design support (Chap. 6) caring about the consistency between architecture and code.

Inconsistency may also affect system variants. A necessary condition for software product lines (defining software variants) is often the following: If a feature model is available for the system, it is typically assumed to be consistent, that is there must be at least one valid combination of features (Chaps. 7 and 8). In Chap. 8, performance is only measured for configurations that are valid according to the feature model. The product implementation derivable from valid combinations of features must also be consistent with further development artefacts such as quality-assurance artefacts. If product implementations evolve, for instance, corresponding test suites must be updated accordingly (Chap. 7).

2.3.2 Correctness

To validate the correctness of a software system, we should ask: *Does the system do what I want it to do?* This question shows that correctness relates to the system's functional requirement specification. A software system is considered correct w.r.t. its requirement specification if it behaves as specified by its requirements. Hence, correctness can also be considered as a kind of consistency, here of code (and other artefacts) with the requirement specification. As correctness is such a central consistency aspect of software systems, it is usually considered explicitly. In most software projects, functional requirements are validated by testing a software. In contrast to validating system functionalities, there is also the possibility to verify them formally. Correctness in the presence of evolution plays a central role in Chap. 7, which is concerned with software testing of evolving SPLs, and in Chap. 11 as this chapter is concerned with the formal verification of evolving automated production systems.

2.3.3 Dependability

Dependability comprises quality aspects such as reliability, availability, safety, and security [Avi+04, LS00]. High dependability allows us to rely on a system functioning as required, even under hampered conditions such as software and hardware faults. The notion of dependability has been discussed very broadly in literature, depending on the different perspectives of various stakeholders. Reference [FCÁ16] gives a literature overview.

Considering *reliability*, we ask: *Does the system show correct behaviour all the time or for a specific time period?* Reliability is closely related to *availability*, which is typically described as the ability of a component or a system to function at a specified moment or interval of time. Reliability is also considered as the probability of success. In addition, dependability comprises *safety*, which shows the degree of hazard prevention that may result from the operation of the system and threatens users or the environment [LG99]. Evolution and safety are discussed in Chap. 10. In contrast, *security* mainly refers to the absence of unauthorised access from users or the environment that threatens the operation of the system [HR06, LG99]. Chapter 9 is mainly concerned with maintaining security in the presence of software evolution.

2.3.4 Performance

Performance of a software system is considered by asking questions like: *Does the system perform the indicated behaviour as fast as required?* Performance engineering comprises all kinds of optimising the timing behaviour and resource consumption of a software system, as well as guaranteeing available or specified resource limitations. Considered aspects are, for example, the throughput, latency, memory usage, and energy consumption of software systems. Performance for the specific case of automated production systems is discussed in Chap. 10. Performance issues can result in loss of productivity for the user. When software engineers start improving the systems's performance, corresponding evolution steps may lead to cost overruns due to tuning or redesign. Moreover, it is likely that tuning may disrupt the original software architecture or its behaviour.

Considering a software system with variants, there are often variants with better or worse performance. Here, checking performance refers to the accessible computation effort and the resulting impact on resource usage and timeliness of a system variant (Chap. 8).

2.3.5 Usability

Users expect a software that is easy to learn, as well as pleasant and efficient to use. Moreover, they appreciate a system that easily recovers from usage errors and whose usage can be easily memorised after some period of not using it. To check usability, the degree to which a software system can be used by specified consumers should be investigated on to achieve quantified objectives with effectiveness, efficiency, and satisfaction in a determined context of use. In Chap. 5, usability is a major aspect in the sense that expectations or assumptions about the usability and the functionality of a system are derived from the users' behaviour.

2.3.6 *Maintainability*

A software system is well maintainable if it can be easily changed with respect to its environment to, for example, correct defects, realise new requirements, or adapt the system to a changed platform. Specific aspects of maintainability are testability, analyzability, and changeability. A software is well testable if its artefacts support testing in given test contexts. Often, testability is a question of good software design featuring strong cohesion and loose coupling. Testability of variant-rich software systems is a key aspect in Chap. 7 as it is concerned with model-based testing of evolving SPLs. A software system is considered analysable if system parts causing deficiencies or failures of the system can be easily identified. In Chap. 11, analysable models are considered to bridge the conceptual gap between requirements and target system implementations. And centrally for software evolution, software shall be easily changeable to be adaptable to continuously occurring changes in the environment with considerable effort.

2.4 Software Evolution

Software system changes show a wide variety, which has been investigated on and classified in the literature, such as [LS80, Cha+01, Buc+05]. In [Buc+05], the authors present a taxonomy for software evolution distinguishing four different dimensions of system change: They consider temporal properties (i.e. when do changes happen), objects of change (i.e. where in the system do we make changes), system properties (i.e. what is changed), and change support (i.e. how is it changed). They do not consider who is doing system changes and why; this has already been done before in [Cha+01]. This split-up of dimensions is driven by the basic idea that activities and processes form the core of software engineering methods. The purpose of taxonomies as the ones found on software evolution is, among others, to provide a framework for comparing and combining individual tools and techniques and to provide an overview of the research domain of software evolution. We take it up in this section: Considering different *kinds of software change* in the following, we will focus on reasons for change, as well as participating artefacts and users, that is the *why* and *what*. Thereafter we consider *evolution processes* where temporal properties, change support, and stakeholders, that is the *when*, *how*, and *who*, are focused. Finally, configuration management is considered to capture all changes of software artefacts that emerge throughout evolution.

2.4.1 Kinds of Software Change

Software changes have been studied for a long time; comprehensive works in this direction are [LS80, Cha+01], where types of software evolution are classified along with the kind of artefacts changed, as well as the reason for change. The authors focus on code versus documentation changes; reasons for change are functionality changes, adaptations to the environment, as well as performance and maintenance issues. Documentation comprises all kinds of software artefacts except of the code.

Early works such as [LS80] and the ISO/IEC standard for software maintenance [Sta14a] propose to distinguish software changes into *corrective*, *adaptive*, *perfective*, and *preventive* modifications.

- Corrective modifications subsume all kinds of *bug fixing* to eliminate system failures and *feature requests* as long as they reflect corrected requirements.
- Adaptive modifications refer to *changes of system environments*, as well as additional *requirement elicitation*. More recently, studies of *adaptive systems* have led to further kinds of evolution activities being runtime adaptations, that is system modifications at runtime [De +13].
- Perfective modifications subsume all kinds of system improvements such as *performance optimisation*, *structure re-engineering or optimisation* (refactoring), and all kinds of documentation activities, especially *knowledge extraction* from the software system.
- Preventive modifications summarise all changes that prevent problems from software systems before they occur.

Software changes may take place continuously, such as planned or ad hoc changes.

Throughout this book, various kinds of system changes are presented: Chap. 4 discusses a variety of concrete evolution steps as they occur in the case studies. Chapter 5 is concerned with detecting and reducing mismatches between stakeholder's mental models during software evolution. The basic problem is that the system may gradually diverge from a given specification or customer demand. This deviation may come from incomplete implementation of requirements—or from changing requirements that are not complemented by a corresponding change of the system. Such deviations shall be reduced. In Chap. 6, continuous software engineering is considered as being a special kind of software evolution. Chapter 7 discusses implementation changes and corresponding updates of quality-assurance artefacts in software product lines such that consistency is preserved. Maintaining performance as a prerequisite for evolving software artefacts is considered in Chap. 8. Analysis strategies are presented that can efficiently assess and predict the system's performance. On this basis, performance improvements over time are considered. Moreover, software variants with the best performance are identified. Chapter 9 is dedicated to maintaining security throughout changing requirements and changing environments such that changes do not affect the system's level of security. The maintenance of safety is addressed in Chap. 10. Capturing and transferring knowledge to next software versions and projects are addressed in

Chaps. 6 and 10; in particular, ad hoc changes with respect to learning are presented in Chap. 10. To be able to distinguish wanted from unwanted system changes, the maintenance of correctness is considered in Chap. 11 by applying formal verification techniques to show the correctness of evolving software systems. Newer revisions of the software must not violate existing software properties and should comply with them even more.

Change may also take place during runtime. A knowledge elicitation technique, well known in software engineering, is the Post-Mortem Analysis (PMA) [Stå+03]. PMA of a system's runtime behaviour simply consists of gathering knowledge about a process and to analyse it in order to improve the next runs of this process in future. An example application of PMA is presented in Chap. 10.

2.4.2 Evolution Processes

Several iterative and incremental software development processes have been proposed, such as the Unified Process [Kru03], V-ModelXT [Vog+15c], and agile software development [Bec99]. *Agile software development* processes already acknowledge and embrace change as an essential fact of life. One of the agile development principles is to welcome changing requirements, even in late development. Furthermore, software development shall be sustainable and software quality shall remain high. How do software development processes actually incorporate evolution? According to [MD08] (referring to [LR03]), the *software evolution process* is a multi-loop, multi-level, multi-agent feedback system that cannot be treated in isolation. A specific form of evolution process is *round-trip engineering* (also called *horseshoe process* [KWC98]) where developers alternate between models and code. This process consists of three phases: The *reverse engineering* phase is needed to understand the structure and behaviour of a larger part of a legacy code by means of models. In the subsequent *restructuring* phase, (a part of) the software is redesigned on the level of models, and finally, *forward engineering* is needed to implement the new design and to integrate it into the existing system.

While a clear separation between development and maintenance has already dissolved in agile software development, this is even more the case in *continuous engineering* [FS17]. Continuous activities are meant to eliminate discontinuities that occur from following development activities in a specific order. Continuous engineering specifically includes continuous improvement and innovation. An early proposed activity that can be considered as continuous innovation activity is that of beta testing, which became a widespread practice, even in industrial software development. It is used to elicit early customer feedback prior to the formal release of software products [Col02]. Following the trend of continuous engineering, software engineers have commonly accepted that software must continually evolve according to changes. Otherwise, the software does not fulfil its ever-changing requirements and therefore will become outdated earlier than expected.

Change impact analysis techniques can identify system parts that are likely to be affected by additional changes. These techniques support knowledge elicitation from change histories to inform all interested stakeholders. On this basis, these techniques can also give an estimation of how costly an intended change will be and how risky it is to make that change. This analysis is used to decide whether it is worthwhile to carry out that change. The risk has a strong relation to software quality. If proper support for measuring quality is available, a measurement report can provide crucial information to determine whether the software quality is degrading and to take corrective actions if this turns out to be the case.

Throughout the book, the following aspects of evolution processes are tackled: The roundtrip model is used in Chaps. 6–8 and 10. In Chap. 6, we show that the small iterations of continuous engineering support lightweight design decision capture and use. Chapter 7 considers an SPL evolution scenario covering a complete family of software products to be evolved. The efficient performance analysis of software variants and versions based on monitoring and model extraction is focused on in Chap. 8. The dynamic nature of running self-adaptive systems and their environments requires continuous validation and verification to assess the system at runtime, which was traditionally done at development time and which requires new and efficient techniques for the runtime case [De +13]. An example for evolving self-adaptive systems is given in Chap. 10. In Chap. 11, regression verification is applied to evolving systems again based on a round-trip model.

2.4.3 Configuration Management

To capture all changes throughout software evolution, emerging changes of software artefacts are usually managed with the help of development tools. *Change management* refers to a systematic consideration of change requests, which may be bug reports and feature requests. To ensure that the most urgent and cost-efficient change requests are prioritised, each request is collected and assessed first and addressed along its priority thereafter. Especially for software product lines where versions of variants may occur, a systematic management of change requests is necessary.

Version management is needed to store and track emerging versions of software artefacts. Moreover, it allows developers to work on these versions concurrently in a coordinated way. To save memory, subsequent versions may be stored in a list of *deltas*. A delta just stores the differences of one version from its successor. Applying these deltas to a root version (usually the newest one), the other versions can be computed. Several developers are allowed to work on the same artefacts concurrently. The version management system tracks the edited artefacts, ensures that changes to one and the same artefact do not get lost, and supports the resolution of conflicting changes. To allow developers working in isolation, the artefacts within the scope of a software system may be duplicated into several *branches* (of the version tree). The ability of branching implies the later facility to merge changes back onto one branch. The usage of branching in the context of continuous integration is tackled in Chap. 6.

Release management is the process by which source code is converted to a final software product, often being built for a specific environment. Version management is usually involved and is recommended but is not a requirement. A reliable release process is as much automatic as possible and supports a quick and frequent deployment, a prerequisite for *continuous integration*. Recently, continuous integration has emerged as a practice to eliminate discontinuities between development and deployment. However, continuous integration is not yet used in aPS (only 33% of companies use it to some extent and 15% by default) [Bou+17b]. In a similar vein, the recent emphasis on *DevOps* recognises that the integration between software development and its operational deployment needs to be a continuous one [FS17]. The concept of continuous deployment, that is the ability to deliver software more frequently to customers, enables frequent customer feedback, which has become very attractive to companies, in the area of production automation; however, it is often not implemented due to confidentiality.

As configuration management may become very complex for software product lines, this problem is the subject in Chaps. 7 and 10. Each variant, or in more detail each feature, can occur in various versions, which have to be integrated in a consistent way. In Chap. 10, the evolution of variants is considered focusing specifically on the continuous correctness of the system.

Chapter 3
Addressed Challenges

Reiner Jung, Lukas Märtin, Jan Ole Johanssen, Barbara Paech, Malte Lochau, Thomas Thüm, Kurt Schneider, Matthias Tichy, and Mattias Ulbrich

Software evolution is a necessity for present-day software development and the operations of enterprise software systems and embedded systems, including production lines. Evolution is driven by changing and new requirements originating from user needs, alterations in the underlying hardware, and environmental changes, such as cloud computing for enterprise systems and modifications of production lines and processes. Current methods and processes in software system engineering are not well suited to handle these drivers of change, as knowledge about the software is predominantly stored in informal documents and not linked with other artefacts. Furthermore, most parts of a software system are only represented in the form of a source code, which carries knowledge only on what to do but not on why to do it.

We address these shortcomings with new ways and forms to describe and specify artefacts used in the development and operation of software systems. Hence, we must use and collect knowledge concerning the software system and its context at runtime and apply it at design time to enrich the evolution. We support the discovery, extraction, and handling of knowledge with novel methods and processes to foster

R. Jung (✉)
Software Engineering Group, Department of Computer Science, Kiel University, Kiel, Germany
e-mail: reiner.jung@email.uni-kiel.de

L. Märtin
Institute for Programming and Reactive Systems, Technische Universität at Braunschweig, Braunschweig, Germany
e-mail: l.maertin@tu-braunschweig.de

J. O. Johanssen
Technische Universität München, Institut für Informatik I1, Garching, Germany
e-mail: jan.johanssen@tum.de

B. Paech
Universität Heidelberg, Mathematikon - Institut für Informatik, Heidelberg, Germany
e-mail: paech@informatik.uni-heidelberg.de

R. Reussner et al. (eds.), *Managed Software Evolution*,
https://doi.org/10.1007/978-3-030-13499-0_3

evolution and make it more reliable and the software maintainable, performant, and secure. To enable these methods and processes, we provide and use new platforms and environments.

During our research, we assessed our methods and processes with two case studies based on the Common Component Modeling Example (CoCoME), resembling a software system for a supermarket chain, and the extended Pick and Place Unit (xPPU), illustrating an industrial plant automation system. CoCoME, which is introduced in Sect. 4.2, includes a fast set of evolution scenarios for the enterprise domain, like adding a webshop or including credit card payments. Similarly, the PPU case study, introduced in Sect. 4.3, provides evolution scenarios originating from industrial production plants. Our aim to incorporate knowledge in software and processes tailored for software and system evolution faces a diverse set of challenges from different perspectives. Firstly, the discovery and externalization of knowledge about requirements, the recording and representation of design decisions, and the learning from past experience in evolution form the human perspective, including that of developers, operators, and users. Secondly, performance and security induce the software quality perspective. Thirdly, round-trip engineering, testing, and co-evolution define the technical perspective. And fourthly, formal methods for evolutionary changes provide the foundation and define the formal perspective. This chapter introduces the challenges we discuss and address in this book, which were researched during the priority programme for managed software evolution:

Tacit Knowledge (Sect. 3.1) The key to evolution is an understanding of changing needs and derived requirements thereof. Unfortunately, stakeholders are often unaware of all aspects and assumptions underlying their needs and requirements. This *tacit knowledge* must be externalised in order to understand requirements and successfully evolve software systems.

Design Decisions (Sect. 3.2) To accommodate changing requirements, software engineers change the software architecture and apply different design patterns.

M. Lochau
Technische Universität Darmstadt, Fachbereich Elektrotechnik und Informationstechnik, Fachgebiet Echtzeitsysteme, Darmstadt, Germany

T. Thüm
Institute for Software Engineering and Automotive Informatics, TU Braunschweig, Brunswick, Germany

K. Schneider
Leibniz Universität Hannover, Fachgebiet Software Engineering, Hannover, Germany

M. Tichy
Institut für Softwaretechnik und Programmiersprachen, Universität Ulm, Ulm, Germany

M. Ulbrich
Institute of Theoretical Informatics, Karlsruhe Institute of Technology (KIT), Karlsruhe, Germany

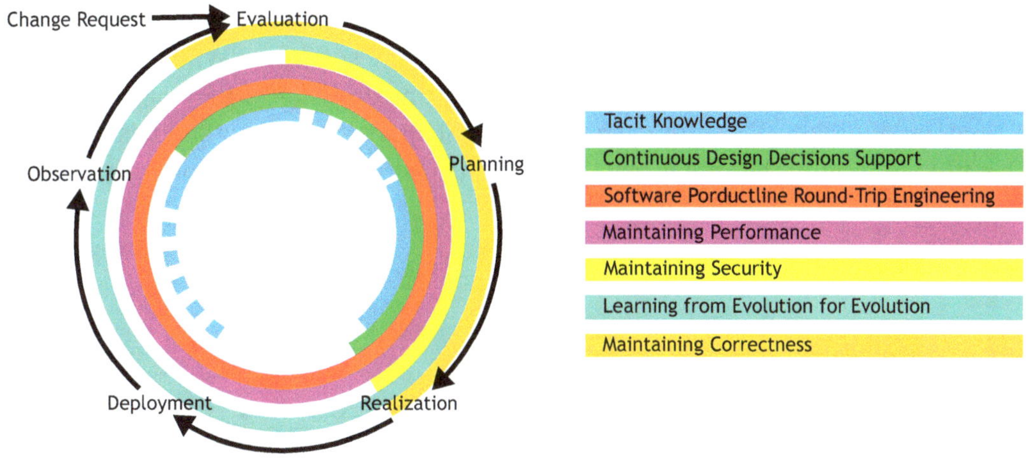

Fig. 3.1 Design for future—addressed challenges

These design decisions could conflict with decisions made in previous iterations of the evolution process, eroding the architecture and harming evolvability. Therefore, it is necessary to support the documentation of and access to design decisions.

Software Product Line Round-Trip Engineering (Sect. 3.3) As depicted in Fig. 3.1, software evolution is a circular process where introducing changes occurs often. Today, software systems are not only subject to reoccurring changes; they also exist in different variants. This is especially the case in embedded systems. Providing a consistent view on versions and variants of product lines introduces new challenges to software evolution.

Maintaining Performance (Sect. 3.4) Being able to predict and forecast performance is necessary for software systems to ensure a timely execution and control over resources. Feature sets from software product lines can result in large numbers of variants, which cannot be evaluated for performance in a timely manner. Furthermore, runtime measurements address only one version of one variant. Both aspects are central challenges in maintaining performance.

Maintaining Security (Sect. 3.5) Keeping a software system secure is a great challenge by its own. It is affected not only by changing requirements within the software system but also by its changing environment. These changes are covered in non-formal documents. Supporting security experts and developers in deriving formal information from non-formal documents and supporting security evaluation throughout evolution are the challenges we motivate in this section.

Learning from Evolution for Evolution (Sect. 3.6) The previous challenges address certain challenges within the evolution cycle. However, we also need to learn and transfer knowledge from one evolution step to another and from one project to another to grow our knowledge on software evolution and improve our processes and software quality. Therefore, we face the challenges of how to process semantically rich changes in past evolution steps and develop methods to understand and exploit this knowledge.

Maintaining Correctness (Sect. 3.7) Software evolution may erode functionality and cause unwanted behaviour alterations in software. While non-formal processes and methods help to mitigate unwanted changes, they cannot detect and correct them. Therefore, we need formal approaches using models to verify software systems, be able to test them for changes and to know how to distinguish wanted from unwanted changes.

3.1 Tacit Knowledge

Long-living software systems face challenges during requirements identification and update due to various reasons. First of all, software systems and the requirements that describe their functional behaviour and non-functional performance change over time. The technical development and the availability of new software and hardware components affect and change existing requirements or even make them obsolete. On top of this, a substantial part of the relevant requirements for software systems remains *tacit*. This means that important knowledge carried by requirement analysts, software users, or other stakeholders remains in their minds. In general, *tacit knowledge* can be described as knowledge that is internalised by a person while its active verbalisation, that is the externalisation of this knowledge, is difficult [PS09].

In contrast to the goal of a complete representation of a software system [Dav93], this results in an incomplete set of requirements. As a consequence, the associated software system remains incomplete as well, which is expressed in different facets. First, software systems are exposed to any type of intrusion. They are in particular vulnerable to attacks in case of a lack of security-related requirements. Second, users of a software system are presented with an unsatisfying set of functionalities that does not match their needs.

Stakeholders of a software system, such as the requirements analyst or the software user, might not be aware of an urgent demand for action or of the associated knowledge that would help to understand a situation in question. Thus, they are unable to verbalise those tacit requirements. This is the reason why an automatic identification and extraction of this tacit knowledge represents an important source of knowledge for the development of long-living and continuously evolving systems.

We envision that tacit knowledge is particularly exposed to being automatically captured, processed, and externalised during the *design time* and *runtime* of a software system: On the one hand, during the design time of a software system, requirements are elicited and described using natural language. In doing so, the use of certain words might indicate implications for the functionality that they describe. For instance, the way a functional requirement is described can pose requirements towards non-functional aspects. On the other hand, during the runtime of a software system, users unconsciously provide insights into the way they interact with the system. Ignoring certain functionalities of a software system or repetitively applying the same usage patterns might hint towards a particular functional requirement that the developers or requirement analysts were previously not aware of.

We want to focus on *tacit knowledge* as an instance of knowledge that is preserved in a software system or its underlying design. Describing tacit knowledge and its building blocks requires defined models. This demand is manifested in one of the SPP1593 themes by calling out for customised meta-models that enable the ongoing development of software systems. We strive for a basic representation of tacit knowledge in the form of ontologies and taxonomies, which can be utilised to detect and describe tacit knowledge. Furthermore, tacit knowledge naturally emerges in an unstructured format produced by heterogeneous instances and actors. Its building blocks remain incomplete and potentially irrelevant, only until they are mapped with existing requirements that relate to the same entity. Addressing the extraction of tacit knowledge requires a platform that can be deployed in a continuously changing environment to visualise building blocks of tacit knowledge. This is one of the SPP1593 themes, that is establishing platforms and environments that enable access to design- and runtime information when it is needed.

By extracting tacit knowledge from both design- and runtime observations, we aim for the following goals. First, we want to enable the creation of software releases that match the requirements of both customers and users and their expectations. Second, we intend to improve and maintain the quality of development for long-living systems through the co-evolution of adequate non-functional mitigation activities. Third, we aim for increasing the software system's usability and an adaption towards the needs of users.

Understanding tacit knowledge poses challenges in their identification due to multiple reasons. First, we expect different kinds of tacit knowledge that can potentially arise during software evolution. Second, the availability of various sources of tacit knowledge plays an important role. Eventually, when it comes to the extraction of tacit knowledge, we see challenges in reducing the mismatch between developers' and security experts' mental model, as well as reducing the mismatch between developers' and users' mental model. Aside from the identification and extraction of tacit knowledge, we face challenges in working with tacit knowledge and its explicit counterpart. In particular, the detection of deviations between specified and derived security knowledge or deviations between expected and observed user behaviour demand attention in their analysis. We summarise this collection of challenges under the following two main challenges and address them in Chap. 5.

Challenge 1 How to identify and extract tacit knowledge to reduce the mismatch between stakeholders' mental models during software evolution?

Challenge 2 How to detect deviations between explicitly elicited requirements and implicitly derived requirements?

3.2 Design Decisions

Continuous Software Engineering (CSE) is a software engineering process in which developers continuously change the software while keeping it in a releasable state [KB17]. CSE means to develop, release, and learn from software in very short rapid cycles [Bos14]. It incorporates agile practices and involves activities such as continuous integration, delivery, and deployment [SAZ17, Joh+18b]. The emergence of CSE is driven by a growing need for flexibility and rapid adaption in the current software environment [FS17]. Thus, CSE provides many techniques for a continuous change. This can also be exploited for continuous design decision support.

Software developers and architects continuously make design decisions while they develop software. When they evolve software, it is important for them to reflect and build on former decisions. Otherwise, they might make inconsistent decisions and are likely to contribute to the erosion of the software architecture or introduce other quality problems. Reflecting on former decisions is particularly important for long-living software systems where many decisions build on one another. Documenting design decisions is important since many different developers are involved at different times and cannot communicate directly.

Design decisions can be made in either a rational or a naturalistic way. Rational decision-making means that developers weigh alternatives and arguments, whereas naturalistic decision-making means that they reuse past experiences to solve a decision problem [ZCM07]. It is often assumed that decision-making in software design is a deterministic and rational process [Fal+11] since software development is an engineering activity. However, this is not so in practice as, for example, Hesse et al. empirically show that naturalistic decision-making is dominant over rational decision-making in the Firefox open-source project [Hes+16]. In naturalistic decision-making, developers do not consider all alternatives and arguments. This is risky as humans tend to overlook what is missing and are subject to cognitive biases [Raz+16]. Thus, developers might anchor on those solutions that first come to mind, omitting more relevant alternative solutions. If the arguments for the decision are not documented, other developers might not understand the decision or might not be convinced. Thus, support for rational decision-making is important. Rational decision-making requires the management of decision knowledge.

Design decision knowledge is the knowledge about design decisions, the problems they address, solution approaches and their alternatives, their context, and their justifications (also called rationale). Decision knowledge vaporizes quickly; that is, if developers do not document decisions immediately, the design decisions are never documented and thus not available later [JB05]. Decisions are often discussed informally and captured partly and distributed: for example, in code, issue comments [Hes+16], commit messages, pull requests [Bru+14], chat messages [Alk+17a, Alk+17b], wikis, and emails; this knowledge is difficult to access later. Thus, developers need support to capture decision knowledge or evolve it from naturalistic decisions and to access it efficiently.

Our long-term vision is an *on-demand decision documentation* as part of the *on-demand developer documentation* suggested by Robillard et al. [Rob+17]. We envision that developers continuously capture and reflect decision knowledge during CSE. Benefits of a continuous capture and reflection on decision knowledge are an improved decision-making process through explicit criteria, the prevention of knowledge vaporization, and consistent future changes.

Our goal is to support developers in this continuous capture and reflection, in particular by performing rational decision-making. The following three developer tasks should be lightweight, that is they should require as little effort as possible: *rational decision-making*, *documentation of decision knowledge*, and its *exploitation*.

There are two major challenges for this support: intrusiveness and inconsistency. It is a challenge to minimize the intrusiveness of a continuous design decision support and to document and maintain decision knowledge consistent with the other artefacts and with former decision knowledge. We summarise and express these challenges under the following two paragraphs and provide solutions in Chap. 6.

Challenge 3 How to integrate rational design decision-making, documentation, and exploitation in software engineering practices? Tool support to manage decision knowledge can be characterized by its intrusiveness in the software development process [Dut+06]. Tools that fit into the development context are less *intrusive* and will more likely be used [KCD09]. Such tools do not require additional effort (e.g. for installing or starting a separate tool) and are thus also lightweight. Rational decision-making, documentation of decision knowledge, and its exploitation should be non-intrusive in the context of the CSE process.

Challenge 4 How to ensure consistency between decision knowledge and artefacts? Consistency means that design decisions are documented and linked to and realized in the artefacts they relate to. To exploit decision knowledge, it is important that the design decisions are *consistent* with former design decisions and with the artefacts, for example with the requirements, architectural software design, and code.

3.3 Software Product Line Round-Trip Engineering

Modern software systems tend to become more and more long living and, therefore, have undergone continuous evolution to ever new versions in order to meet constantly changing requirements. For instance, the initial version of the PPU case study only comprises a stack with multiple slides for sorting different work pieces according to their types, as well as a crane and a stamp. Later on, the PPU undergoes several evolution scenarios in order to adapt to changing requirements and platforms (e.g. the ramp is later replaced by a standard ramp to support application scenarios without sorting). As a consequence, all PPU (software) artefacts (potentially) affected by those changes have to be adapted to support the new versions.

In addition, modern software systems are highly configurable, thus comprising many different variants being custom-tailored to specific needs. For instance, the modular architecture of the PPU supports many different variants in order to adapt to different environments, platforms, and customers' requirements. Such a collection of similar yet well-distinguished variants of the same core product is frequently called a product family. Software product line engineering (SPLE) is an established methodology for handling the additional complexity caused by the increasing variability of modern (software) systems by means of variability-aware engineering and quality-assurance techniques. To this end, SPLE aims at systematically exploiting knowledge about commonality and variability among all kinds of engineering artefacts (e.g. design and test models, implementation code, and test cases) in a family of similar products.

Finally, modern software systems are, in most cases, an integral part of larger socio-technical systems, thus requiring accurate quality assurance to reduce the risk of fatal errors. Model-based testing is a widely used black-box testing technique for automated quality assurance, where a test model serves as a behavioural specification of the expected behaviour of the (potentially inaccessible) implementation code to be tested. For instance, the PPU behaviour is specified using statechart models, which can be used to automatically derive test cases covering a predefined set of test goals for systematically investigating the different runs of the PPU.

Although very promising concepts and tools exist in recent research for tackling all those three kinds of engineering challenges separately, a comprehensive approach integrating the different solutions into one conceptual framework is still an open issue. In particular, a corresponding round-trip engineering methodology has ensured an effective and efficient quality assurance of evolving, variant-rich software systems in a systematic and consistency-preserving way. To this end, a structured process for artefact co-evolution is required for all possible kinds of evolution scenarios of engineering- and quality-assurance artefacts involved.

Our vision is to define a comprehensive methodology for round-trip engineering and model-based testing of evolving, variant-rich software systems. To realize this vision, we first have to extract and integrate variant/version information in an automated way from evolving model-based product-line engineering and quality-assurance artefacts. Based on this additional information, we pursue to define criteria for detecting and avoiding inconsistencies between those different design-, implementation- and quality-analysis artefacts.

To achieve our goals, we have to address several challenges with respect to the three guiding themes of the SPP, namely *Knowledge Carrying Software*, *Methods and Processes*, and *Platforms and Environments for Evolution*. In particular, we address two essential challenges.

Challenge 5 How to automatically extract and integrate variant/version information in model-based SPL engineering and quality assurance?

Challenge 6 How to avoid inconsistencies in different design-, implementation- and quality-analysis artefacts?

By addressing these research questions, we contribute to the different guiding themes of the SPP in various ways.

3.4 Maintaining Performance

Performance is a key quality characteristic of software systems, describing its properties with respect to timeliness and resource usage. Typical performance measures include response times and throughput of a software system. Insufficient performance has a negative impact on the service quality of software systems, which in turn affect key business indicators such as revenue. Performance issues in enterprise applications and web services can limit employee productivity and cause customers to switch to other services. In production systems, insufficient performance can limit production output and may reduce the quality of products, harm employees, and damage facilities and products. Therefore, performance needs to be addressed throughout the entire software life cycle from development to operations via suitable performance analysis methods, techniques, and tools.

Researchers have developed a wide range of performance analysis methods in the past, which allow to assess single versions and variants of a software product. However, today's software is often highly configurable and evolves frequently. Different *versions* replace each other over time, while multiple *variants* co-exist at the same time. Especially in the context of product lines, which play an important role in production systems and handheld devices, variants can be numerous as all potential feature combinations must be evaluated separately. For example, different variants of the Pick-and-Place Unit (PPU) can be configured by choosing from the defined relationship of mandatory, optional, and alternative features, such as alternative cranes and stamps, as well as a set of supported workpieces. Furthermore, modern software is often developed with agile development methods and processes that create new versions for every feature, resulting in a high frequency of changes. For example, Common Component Modeling Example (CoCoME) includes a definition of design and runtime evolution scenarios such as the addition of new features or platform migrations based on changing requirements and runtime reconfigurations. Therefore, the number of versions and variants, as well as the different and evolving types of artefacts (models, code, measurements, etc.) pose challenges on performance analysis strategies.

Our vision is to address the performance of variants and versions in an efficient way throughout the software life cycle. This supports software engineers and administrators as they can predict software performance at design time and evaluate it at runtime.

Performance is influenced by design, configuration, implementation and deployment. Therefore, performance analysis must be part of the design process. At runtime, the effects of these influence factors become apparent and allow to further understand their performance impact. We envision to use knowledge derived from runtime observations to enrich and improve performance assessments.

Performance evaluation of potential variants is excessively time consuming, for example the PPU feature tree allows for X variants, which limits the ability to apply performance prediction approaches. However, performance is a key element also in software product lines. Our vision is to reduce the necessary effort through a smart selection of variants, modularization, reuse and knowledge gained during runtime of previous versions of the variants.

Our goal is to provide continuous support for addressing performance concerns for versions and variants via respective performance analysis strategies. They must be able to provide answers to performance questions by engineers in a timely manner.

Variants can comprise minor deviation from each other or result in very different software systems. Each difference in the architecture can influence the performance of a component, as the communication changes between components. Unfortunately, to test and evaluate every potential variant is time consuming and impede development due to long evaluation cycles. In Chap. 8, we want to address this challenge.

Challenge 7 How to efficiently analyse the performance of all variants of a software system?

While variants are different software assemblies that exist in parallel, versions reflect differences over time as the software evolves. During the evolution, engineers need to address performance either due to current performance issues that they have to solve or in order to fulfil performance requirements in the future. This leads us to the challenge.

Challenge 8 How to exploit evolving artefacts for the performance analyses of software throughout its life cycle?

3.5 Maintaining Security

The security of software systems is a highly important quality aspect. This is motivated by the fact that today an increasing amount of personal data are handled by software. A vast amount of people not affiliated with security or inner workings of information technology (IT) is trusting that the data are processed securely.

In detail, in many cases this means compliance with the most common security requirements like integrity, authenticity, availability, and privacy.

Moreover, an increasing amount of systems exist that tend to collect data of a whole human life span and/or collect data throughout the day. For example, cloud storage services like Dropbox can store not only a theoretically unlimited amount of data but also an unlimited amount of revisions. Social networks like Facebook are able to record a whole life. Smartphones or smartwatches are with us the whole day and continuously mine data through quite a few sensors and also pre-analyse data like determine a person's position by combining GPS data, names of available Wi-Fi spots, and assigned IP addresses.

On top of that, a growing number of information processing, mostly Internet-connected systems, is pervading our daily lives, like most *smart* or *IoT* devices, such as smart light bulbs, smart light switches, or simply smart speakers/assistants like Google Home or Amazon Echo. There are hardly any instances where these systems do not rely on servers or services that are Internet based. In a world of interconnected systems, your system is also connected to an unpredictable number of attackers.

There actually is a big number of systems that were developed or deployed a long time ago, and there will be even more in the future. As a result, data that pervades all of our lives is in the hands of an opaque mesh of systems connected through the Internet. And even if one person wants to avoid her data being stored in such services, it is a desperate situation when her friends store, for example, photos or other personal data in their cloud services.

Today we must experience that current systems fail to keep their promise. Hacks, vulnerabilities, and data breaches had already happened in a magnitude that has never been seen before. Examples are Heartbleed (OpenSSL), Krack (WPA2), 68 million password hack (Dropbox), PlayStation network hack (77 million customer data), and the CPU bugs leading to the Spectre/Meltdown attacks that affect nearly every processor in end-user systems rolled out since 1995.

The vision is to incorporate security relevant knowledge accompanying the ordinary system design. Ordinary system development runs through different levels of abstractions, and so there are possibilities for wrong decisions at early development stages. Especially caused by the fact that most systems tend to be interconnected and new attacks come up rapidly, not only system development should be accompanied in early stages like design decisions but also the system's context needs to be touched, like current security knowledge and knowledge about attacks and mitigations.

To achieve this goal, knowledge needs to be gathered (semi-)automatically. The knowledge must include new attacks (or new attack vectors), mitigations, precautions, and best practices relevant for a given system and domain. Even when a *secure system design* has been obtained, the runtime behaviour of the system is also important. On the one hand, there is a number of security requirements that cannot be checked fully at design time, at least when they rely on runtime data, for example consider a deployment context or access-control-related user data. On the other hand, as argued before, there might be a high risk that a system with an initially secure design is attacked during runtime using an unforeseen attack. In this case, one might want to detect this via anomaly detection techniques. At least, one might want to react at runtime by adapting a system. To reach this goal, continuous monitoring of the system seems inevitable. The result shall be detection of unwanted behaviour regarding the security design and also adapting the system to mitigate threats.

Challenge 9 How can security knowledge, available via diverse non-formal sources, be incorporated and utilized for a long-living system design?

Challenge 10 How can developers and security experts be supported to react to context evolution, which may compromise the system's security design or compromise the system at runtime?

3.6 Learning from Evolution for Evolution

Learning is the process of changing one's behaviour through knowledge acquisition. New knowledge is generated during both the *design and construction phase* and the *operation phase* of a long-living software system. Making this knowledge accessible in *Knowledge Carrying Software* is one of the guiding themes of the priority programme. Knowledge can be learned and applied through the whole evolution cycle. But much knowledge is either implicit and never documented or missing completely.

There are multiple reasons for this; for example, tight time and cost restrictions can prevent software engineers from creating documentation in the first place. Bad requirements engineering practices can also lead to this outcome. Furthermore, creating formal documentation, for example in the form of models, is a complex task that might be perceived as tedious and cumbersome. Creating this kind of formal documentation also requires a high level of expertise. Documentation might also be wrong or become out of date. Oftentimes tests are also used to ensure correctness of software and to document it, but for practical reasons tests cannot cover the entire behaviour of a system. Thus, knowledge is often not documented and scarcely available.

Missing knowledge about the system and its environment greatly hampers the evolution of long-living software systems. Reasons for this are that detailed knowledge of a software system is an essential prerequisite for an effective software evolution and for ensuring the correctness of a software system.

Our vision is to semi-automate the learning of knowledge and its application for the evolution of model-based long-living software systems. We can then use this knowledge to support software engineers who would not otherwise have access to this knowledge. This support comes in the form of ensuring correctness and recommendations about future evolutions, as well as assessing the effort required for changes. For this we need to identify evolutions in the past and present, assess their impact on the systems, and use the gained knowledge to derive future evolutions, for the same system or different systems. Our automatically extracted knowledge will enable the development off *Knowledge Carrying Software*. This extracted knowledge can be about past evolutions or about the current behaviour of the system, for example in the form of automatically learned behavioural models. Our results will be implemented in software tools that can be used as *Platforms and Environments* for evolution. One example is the SiLift tool (cf. Sect. 10.1.1) for identifying historical evolution steps, which is the foundation for other software tools in this chapter.

Our goal is to automatically create knowledge about a system or its past evolutions. This knowledge shall then be used to support future evolutions of that system or similar systems. Knowledge about past evolutions is contained in artefacts stored in software repositories. These past evolutions need to be extracted and then processed so that the engineer can readily use this knowledge. Similarly, knowledge about the current system might be derived from the actual running system, for example to create models about a system's functional or non-functional behaviour. The derived knowledge shall then be utilized by recommending, selecting, or deriving evolutions of the system or similar systems such that those systems correctly realize changed functional requirements or improve their non-functional behaviour due to the evolution.

Realizing those goals poses several challenges. We group these challenges into those concerning the analysis of *past* and *future* evolutions.

Challenge 11 How to identify and process semantically rich changes from past software evolutions?

Past changes in model-based systems come in the form of models under version control (e.g. git). These models and their versions can be numerous and describe the system under different viewpoints. However, simple graph differences on the abstract syntax level are too fine-grained and lack the semantics of changes on higher level representations. Consequently, the first challenge is to identify past software evolutions by computing and grouping the corresponding model differences and give those evolutions semantics on the modelling language level.

Those semantically rich software evolutions can then be used to drive future software evolutions—leading us to the second challenge.

Challenge 12 How to exploit past software evolutions to improve future software evolutions?

This second challenge has multiple variants. One variant is related to the co-evolution of different viewpoint models of the system. Here, a system can exploit past evolutions to recommend co-evolutions of viewpoints if a user changes a single viewpoint.

Another variant is to use knowledge about past evolutions to establish a knowledge-carrying network. This network could exchange experiences of past evolutions between similar systems characterized by their behaviour and context and use this knowledge to support the engineer in evolving systems. A final variant addresses maintainability of long-living systems. Here, knowledge about past evolutions could be used to estimate the maintainability of information systems and automated production systems.

3.7 Maintaining Correctness

Evolution is usually driven by the need to change a particular part of the system, for example in order to repair a malfunction or to add or improve features. The challenge is to ensure that other aspects of the system that are not targeted by the change are not modified. Unfortunately, system evolution might invalidate properties a system had achieved before and is a threat to the system's safety, security, performance, maintainability, and other system properties. In particular, evolution may threaten the trust that an earlier version of the system has gained in earlier testing phases or by formal verification. Also, if a system has run flawlessly for a decade, this generates some amount of (informal) trust in the correctness of the system.

The goal of *formal verification* within the context of software evolution is to prove that system properties are not lost due to introduced changes. The properties to be maintained can either be formulated explicitly as formal specification (or modelling) artefacts, or they can be present implicitly in form of the code that drives the existing system.

Knowledge about the system is present both in specification artefacts and in the code of the program run on the system. If formal verification is able to prove that a new revision also has these explicit or implicit properties in the code, then verification serves as a preservation means for the trust into systems - and management of knowledge. The task for the formal analysis of a system evolution step can be partitioned into two disjoint sub tasks:

1. *Analysis of system aspects that are intended to be retained.*
   This analysis is used to establish that defined parts of the system behave as before the change in defined cases. It transfers all properties of the retained part of the system behaviour onto the new revision without requiring to explicitly state them.
2. *Analysis of system aspects that are intended to be changed.*
   Almost every evolution step (if it is not a pure software refactoring) contains an intentional change for some part of the observable behaviour. The above analysis does not help in this case; we cannot (solely) rely on the old revision as specification for the intended behaviour after the evolution step, but we need to specify the intended properties of the system explicitly.

Both aspects of formal verification for evolving systems are challenging in themselves, and it is interesting to observe how they can accompany an evolutionary process spanning over evolutionary steps.

It is important to observe that for the analysis of automated production systems, these cannot be reduced to their software alone—instead, it is imperative that models of the contextual hardware are taken into consideration as well: Interdisciplinary modelling is important to make the context and environment part of the verified system. In Chap. 11, we focus on the preservation of safety properties throughout the evolution of automated production systems. Similar techniques for proving the preservation of properties are in principle also thinkable for security, performance, or other properties—but have not been investigated within this programme. The aspects of embedding formal evolution analyses into a user-friendly development process is outlined in Sect. 10.2.

We envision a software evolution process that is naturally and fully accompanied by (automatic) formal verification steps, thus guaranteeing that desired system properties are always maintained during evolution. The engineers responsible for designing and implementing an evolution step will be provided with expressive and usable specification languages with which they can specify which parts of the systems should remain untouched and which parts should expose a different behaviour. These specification techniques allow the engineer to specify desired behaviour both incrementally (as differences to behaviour of the earlier version) and interdisciplinary (concerning not only the software but also the context and the hardware). While a formal verification is the more far-reaching goal, the obtained specification artefacts can also serve as oracles for testing as a more conventional technique of verification.

To realise this vision, appropriate specification languages and techniques and according verification techniques are required that enable the application of formal verification within the evolutionary process. The first goal is therefore to provide the right specification and verification techniques for a formal verification for evolution. The specification techniques must allow for a multi-disciplinary approach going beyond the software and comprising also the hardware and must take special needs of the applications into account. They must also operate incrementally. The corresponding automatic verification techniques must be powerful enough to discharge typical verification conditions within reasonable time and fully automatically.

The two research questions for this research field arise naturally from the partitioning of the analysis tasks described earlier in this section. They correspond to the duality of the nature of an evolution step requiring that some chosen system properties are retained while others may change (in a chosen fashion).

Challenge 13 How to model, specify, and verify that a system retains desired behaviour during evolution?

Challenge 14 How to model, specify, and verify intentionally changed behaviour during system evolution?

Chapter 4
Introduction to Case Studies

Safa Bougouffa, Kiana Busch, Robert Heinrich, Christopher Haubeck, Suhyun Cha, Ralf Reussner, and Birgit Vogel-Heuser

This chapter introduces the case studies used in the DFG Priority Programme *Design For Future – Managed Software Evolution* (SPP 1593). Section 4.1 gives an overview of evolution in information systems and automated production systems. An open community case study for software architecture modelling and evolution, the Common Component Modeling Example, is introduced in Sect. 4.2. An open demonstrator for automated production systems, the Pick and Place Unit (PPU) and its extension (xPPU), is introduced in Sect. 4.3. Finally, both case studies are integrated as Industry 4.0 demonstrator and introduced in Sect. 4.4.

4.1 Evolution of Long-Living Systems to an Industry 4.0 Case Study

Many industrial information systems are operated over decades. During operation, they face various modifications, for example due to emerging requirements, bug fixes, and environmental changes, such as legal constraints or technology stack updates. In consequence, the systems change and evolve continually.

S. Bougouffa (✉) · S. Cha · B. Vogel-Heuser
Technische Universität München, Lehrstuhl für Automatisierung und Informationssysteme, Garching, Germany
e-mail: safa.bougouffa@tum.de; suhyun.cha@tum.de; vogel-heuser@tum.de

K. Busch · R. Heinrich (✉) · R. Reussner
Institute for Program Structures and Data Organization, Karlsruhe Institute of Technology (KIT), Karlsruhe, Germany
e-mail: kiana.busch@kit.edu; robert.heinrich@kit.edu; reussner@kit.edu

C. Haubeck
Universität Hamburg, MIN-Fakultät, Fachbereich Informatik, Hamburg, Germany
e-mail: haubeck@informatik.uni-hamburg.de

R. Reussner et al. (eds.), *Managed Software Evolution*,
https://doi.org/10.1007/978-3-030-13499-0_4

Supporting software evolution is a competitive advantage in software engineering. A variety of methods aim at supporting different aspects of software evolution. However, it is hard to assess their effectiveness and to compare them due to divergent characteristics [Hei+15a]. Empirical research in terms of case studies and controlled experiments is useful to validate these methods. However, empirical studies on software evolution are rarely comprehensive.

To study evolution comprehensively, we believe it is important to collaborate by joint research. Joint research supports sharing of knowledge and resources [SDJ07]. In particular, this allows replicating studies, which in general is important to confirm and to strengthen the results of empirical research [JG12] and thus enhance evidence. Our goal is to support joint research by collaboration and replication in empirical studies based on common evolution scenarios and artefacts. Currently, empirical studies on software evolution are seldom comparable as they vary in analysed subjects and execution process. Furthermore, these studies are rarely reusable as important artefacts (e.g. requirements, design decisions, architectural knowledge, or context knowledge) are often not provided to the community. A common basis for study collaboration and replication is missing. To overcome these shortcomings in the SPP1593, two case studies are used: the Common Component Modeling Example (CoCoME) as a community case study for software architecture modelling and evolution and the Pick and Place Unit (PPU) and its extension (xPPU) as a community case study for automated production systems' evolution. CoCoME represents a knowledge base for collaborative empirical research on information system evolution [Hei+15a]. The knowledge base for the evaluation process can be exploited and extended by researchers with different backgrounds and research interests. It provides assistance on diverse characteristics that are important for software evolution, like artefacts in different revisions, comprehensive evolution scenarios, and coverage of different life-cycle phases (development-level evolution and operation-level adaptation). The xPPU represents a lab-size demonstrator for investigating research on evolution in machine and plant automation [LFV13]. The original PPU featuring 13 evolution scenarios is limited in size and complexity, but it has been extended with its functionality, together with the additional structure with over 10 evolution scenarios. Different evolution scenarios are provided [LFV13] to demonstrate its various change reasons, for example changing requirements, fixing of failures, and unanticipated situations on site. The xPPU evolution scenarios are provided to meet research requirements of the community, together with their artefacts such as system architecture, models, runtime data and code.

The community case studies aim at providing several benefits to researchers:

- By building upon existing specifications and settings, less effort in scenario definition, study setup, and execution is required.
- A common case study increases the comparability of evaluation results with those of other researchers and leads to increased evaluation confidence.
- A common case study also increases community acceptance by interaction with other researchers.

Unlike information systems, automated Production Systems (aPS) consist of artefacts of multi-disciplines and are all closely interwoven; the software for an aPS is strongly influenced by the hardware, which is implemented by mechanical and electrical/electronic components. Usually the complexity of the software and the system itself is very high; therefore, it is not obvious how a change in one discipline is affecting the software, context or platform of the system. [Jäg+11] even though maintainability is an important aspect for a long-living system.

The three disciplines involved in aPS are regarded as three different aspects of context, platform, and software [Leg+14]. Context includes the mechanical aspects of the system, such as pure mechanical components, sensors, and actuators. Platform represents electric/electronic aspects, which manage signal flows from or to the interfaces of the Programmable Logic Controller (PLC). Software reflects software engineering aspects, which consist of data-processing functions using the flow-in information to generate the flow-out information. The software of the aPS has been implemented in IEC 61131-3 [Int09], to be run on PLCs.

Modularity, which is one of the key aspects to enable evolution of software-intensive systems [PCW84], is still rarely fully applied in aPS [Vog+17b]. Moreover, fundamental methods such as variability modelling and tracing, which enable software evolution, are still limited to the software domain of the cyber-physical systems. However, aPS impose special requirements on the development and maintenance process. For instance, mechatronic components are designed to function for several years. However, it is predictable that their development and maintenance will change over their utility lifetime. To allow for later adaptions to the functionality of these components, suitable means should be considered during the development. As software can be adapted more easily than mechanical or electrical parts, changing the control software of aPS may solve adaption requirements. However, these changes may result in code smells, as they are usually conducted quickly on site by technicians.

aPS are supposed to operate for decades. During operation, they are ageing. For instance, as a result of physical effects like wear, tear, and corrosion, life expectations of mechanical components are affected. These components have to be maintained after some years, known as re-engineering and modernisation (cp. Fig. 4.1). There are other reasons for ageing such as changing requirements and system specifications, market requirements, new technologies or legal requirements. Many of those changes can be realised by adapting the control software, which is done more frequent and even during runtime.

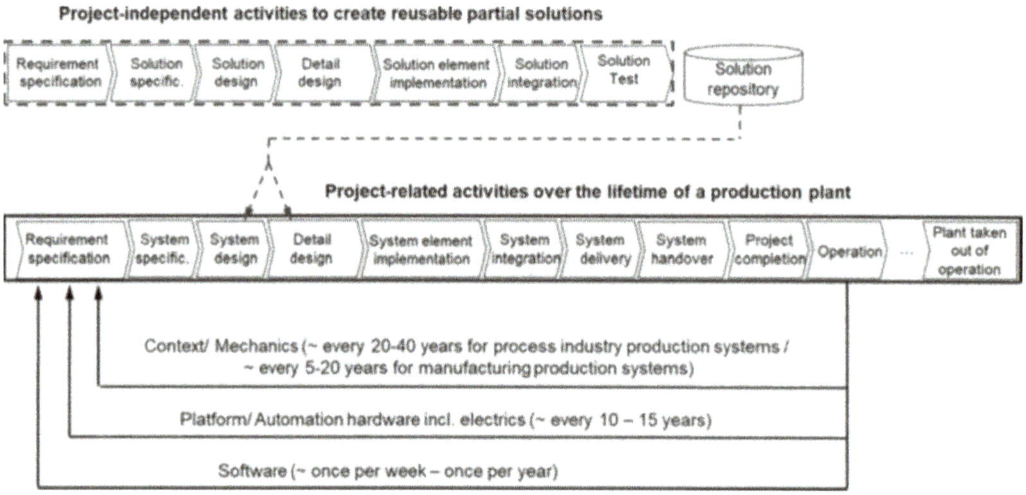

Fig. 4.1 V-Model XT integrated into the life cycle of different disciplines in aPS distinguishing between project-independent activities (top) and project-related activities (bottom) [Vog+15c]

<table>
<tr><th colspan="2">Scenario category: / Causal Order of changes and change criteria</th><th>Ia</th><th>Ib</th><th>Ic</th><th>Id</th><th>IIa</th><th>IIb</th><th>IIc</th><th>III</th><th>IVa</th><th>IVb</th><th>IVc</th><th>Va</th><th>Vb</th><th>Vc</th><th>Vd</th><th>VIa</th><th>VIb</th><th>VIc</th></tr>
<tr><td colspan="2">PPU scenario (cp. Table 2)</td><td>Sc11, Sc12 (*)</td><td>Sc12d (#)</td><td>Sc1 (*)</td><td>Sc12c (#)</td><td>Sc13 (*)</td><td>Sc1 (*)</td><td>Sc2, 4.4b, 6 (*)</td><td>Sc6 (*)</td><td>Sc4b (*)</td><td>Sc1 (*)</td><td>Sc12c (#)</td><td>Sc11, Sc12</td><td>Sc12d (#)</td><td>Sc1 (*)</td><td>Sc12c (#)</td><td>Sc13 (*)</td><td>Sc1 (*)</td><td>Sc12c (#)</td></tr>
<tr><td colspan="2">(a) Requirements of the plant's management (informal)</td><td colspan="11">1.</td><td colspan="7">unchanged</td></tr>
<tr><td colspan="2">(b) Semi-formal system requirements specification (SRS)</td><td colspan="7">2.</td><td colspan="11">omitted</td></tr>
<tr><td rowspan="3">Arti-fact</td><td>(c) Software of the aPS</td><td>3.</td><td></td><td></td><td></td><td colspan="3">4.</td><td rowspan="3">2.</td><td colspan="3">3.</td><td>1.</td><td></td><td></td><td></td><td colspan="3">2.</td></tr>
<tr><td>(d) electrical parts of the aPS</td><td></td><td>3.</td><td></td><td rowspan="2">3.</td><td>3.</td><td></td><td rowspan="2">3.</td><td>2.</td><td></td><td rowspan="2">2.</td><td></td><td>1.</td><td></td><td rowspan="2">1.</td><td>1.</td><td></td><td>1.</td></tr>
<tr><td>(e) mechanical parts of the aPS</td><td></td><td></td><td>3.</td><td></td><td>3.</td><td></td><td>2.</td><td></td><td></td><td>1.</td><td></td><td>1.</td><td></td></tr>
<tr><td colspan="2">Anticipation of Change (Buckley et al., 2005)</td><td colspan="7">yes</td><td colspan="11">no</td></tr>
<tr><td colspan="2">Time of change</td><td colspan="7">offline</td><td colspan="11">online</td></tr>
</table>

Fig. 4.2 Categories of evolution scenarios with references to PPU case study examples in Section 3 [Vog+15c]

Evolution of aPS can be initiated by different reasons for change, which can affect the software, mechanical, and/or electrical and electronic parts. A classification of evolution was introduced in [Vog+15c], which distinguishes causal orders of change by which the aPS is affected (see Fig. 4.2). The evolution categories can be related to the history of change and anticipation of change [Buc+05, KVF04]. Anticipated changes include changes during the development of the system and also during operation in case of a model-based approach (i.e. offline changes). Moreover, changes during commissioning and operation are categorised as unanticipated changes (i.e. online changes), as they are implemented directly in the aPS during runtime.

In order to blur the boundaries between pure information systems and automated production systems, recent trends in industrial digitalization, known as Industry 4.0, were established. According to Vogel-Heuser et al. [Vog+15c], the proportion of software in automated production systems is increasing and the demand for highly customizable production systems will require higher involvement of multiple engineering disciplines. Consequently, research demonstrators in Industry 4.0 are required to study evolution cycles in these heterogeneous environments.

There exist demonstrator systems for Industry 4.0 environments targeting specific problems where the automation aspect is dominant [VH16]. The software systems interacting with the physical parts of these prototypes do not comprehend the complexity of information system in real-world scenarios. Additionally, a community case study is supposed to be a standardised or at least widely used reference for projects with the same research topics. This requires a demonstrator that not only is easily accessible and expendable but also comprehends the most significant aspects of evolution in Industry 4.0 scenarios. Therefore, both case studiesCoCoME and xPPU are integrated as Industry 4.0 case study.

4.2 Introduction of the CoCoME Case Study

CoCoME represents a trading system as it can be observed in a supermarket chain handling sales. This includes processing sales at a single store of the chain, like scanning products or paying, as well as enterprise-wide administrative tasks, like inventory management or reporting. Each store of the CoCoME supermarket chain contains several cash desks, whereas the set of cash desks is called cash desk line (visualised by the dashed line) (Fig. 4.3). The cash desk is the place where the

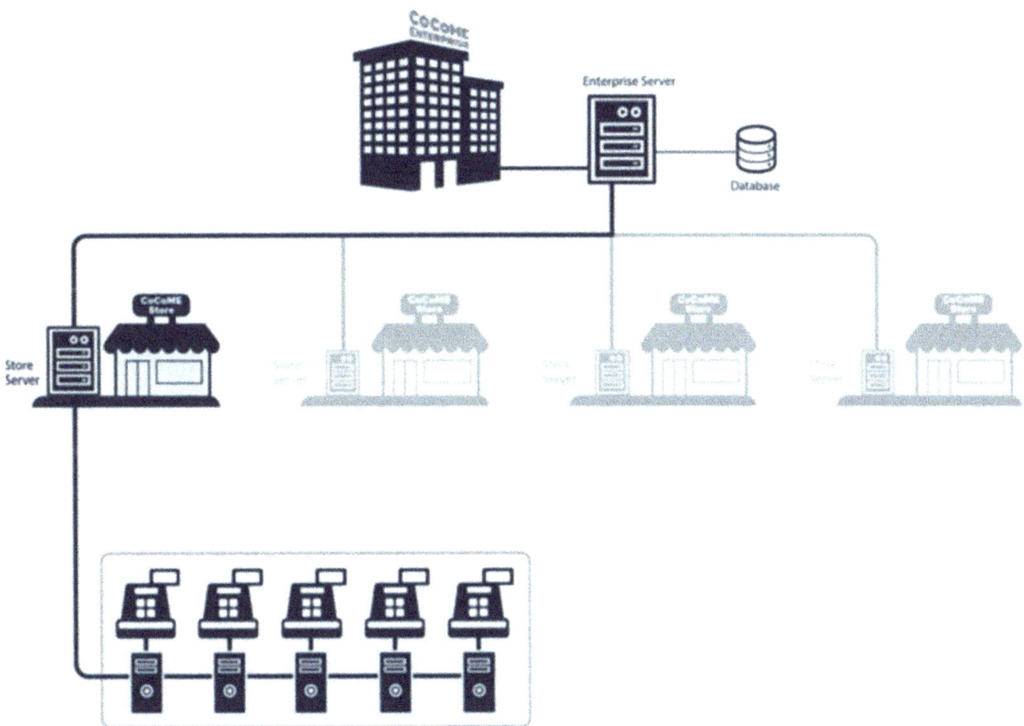

Fig. 4.3 Overview of the CoCoME structure

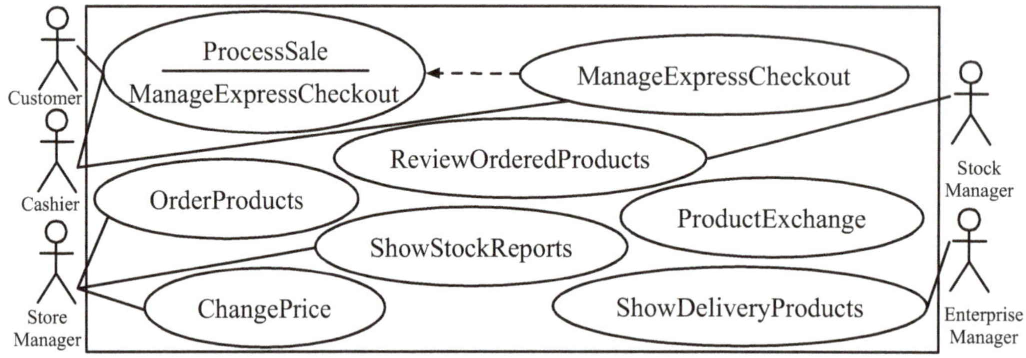

Fig. 4.4 Basic use cases of CoCoME [Her+08b]

cashier scans the goods that a customer wants to buy. The central unit of each cash desk is the cash desk PC. The cash desk line is connected to a store server. A set of stores is organised in the CoCoME enterprise where an enterprise server exists to which all stores are connected.

A detailed description of the basic use cases supported by CoCoME is given in [Her+08b]. In the *ProcessSale* use case, the cashier detects the products that a customer wants to buy and payment is performed at the cash desk (Fig. 4.4). If the conditions for express checkout [Her+08b] are fulfilled, a cash desk automatically switches to express mode in the *ManageExpressCheckout* use case. Product items can be ordered by the store manager in the *OrderProducts* use case. In the *ReceiveOrderedProducts* use case, products that arrive at the store are checked and inventoried by the stock manager. The store manager generates stock-related reports in the *ShowStockReport* use case. The *ShowDeliveryReports* use case provides the mean times a delivery from each supplier to a considered enterprise takes to the enterprise manager. The store manager can change the sales price of a product in the *ChangePrice* use case. In the *ProductExchange* use case, products are shipped from one store to another if a store runs out of a certain product. In this use case, no human actor is involved. Only the system is involved.

CoCoME uses Java SE in combination with Java Database Connectivity (JDBC), Java Persistence API (JPA), and Java Message Service (JMS) (Fig. 4.5). JMS is used to provide a way for communication between the components. The main component is the TradingSystem component. It consists of the TradingSystem::CashDeskLine component and the TradingSystem::Inventory component. The TradingSystem::CashDeskLine in turn consists of several CashDesk components representing the physical cash desks in a store with their corresponding components like the CashBox, BarcodeScanner, and CardReader. There is one Coordinator component per store, which receives sales events from the cash desks and changes the express mode state if needed. The TradingSystem::Inventory consists of the Console component, which provides a user interface for store-related operations through its Store component. The Console::Reporting component provides the user interface to retrieve enterprise or store reports. The central component of the TradingSystem::Inventory is the Application component. It provides the cash desk

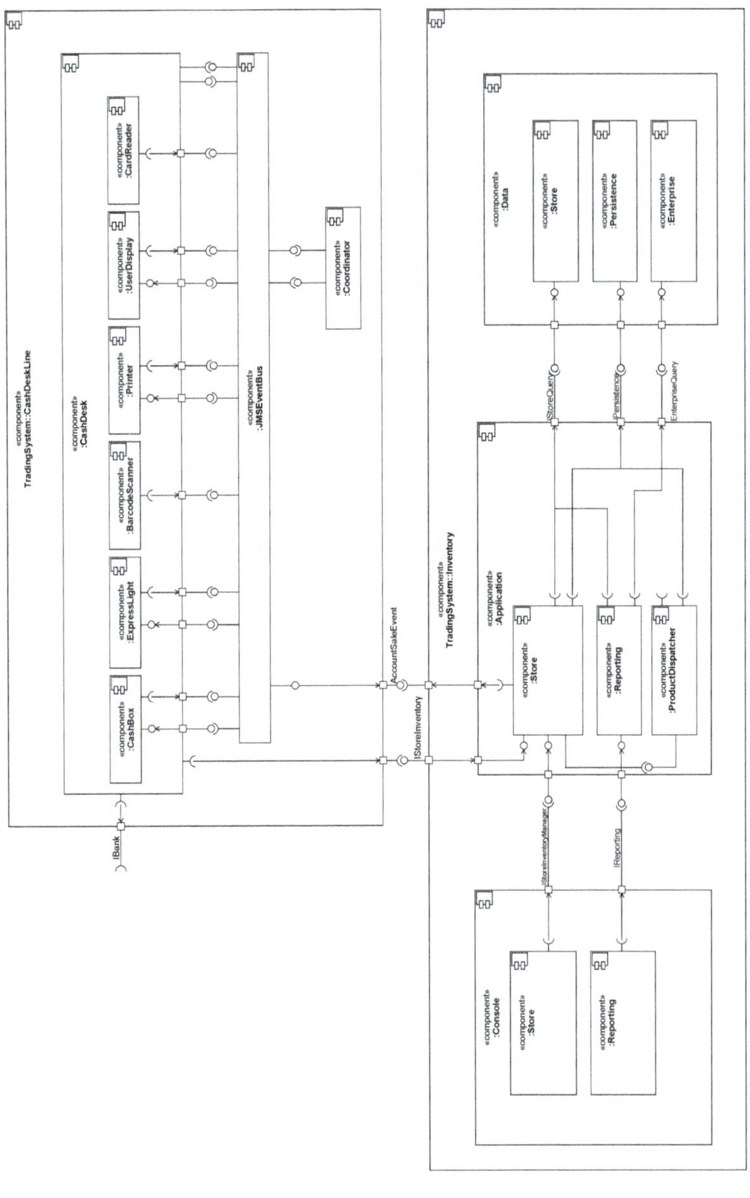

Fig. 4.5 Initial software architecture of CoCoME [HRR16]

and the store user interface and the operations to retrieve data and to book sales. The data are transferred in the form of Transfer Objects to provide an abstraction layer between the database and the other components. To retrieve the reporting information for the presentation layer, the Application::Reporting component provides the needed interface. There is also a ProductDispatcher component available to dispatch needed stocks from one store to another if necessary. A connection to the underlying database is realised by the Data component, which relies on JDBC and JPA to persist and retrieve data. It is divided into three sub-components, Store, Enterprise, and Persistence. The Store and Enterprise components are only used to query store or enterprise data, whereas the Persistence component writes objects to the database.

A detailed description of the initial requirements, architecture, and system behaviour in form of sequence diagrams is given in [Her+08b]. In the course of the DFG Priority Programme 1593, CoCoME faces changes by various evolution scenarios. Detailed description of changes to requirements, architecture, and system behaviour is given in [HRR16].

Since CoCoME has been applied and evolved successfully in various research projects, like SLA@SOI and Q-Impress funded by the European research council, several variants exist that span different platforms and technologies. Furthermore, various development artefacts are available, such as requirement specification or design documentation, that changed over time. CoCoME is well suited to serve as a study subject because the supermarket context is commonly comprehensible and the complexity of the system is appropriate. As CoCoME is a distributed system, several quality properties are affected by evolution.

In SPP 1593, a hybrid cloud-based variant of CoCoME has been developed based on the initial CoCoME specification [Her+08b] by implementing various evolution scenarios. The frontend of the hybrid cloud-based variant of CoCoME uses Java Server Faces (JSF) to implement the user interface (Fig. 4.6). In the WebFrontend::UseCases component, the presentation logic is implemented, which uses the components in the TradingSystem component to store the data retrieved from the ServiceAdapter. The ServiceAdapter component defines and implements an interface for database access and internally uses JDBC and JPA to access the underlying database. To query the database, the ServiceAdapter provides a Representational State Transfer (REST) style interface over Hypertext Transfer Protocol (HTTP).

Additional abstraction layers are introduced for the communication between the presentation layer and the business logic. These layers are located in the WebService component. The inner structure of the TradingSystem was nearly left unchanged. One exception is the event bus. Instead of the JMS event bus, the Context and Dependency Injection (CDI) event bus is used. Another change is that the components in Data now use the ServiceAdapter instead of the database directly. This allows for more flexibility in the cloud context. The newly introduced WebService::CashDesk component provides the frontend with a way to access the cash desk components. It is designed as a wrapper around the business logic so the method of accessing the business logic can be exchanged just by exchanging the wrapper classes. This is also the purpose of the WebService::Inventory component.

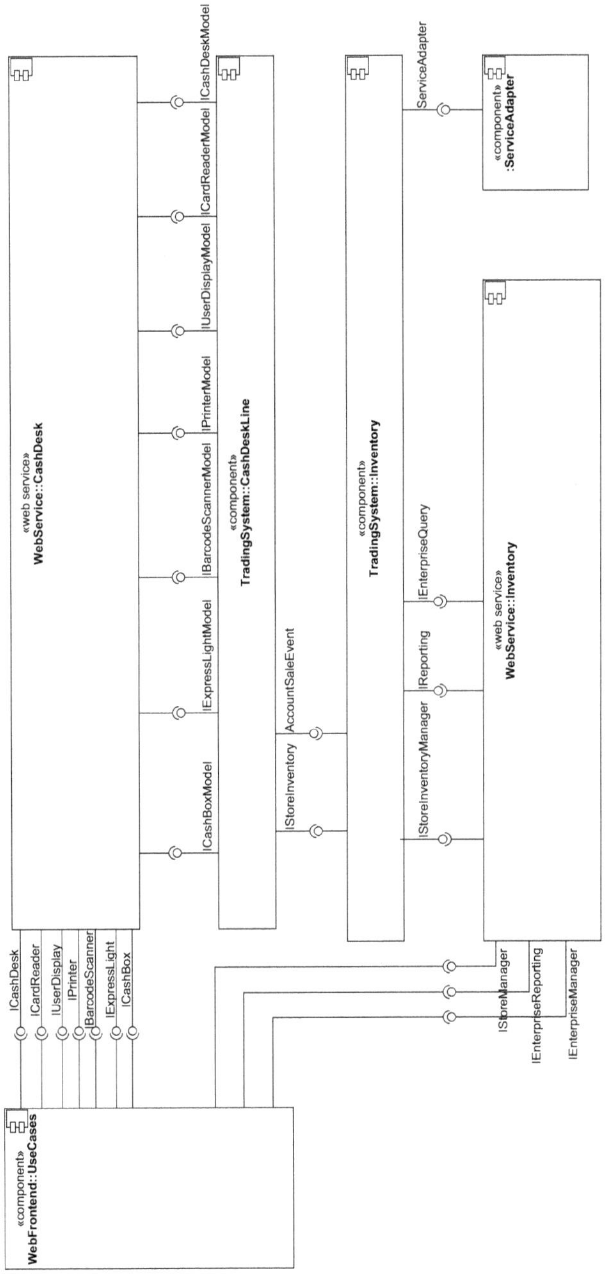

Fig. 4.6 Architecture overview of the hybrid cloud-based variant of CoCoME (coarse structure) [HRR16]

The WebService::Inventory contains the Enterprise component to enable the frontend to access enterprise-related information. This is necessary to enable several tasks needed for database administration like the listing of all stores in a specific enterprise. Design details are given in the technical reports [HRR16] and [HKR18].

We specified and implemented distinct evolution scenarios covering the categories adaptive and perfective evolution. Corrective evolution is not considered in the scenarios as this merely refers to fixing design or implementation issues. An adaptive evolution of the hybrid cloud-based variant of CoCoME is reflected in the scenarios Platform Migration, Microservice Architecture and Container Virtualization due to evolving technology. Perfective evolution is represented in the scenarios Adding a Pick-Up Shop, Adding a Mobile App and Adding Payment Methods by emerging user requirements. Furthermore, in order to accommodate the self-adaptiveness of modern software architectures, reconfiguration during system operation is addressed in the scenario Database Migration.

4.2.1 Platform Migration

The CoCoME enterprise must reduce operating costs of the resources and, therefore, migrates some resources to the cloud. The enterprise server and its connected database are now running in the cloud. The introduction of the cloud enables flexible adaptation and reconfiguration of the system. However, putting the system into the cloud causes new challenges regarding quality properties that must be considered in development and operation. For example, a look back in the recent past shows that privacy is one of the most important quality properties for cloud-based systems.

The evolution scenario Platform Migration transfers the initial variant of CoCoME to the hybrid cloud-based variant. As mentioned before, for the design of the hybrid cloud-based variant, additional abstraction layers are introduced for the communication between the presentation layer and the business logic. These layers are located in the WebService::CashDesk and WebService::Inventory components. The WebService::CashDesk component provides the frontend with a way to access the cash desk components. The WebService::Inventory component enables the frontend to access enterprise-related information. Wrappers are designed around the business logic, so the method of accessing the business logic can be exchanged just by exchanging the wrapper classes.

4.2.2 Adding a Pick-Up Shop

In this scenario, an online shop is added where the customers can order online and pick up the goods at a chosen store. This design-time modification includes adding new use cases and modifying existing design models.

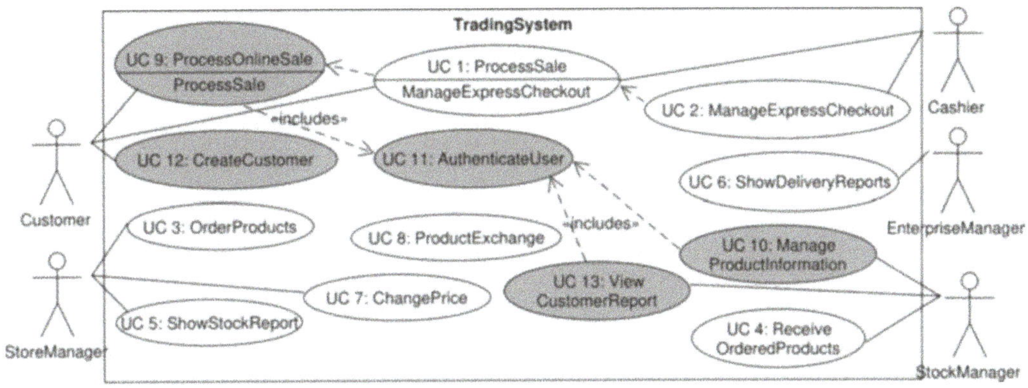

Fig. 4.7 Use cases of the pick-up shop [HRR16]

The CoCoME enterprise is in competition with online shop vendors (such as Amazon and Taobao). In order to increase its market share, the CoCoME enterprise management decides to offer a pick-up service for goods to address emerging customer requirements. The customers can order and pay online. The goods are delivered to a pick-up place (i.e. a store) of her/his choice. If the order has not been paid online, the goods have to be paid at the pick-up place (either per credit card or cash).

Existing use cases are extended, and new use cases are added to cover the pick-up shop's functionality (Fig. 4.7). In the *CreateCustomer* use case, a customer creates a new customer account for the pick-up shop. Users can be authenticated at the pick-up shop by the use case *AuthenticateUser*. The use case *ProcessOnlineSale* extends the existing use case *ProcessSale* by enabling a customer of the shop to select the products he/she wants to buy and to perform payment via credit card. Product information stored in the system can be changed by the stock manager in the *ManageProductInformation* use case.

For implementing the pick-up shop, the hybrid cloud-based variant had to be modified and extended to fit the needs arising from an online shop (Fig. 4.8). The first extension is to implement a service for customers to register and log in. This functionality requires the ServiceAdapter to store the login information and additional data like credit card data and the customer's preferred store in the data store.

The second modification is to include the services for the creation, modification, and authentication of customers into the business logic tier. To this end, the Inventory component is extended by a new UserManager component. This component implements the communication with the ServiceAdapter to retrieve, modify, or create the user and customer data.

The ShoppingCart component keeps track of all items that the customer wants to buy and is responsible for calculating the total price of these items. When the customer is done adding items to the ShoppingCart and proceeds, the sale is persisted by the CheckOut component.

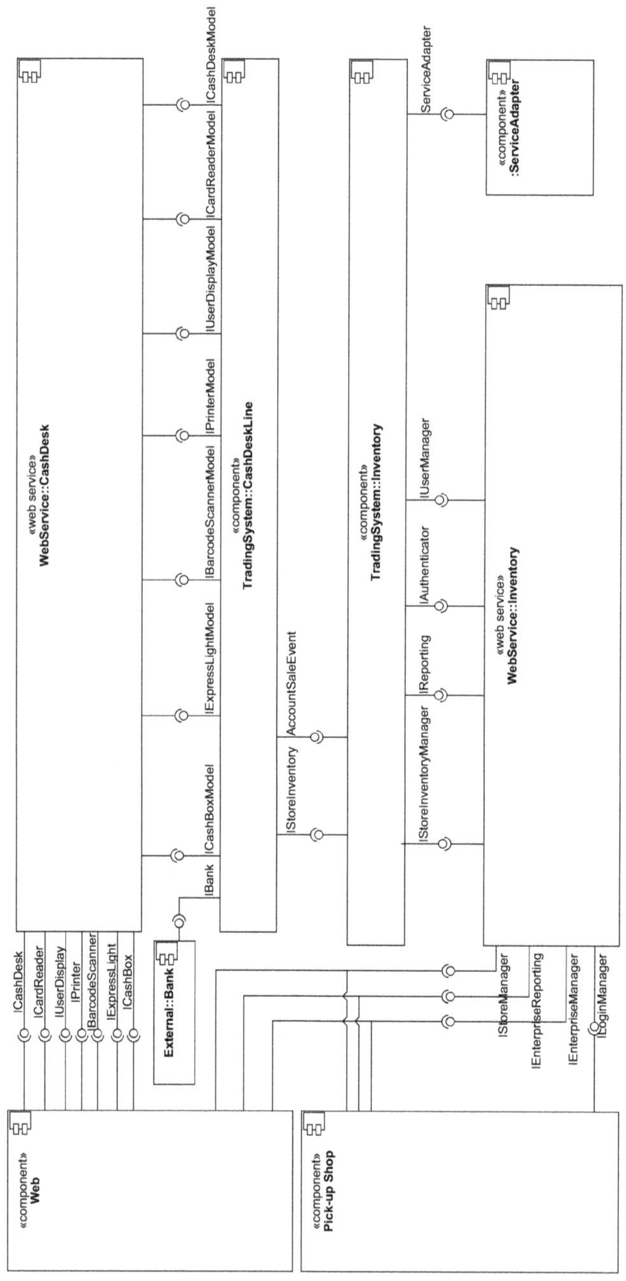

Fig. 4.8 Architecture overview with pick-up shop extension (coarse structure) [HRR16]

By introducing the pick-up shop as web application, the CoCoME system changes from a closed system (only employees can access but not the customers, and access depends on the location, e.g. a store) to an open system (all customers can accessed via the Internet). This raises certain consequences such that the number of users is not restricted any longer. Hence, various quality properties are affected, for example privacy, security, performance, and reliability.

4.2.3 Database Migration

After a while, the CoCoME enterprise starts a big advertisement campaign. Advertisements lead to an increased amount of sales. Thus, the performance of the system may suffer due to limited capacities of the cloud provider currently hosting the enterprise database. Migrating the database from one cloud provider to another may solve the scalability issues.

Especially in the cloud, the application usage, performance, pricing, and privacy are closely interrelated. The application usage impacts on the application's performance and pricing. Continuously appraised elasticity rules trigger the migration and replication of a cloud application's software components among geographically distributed data centers. Both migration and replication may lead to violation of privacy policies that prescribe certain geo-locations. Furthermore, a cloud application may also face performance/availability trade-offs as replication is often done for improving the system's overall availability, not just performance, which again might violate privacy policies.

This scenario represents a reconfiguration at runtime. Migrating the database may cause a privacy issue due to violations of privacy constraints. According to a privacy constraint[1] of the European Union (EU), sensitive data must not leave the EU. Since the CoCoME enterprise is located within the EU, its databases containing customer data must be hosted on data centers within the EU. This scenario is about the dynamic analysis of cloud applications at runtime to identify upcoming quality flaws. It includes model-based observation and prediction techniques in flexible environments.

4.2.4 Adding a Mobile App Client

In order to outperform its competitors and expand its market share, the CoCoME enterprise decides to offer a mobile app client. In this perfective evolution scenario, a mobile client is added where the customers can order through their mobile phones and pick up the goods at a chosen store. Figure 4.9 depicts the mod-

[1] http://eur-lex.europa.eu.

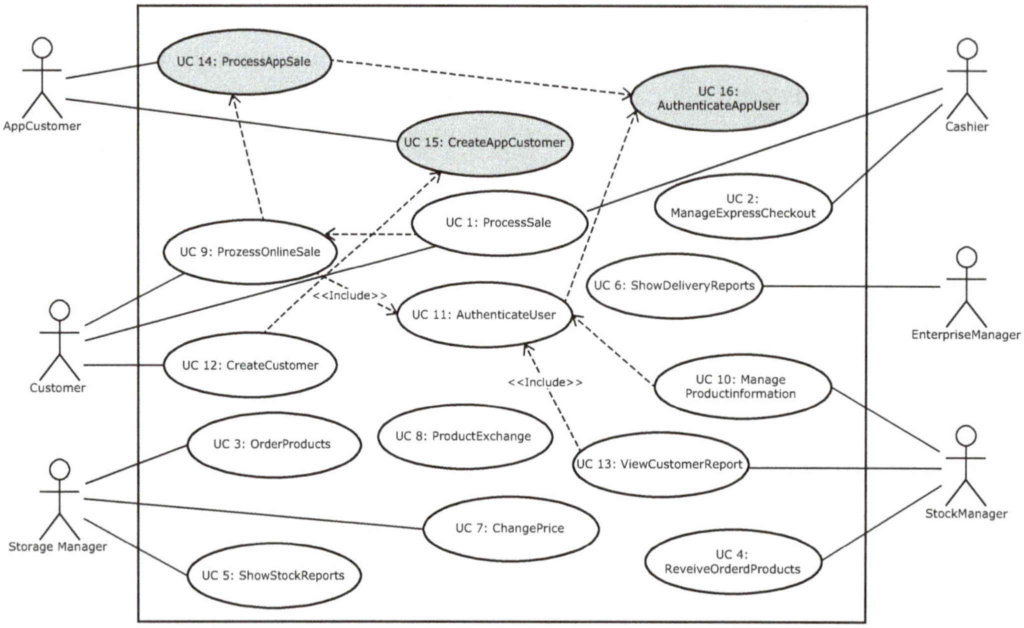

Fig. 4.9 Use cases of the mobile app [HKR18]

ifications regarding the use cases of CoCoME. In the *CreateAppCustomer* use case, a customer creates a new customer account for the mobile app. Customers can be authenticated on the app by the use case *AuthenticateAppUser*. The use case *ProcessAppSale* extends the existing use case *ProcessSale* by enabling the customer to buy products using a mobile app. This scenario introduces mobile communications to the CoCoME system, which may affect quality properties like privacy, security, performance, and reliability.

This design-time modification is based on the pick-up shop scenario but implements a mobile frontend (Fig. 4.10). The backend of CoCoME does not face any changes. An AppShopAdapter is introduced to bridge the technology gap between the web services of CoCoME and the technology used by the mobile app client. The AppShopAdapter consumes the three web services WebService::Inventory::LoginManager, WebService::Inventory::Store, and WebService::Inventory::Enterprise and provides a Rest API, which is used by the AppShop. The Rest API contains the service endpoints. Further design details are described in the technical report [HKR18].

4.2.5 Microservice Architecture

The architectural style of CoCoME is changed to microservices for reducing the coupling between the services of CoCoME and enable independent deployment, as well as reuse. In this adaptive evolution scenario, the functionality of CoCoME remains the same while changing the architectural paradigm of the system. This

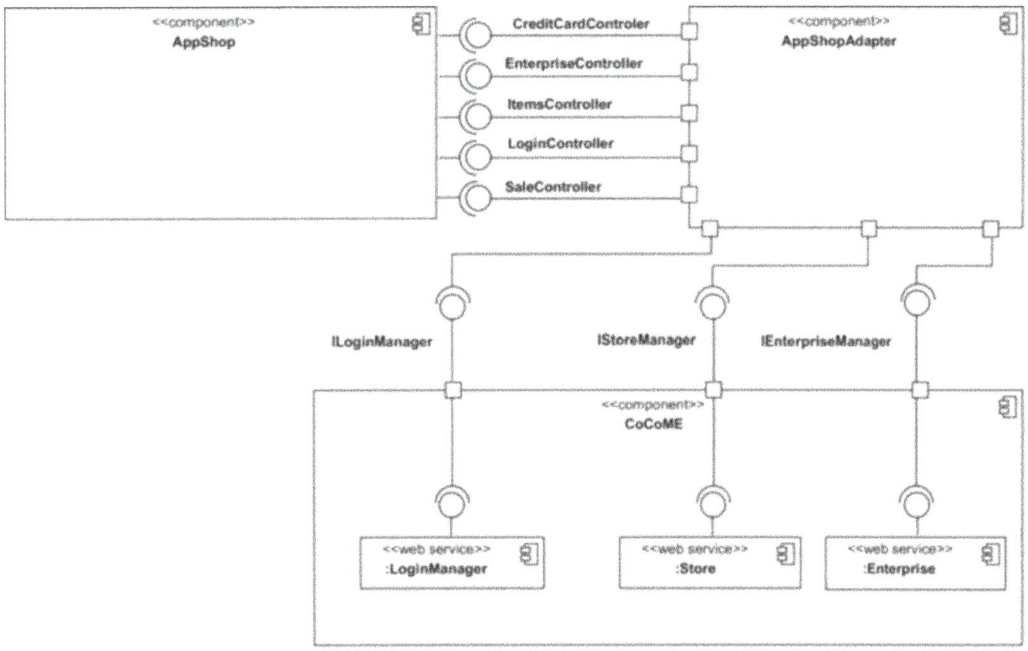

Fig. 4.10 Architecture overview with mobile app extension (coarse structure) [HKR18]

design-time modification introduces a collection of loosely coupled microservices where each microservice is internally structured in a layered fashion. Each microservice has its own graphical user interface (GUI) and business logic. Each microservice, except for Reports, has its own database. The CoCoME system (before structured by technical layers) is decomposed into four microservices for managing the orders, reports, stores, and products (Fig. 4.11).

In addition to the four microservices, a Frontend service is introduced. The Frontend service is required to provide a unique GUI and entry point for users. When a user requests a service, for example by clicking a button on the GUI, the request is delegated by the Frontend service to the corresponding microservice. Thus, the Frontend service handles the orchestration of the microservices. Furthermore, the Frontend service is responsible for identity and access management.

The evolution of the architectural style shifts complexity from software design into system operations. While the individual complexity of a microservice is reduced compared to intermeshed services, additional complexity is introduced for the orchestration of the single microservies. Moreover, quality properties like performance and privacy are affected by this evolution scenario.

4.2.6 Container Virtualization

In this scenario, the deployment and operation of the CoCoME system is facilitated by introducing container-based virtualization with Docker. Docker eases the integration of CoCoME into build and deployment pipelines. In this adaptive evolution

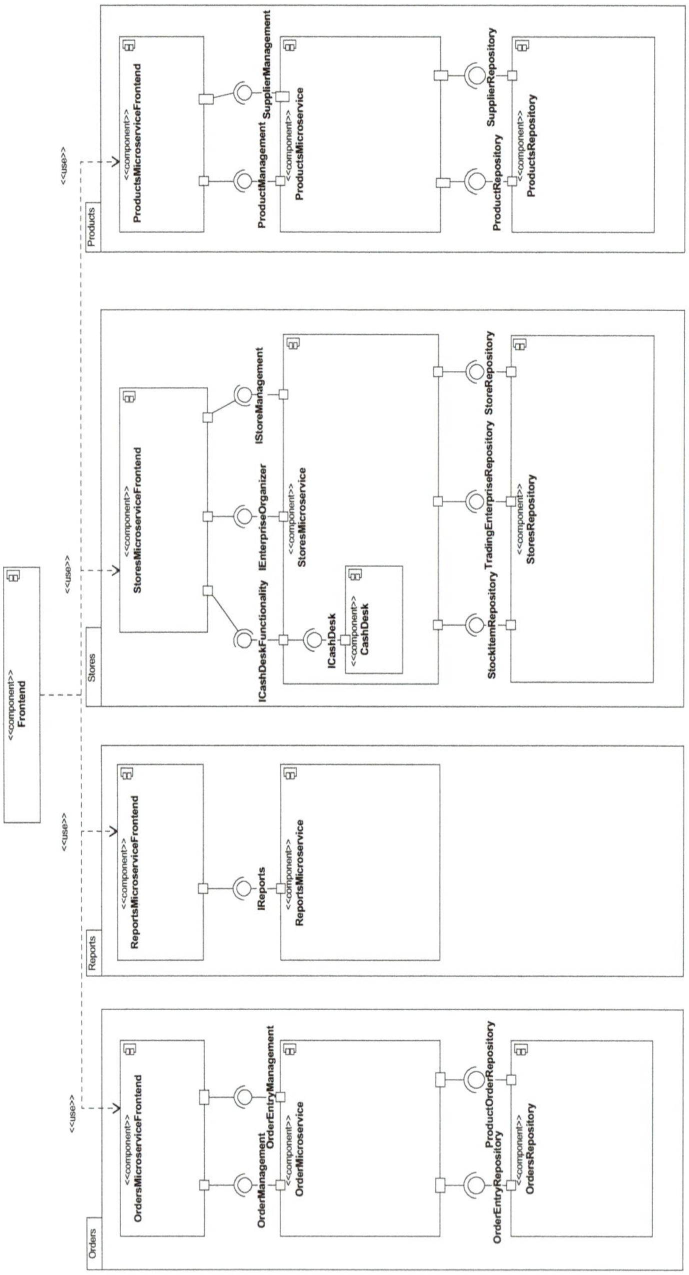

Fig. 4.11 Overview of the microservice architecture of CoCoME [HKR18]

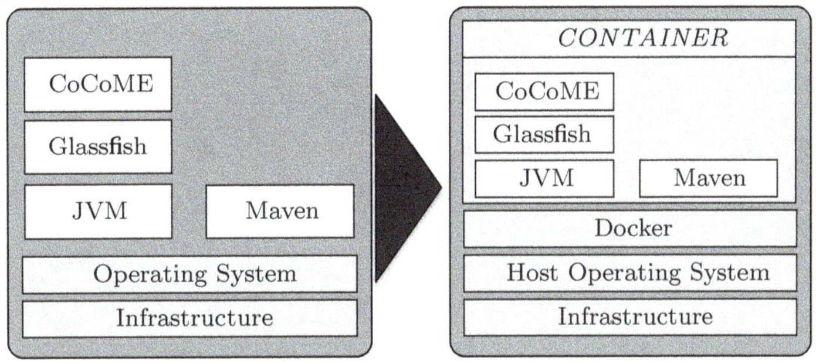

Fig. 4.12 Extended technology stack CoCoME [HKR18]

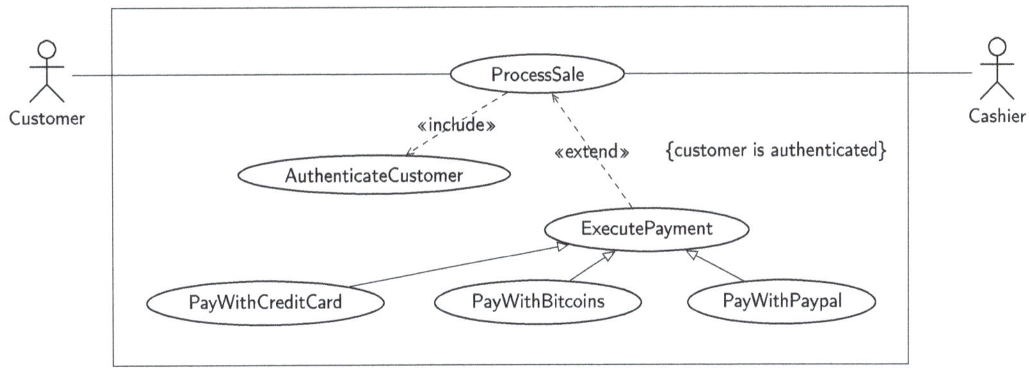

Fig. 4.13 Use cases of CoCoME payment possibilities

scenario, the functionality of CoCoME remains the same, while the technology stack is extended (see Fig. 4.12). The given CoCoME stack is moved into the Docker Daemon, which runs a Linux distribution. This evolution scenario provides a platform independent CoCoME that does not require any preconditions like installing or updating software. By using Docker, a version of CoCoME can be instantiated on any device without installing additional software. Furthermore, the building and deployment of CoCoME can be automated and be sped up.

4.2.7 Adding Payment Methods

Currently, customers can only pay via credit card. In this scenario, the CoCoME sales systems is extended with new payment possibilities such as PayPal and Bitcoins (Fig. 4.13).

Customers are then enabled to select between various payment options. Payments are initiated by the TradingSystem::CashDeskLine component (Fig. 4.8). This component communicates with an external bank (External::Bank::TrivialBankServer component) via the IBank interface. The IBank interface defines the methods *validateCard* and *debitCard*. In this scenario, a generic IPayment interface is introduced

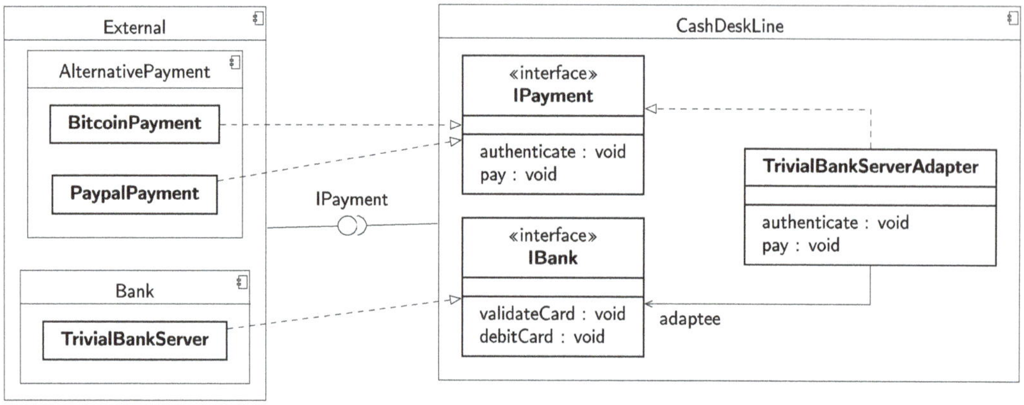

Fig. 4.14 Excerpt of the CoCoME architecture after adding new payment possibilities

that defines the *authentication* and *payment* methods. The IPayment interface is implemented by the PaypalPayment and the BitcoinPayment components (as part of the External::AlternativePayment component). In order to still provide the customer with the possibility to pay via credit card, the IPayment interface needs to be mapped to the IBank interface. For this purpose, the adapter design pattern is chosen. Figure 4.14 shows the resulting architectural structure.

4.3 Introduction of the PPU and xPPU Case Studies

The PPU and xPPU represent a laboratory plant for automated production system. The case studies handle and manipulate workpieces (WP) of different material (Fig. 4.15). An order for WPs is initially processed at a material storage. Afterwards, the PPU and xPPU distribute and manipulate the WPs that are detected by many different kinds of control hardware. Finally, WPs are sorted based on their material in product storage and delivered.

The original PPU consists of four equipment modules: stack, crane, stamp, and conveyor. WPs, which are the target of the process of the plant, are stored at the stack. These WPs are processed differently depending on their type in which the WP is either directly transported to the conveyor by the crane or moved to the stamping unit followed by transported to the conveyor. Sorting ramps possibly differ also depending on the WP type. The xPPU have additional features, such as a reordering module for logistic flexibility, so-called picalpha; reinforced security and safety; product recognition using radio-frequency identification (RFID); manual operating mode; and Industry 4.0 interface (Fig. 4.16).

In the xPPU, production, material, and product managers are responsible for controlling the plant status, material status, as well as the resulting product status respectively (Fig. 4.17). When the order is initialised, the production manager control the processes the plant conduct regarding the material and resulting product. The processes (i.e. basic control functionality) can be manipulating WP (i.e. stamping)

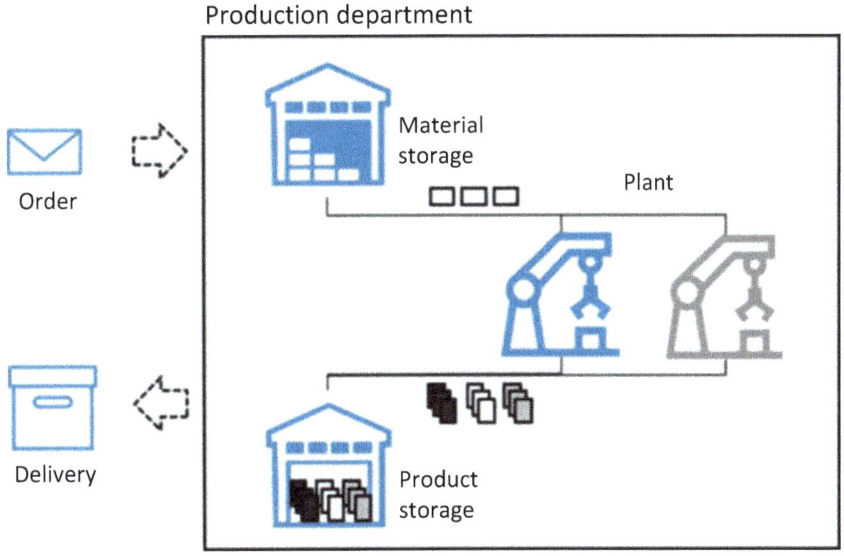

Fig. 4.15 Overview of the PPU and xPPU production chain

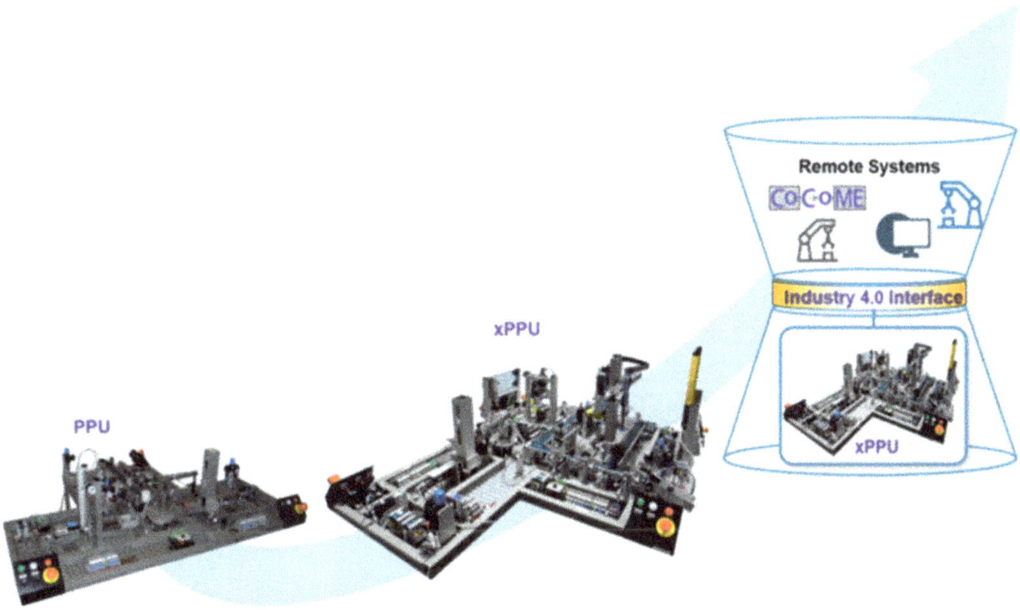

Fig. 4.16 Overview of the PPU, xPPU, and Industry 4.0 case studies

or sorting WP in different ramps according to their material. The plant operator is responsible for selecting the mode of operation for the plant (i.e. manual or automatic), as well as monitoring the status of the plant regarding fault and emergency handling. By enabling Industry 4.0 interface to the xPPU, remote operator and system can access the plant over the web or mobile application and execute processes. The use case for the Industry 4.0 interface is further detailed in Sect. 4.4.1.

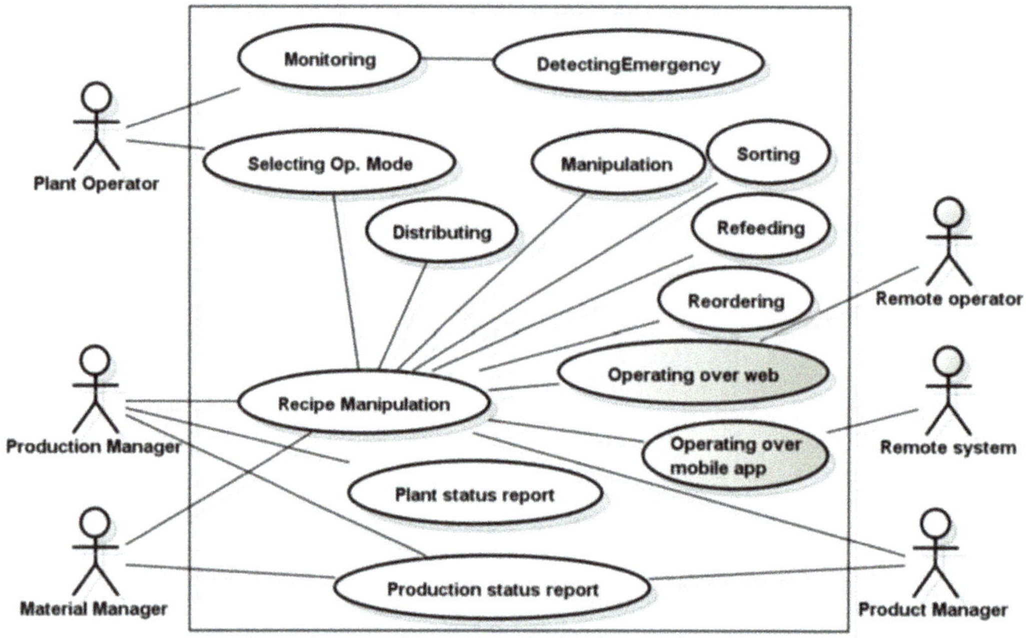

Fig. 4.17 Basic use cases of xPPU (highlighted use cases are from enabling Industry 4.0 interface)

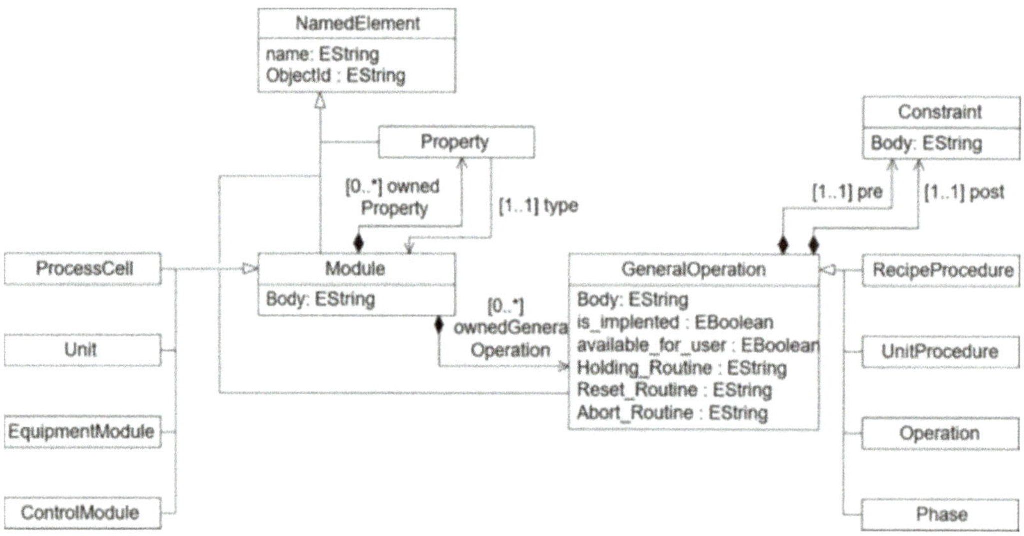

Fig. 4.18 Excerpt of the meta-model developed based on ISA88 [Com+95]

The meta-model used for modelling the system architecture of the xPPU is based on ISA88 standard [Com+95] (Fig. 4.18), which is a reference model for providing the essential fundamentals for batch process control (Fig. 4.19). The two central classes are the Module and the GeneralOperation. The Module corresponds to the physical assets of an enterprise. The GeneralOperation represents the procedural elements from the ISA88 standard. Both classes inherit the name and ObjectId from the NamedElement class. The Module can have multiple relations to the class

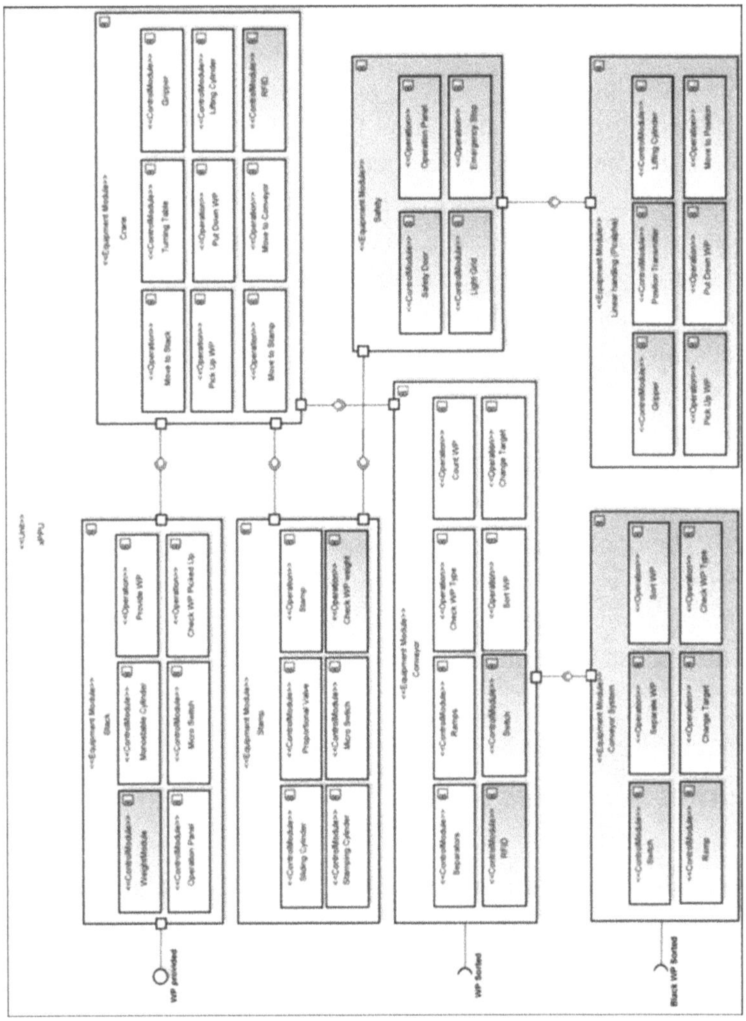

Fig. 4.19 Functional and structural view on the system architecture of PPU and xPPU (highlighted are the extended parts)

Property, which refers through a type relation to an existing Module. Moreover, a Module, which is already available and implemented in the overall model, can thus be referenced and used several times, which allows the creation of a repository (i.e. area repository). In addition, the Module is also related to GeneralOperation, which allows the procedural elements to be assigned to the physical plant components. GeneralOperation has two compositional relations to Constraint via a pre and post relation, which respectively express pre-conditions and post-conditions of procedural elements to be checked before and after the execution of a GeneralOperation. Furthermore, the physical assets in terms of process cells, units, equipment modules, and control modules inherit from the class Module. In the same manner, procedural elements in terms of recipe procedure, unit procedure, operation, and phase inherit from the class GeneralOperation.

In order to provide use cases and allow the comparison of different solutions, 24 evolution scenarios have been developed during the SPP 1593. Detailed documentation of the xPPU evolution scenarios are documented with structural and behavioural models, PLC control code, Matlab/Simulink simulation projects, and mechanical CAD files [Vog+14b] and are publicly available to the community on github.[2] The evolution scenarios were extended regarding more sophisticated requirement modelling, as well as fault handling functionality Chap. 12.

The xPPU is also used by the research community outside the SPP1593 to identify inconsistency [Fel+16], control parameter optimization [Zou+18], and in-place traceability [Ale+17]. The xPPU is connected to a PLC through EtherCAT, allowing the process of signals from the xPPU and the control of actuators accordingly (Fig. 4.20). The control software runs on a PC with a particular environment (e.g. CODESYS or TwinCAT). Furthermore, the PLC is connected to an Open Platform Communications (OPC) server that allows accessing the plant by OPC clients such as the Industry 4.0 interface.

4.3.1 *Evolution Scenarios of the PPU*

In Table 4.1, 13 sequential evolution scenarios of the PPU are depicted, which cover different combinations of platform, context, and software changes.

- Scenario Sc0: The initial scenario is the evolution scenario Sc0 where the stack, the crane, and a slide exist. The stack pushes a single black plastic WP out of the stack into the crane's pick-up position. At the pick-up position, the crane picks up single WPs by moving the crane down and by using a vacuum gripper to suck the separated WP. Upon rotation of 90°, the crane reaches the slide's position, where the WP has to be placed. After moving down, the vacuum gripper releases the WP, which then glides down the slide.

[2]https://github.com/x-PPU.

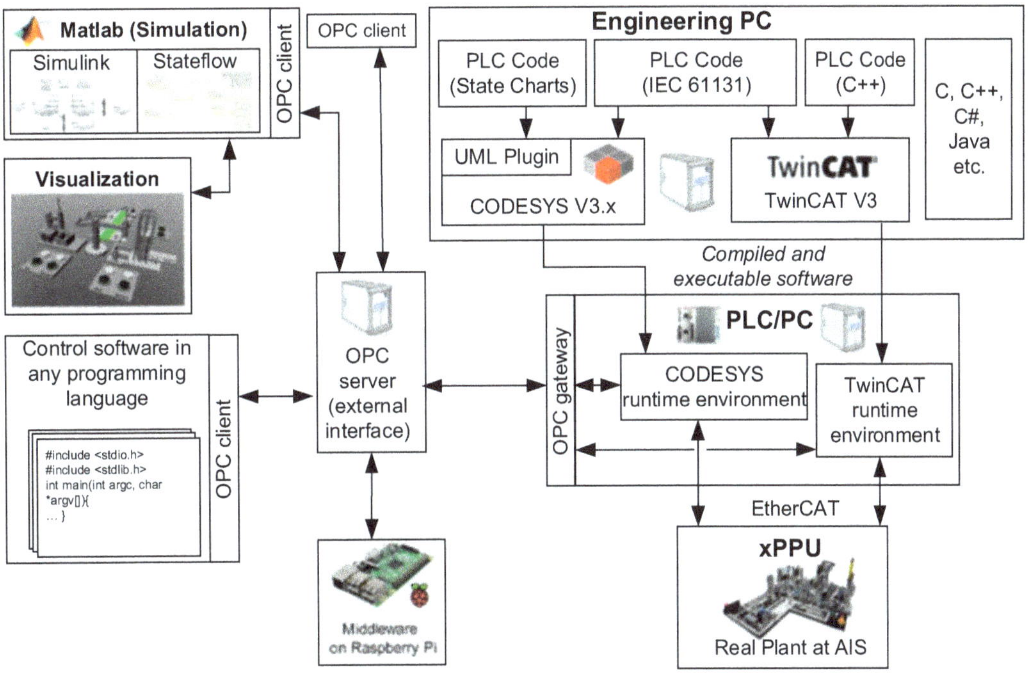

Fig. 4.20 Environment frame of engineering and access to xPPU

- Scenario Sc1: Within this scenario, the slide was replaced with a Y-shaped slide to increase the capacity of the slide to five WPs. the evolution in this scenario affect only the context as solely mechanical component was added.
- Scenario Sc2: Within this scenario, the PPU processes black plastic WPs, as well as metallic WPs. In order to distinguish between the processed WPs, an additional inductive sensor was installed at the stack.
- Scenario Sc3: For tractability reasons, a stamp module was added within this scenario to allow the labelling of the WPs. The stamp is located at position 180° of the crane. Once the WP is detected at the stack, the crane picks up the WP and turns to the stamp position to place it at the magazine, which then retracts to position the WPs under the stamp. The stamp moves down to press the WPs for a while and retracts. The magazine extrudes, and the crane then picks the WPs and place them at the slide. The evolution in this scenario results in modification of all dimensions of the crane.
- Scenario Sc4a: To increase availability, inductive sensors are installed for crane positioning replacing micro switches as they are more robust against pollution. The inductive sensors provide the same signals as the old position sensors. Therefore, the software is not affected; only the crane platform is modified.
- Scenario Sc4b: To increase the reliability of crane positioning, micro switches were installed in addition to the existing inductive sensors. As a result, each inductive sensor has a redundant micro switch.
- Scenario Sc5: Within this scenario, the crane behaviour is changed to allow the processing of more than one WP at a time. As soon as the crane places a metallic WP at the stamp, the stack checks if a plastic WP is available for pickup. In this

Table 4.1 Evolution scenarios of the PPU

Sc	Cause of evolution	Stack			Crane			Stamp			Ramp			Conveyor			Realization
		C	P	S	C	P	S	C	P	S	C	P	S	C	P	S	
0	Increasing throughput of workpiece	*A*	*A*	*A*	*A*	*A*	*A*	–	–	–	*A*	*A*	*A*	–	–	–	New development of the machine
1	Increasing capacity of the output storage	○	○	○	○	○	○	–	–	–	*M*	○	○	–	–	–	Y-shape of the ramp
2	Additional processing of metallic workpieces	*A*	*A*	*A*	○	○	○	–	–	–	○	○	○	–	–	–	Inductive sensor
3	Labelling of a workpiece	○	○	○	*M*	*M*	*M*	*A*	*A*	*A*	○	○	○	–	–	–	Addition of a stamp unit
4a	Decreasing failure due to sensor pollution	○	○	○	○	*M*	○	○	○	○	○	○	○	–	–	–	Replacement of crane sensors
4b	Increasing reliability of crane positioning	○	○	○	*M*	*M*	*M*	○	○	○	○	○	○	–	–	–	Sensor redundancy through inductive sensor and micro switch
5	Increasing throughput of workpiece	○	○	○	○	○	*M*	○	○	○	○	○	○	–	–	–	Optimised crane behaviour through the use of the stamp as a buffer
6	Further increasing in throughput of workpiece	○	○	○	*M*	*M*	*M*	*A*	○	○	○	○	○	–	–	–	Additional mechanical buffer
7	Recognition of additional workpiece	*A*	*A*	*A*	○	○	○	○	○	○	○	○	○	–	–	–	Installing of a light sensor
8	Different processes for different workpieces	○	○	○	○	○	○	*A*	*A*	*M*	○	○	○	–	–	–	Different pressure profiles at the stamp unit

9	Logistics optimisation	o	o	o	o	o	o	o	o	o	*M*	*M*	*M*	*A*	*A*	*A*	Replacement of the Y-slide by a conveyor belt with individual ramp
10	Increasing output storage	o	o	o	o	o	o	o	o	o	o	o	o	*A*	*A*	*A*	Two additional ramps on the conveyor belt
11	Different storage locations	o	o	o	o	o	o	o	o	o	o	o	o	*M*	*M*	*M*	Successive filling of ramps
12	Correct sorting of workpieces in ramps	o	o	o	o	o	o	o	o	o	o	o	o	o	o	*M*	Specified sorting of the workpiece
13	Increasing the precision of the crane	o	o	o	*M*	*A*	*M*	o	o	o	o	o	o	o	o	o	Analogue sensor

Sc Scenario, *A* Added, *M* Modified, *o* no changes, *C* Context, *P* Platform, *S* Software

case, the crane uses the stamping time to transport the plastic WP to the slide. The realised evolution only affects the software of the crane.

- Scenario Sc6: Within this scenario, a mechanical buffer was mounted next to the stamp, which allows another metallic WP to be placed next to the stamp even if the stamp is processing metallic WP. The behaviour of the crane is similar to Sc5.
- Scenario Sc7: Within this scenario, the PPU processes additional white plastic WP. Therefore, the stack was modified with additional optical digital sensor to detect the brightness of the WP. Combining the already existing inductive sensor with the new sensor, the stack is able to differentiate all kinds of WPs. The white plastic WPs are stamped like metallic ones. Black WPs are transported directly to the slide.
- Scenario Sc8: Due to the fragility of white plastic WPs compared to metallic ones, the stamp was modified with two different pressure profiles each for specific types of WP. Therefore, the present two-way valve was replaced by a proportional valve that handle analogue values.
- Scenario Sc9: Within this scenario, a conveyor was installed in the place of the slide. The crane now places the WPs directly on the conveyor, which transports WPs to a slide mounted at the end of the conveyor.
- Scenario Sc10: Additional two output slides were added in this scenario at the side of the conveyor. Therefore, to separate the WPs, two pneumatic pushers are mounted at the opposite side of the conveyor, facing towards the two slides. Right before each pusher, an optical sensor is attached to detect whether a WP is available. The slide mounted at the end of the conveyor is filled first, then the mid slide, and finally the slide at the beginning of the conveyor (first slide).
- Scenario Sc11: Within this scenario, only one type of WPs is separated into one slide. Therefore, two inductive sensors are installed in front of the optical sensors right before the two slides on the side. In the first slide, white WPs are separated; on the mid slide, metallic WPs are separated; on the last slide (at the end if the conveyor) black WPs are sorted.
- Scenario Sc12: In this scenario, the sorting order of WPs is changed at slides. Now WPs have to be mixed in all slides. The change in this scenario only affects the software.
- Scenario Sc13: Until this scenario, the positioning of the crane is done using digital position sensors. To increase the accuracy and to avoid spending cables and terminal blocks, the digital sensors are replaced by analogue sensors (potentiometer).

4.3.2 Incremental Evolution Scenarios

Within scenario 11, the sorting of WPs at the conveyor is targeted. The scenario follows a specific sorting regarding the WP types. The first ramp collects white WPs, the second ramp collects metal WPs, and the third ramp collects black WPs. The change is implemented by checking the type of WP with a diffuse and inductive sensor after the WP is placed on the conveyor belt. When a white WP is identified, the first pneumatic cylinder pushes the WP in the first ramp, and after another sensor check the metal WPs are pushed in the second ramp by the next cylinder. Black WPs pass both the lateral ramps and are transferred to the ramp at the end of the conveyor. According to the categories of changes, scenario 11 is a change of category 5 without adaption of the requirement and specification.

Because of the various possibilities to sort WPs, this scenario is used to implement so-called mini-scenarios. Mini-scenarios are evolution scenarios of the PPU that only have a very limited impact on the whole system. The mini-scenarios were introduced because some technologies such as verification are not feasible for large change. The mini-scenarios reflect ad hoc changes that are often instantaneously performed to quickly react to avoid standstills of the production system. The mini-scenarios are simplifications in the material flow of scenario 11 and are implemented as simple code adaptations of the software code. Table 4.2 shows the implemented mini-scenarios. Scenario 11a and 11b simplify the material flow of the PPU by exclusively using only one ramp. In scenario 11c, two ramps are used by an alternating pattern that arise a very unique material flow. Scenario 11d and 11e are preliminary stages to the original scenario 11 by sorting just one or two WPs in a specific ramp. The mini-scenarios can be used to investigate approaches that consider undocumented or unknown changes during operation. The platform and context are not affected by any mini-scenario, and the changes in the behaviour arising out of the software modification are much smaller than in the other evolution scenarios. Therefore, these scenarios can, for example, be used to evaluate approaches that try to ensure consistency between specifications, models, and the running system and consider transformation of models or focus on atomic modification steps.

Table 4.2 Mini-scenarios: limited software modifications of the sorting of conveyor belt

Scenario	Cause of evolution	Conveyor belt			Realization
		C	P	S	
11	Specific sorting regarding workpiece type	○	○	*M*	White workpieces are stored in Ramp 1, metal in Ramp 2, and black in Ramp 3
11a	Exclusive use of Ramp 1	○	○	*M*	All workpieces are stored in Ramp 1
11b	Exclusive use of Ramp 2	○	○	*M*	All workpieces are stored in Ramp 2
11c	Use of two ramps	○	○	*M*	All workpieces are alternatively stored in Ramp 1 and Ramp 2
11d	Sorting of one workpiece type	○	○	*M*	White workpieces are stored in Ramp 1, and the others in Ramp 2
11e	Sorting of two workpiece types	○	○	*M*	White and black products are stored in Ramp 1 and the others in Ramp 2

M Modified, *o* no changes, *C* Context, *P* Platform, *S* Software

4.3.3 Evolution Scenarios of the xPPU

In Table 4.3, extended sequential evolution scenarios of the xPPU are depicted.

- Scenario Sc14: Within this scenario, the xPPU processes additional metallic WPs of different weights. Therefore, the stack was modified with a **weighting module** to distinguish between the processed WPs based on their weight. The introduction of new WPs will also affect the crane's behaviour. During the transportation of different WPs by the crane to the stamp or the conveyor, the heavier WPs need more time to stop oscillating after the crane's rotation. This latter modification can be adapted by modifying the software. Furthermore, the stamp is modified with different stamping pressures (e.g. heavy, medium, and light pressure).
- Scenario Sc15: To allow re-feeding of WPs that are detected as being faulty, the xPPU was extended with a **conveyor system** containing three additional conveyors.
- Scenario Sc16: Within this scenario, the xPPU allows the processing of WPs in priority at the conveyor system. A **picalpha module** was mounted on the first conveyor of the conveyor system, which has a handling module for reordering WPs by picking and placing the WP ahead in a different position.
- Scenario Sc17 and Sc18: With the evolution in these scenarios, the xPPU is extended with a **safety door** for the prevention of accidents at the stamp, as well as a **light grid** to prevent accidents at the picalpha module. The mounted hardware incorporates emergency stop buttons, as well as additional control elements.
- Scenario Sc19: The xPPU in this scenario has an additional control button to switch between automatic operating mode and the additional **manual mode**. Within the manual mode, the operator is allowed to control the xPPU in any required function sequence.
- Scenario Sc20: Within this scenario, the xPPU was extended with **energy monitoring hardware**. This hardware allow to measure the energy consumed by the different clamps. Therefore, three Wattmeter were installed. Not only does it allow to measure the electric energy consumed by the plant, but with flow sensor it is also possible to measure the air pressure and the air flow through the xPPU. This information can be used to optimise the plant focusing on energy-saving aspects. It also allows to monitor if some parts consume more energy than usual, which might lead to the conclusion that these parts have to be replaced due to malfunction.
- Scenario Sc21: Within this scenario, the xPPU has four **valve blocks** that allow to turn off the air flow on some xPPU modules. This feature allows to simulate failures in the air flow, as well as turn off the air pressure in specific hardware parts for safety reasons.
- Scenario Sc22: To enable more flexible production management, the xPPU was extended with two **RFID-Reader/writer**. One was mounted at the crane parallel to the gripper position, and the other on the conveyor belt. Each WP now was

Table 4.3 Evolution scenarios of the xPPU

Sc	Cause of evolution	Stack			Crane			Stamp			Ramp			Conveyor			xConveyor			Realization
		C	P	S	C	P	S	C	P	S	C	P	S	C	P	S	C	P	S	
14	Distinction of workpieces by their mass	*M*	*M*	*M*	○	○	○	○	○	○	○	○	○	○	○	○	–	–	–	Weighing module to enable the measurement of mass
15	Implementation of more complex processes	○	○	○	○	○	*M*	○	○	○	*M*	○	○	*M*	*M*	*M*	*A*	*A*	*A*	Conveyor system to enable re-feeding workpieces into the manufacturing process
16	Workpiece processing by priority at conveyor system	○	○	○	○	○	○	○	○	○	○	○	○	○	○	*M*	○	○	*M*	Implementing handling module
17	Prevention of human hazard situations at stamp	○	*M*	○	○	*M*	○	*M*	*M*	*M*	○	*M*	○	○	*M*	○	○	*M*	○	Implement safety door and emergency stop switching module
18	Prevention of human hazard situations at the conveyor system	○	*M*	○	○	*M*	○	○	*M*	○	○	*M*	○	○	*M*	○	*M*	*M*	*M*	Implement light grid and emergency stop switching module
19	Additional operating mode (manual)	○	○	*M*	○	○	*M*	○	○	*M*	○	○	*M*	○	○	*M*	○	○	*M*	Push buttons are added to allow manual operations

(continued)

Table 4.3 (continued)

Sc	Cause of evolution	Stack			Crane			Stamp			Ramp			Conveyor			xConveyor			Realization
		C	P	S	C	P	S	C	P	S	C	P	S	C	P	S	C	P	S	
20	Monitoring energy consumption (electrical energy and compressed air)	*M*	o	*M*	*M*	o	*M*	*M*	o	*M*	*M*	o	*M*	*M*	o	*M*	*M*	o	*M*	Additional energy monitoring hardware
21	Decreasing air pressure for fault detection and isolation	o	*M*	*M*	o	*M*	*M*	o	*M*	*M*	o	*M*	*M*	o	*M*	*M*	o	*M*	*M*	Additional valve blocks
22	Enabling more flexible production management	*M*	*M*	*M*	*M*	*M*	*M*	o	o	o	o	o	o	*M*	*M*	*M*	o	o	o	RFIDs are added to the crane and conveyor
23	Networked PLC, distributed platforms	o	*M*	*M*	o	*M*	*M*	o	*M*	*M*	o	*M*	*M*	o	*M*	*M*	o	*M*	*M*	One PLC per machine part, that is crane, stamp, and stack
24	Web connectivity of xPPU	o	o	o	o	o	o	o	o	o	o	o	o	o	o	o	o	o	o	Enable OPC connection to xPPU

Sc Scenario, *A* Added, *M* Modified, *o* no changes, *C* Context, *P* Platform, *S* Software

labelled with an RFID tag, which contains specific information about the WP (e.g. weight and date of labelling).

- Scenario Sc23: Within this scenario, the xPPU is controlled in a decentralised way by a set of (PLCs). **Four different controllers** where used. One for the crane, stamp, stack, and conveyor belt and three for each conveyor of the conveyor system.
- Scenario Sc24: Within this scenario, an Open Platform Communications Unified Architecture (**OPC UA**) connection was enabled to read and write data information from the xPPU to an online server. The OPC UA standard is a collaboration partner of IEC 61131-3 officially[3] and enables flexible process planning as a feature of Industry 4.0. The read and write data information is used to monitor and control the xPPU. Using OPC UA allows us to monitor many variables and values of the xPPU and still have a quick response time. Third-party programs can access the online server and, therefore, the data and use them for monitoring purposes, data gaining, and big data mining purposes. With specified algorithms, statements can be made on the reliability of hardware parts. Also, the usage of each hardware part can be optimised, reducing maintenance work, energy consumption and, therefore cost.

4.4 Industry 4.0 Case Study

In this section, we present the Industry 4.0 community case by integrating both community case studies xPPU and CoCoME (cp. Fig. 4.16). This new case study implements common use cases in Industry 4.0 environments, such as ordering a customizable product, creating a production plan for a customizable product on multiple abstraction layers, and observing the progress of batch size one productions. We enabled event-based communications between information system and automated production components by providing a web-service-based communication model. The Industry 4.0 case study allows to define and emulate the automated production systems in a web-based frontend. Moreover, an automated production system (i.e. the xPPU) is interconnected to an information system (i.e. CoCoME) by a REST-based web services.

4.4.1 Industry 4.0 Interface of the xPPU

aPS are mostly controlled by PLCs, which are programmed in order to execute specific tasks. A program code is loaded onto the PLC through dedicated connection with the computer (i.e. EtherCAT). The PLC then performs, in a cyclic execution,

[3] https://opcfoundation.org/markets-collaboration/plcopen/.

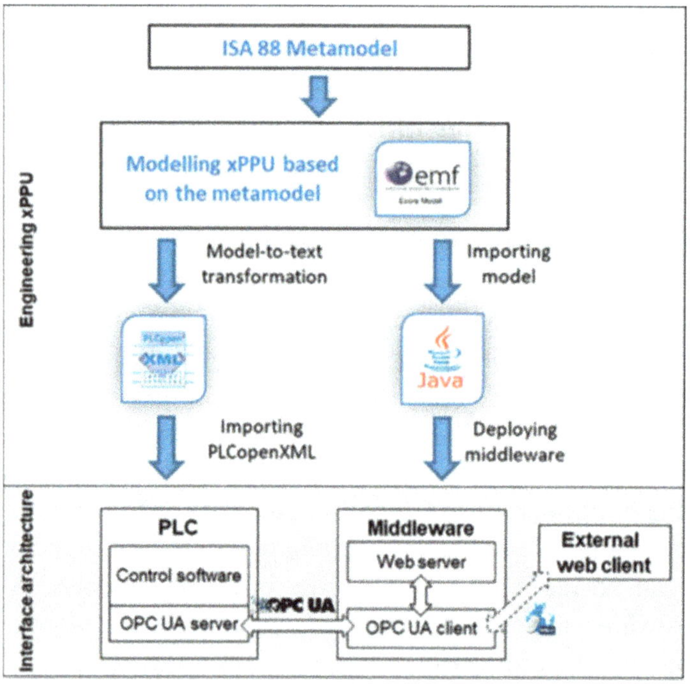

Fig. 4.21 Overview of the concept of dynamic reconfiguration and generation of the Industry 4.0 interface [Bou+17a]

the processing of internal operations, reading of inputs, execution of the program, and updating of outputs. In [Bou+17a], a design concept that enables flexible entry of orders in a production system during its operation, through dynamic reconfiguration of orders and process planning via a remote interface, was introduced. The developed concept allows dynamic services to the CoCoME via web services. The remote interface of the xPPU is considered as an evolution scenario that also affects the environment frame of the xPPU (cp. Fig. 4.20).

A model-based approach was used for the implementation of the PLC code, which controls the plant itself, and a middleware application that enables external access for interacting with the plant (Fig. 4.21). The model-based approach aims at configuring a model of a planned or an existing aPS and allowing a continuous extension and modification of the model. In case of additional functionalities or changes of the system, the model-based approach allows the engineer to efficiently perform modifications within the model.

The underlying meta-model is based on the ISA88 standard [Com+95]. Based on the ISA88 standard, an editor for modelling the plants was implemented. Using this editor the PLC control code is generated together with the industry 4.0 interface, allowing remote access and control through executing available services of the plant. It is designed to enable flexible entry of orders during the operation of the aPS through dynamic reconfiguration of orders and process planning. The aPS should independently check whether the services can be performed from a technical perspective. For the verification of the technical limits, pre-conditions and post-conditions are stored within the offered services.

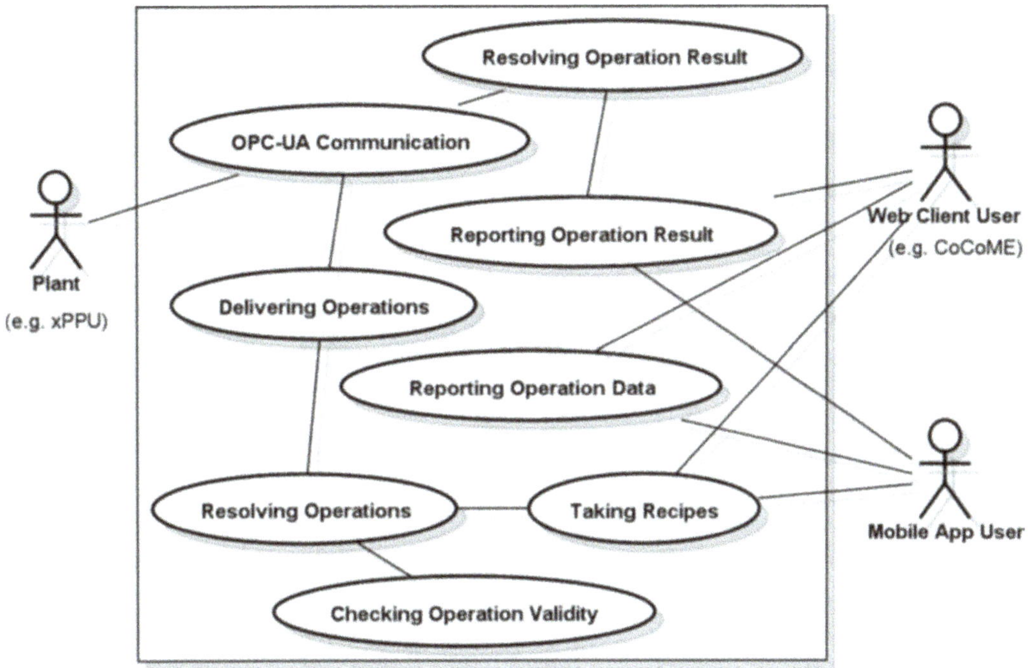

Fig. 4.22 Use cases of the Middleware

One of the main features of Industry 4.0 is connectability of the plant. Thus, besides the use case of the plant (cp. Fig. 4.17), it also includes the Middleware interconnect between the plant (i.e. xPPU) and the users (Fig. 4.22). Over this interconnection, it takes the execution orders from the user side and delivers them to the plant side. Users can be an external operator to execute the system from the remote site or another system to be connected with the plant. From the plant, information regarding the status of the plant or the execution of the operations is delivered to the user side. The communication between the PLC of the xPPU and the Middleware is established over an OPC-UA architecture, which is the official collaboration partner of IEC 61131-3. Middleware executes an OPC-UA client to connect to the OPC-UA server in the PLC and communicates with the PLC over this connection.

For the user side, RESTful (Representational State Transfer) web service is implemented to provide simpler and more lightweight access (Fig. 4.23). Thus, users can have access using an HTTP request (GET or POST) over a web-client application and execute their desired functionality, such as getting a history list, getting variable values, executing a single operation, or executing batch operations. This interface is also implemented in a mobile application form and provided to the users. The Middleware is available for the community on github.[4]

[4]https://github.com/x-PPU/I4.0_Interface.

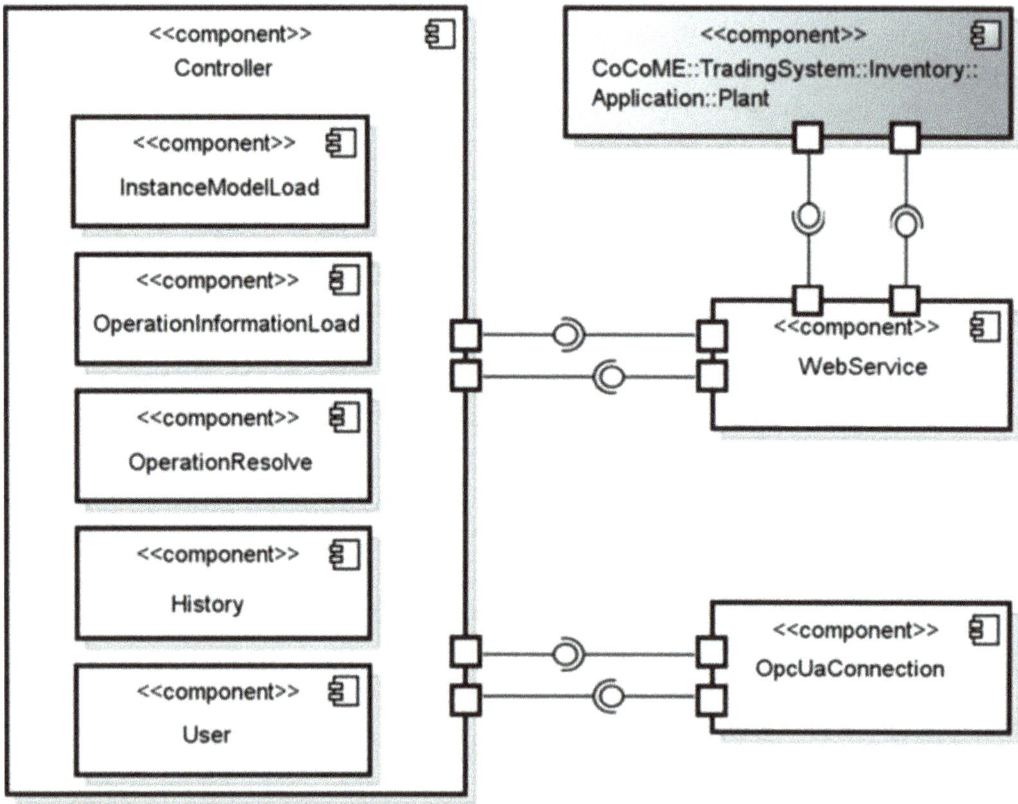

Fig. 4.23 Overview of the Middleware architecture (highlighted are the connection to CoCoME)

4.4.2 Integration of CoCoME and xPPU to Form an Industry 4.0 Case Study

The integration of both case studies, CoCoME and xPPU, can be considered as a further evolution scenario for CoCoME [Bic+18]. The integration of CoCoME and xPPU is based on the hybrid cloud-based variant of CoCoME. Figure 4.21 in the previous subsection shows that the xPPU plant provides a REST interface. The REST interface allows retrieving data and executing the production operations. CoCoME is extended to communicate with this interface (Fig. 4.24).

The main goal of integrating both case studies is to support the *OrderCustomProduct* use case (Fig. 4.25). In this use case, the customer can order individualised products in a store, which are then forwarded to the CoCoME enterprise. In the *DefineProductRecipe* use case, the enterprise manager creates a product recipe based on the order as an ordered list of the needed plant operations, and the CoCoME enterprise triggers the production. In the *SpecifyProductionPlant* use case, the plant operation templates are defined by the plant manager and then forwarded to the connected plants. The production units of the plants use this list to execute the appropriate operations [Bic+18].

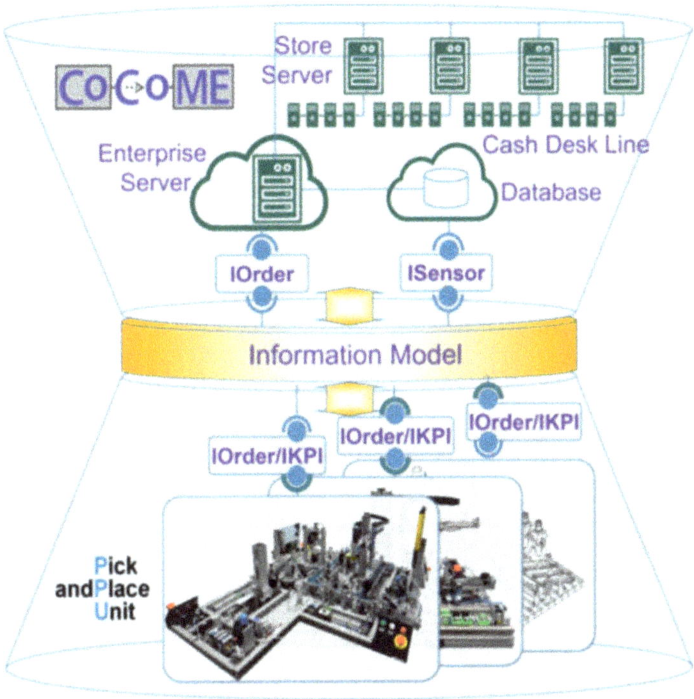

Fig. 4.24 Overview of the integration of CoCoME and xPPU enlarged from [Vog+09, VPF17]

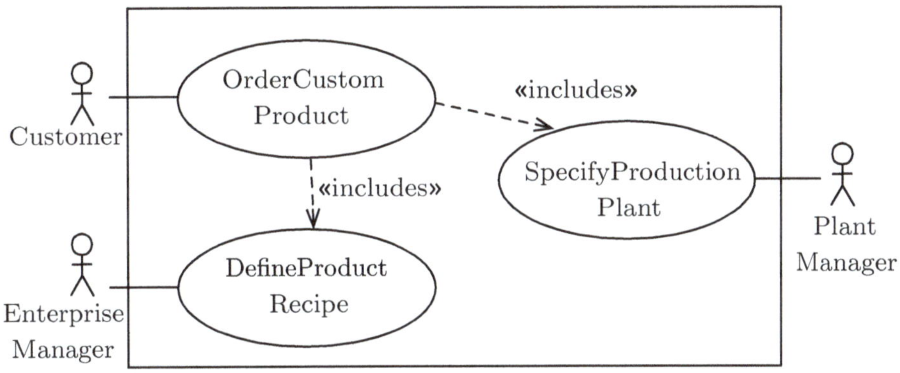

Fig. 4.25 Overview of the use cases for CoCoME after the integration of CoCoME and xPPU, adapted from [Bic+18]

Figure 4.26 illustrates our extensions to a hybrid cloud-based variant of CoCoME to enable the integration of CoCoME and xPPU. In the following, we describe the new components and the relevant changes to the existing components. The `TradingSystem::CashDeskLine::Configurator` component and the corresponding `WebService::CashDesk::Configurator-Service` component enable the customer to configure the custom products. The `TradingSystem::Inventory::Application::Production` component schedules the production order. The `TradingSystem::Inventory::Application::Plant` component provides the functionalities of plant servers,

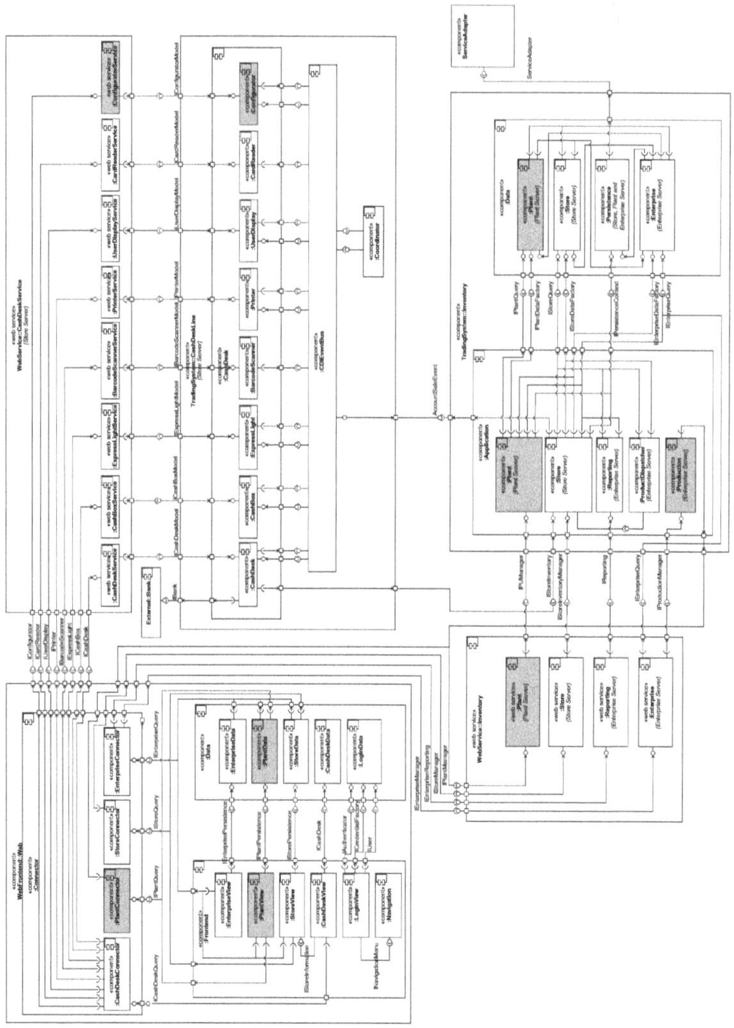

Fig. 4.26 Architecture overview of the Industry 4.0 variant of CoCoME [Bic+18]

such as creating production unit types. The `TradingSystem::Inventory::Data::Plant` involves various data structures, for example for production units. Additionally, we had to extend the `TradingSystem::Inventory::Data::Enterprise` to include further data structures, such as ordering plant or production operations. The `TradingSystem::Inventory::Data::Store` component was extended to manage customised products. The `WebService::Inventory::Plant` component represents the web service of the `TradingSystem::Inventory::Application::Plant` component. Further, we extended the `WebService::Inventory::Store` and `WebService::Inventory::Enterprise` components by the event-based messaging and the corresponding operations for the added data structures. The `WebFrontend::Web::PlantView` component provides the plant manager web-based views managing the production unit and plant operations. The `WebFrontend::Web::EnterpriseView` enables enterprise manager to manage the production order, plants, and custom products. Further, the `WebFrontend::Web:: EnterpriseView::Store` allows configuring and managing custom products. A detailed descriptions of the components of the industry 4.0 variant of CoCoME are given in the technical report [Bic+18].

Part II
Knowledge Carrying Software

Chapter 5
Tacit Knowledge in Software Evolution

Jan Ole Johanssen, Fabien Patrick Viertel, Bernd Bruegge, and Kurt Schneider

Requirement elicitation is an essential activity to identify functional and non-functional requirements of a software system. In long-living software systems, requirements identification and update are particularly challenging. This typically results in an incomplete set of requirements. The reasons for this lie in continuous changes over the lifetime of the software system, followed by a substantial part of the requirements that remains unspoken: Users, and generally any stakeholder of a software system, might not be consciously aware of new or evolved needs or of the associated reasons. As a result, they are unable to express and verbalise requirements that relate to this knowledge, which is called *tacit knowledge*. This chapter details the identification and externalisation of tacit knowledge during both the design time and run time of a long-living and continuously evolving system. The overall goal is to detect deviations between explicitly elicited requirements and implicitly derived requirements. We discuss two cases in which the identification and externalisation of tacit knowledge is crucial for high-quality software systems.

In the first case, tacit knowledge about security is identified and externalised by heuristics as an example for non-functional requirements elicited during design time. Previously externalised knowledge is encoded in heuristics and filters for machine learning, which classify general requirements into more and less security-related ones. As a consequence, security experts can focus their time and effort on the more security-related requirements. In the long term of a long-living software system, externalising and reusing tacit security knowledge will be embedded in a cyclic learning process.

J. O. Johanssen (✉) · B. Bruegge
Technische Universität München, Institut für Informatik I1, Garching, Germany
e-mail: jan.johanssen@tum.de; bruegge@in.tum.de

F. P. Viertel · K. Schneider
Leibniz Universität Hannover, Fachgebiet Software Engineering, Hannover, Germany
e-mail: fabien.viertel@inf.uni-hannover.de; kurt.schneider@inf.uni-hannover.de

R. Reussner et al. (eds.), *Managed Software Evolution*,
https://doi.org/10.1007/978-3-030-13499-0_5

The second case focuses on tacit knowledge captured during the run time of a system to improve the functional aspects of a software system. Usage monitoring allows to understand the difference between the specified and observed behaviour of a user. A system is inconsistent or incomplete if the requirements are incorrectly implemented or an important feature has not yet been identified and implemented. Traditional approaches address these problems only by using bug reports and change requests. We claim that the identification and extraction of tacit usage knowledge help to reveal misunderstandings and leads to feature requests without the active verbalisation by the users of the software system.

5.1 Toward Identification and Extraction of Tacit Knowledge

Software systems are built on a set of requirements established during requirements engineering. Requirements elicitation is a major activity of requirements engineering aiming at a complete representation of the system under development and its *external* behaviour [Dav93].

Long-living systems face challenges even if state-of-the-art requirement elicitation practices are applied. A component without confidential data but with Internet access may turn into a security-related one when it is connected to yet another component that contains customer data. Likewise, a simple view may be easy to use in its initial version, but during the system's lifetime, new visual components are added, affecting the way the interface was originally designed. Each set of requirements may look simple by itself; however, in combination, they may require specific attention. Even a system that is initially considered secure or user-friendly may eventually become vulnerable or confusing by the continuous changes of the long-living system.

Developers may have some understanding of security or usability concerns but only a very limited knowledge for recognising related aspects. When they implement new functionality or integrate components, they may not recognise implicit vulnerabilities or usability problems. They would need a hint or *breakdown* to raise their attention. In addition, existing requirements relate to and have an impact on more aspects than initially defined. At the same time, the attempt to obtain a complete specification of requirements often leads to analysis paralysis [Bro+98]: The intention to analyse an aspect in its entirety slows down the process and finally paralyses it. In this chapter, we focus on the aspects of the following requirements:

- **Non-functional requirements** and their impact that neither customers nor developers are aware of during requirements elicitation at design time.
- **Functional requirements** that evolve during the run time of a software system that end users are unable to express.

Tacit knowledge is knowledge deeply ingrained in a person's mind [PS09]; a person will apply such knowledge repeatedly but may not be able to verbalise this given knowledge. For example, security experts avoid code injection vulnerabilities as part of their expertise. Likewise, developers keep the user interface simple and easy to use without explicit requirement. When their activity of competence is interrupted while they apply this tacit knowledge—the breakdown—they will remember the rationale. In many cases, domain experts are not even aware that their expertise depends on this knowledge and that this knowledge might be useful for others. We follow the hypothesis that the utilisation of tacit knowledge allows the requirements of long-living systems to be kept consistent and complete throughout the lifecycle of the system. We analyse two perspectives on tacit knowledge: design time and run time.

A Design Time Perspective on Requirements. Systems evolve over time. During the initial design phase, certain aspects might be considered irrelevant. For instance, a supermarket system designed without the Internet in mind would not consider attacks or vulnerabilities that arise when the system is extended to an online store during its evolution. Thus, security requirements and the awareness for security-related aspects of functional requirements may have not been considered during the initial design phase. To cope with this situation, developers extend the functionality but often overlook the need to adapt associated non-functional requirements, such as security, that result from the change. Over time, this neglect will turn an initially secure system into an insecure and vulnerable one.

A Runtime Perspective on Requirements. Information on users and on how they practically employ a system might not be present during requirement elicitation. Therefore, systems might not deal well with users, and previously made decisions require refinements. In addition, new requirements are demanded since they become relevant only when the software is used during a later point in time. Users and their intention change over time, which results in changed requirements that evolved by frequently using the software. Two approaches were developed to handle the lack of usage knowledge, that is how software is being utilised by end users: To support requirements elicitation, the concept of a stakeholder was introduced to software engineering [Con94]. Stakeholders represent the interests of clients, customers, and developers—but often neglect the interests of end users and are difficult to identify if a user has not been able to participate in the requirements elicitation [SFG99, Con94]. In the field of human-computer interaction—and in other fields such as marketing [Jen94]—another approach was established to deal with not yet existing users: personas, so-called "hypothetical archetypes" [Coo99], refer to a fictional and synthetic character that one would imagine a user *could* look like, focusing on certain characteristics. Personas are derived from a limited population sample and reflect specific characteristics of users.

We present evolutionary approaches for both perspectives, namely to identify neglected non-functional requirements, such as security during design time, and to identify functional requirements by observing real users during run time. Both approaches share similar challenges: discover, understand, and transform users' tacit knowledge into explicit knowledge.

To transform tacit knowledge to explicit non-functional requirements during design time, we describe an approach that identifies security-related requirements semi-automatically using natural language processing. Our approach is able to retrieve vulnerabilities from requirements written in natural language based on security incidents.

We describe a formative approach for understanding users from runtime information, which begins with personas as the starting point for the classification of real users. This is similar to a *greedy* algorithm, which starts with a local optimum—an assumption of how a hypothetical stakeholder [RC03] could look like—and continues searching for a better user understanding.

Both approaches apply iterative and evolutionary procedures. We begin with an empty starting situation, for example knowing nothing about security requirements or the user's preferences. Both approaches aim to improve the current set of requirements for a given problem and the understanding of the real users by continuously transforming tacit knowledge into explicit knowledge. Ultimately, this process will result in:

- Increasing the system's usability and customisation towards the needs of users by software releases that better fit the requirements of customers and the expectations of users
- Improving and maintaining the quality of development for long-living systems by co-evolving non-functional requirements, such as security or usability

The chapter is structured as follows. In Sect. 5.2, we provide an overview of the foundations of tacit knowledge. In Sects. 5.3 and 5.4, we introduce our approaches and highlight their application in a concrete example. The approaches address the two main challenges as described in Sect. 3.1: identification and extraction of tacit knowledge, as well as detection of deviations in requirements. In Sect. 5.5, we present related work. Section 5.6 provides a summary, outlook, and suggestions for further reading.

5.2 Foundations

The aim of software engineering is to establish activities for specifying, developing, and managing software evolution. However, these activities usually cannot capture every aspect required for a complete specification. One reason for the incompleteness of the specification lies in the inability of stakeholders to express their requirements—even though they are aware of a *need*, generally referred to as *tacit knowledge*.

Polanyi builds his definition of tacit knowledge on the fact that "we can know more than we can tell" [PS09]: In his book *The Tacit Dimension*, he further coins the term tacit by describing it as a skill, positioning the term closely to physical actions such as riding a bicycle or playing an instrument—actions that are learned over a long period and apparently impossible to describe in words. Polanyi systematically describes the inner workings of a human when experiencing or, more precisely, externalising tacit knowledge. He identifies the *functional* relationship and structure of tacit knowledge, which allow to disassemble the individual parts of tacit knowledge. Further, semantic and ontological aspects lead to the *phenomenal* structure of tacit knowing.

Gigerenzer [Gig08] uses the comparison of a native speaker that—while they can find a sentence to be grammatically correct—they are usually unable to verbalise the underlying grammar; he calls this *gut feeling* and uses the term interchangeably with intuition and hunch [Gig08]. Gigerenzer continues to exemplify that humans tend to choose logically unlikely alternatives when asked for predicting the likelihood of two alternatives—the *conjunction fallacy*. They base their decision on impressions rather than mathematical *rationale* [Gig08].

In his book *The Reflective Practitioner: How Professionals Think in Action*, Donald A. Schön recognises similar patterns in working environment settings [Sch83]. He coins the phrase that *our knowing is in our action* [Sch83]. He develops the term *tacit knowing in action* by noticing that practitioners are continuously making decisions during their day-to-day work, such as the assessment of situations or quality criteria, without paying attention to the act of decision-making. However, sometimes they are interrupted during this process and reflect on their action: By extracting the underlying features of their judgements to criticising existing approaches, they arrive at an improved embodiment [Sch83].

Nonaka and Takeuchi provide an extensive examination of the differences between *explicit* knowledge, that is written down in rules, definitions, or handbooks, and *implicit* knowledge, that is experiences of an individual that are based on personal values and motivated by cultural aspects [NT12]. In their book *The Knowledge-Creating Company*, the authors describe the dynamic interplay between these two knowledge types as the key for knowledge creation in companies. They establish a spiral model that contributes to the social process of knowledge sharing that heavily depends on a collaborative interaction and leads to the externalisation of knowledge, which makes it useful for companies.

Tacit knowledge is investigated in multiple fields, such as social, psychological, or physiological science. Understanding and externalising tacit knowledge can be valuable for other disciplines as well. For instance, Schneider acknowledges that specific techniques are needed to capture requirements and additional information when and where they surface: in natural language requirements specifications or by observing activities by experts [Sch09].

5.3 Tacit Knowledge During Design Time

Tacit knowledge is not easily available for extraction, externalisation, and use by others. A person with tacit knowledge acts in a knowledgeable way but is not able to explain that knowledge. In the first part of this section, we describe a case in which requirement engineers and developers deal with requirements. Since they are usually not security experts, their experience in security is limited. Security experts are knowledgeable about security but may be unable to apply that knowledge to a given set of requirements. A large part of their security knowledge remains tacit.

They need a breakdown in order to shift tacit knowledge to their conscience and apply it. In the following heuristic approach, we use natural language processing, ontologies, and frames to guide and focus the attention of security experts to use cases (UCs) that are more security-related than others. This is supposed to reduce their effort and help them focus on the most rewarding requirements for identifying security problems.

This focus and contextualisation can help to externalise their respective tacit knowledge. The externalised knowledge will also be stored for future use: It can help improve the above-mentioned heuristic filtering mechanisms, thus improving the automated part of classification.

5.3.1 Security in Requirement Documents

Security is an important quality aspect. It is not obvious whether a requirement is security relevant or not. It will depend on other requirements and on the environment that the software is used in: Depending on laws, different levels of security will be required. Knowledge about security incidents or innovations in attacks has a major influence on security. All these aspects are in constant flux and need to be monitored to keep a long-living system secure.

Most customers and requirement engineers are not security experts. In the requirement elicitation phase, some of them rely on their *gut feeling* in judging the security relevance of requirements. This gut feeling or *experience* indicates certain knowledge that is, however, difficult to grasp. Developers consider a requirement security-related, but they cannot say why. It just looks suspicious to them. From their perspective, the reason for that suspicion is *tacit knowledge*.

Use cases and a specification document are artefacts resulting from requirement activities. Use cases support the understanding of requirements and describe what the system should do. In most cases, they are written in natural language, which makes them more comprehensible for customers. Due to the large number of requirements and use cases involved in a large long-living software system, checking entire specifications and all use cases for security concerns would be very laborious and, in most of the cases, impossible for economic reasons.

Therefore, we developed a semi-automatic approach for the classification of natural language requirements with a special focus on use cases. As a result, only parts of those artefacts are classified as security-related and then need an in-depth investigation by security experts.

Even security experts cannot cover all relevant security knowledge to determine whether a requirement is security-related or not. While developers and requirements engineers are not aware of security concerns, security experts may not be able to identify a concrete problem with respect to their large internalised knowledge about potential attacks. Again, a lot of tacit knowledge needs a breakdown to come to the foreground.

This observation led us to the following research questions [Gär+14]:

- **RQ1**: How can security knowledge be organized in a way that it can be used for assessing the requirements of a long-living software system?
- **RQ2**: How can requirements engineers identify security-critical issues in natural language requirements semi-automatically?
- **RQ3**: How can requirements engineers be supported to extract proper security knowledge from identified security-critical issues in requirements?

We need a security knowledge model to use and collect security-related knowledge. Our approach uses heuristics to identify security vulnerabilities.

Our goal is to support the security assessment of requirement while using security knowledge of reported security incidents. We focus on use cases. In Sect. 5.3.2, we show how related knowledge is modelled. Requirements are classified semi-automatically. Among other techniques, we use Natural Language Processing (NLP). The classification is performed based on the semantic of words in a requirement. In Sect. 5.3.3, the approach is described in detail. We describe the identification of security issues by heuristics in the remainder of this section. Furthermore, we explain the extraction of security knowledge from informal sources, such as conversations. The knowledge base is filled from those sources. Section 5.3.4 presents an evaluation on the case study using the iTrust medical health care system.

5.3.2 *Modelling of Security Knowledge*

Security faces the challenge of unknown unknowns [MH05]: *we do not even know what we don't know*. It is impossible to say which knowledge will be relevant in the future. Relevant security knowledge, for example on new attacks, changes rapidly over time.

Trustworthy data should be securely encrypted. Data Encryption Standard (DES) met this requirement. In the mid-nineties, attacker knowledge revised that perception. Nowadays, DES is considered insecure, so that another encryption such as the extension Advanced Encryption Standard (AES) must be used to meet the above-mentioned requirement of *securely encrypting* data. To prevent a leak of data integrity, we use reasoning techniques to detect these data flows. A detailed description of this procedure is provided in Sect. 5.3.3 Therefore, security knowledge must be maintained by human interaction iteratively.

Security Ontology

Security knowledge consists of knowledge about security incidents, operator obligations, and security guidelines—to name just a few. We collected various taxonomies and ontologies for modelling incident-centric security knowledge from literature and derived an ontology covering the most important parts. According to Schreiber, there are general ontologies and domain- and task-specific ontologies [Sch08]. The creation of ontology includes the definition and hierarchical ordering of important terms, their properties and relations, as well as their instances.

Our ontology is derived from literature and is a general security ontology. The upper part of that ontology consists of generic terms and concepts related to security, such as assets, vulnerabilities, and attacks. The lower part of the ontology details those concepts with respect to the specifics of a given long-learning system. For example, customer data are considered an asset, and the WiFi connection in a CoCoME store may cause vulnerability.

For identifying the hierarchical structure of the upper ontology, a systematic literature review was applied to identify security-related terms and their relations. We addressed publications about concrete ontologies of security knowledge from the area of threat modelling, risk analysis, computer and network security, software vulnerabilities, and information security management. Furthermore, we consider publications covering information systems, cyber-physical systems, distributed systems, and agent-based systems. The named security concepts of these publications are considered for the concepts of our security ontology. To focus on security issues in requirements engineering, publications should primarily consider the technical security aspects of systems (e.g. protocols and encryption algorithms). Further publications that describe applicable approaches were considered for capture and enrich security knowledge. For the automatic search on digital libraries we used the terms security, information system, software, ontology, and meta-model. To find similar work that we did not find within the automatic search, the references of the found work was checked for relevance. Publications until the beginning of February 2015 were considered. All found publications were selected based on the criteria in the following steps.

First step

- Publication exists in full text and is written in English.
- Publication describes a realised, practical applicable approach.
- Publication addresses the modulation, application, or acquisition of security knowledge in software engineering.

Second step

- Publication describes the terms of an ontology with respect to security and their relations.
- The ontology presented in the publication is universally valid.

Third step

- The ontology describes a specific approach to capture knowledge related to security.
- A concrete knowledge source is considered for the extraction of knowledge.

Table 5.1 Publications considered for the creation of ontology [Gär+14]

Publication	Principal security concepts
Howard et al. [HL98]	Action, target, access, tool, vulnerability, result, objective, attacker
Jung et al. [JHS99]	Asset, vulnerability, threat, security control, risk probability, asset value, impact, EC environment
Mouratidis et al. [MGM03]	Constraints, secure entity (goals, tasks, resources), secure dependency
Undercoffer et al. [UJP03]	Attack, system component, input, consequence, means, location
Alvarez et al. [ÁP03]	Entry point, vulnerability, service, action, input length, http headers, http verb, target, scope, privileges
Swiderski et al. [SS04]	Asset, entry point, trust level, attack, attacker, vulnerability, countermeasure
Herzog et al. [HSD07]	Asset, threat, vulnerability, countermeasure
Tsoumas et al. [TG06]	Asset, risk, threat, attack, threat agent, vulnerability, impact, countermeasure, controls, security policy, stakeholder
Karyda et al. [Kar+06]	Asset, countermeasure, objective, person, threat
Barnum et al. [BS07]	Vulnerability, weakness, method of attack, attack consequence, attacker skill, solution and mitigation, resource, context
Fenz et al. [FE09]	Asset, organisation, security attribute, threat, threat source, threat origin, vulnerability, control, severity scale
Elahi et al. [EYZ09]	Vulnerability, effect, attack, security impact, malicious goal, attacker, countermeasure, malicious action, component, actor
Simmons et al. [Sim+09]	Attack vector, operational impact, defence, informational impact, target (network, application, etc.)
Guo et al. [GW09]	Attack, countermeasure, consequence, attacker, vulnerability, IT product
Miede et al. [Mie+10]	Attack, countermeasure, asset, vulnerability, threat, security goal
Eichler [Eic11]	Asset, threat, damage scenario, protection requirements, safeguard, module

The resulting publications, including their security concepts, are listed in Table 5.1. We identified ontology assets, entry points, trust level, system components, attack, vulnerability, threat and countermeasure. These components are mentioned in several of the considered publications, which leads to the structure of our ontology. In the following, the components and their relations will be described and explained with examples.

- An asset is an item of interest worth being protected (e.g. username and password).
- Entry points define the interfaces to interact with the system. They provide access to assets (e.g. login website, email, input field).
- A trust level describes which role has access to an asset using a specific entry point (e.g. user, administrator).

- System components model the regarded system focusing on assets and entry points. This includes hardware, as well as software components (e.g. database, logging).
- An attack is a sequence of malicious actions that are performed by an attacker aiming at assets (e.g. cross-site scripting, denial-of-service attack).
- Vulnerability is a system property that facilitates unintended access or modification of assets. It violates an explicit and implicit security policy. Entry points may have or provide access to vulnerabilities (e.g. improper neutralisation of input, missing encryption of sensitive data).
- A threat is the possibility to perform a successful attack on a specific asset. Successful attacks exploit at least one vulnerability to cause damage (e.g. execute unauthorised code or commands, expose sensitive data).
- A countermeasure mitigates a certain threat by fixing the respective vulnerability (e.g. input validation, encryption of sensitive data).

In Fig. 5.1, the upper parts of the ontology are displayed. This upper security ontology has to be refined in terms of concepts and in terms of instances. For example, there are various assets of a system, such as username or password, that have to be considered. The concept assets of the ontology have to be instantiated by these concrete assets.

Representation of Knowledge

To monitor different knowledge sources, it is necessary that the knowledge they provide is represented in a uniform manner. Each knowledge item, such as security incidents and use cases, has to be transformed into separate analysis models. They form the so-called security abstraction model. A security abstraction model represents a scenario that describes the use case with respect to security. It has been defined based on the knowledge structure of our security ontology. As an example, the description of a use case is that "a user enters his password into the web form". It contains "user" as trust level, "password" as the related asset, and "web form" as

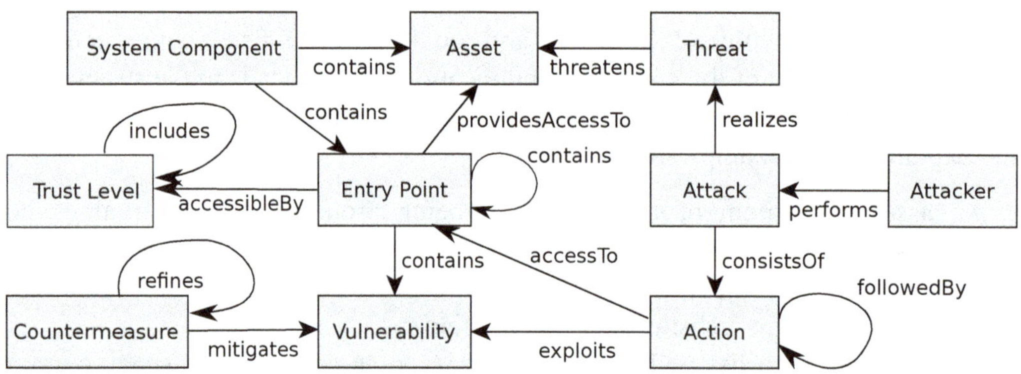

Fig. 5.1 Security ontology [Gär+14]

Table 5.2 Step of use case in an abstraction model

Concepts	Use case
Trust level	User
Assets	Password
Entry point	Web form

the entry point to that asset. Table 5.2 shows the textual representation of a use case step. The model can contain one to multiple of these scenario steps.

5.3.3 Identification and Extraction of Tacit Security Knowledge

In general, our approach consists of two steps: (1) the identification of security vulnerabilities in requirements and (2) the extraction and enrichment of security-related knowledge. For applying our approach, the security ontology has to be manually enriched with security-related terms and their relations to each other by a domain or security expert. To consider requirements and security incidents for the security assessment, the transformation into the previously mentioned analysis model is necessary. These models will be generated automatically in the security assessment approach with the consideration of word similarity and relations between words which are part of both a use case and the ontology.

In the security requirement assessment process, use cases will be classified with respect to the enriched security knowledge through heuristic findings. These heuristics will be described in this section. The automatically generated results of the classification and the heuristic findings will be passed to the requirements engineer, who is now able to enrich the existing security knowledge based on the findings of the security assessment. These findings now represent knowledge consisting of security-related terms that are extracted from the security assessment process and that are not part of the security knowledge base. The requirements engineer can now enhance the knowledge base with this information.

Classification of Words

In general, use cases are written in natural language. Therefore, we use natural language processing for their security assessment. Semantic similarity is defined as the similar meaning of two potentially syntactical different words [Sch94a]. We focus on nouns in the requirements and incidents. To identify the nouns, a statistical part-of-speech tagger is inevitable [PPM04]. If a security affiliation exists for these nouns, they will be assigned to the attribute system component, entry points, asset, and trust level of the security abstraction model. The modelled security knowledge supports the assignment of extracted words to the attributes.

The semantic similarity between nouns can be measured based on the structure and content of *WordNet*. In WordNet, the nouns are organised in hierarchies [Fel98]. We adapt the method of the lowest common subsume (LCS) [JC97]. The concept of LCS is a tree-like lexical taxonomy in which the similarity of words will be described by the shortest path between them in the tree. If the information content of the LCS is above a predefined threshold, the similarity between two words is very low. Otherwise, both words are semantically similar. To get the LCS of two words, the paths by using their hypernyms listed in WordNet will be derived.

Measurement of Similarity Between Security Abstraction Models

To identify the alignment of security, we utilise the Needleman-Wunsch algorithm [NW70]. The algorithm is originally used to determine the similarity of amino acid sequence of two proteins: All possible pairs of sequences could be represented as a two-dimensional array. The similarity of two sequences is represented as a pathway through the array. A smallest match when comparing a pair of amino acids can be used, one from each protein. The maximum match is defined as the largest number of amino acids of one protein that can be matched with those of another protein.

This comparison was transferred to the comparison of security abstraction models with use cases. To detect whether a use case is security relevant or not, all steps included will be compared to the collected security knowledge in the form of steps of a security abstraction model. For this assessment, the previous explained LCS method of semantic similarity is used. If the calculated LCS-value is above a given threshold, there is likely a vulnerability in a given use case. The results of every assessment are stored in a two-dimensional matrix, which is created for every security abstraction model comparison. The matrix cells contain LCS-values for the indication of similarity of two specific steps. In Table 5.3, an example of a comparison of a use case with the steps UC1 and UC2 and a security incident (SI) with the steps SI1 and SI2 are shown.

(Semi)-Automatic Acquisition of Tacit Knowledge

We interleaved the refinement and knowledge enrichment of the knowledge base in the security relevance assessment of use cases as an active learning mechanism. The requirement engineer actively decides to acquire potentially new security

Table 5.3 Extract of the comparison of two security abstraction models

		Security incident	
		Step SI1	Step SI2
Use case	Step UC1	0.5	1.5
	Step UC2	1.0	0.1

knowledge, such as the modification, reinforcement, and refinement of existing knowledge.

For this enrichment, there are two different results of classification, which process different information. The first are the true positives. In our approach, these are use cases that would be correctly classified as security-related. They enhance the knowledge through correctly classified terms. For example, if in the sentence "The user enters an identification number and a pin" the pin will be identified as security-related, we conclude via the existing linguistic dependency between pin and identification number that both are security-related. Besides classifying this sentence, the new insight can also be added as additional knowledge to the knowledge base.

The knowledge base can even be extended by false positives. They will be considered for specifying the terms for a certain domain. For this purpose, falsely classified scenario steps identified by the similarity computation concluding the attributes (system component, asset, entry point, and trust level) will be considered. If the value of similarity for an attribute is under a predefined threshold, there is an uncertainty for the classification. Therefore, the requirement engineer can actively manage whether a term should be excluded or included for the security classification approach. Afterwards, the learned security knowledge can be enriched by a security expert with additional security information (e.g. security standards and guidelines). Explicit security knowledge and precision grow over time.

5.3.4 *Tacit Security Knowledge Examples*

We applied our approach to the CoCoME case study. However, there is only a limited number of security-related requirements in CoCoME. Most of those had to be introduced for demonstrating the feasibility of our approach. Although intentionally inserted problems may be useful for concept demonstration, there are obvious threats to validity.

Therefore, we decided to strengthen the evaluation by using a second, larger example provided by others. The iTrust medical system case study is used by many researchers as a benchmark for security. Since it resembles CoCoME in many aspects, findings are relevant for the application domain represented by CoCoME.

In iTrust, a medical health care system [11], patients are able to manage their health records, such as medical items, and personnel can organise their work. If sensitive patient data are stored, only a limited number of people should be allowed to receive insights into this data. Therefore, security is inevitable to prevent access by intruders. Version 23 of iTrust consists of 55 use cases written in natural language, and the health care system is developed as web application. Our goal is to evaluate whether our approach can support requirements engineers through the security assessment of requirements.

Ten of the use cases of iTrust were selected as initial security knowledge for the requirement elicitation. These use cases distinguish themselves from each other

Table 5.4 Derived misuse cases of the iThrust system [Gär+14]

Concept	Individuals
MUC1	
Asset	Initial password, security key
Entry point	Email
Trust level	User
MUC2	
Asset	Address
Entry point	Address field, health record, view, display
Trust level	Patient, health care personnel

in such a way that they have at least one different actor and cover a different functionality of iTrust.

Unfortunately, there is no security incident documentation in iTrust. Nevertheless, a security incident can also be seen as a use case for the attacker, whereas for the requirements engineer it would be a misuse case (MUC). Therefore, we created misuse cases with respect to the ten initial use cases. In our example, an MUC represents the steps of a specific security incident, which is created based on known security incidents that occurred in the past.

A security ontology was set up on the use cases and misuse cases. The terms of the medical health care domain were considered to embed the domain-specific knowledge in our knowledge base. Furthermore, the individuals of the misuse cases listed in Table 5.4, like system components, assets, trust levels, and entry points, were added as well.

Through the analysis of use cases, we identified for use case 1 (UC1) and use case 6 (UC6) that they are ambivalent because there exists an misuse case, which malicious users follow to attack the use cases. UC1 describes the sending of the initial password for a user account, which is required to login to iTrust, to a user via email after the creation of the account by the medical personnel. This leads us to misuse case 1 (MUC1), in which a hacker intercepts the email and uses the password to have access to the iTrust system. This procedure is called *hijacking*. In UC6, the patient can manage their visits to health care professionals (e.g. doctors) and is able to see a list of health care professionals who have insights into their patient data. This leads to MUC2, in which the address fields of the patient view contain vulnerability that enables cross site scripting (XSS). XSS is one of the most dangerous vulnerabilities in web applications. An improper neutralisation of input enables XSS. An attacker is able to inject malicious browser-executable content into the patient view to steal sensitive data (e.g. medical identification number or password). The named misuse cases are listed in Table 5.4.

For the evaluation of our approach, we split the evaluation into two iterations. For the first iteration, we considered 35 use cases in addition to the ten initial use cases for the security assessment. The results of the heuristic approach were compared to the results of the manual and previously done requirements elicitation. Based on the true and false positives, security knowledge refinement was performed.

Table 5.5 Evaluation results [Gär+14]

		ACC	FPR	FNR
1st iteration (n = 44)				
Our approach	MUC1	0.90	0.10	0.00
	MUC2	0.64	0.55	0.15
Naïve Bayes	MUC1/2	0.61	0.00	0.89
SVM	MUC1/2	0.57	0.00	1.00
k-NN	MUC1/2	0.57	0.15	0.83
2nd iteration (n = 55)				
Our approach	MUC1	0.98	0.00	0.14
	MUC2	0.84	0.14	0.23
Naïve Bayes	MUC1/2	0.71	0.11	0.67
k-NN	MUC1/2	0.76	0.00	0.68

In the second iteration, the refined knowledge was used for the heuristic security assessment of use cases.

For evaluating our approach, we compared its performance to the results of Naïve Bayes, Support Vector Machine (SVM), and the k-nearest neighbors algorithm (k-NN). As quality facets, we considered the accuracy (ACC), false positive rate (FPR), and false negative rate (FNR). Under the ACC, we understand the degree of correctly classified use cases with respect to all of them. The false positive rate is defined by the number of falsely classified security-related use cases. Conversely, the false negative rate measures the falsely classified use cases as non-security-related.

In the training phase, the initial use cases are labelled while considering the misuse cases. If an misuse case is related to a use case, the use case is labelled as security-related. Otherwise, it is labelled as non-security-related. A low FNR implies that most of the use cases were found, which is desired. In the first iteration, SVMs has an FPR of 1.0, which means that no security-related use cases were found. Therefore, we were not able to refine knowledge based on heuristic findings. Thus, we did not consider SVMs for further iterations. Viewing the results of iteration 2, our approach in fact got ACC 0.98 for MUC1 and 0.84 for MUC2, as well as an FNR for MUC1 with 0.14 and for MUC2 with 0.23 as the best results. Only the FPR of MUC2 with 0.14 is higher than the other approaches. The results are listed in Table 5.5. Nevertheless, this fact is regardless for the context of requirements elicitation. It is required to find all of the security-related use cases, which is affected by the FNR. Afterwards a security expert can sort out false positives to achieve only security-related use cases.

5.4 Tacit Knowledge During Run Time

The requirement elicitation phase examines a software system in its completeness, striving for a complete and correct description. This is usually being done by developers through discussions with stakeholders, which are typically represented by customers or the initiator of a software project. However, the end user of a system might pose different requirements. This is why requirement elicitation also includes interviews with the end users of a software system. In particular, user feedback is valuable in case it is collected during the run time of a system. Therefore, capturing knowledge about how a software system is utilised in the field carries valuable knowledge and represents an important aspect in software evolution.

The idea of collecting and improving software systems based on user feedback is further encouraged by recent activities that evolved under the umbrella of Continuous Software Engineering (CSE). At the core of its encompassing activities, continuous delivery allows to distribute software increments in short cycles to users, reducing the time between a developer's change in the form of a commit pushed to a software repository and the execution of its corresponding software artefact by an end user within the target environment [Bos14, FS17].

In the remainder of this section, we establish a perspective on tacit knowledge during run time. We present an approach on how tacit usage knowledge can be extracted from observed user behaviour. Therefore, we introduce the application domain, which we limit to users of mobile applications, and elaborate on the taxonomy of feedback, which we use synonymously to usage knowledge—referring to any knowledge that resulted from observing user behaviour. We conclude this section by describing preliminary results of a current research project.

5.4.1 Usage Knowledge in Software Evolution

Systems are designed by developers and their interpretation of how users utilise software, as described in Sect. 5.4.2. Information on users and on how they employ a system is rarely present during requirement elicitation. The feedback and behaviour of users reveal insights that help to evolve a long-living software system, in particular regarding the following shortcomings:

- Existing requirements are no longer applicable and need to be refined.
- New requirements are demanded that have not been considered during the initial phase of requirements elicitation.
- New user groups evolved, and users' intentions and requirements changed over time, which results in the need to adapt existing requirements.

Current software engineering practices apply iterative development processes that allow for the integration of users' feedback. This feedback can be divided into two groups [MHR09]: feedback that has been provided explicitly by the user—*conscious feedback*—and feedback that they provide indirectly and thereby implicitly—*unconscious feedback*—as an integral part of the application usage. Figure 5.2 depicts the taxonomy of conscious and unconscious feedback.

Conscious feedback is usually utilised during software evolution and is a rich source of usage knowledge. Users try to reach out to the developers, for example in form of an app store review, via mail, or through any other social media platform.

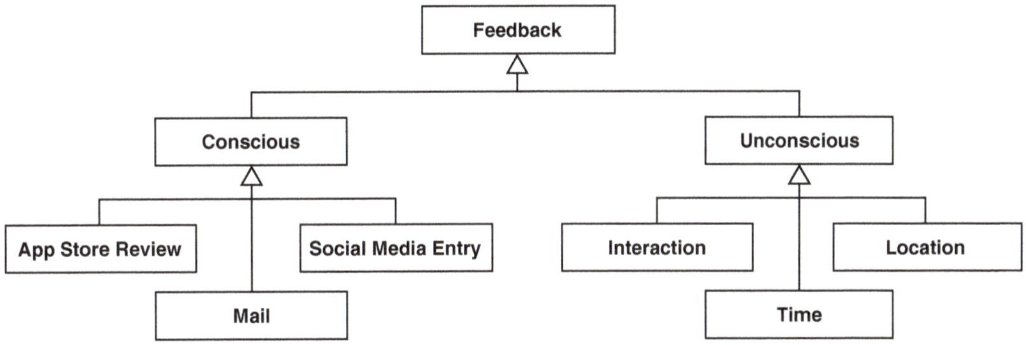

Fig. 5.2 A taxonomy of feedback provided by the end users of a mobile application

They relay their experience and clearly address a problem they had encountered. The utilisation of unconscious feedback requires a more advanced procedure of usage knowledge understanding since interactions, such as clicks or taps, or contextual information, such as time and location, need to be processed; well-adjusted methods can be used to retrieve such precise information about user interaction [Joh+18a].

It is unconscious feedback that enables the detection of tacit usage knowledge that can be utilised for software evolution. Tacit knowledge in the context of usage knowledge goes beyond user analytics. It describes the users' feelings, ideas, and insights about a software system that they are unable to express in conscious feedback such as written text. In particular, it is knowledge that they apply without knowing it, which might not follow the way the system was designed in the first place.

We want to inspect runtime tacit knowledge with a concrete example. Imagine a mobile application that offers users the possibility to read news articles that are presented in full screen. The developers implemented two possibilities to enable the navigation between entries: (a) using a swipe gesture or (b) selecting a dot at the bottom of the page that represents every news entry currently available. First-time users might only use the dots to navigate since it is the most obvious way. However, this is tedious since the dots are tiny and hard to spot. It is only until the moment the users discover the swipe gesture that they learn a new, more intuitive and convenient way of navigation. When developers understand the users' interaction with the application, they are able to react and either improve the button navigation or add a distinct introduction to the swipe navigation. Similarly, as an additional example, navigating through a vertical list of entries on a mobile device can be accomplished in different ways: Users may perform (a) a long-lasting, exaggerated gesture or (b) multiple precise, yet repetitive, short swipes to move through the list. While the first behaviour indicates easily readable content, the latter one might be interpreted in a way that the list's content is hardly understandable and requires the full attention of a user.

5.4.2 Modelling of Knowledge

In our following analysis, we assume four main entities as illustrated in Fig. 5.3: The *User* is the main actor who uses the *Application*, which represents a software system.

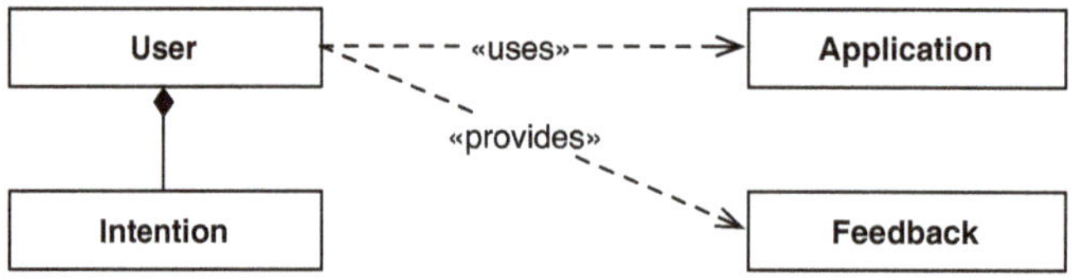

Fig. 5.3 Analysis of the application domain of usage knowledge

After and during the application usage, they provide *Feedback*, which can be further differentiated, as depicted in Fig. 5.2. The feedback is based on the user's *Intention*. This intention represents the user's idea of how they expect the application to accomplish a given task and how to behave given a certain interaction model posed by the application. To capture the intangible concepts of a user's intention, Norman introduced the *Conceptual Model*, which aims to formalise different perspectives on a similar issue [ND86]. He describes a relationship between the conceptual model and the *Mental Model* of every stakeholder that interacts with an application. In Fig. 5.4, we sketch involved models, in which the actual reality is represented by the conceptual model, which might be interpreted in different ways.

According to Norman, two models are derived from the conceptual model: a *System Model* and a mental model. Both of them are related to and formed by a variety of models. The system model is the result of the discussions of domain experts while applying domain knowledge. They create artefacts—the software increments—in accordance with their understanding of a design, functional, and object model. The mental model encompasses the users' perception on that specific artefact. The mental model depends on educational, cultural, or other general knowledge models that can be summarised under tacit knowledge. Eventually, it is the *User Interface* that brings both models together. The overall goal is to achieve

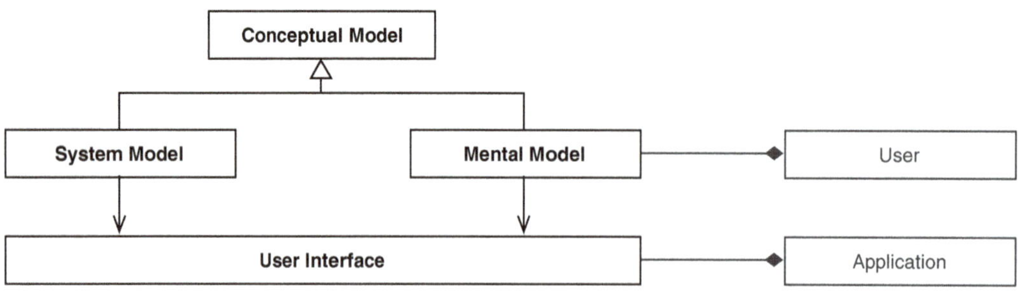

Fig. 5.4 Interpretation of the conceptual model as a system model and mental model [ND86] and their combination with the application domain coloured in grey on the right part of the figure

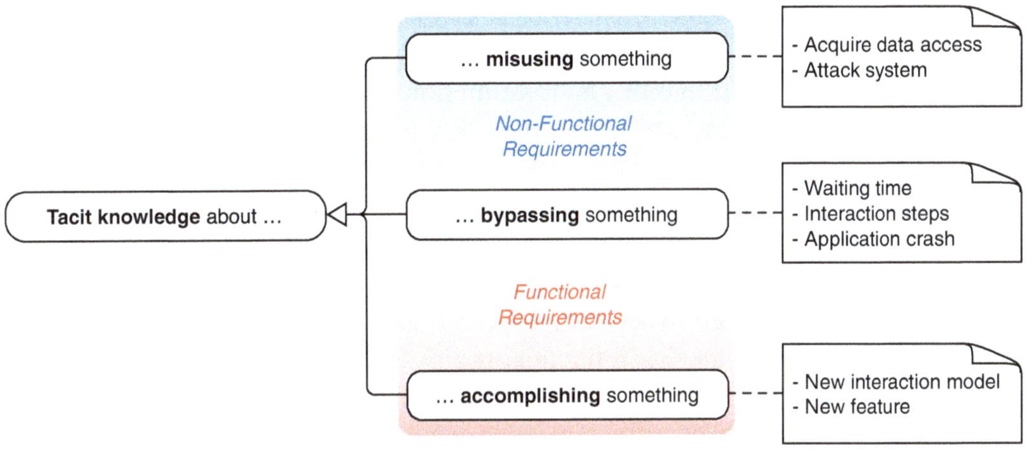

Fig. 5.5 Categories of tacit knowledge in the context of software evolution

a natural mapping [Nor13] that is characterised by a minimal amount of model disagreement. The disagreement of the system model and the mental model might be measured in the user's interaction with the application's user interface, which is built from the developer's system model.

The user's intention is closely bound to the tacit knowledge that users are unable to describe. As shown in Fig. 5.5, tacit knowledge can be categorised into three groups, though there might be more ways of distinguishing tacit knowledge in software evolution.

5.4.3 *Identification and Extraction of Tacit Usage Knowledge*

For the identification and extraction of tacit usage knowledge during run time, we propose a semi-automated approach. First, the occurrence of potential tacit knowledge needs to be detected, which should be accomplished using machine learning—we introduce the concept of runtime personas for this purpose in the next section. Second, in the event of tacit knowledge detection, a request for more qualitative feedback is posted. Third, a manual step of integrating the detected situation of tacit knowledge with the qualitative feedback of users is performed. Steps 2 and 3 are described as the extraction of tacit usage knowledge in the last part of this section.

Runtime Personas

Tacit knowledge needs to evolve; it is not existent at the moment a user starts using a software system. It develops over time, figuratively, though the temporal aspect can be part of the consideration. Other characteristics that indicate the familiarity of a user with the system might be clicks or any other quantifiable value summarized under unconscious feedback.

We apply Polanyi's terminology and assumptions for describing the identification of tacit knowledge. He introduces the *proximal* term and the *distal* term [PS09]. Proximal terms are considered the origin of an action, a starting point, or any event, such as interaction with the user interface, that eventually leads to a result. Such a result is described by the distal term, which can be any end point, intention, or goal, such as the execution of a software feature. During the first step of our approach, we aim to identify the connection between these two terms, which previously remained tacit. Polanyi states that there is a fluctuating link between the two of them, which eventually ends in a bold, established relationship—the tacit knowledge. Figure 5.6 illustrates this evolvement of tacit knowledge separated over a time span of different observations during the run time of a software system.

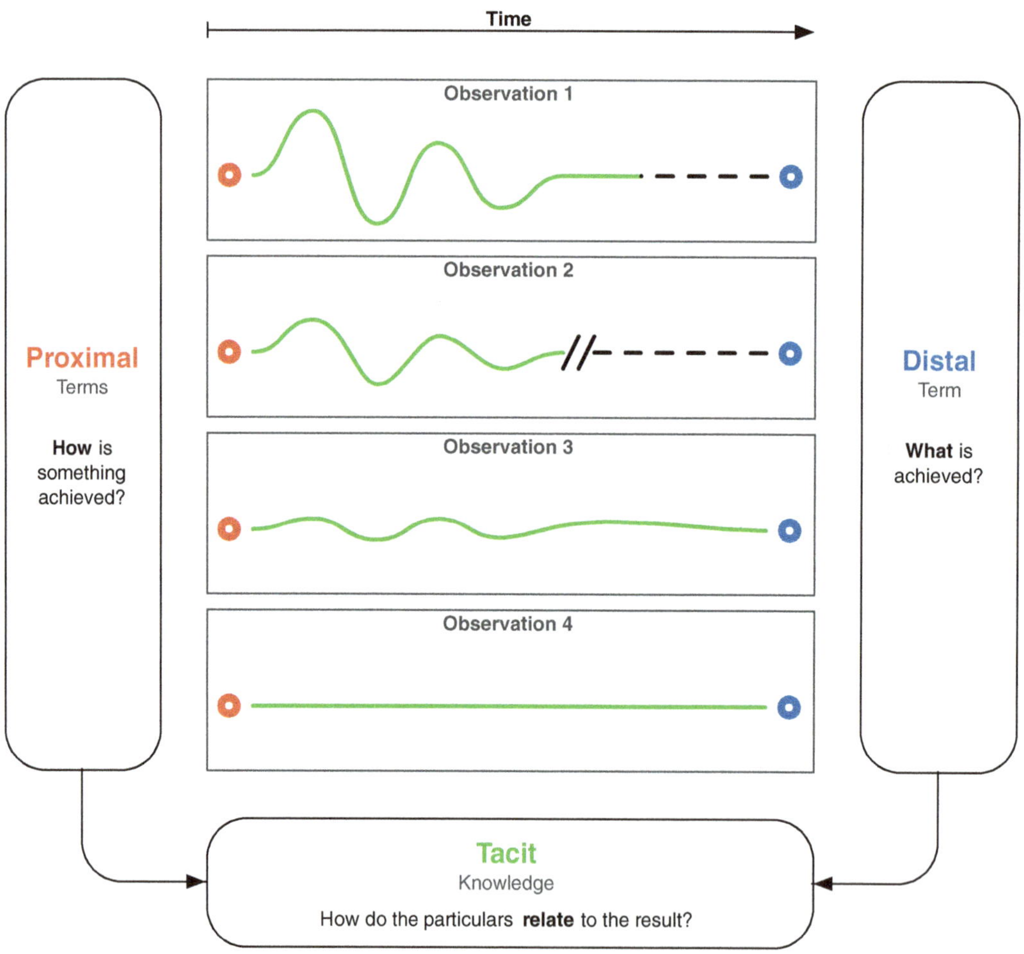

Fig. 5.6 The relation between the proximal terms (red), distal term (blue), and tacit knowledge (green). The proximal terms, for example taps by the users, are eventually mapped to the distal term, for example the feature execution. According to Polanyi [PS09], tacit knowledge can be understood as the established mapping between the proximal and distal terms

Polanyi argues that "we are aware of the proximal term of an act of tacit knowing in the appearance of its distal term" [PS09] and continues to define this finding as the *phenomenal* structure [PS09]. Consequently, if we identified the distal term of a given tacit knowledge while users established a mature connection between both terms, we might be able to derive the proximal terms that are of great value to start understanding software usage. For the purpose of collecting and allocating observations, we introduce the concept of **Runtime Personas**. According to Polanyi, tacit knowledge is a person-related concept, which matches the persona definition. Run time personas form a container to capture the evolvement and eventually the discovery of tacit knowledge. The evolvement of a run time persona is initiated with traditional personas as a first, optimal representation of tacit knowledge, while it gets enriched throughout multiple stages and new findings.

This process can be understood best by giving an example aligned with Fig. 5.6. The distal term defines the results of an action—the consequence or outcome, depending on the observation. In the context of software engineering, this could be the execution of a feature, in particular related interactions with the user interface. Referring to our initial examples, the distal term could be expressed in consuming a list of information on a mobile application. It is the proximal terms, the *particulars*, that a user may not be able to tell when using the software system. In our example, it manifests itself in the way the user interacts with the list to traverse the list's content. The challenge lies in the discovery of the connection between this interaction and the usage of the list, namely its corresponding distal term. Traditional personas [Coo99] serve as the starting point. They describe a person's characteristics that qualify them for the usage of a feature, in particular reaching the previously defined distal term. Further, they encapsulate the observations resulting from the asymptotic process of information extracting. For instance, *Observation 1* refers to a situation in which it is not clear if a user's interaction leads to a feature usage. *Observation 2* seems promising, but indications stopped before it could be clearly mapped to the usage of the feature. *Observation 3* represents the first time that a definite correlation between the proximal and distal terms could be established, while it still includes some fluctuations. Finally, *Observation 4* encompasses a clear link between the two terms, allowing for the derivation of tacit knowledge.

Extraction of Tacit Usage Knowledge

Adapting Polanyi's hypothesis of the phenomenal structure of tacit knowledge to the context of usage knowledge in software systems, users are aware of their interactions from which they are attending to accomplish the feature—in appearance of that specific feature. This allows for extracting the tacit knowledge in the event of *Observation 4*.

We propose utilising a modal window that asks the user for qualitative feedback, as shown in Fig. 5.7. It is triggered as soon as a distinct relation between proximal and distal terms is detected. In particular, we imagine gaining insights with regard to the following questions:

Fig. 5.7 Mockup of requesting feedback from user

- What has the user been trying to do?
- How did the user try to achieve it?
- Did the user experience any problems during this process?

The qualitative feedback enables the developer to understand and externalise the tacit knowledge carried out by the users during run time. For integrating the usage observation with the qualitative feedback, we propose the introduction of a dashboard [Joh+17b]. The dashboard is a central component of the **CURES** project. Within this dashboard, we envision to visually display categories of equivalence classes—either based on the usage knowledge or by groups of distal terms, namely the performed features. This allows the developers to augment information from multiple feedback and find an optimal solution for integrating the new findings [Joh+17a].

A further extension to encourage users to provide more detailed information about the performed action could include a predefined selection of features—the distal term—potentially involved in the process. However, this would require the possibility to make a distinction in features used, in particular features offered by the software system.

Besides the integration and utilisation of the tacit runtime knowledge during design time tasks by the developer, recurring patterns of tacit knowledge can be caught during run time and utilised by the developer. For example, referring to Fig. 5.5, in case a user wants to bypass several process steps that in general cannot be removed from the application, the system could still provide a shortcut functionality as soon as this situation is detected.

5.4.4 Tacit Usage Knowledge Examples

We focus on the automatic creation of run time personas from usage behaviour within mobile applications. In this section, we describe examples of tacit usage knowledge from a current research project [Frö18].

We prepared an open-source mobile application with several modifications to record explicit usage data, such as interactions with the user interface in the form of taps and gestures, as well as other sensor data, such as gyroscope and tap pressure. We designed a catalogue of tasks to stimulate interaction within the application; for example, we asked to use a specific functionality of the application or to find out particular information that required them to navigate through several views of the application. The tasks were carefully chosen to encompass typical routines of user interactions, as well as aspects that allow to recognise the users' behaviour in unexpected situations. Based on the task execution by more than 100 individuals, we trained multiple classifiers to derive the following characteristics for our run time personas.

- *Person-related information* aims to characterise attributes that are highly individual to users, such as age groups distinguished by age ranges or their proficiency and skills in dealing with mobile applications, distinguished in beginner and expert groups.
- *Application-related information* aims to define the user's familiarity with the application at hand. This is reflected in attributes such as the familiarity level, while we distinguish between a beginner and expert level, and their mental phase with respect to the application usage, that is if they are exploring the interface or if they are productively working and interacting with its functionality.
- *Application-related usability issues* aim to reflect users' behaviour given a situation in which they encounter an unexpected system behaviour, such as inconsistencies in the user interface or missing user interaction elements in the user interface.

So far, based on the current evaluation of usage data, we receive good results on detecting situations in which users encounter an application-related usability issue. We hypothesise that this is based on the fact that they only occur during a short period of time, which is revealed in a distinct set of obvious changes in user behaviour. The exact characteristics of the features remain yet unknown. Equally promising results can be reported for detecting application-related information.

Here, the detection of the productivity status of a user results in especially good results. However, we assume a systematic error in measuring the productivity of a user. Currently, we label a behaviour as productive in case the user is *on their way* to using a functionality. In case they are *moving away from it*, for example navigating towards a view that is not related, leaving no further space to use the functionality, we consider their status as exploring. The results of the classifier depend on a threshold for distinguishing between these two states. Measurements for person-related information highly depend on the splitting of both the test and training data for the individual classifiers.

We observe that application-related information can be suitable for automatically deriving run time persona attributes. We hypothesise that this is because of their inherent semantic relation to the user interaction. Person-related information, on the other hand, is more challenging in its extraction and consequently is less accurate to detect. Multiple reasons for its low predictability might be found in the way of data collection.

In general, the presented approach to collect run time personas' characteristics and the resulting classifiers need to be treated with caution. Firstly and most importantly, the approach would highly benefit from even more individuals who provide usage data. In our model under consideration, we have an unbalanced distribution of person-related information. This could be the reasons why the models for person-related information might perform worse than the application-related information. We also acknowledge a high bias of the sample application that was used to collect the usage data. We tried to minimise this effect by tailoring the task scenarios around general user interface interactions that are typical for a majority of mobile applications. Overall, we suppose that several machine learning features for training a model remain undiscovered. Therefore, future research is required to find more machine learning features that reveal the main behaviour characteristics of an action.

5.5 Related Work

Tacit knowledge is present during various aspects of software evolution. For instance, it has been shown that developers share important rationale through chat messages to perform development tasks [Alk+17a, Alk+17b]. This observation fosters our assumption that there is more knowledge in existing artefacts that has not yet been externalised. In particular, LaToza et al. highlight knowledge that resides in developers' minds regarding the application of tools and activities to perform code tasks during software development [LVD06]. This chapter sets the focus on tacit knowledge to improve requirements elicitation by capturing additional information during the design and run time of a software system. In the following, we present existing work.

AlHogail and Berri [AB12] propose the development of architecture to preserve security knowledge within an organisation. They plan to perceive and distribute security knowledge to tackle the problem of availability of security experts in software projects. This enables a faster reaction on security incidents. To preserve security knowledge, a template is used. Tsoumas and Gritzalis [TG06] present a security management approach for information systems containing security knowledge of different sources. Several approaches deal with the management of security knowledge in ontologies [Ras+01, KR07, BKK05]. Lee et al. [Lee+06] introduce an approach for the extraction of relevant concepts from documents to build a problem domain ontology. Jung et al. [JHS99] developed a reasoning approach to use past security accidents in the risk analysis of e-commerce systems. To apply this approach, the problem must be formatted into a specific case representation, which makes additional effort necessary.

Most of the approaches are not considering the evolution of security knowledge intensively. The support of requirements engineers who use past events from gathered security knowledge in the context of requirements elicitation was not taken into account in most approaches. Furthermore, cases in which knowledge changes over time were also not considered.

When switching the perspective from a software architect or requirement analyst to end users, for example the users of a software system, the runtime aspects of a software system provide a rich source of tacit knowledge. Following Roehm et al.'s findings, developers try to make use of this by putting themselves in the shoes of users to understand program behaviour and get first ideas to further act on it [Roe+12].

By applying a semi-automatic approach, Damevski et al. mine large-scale datasets of IDE interactions [Dam+17]. Therefore, they aim to identify inefficient applications of IDE usage patterns relying on their observations of developers' activities during their daily development tasks. They begin with an automated approach that—after preparing the input data—encompasses a sequential pattern mining and filtering activity. Hereafter, clusters are created to determine common workflows of developers, which are verified by the authors and a developer survey. The approach of Damevski et al. shares a concrete process model to derive knowledge from usage behaviour for the specific domain of integrated development environments (IDEs). Our approach presented in Sect. 5.4 reflects the core idea of the approach presented by Damevski et al. In particular, we try to identify common usage patterns of a software increment.

Zhang et al. present a *quantitative bottom-up data-driven approach to create personas* in their paper *Data-Driven Personas: Constructing Archetypal Users with Clickstreams and User Telemetry* [ZBS16]. Their approach on creating personas solely relies on click streams, while we want to incorporate other data as well, such as the location or any meta data that describes *how* and *when* clicks occurred in order to provide additional semantics.

Almeida et al. acknowledge the presence of poorly designed applications that prevent users from using them and sustainable maintenance and evolution [Alm+15]. They introduce a usability smell catalogue that allows for their identification, as well as refactoring the problems in question. Similarly, we strive to find *behavioural smells* that provide information about the users [Joh18].

Gadler et al. apply log mining to derive the use of a system; utilising Hidden Markov Models, they automatically represent user's intention [Gad+17]. We want to apply a similar approach to understand the users' intention when interacting with a new software increment.

5.6 Conclusion

To conclude this chapter, we provide a brief summary of tacit knowledge in software evolution, an outlook on future challenges, as well as further reading suggestions.

5.6.1 Summary

We described two approaches to identify and extract tacit knowledge during the design time and run time of software systems. During the development of the approaches introduced in Sects. 5.3 and 5.4, we encountered various lessons learned, which we summarise subsequently.

We acknowledge that requirements which become new features might be relevant for security. Identifying tacit knowledge in the form of security knowledge is a difficult task for which a good understanding of security and the domain of the software is necessary. Nature language processing can support the requirement engineer during this task.

Extracting tacit usage knowledge during run time raises various challenges. As indicated in Fig. 5.6, potentially *wrong* usage behaviour might eventually transition into a pattern that is of interest and relevant for a new feature or functionality of an application. This learning phase needs to be a core element in the detection of usage behaviour, making it an important reference that points to the tacit knowledge. Likewise, it is important to distinguish tacit knowledge from any kind of *noise* effects. Eventually, we learned that only a limited set of new features can be detected, while the quality of insights highly depends on the application in question.

Further discussions on security and its maintenance are described in Chap. 9. Linking the tacit usage knowledge to other knowledge types, such as decision knowledge described in Chap. 6, provides new possibilities to further support software evolution.

5.6.2 Outlook

Tacit knowledge in the domain of software evolution promises future research areas to improve processes and software quality. In the following, we elaborate on multiple aspects of design and runtime tacit knowledge that we propose to continue to work on in the future.

We developed an approach to identify security-related requirements semi-automatically using natural language processing. The success of our approach depends on the quality of security knowledge. Detailed knowledge leads to a more helpful base of security knowledge for our approach. One challenge is to retrieve and model the security knowledge to make it accessible for further requirement elicitation. Our approach can identify vulnerabilities in requirements written in natural language based on security incidents. With the iThrust case study, we have shown that our approach performs better than other approaches, such as Naïve Bayes, k-NN, and SVMs. To apply our approach in an industrial setting, we have to evaluate the level of detail that is used to document security incidents. Furthermore, we need to investigate if intermediate feedback on security issues in requirements improves the elicitation of security requirements.

A general, major challenge for future research efforts regarding runtime tacit knowledge will be the detection of deviations between explicitly elicited requirements and implicitly derived requirements based on users' behaviour. In particular, creating a traceability link between these requirement sources still poses a challenge in the exploration of tacit usage knowledge.

Two additional challenges should be investigated to further evolve software engineering regarding tacit knowledge during run time. We found a challenge in detecting actual error conditions. In particular, this requires to decide whether a behavioural pattern or sequence is relevant or if it is simply *noise*, which is irrelevant for the evaluation (see *Observation 1* and *Observation 2* in Fig. 5.6). This challenge results in a fundamental question: Is every behaviour relevant and is there such a thing as noise? Furthermore, the actual interaction with users, as described in Sect. 5.4.3, needs to be clearly defined. This includes the question on when a user can be interrupted in order to retrieve their state, that is what they have been doing, how they were doing it, and if they experienced any problems (see Fig. 5.7). We identified two requirements that need to be fulfilled to spot the appropriate moment to interrupt a user and thereby prevent negative interruptions. First, a user should only be interrupted if it can be guaranteed that it will not interfere with their current workflow. Second, no critical process should be disturbed. Both requirements, however, pose new challenges. A balance needs to be found to keep a minimal time span between the interaction and the interruption. A delay, though, results in the problem that traceability should be guaranteed; that is, the users' feedback should be allocated clearly to an interaction. We envision to develop a tacit knowledge characteristic similar to the properties defined in database transactions: atomicity, consistency, isolation, durability [HR83].

5.6.3 Further Reading

In the project SecVolution, Bürger et al. presented a framework that analyses the environment, security-related requirements, and observations to provide an automated reaction to observed changes and to ensure a certain security level for long-living information systems [Bür+18].

As part of our previous work, we developed a prototype called FOCUS for the documentation of non-functional requirements while using execution traces, as well as video screencasts underlined by audio comments [Sch06]. The documentation can be created as a by-product via recording the application of a task [Sch06].One field for using our tool is security. Therefore, we have enhanced this documentation by a semi-automated approach to analyse security vulnerabilities based on remote code exploits for Java applications [VKK17]. The analysis enables the localisation of a source code vulnerability while distinguishing a penetration test recording with a recording of the regular behaviour of the same application. Gärtner et al. developed a tool-based approach, which provides heuristic feedback on security-related aspects of requirements to document decisions [Gär+14]. For this purpose, a decision model is used to systematically capture and document requirements, design decisions, as well as related rationale.

Pagano and Roehm described the difference between expected and observed user behaviour based on different perceptions of the conceptual model [Pag13, Roe15], an aspect that we address in Sect. 5.4.2. Roehm et al. investigated derivations in the descriptions of use cases with observed behaviour of users by applying machine learning techniques [Roe+13a]. The interaction with user interface elements is investigated by Roehm et al. using an approach to associate user interactions with application bugs to enable failure reproduction [Roe+13b].

We provide and maintain the source code and further explanation of tools and platforms for usage knowledge understanding in an online repository.[1]

[1] https://github.com/cures-hub.

Chapter 6
Continuous Design Decision Support

Anja Kleebaum, Marco Konersmann, Michael Langhammer, Barbara Paech, Michael Goedicke, and Ralf Reussner

In this chapter, we elaborate on how design decisions are made, documented, and exploited during software evolution. We emphasise the importance of design decisions, in particular in the context of continuous software engineering. We detail the challenge of the *intrusiveness* of rational decision-making, documentation, and exploitation of design decisions and the challenge of ensuring *consistency* between design decisions and software artefacts.

The main contributions of this chapter are three approaches to a continuous design decision support: First, we present an approach that supports developers in design decision-making using a catalogue of design patterns. Second, we present an approach to support the awareness for documented design decisions by integrating the decision documentation with the underlying source code. Third, we present how short-cycled practices in continuous software engineering can be used to support the documentation and exploitation of design decisions.

A. Kleebaum · B. Paech (✉)
Universität Heidelberg, Mathematikon - Institut für Informatik, Heidelberg, Germany
e-mail: anja.kleebaum@informatik.uni-heidelberg.de; paech@informatik.uni-heidelberg.de

M. Konersmann
Institute for Software Technology, Research Group Software Engineering, Universität Koblenz-Landau, Koblenz, Germany
e-mail: konersmann@uni-koblenz.de

M. Goedicke
paluno – The Ruhr Institute for Software Technology, Specification of Software Systems, Universität Duisburg-Essen, Essen, Germany
e-mail: michael.goedicke@s3.uni-due.de

M. Langhammer · R. Reussner
Institute for Program Structures and Data Organisation, Karlsruhe Institute of Technology (KIT), Karlsruhe, Germany
e-mail: michael.langhammer@alumni.kit.edu; reussner@kit.edu

R. Reussner et al. (eds.), *Managed Software Evolution*,
https://doi.org/10.1007/978-3-030-13499-0_6

All three approaches contribute to the guiding themes *knowledge carrying software* and *methods and processes for evolution* of the priority program.

6.1 Introduction

Continuous Software Engineering (CSE) is a software engineering process in which developers continuously change the software while keeping it in a releasable state [KB17]. CSE means to develop, release, and learn from software in very short rapid cycles [Bos14]. It incorporates agile practices and involves activities such as continuous integration, delivery, and deployment [SAZ17, Joh+18b]. The emergence of CSE is driven by a growing need for flexibility and rapid adaption in the current software environment [FS17].

Software developers and architects continuously make design decisions while they develop and evolve software. They make decisions on the requirements to be addressed, the design artefacts (e.g. architectural components, packages, interfaces, classes, and methods) to be created or the design patterns to be applied. For example, it is a design decision to apply an adapter design pattern instead of changing an existing interface when adding new features to a software. The knowledge of the developers on the design decisions they make is called *decision knowledge*. In particular, decision knowledge comprises the knowledge about the problems, the decisions they address, solution approaches, their context, and rationale in terms of arguments, criteria, and the assessment of solution alternatives.

Decision knowledge should be communicated within a development team so that every developer knows and considers existing decisions [Bru+14]. When developers evolve software, it is important for them to reflect and build on former decisions. Otherwise, they might make inconsistent decisions and are likely to contribute to the erosion of the software architecture or introduce other quality problems [Cle+13, Cap+16]. Reflecting on former decisions is particularly important for long-living software systems where many decisions build on one another.

The documentation of decision knowledge is important for several reasons: First, many different developers might be involved at different times. Thus, they cannot communicate directly and rely on documented decision knowledge when they reflect on former decisions. That means that the documentation of decision knowledge is important to prevent knowledge vaporisation [Cap+16]. Decision knowledge vaporises quickly; that is, if developers do not capture decision knowledge immediately, it will never be captured and thus will not be available later [JB05]. Tacit decision knowledge (cf. Chap. 5) enlarges the risk of misunderstandings and errors during evolution or maintenance. Second, the documentation of decision knowledge makes the criteria for the design decisions explicit that might otherwise be overlooked. This promotes a more rational decision-making process. Third, documented decision knowledge is valuable to support future changes. It supports change impact analysis, requirement validation, and long-term maintenance and keeps developers informed about underlying architectural decisions [Cle+13].

While there is clearly a need for decision knowledge documentation, in practice this is often not performed [APM16]. In practice, decisions are mostly made and documented in a naturalistic way [ZCM07, Hes+16]. This means that only a part of the decision knowledge—often only the decision—is documented, which impairs the rational decision-making. Humans tend to overlook what is missing and are subject to cognitive biases [Raz+16]. Furthermore, if the arguments for the decision are not documented, other developers might not understand the decision or might not be convinced.

Recently, various techniques emerged that try to reconstruct decision knowledge by mining written text from informal sources such as chat messages, which is referred to as *extractive summarisation* [NHJ16]. These techniques are promising in identifying decision knowledge; however, the knowledge may be incomplete, outdated, or hard to access later. In other cases, the knowledge is not captured at all but only resides in the developers' heads as tacit knowledge. Researcher attempt to infer tacit knowledge by *abstractive summarisation* of software artefacts such as source code changes [Cor+14]. However, Robillard et al. confirm that it is unlikely to infer complex information such as rationale by mechanical extraction of facts from software artefacts [Rob+17]. Therefore, summarisation techniques only partially help to reconstruct decision knowledge in case they are applied retrospectively. Decision knowledge needs to be explicitly documented in order to preserve it. It is important to note that easy exploitation of the decision knowledge motivates developers to document it, as the developers themselves can profit from the documentation [BB08].

CSE provides many practices for a continuous change [KB17]. These can be used for a continuous design decision documentation. Our long-term vision is an *on-demand decision documentation* as part of the *on-demand developer documentation* suggested by Robillard et al. [Rob+17]. We envision that developers continuously capture and reflect decision knowledge during CSE. Our goal is to support developers in this continuous capture and reflection, in particular by performing rational decision-making. The following three developer tasks should be lightweight; that is, they should require as little effort as possible: *rational decision-making*, *documentation of decision knowledge*, and its *exploitation*.

6.1.1 Challenges for a Continuous Design Decision Support

Tool support to manage decision knowledge can be characterised by its intrusiveness in the software development process [Dut+06]. Tools that fit into the development context are less *intrusive* and will more likely be used [KCD09]. Such tools do not require additional effort (e.g. for installing or starting a separate tool) and are thus also lightweight. For example, a developer can capture the design decision for applying an adapter design pattern within a commit message instead of in a separate tool. Rational decision-making, documentation of decision knowledge, and its exploitation should be non-intrusive in the context of the CSE process. It is a challenge to minimise the intrusiveness of a continuous design decision support.

Challenge regarding intrusiveness: how to integrate rational design decision-making, documentation, and exploitation in software engineering practices

To exploit decision knowledge, it is important that the design decisions are *consistent* (a) with former design decisions and (b) with the artefacts, for example, with the requirements, architectural software design, and code. Consistency means that design decisions are documented, as well as linked to and realised, in the artefacts they relate to. For example, the design decision to apply the adapter design pattern should be linked to the code that implements the pattern. Then developers can reflect on this decision when they change the code. Developers need to reflect former decision knowledge during decision-making, so that the design decisions are consistent with each other. There are two types of former decision knowledge: First, general decision knowledge is documented in *external knowledge bases* (e.g. about design patterns). Second, new design decisions build on former decision knowledge *specific to the software development project*. Especially in long-living software systems, much decision knowledge accumulates. Documented decision knowledge might be invalidated during software evolution and needs to be updated. Not only decisions need to be consistent with each other. The decision knowledge also needs to be consistent with the artefacts. Moreover, the design artefacts, for example architectural software design and code, also need to be consistent with each other to ensure that the decisions are actually implemented. It is a challenge to document and maintain decision knowledge consistent with the other artefacts and with former decision knowledge.

Challenge regarding inconsistency: how to ensure consistency between decision knowledge and artefacts

6.1.2 Solution Approaches for Design Decision Challenges

In this chapter, we present approaches that address both challenges. The approaches try to find a balance between intrusiveness and consistency support. A more powerful support typically requires separate tools, which are more intrusive. Also, the approaches focus on different kinds of decision knowledge. The first approach promotes rational decision-making by providing software designers with a catalogue of questions that support them in choosing a design pattern. Thus, this approach focuses on *consistency with external decision knowledge, which is presented in a separate tool*. The second approach focuses on the *consistency among decisions within a project, architecture, and code*. It ensures that design decisions are documented and related to design and implementation artefacts. Thus, this approach improves the consistency relation between these artefacts. It incorporates the decision knowledge captured by the design pattern approach. The third approach provides *non-intrusive integration* of the documentation and exploitation support during CSE and *lightweight traceability for consistency*. During CSE, developers usually manage code and other development knowledge in a Version Control System (VCS) and issues in an Issue Tracking System (ITS) [Sai+17]. The third approach integrates the documentation and exploitation of decision knowledge into practices relating to the VCS and ITS. Thus, it does not require a separate tool. It uses *extractive and abstractive summaries* to support the transition from naturalistic to rational decision knowledge documentation. Furthermore, it identifies relevant decision knowledge based on traceability links to support *consistent decision-making*. These approaches showcase different ways to support decision-making, documentation, and exploitation. The choice of one of them depends on the context.

6.1.3 Structure of This Chapter

This chapter is structured as follows: Sect. 6.2 sketches the Decision Documentation Model (DDM) as a foundation of this chapter. The DDM allows developers and architects to document decision knowledge incrementally and collaboratively. Section 6.3 presents the approach that supports the decision-making regarding design patterns using a pattern catalogue and documenting such decision knowledge. Section 6.4 presents the approach to support the documentation and consistency by integrating design decision models with program code. In Sect. 6.5, the approach focusing on short-cycled CSE practices is introduced. Section 6.6 presents related work. Section 6.7 discusses and concludes this chapter and provides an outlook. Section 6.8 provides references for further reading.

6.2 Foundations

We represent decision knowledge based on the DDM by Hesse and Paech [HP13]. According to the DDM, decision knowledge is documented as *decision components*, which can be nested and refer to other knowledge. Figure 6.1 shows the key decision components of the DDM (depicted with yellow background), as well as additional decision components used in the pattern catalogue in Sect. 6.3 (depicted with white background). In Fig. 6.1, *decision component* is an abstract class that can only be instantiated through its subclasses. Related knowledge elements can be decision knowledge or software artefacts such as requirements, architectural design, code, and test cases. Decision components are the decision *problem* to be solved (issues or goals), *solution* (alternatives or claims), *context* information (assumptions, constraints, or implications), and *rationale* (arguments or assessments). The DDM subsumes decision elements used in other approaches [PDH14] but does not prescribe any components for decision documentation. Therefore, it supports incremental documentation of decisions and in particular both naturalistic and rational decision-making. Any part of the decision knowledge can be captured as soon as it is available. In addition, any number of stakeholders such as developers, architects, and requirement engineers can collaborate while documenting decisions. Each stakeholder contributes that part of the decision knowledge they know best. The requirement engineer can, for example, add constraints, which have to be reflected for a particular solution.

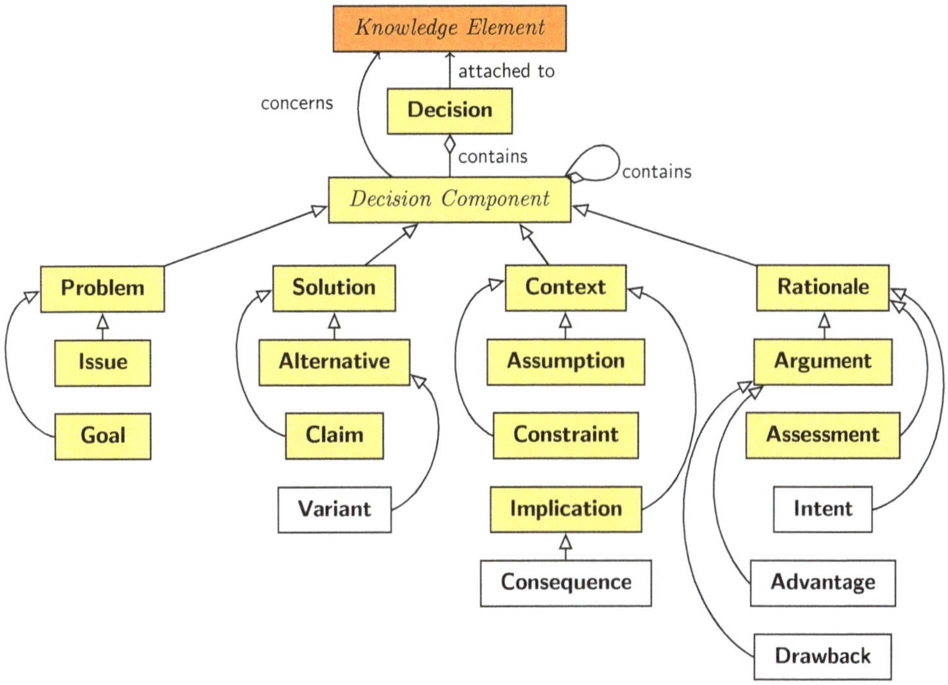

Fig. 6.1 Decision documentation model (DDM) adapted from [HP13]

The DDM has been applied in an empirical study on Firefox issue reports [Hes+16]. This showed that the DDM can adequately reflect the decision knowledge captured in issue trackers. The dominance of naturalistic decision-making in this study confirms the need for an incremental and collaborative decision documentation. In addition, the DDM has been applied in a case study on design session transcripts [HP16]. This confirmed that the DDM also adequately reflects decision-making in a team. In particular, the usage of the DDM made complex decision knowledge structures in the design sessions explicit.

6.3 Using a Design Pattern Catalogue to Make Design Decisions

In this section, we explain the *Architectural Modelling with Design Decision Documentation (AM3D)* [Dur14] approach that supports software architects and software developers in the process of decision-making. For this purpose, it uses a pre-defined pattern catalogue that contains patterns and pattern-specific questions as main artefacts. Software architects using the approach need to answer a set of questions to get the correct pattern that solves their current problem. Compared to the classical software architecture process, the advantage of this approach is that the design decisions become more rational and less naturalistic. Furthermore, the design decisions are documented and made explicit and thus are easier to understand by other software architects and software developers. The AM3D approach supports rational decision-making consistent with former external decision knowledge. In the following, we describe the approach in detail and apply it to the Common Component Modeling Example (CoCoME) case study. The details of the pattern catalogue and the decision-making process are presented in the dissertation of Durdik [Dur14].

This section is structured as follows: Sect. 6.3.1 explains the motivation for using a pattern catalogue. In Sect. 6.3.2, we explain how a pattern catalogue can be used for decision-making. In Sect. 6.3.3, we show how the presented approach can be applied to our current example.

6.3.1 Motivation for Using a Pattern Catalogue

In the domain of software engineering, patterns are widely used to solve common problems. In the last decades, various pattern catalogues have been introduced, for example by Gamma et al. [Gam+95] and Buschmann et al. [Bus+96]. If software architects and software developers need to solve a specific problem, they can often use one of the already existing patterns. Choosing the correct pattern for a given problem, however, is not an easy task as there are many patterns solving similar problems. Another problem that arises using patterns is that they are often used wrongly. Hence, choosing the correct pattern and using it correctly is a difficult and error-prone task.

6.3.2 Decision-Making Process Using a Pattern Catalogue

In this section, we explain the decision-making process, which is used to choose the correct pattern. This includes the presentation of the pattern catalogue and the activities to make the design decisions explicit.

Most sources of patterns, such as [Gam+95], contain patterns in a free-text form. The advantage of these sources is that one can learn about patterns, their benefits, their usage, and others. However, their disadvantage is that the information is not structured, and it takes a lot of time to gain knowledge about patterns that can be used to solve a specific problem. Often, it is also unclear which pattern form shall be chosen to solve a given problem.

The design pattern catalogue of the AM3D approach aims to overcome these disadvantages. Its main purposes and goals that are relevant for the decision-making process are (1) to present structured information about patterns, (2) to allow for semi-automated documentation of the pattern usage, and (3) to support goal-oriented requirement engineering.

The three main information parts stored in the pattern catalogue are (1) general information about the pattern, (2) questions annotated to the pattern, and (3)

Table 6.1 Information about a pattern stored in the pattern catalogue [Dur14]

Category	Detailed attribute	Short description
General information	Name	A name for the pattern
	Type	A type for the pattern, for example object-oriented pattern or security pattern
	Category	The category of the pattern, usually described by pattern authors; for instance, *behavioural* patterns are a category by Gamma [Gam+95]
	Information source	The original source of the pattern
	ID	A unique identifier for the pattern
	Goal	A high-level description of the pattern's goal, respectively the problem that can be solved using the pattern
	Description	A brief description of the pattern, which is intended for users in order to understand the concept of the pattern
	Advantages	Advantages of the pattern, which come with the usage of this pattern
	Drawbacks	Highlighting problems/drawbacks of the pattern
	Keywords	Keywords to characterise the pattern
	Quality attributes	The pattern's impact on quality dimensions of the software system, for example performance increased/decreased
	Relationships	Relations to other patterns, divided into three dimensions: (1) recommended co-patterns, (2) similar patterns, and (3) excluded patterns
	Variants	Variants of the pattern
Question annotations	Goal	Questions on the goal of the user, that is whether the user likes to solve a problem in a specific way
	Intent	Questions on the intent of the user, that is whether the user intents to have a specific behaviour in a software system
	Consequence	Questions on consequences, that is whether some consequences are acceptable if a specific pattern is used

the structure of the implementation as a Unified Modeling Language (UML)-like diagram. Table 6.1 shows the details for the general information and the questions. The questions are divided into the following four categories: (1) questions regarding the goal of the pattern, (2) questions regarding the advantages of the pattern, (3) questions regarding the drawbacks of the pattern, and (4) questions regarding variants of the current pattern.

Table 6.2 Questions for the façade pattern [Dur14]

Type	Question
Goal	Would you like to provide a unified interface to a set of interfaces in a subsystem?
Intent	Would you like to minimise the communication and dependencies between subsystems?
	An additional functionality wrapped into the unified interface is not your intent? (otherwise → proxy)
	Is a stateless unified interface your intent? (otherwise → proxy)
	Is it desired that subsystem classes know nothing about the façade object(s)? (otherwise → mediator)
	A new interface for an object is not your intent? (otherwise → adapter)
Consequence	Is a potential performance bottleneck not an issue?

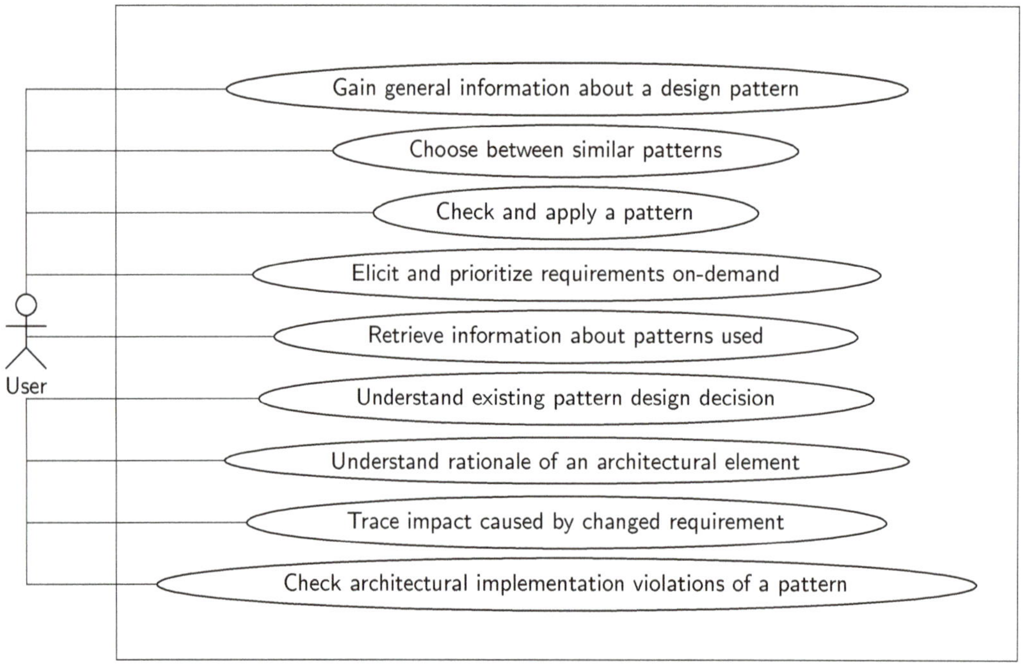

Fig. 6.2 Use cases for the pattern catalogue [Dur14]

As an example, questions for the façade pattern are shown in Table 6.2. The structured information about the patterns allows to ask structured questions to the users and to present appropriate patterns for the problem that the users want to solve.

The pattern catalogue can be used in multiple use cases during the development process. The use cases are shown in Fig. 6.2. In this chapter, we focus on the main use case *check and apply a pattern*, which involves making the design decision for a specific pattern and documenting this decision. The remaining use cases are explained in [Dur14]. Figure 6.3 shows the activity diagram of the use case. The first step is to analyse the problem based on the given requirements. The second step

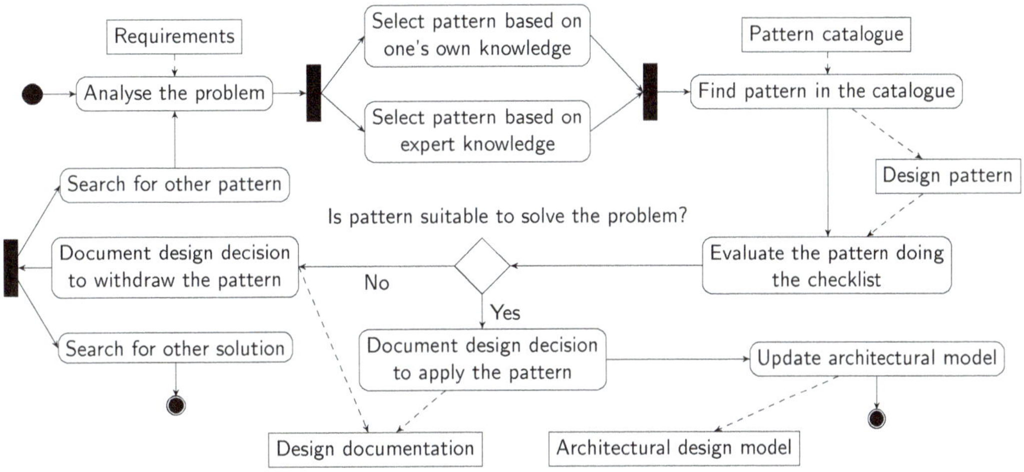

Fig. 6.3 Activity diagram of checking and applying a pattern [Dur14]

is to pre-choose a pattern based on one's own knowledge or based on an expert's knowledge. Next, the pattern catalogue is used to find and evaluate the pattern. The evaluation is done by using the checklist, which is attached to the pattern, that is the questions for the pattern are evaluated again to clarify whether the chosen pattern is a correct one for the given problem. If the pattern is suitable to solve the problem, the design decision has been made. The next steps are to document the decision and to update the architectural model with the newly chosen pattern. If the pattern is not suitable, the decision that the pattern has not been chosen and the reason why are documented. Then the iteration starts from the beginning by re-analysing the problem and looking for a different pattern. If, however, no pattern can be found that solves the problem, another solution needs to be found, for example clarifying the requirements.

In summary, the AM3D process guides users through the process of decision-making. It also stores the answers and the decision in a model, that is the decision knowledge is made explicit and is documented. The main advantages of using the catalogue and the structured process are as follows: (1) The rationale and other decision knowledge of the design decisions to apply a specific pattern is documented. (2) Through systematic pattern evaluation with the help of question annotations, software developers and software architects are supported in applying design patterns and design pattern variants correctly.

The AM3D approach has been evaluated in a controlled experiment with 20 students [Dur14]. During the evaluation, the technical questions concerning the patterns have been evaluated as well. For the evaluation, the approach was compared to a standard pattern catalogue. During the evaluation, the students had to face two scenarios: In the first scenario, a new design decision had to be made, whereas in the second scenario an existing decision had to be re-evaluated. The students who used the AM3D approach had better results in both scenarios. The results for the first scenario are statistically significant, while the results for the second scenario are not.

6.3.3 Application to the Case Study

In this section, we show an application of the AM3D approach to a CoCoME evolution scenario. In this scenario, the CoCoME sales system is extended by new payment possibilities. Up to now, customers could only pay via debit card. Payments are initiated by the CashDesk component. Currently, this component communicates with an external bank (`TrivialBankServer` component) via the `IBank` interface. The `IBank` interface defines the methods `validateCard` and `debitCard`. Figure 6.4 shows an excerpt of the CoCoME architecture as a Palladio Component Model (PCM) repository diagram [BKR09].

Requirements for modern payment possibilities such as PayPal and Bitcoins arise. The new payment possibilities are to be implemented, while the existing payment possibility using a bank server will still be supported. We focus on the latter case and assume that the decision process is executed using the AM3D approach.

In this scenario, the generic `IPayment` interface is introduced that defines the `authenticate` and `pay` methods. For using the existing component `TrivialBankServer` together with the new `IPayment` interface, the adapter pattern and the façade pattern are taken into account by software architects. Hence, they need to evaluate the two patterns using the design pattern catalogue. First, the façade pattern is evaluated. As we can see in Table 6.2, however, the first question for the façade pattern is answered with *no* because no unified interface to a set of interfaces needs to be provided. Thus, the architects know that the façade pattern is not the correct pattern in this case. As a next pattern, the adapter pattern is evaluated. Therefore, the questions in Table 6.3 are used. Even though the questions are technical and quite detailed, the evaluation showed that they can be answered correctly by intended users of the AM3D approach. As all the questions for the adapter pattern can be answered with yes, the architects know that they can use the adapter pattern for the implementation. The decision knowledge is illustrated

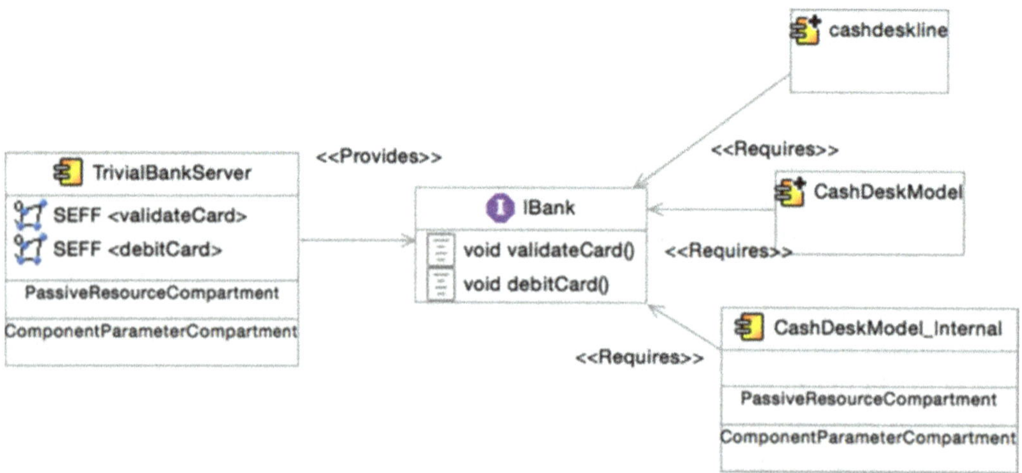

Fig. 6.4 An excerpt of the CoCoME architecture in PCM before the evolution scenario

Table 6.3 Questions for the adapter pattern

Type	Question
Goal	Would you like to convert an interface of a class (or an object) into another interface that clients expect?
Intent	Would you like to make interfaces of incompatible classes compatible?
	Would you like to change the interface of an existing object (a new interface design for an object)? (otherwise → proxy or decorator)
Consequence	Are you aware of the size of the code you have to write and maintain to adapt the class?

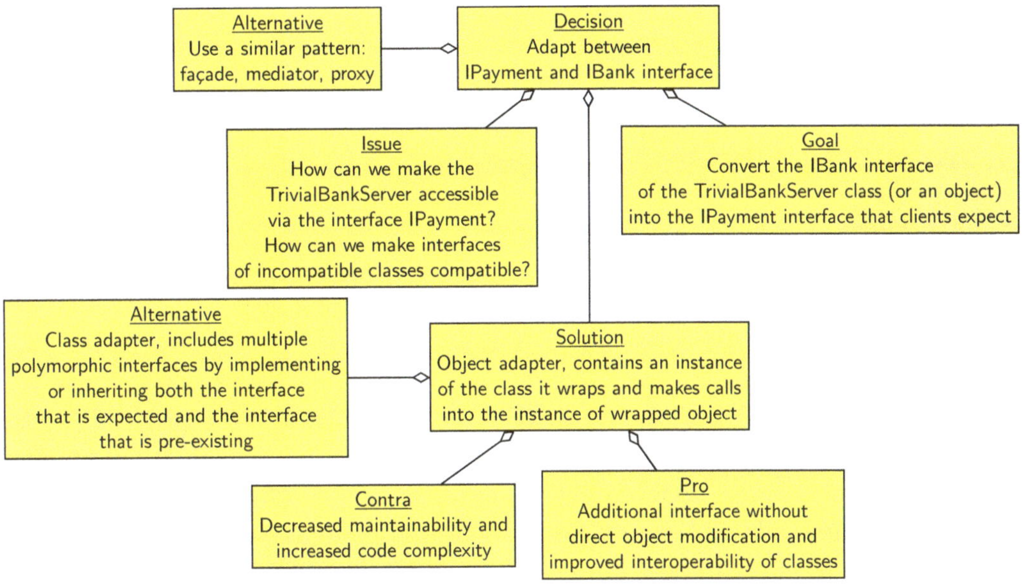

Fig. 6.5 Decision knowledge for the adapter pattern according to the DDM

in Fig. 6.5 (according to the DDM, cf. Sect. 6.2). From the pattern catalogue, they also get an example for the adapter pattern and adapt it to the CoCoME components and interfaces. They adapt the existing `IBank` interface using the `TrivialBankServerAdapter` component in order to make the component `TrivialBankServer` compatible with the new `IPayment` interface. Figure 6.6 shows the resulting architectural structure.

6.4 Integrating Design Decision Models with Program Code

During the evolution of software systems, documented design decisions are often not updated. The documented design decisions, design artefacts, and the program code are then no longer consistent. Even worse, the documented design decisions may be misleading, when they document a revised decision, and are neither updated

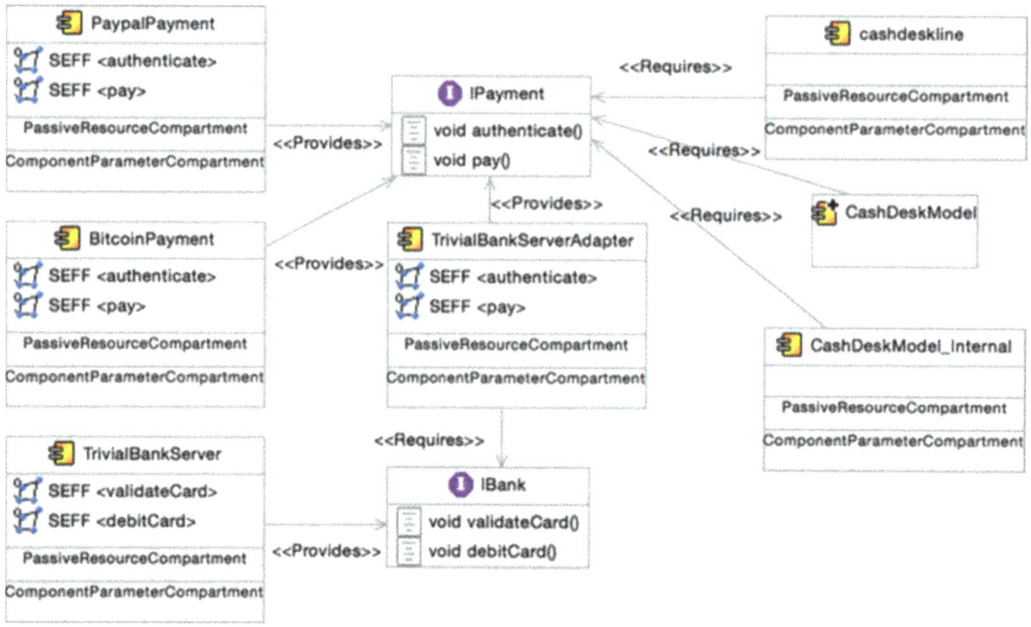

Fig. 6.6 An excerpt of the CoCoME architecture in PCM after the evolution scenario

nor marked as outdated. In this section, we describe an approach to integrate decision knowledge and software architecture information with program code. The tool *Codeling* [Kon18, Kon16] implements an approach for integrating model information with program code. Codeling is used to create bidirectional translations between program code and abstract models of that code. By documenting design decisions within the program code and relating them to architectural design artefacts, the documentation of design decisions is visible during the development and evolution of a system. The goal is to improve the documentation of decision knowledge, the consistency between software models and code, the evolvability, and the understandability of the software.

In Codeling, we create mappings between the concepts of architecture implementation languages and abstract software models. As an example, we define mappings between components defined in the UML and components defined with the Java programming language extended with a component framework. These are the artefacts to which decision knowledge is attached according to the DDM (Fig. 6.1). Therefore, Codeling can document design decisions that were made using the approach described in Sect. 6.3. We use these mappings to automatically propagate changes in the model or the program code to the other representation. As the mapping between these artefacts and program code is established with Codeling, it is possible to attach decision knowledge to these program code elements. When all modelled information has a representation in the program code, a separate model document is not necessary any more. It can be extracted from the program code using the defined mappings.

In Sect. 6.4.1, we briefly describe Codeling and its application to software architectures. Here, we address the challenge to ensure consistency between architectural software design and code. Section 6.4.2 extends the approach with a notation for decision knowledge. Here, we extend the consistency relation between architectural design and code with design decision knowledge. We also address the challenge to integrate the documentation of decision knowledge into software engineering practices, especially into coding and modelling. Section 6.4.3 shows the application of Codeling on the current example of Sect. 6.3.3.

6.4.1 Integrating Architecture Models with Code

Specifications of software architectures can be seen as abstract views on relevant design decisions. The goals of architecture specifications are diverse, generally centering on the design, communication, or analysis of the subject of specification. A set of abstract concerns commonly agreed upon seems to exist for defining software architectures, as manifested by the standard ISO/IEC 42010 [ISO11b]. These include the general structure of a system, usually expressed in components, interfaces, and their interconnection. They are often accompanied by abstract behaviour descriptions or quality aspects. During software development, the architecture is realised in the software artefacts, including the program code, configuration, and the use of existing platforms. The goal of the implementation is an executable system. The implementation of software architecture is driven by industry standards and platforms that define standard elements such as components and interfaces. Languages for architecture specification and for architecture implementation have common concerns (see e.g. [MBG10]), typically at least the definition of components, interfaces, and their interconnections. However, they have different foci and include different types of architectural designs and different details added to the architectural description.

Codeling creates a systematic mapping between architecture specification model elements, relations, and attributes and their implementation based on standardised or project-specific architecture implementation languages. These mappings specifically define places where arbitrary other code can be added. This kind of mapping allows to extract architecture specification models from program code and to propagate changes in these models back to the code.

Codeling comprises three parts. Figure 6.7 sketches an overview of these parts and their relations. The figure describes artefacts of the approach with rounded boxes and translations between these artefacts with arrows. The parts are used to bidirectionally translate between program code and a specification model expressed in an architecture specification language. The parts are underlined in Fig. 6.7.

Intermediate Architecture Language The Intermediate Architecture Language (IAL) mediates between architecture implementation models and architecture specification models. The IAL is implemented with an Ecore-based [Ste+09] meta model. It has a small core with the common elements of architecture languages. The core is extended with profiles [Lan+12] to represent, for example different kinds of

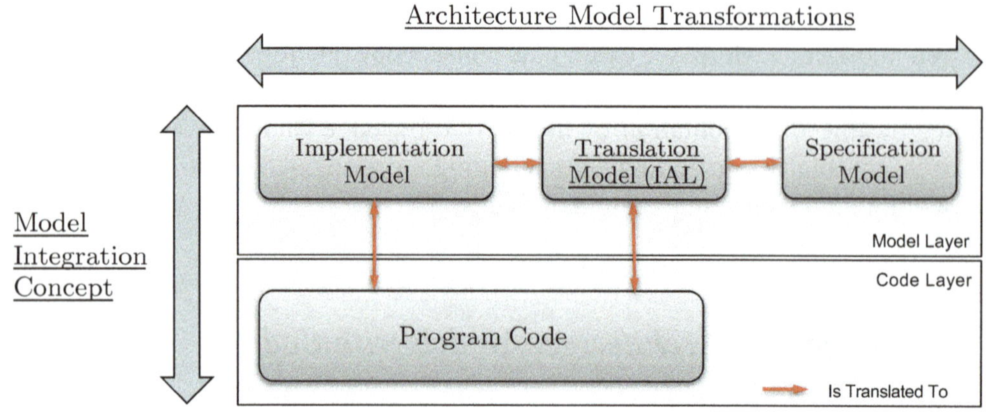

Fig. 6.7 The parts of *Codeling* for integrating architecture model information with program code

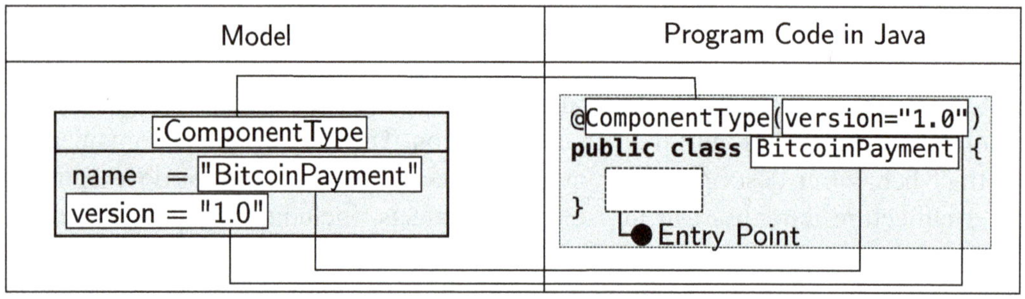

Fig. 6.8 An exemplary bidirectional model-to-code mapping from the MIC

interfaces, component hierarchies, or quality attributes. Models that are expressed with the IAL are called *translation models*.

Model Integration Concept The Model Integration Concept (MIC) describes bidirectional formal mappings between program code structures and an implementation model. The implementation model is a model representation of the architectural aspects of the code. For example, a Java type declaration with a specific annotation might represent a component type, and annotation parameters represent attributes of this component. Figure 6.8 gives an example of two combined mappings. A modelled component type is represented as a Java type declaration with the annotation *ComponentType*. The type's name is mapped to the component type's name. The modelled attribute *version* and the value are mapped to an annotation parameter assignment. Bidirectional model-to-code mappings in the MIC may include *entry points*. Within entry points, arbitrary other program code can be inserted.

In Codeling, the program code also contains information that is not part of an architecture implementation language but is only subject to a specification language. For example, many architecture implementation languages do not describe hierarchical architectures. The hierarchy information is added to the program code, for example using package structures. This information is forwarded directly to the translation model using the MIC. The MIC implements bidirectional transformations. Therefore, changes in the model are propagated to code changes.

For Codeling, we have developed a set of translation templates between models and code. They generically describe how modelled objects, attributes, and references can be represented in program code, so that bidirectional translations can be implemented. Codeling consists of a tool to generate automated translations, by relating these templates to specific meta-model elements [Kon18]. The tool then generates translation classes in Java, which are executable within Codeling.

Architecture Model Transformations Bidirectional architecture model transformations translate between implementation models, translation models, and specification models. Architecture implementation models are translated into specification models. Changes to a specification model are propagated to the corresponding implementation model.

6.4.2 Design Decisions, Rationale, and Patterns in the IAL

Section 6.3 presents the specification language *AM3D* for design decisions and rationale applied to PCM diagrams. To integrate design decisions and rationale with Codeling, (a) the IAL must be able to handle this information. This makes design decision information available to Codeling. Then (b) transformations must be created between the AM3D and the IAL to make the information available to the existing tool environment of AM3D. Finally, (c) mappings must be created between the IAL and the program code.

The IAL can handle decision knowledge (a) via corresponding profiles. These are language extensions for expressing design decisions with rationale. Decisions can either be decisions for the existence or design of specific components or the decision for implementing a specific architectural pattern. Decisions are accompanied by rationale. The rationale can be expressed with informal text or by answering questions of a catalogue, as it is described in Sect. 6.3. We also added meta-model elements for describing instances of architecture patterns and the roles of components and connectors within them, as described in Sect. 6.3. We implemented transformations between the IAL and AM3D (b) with triple-graph grammars[1] (TGG) [Sch94b]. TGGs describe a bidirectional relationship between language elements. For example, they can be used to define that a decision element in the IAL corresponds to a decision element in AM3D. Automated synchronisation rules can be derived from these relationships.

Mappings between decision knowledge expressed in the IAL and Java program code (c) have to be designed in the context of the MIC. A simplified example for expressing the modelled decision knowledge in program code with the MIC is given

[1]The IAL meta model with the design decisions and pattern profiles and transformations between the IAL and AM3D are available under https://codeling.de.

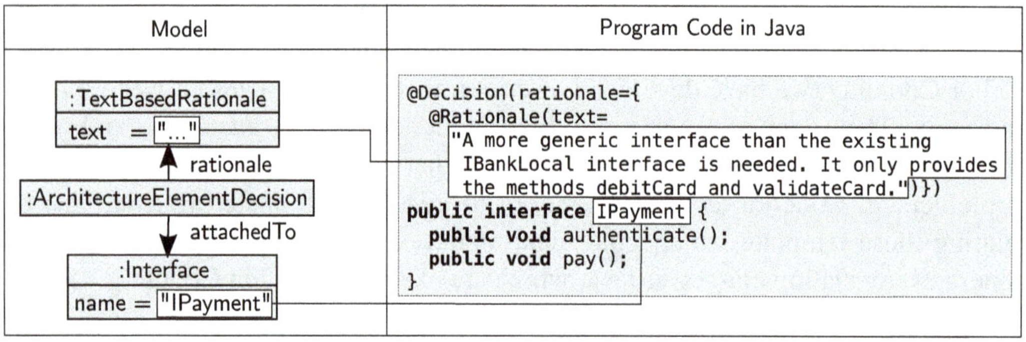

Fig. 6.9 A bidirectional example model-to-code mapping of a decision for an architectural element with text-based rationale

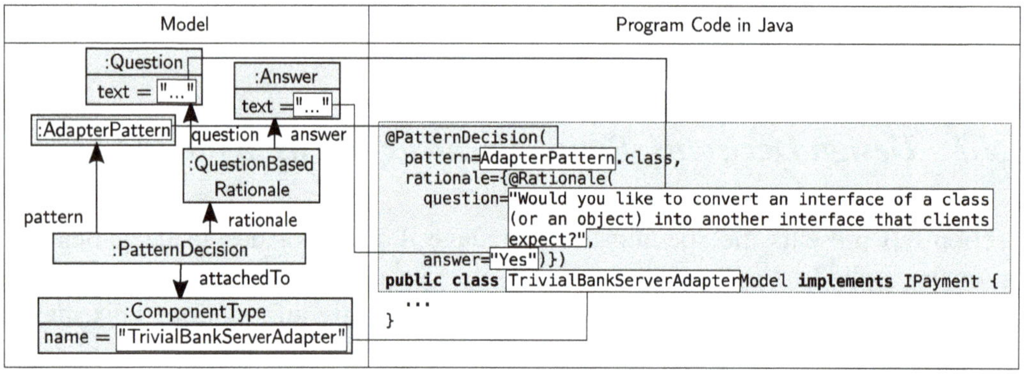

Fig. 6.10 A bidirectional example model-to-code mapping of a pattern decision with question-based rationale

in Fig. 6.9. The figure shows an interface. The modelled interface is represented with an interface definition in Java. The name of the Java interface is mapped to the value of the attribute *name*. A decision with a text-based rationale is attached to the interface. The attached decision is defined as an annotation attached to the Java interface. The rationale is an annotation parameter. The model instantiation of the rationale is a *TextBasedRationale* with a text that contains the actual, informal rationale. The code equivalent is an instantiation of the annotation `Rationale` with the parameter `text` with the respective content.

Figure 6.10 shows an exemplary mapping between a question-based decision for an architectural pattern and a respective code representation. The model shows a pattern decision attached to a component type. The pattern decision relates to an instance of the adapter pattern. The rationale is based on the answering of questions in a catalogue. The component type is represented as a Java type declaration with the name of the component type and the suffix *Model*. The pattern decision is represented as an annotation attached to that type. It has two annotation parameters: The pattern references the type `AdapterPattern`. This type is defined in a library. It represents the corresponding pattern. This mechanism allows for type-safe references because the referenceable types need to implement a specific interface.

In this example, the rationale is represented by the parameters `question` and `answer` of the annotation `Rationale`.

In four case studies, Codeling has shown its applicability and usefulness for improving the consistency between architecture models and code, and the understandability and evolvability of software architectures [Kon18, Chapter 10]. In these case studies, Codeling has been used to extract software architecture models from code, propagate changes in architecture models to the code, and to migrate between architecture languages. Besides architectural structure, the integrated information in these case studies also include performance annotations on operations. They indicate the expected performance of an operation for simulation purposes. This is comparable to design decisions as they are presented in this section. In this section, design decisions are also attached to structural elements and have no operational semantics for the software. Therefore, the approach presented here can document design decisions integrated with the program code and improve the understandability and the evolvability of the software architecture, including the design decisions.

6.4.3 Application to the Case Study

In the context of the case study used in this chapter, Codeling is used to create a PCM view upon the CoCoME architecture with AM3D extensions. Figure 6.4 in Sect. 6.3.3 shows an excerpt of the PCM repository as it is extracted with Codeling. The full repository diagram is shown in Fig. 12.4 on page 350. Table 6.4 gives an overview of the mapping between the CoCoME code, the corresponding architecture implementation language, and PCM meta-model elements. The table contains

Table 6.4 Overview of the mapping between PCM meta-model elements, CoCoME meta-model elements, and program code structures

PCM meta-model element	CoCoME meta-model element	Program code structures
Basic component with the name "Model"	"Model" component	Type declaration with the name "Model"
Basic component with the name "Console"	"Console" component	Type declaration with the name "Console"
Basic component with the name "Server"	"Server" component	Type declaration with the name "Server"
Composite component	Component with children	Package declaration with package or type declarations as subcomponents
Operation provided role	Provided interface	Implemented interface
Operation required role	Required interface	Interface instance given to type via constructor

the mappings relevant for adding design decisions and rationale to component and pattern decisions.

First, we developed a meta model for describing the CoCoME architecture. This was necessary because the original CoCoME implementation does not follow any standard for implementing components but uses a custom style for describing architectural elements and their interconnections using plain Java. For example, it defines three different types of components: *model* components, *console* components, and *server* components. Instances of these component types are implemented using Java type declarations with names that end with that specific suffix. The different component types indicate different roles of the corresponding components within the program. Second, we implemented bidirectional model-to-code transformations between the CoCoME program code and the newly created meta model for the CoCoME architecture.

Next, we created mappings between the CoCoME architecture meta model and the IAL using triple-graph grammars. Design decisions and their rationale are information that can be attached to their corresponding code elements. Figures 6.9 and 6.10 show examples of this set of transformations between models and code. In the CoCoME example, a new interface `IPayment` is introduced because the existing `IBank` interface did not provide the necessary operations. This decision is attached to the new Java interface in Fig. 6.9. The informal text of the text-based rationale is added as annotation member value. Another change in the CoCoME example is the introduction of an adapter, following the adapter pattern, to make the TrivialBankServer accessible via the interface `IPayment`. Figure 6.10 shows the integration of a pattern decision with a question-based rationale. The listing shows how the pattern decision is documented with annotations in the Java code. The implementation of the pattern is not shown in this figure, for readability reasons. Documented design decisions have no operational semantics, which means that it is not necessary to evaluate them at run time. A pattern decision references a pattern in an annotation parameter. Here, only the decision is defined. The actual implementation of the pattern is not evaluated with this mapping. However, such mappings can be created with the MIC. For example, such translations would ensure that a component type, which has the role of an adapter in an adapter pattern, implements the respective interface and has a reference to the adaptee. The actual behaviour of the adapter can then be implemented in entry points of the code representation.

The model-to-code translations and model-to-model translations have to be defined by a developer. Codeling contains tools to support the definition of bidirectional model-to-code transformations with templates and a code generator. Once defined, the automated translations can be used with Codeling to create an architecture model of the CoCoME code with decision knowledge in PCM with AM3D extensions. Changes in the model are automatically propagated to the program code.

In summary, Codeling addresses the challenge of the consistency between architectural knowledge and the program code. Besides other information, this architectural knowledge includes architectural structure, design decisions, and architectural patterns. The approach also addresses the challenge to integrate the documentation of decision knowledge into software engineering practices, especially into coding and modelling. The main advantage is that design decision models are documented at the code level, so that the decisions are available to developers and are included in the VCS.

6.5 Continuous Management of Decision Knowledge

The approach presented in this section integrates the documentation and exploitation of design decisions into the work of the developers, in particular the usage of VCS and ITS. We refer to it as Continuous Management of Design Decisions (ConDec).

We address both challenges in this section. In Sect. 6.5.1, we detail the relevant knowledge elements of the DDM introduced in Sect. 6.2. Section 6.5.2 presents the main ideas on how to use short-cycled CSE practices to trigger developers so they would document and exploit decision knowledge. Section 6.5.3 describes the application to the case study.

6.5.1 *Integrating Design Decisions into CSE*

The knowledge meta model is shown in Fig. 6.11. Software artefacts contain knowledge that we classify into system and project knowledge [PDH14]. *System knowledge* concerns the software itself (e.g. code, requirements, design, test cases), whereas the knowledge about its development and evolution is summarised under the term *project knowledge*. *Decision knowledge* can relate to both knowledge types.

In CSE, features are more prominent than components [Bos14]. Thus, we focus on features and code as essential system knowledge elements in CSE. Features represent both functional and non-functional requirements. Features can be split into

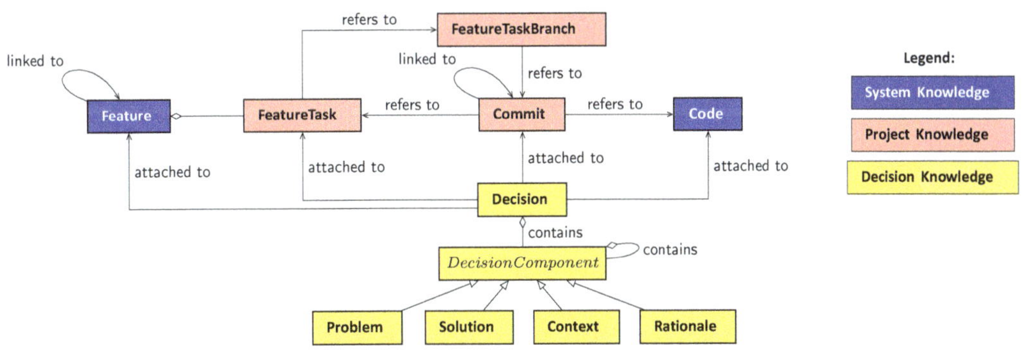

Fig. 6.11 Relationship between features, tasks to implement the feature (feature task), code, commits, and decision knowledge

sub-features or grouped into bigger features. We refer to the tasks that developers fulfil to implement a feature as *feature tasks*. Short-lived branches can be used to encapsulate the actual development work [Kru+14]. We refer to these branches as *feature task branches*. A feature task branch comprises one or more commits that refer to code. When a feature task branch is merged into another branch, a merge commit is created. The difference between merge commits and normal commits is that the merge commit has two parent commits [CS14]. Feature tasks, feature task branches, and commits are types of project knowledge. We use the DDM explained in Sect. 6.2 to represent the decision knowledge.

We assume that tracing between features, feature tasks, commits, and code, as well as decision knowledge, is possible (cf. the relationships in Fig. 6.11). Tracing can be accomplished either using (a) textual annotations such as decision annotations [Hes+15] or task identifiers in the commit messages, (b) distinctly documented trace links (e.g. within a table), and (c) trace retrieval techniques [Cle+13]. A tracing possibility is the prerequisite for developers to consider and ensure the consistency of decision knowledge and artefacts. Tracing enables developers to simultaneously reflect decision knowledge and artefacts. Developers can explore code and decision knowledge that evolved during the implementation of a feature. Likewise, developers can see decision knowledge and features relevant to a certain piece of code.

Evidently, there are other CSE artefacts that can contain relevant knowledge, for example user feedback, pull requests, or chat messages. We consider the artefacts in Fig. 6.11 as the minimal set of CSE knowledge artefacts.

In the following, the implementation of this meta model is introduced: Feature tasks are often called *tickets* and managed in an ITS [Sai+17]. We store both feature tasks and features in the ITS, whereas code and commits are stored in a VCS. In the ITS, developers can create distinct decision knowledge elements linked to the respective features and feature tasks. In the VCS, developers textually capture decision knowledge in commit messages and code. We encourage developers to mark it as such knowledge using *decision annotations* (cf. Sect. 6.5.3, Listing 6.1), as suggested by Hesse et al. [Hes+15]. The identifier of the feature task is added to the commit message. This satisfies the finding by Codoban et al. [Cod+15] that a good commit message expresses the rationale of the change and provides a link to requirements. Therefore, we use decision annotations, feature task identifiers in the commit messages, and distinctly documented trace links to establish tracing.

A first tool to capture these kinds of decision structures is the tool DecDoc, which is based on the DDM and allows to document design decisions collaboratively and incrementally [HKR16]. DecDoc supports the capturing of distinct decision knowledge elements, as well as implementation decisions, as annotations in the code. The DDM and DecDoc were evaluated by a retrospective analysis of decision-making processes of professional software designers [HP16]. The evaluation showed that it is feasible to document complex decision knowledge in DecDoc from collaborative and incremental decision-making processes [HKR16]. In order to be less intrusive, we now develop the ConDec tool support, which directly integrates into the ITS (JIRA) and VCS (Git) [Kle+18b]. ConDec comprises the features of DecDoc and more features, such as the capture of decision knowledge when committing code as part of the commit message.

6.5.2 Decision Knowledge Triggers

CSE involves implementing and delivering many small increments. Practices advancing these increments are ideal to integrate *decision knowledge triggers*, that is techniques that trigger developers to capture and use decision knowledge. They are ideal because they are regularly performed by developers. Furthermore, they comprise practices that indicate that developers either *start* or *finish* work (Table 6.5). Practices that indicates *start* are to open a feature task and to create a feature task branch. Practices that indicate *finish* are to commit code, merge a feature task branch, or close a feature task. Before performing a *finish* practice, developers might have made important decisions. Thus, when developers perform a *finish* practice, we want to trigger them to explicitly capture decision knowledge. When developers perform a *start* practice, we want to trigger them to use existing decision knowledge to make sure they *consider consistency between old and new decisions*.

Figure 6.12 shows a state diagram of decision knowledge in CSE. The labels of the transitions indicate the type of CSE practice (*start* or *finish*) that developers perform. The *start* transitions always involve that developers make decisions. In

Table 6.5 CSE practices to trigger developers to document and exploit decision knowledge

Tool	CSE practice	Type
ITS	Start feature task	*start*
	Close feature task	*finish*
VCS	Create feature task branch	*start*
	Commit code	*finish*
	Merge branches	*finish*

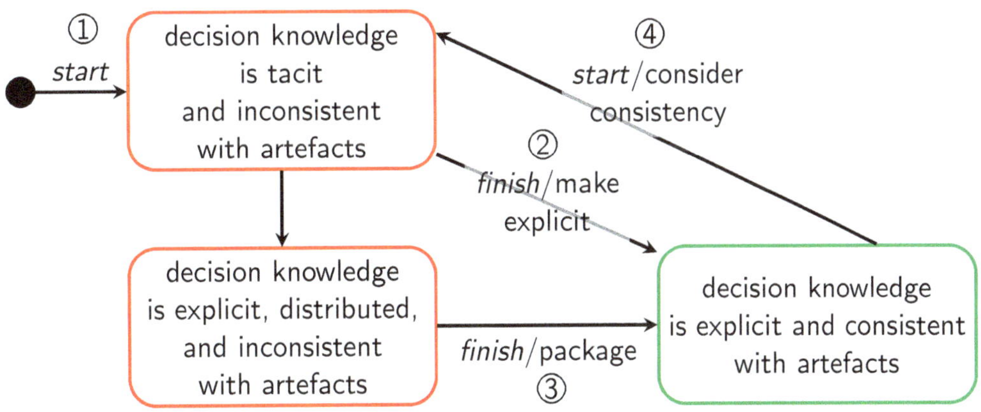

Fig. 6.12 State diagram of decision knowledge and artefacts. The state on the lower right side is the preferred state

addition, the tasks on the right side of the labels (*make explicit*, *package*, and *consider consistency*) need to be performed by developers for certain transitions. The ConDec approach supports these tasks: The integration of tool support into short-cycled start and finish practices *triggers* developers to explicitly capture decision knowledge consistent with artefacts and exploit it afterwards.

At the beginning of the work, decision knowledge is often *tacit* in the head of a few developers (Fig. 6.12-①). If decisions are not tacit, they are often discussed informally and captured partly and in a distributed manner, such as in issue comments [Hes+16], commit messages, pull requests [Bru+14], wikis, emails, chat messages [Alk+17a], or Internet relay chat channels [Alk+18]. We refer to this decision knowledge as *distributed knowledge*. This knowledge is hard to access later and might even be outdated. Therefore, we consider tacit and distributed knowledge as inconsistent with artefacts (cf. Fig. 6.12, left). Decision knowledge and artefacts become inconsistent as soon as they are created or changed. Transitions between consistent and inconsistent states are frequently recurring during CSE, while some artefacts are in a consistent and others in an inconsistent state at the same time. We describe the techniques behind the decision knowledge triggers in the following.

Making Tacit Decisions Explicit

Many decisions remain tacit, that is they are not captured anywhere but are already incorporated in the software. We present developers with *abstractive summaries* of changes to software artefacts when they perform a finish practice (Fig. 6.12-②). By presenting *abstractive summaries*, we want to trigger developers to make tacit decisions explicit, that is to reconstruct decision knowledge. This approach builds on the summarisation of source code changes, as suggested by Cortés-Coy et al. [Cor+14]. Tool support extracts change sets by comparing the code before and after the change. These change sets are the basis for generating an abstractive summary.

Packaging Distributed Decision Knowledge

Developers are presented with relevant distributed decision knowledge when they finish an implementation, as indicated through a finish practice (Fig. 6.12-③). They can check whether the decision knowledge really reflects the changes made. Thereby, we want to trigger them to package the most important decisions and to link them to the corresponding feature, feature task, or commits.

We present relevant distributed decision knowledge as *extractive summaries* using two techniques: (1) Developers can explicitly mark decision knowledge using decision annotations, as presented by Hesse et al. for code [Hes+15] and Alkadhi et al. for chat messages [Alk+17b]. Similarly, they are enabled to apply such decision annotations in other CSE artefacts, for example in comments to feature tasks, pull requests, or wiki pages. (2) We mine the unstructured distributed decision knowledge by machine learning techniques similar to Rastkar and Murphy [RM13], Rogers et al. [Rog+14], Bhat et al. [Bha+17], and Alkadhi et al. [Alk+17a, Alk+18]. All of these techniques require a gold standard to train a supervised classifier. It needs to be investigated to which extent such gold standards can be generalised to identify decision knowledge from different types of CSE artefacts.

Criteria for relevance for inclusion in extractive summaries could be a direct reference (e.g. decisions captured in the code to be committed) or an indirect reference (e.g. decisions mentioned in a recent chat message or feature task comment by the developer).

Considering Consistency Between Decisions

To ensure consistency between decisions, we focus on practices that indicate that a decision is to be taken (Fig. 6.12-④). One example is when a developer sets the status of a feature task from *open* to *in progress*.

By presenting relevant decision and system knowledge, we want to trigger the developers to take previous decisions into account when working on the new feature task. This supports developers during the implementation of features. Criteria of relevance are derived from the trace links in Fig. 6.11. For example, relevant decision knowledge and code are those from other feature tasks that are related to the same feature.

6.5.3 Application to the Case Study

In the following, we use the CoCoME evolution scenario described in Sect. 6.3.3. In this scenario, the CoCoME sales system is extended with new payment possibilities. That is, one feature should enable the CoCoME customer to pay via Bitcoins and another feature to pay via PayPal. First, the requirement engineer (product owner) creates a feature task to implement the Bitcoin payment feature. The feature task is assigned to developers, who set the status from *open* to *in progress* and create a feature task branch to work on this feature task. Thus, they perform a start practice, as indicated in Fig. 6.12-①. The developers collaboratively discuss the design. One developer suggests extending the `IBank` interface with new payment methods, while another developer states that there are bank regulations that forbid to easily change that interface. The developers decide that a new `IPayment` interface could be added. Thus, the developers create the `IPayment` interface that contains the `authenticate` and `pay` methods.

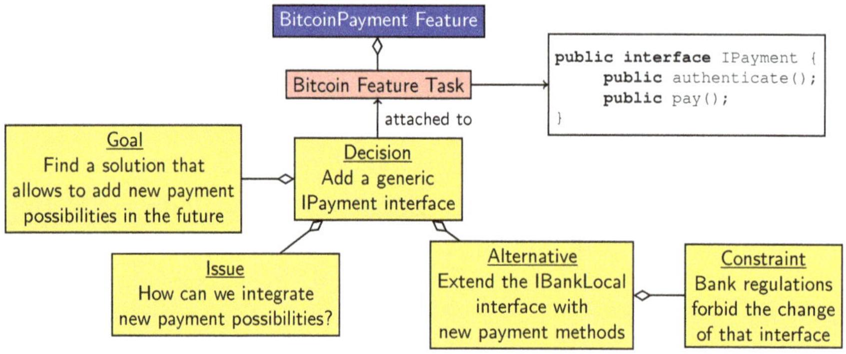

Fig. 6.13 Decision for adding the IPayment interface and related knowledge

Scenario for the Explicit Documentation of Decision Knowledge

The developers explicitly document decision knowledge consistent with artefacts. One possibility to document decision knowledge is that the developers write it in the code using decision annotations (Listing 6.1). Similarly, the developers can document the decision knowledge in the commit message or in the ITS. Consequently, the decision knowledge is consistent with the feature, feature task, and code, as depicted in Fig. 6.13. The knowledge can be accessed from each of these artefacts. For this purpose, it does not make any difference whether the developers document the decision knowledge in the VCS or ITS.

Scenario for Making Tacit Decisions Explicit

Imagine the developers did not document the decision *Add a generic IPayment interface* in the decision annotations (Listing 6.1). However, the decision knowledge resides tacitly in the head of the developers. When the developers commit the code changes, they perform a finish practice (Fig. 6.12-②). Since the code change

Listing 6.1 Example for using decision annotations during implementation

```
/* @Decision Add a generic IPayment interface
 * @Issue How can we integrate new payment possibilities?
 * @Goal Find a solution that allows to add new payment
     possibilities in the future
 * @Alternative Extend the IBank interface with new payment
     methods
 * @Constraint Bank regulations forbid the change of that
     interface */
public interface IPayment {
    public authenticate();
    public pay();
}
```

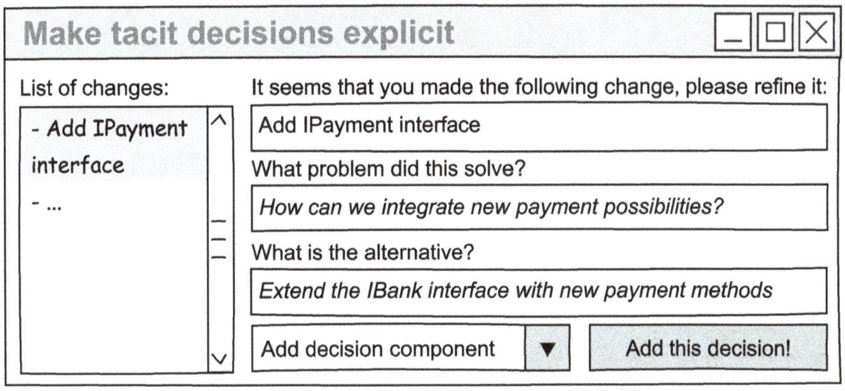

Fig. 6.14 A summary of changes illustrated as a sketch. The italic text is manually added by the developers

contains the addition of a new interface, the summary *Add IPayment interface* is suggested to them (Fig. 6.14). The developers approve that the summary of the change belongs to an important decision and reconstruct additional information on the decision problem (issue) and its alternatives. In particular, this supports developers to reflect about naturalistic decisions.

Scenario for Packaging Distributed Decision Knowledge

Imagine the developers did not document the decision knowledge as depicted in Listing 6.1 but discussed it in a written form, for example in the comments to the feature task, chat messages, Internet relay chats, or pull request for the feature task branch. Developers perform a finish practice when they close the respective feature task (Fig. 6.12-③). Tool support extracts relevant distributed decision knowledge from the original source (i.e. comments to the feature task, chat messages, Internet relay chats, or pull request). For example, the distributed decision knowledge is expected to be relevant when it was recently mentioned by the same developers. Further, the decision knowledge is classified by a machine learning approach and presented to developers, as shown Fig. 6.13. Since the developers discussed the addition of an IPayment interface, the decision *Add a generic IPayment interface* is suggested to them. Developers acknowledge that *Add a generic IPayment interface* is a decision they made and that the related decision knowledge is correct. The decision knowledge is stored inside of the ITS and gets linked to the feature task (Fig. 6.13).

Scenario for Considering Consistency Between Decisions

Imagine that the implementation of the Bitcoin payment feature task was finished and the decision knowledge is documented, as shown in Fig. 6.13. The feature

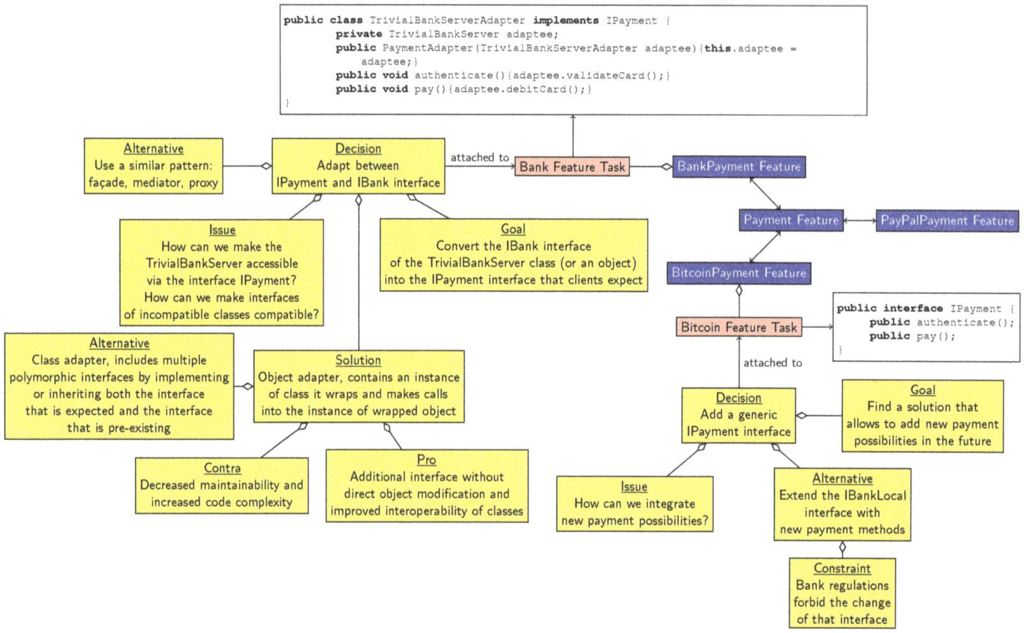

Fig. 6.15 Important decision knowledge related to the implementation of the payment feature

task to implement the PayPal payment feature is assigned to other developers. Figure 6.15 shows how decision knowledge is visualised in the context of related artefacts. When the developers set the status of the new feature task to implement the PayPal payment feature from *open* to *in progress*, they perform a start practice (Fig. 6.12-④). Since this feature is linked to the Bitcoin payment feature (Fig. 6.15), the code of the `IPayment` interface, as well as the decision knowledge *Add a generic IPayment interface*, is presented to the developers. Thus, they will learn about the integration of new payment possibilities and make decisions consistent with this previous one. The decision knowledge for the usage of the adapter pattern (cf. Sect. 6.3.3) can also be accessed.

6.6 Related Work

In this section, we discuss related work regarding the challenges of ensuring the consistency and minimising the intrusiveness of the design decision documentation.

6.6.1 Documentation Consistent with External Decision Knowledge

The following section summarises related work for the AM3D approach by Durdik [Dur14]. One of the most related approaches to the AM3D approach is Software

Engineering Using Rationale (SEURAT) by [BB08] including its extension presented by Wang and Burge [WB10]. It supports architects and developers by finding a pattern for a given problem. The design rationales and the design decisions during the decision-making are stored. Furthermore, SEURAT includes questions that have to be answered during the decision-making process in order to find the correct pattern. The purpose of these questions, however, is different from that of the AM3D approach. In SEURAT, the questions are used to find information, which is required before the decision can be made. They also specify which source of information is used to answer them.

Zimmermann et al. [Zim+08, Zim11] introduce a decision framework. The approach is based on reusable architectural decision models. The goal of the approach is to support developers and architects during the decision-making process, in particular during the phases decision identification, decision-making, and decision enforcement. The main focus of the approach by Zimmermann et al., however, is on the reuse of decisions and decision-related information itself, while AM3D focuses on the reuse of solutions.

The AM3D approach is not an expert system approach (see Table 3.1 in Durdik [Dur14]). The main difference between an expert system and the AM3D approach is that AM3D goes beyond a typical expert system as it helps users not only by finding a suitable solution but also by evaluating the solution, comparing it with other solutions, and documenting the found solution together with its decision rationales. However, Durdik [Dur14] pointed out that some expert system approaches, such as Garbe et al. [Gar+06], are also related to the AM3D approach as they use questions in order to choose a software pattern for a given problem.

6.6.2 Documentation of Decision Knowledge Consistent with Architecture and Code

There is also related work regarding the relationship between models and code. The field of model/code co-evolution describes how models and code can evolve together. Work in this area usually focuses on one specific type of model. For example, Langhammer [Lan17] describes an approach for the co-evolution of Palladio architecture models and Java program code. Langhammer describes rules that preserve a consistent relationship between the architecture model and the program code during changes on either side. The Codeling approach, presented in Sect. 6.4, instead allows for co-evolution between arbitrary object-oriented program code and model languages, as long as the latter can be represented with a specific subset of the Ecore meta model [Kon18].

Approaches for the co-evolution of models and code often do not consider the evolution of the underlying languages. Rocco et al. [Roc+14] explicitly describe language evolution as an aspect of model/code co-evolution. When a system is modelled using meta models and a corresponding code is generated, the evolution of the meta model is a challenge. Such changes can break the code generators. This is a case of model/code co-evolution: The meta model can be regarded as model, and the code generator can be regarded as code in the context of model/code co-evolution. The authors propose a co-evolution approach where model changes are propagated via well-defined transformations, which operate on the code and take the model difference as input. This approach can be used to handle architecture language evolution regarding model editors but not regarding the code that implements a system's architecture.

The synchronisation between models and between models and code is the focus of the research in (in)consistency management [Fel+15]. These approaches assume that two views upon a shared body of information overlap. When one view is changed in the overlapping part, these changes should be propagated to the other view. Consistency management deals with methods and tools to re-establish synchronisation. Existing consistency management approaches focus on coarse-grained program code structures, such as code files or classes and relate them to model elements. Konersmann [Kon18] argues that a more fine-grained abstraction level is necessary and implements such consistency relationships in Codeling. Vitruv [KBL13] is a more general approach to keep different views consistent. It bases on coupling EMOF-specified meta models. For the coupling of the Palladio meta model for architectural specification with Java, see the PhD thesis of Langhammer [Lan17].

In 1995, Murphy et al. [MNS95] presented an approach to bridge the gap between program code elements and higher-level software models. In their approach, a mapping is created between higher-level model elements and program code elements. The approach of Murphy et al. is limited to mappings between model elements and program code files, neglecting the structures within the code files. Approaches need to address structures within the code files to add decision knowledge to specific architecture elements in the code.

6.6.3 Non-intrusive Documentation of Decision Knowledge

A documentation technique is lightweight if developers require only little effort to document knowledge. In addition, a non-intrusive documentation technique enables developers to document knowledge in a lightweight way as part of their development practices. In the following, we discuss both lightweight and non-intrusive techniques.

There are several models to represent decision knowledge, for example *Question, Options, Criteria* by MacLean et al. [Mac+96] and the *Decision Representation Language* by Lee [Lee91]. In this chapter, we use the DDM to represent decision knowledge (cf. Sect. 6.2). The main difference in comparison to former models is that developers can explicitly model context knowledge in a fine-grained way and that all components of a decision can be nested and refined. The *collaborative and incremental nature of the DDM* allows for a flexible documentation of decision knowledge in contrast to filling out static text templates. The DDM is suitable to represent decision knowledge from informal and thus lightweight decision-making processes [HP16, Hes+16].

Hesse et al. [HKR16] investigate whether other approaches (implemented in tools) allow to document decision knowledge in a collaborative and incremental way. They identified that Archie [Cle+13] and SEURAT [BB08] are most similar to the tool DecDoc. The main differences are that SEURAT does not support naturalistic decision-making and Archie does not support shared documentation. Alexeeva et al. provide a literature overview of 56 decision documentation approaches [APM16]. They identified that the approaches are concerned with the following goals: documentation, consistency, evolution, extraction, impact analysis, reuse, sharing, traceability, and visualisation. Twelve of the approaches have the goal of enabling architecture consistency or compliance checks and thus address the consistency challenge of this chapter. However, the usage of these existing approaches requires developers to perform additional steps. Instead, the ConDec approach (Sect. 6.5) is integrated into developers' daily practices, such as committing code. In this regard, the ConDec approach is less intrusive.

A lightweight approach to document decision knowledge are *decision annotations*. Decision annotations enable developers to classify information as decision knowledge. Hesse et al. [Hes+15] use decision annotations to capture decision knowledge in code. Alkadhi et al. present an approach to capture decision knowledge in chat messages using such annotations [Alk+17b]. The ConDec approach also uses decision annotations in commit messages and issue comments. The importance of rationale in commit messages is confirmed by Codoban et al. [Cod+15]. They criticise that commit messages as often being non-informative. Our approach combines annotations to important artefacts like code or commit messages with explicit decision models, as the former eases the capture and the latter eases the understanding of decisions.

Perhaps the most lightweight approach to capture decision knowledge is using informal, non-structured *natural language*. Recently, various approaches emerged that try to automatically identify and extract decision knowledge captured in non-structured natural language. For this purpose, they use machine learning techniques. Alkadhi et al. show how to automatically identify decision knowledge in chat messages [Alk+17a] and Internet relay chat channels [Alk+18]. Rogers et al. mine decision knowledge from bug reports [Rog+14], whereas Bhat et al. focus on issue comments in general [Bha+17]. The ConDec approach allows for the informal documentation of decision knowledge and integrates mining techniques into the daily work of the developers instead of applying them retrospectively. As part of their future work, Rogers et al. [Rog+14] and Bhat et al. [Bha+17] state that they are planning to integrate mining features into existing knowledge management tools. The ConDec approach picks up this idea, as described in previous sections.

Saito et al. [Sai+17] and Rastkar and Murphy [RM13] also exploit *knowledge documented in artefacts of the ITS and VCS* . Similar to them, the ConDec approach also uses commits to link code in the VCS to tasks in the ITS. The meta model in Fig. 6.11 makes these relationships explicit and shows how decision knowledge refers to these artefacts. Saito et al. [Sai+17] developed an approach to retrospectively link commits to tasks. After applying their approach, they found that still 20% of the tasks were not documented in the ITS as issues but directly communicated to developers. The ConDec approach does not address such undocumented tasks but supports developers to make tacit decision knowledge explicit. In the approach by Rastkar and Murphy [RM13], extractive summaries of issues that relate to a certain piece of code are presented to the developers. The summaries are supposed to provide developers with the rationale for code changes. Unlike Rastkar and Murphy, the ConDec approach creates summaries during finish practices in order to trigger developers to document important decision knowledge.

6.7 Conclusion

This chapter presented three approaches regarding the elicitation, documentation, and exploitation of design decisions in the context of CSE and long-living, evolving software systems. These approaches focused more on either the challenges of intrusiveness or consistency.

The AM3D approach supports architects and developers in making rational design decisions *consistent with external decision knowledge, which is presented in a separate tool*. In addition, the Codeling and ConDec approaches focus on ensuring *consistency among decisions within a project, architecture, and code*. While the AM3D approach leaves open where to document the knowledge, the Codeling and the ConDec approaches use annotations. In the ConDec approach, *lightweight traceability* is established, whereas the Codeling approach uses *transformations (formal mappings) between architecture and code*. These transformations are more powerful than traceability links since transformations can be used to create decision models that are interrelated with architecture models and the corresponding code. Hence, changes in the models can be propagated to the code. However, transformations are more intrusive than traceability links because they require extra notations. In addition to using annotations, the ConDec approach also captures decision knowledge in commit messages and in the ITS. Further, the ConDec approach uses short-cycled CSE practices to support developers in documenting and exploiting decision knowledge. The presentation of decision knowledge supports developers in making consistent design decisions and design decisions consistent with the software artefacts. In particular, ConDec also needs to find a balance between (a) the extent to which it can support developers in documenting decision knowledge consistent with former decisions and artefacts and (b) the intrusiveness of the presentation of knowledge. Thus, there is a trade-off between lightweight capturing or having powerful consistency checks that need to be considered when setting up a software development project.

The presented approaches are a first step towards extending CSE with a *continuous management of decision knowledge*. The following enhancements are desirable. Durdik [Dur14] pointed out future work for the AM3D approach. For instance, the AM3D approach can be extended to support behavioural models; that is, behavioural information contained in design patterns can be supported. Currently, the AM3D approach only supports component-like models. In Codeling, the information about pattern instantiations is integrated with program code. This integration only contains the decision and the name of the instantiated pattern. In the future, the implementation should be generated accordingly to actually implement the pattern, where possible. The ConDec approach is implemented in tools [Kle+18b]. We will evaluate the tool support during CSE projects that are part of a practical course at university. We will assess to which extent decision knowledge triggers support developers during CSE. In particular, we will investigate which knowledge is worth capturing. Furthermore, we will clarify how to maintain the knowledge in order to keep it useful and how to access the relevant parts of knowledge.

6.8 Further Reading

Using a Design Pattern Catalogue to Make Design Decisions The main idea and details about the AM3D approach are presented in the dissertation of Durdik [Dur14]. Durdik and Reussner [DR13] explain the rationale for using design patterns and pattern documentation. The ADVERT approach, which uses AM3D for design decision-making, is explained in [Kon+13].

Integrating Design Decision Models with Program Code The integration of architecture models with code is subject to the work by Konersmann [Kon18]. It is based on the idea of embedded models by Balz [Bal11]. The tools for creating and executing translations between architecture-related program code and models are available on https://codeling.de. Konersmann et al. describe variants of this approach, for example for integrating deployment model information [KH16] or behaviour models [KG15] with program code, and the use of integrated model information for locating and understanding errors [Kon14].

Continuous Management of Decision Knowledge The integration of project and system knowledge, in particular the joint management of decisions and work items, is thoroughly discussed by Paech et al. [PDH14]. The DDM was first introduced in [HP13]. Hesse et al. performed several studies that demonstrated the feasibility of the DDM to represent complex decision knowledge. In [Hes+14], they use the DDM to document decisions that address security requirements. In [HP16], they investigated the decision-making process during design sessions. In [Hes+16], they empirically investigated informal decision knowledge from the ITS of the Firefox open-source project. They found that the documented knowledge mostly concerned the decision context and that naturalistic decision-making is dominant over rational decision-making for both bug reports and feature requests. Hesse et al. describe their implementation of the DDM in [HKR16, Hes+15].

The ConDec approach is described by Kleebaum et al. [Kle+18a, Kle+18b]. Johanssen et al. in particular address the visualisation of decision knowledge in relation to usage knowledge [Joh+17b]. Tool support for the documentation and exploitation of decision knowledge in the ITS and VCS is available on https://github.com/cures-hub.

Chapter 7
Model-Based Round-Trip Engineering and Testing of Evolving Software Product Lines

Malte Lochau, Dennis Reuling, Johannes Bürdek, Timo Kehrer, Sascha Lity, Andy Schürr, and Udo Kelter

Modern software systems tend to be more and more long living and, therefore, have to undergo continuous evolution to cope with new, and often initially unforeseen, user requirements, application contexts, and execution platforms. In practice, the necessary changes applied to respective design-, implementation-, and quality-assurance artefacts are often performed in an ad hoc, and mostly manually conducted, manner, thus lacking proper documentation, consistency checks among related artefacts, and systematic quality-assurance strategies.

These issues become even more challenging in case of variant-rich software systems such as software product lines, where even small changes may (intentionally or

M. Lochau (✉) · J. Bürdek · A. Schürr
Technische Universität Darmstadt, Fachbereich Elektrotechnik und Informationstechnik, Fachgebiet Echtzeitsysteme, Darmstadt, Germany
e-mail: malte.lochau@es.tu-darmstadt.de; johannes.buerdek@es.tu-darmstadt.de; andy.schuerr@es.tu-darmstadt.de

D. Reuling
Praktische Informatik/Softwaretechnik, Fachbereich Elektrotechnik und Informatik, Universität - GH - Siegen, Siegen, Germany
e-mail: dreuling@informatik.uni-siegen.de

T. Kehrer
Institut für Informatik, Humboldt-Universität zu Berlin, Berlin, Germany
e-mail: timo.kehrer@informatik.hu-berlin.de

S. Lity
Institut für Softwaretechnik und Fahrzeuginformatik, Technische Universität Braunschweig, Informatikzentrum, Braunschweig, Germany
e-mail: lity@isf.cs.tu-bs.de

U. Kelter
Praktische Informatik/Softwaretechnik, Fachbereich Elektrotechnik und Informatik, Universität - GH - Siegen, Siegen, Germany
e-mail: kelter@informatik.uni-siegen.de

R. Reussner et al. (eds.), *Managed Software Evolution*,
https://doi.org/10.1007/978-3-030-13499-0_7

erroneously) affect a high number of similar product variants simultaneously. Again, the idealistic assumption that a software product line is designed, implemented, and assured in its entirety from scratch prior to the initial delivery any individual product variant to costumers is often unrealistic in practice. In particular, three (potentially concurrently) evolving sets of related product-line artefacts have to be taken into account:

1. A *product-line architecture* typically consists of a configuration model, configurable product-line implementation source code, as well as further design- and quality-assurance artefacts from which respective variants are automatically derivable for a given product configuration.
2. A *product family* consists of materialised software variants corresponding to valid product configurations of the product line as delivered to the customers.
3. A set of *product-specific quality-assurance artefacts* (e.g. test cases) that permit sufficient assurance of every software variants of the product line prior to their delivery and initial execution by the customer.

As a consequence, during product-line *evolution* and *co-evolution* scenarios, developers are faced with multiple diverse yet highly interrelated notions of artefact-consistency preservation, namely consistency between (1) product-line architecture artefacts and (2) respective software variants of the product family, as well as consistency between (3) configuration-specific quality-assurance artefacts and (2) corresponding software variants.

In this chapter, we describe a model-based framework for systematic and (semi-)automatic round-trip engineering of continuously evolving software product lines incorporating all possible evolution and co-evolution scenarios of product-line engineering and quality-assurance artefacts. To this end, we lift the corresponding *forward-* and *re-engineering* scenarios known from classical round-trip engineering to product-line engineering, respectively. In particular, we consider a product-line architecture to consist of a feature diagram serving as a configuration model, a STATECHART model superimposing all product-variant behaviours into one behavioural product-line specification, and a preprocessor-based C-code product-line implementation comprising all software-variant implementations. As quality-assurance methodology, we consider model-based testing, where test suites are automatically generated for product-line implementations with respect to a given set of test goals on the corresponding product-line STATECHART test model, to be covered on all derivable software variants. Our methodology combines two key techniques from model-based software engineering, namely:

- *Model differencing* and *model merging* for automatically comparing and integrating software variants and versions in a systematic way into one unified yet evolving product-line representation, and
- *Knowledge-carrying software* for integrating information about variant- and version-specific software artefacts into engineering and quality-assurance processes at different levels of abstraction

This combination ensures consistency of interrelated engineering- and quality-assurance artefacts throughout the entire life cycle of evolving product lines. In addition, the approach facilitates the application of efficient family-based analysis strategies, initially developed for software variants already organised in product lines, to both variant- and version-rich software systems, as well as arbitrary combinations thereof.

To summarise, the contribution of this chapter consists of an integrated approach that combines different recent techniques and tools from model-based software engineering and software product-line engineering into one novel conceptual framework for product-line round-trip engineering. The methodology is illustrated by a running example by means of an extract from the extended Pick and Place Unit (xPPU) study, and we further describe available tool support for the different techniques.

This chapter is organised as follows. In Sect. 7.1, we first describe the necessary background on product-line engineering and model-based testing and introduce a running example by means of an extract from the xPPU case study. Based on these foundations, we summarise the challenges in round-trip engineering and model-based testing for quality assurance of evolving software product lines, as addressed in the remainder of the chapter. The main part of this chapter is separated into two consecutive sub-parts: in Sect. 7.2, we first describe evolution scenarios of the different engineering and quality-assurance artefacts separately and, in Sect. 7.3, we then explain co-evolution scenarios to ensure consistency among concurrently evolved yet interrelated artefacts. Section 7.4 concludes and gives a sketch of a road map for future research. Finally, Sect. 7.5 summarises recent publications describing in detail the different approaches summarised in this chapter.

7.1 Foundations

In this section, we first describe the necessary background and basic notions from the research fields of model-based software engineering and testing, especially in the context of software product lines, as used throughout this chapter. Based on these concepts, we describe the major challenges in handling evolution and co-evolution scenarios in product-line engineering and model-based testing, in order to facilitate a comprehensive methodology to support model-based round-trip engineering and quality assurance of evolving software product lines.

7.1.1 Model-Based Software Development and Testing

As our running example, we consider an excerpt from the extended Pick and Place Unit (xPPU) case study [Vog+14b], which is used in the following to illustrate the proposed methodology. For a detailed description of the xPPU case study, we refer the interested reader to Sect. 4.3.

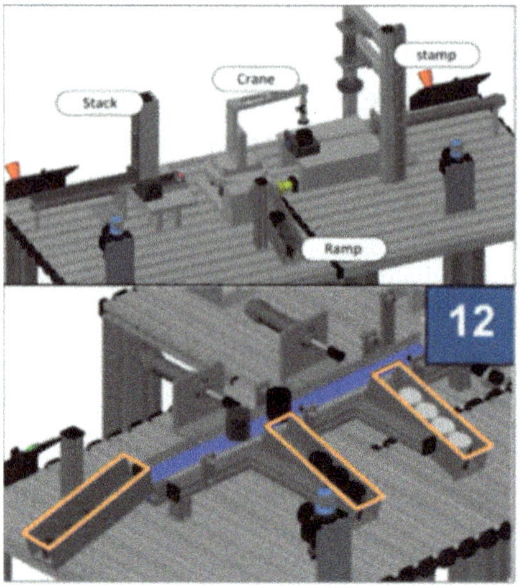

(a)

	v1	v2	v3
1	Initialize	Initialize	Initialize
2	Add Error Handling	Add Error Handling	-
3	-	-	Add Error Handling
4	-	Remove Error Handling	-
5	-	-	Delete Variant

(b)

Fig. 7.1 (**a**) xPPU evolution scenario. (**b**) Overview of xPPU evolution steps

Extended Pick and Place Unit (xPPU) The xPPU is a bench-scale demonstrator for software systems in the automation-engineering domain. As depicted in Fig. 7.1a, the xPPU is a configurable system consisting of several different hardware components for handling and transporting Workpieces (WP) with cylindrical shapes (e.g. bottles). In this way, the xPPU is adaptable to different application scenarios. In particular, the xPPU is able to handle three types of WP: *light plastic*, *dark plastic*, and *metal*. To this end, an xPPU comprises a *Stack* working as WP input storage, a *Ramp* working as a WP output storage, a *Stamp* for labelling WP, and a *Crane* for transporting WP between working positions.

The PLC-based control software of the xPPU has been developed in a model-based way, by employing a combination of structural and behavioural modelling languages as defined by the EN 61131-3 standard for automation-engineering software [Gro11]. Model-based development of automation-control software helps to cope with inherent complexity and mission criticality, as apparent in this and similar application domains, by facilitating automated generation of high-quality and platform-specific implementation code, as well as model-based quality-assurance techniques such as model-based testing.

Model-Based Testing Model-based testing is a widely used black-box testing technique that abstracts from internal implementation details of software components or -systems under test [UL07]. To this end, a *test model* serves as a behavioural specification of the expected behaviour of the (potentially inaccessible) implementation code to be tested. Behavioural conformance of an implementation to a given test model is investigated by experimental execution scenarios (i.e. *test cases*). Hence, *test models* are utilised in two ways during model-based testing:

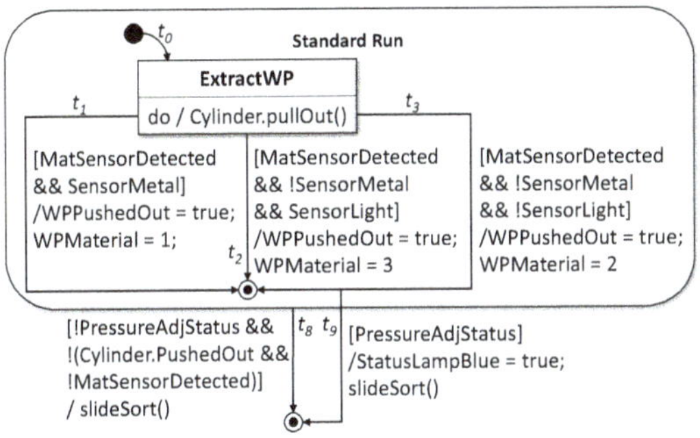

(a)

```
1  ...
2  while (!WPStockEmpty) {
3    Cylinder.pullOut();
4    if (MatSensorDetected && SensorMetal)
5      t1: WPPushedOut = true; WPMaterial = 1;
6    else if (MatSensorDetected
7        && !SensorMetal && SensorLight)
8      t2: WPPushedOut = true; WPMaterial = 3;
9    else if (MatSensorDetected
10       && !SensorMetal && !SensorLight)
11     t3: WPPushedOut = true; WPMaterial = 2;
12
13   if (PressureAdjStatus)
14     t9: StatusLampBlue = true; slideSort();
15   else if (!PressureAdjStatus && ...)
16     t8: slideSort();
17 }
18 ...
```

(b)

Fig. 7.2 Extract from a xPPU variant. (**a**) Test model. (**b**) Code

- The test model is used as input for testing tools for automatically *generating* test cases, *executing* those test cases on the system under test, and *evaluating* test-execution results with respect to the expected behaviour (*test oracle*) as stated by the test model.
- The test model is used to measure *adequacy* of an (either already existing or pro-actively generated) set of test cases (i.e. a *test suite*). For instance, a *coverage criterion* may be applied to identify a set of *test goals* in the test model, each to be satisfied by at least one test case of the test suite.

Figure 7.2 shows an extract from the test-model specification of the xPPU in terms of a STATECHART model [UL07]. STATECHARTS (and respective dialects) offer a widely used visual modelling language that constitutes a particularly well-established specification formalism for concisely capturing functional specifications of reactive control-software systems at system and component levels. STATECHARTS are also widely applicable as a basis for automated generation of implementation code, as well as for model-based test-case generation and test-coverage measurement [UL07, Rös+14, Loc+14].

The xPPU behaviour, as abstractly specified in the STATECHART model in Fig. 7.2, constitutes handling of three different types of WP: *light plastic*, *dark plastic*, and *metal*. Each of those types of WP are transported from the *Stack* via the *Crane* to the *Stamp*. *Light* WP are stamped using *adjustable pressure*, whereas *dark* WP and *metal* WP are stamped using *standard pressure*. To this end, variable *PressureAdjStatus* determines whether adjustable pressure or standard pressure is used based on the material of the incoming WP. Finally, all WPs are transported to the *Slide* and sorted according to their specific type. The behaviour specified in the test model in Fig. 7.2a corresponds to one particular *implementation variant* of the xPPU, as shown in the (simplified) code-listing excerpt in Fig. 7.2b. Whenever a new WP arrives in the xPPU (see Line 2), the *Cylinder* pulls it from the *Stack* (see Line 3). Lines 4–11 implement the control logic for identifying and handling the three different types of WP, as described above.

When using STATECHARTS as test models, test cases correspond to valid and complete transition paths in the state-transition graph (i.e. paths corresponding to valid executions from the initial state to a final state). A test-case execution thus defines a sequence of input stimuli to be injected into the system under test, together with a corresponding sequence of observable output behaviours expected from the system under test for those inputs as given by the transition labels in the test-model specification. Similar to code-coverage criteria, coverage criteria for STATECHART models aim to investigate different possible control flows (e.g. state and transition coverage), as well as data-flow aspects (e.g. def-use coverage) of the implementation under test [UL07].

For example, applying *transition coverage* to the xPPU test model in Fig. 7.2 ensures that a test suite contains at least one test case for investigating the correct handling of each type of WP. The code parts corresponding to the three test goals $t1$, $t2$, $t3$ correspond to the three transitions in the test model (see Fig. 7.2a) and are marked with respective code labels (see Fig. 7.2b). For instance, a test-case execution examining the handling of *light plastic* WP with *adjustable pressure* requires as expected output the corresponding status lamp to be switched on (test goal $t9$ in Line 14). After that, all types of WP are transported to the slide, where they are finally sorted according to their specific type (test goals $t9$ and $t8$ in Line 14 and 16, respectively).

To summarise, a *test suite* achieving complete transition coverage on the xPPU test model in Fig. 7.2a requires at least three test cases, for instance:

- Test case $tc_1 := (t_0, t_1, t_8)$ for handling *metal* WP
- Test case $tc_2 := (t_0, t_2, t_9)$ for handling *light plastic* WP using *adjustable pressure*, and
- Test case $tc_3 := (t_0, t_3, t_8)$ for handling *dark plastic* WP

Product Families Besides the particular xPPU variant described so far, the modular architecture of the xPPU supports many further variants in order to adapt to different environments, platforms, and customer needs. Such a collection of similar yet well-distinguished variants of the same *core product* is frequently called a *product family* [Ape+13]. For presentation purposes, we limit our considerations in the following to two further variants from the *xPPU product family*, referred to as *v2* and *v3*, and the previously described variant is denoted as *v1*, respectively. In contrast to variant *v1*, variant *v2* has reduced functionality; namely, it cannot handle *light plastic* WP differently and always uses *standard pressure* for stamping. Figure 7.3 shows the corresponding extract from the test model and the respective implementation code of variant *v2*. Here, the handling of *metal* WP is equal to that of variant *v1*, whereas the handling of *light plastic* and *dark plastic* are the same in *v2*, contrary to different behaviours for each *plastic* WP in case of variant *v1*. Hence, a test suite achieving complete transition coverage on the test model of variant *v2* requires at least two test cases, for instance

- test case $tc_1 := (t_0, t_1, t_8)$ may be (re-)used from the test suite of variant *v1*, whereas

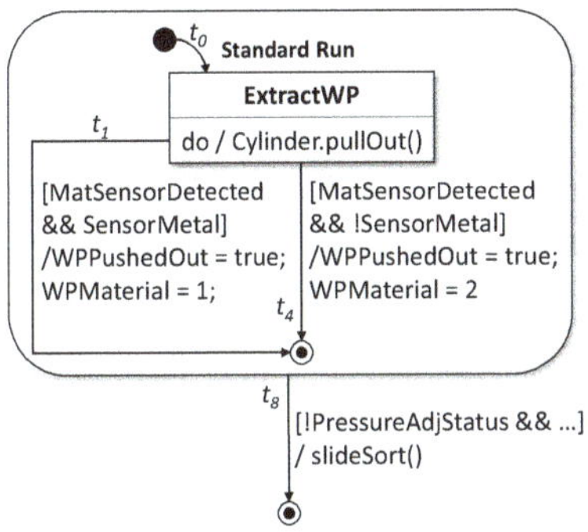

(a)

```
...
while (!WPStockEmpty) {
  Cylinder.pullOut();
  if (MatSensorDetected && SensorMetal)
    t1: WPPushedOut = true; WPMaterial = 1;
  else if (MatSensorDetected && !SensorMetal)
    t4: WPPushedOut = true; WPMaterial = 2;

  if (!PressureAdjStatus && ...)
    t8: slideSort();
}
...
```

(b)

Fig. 7.3 A second xPPU variant. (**a**) Test model. (**b**) Code

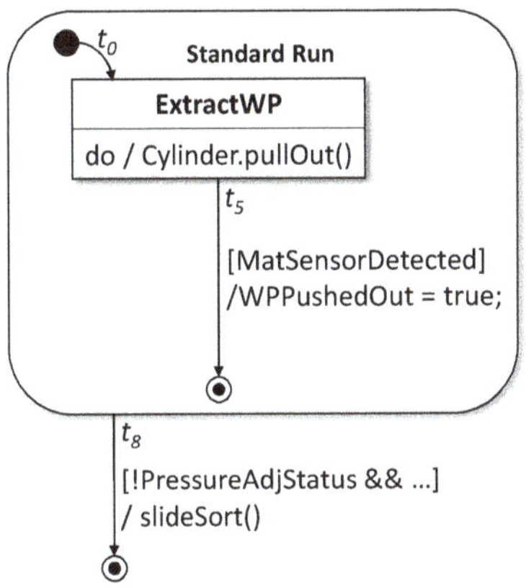

(a)

```
...
while (!WPStockEmpty) {
  Cylinder.pullOut();
  if (MatSensorDetected)
    t5: WPPushedOut = true;

  if (!PressureAdjStatus && ...)
    t8: slideSort();
}
...
```

(b)

Fig. 7.4 A third xPPU variant. (**a**) Test model. (**b**) Code

- test case $tc_4 := (t_0, t_4, t_8)$ is a new test case, additionally required to examine equal handling of *light plastic* and *dark plastic* WPs in variant *v2*.

In contrast to the reusable test case t_1, the other test cases t_2, t_3 derived for testing variant $v1$ are not applicable for testing variant *v2*.

Finally, variant v_3 constitutes a very basic xPPU, which is only able to handle *metal* WP and which has no *Stamp* (see Fig. 7.4). As a consequence, for testing variant $v3$ (again, aiming at transition coverage of the respective test model of variant *v3*), only one single test case, for instance

- test case $tc_5 := (t_0, t_5, t_8)$

is required, which differs from all the previously derived test cases due to the essential behavioural differences of variant *v3*, as compared with variant *v1* and *v2*. Next, we describe how principles from product-line engineering can help to systematically exploit commonality among the members of a product family during both software development and quality assurance (e.g. for reasoning about test-case reuse among variants).

7.1.2 *Model-Based Product-Line Engineering and Testing*

Software product line engineering (SPLE) is an emerging methodology that has been successfully applied in various industrial application domains [Wei08]. SPLE offers a practicable possibility to handle the increasing variability during engineering and quality assurance of automation-control software, as described for the xPPU example. To this end, SPLE aims at systematically exploiting knowledge about commonality and variability among all kinds of engineering artefacts (e.g. design- and test models, implementation code, and test cases) in a family of similar products [PBL05a, CN01]. An explicit specification of common and variable parts among the different variants is based on their supported *features*, denoting configuration parameters (i.e. user-visible characteristics of products) in the *problem space* of a product family. For automated derivation of product variants complying to a given configuration, features are further related to software building blocks by means of reusable engineering artefacts in the *solution space*, being composable into respective implementation variants. In the following, we first describe the idealistic view on product-line engineering based on the assumption that the whole product line is developed from scratch before finally being delivered to the customer.

Problem Space For the problem-space specification, SPLE usually employs *feature models* to describe the set of available features, together with constraints among those features to be satisfied by a feature selection to constitute a *valid product configuration*. Figure 7.5a shows the feature model for the xPPU product line using the visual Feature Oriented Domain Analysis (FODA) notation (frequently called *feature diagrams*) [Kan+90a]. A feature model organises the set of supported features as nodes in a tree-like hierarchy, inducing dependencies of child features to its parent features (i.e. the selection of a feature requires the selection of its parent feature in a valid configuration). Singleton child features are either *mandatory* (i.e. they must be selected whenever their parent features are selected in a valid configuration) or *optional*. For instance, a valid xPPU configuration *must* contain a *Crane* device and *at least one Slide* and *must* handle *at least one* type of *Work Piece*, whereas the *Stamp* is *optional*. Besides singleton child features, mutually

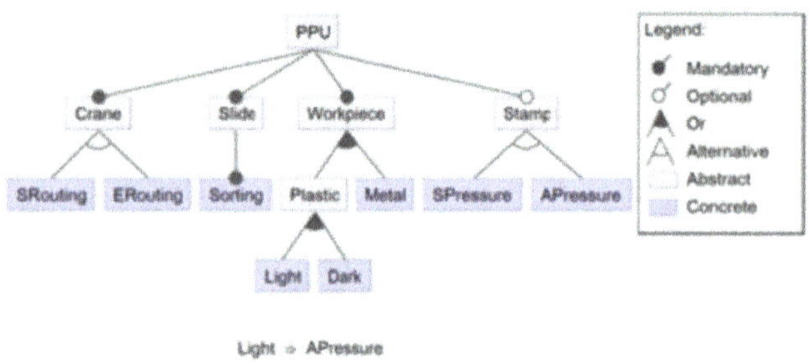

(a)

	Metal	Dark	Light	SPressure	APressure	Sorting	SRouting
V1	x	x	x		x	x	x
V2	x	x		x		x	x
V3	x			x		x	x
V4	x				x	x	x
V5		x			x	x	x
V6			x		x	x	x
V7	x	x			x	x	x
V8	x		x		x	x	x
V9		x	x		x	x	x
V10		x		x		x	x

(b)

Fig. 7.5 Extract from the xPPU feature model and valid configurations. (**a**) xPPU feature model. (**b**) xPPU variants

dependent sibling child features may be assembled into *feature groups*, being either *or groups* (i.e. *at least one* of its features must be selected if the parent feature is selected), or *alternative groups* (i.e. *exactly one* feature must be selected). For instance, a *Crane* either uses *Standard Routing*,or *Extended Routing*, whereas the set of types of supported *Plastic* WP may include *Dark*, *Light*, as well as both in combination. Finally, further dependencies between hierarchically unrelated features can be expressed using *cross-tree constraints* (e.g. *Work Pieces* made of *Light Plastic* require a *Stamp* with *Adaptive Pressure*). The set of all valid configurations according to the xPPU feature model is given in Fig. 7.5b. Please note that—due to space limitations—we omitted the second half of configurations, which only differs from the given ones by having *ERouting* selected instead of *SRouting*. Further note that the first three configurations correspond to the xPPU variants $v1$, $v2$, and $v3$, as described above.

In the next step of SPLE, a *mapping* of configuration-specific solution-space artefacts onto corresponding feature selections is defined, in order to relate configurations to respective parts in configurable test models and implementation code of the product line.

Solution Space Features not only denote configuration parameters in the problem space but also refer to *variation points* within engineering artefacts in the solution space, potentially at all levels of abstraction [Ape+13]. Here, we use an annotation-based approach for a product-line representation of a product family, by integrating variability information into solution-space artefacts (i.e. test models, implementation code, and test artefacts).

Presence Conditions for Variant-Knowledge At the level of design- and test models like STATECHARTS, variant-specific model elements (here: transitions) are equipped with annotations over propositional feature expressions, representing *presence conditions* for well-defined variation points in the solution space. Those *model templates* therefore virtually include (or superimpose) any possible model variant of the product line into one model, constituting a so-called *150% model*. Hence, a configuration-specific *model variant* (i.e. a 100% model) can be obtained from a 150% model by projecting only those model elements whose presence conditions are satisfied by the respective feature selection of the configuration [CE00]. Figure 7.6a depicts the 150% test model for the xPPU product line, where the respective test-model variants for the configurations $v1$, $v2$, and $v3$ correspond to the model variants, as described above.

A similar principle is frequently used in practice for integrating variation points into source-code artefacts of product-line implementations: conditional-compilation directives such as `#if` macro, as provided by the C preprocessor, allow for marking variable code parts (variation points), again, by using propositional formulae over (Boolean) feature variables as presence conditions [Käas+11]. Figure 7.6b depicts the variable implementation source code of the xPPU example corresponding to the aforementioned 150% test-model extract.

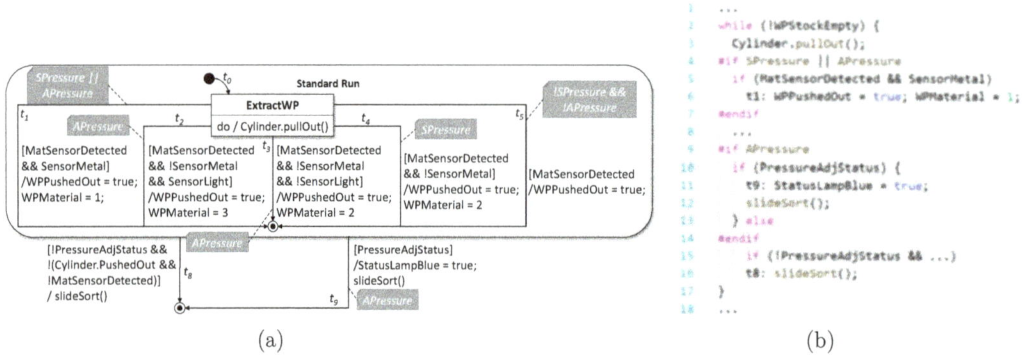

Fig. 7.6 150% xPPU Test model. (**a**) Test model. (**b**) Code

Family-Based Product-Line Testing The additional knowledge in a product-line representation provided by the feature model and corresponding feature mappings onto a 150% test model provides opportunities for improving the efficiency of quality assurance of product families. To this end, *family-based product-line analysis strategies* aim at analysing whole product families at once instead of using a variant-by-variant approach [Thü+14a]. In particular, *family-based test-suite generation* potentially reduces the overall number of test-generator runs and therefore the number of required test cases for covering all members of a product family, as compared to considering every variant one by one, as described above [Bür+15a]. For this, the additional information provided by the presence conditions in 150% test-model specifications supports automated reasoning about (re-)usability of derived test cases among different variants. To do so, the set of presence conditions attached to those transitions located on the path being traversed in the test model by a test case for reaching a particular test goals is conjugated to form a presence condition for that particular test case (i.e. a so-called *Software product line (SPL) test case*). The presence condition of an SPL test case, therefore, characterises exactly the set of configurations for which that test case is applicable. Based on this notion, we call a set of SPL test cases an *SPL test suite*, and an SPL test suite is further called *complete* if for each test goal in the 150% test model (being selected by a given coverage criterion as usual) and for each test-model variant there exists at least one SPL test case covering that test goal and whose presence condition is satisfied by the configuration of that variant (see [Bür+15a, Loc+14] for a precise definition).

As an example, applying family-based SPL test-suite generation to the 150% test model of the xPPU example (see Fig. 7.6) for transition coverage may result in the following *complete SPL test suite*:

- SPL test case $tc_1 := (t_0, t_1, t_8)$; [*SPressure* || *APressure*]
- SPL test case $tc_2 := (t_0, t_2, t_9)$; [*APressure*]
- SPL test case $tc_3 := (t_0, t_3, t_8)$; [*APressure*]
- SPL test case $tc_4 := (t_0, t_4, t_8)$; [*SPressure*], and
- SPL test case $tc_5 := (t_0, t_5, t_8)$ [*!SPressure* && *!APressure*].

Here, the feature expressions given in brackets denote the respective presence conditions (i.e. test case t_1 is applicable to the variants $v1$ and $v2$; test cases t_2, t_3, t_4 are applicable to variant $v1$; and test case t_5 is applicable to variant $v3$). Hence, the resulting test cases exactly correspond to those previously derived by using a variant-by-variant approach but now carry additional information about the respective implementation variants of the xPPU product line to which they are applicable. Hence, test cases being reusable among different product variants are generated only once using a family-based approach, thus reducing the number of (redundant) test-generator calls, as compared to a variant-by-variant approach.

7.1.3 Product-Line Round-Trip Engineering and Artefact Co-evolution

In practice, those idealistic 150% product-line representations, on which family-based analysis strategies heavily rely, are usually not—or only partially—available. This is due to the fact that product lines are, in most cases, not developed *pro-actively* from scratch in a *forward-engineering* manner but rather continuously evolve over time and therefore comprise not only variability *in space* (by means of simultaneously existing variants) but also variability *over time* (by means of sequences of subsequent versions). Hence, most product lines are developed *re-actively* (i.e. by starting with an initial minimum product line comprising a small set of core variants, which is then continuously revised throughout their life cycle to adapt to ever-changing needs) or in an *extractive* way (i.e. by *reverse engineering* a product-line representation from an existing product family) or by combining both styles [Ape+13].

For instance, Fig. 7.1a illustrates a possible evolution scenario of the xPPU product line: the core xPPU initially comprises a *Stack* with multiple *Slides* for *Sorting* WP according to their types, as well as a *Crane* and a *Stamp*. Later on, in evolution scenario 12, an alternative *Standard Ramp* without *Sorting* will become available. As a consequence, all product-line artefacts (potentially) affected by those changes have to be adapted to support the new variants, namely the feature model, the 150% design- and test-model specification, the variable implementation code artefacts, the respective model- and implementation variants, and the accompanying model-based SPL testing artefacts.

Figure 7.7a provides an overview of the different model-based product-line engineering and testing artefacts under consideration, together with possible evolution step and resulting co-evolution scenarios (which will be referred to as ①–⑥ in Sect. 7.3) corresponding to respective forward- and re-engineering steps potentially arising during product-line round-trip engineering. To summarise, we consider three different kinds of artefacts and use the following terminology for this different artefacts throughout this article.

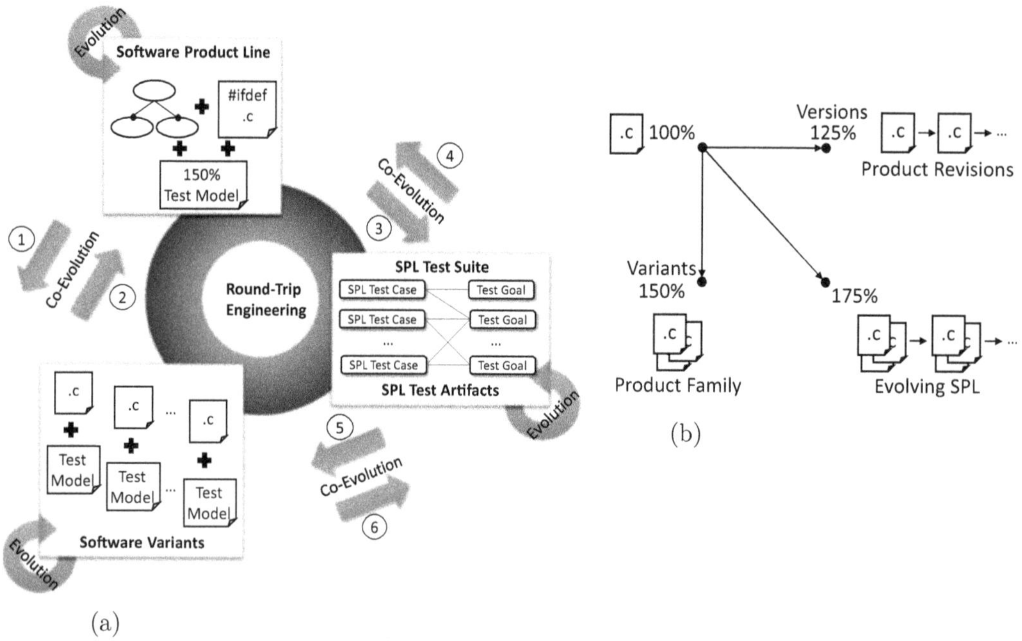

Fig. 7.7 Overview of SPL evolution. (**a**) Product-line round-trip engineering. (**b**) Dimensions of variability

- **Software Product Line Artefacts.** The problem-space artefacts of product lines include the feature model, given as a feature diagram in FODA notation; the solution-space artefacts consists of the 150% implementation, given as C code with preprocessor macros over feature conditions, as well as a 150% test-model specification, given as STATECHART models annotated with feature conditions.
- **Software Variants.** The set of software variants include variant implementations given as (plain) C code, as well as corresponding test-model variants given as (plain) STATECHART models, each of them related to a particular product configuration of the product line.
- **Product-Line Testing Artefacts.** The set of model-based testing artefacts include the set of test goals on the 150% test model, as well as a complete SPL test suite with respect to the set of test goals.

Throughout the life cycle of a product-line, all three kinds of artefacts potentially undergo continuous *evolution* in terms of *changes* imposing *revisions* of artefacts and therefore new *versions* of the entire product line. Due to the complex interrelations between the different kinds of artefacts, an accompanying *co-evolution* of other artefacts is required in order to ensure artefact consistency in handling (potentially concurrent) evolution steps at any level throughout the entire life cycle of the product line. Concerning model-based engineering and quality assurance of evolving software product lines using model-based testing in particular, the major challenge to be solved can be summarised as follows:

Every (supported) version of all valid software variants of an evolving product line has to be sufficiently (re-)tested (covered) prior to its (re-)delivery to the customer and/or its initial execution or restart.

As illustrated in Fig. 7.7b, we therefore distinguish three *dimensions* of integrated representations of artefact variability in evolving software product lines based on the initial artefact (i.e. 100% representation), namely:

- All existing *versions* of the same artefact in a 125% presentation
- All existing *variants* of the same artefact in a 150% representation, as well as
- All existing *variants and versions* of the same artefact in a 175% representation

In the following, we describe in detail the different possible scenarios of product-line evolution (Sect. 7.2) and co-evolution (Sect. 7.3), as depicted in Fig. 7.7a.

7.2 Evolution

In this section, we discuss different possible *evolution scenarios* of model-based product lines and describe techniques to properly handle the impact of those evolution scenarios on the different kinds of product-line artefacts.

7.2.1 Evolution of Software Variants

Under idealistic circumstances, evolution of software product lines would be conducted in a properly preplanned, offline, and forward manner as follows:

- **Step 1:** updating the feature model
- **Step 2:** adapting the solution-space and model-based testing artefacts and the corresponding feature mappings affected by the update
- **Step 3:** deriving updates of software variants for those product configurations affected by the changes, and
- **Step 4:** (re-)generating and (re-)executing test cases required for ensuring the correctness of the changes on the affected software variants

In practice, evolution usually takes place at the level of particular variants rather than at the level of the whole product-line representation [Nev+15]. For instance, a *clone-and-own approach* is frequently used to make changes to a particular model-/program variant and then to propagate those changes by copying and pasting/replacing the affected model/code parts in other variants for which the change is also relevant [Ape+13]. However, if not conducted carefully, such an ad hoc approach is inherently prone to causing continuous decay of the overall product-line structure (e.g. causing either redundant-code or missing-code anomalies in a

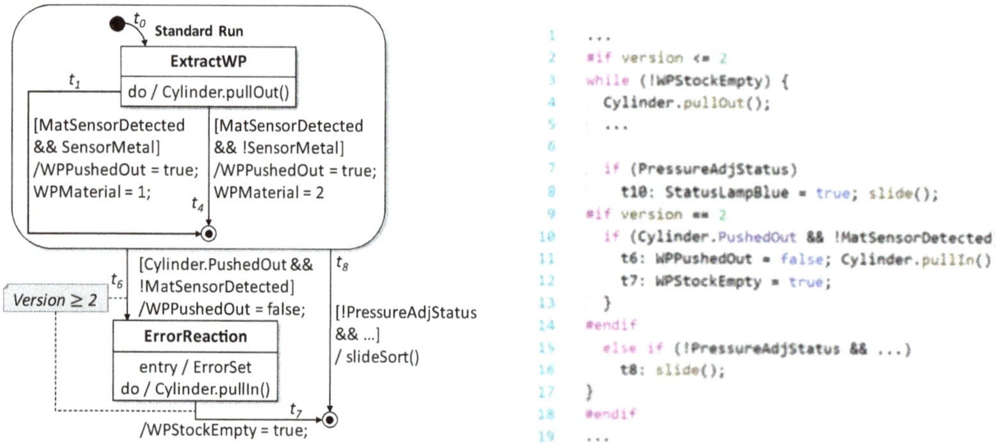

(a) (b)

Fig. 7.8 Test model of variant 2 in version 2. (**a**) Test model. (**b**) Code

particular variant), which, in the worst case, may lead to inconsistent and erroneous variant implementations and/or quality-assurance artefacts.

Figure 7.1b summarises the evolution steps of the xPPU product line considered in the following examples. Consider variants $v1$, $v2$, and $v3$, as described in the previous section, to constitute the *initial version 1* of the xPPU product line. In a first evolution step, leading to *version 2* of the xPPU product line, a *revision* of the xPPU functionality takes place, resulting in adding error-handling capabilities. To this end, a new model fragment, comprising the additional state *ErrorReaction* and corresponding *transitions* for error handling, is added to those test-model variants affected by this change. In particular, the new behaviour is supposed to be added to the existing variants $v1$ and $v2$ of the xPPU product line, whereas variant $v3$ remains without error handling. Figure 7.8 depicts the updated version of the test model of variant $v2$, now containing the newly added model fragment, where a similar change is applied to the respective test model of variant $v1$ (e.g. by applying clone and own of the new fragment from $v2$ to $v1$ or vice versa). In order to master those kinds of product-line evolution scenarios in a model-based setting, we are faced with two major challenges, namely:

- Evolution steps are often conducted in an ad hoc manner and without a proper documentation. Hence, in order to *understand* and *propagate* those changes to other affected variants as well, they have to be properly *represented* in a well-defined way.
- Evolution steps are potentially conducted to all possible artefacts of product-line representations. This may impact the integrity and consistency of further artefacts at the same level, as well as at any other level of representation. Hence, in order to *make explicit* those changes for subsequent engineering steps (e.g. family-based quality assurance), they have to be properly *integrated as additional knowledge* into product-line artefacts.

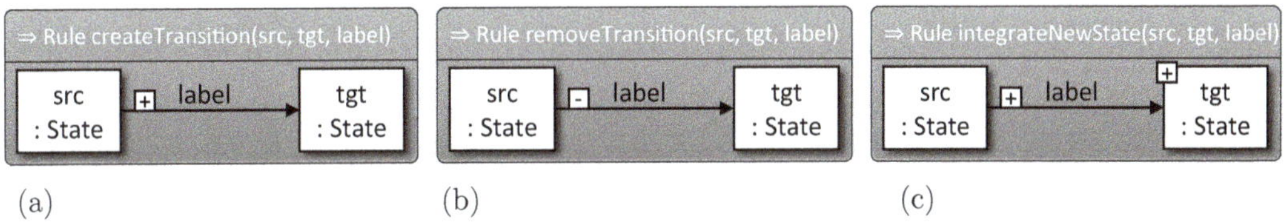

Fig. 7.9 Edit operations for statecharts (Abstract syntax). (**a**) Create transition operation. (**b**) Remove transition operation. (**c**) Integrate state operation

To cope with these challenges, we utilise and combine two techniques, namely (1) *model differencing and model patching* from model-based software engineering [Men02] and (2) *annotation of presence conditions* from product-line engineering [CE00] (Fig. 7.9).

Model Differencing and Model Patching Model-differencing approaches are used for deriving and representing common and differing parts between model versions/variants [Men02]. Here, we employ model differencing techniques for handling variants and revisions of product-line modelling artefacts. To this end, *state-based differencing* of two given versions/variants, $v1$ and $v2$, of a model aims at identifying similar parts within $v1$ and $v2$ on the basis of the current states of both models. We refer to Sect. 10.1.1 for an in-depth description of model-differencing and patching techniques and will only briefly describe the corresponding notions and concepts in the following.

There are various different techniques to decide whether element a of model $v1$ and element b of model $v2$ are considered *similar*. For instance, equality of (unique) *identifiers* or *names* of elements are frequently used criteria for comparing model elements. Based on those criteria, a pair (a, b) of model elements considered similar is called a *correspondence*, where a and b are said to correspond to each other. A *matching* between models $v1$ and $v2$ is a set of (all) correspondences between the elements of $v1$ and $v2$. Given such a matching, a *directed delta* (*difference*) comprising a set of change actions from model $v1$ to model $v2$ can be derived as follows:

- Each model element of $v1$ (or $v2$, respectively) not matched to any other model element leads to a change action that deletes (or creates, respectively) this element.
- Each non-identical property (e.g. a name) of two corresponding elements yields a change action overwriting this property with the value apparent in model $v2$.

Each change action derived this way into a directed delta corresponds to a low-level change being observable between both models, where, however, the actual modification may have been applied in a different way in case of ambiguity (see Sect. 10.1.1 for details). In addition, those corresponding low-level changes consider both models simply as plain directed graphs without considering any further well-formedness rules or necessary abstractions needed for understanding the impact of evolution steps. Instead, model differences should be represented in

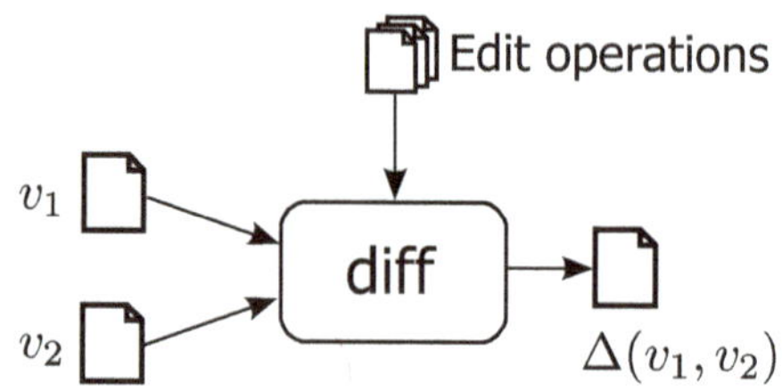

Fig. 7.10 High-level model differencing

a structured and preferably human-readable way (e.g. in terms of *edit operations* corresponding to editing commands in a visual modelling environment). To this end, we further consider *high-level differencing* based on such edit operations for a suitable representation of model differences [KKT11] (see Fig. 7.10). An edit operation groups (several) change actions into one *change set* leading to a so-called *lifting* of differences to a higher abstraction level. Hence, each edit operation obeys an interface consisting of two parts:

- A *difference* $\Delta(v_1, v_2)$ consists of a sequence of *edit steps* $s_1 \dots s_n$ that when applied to model variant/version $v1$ in exactly this order will yield model variant/version $v2$.
- An *edit step* invokes an *edit operation* and supplies appropriate actual parameters for applying the respective changes to a given model.

Edit operations may be defined and implemented using recent techniques, for instance, declarative graph transformation rules [KKT11]. Simplified rules for edit operations on STATECHARTS are presented in Fig. 7.9, being depicted in their abstract syntax. The first two *atomic* operations in Fig. 7.9a and b specify how to create (delete) a given transition, labelled by *label*, between a source state *src* and a target state *tgt*. Based on these atomic operations, a sample *complex* edit operation for creating a new state and connecting this state by a new transition to an existing one is presented in Fig. 7.9c. This complex operation therefore allows to integrate and connect a new state into an existing model by one edit single operation.

For instance, regarding our xPPU example, the difference $\Delta(PPU2_{v1}, PPU2_{v2})$ describing the evolution from version 1 of the test-model variant $v2$ (see Fig. 7.3a) to version 2 (see Fig. 7.8) may be given as follows:

- *IntegrateNewState(*S_0*,ErrorReaction,*t_6*)*: A new state *ErrorReaction* is added and integrated via the (new) transition t_6.
- *CreateTransition(ErrorReaction,Final,*t_7*)*: A new transition t_7 is created, from the previously created state *ErrorReaction* to the existing final state.
- *AddAnnotations(*t_6*,*t_7*, Version* ≥ 2*)*: Both new transitions t_6 and t_7 are annotated with version information as the new error functionality is only available in version 2 and subsequent versions (see below for more details).

Hence, a high-level difference allows for a proper representation of evolution steps. Furthermore, such a representation can be used for propagating (parts of) changes between different versions/variants, denoted as *model patching* [KKT13]. To this end, we utilise difference $\Delta(v1, v2)$ between two models $v1$ and $v2$ as a *patch* (or edit script) on a third model $v3$ as follows:

- Actual parameters for each edit step $s_k \in \Delta(v1, v2)$ are to be adapted to model $v3$ as elements and/or properties available in $v1$ may not be (identically) available in model $v3$. To do so, a matching between models $v1$ and $v3$ is computed for finding corresponding (and thus appropriate) parameter values, as described earlier.
- Sequential dependencies between edit steps $s_i, s_k \in \Delta(v1, v2)$ are to be derived for computing a (partial) ordering among patch operations. For instance, in $\Delta(PPU2_{v1}, PPU2_{v2})$, the creation of state *ErrorReaction* has to precede the creations of transition t_7 requiring this state as a source state.

Based on this construction, we can apply an (adapted) patch to other models for propagating changes among variants and/or versions [KKR14]. In case of the xPPU example, we may apply patch $\Delta(PPU2_{v1}, PPU2_{v2})$ to xPPU variants $v1$ and $v3$ for introducing error handling (see evolution steps in Fig. 7.1b), instead of manually (re-)creating these changes for all variants [KKR14].

Presence Conditions for Version-Knowledge In the previous section, we already explained the idea of using presence-condition annotations to represent variation points as additional knowledge within solution-space artefacts of software product lines. Based on this concept, a so-called 150% model (e.g. a STATECHART test model for the whole product line) can be defined that superimposes all model variants (i.e. all 100% test models of any derivable software variant) of the product line. In this regard, presence conditions annotate variable model parts with *variant-information* (i.e. propositional conditions over feature-selections), for which they are relevant. In a similar way, presence conditions may be employed to denote *version-information* and to propagate this information among engineering- and quality-assurance artefacts throughout the whole life cycle of an evolving product line. To this end, we introduce (atomic) presence conditions of the form

$$\textit{Version}\ \texttt{relop}\ k,$$

where $\texttt{relop} \in \{<, \leq, \geq, >\}$ as usual, to denote ranges of version numbers (revisions), in which an annotated artefact is—or has been—present in a model- or code fragment of the product line. In order to keep the following presentation graspable, we limit our considerations to a globally consistent and linearly increasing version-history, represented by a single (Integer-valued) meta-variable *Version*. Starting at initial version 1, *Version* is constantly increased by the value 1 after every new revision. We further assume that each revision may include multiple, yet non-conflicting, changes to the same and to different artefacts. Based on the notion of atomic presence conditions, arbitrary *version-history intervals* can be expressed using logical connectives $\wedge$ and $\vee$ as usual (please note that we will use $\wedge$ and $\vee$ in models and `&&` and `||` in code interchangeably in the following). For instance, an artefact annotated with the presence condition

$$(\textit{Version} \geq 2 \wedge \textit{Version} < 6) \vee \textit{Version} \geq 7$$

was not part of the initial version 1 but has been newly added to a model/code artefact in *version 2* but was later (temporarily) removed again in *version 6* and is, from *version 7* on up to the current version, again part of the model/code artefact. As a consequence, artefacts without version annotations are implicitly annotated with the presence condition $Version \geq 1$ (i.e. the artefact existed from version 1 until the current version).

Similar to the integration of all 100% model/code *variants* of a product line into one 150% model/code representation using presence conditions over feature-selections, all 100% model/code *versions* of one single variant can be integrated into one superimposed model using presence conditions over version-intervals. For convenience, we will call the latter representation a *125% model/code* artefact in the following (assuming that differences among different versions are considerably smaller than those between variants). Reconsidering the example in Fig. 7.8a, this model constitutes the 125% test model of xPPU variant *v2*, including both initial version 1 without error handling and version 2 (and all later versions up to the current version) with error-handling capabilities. The model fragment for error handling, consisting of the transitions t_6 and t_7, as well as the state *ErrorReaction*, is therefore annotated with presence condition $Version \geq 2$, whereas all other model elements are not annotated and thus are present in all versions since the initial version. The corresponding 125% code fragment of variant $v2$ is depicted in Fig. 7.8b, where the `#if` block (Lines 9–14) marks the code parts for error handling added during revision 2 of the implementation. Similar updates have been likewise applied to the STATECHART model and respective implementation code of variant $v1$, whereas variant $v3$ has not been affected by this revision.

Concerning the next evolution step, assume the new error handling later to be considered useful also for variant *v3* and therefore added to the respective STATECHART model and implementation code of variant *v3* during *revision 3* of the xPPU product line. As a consequence, the 125% test model of variant *v3* now also contains the model fragment for error handling, as previously added to variants *v1* and *v2*, whereas this fragment is now annotated with the presence condition $Version \geq 3$ and likewise for the implementation code of *v3*. In contrast, variants *v1* and *v2* remain unchanged during revision 3.

In revision 4 of the xPPU product line, however, error handling is removed, again, but only from variant $v2$ as it has been shown to be inappropriate for this particular xPPU configuration, whereas it remains in variants $v1$ and $v3$. Figure 7.11a shows the 125% test model of variant *v2* after revision 4, in which the presence conditions of the transitions have been updated, accordingly, to

$$Version \geq 2 \land Version < 4,$$

and, similarly, for the 125% implementation code of variant $v2$.

Finally, let us consider a special case of product-line revision in which the presence/absence of entire variants changes as part of an evolution step. For instance, as part of revision 5, it has been decided that variant $v3$ is no more supported by the xPPU product line. Hence, *all* solution-space artefacts related to

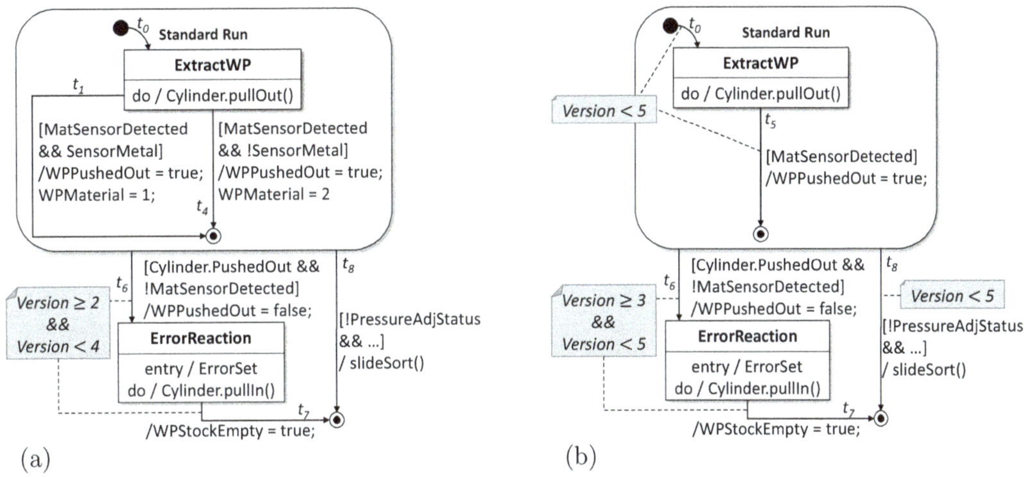

Fig. 7.11 Further evolution steps of variants 2 and 3. (**a**) Test model of variant 2 in version 4. (**b**) Test model of variant 3 in version 5

$v3$ are disabled from version 5 on for variant $v3$, as illustrated in the corresponding 125% model in Fig. 7.11b (and similarly, for the implementation code of variant $v3$). In contrast, variants $v1$ and $v2$ are unaffected by revision 5.

To generalise, updating a presence condition φ of a product-line artefact of a 125% representation to presence condition φ' as a result of a revision k consists of three possible cases:

- $\varphi' := \varphi \vee Version \geq k$ if the artefact is *added* during revision k
- $\varphi' := \varphi \wedge Version < k$ if the artefact is removed during revision k, and
- $\varphi' := \varphi$ if the artefact remains unchanged during revision k

which can be automatically derived from respective model/code difference-rule applications, as described above.

7.2.2 *Evolution of Software Product Lines*

As described before, an idealistic view on product-line evolution should always start with the evolution of the problem-space specification (i.e. the feature model), followed by necessary adaptations to solution-space engineering artefacts (i.e. 150% models and code).

Evolution of Problem-Space Artefacts Based on the *syntactic differences* between a feature model and its revised version due to a feature-diagram edit applied during product-line evolution, the *semantic impact* may be classified in terms of the potential changes of those edits caused on the set of valid configurations (i.e. depending on whether valid configurations may become valid and/or vice versa) [Bür+15b, TBK09].

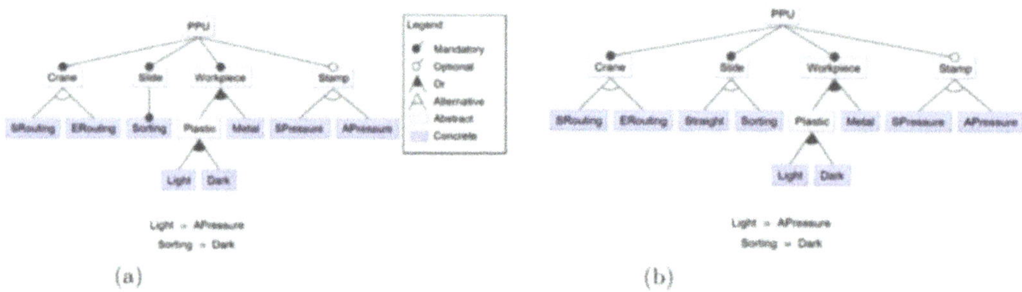

Fig. 7.12 Feature-model evolution scenarios. (**a**) Feature model version 2. (**b**) Feature model version 3

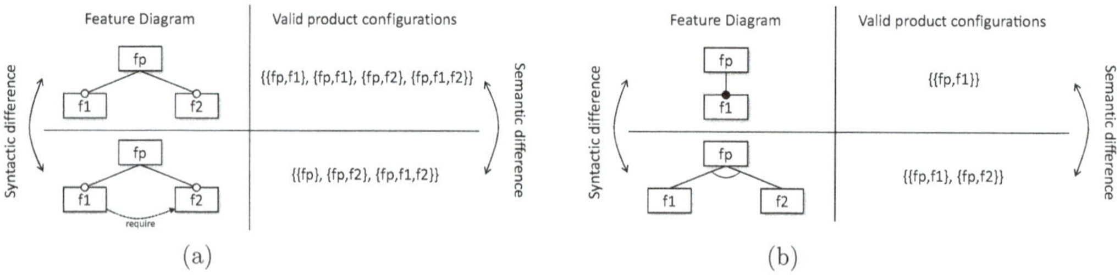

Fig. 7.13 Feature-model edit operations. (**a**) Operation 1. (**b**) Operation 2

As a first example of feature-model evolution, consider the feature-diagram edit from the initial model version in Fig. 7.5a to the new version in Fig. 7.12a. Here, the additional cross-tree constraint *Sorting* $\Rightarrow$ *Dark* has been added to restrict the set of valid configurations of the xPPU product line. Semantically, this edit removes variant *v3* from the set of valid configurations, which has been referred to as *revision 4* from the perspective of software-variant evolution in the previous subsection. A corresponding model-differencing rule for this kind of (atomic) edit operation (see Fig. 7.13a) is therefore classified as *specialisation* step.

As a second example, consider the feature-diagram revision from the model version in Fig. 7.12a to the new model version in Fig. 7.12b. This change consists of a *complex* edit operation involving two *atomic* edits: (1) adding a new feature node *Straight* to parent feature *Slide* and (2) converting the two sibling singleton feature node *Straight* and *Sorting* into an *alternative group*. This edit now enables customers, in addition to the previous variants, to further configure xPPU variants having a *Standard Ramp* with only one *Slide* (i.e. without *Sorting* of WP). The corresponding model-differencing rule for this kind of (complex) edit operation (see Fig. 7.13b) is therefore classified as *generalisation* step.

In addition to the classification of the semantic impact of feature-model edits, the differencing information can, again, be used to annotate model parts with version-information in a similar way, as already described above for STATECHART models and implementation code. The resulting feature model, unifying variant, and version information at the same level of abstraction are also referred to as Hyper-Feature-Models [SSA14].

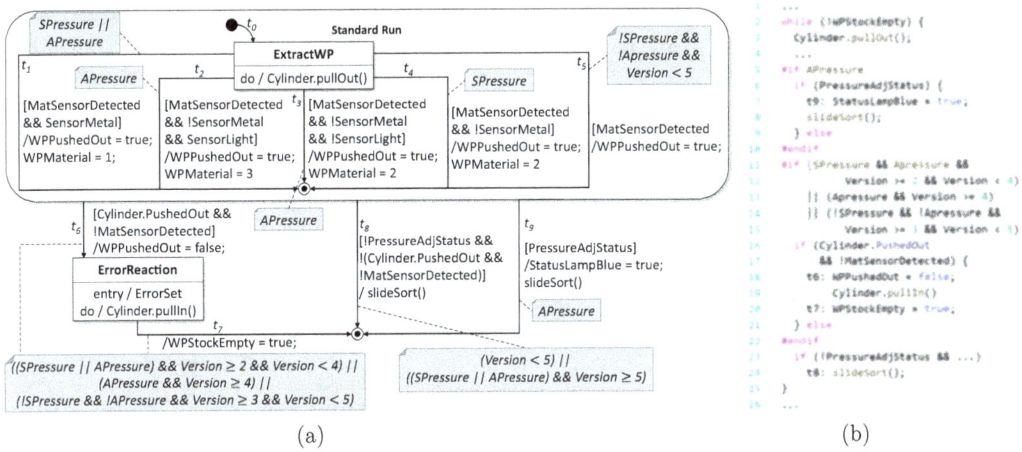

Fig. 7.14 175% test model. (**a**) Test model. (**b**) Code

Evolution of Solution-Space Artefacts The evolution of solution-space artefacts can be handled with similar techniques, as already described for software-variant evolution (i.e. by combining model differencing and presence-condition annotations). However, during the evolution of entire product lines, solution-space representations following the idea of 150% models/code now have to integrate all versions of all model variants by superimposing the 125% model-/code-parts of all variants. In those models, presence conditions have to relate variant- and version-information in a consistent way, in order to express which model-/code parts are (or have been) present in which model-/code variant in which version of the product line. Consequently, we call this kind of representation 175% model/code. We, again, refer to Fig. 7.7b for an overview of the terminology for the different kinds of representations described so far.

As an example, reconsider the five revisions of the xPPU product line, as described previously at the level of software variants, now being applied at the level of the product-line representation. The resulting 175% STATECHART model, including all five revisions of all three variants, is depicted in Fig. 7.14. Most remarkably, the presence conditions

$$((SPressure \vee APressure) \wedge Version \geq 2 \wedge Version < 4) \vee$$

$$(APressure \wedge Version \geq 4) \vee$$

$$(!SPressure \wedge !APressure \wedge Version \geq 3 \wedge Version < 5)$$

of the transitions $t6$ and $t7$ precisely reflect the version-history of error handling in the xPPU product line from version 1 to version 5 as follows:

- The clause in row (1) states that error handling is available in product configurations corresponding to variants $v1$ and $v2$ from version 2 to version 3.

- The clause in row (2) states that error handling is no more available in the product configuration corresponding to variant $v2$ from version 4 but remains available in variant 1.
- The clause in row (3) states that error handling is available in the product configuration corresponding to variant $v3$ from version 3 to version 5 (in which the entire variant is finally removed from the xPPU product line).

Similarly, transition *t5* is annotated with the presence condition

$$(!SPressure \wedge !Apressure) \wedge Version < 5$$

to denote that this transition is present in variant $v3$ from the initial version up to version 4 as it is removed during revision 5. Finally, the annotation

$$(Version < 5) \vee ((SPressure \vee APressure) \wedge Version \geq 5)$$

ensures that transition *t8* will be removed from variant 3 in version 5 but will remain in variants 1 and 2.

The 175% implementation code in Fig. 7.14b shows the corresponding code parts of transitions t6, t7, t8, and t9. Here, the code parts nested in the `#if` block in Lines 5–10 are present in all versions of all variants having feature *APressure* selected, whereas the `#if` block in Lines 11–22 conditionally adds code for error handling, depending on the particular variant and version under consideration.

7.2.3 Evolution of Model-Based Testing Artefacts

Concerning model-based testing artefacts of evolving software product lines, we have to adapt the notions of SPL test case and (complete) SPL test suite [Bür+15a], accordingly, to also take version-information into account, as provided by a 175% test model. To this end, the presence condition of an SPL test case now incorporates both variant- and version-information, thus denoting the set of variants together with a sub-range of their versions required for the test case to be applicable.

As an example, instead of using an automated test-generation tool, consider a tester to manually add a test case to a test suite for the xPPU product line. Based on the 175% test model, the corresponding presence condition for that test case can be derived by conjugating the corresponding presence conditions of those transitions traversed by this test case. For instance, the test case

$$tc3 := (t0, t3, t8)$$

corresponding to the path $t0, t3, t8$ with presence condition *true* from transition $t0$, *APressure* from transition $t3$, and

$$(Version < 5) \vee ((SPressure \vee APressure) \wedge Version \geq 5)$$

from transition $t8$ results in the conjugated presence condition:

$$(t0)\ (true) \wedge$$
$$(t3)\ (APressure) \wedge$$
$$(t8)\ ((Version < 5) \vee ((SPressure \vee APressure) \wedge Version \geq 5)).$$

In addition, the notion of complete SPL test suite has to be likewise enhanced, now requiring that every test goal is covered on every *variant* and *version*, including this test goal, by at least one SPL test case being applicable to this particular *version* of that *variant*. Table 7.1 shows a minimal set of test cases required for complete test coverage of the 175% test model, as shown in Fig. 7.14b. Each row corresponds to a test case, represented by a path through the test model, together with the presence condition and the set of test goals covered by that test case in the respective variants and versions. For example, test case *tc1* covers the test goals *t0*, *t1*, and *t8* on variants *v1* and *v2* in all their versions. Hence, test goal *tc1*, which is only present in variant *v1* and *v2*, is completely covered by this test case on all versions in which it occurs. In contrast, test goals *t0* and *t8* are also present in version $v3$, thus requiring a further test case *tc6*, covering test goals *t0* and *t8* on variant *v3* in all of its versions. In addition, the test case also covers test goal *t5*. The further test cases of the given test suite can be derived accordingly.

As illustrated by this example, the derivation and evolution of model-based testing artefacts (i.e. test goals and corresponding SPL test suites) requires additional knowledge as provided by the feature model and the 175% test model, which will be described in the following section about *co-evolution*.

7.3 Co-evolution

In this section, we discuss the co-evolution scenarios ①–⑥ of model-based product lines, as depicted in Fig. 7.7a, and describe how to ensure consistency among the different product-line engineering- and quality-assurance artefacts involved.

7.3.1 Co-evolution of Software Product Lines and Product Variants

Co-evolution scenario ① is concerned with the evolution of software variants due to changes in the software product line. Following a brute-force approach, all existing model/code variants might be simply re-generated by deriving from the respective 175% model/code the corresponding 100% representations according to

Table 7.1 175% test suite

Test case	Presence condition	Variants	Versions	Goals
$tc_1 = (t_0, t_1, t_8)$	(SPressure ∨ APressure) ∧ ((Version < 5) ∨ ((SPressure ∨ APressure) ∧ Version ≥ 5))	v1, v2	1, 2, 3, 4, 5	t0, t1, t8
$tc_2 = (t_0, t_2, t_9)$	APressure	v1	1, 2, 3, 4, 5	t0, t2, t9
$tc_3 = (t_0, t_3, t_8)$	APressure ∧ ((Version < 5) ∨ ((SPressure ∨ APressure) ∧ Version ≥ 5))	v1	1, 2, 3, 4, 5	t0, t3, t8
$tc_4 = (t_0, t_4, t_8)$	SPressure ∧ ((Version < 5) ∨ ((SPressure ∨ APressure) ∧ Version ≥ 5))	v2	1, 2, 3, 4, 5	t0, t4, t8
$tc_5 = (t_0, t_1, t_6, t_7)$	(SPressure ∨ APressure) ∧ (((SPressure ∨ APressure) ∧ Version ≥ 2 ∧ Version < 4) ∨(APressure ∧ Version ≥ 4) ∨ (!SPressure ∧ !APressure ∧ Version ≥ 3 ∧ Version < 5))	v1 v2	2, 3, 4, 5 2, 3	t0, t1, t6, t7 t0, t1, t6, t7
$tc_6 = (t_0, t_5, t_8)$	(!SPressure ∧ !APressure) ∧ Version < 5) ∧ ((Version < 5) ∨ ((SPressure ∨ APressure) ∧ Version ≥ 5))	v3	1, 2, 3, 4	t0, t5, t8
$tc_7 = (t_0, t_5, t_6, t_7)$	(!SPressure ∧ !APressure) ∧ Version < 5) ∧ (((SPressure ∨ APressure) ∧ Version ≥ 2 ∧ Version < 4) ∨(APressure ∧ Version ≥ 4) ∨ (!SPressure ∧ !APressure ∧ Version ≥ 3 ∧ Version < 5))	v3	3, 4	t0, t5, t6, t7

the corresponding product configuration and the new version number of the evolved product line.

For instance, in the first evolution step applied to the 150% xPPU test model shown in Fig. 7.6a, error handling has been added to the variants *v1* and *v2* (see Fig. 7.1b). As a consequence, one may simply re-generate the corresponding 100% model variants of all possible configurations to ensure consistency with the product line. However, in this way, also those model variants not affected by any changes would be re-generated, which becomes highly inefficient in case of larger product lines with hundreds or even thousands of possible configurations. To avoid this, the additional information gained from model differences and respective presence conditions in 175% representations allow for a more fine-grained change-impact analysis, as will be described in the following.

Problem-Space Co-evolution Scenario ① As described in the previous section, a semantic classification of syntactic feature-model edits can be helpful in proving the potential impact of problem-space evolution on the validity of existing software variants:

- *Generalisation* indicates that (1) all existing variants still correspond to a valid configuration and (2) new variants corresponding to previously invalid configurations may be derivable after the feature-model update.
- *Specialisation* indicates that (1) some existing variants may become invalid and (2) no new variants are derivable after the feature-model update.
- *Refactoring* indicates that the set of valid variants does not change after the feature-model update.
- *Arbitrary edit* indicates that (1) some existing variants may become invalid and (2) new variants may be derivable after the feature-model update.

Based on this information, further investigations on the change impact with respect to the validity or invalidity of particular configurations can be conducted in a systematic and automated way (e.g. using constraint solvers [TBK09]). For instance, the edit applied to the initial version of the xPPU feature diagram in Fig. 7.5a, leading to the new version in Fig. 7.12a, constitutes *specialisation* as variant *v3* becomes invalid. In contrast, the second feature-diagram evolution, leading to the version in Fig. 7.12b, is *generalisation* as we add the new optional kind of *Straight* slide, which leads to a new set of variants having this slide, optionally in addition to the old ones. In these cases, where new variants arise, the 175% test model can be used to derive additional test cases for specifically assuring the corresponding implementation variants. Otherwise, in cases of variants becoming invalid, the presence-condition information attached to existing test cases can be used to remove invalid test cases from SPL test suites.

Solution-Space Co-evolution Scenario ① As described in the previous section, evolution of solution-space artefacts potentially causes changes in parts of 175% model/code representations. Hence, assuming that an evolution scenario yields a new *version k* of the product line, a closer investigation of the presence conditions after updating 175% models/code to version *k* provides information about affected software variants. In particular, for an artefact annotated with a presence condition having a newly added sub-clause of the form

$$(\varphi \wedge \mathit{Version}\ \texttt{relop}\ k),$$

with φ being a propositional formula over features as described previously, two cases arise:

- If `relop` is equal to $<$, then the artefact has been removed during revision k from all variants satisfying φ
- If `relop` is equal to $\geq$, then the artefact has been added during revision k to all variants satisfying φ, respectively.

Based on this information, the overall subset of variants affected by changes on solution-space artefacts performed in revision k can be obtained without additional effort. In addition, the corresponding updates to 100% model/code representations of the affected variants can be conducted automatically (e.g. by means of patches derived from this information).

For instance, consider the transitions $t6$ and $t7$ added for error handling to the 150% test model in Fig. 7.14. For variant $v3$, these transitions become present in versions 3 and 4 due to the sub-clause

$$(!\mathit{SPressure}\ \wedge\ !\mathit{APressure} \wedge \mathit{Version} \geq 3 \wedge \mathit{Version} < 5)$$

in the presence condition of $t6$ and $t7$ in the updated 175% model.

In contrast to co-evolution scenario ①, scenario ② is concerned with the evolution of software product lines due to changes directly applied to individual software variants. Again, we consider co-evolution of both problem-space and solution-space artefacts.

Problem-Space Co-evolution Scenario ② Given an (evolving) set of software variants corresponding to a set of all valid configurations of a product family, the problem of deriving a corresponding configuration model (e.g. a feature diagram) that precisely captures this set of valid configurations is frequently known as *feature-model mining* or *product-line extraction*. We will not go into detail about this particular evolution scenario but rather refer to recent literature about different techniques addressing this problem [Alv+08, MBB16].

Solution-Space Co-evolution Scenario ② Given a set of N software artefacts (e.g. models or code) corresponding to a set of valid software variants of a product family, the problem of deriving an integrated representation superimposing similarities among those representations is frequently referred to as N-way merging [RC13].

N-way Model Merging and Model Integration An overview of the three steps performed during N-way merging in general is depicted in Fig. 7.15 and can be described as follows.

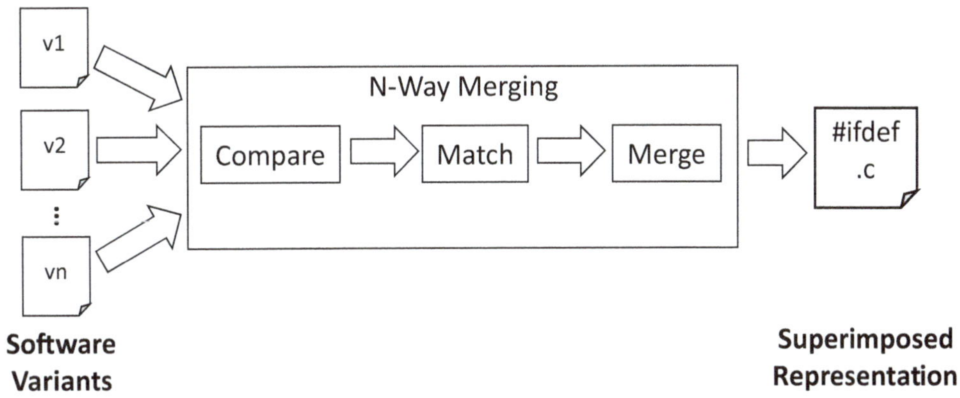

Fig. 7.15 N-way merging

- **Compare.** In this step, elements (e.g. code lines or model parts) of the different models are compared and their similarity is measured with respect to a given *similarity criterion*. Thus, for each possible set of presumably similar elements originating from different models, a similarity value between 0 and 1 is computed. To this end, the same element properties may be used, as already previously described for model differencing (e.g. the types and names of elements).
- **Match.** Based on the compare values, those subsets of elements are being matched (i.e. considered to be same) that constitute the (presumably) most similar elements among the different models. As a result, a complete match contains a complete partitioning of all model elements from all N models. Although various different matching algorithms can be used in this step, a frequently applied greedy-based heuristic incrementally selects further subsets of unmatched elements having the best remaining similarity value, until all elements are finally matched. Similar to the notions already described in the previous section about model differencing, elements matched for merging are referred to as corresponding (see Sect. 7.2).
- **Merge.** In the merge step, all previously matched elements are integrated into the resulting merged model. To this end, the *union-merge operator* is frequently used in practice, which is based on the assumption that all matched elements are complementary (i.e. being literally the same element appearing in different variants and/or versions) and should therefore be *unified* into one element within the superimposed representation. In contrast, unmatched elements (i.e. residing in singleton subsets after matching) are inserted as singleton elements without any unification with other elements.

As described previously, one key aspect of our approach is to use presence conditions for representing variant- and version- information in a uniform and declarative way. In order to facilitate consistency-preserving artefact co-evolution, we automatically integrate presence conditions during the merging step of N-way merging. In particular, we integrate variability information using *variation*

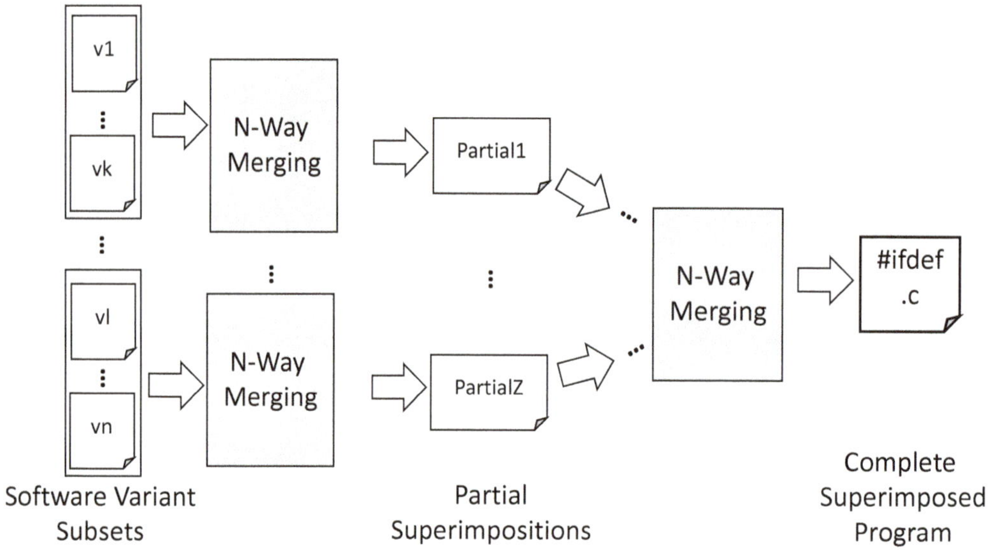

Fig. 7.16 Incremental N-way merging of software variants

points/revision points in terms of conditional model/code fragments over presence conditions rather than (meta-)annotations, as described previously. This alternative representation enables a seamless application of many recent family-based analysis techniques and tools, which are mostly based on this so-called *variability encoding* [Ape+13].

Based on the technique of N-way merging, the following basic co-evolution scenarios can be handled in an automated way:

- Given a set of N 100% models/code artefacts corresponding to the different versions of the same model/code variant, N-way merging results in a 125% representation.
- Given a set of N 100% models/code corresponding to the different variants of the same model/code version, N-way merging results in a 150% representation.

In the case of multiple subsequent versions of either a software variant or an entire product line, the set of N representations is usually not available all at once but rather emerge over time due to evolution scenarios. Hence, merging has to be applied incrementally and/or on subsets (see Fig. 7.16). To this end, the availability of integrated variability-information in terms of variation points/revision points within (partially merged) models allows for incrementally matching and merging further variants and/or versions into product-line representations throughout the entire life cycle of evolving product lines. Based on the technique of incremental N-way merging, advanced co-evolution scenarios can be handled, such as the following:

- Given a 125% representation comprising the different versions of one particular variant up to revision $k - 1$ and a 100% representation as a result of revision k of that variant, their merging yields a 125% representation comprising all versions of that variant up to revision k.

- Given a set of N 125% representations comprising the different versions of a set of N variants, their N-way merging yields a 175% representation comprising all variants with all their versions.
- Given a set N 150% representations comprising the different versions of a product line, their N-way merging yields a 175% representation comprising all these variants with all their versions.

As an example, recall the evolution scenario of version 1 of the 150% test model in Fig. 7.6, leading to version 2, which shall be now conducted at the level of variants. During the revision leading to version 2, the test models of the variants $v1$ and $v2$ (see Fig. 7.8) are evolved to now contain error handling, whereas the test model of variant $v3$ (see Fig. 7.4) remains unchanged. We now consider this evolution scenario at the level of the implementation code, and we focus on the code parts implementing the transitions below the so-called *standard-run* state (see Fig. 7.14). To this end, we consider the representation of source code in terms of CFA, constituting a program abstraction frequently used by many program-analysis and testing tools [Bür+15a]. States (or nodes) of a CFA correspond to control-flow locations (i.e. lines of source code) in a given program, whereas edges denote different kinds of basic imperative control flows (i.e. control-flow sequences, control-flow branches, and control-flow loops) as usual, being either labelled with (basic blocks of) program statements or expressions, respectively. This representation allows us to apply principles from model differencing and model merging, as described above, to STATECHART models, as well as to implementation code in a similar way. Figure 7.17d shows the corresponding extract from the CFA of the 175% code of the product line in version 1, whereas Fig. 7.17a–c shows similar

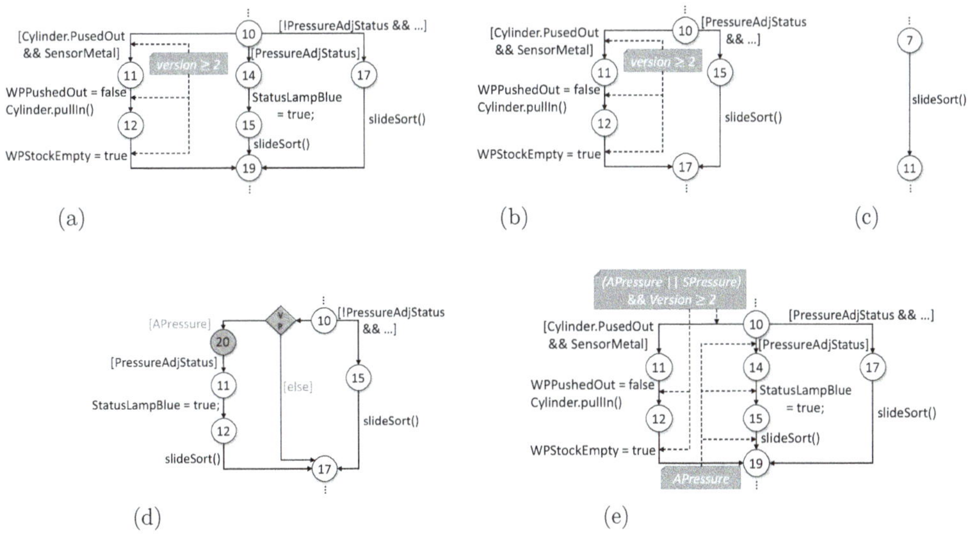

Fig. 7.17 Incremental N-way CFA merging. (**a**) CFA of v1 in Version 2. (**b**) CFA of v2 in version 2. (**c**) CFA of v3 in version 2. (**d**) 175% CFA in version 1. (**e**) 175% CFA in version 2

extracts from the 100% CFA representations of variants $v1$, $v2$, and $v3$ after revision 2. Figure 7.17e therefore depicts the 175% CFA resulting from merging the 175% CFA representation and the 100% CFA representation, thus yielding the 175% CFA representation after revision 2. Hence, by (incrementally) applying N-way merging in this way, similarities among variants and/or versions are reflected in the resulting 175% CFA. For instance, path 10-17-19 is present in all variants and all versions, whereas path 10-14-15-19 is present in all versions of variant $v1$ (having feature *APressure*), and path 10-11-12-19 (for error handling) is only present in version 2 of variants $v1$ and $v2$.

7.3.2 Co-evolution of Software Product Lines and Model-Based Testing Artefacts

Concerning scenario ③, the co-evolution of model-based testing artefacts according to evolving product-line representations can be conducted in a straightforward manner. Based on the combined variant/version-information in the updated 175% test-model specification, family-based test generation can be applied for updating the SPL test suite in order to become consistent with the latest revision. Concerning the application of test cases selected for retesting variant implementations being potentially affected by the changes, again, the additional information in the updated 175% implementation code can be used for change-impact analysis similar to principles known from regression testing [Loc+12].

For instance, concerning the SPL test suite, as shown in Table 7.1, the additional test case *tc5* has to be added to the test suite after adding error handling to variants *v1* and *v2* during revision 2. In addition, after removing variant *v3* during revision 5, test cases *tc6* and *tc7* both become invalid as they are only executable on that variant.

Concerning scenario ④, co-evolution of manual updates of SPL test suites and corresponding product-line representations can be conducted by deriving variant/version-information for newly added test cases from the the 175% test model.

For instance, a tester may decide to add the additional test case $tc8 = (t0, t1, t9)$ into the SPL test suite, as shown in Table 7.1, to test the correct interplay between transitions *t1* and *t9* in variant *v1*. The corresponding presence condition obtained from the respective path in the 175% test model is given as

$$(SPressure \vee APressure) \wedge APressure,$$

thus being valid for any version of all variants having feature *APressure* selected. In contrast, test case $tc9 = (t0, t4, t9)$ is invalid as the presence condition $(SPressure \wedge APressure)$ contradicts the feature model in all versions of the xPPU product line.

Similarly, the impact of manual removals of test cases from SPL test suites on the test coverage can be investigated on the 175% test model. For instance, if test case *tc2* is removed from the SPL test suite, as shown in Table 7.1, test goal *t0* is no longer covered in any version of all variants containing this goal.

7.3.3 Co-evolution of Product Variants and Test Artefacts

Finally, co-evolution scenarios ⑤ and ⑥ can be handled by sequentially composing the different scenarios for co-evolving product-line representations, as described above, namely:

- Scenario ⑤ can be handled by first conducting scenario ④ and then scenario ①.
- Scenario ⑥ can be handled by first conducting scenario ② and then scenario ③.

7.4 Conclusion

In this chapter, we described a model-based framework for systematic round-trip engineering and quality assurance of continuously evolving software product lines. The presented methodology utilises two major techniques from model-based software engineering, namely:

- *Model differencing* and *model merging* for automated comparison and integration of software variants and versions of an evolving software product line, and
- *Knowledge-carrying software* for the integration of additional information about variant- and version-specific software artefacts into engineering and quality-assurance processes.

This combination ensures consistency among engineering and quality-assurance artefacts throughout the entire life cycle of evolving product lines and facilitates the application of efficient *family-based* product-line analysis strategies to both variant- and version-rich software systems, as well as arbitrary combinations thereof.

To conclude this chapter, we briefly outline a road map for possible future research directions based on the proposed framework.

Besides the model/code artefacts and the corresponding knowledge on product-line representations, as discussed throughout this chapter, further types of artefacts and meta-information annotations might be considered in a similar way due to the generality and generic nature of the presented approach and tools.

In addition to model-based testing, further quality-assurance techniques (e.g. model checking, NFP analysis, etc.) might be lifted in a similar way to become applicable for family-based analyses of both variants and versions in a unified way.

Finally, other kinds of evolution scenarios and co-evolution scenarios might be taken into account. For instance, in practice, a large repository of continuously evolved legacy test cases exists for which corresponding variant-/version-knowledge is often not available, incomplete, and error prone. Hence, precise techniques for reverse-engineering (or learning) variant-/version-information from those existing artefacts is a crucial open issue for future research.

7.5 Further Reading

Further details about tool support and experiences gained from experimental evaluation results obtained for the different techniques can be found in recent publications summarised in the following. In addition to the references already provided in the different subsections of this chapter, the following references also contain further information about related work on the different approaches considered in this chapter.

A survey about different product-line analysis techniques, including family-based Analysis, can be found in [Thü+14a]. In particular, a tool implementation of the family-based test-suite generation approach based on the software model checker CPACHECKER [Bey+04, D B+13] can be found in Bürdek et al. [Bür+15a], and evaluation results for applying the approach to the PPU case study can be found in Lochau et al. [Loc+14]. The evaluation results show remarkable gains in efficiency under stable effectiveness of applying family-based test generation, as compared to a variant-by-variant approach. This tool can be extended, accordingly, to handle combinations of variant- and version-knowledge, as described in this chapter.

The representation of variability information by means of presence-condition annotations has been initially proposed by Czarnecki et al. as part of their template-based approach for product-line modelling [CE00].

An alternative approach for conceptually integrating variant- and version-information into one representation based on the delta-modelling approach has been proposed by Lity et al. in [Lit+18]. A detailed description of re-engineering the xPPU case study as a product line for model-based testing can be found in [Lit+15]. A general description of challenges in testing product lines can be found in [McG01].

An overview on model-versioning techniques and tools may be found in [ASW09]. Concerning model differencing techniques, in particular as described in this chapter, a dedicated overview can be found in [Kol+09]. Among others, the SILIFT framework allows for a rule-based specification of corresponding model-transformation operators, being applicable to arbitrary input models in a generic way [KWN05]. Among others, this tool has been successfully applied to efficiently and effectively compute and classify differences between FODA feature diagrams, as described in this chapter [Bür+15b]. This approach is, in general, adaptable to any Eclipse Modeling Framework (EMOF)-based modelling language, such as STATECHART test models, as considered in this chapter. This tool can be extended, accordingly, to also compute model differences and N-way model merges of other product-line artefacts like STATECHART test models and CFA-based representations of implementation code, as described above. Finally, further reading on model-merging notions and techniques can be found, among others, in [Men02] as well as in [RC13].

Chapter 8
Performance Analysis Strategies for Software Variants and Versions

Thomas Thüm, André van Hoorn, Sven Apel, Johannes Bürdek, Sinem Getir, Robert Heinrich, Reiner Jung, Matthias Kowal, Malte Lochau, Ina Schaefer, and Jürgen Walter

---

T. Thüm (✉) · M. Kowal · I. Schaefer
Institute for Software Engineering and Automotive Informatics, TU Braunschweig, Brunswick, Germany
e-mail: t.thuem@tu-braunschweig.de; m.kowal@tu-braunschweig.de; i.schaefer@tu-braunschweig.de

A. van Hoorn
Institute of Software Technology, University of Stuttgart, Stuttgart, Germany
e-mail: van.hoorn@informatik.uni-stuttgart.de

S. Apel
Chair of Software Engineering I, Department of Informatics and Mathematics, University of Passau, Passau, Germany
e-mail: apel@uni-passau.de

J. Bürdek · M. Lochau
Technische Universität Darmstadt, Fachbereich Elektrotechnik und Informationstechnik, Fachgebiet Echtzeitsysteme, Darmstadt, Germany
e-mail: johannes.buerdek@es.tu-darmstadt.de; malte.lochau@es.tu-darmstadt.de

S. Getir
Institut für Informatik, Johann-von-Neumann-Haus, Humboldt-Universität zu Berlin, Berlin, Germany
e-mail: getir@informatik.hu-berlin.de

R. Heinrich
Institute for Program Structures and Data Organization, Karlsruhe Institute of Technology (KIT), Karlsruhe, Germany
e-mail: robert.heinrich@kit.edu

R. Jung
Software Engineering Group, Department of Computer Science, Kiel University, Kiel, Germany
e-mail: reiner.jung@email.uni-kiel.de

J. Walter
Chair of Computer Science II, Universität Würzburg, Würzburg, Germany
e-mail: juergen.walter@uni-wuerzburg.de

R. Reussner et al. (eds.), *Managed Software Evolution*,
https://doi.org/10.1007/978-3-030-13499-0_8

Adaptation is heavily used for today's software in two dimensions. First, developers frequently release new *versions* of software to meet new or changed requirements (aka. software evolution [BR00]). Second, developers simultaneously develop *variants* of software to meet contradictory requirements (aka. configurable software or software product lines [CE00, Ape+13]). While versions typically replace existing versions, variants co-exist to meet certain requirements each. Both variants and versions give rise to software variation. Performance—capturing software quality properties with respect to timeliness and resource usage—is of particular relevance to software design, operations, and evolution. It has a major impact on key business indicators. Consequently, during the software's life cycle, developers and operators need to be aware of performance.

Over the last decades, the community has developed methods, techniques, and tools to analyse performance in different design and operations stages, combining model-based and measurement-based approaches [WFP07, Bru+15]. Figure 8.1 depicts the artefacts and activities being involved in model-based performance analysis in combination with measurements. architectural models for the software versions and variants, for example using Unified Modeling Language (UML), can be augmented by performance-relevant information, for example using UML profiles such as MARTE [Obj11]. These models can be used to predict performance indices of the respective versions and variants, for example CPU utilisation and response times. Two common approaches are used for prediction [CMI11]: (1) simulating the models and (2) transforming the architectural models to analytical models, for example queuing networks or Petri nets and solving or simulating these models using respective tools. Once implementation artefacts become available, performance indices can be obtained by measurements, for example using profilers or application performance management (APM) tools [Heg+17]. Once measurements are available from implementation artefacts, performance models can also be

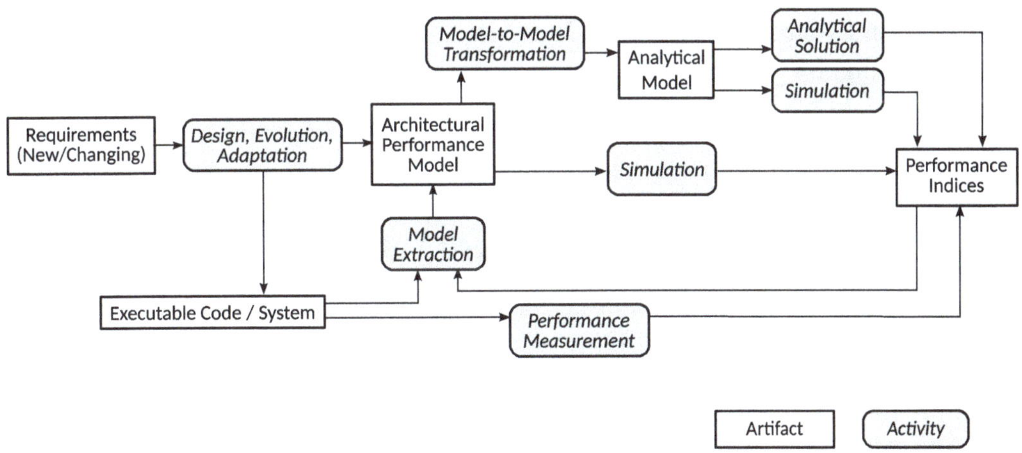

Fig. 8.1 Performance engineering taxonomy including alternative performance evaluation methods

extracted automatically. These extracted models can also be used during runtime, example to react dynamically to changing environmental conditions, such as changing workload characteristics [CMT16].

Even though variants and versions are quite different in their purpose, their software variation challenges software analyses in a similar manner. In particular, it is often infeasible to analyse all variants and all versions of a software, especially for performance analyses, because of several reasons. First, even when applied automatically, performance analyses are time-consuming due to the necessity to execute the software under test using different workloads [WFP07]. Second, the sheer number of variants and versions of today's software renders it infeasible to analyse all of them separately due to combinatorial explosion [Thü+14a]. Even though variation is often low between certain variants and versions, a small change can have a huge impact on the performance of the overall software. Hence, we cannot just measure the performance of one variant or version and, thus, need strategies to systematically cope with software variation.

Ideally, the performance of software variation would be analysed with an automated process that incorporates the knowledge of previous performance analyses steps. We envision a process in which a stakeholder identifies a performance-related concern. Then a magic box automatically selects a strategy to answer the concern, including a mixture of predictions, as well as offline and online tests. When applying this strategy, results are not only propagated to the stakeholder but also to a knowledge base. While the stakeholder acts on the results by evolving the system or refining concerns, the growing knowledge base is used by the magic box in the next iteration.

In this chapter, we report on our experiences with performance evaluation strategies for software variation. We elaborate on strategies to efficiently analyse the performance of software variants in Sect. 8.1 and of software versions in Sect. 8.2. We are using both case studies introduced in Chap. 4 for illustration. Section 8.1 is exemplified using the Pick-and-Place Unit (PPU) case study, while Sect. 8.2 uses the Common Component Modeling Example (CoCoME) case study. We conclude our discussions by giving a unified view over performance analysis strategies for software variation and a discussion of future challenges in Sect. 8.3.

8.1 Analysis Strategies for Software Variants

Numerous strategies are known to analyse software variants [Thü+14a]. However, not all of them are applicable for performance evaluation, as some strategies can be used only for static analysis and not to actually run the software variants. We report on our experience in applying complementary strategies to analyse the performance of software variants. In Sect. 8.1.1, we elaborate on approaches that try to focus on the most relevant variants by sampling the large variant space. As we use test cases to measure the performance of variants and as manually creating those is laborious, we discuss how to generate test suites that cover all variants in Sect. 8.1.2.

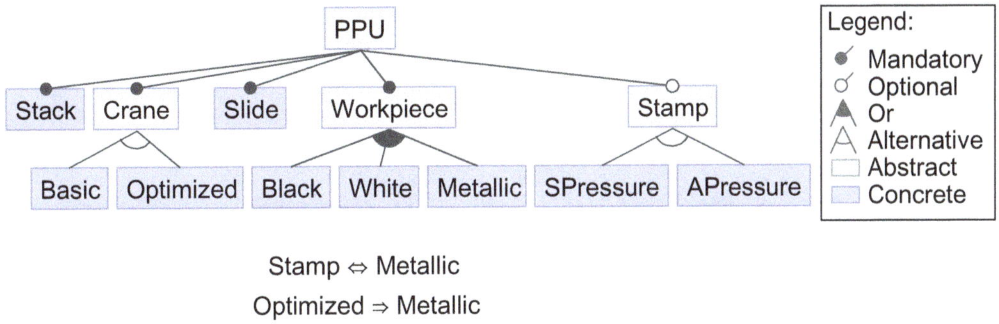

Fig. 8.2 Excerpt of the feature model of the PPU

Finally, in Sect. 8.1.3, we discuss a strategy to predict the performance of variants analytically without the need to measure the performance of every variant. That is, the techniques discussed in Sects. 8.1.1 and 8.1.2 may or may not be combined, whereas the technique presented in Sect. 8.1.3 is applied in isolation.

Pick-and-Place Unit as a Motivating Example A feature model typically has a tree-like graphical representation depicting the hierarchically arranged set of features. Relationships in the feature model regarding parent and child features are expressed with the common notation of *mandatory*, *optional* features and *or-*, *alternative* groups and their underlying semantics (cf. legend in Fig. 8.2 for the graphical representation) [Kan+90a, CE00]. *Abstract* features do not contain realisation artefacts and are only used for structural purposes [Thü+11]. A feature model of the PPU case study system, as introduced in Chap. 4, is shown in Fig. 8.2. The PPU can process up to three different kinds of workpieces (WPs): *White*, *Black*, and *Metallic* workpieces. A *Stack* stores all workpieces before they are processed by the *Crane*. *Basic* and *Crane* are two alternative implementations of the crane behaviour differing in the processing times of workpieces. In addition, the optimised implementation requires a stamping module, making the metallic workpiece type necessary. Finally, all workpieces are transported to the *Slide*, awaiting packaging or further processing in other automation systems. For illustration, we describe three selected variants in more detail in the following.

Variant 1 is the minimal system configuration consisting of the concrete features *Stack, Basic, Slide,* and *Black*. The *Black* workpieces are transported from the *Stack* to the *Slide* by the *Crane*. This process is repeated until no more workpieces are present.

Variant 5 can distinguish between two different types of workpieces (*Metallic* or *Black*). While *Black* workpieces are treated as in Variant 1, metallic pieces take a different route through the system. They are transported by the *Crane* to the new stamp component (i.e. *SPressure*). After the stamp process is finished, these pieces are also transported to the *Slide*.

Variant 9 is identical to the previous variant on the hardware level. The crane implementation is optimised (cf. feature *Optimised*) as the crane no longer waits at the stamp for the stamping process to be finished. Instead, the crane moves back to the stack to pick up the next black workpiece (if present) and transports it to the slide. Afterwards, the crane fetches the stamped workpiece and transports it to the slide.

8.1.1 Sample-Based Analysis of Software Variants

As said previously, configurable systems may have configuration spaces of substantial size, so identifying which variant performs best in a concrete setting is difficult. In the worst case, the size of the configuration space of a configurable system is exponential in the number of features. While, in practice, the actual number of desired or relevant software variants is considerably smaller, typically, configuration spaces of real-world systems are still huge [Ber+13]. In fact, even enumerating all valid variants—not to speak of performing any measurements—is often computationally intractable. Due to the small size of our example, enumerating all variants is possible though, as we illustrate in Table 8.1.

To learn about the performance behaviour of individual variants, practitioners resort typically to *sampling*. The idea is not to analyse all variants of a given configurable system individually, but just a *sample set*, which is smaller and can be analysed in feasible time. For the purpose of our example, let us assume that we analyse variants 1, 4, and 9 (cf. Table 8.1). The key idea of a sampling-based approach is not just to work with the performance data of the sample set but to use them also to learn about the performance behaviour of other variants not in the sample set, say variants 7 and 10, in our example. In other words, we want to *predict* the performance behaviour of all (or some) variants of a system based on the performance measurements we did on a sample set.

Sampling Strategies There are various strategies to select a proper sample set and to generalise the measurements to the other variants of the system. Let us illustrate some key strategies here by means of the example of Table 8.1, which includes a performance value for every variant of the PPU case study. An interesting observation is that there are only three different kinds of variants: variants that can process 0.12 workpieces/s, 0.03 workpieces/s, and 0.09 workpieces/s. Interestingly, in our sample set (variants 1, 4, 9), there is no variant with the value 0.09. While this is not necessarily a problem, we will we discuss it shortly as it illustrates that selecting variants for the sample set is a crucial step.

In the literature, there are several strategies for selecting sample sets [Med+16]. One notable strategy—beyond mere *random sampling*—is *t-wise coverage* sampling [JHF12]. The idea is that the variants of the sample set should contain or *cover* certain features and combinations of features. *Feature-wise* ($t = 1$) sampling means essentially that every feature of the configurable system should be selected in, at least, one variant and deselected in, at least, one variant of the sample set. In our exemplary sample set, this is not the case as, for example, feature *APressure* is not in any of its variants. In contrast, sets 1, 11, and 12 are a valid feature-wise sample

Table 8.1 Variants of the pick-and-place unit and their performance values

Variant	Concrete features	Performance (in workpieces/s)
1	Stack, Basic, Slide, Black	0.12
2	Stack, Basic, Slide, White	0.12
3	Stack, Basic, Slide, Black, White	0.12
4	Stack, Basic, Slide, Metallic, SPressure	0.03
5	Stack, Basic, Slide, Black, Metallic, SPressure	0.09
6	Stack, Basic, Slide, White, Metallic, SPressure	0.03
7	Stack, Basic, Slide, Black, White, Metallic, SPressure	0.09
8	Stack, Optimised, Slide, Metallic, SPressure	0.03
9	Stack, Optimised, Slide, Black, Metallic, SPressure	0.12
10	Stack, Optimised, Slide, White, Metallic, SPressure	0.03
11	Stack, Optimised, Slide, Black, White, Metallic, SPressure	0.12
12	Stack, Basic, Slide, Metallic, APressure	0.03
13	Stack, Basic, Slide, Black, Metallic, APressure	0.09
14	Stack, Basic, Slide, White, Metallic, APressure	0.03
15	Stack, Basic, Slide, Black, White, Metallic, APressure	0.09
16	Stack, Optimised, Slide, Metallic, APressure	0.03
17	Stack, Optimised, Slide, Black, Metallic, APressure	0.12
18	Stack, Optimised, Slide, White, Metallic, APressure	0.03
19	Stack, Optimised, Slide, Black, White, Metallic, APressure	0.12

but still do not contain a variant with the value 0.09. *Pair-wise* ($t = 2$) sampling requires that for each pair of features there is at least one variant, in which both are selected and both are deselected and each feature is selected while the other is deselected. Our exemplary sample set does not attain pair-wise coverage either as it does not even cover all features. The pair-wise sample sets 1, 2, 3, 6, 9, 12, 16, and 19 would be sufficient for our example. Selecting higher values of t increases coverage but also leads to larger sample sets.

Learning from Sample Sets Given a sample set, there are several approaches that aim at learning the influences of individual features and their combinations on performance to allow predictions of the performance behaviour beyond the sample set [Sie+12a, Guo+13, Sar+15, Sie+15, Nai+17]. A simple approach is to approximate the performance of every individual feature [Sie+12a]. This can be achieved easily by a comparative measurement: measuring a basic variant with and without the feature in question and assigning the difference in performance behaviour to that very feature. As an example, let us assume that we measured (denoted using function Π) the processing time of variants 6 and 7 of our PPU case study (in workpieces per second):

$\Pi(\text{Stack, Basic, Slide, White, Metallic, SPressure}) = 0.03$
$\Pi(\text{Stack, Basic, Slide, Black, White, Metallic, SPressure}) = 0.09$

The difference in observed throughput is 0.06, which we consider as the influence of the feature black (as it is the only feature in which the two configurations differ). This way we can assign every feature a value. Based on the values for individual features, we can already make predictions, which are rather imprecise, though. For example, if want to predict the combined influence of the features black and white, we would just add their individual influences, say $0.06 + 0.09 = 0.15$ (assuming the individual influence of white is 0.09).[1] The point is that this prediction may be wrong (in fact, it is very likely wrong). The reason is that the two features may *interact* interfering at the level of processing time (or other properties).

Feature Interactions Let us revisit the prediction procedure: Essentially, it takes the influences on the processing time of individual features and adds them up according to the variant whose processing time shall be predicted. However, due to feature interactions, the influences of the features involved do not necessarily add up, as we have seen for the features black and white. To identify the interaction between the two, we need to measure a variant that has both features selected, in addition to the measurements that we already have. This way we can pinpoint the interaction, which amounts, say, to a decrease of 0.03 workpieces/s. Knowing the influence of this interaction, we can make a more precise prediction, which is $0.06 + 0.09 - 0.03 = 0.12$.

So incorporating feature interactions improves the accuracy of the prediction procedure. The downside is, to identify all feature interactions of a configurable system, we need again to measure a possibly exponential number of system variants. This is where the sampling strategies come into play. Using, for example, pair-wise sampling presumes that the most relevant interactions are among pairs of features, which are covered by pair-wise sampling.

Experiences and Further Reading In the course of SPP 1593, we extended the tools FeatureIDE and SPL Conqueror. FeatureIDE is an Eclipse-based development environment for feature-oriented software development [Thü+14b, Mei+17], in which we integrated numerous sampling algorithms [AlH+16b, AlH+16a]. We used FeatureIDE to compute the samples for our running example. SPL Conqueror bundles various sampling and learning strategies for the performance prediction of configurable systems [Sie+12b].[2] In a number of studies, we applied it successfully to real-world configurable systems from different domains, including databases,

[1]Note that for other properties of interest, other ways of combining influence may be preferable, for example taking the minimum of two values for reliability.

[2]https://www.infosun.fim.uni-passau.de/se/projects/splconqueror/.

compilers, video encoders [Sie+12a, Sie+13, Sie+15], and scientific computing codes [Gre+14, Gre+17]. We further extended the whole approach, including the notion of feature interaction, to settings where numeric parameters are used to configure the system (e.g. cache size) [Sie+15], which may also interact in various ways [SSA17]. As for the learning procedure, we support classification and regression trees, linear regression, random forests, and others. As for sampling, we experimented with various coverage criteria [Med+16], as well as progressive and projective sampling [Sar+15]. Recently, we also surveyed the extensive literature on product sampling based on feature models [Var+18]. Our literature overview can be used by practitioners and researchers to find suitable sampling algorithms based on the available input, such as feature model and source code, and desired coverage criteria, such as feature interaction coverage or code coverage.

8.1.2 Family-Based Test-Suite Generation for Software Variants

The idea of sample-based performance prediction, as described in the previous Section, is to estimate performance values of all possible variants of a configurable software system, by only investigating a subset (sample) of variants. This approach enables a reduction of the overall effort required for performance analysis, as compared to explicitly considering every possible variant one by one. However, the accuracy of the predicted data naturally depends on the quality of the performance measurement data available for the sample set. Hence, experimental executions of the sampled variants are required in order to gather realistic and reliable performance measures for embedded software systems such as the PPU. To this end, the collected measurement data should rely on a high diversity of possible system behaviours, covering a high fraction of default, exceptional, and even fail-safe execution scenarios. Model-based coverage-driven testing constitutes a well-suited approach to systematically exercise the behaviours of software systems in an automated manner [UL07].

Model-Based Testing The term (software) testing in its most general form refers to any activity being concerned with investigating (and assuring) quality aspects of a given software system [UL07]. In particular, *dynamic* testing involves experimental executions of *test cases* by executing the software under controlled conditions, in order to investigate the output behaviours for particular input stimuli. The observed behaviours may comprise *functional* aspects (e.g. comparing the observed outputs to the ones expected for the inputs), as well as *non-functional* aspects (e.g. the amount of response time required by the system to produce the outputs).

Concerning model-based testing in particular, a behavioural specification (*test model*) of the software is used to automatically derive a set of test cases into a *test suite*. Test cases are usually selected into a test suite with respect to a given coverage criterion, defining a set of test goals, each to be satisfied by at least one test case of a test suite.

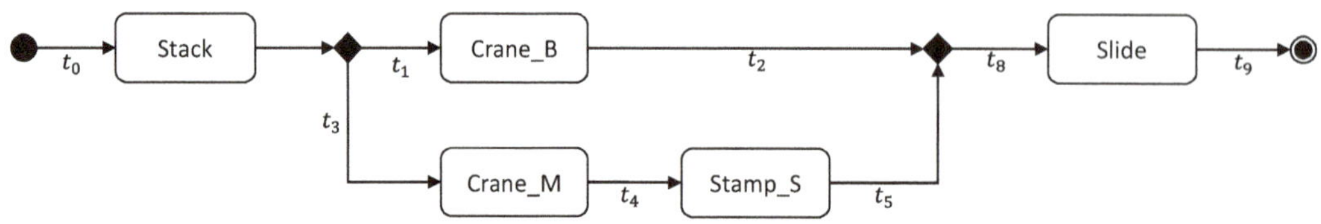

Fig. 8.3 Test model of variant 5 of the pick-and-place unit

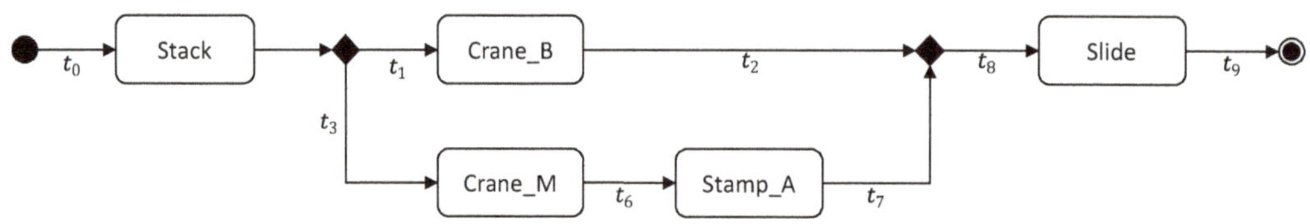

Fig. 8.4 Test model of variant 13 of the pick-and-place unit

Figure 8.3 shows an excerpt of a simplified test model for Variant 5 of the PPU, given as a UML activity diagram. However, the technique described in the following is not limited to a particular behavioural modelling language but is likewise applicable, for instance, to UML state machines and similar formalisms. The model describes the scenarios for the treatment of *Black* workpieces (branch with action *Crane_B*), as well as *Metallic* workpieces (branch with action *Crane_M*, followed by *Stamp_S*) both coming from the *Stack* and subsequently going to the *Slide*. A test case, therefore, consists of a sequence of actions from the initial action to the final action of the activity, connected via a path of control-flow edges. For brevity, we omit further details about the actions performed and the edge labels in the following examples (cf. [Loc+14] for further details). As coverage criterion, we consider edge coverage, where the set of test goals is annotated as $t_0, t_1, \ldots, t_9$ in Fig. 8.3. A test case derived from the test model for reaching, for instance, test goals t_9 may be given as the sequence $T1 = (t_0, t_1, t_2, t_8, t_9)$. This test case also covers test goals t_0, t_1, t_2 and t_8, whereas test goals t_3, t_4 and t_5 of the alternative branch remain uncovered. Hence, in order to also cover the alternative branch, a further test case $T2 = (t_0, t_3, t_4, t_5, t_8, t_9)$ is required such that a test suite consisting of $T1$ and $T2$ achieves complete edge coverage.

Considering Variant 13 of the PPU (cf. test model variant in Fig. 8.4), the behaviour corresponding to test case $T1$ remains the same (and may, therefore, be reused for also testing this variant). In contrast, the behaviour of $T2$ is not valid any more as metallic workpieces are now treated differently by the *Stamp*, thus requiring an additional test case $T3 = (t_0, t_3, t_6, t_7, t_8, t_9)$. Nevertheless, re-generating a test suite anew from scratch for every individual variant in order to finally achieve complete coverage on all variants tends to become inefficient [Bür+15a]. This is due to the high amount of similarity among the variants leading to a potentially high number of redundant test cases. In addition, in case of configurable software of realistic sizes, this approach even becomes impossible as the number of variants potentially grows exponentially in the number of features.

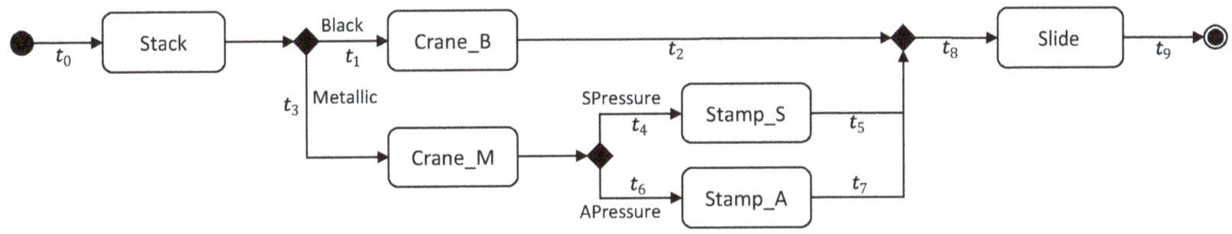

Fig. 8.5 150% test model of the pick-and-place unit

Table 8.2 Test models for variants of the pick-and-place unit

	Features				Edges									
Variant	Black	Metallic	SPressure	APressure	t_0	t_1	t_2	t_3	t_4	t_5	t_6	t_7	t_8	t_9
1	x				x	x	x						x	x
4		x	x		x			x	x	x			x	x
5	x	x	x		x	x	x	x	x	x			x	x
12		x		x	x			x			x	x	x	x
13	x	x		x	x	x	x	x			x	x	x	x

Family-Based Test-Suite Generation Family-based product-line analysis in general [Thü+14a] and family-based test-suite generation in particular [Bür+15a] aim to automatically achieve complete test coverage for all variants without considering every variant individually. To this end, a so-called 150% test model is used that superimposes all test-model variants into one integrated test model. An excerpt from the 150% test model of the PPU example is shown in Fig. 8.5, comprising behaviours for variants 1, 4, 5, 12, and 13. Variable parts (e.g. edges in this example) of a 150% model are augmented with *presence conditions* (i.e. propositional formulae over Boolean feature variables), denoting those subsets of configurations, in whose corresponding test-model variants the respective part is present.

Table 8.2 summarises for the set of all variants which edges (and, therefore, which test goals) are present (or relevant) in which variant. This additional information can be utilised during test-case generation for reasoning about the reuse of test cases while covering test goals in different variants. For instance, test goal t_1 is only present in variants with feature *Black* being selected (i.e. variants 1, 5, and 13), whereas t_0 is present in all variants. The aforementioned test cases $T1$ (requiring feature *Black*) and $T2$ (requiring features *Metallic* and *SPressure*), therefore, together cover test goal t_0 on variants 4 and 5, but they are both not valid for variants 12 and 13 (requiring feature *APressure* to be selected). Hence, a third test case, $T3 = (t_0, t_3, t_6, t_7, t_8, t_9)$, is to be derived to finally cover test goal t_0 on all variants in which it occurs.

The possible reuse of test cases among variants sharing similar paths achievable by family-based test-suite generation potentially reduces testing effort as compared to variant-by-variant testing. For instance, applying variant-by-variant test-case derivation to the PPU example in Table 8.2 at least produces an overall number of seven test cases (i.e. $1(V1)+1(V4)+1(V5)+2(V12)+2(V13) = 7$) according to the number of paths within the different test-model variants. In contrast, when

Table 8.3 Test suite for complete transition coverage of the pick-and-place unit test model

TC	Path	Features				Variants				
		Black	Metallic	SPressure	APressure	V1	V4	V5	V12	V13
T1	t_0, t_1, t_2, t_8, t_9	x				x		x		x
T2	$t_0, t_3, t_4, t_5, t_8, t_9$		x	x			x	x		
T3	$t_0, t_3, t_6, t_7, t_8, t_9$		x		x				x	x

applying the family-based test-generation strategy, three test cases are sufficient to achieve complete edge coverage on all variants, as illustrated in Table 8.3. Based on this information, two variants are sufficient to execute the resulting three test cases (e.g. variants 5 and 12).

Experiences and Further Reading Besides the PPU case study, the presented technique has been applied to other application domains, including medical-device control software, Linux-kernel drivers, and embedded-system utility software. For those experiments, we observed similar results concerning efficiency improvements as compared to variant-by-variant testing. Corresponding tool support utilises the temporal model checker SPIN for model-based (black-box) generation from UML state charts [Loc+14], as well as the software model checker CPACHECKER for white-box text generation from product lines implemented in C using compile-time variability (C pre-processor) [Bür+15a]. Our experience gained from the various experimental results show that remarkable efficiency improvements of family-based coverage-driven test generation, as compared to a variant-by-variant approach, can be observed in almost all cases, at least up to a certain product-line size (concerning, e.g., the number of features and amount of code). Beyond this critical threshold, the additional effort required, for example for presence-condition analysis, may obstruct the applicability of family-based analyses. Finding a good trade-off between reuse of analysis information and scalability of family-based product-line analysis strategies therefore is the most emerging issue for future research.

8.1.3 Family-Based Analysis of Software Variants

While Sects. 8.1.1 and 8.1.2 focused on how to measure and predict the performance of variants, an orthogonal way is to build and analyse a performance model. Performance models are well understood for single systems, but applying them to each variant separately involves redundant effort. Similar to the test-suite generation of Sect. 8.1.2, we apply a family-based strategy to analyse performance models of software variants efficiently.

We extend the UML activity diagrams that are already used as test models in Sect. 8.1.2 by quantitative performance information. For instance, Fig. 8.6 depicts Variant 5 of the PPU enriched with such performance annotations. In particular, we assume that the following parameters are provided: (1) rate of arrivals of workpieces

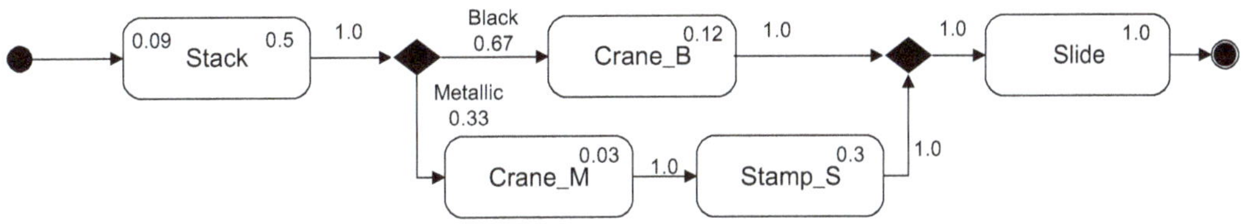

Fig. 8.6 Variant 5 of the pick-and-place unit with performance annotations

into the system, denoted by λ; hence, $1/\lambda$ is taken to be the average time between two successive arrivals at the system (cf. Fig. 8.6, top-left corner of the initial node), and (2) rate of processing a workpiece by each node, denoted by μ (cf. Fig. 8.6, top-right corner of a node). Finally, we require annotations on the edge connecting nodes. Specifically, an edge between nodes V_i and V_j must be annotated with the probability that a workpiece processed by node V_i goes to V_j. We call this model a performance-annotated activity diagram (PAAD). Once the annotations are made, the PAAD is amenable for an automatic performance evaluation. In particular, we can interpret a PAAD as a continuous-time Markov chain with an underlying Jackson-type queuing network [Jac63]. The evaluation is executed by solving the following system of equations: $(I - P^T)\gamma = \lambda$. P is the routing probability matrix, I is the identity matrix, λ is a vector based on the defined arrival rates, and γ is a vector containing the effective arrival rates that we are interested in. For instance, the considered PPU variant gives us

$$P = \begin{bmatrix} 0.0 & 0.67 & 0.33 & 0.0 & 0.0 \\ 0.0 & 0.0 & 0.0 & 0.0 & 1.0 \\ 0.0 & 0.0 & 0.0 & 1.0 & 0.0 \\ 0.0 & 0.0 & 0.0 & 0.0 & 1.0 \\ 0.0 & 0.0 & 0.0 & 0.0 & 0.0 \end{bmatrix} \quad \lambda = \begin{bmatrix} 0.09 \\ 0.0 \\ 0.0 \\ 0.0 \\ 0.0 \end{bmatrix} \quad \mu = \begin{bmatrix} 0.5 \\ 0.12 \\ 0.03 \\ 0.3 \\ 1.0 \end{bmatrix}$$

Once we solve the system for γ, the steady-state behaviour of the network is fully characterised and we can interpret the results of the analysis in terms of user-perceivable performance properties of the system [Ste09]:

- *Throughput:* the number of workpieces that a node can process in a given amount of time (i.e. γ)
- *Utilisation:* the probability that a node is busy processing a workpiece (i.e. γ/μ whereas μ is the service rate)
- *Queue length:* the number of jobs waiting at a node, including those in service (i.e. $\gamma/\mu/(1 - \gamma/\mu)$).

For instance, the utilisation of each node in Fig. 8.6 is computed with 18% for the *Stack*, 50% for the *Crane_B*, 100% for the *Crane_M*, 10% for the *Stamp*, and 9% for the *Slide*. However, we have to solve the system of equations for each variant separately since it is not possible to reuse the numerical computations across variants. Even varying the exogenous arrival rate λ by 0.01 forces us to do a re-computation.

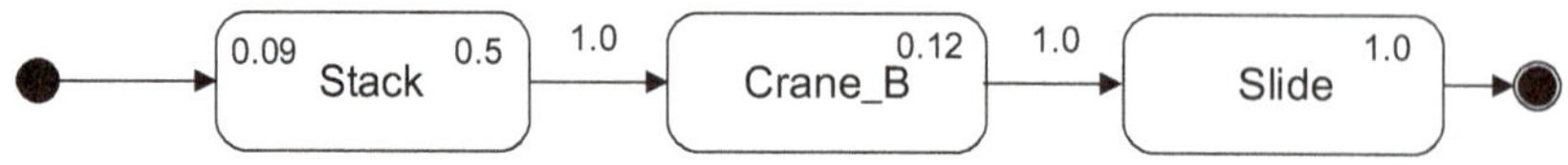

Fig. 8.7 Variant 1 of the pick-and-place unit with performance annotations

In SPP 1593, we developed a family-based performance analysis that solves the system of equations once and enables us to reuse the results across all variants. The analysis requires the construction of a 150% model of the system. Thus, we need a variability modelling mechanism in order to incorporate the individual variants into a 150% model. For this purpose, we introduced the concept of delta modelling in our approach. Delta modelling is a modular yet flexible variability modelling method on the implementation artefact level and allows capturing closed and open variant spaces. Each delta contains a set of basic operations to be performed on a PAAD, such as the addition and the removal of nodes and edges, or the modification of parameters, such as the probability of an edge and service rates in nodes. In addition, we have a core that can be an arbitrary variant of the system. Hence, applying a delta to the core yields a new variant of the system and in our case a new PAAD, which has performance characteristics that can again be numerically analysed using the product-based evaluation.

The PAAD in Fig. 8.6 represents the core of the PPU. Next, we can define a delta comprised of several transformations, that is removal of the nodes *Crane_M* and *Stamp_S* and their connecting transitions, as well as setting the probability from *Stack* to *Crane_B* to 1.0. An application of this delta to the core gives us the most basic variant of the PPU, depicted in Fig. 8.7.

We are able to model all variants of the PPU using delta modelling. Merging all deltas and the core gives us the 150% model of the system (cf. Fig. 8.5, where performance annotations are omitted). Similar to the analysis of a single variant, we can derive the routing probability matrix and vectors for arrival and service rates from the 150% model. However, each value that is different in multiple variants (i.e., depends on a delta) is now represented by a variable (i.e., symbolically rather than by a concrete value). For instance, let us consider three variants of the PPU comprised of our core (cf. Fig. 8.6), the most basic variant (cf. Fig. 8.7), and the variant introducing the second stamping module *Stamp_A* leading to the 150% model, as depicted in Fig. 8.5. The respective matrix and vectors containing symbols for each changed value are as follows:

$$P_s = \begin{bmatrix} 0.0 & p_{C_B} & p_{C_M} & 0.0 & 0.0 & 0.0 \\ 0.0 & 0.0 & 0.0 & 0.0 & 1.0 & 0.0 \\ 0.0 & 0.0 & 0.0 & p_{S_S} & 0.0 & p_{S_A} \\ 0.0 & 0.0 & 0.0 & 0.0 & p_{Sl} & 0.0 \\ 0.0 & 0.0 & 0.0 & 0.0 & 0.0 & 0.0 \\ 0.0 & 0.0 & 0.0 & 0.0 & p_{Sl_2} & 0.0 \end{bmatrix} \qquad \lambda_s = \begin{bmatrix} \lambda_{Stack} \\ 0.0 \\ 0.0 \\ 0.0 \\ 0.0 \\ 0.0 \end{bmatrix} \qquad \mu_s = \begin{bmatrix} 0.5 \\ 0.12 \\ \mu_{C_M} \\ \mu_{S_S} \\ 1.0 \\ \mu_{S_A} \end{bmatrix}$$

We solve the system of equations, but we are not able to receive concrete performance properties in terms of throughput or utilisation for individual variants at this point since the equations are solved symbolically and still contain the unknown variables from the routing matrix and the rate vectors (e.g. for utilisation):

$$Util = \left[2 * \lambda_{Stack}, \frac{25 * \lambda_{Stack} * p_{C_B}}{3}, \frac{\lambda_{Stack} * p_{C_M}}{\mu_{C_M}}, \ldots, \frac{\lambda_{Stack} * p_{C_M} * p_{S_A}}{\mu_{S_A}} \right]$$

As a final step, we have to insert the probabilities and rates of a specific variant into the symbolic solution yielding the desired concrete performance value and thus the same result as analysing each variant separately. The family-based analysis is significantly more efficient considering computation times for a given large variant space. Numerical experiments show that it can be up to two orders of magnitude faster [KST14]. The computational benefit results from the expensive process of solving the system of equations over and over again for each variant in isolation, which is not necessary in our proposed family-based analysis. In addition, the computation time giving us the symbolic solution is independent of the number of variants that are analysed afterwards. Each symbol may stand for an infinite number of values resulting in an infinite number of variants that can be analysed with the symbolic solution.

Assuming, for instance, that we wish to study the impact of different arrival rates λ into the PPU, Fig. 8.8 (left part) shows the utilisation at every node for Variant 0. The results indicate that *Crane_B* is the bottleneck of the system because its utilisation is consistently the highest. Figure 8.8 (right part) shows a similar analysis for the core (i.e. Variant 3). In this case, the bottleneck is the *Crane_M* node transporting metallic workpieces to the stamping module, which takes significantly longer compared to processing a black workpiece directly to the slide. Another scenario would be to study the distribution of black and metallic workpieces processed by the PPU in order to identify an optimal system solution. In the standard configuration, the PPU processes 2/3 black and 1/3 metallic workpieces. We can

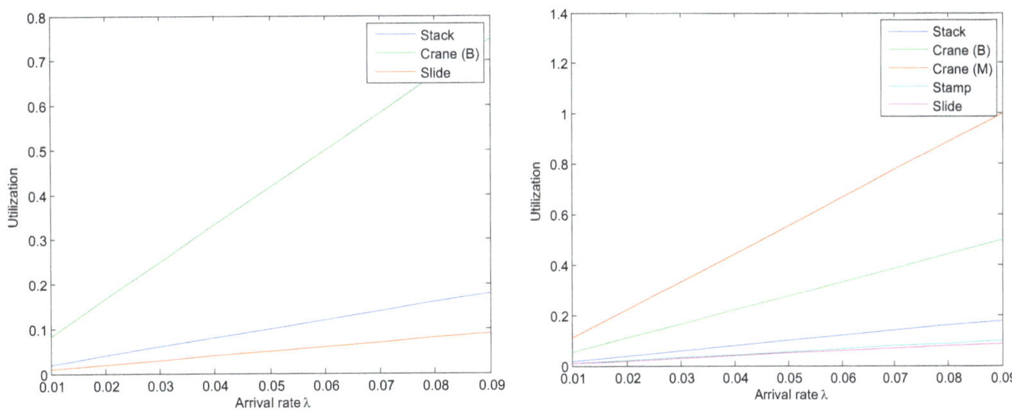

Fig. 8.8 Utilisation of variants 0 and 3 with a varying arrival rate λ

change this by simply varying the routing probabilities leading from the stack to the different cranes and look at the performance impact afterwards. We just have to plug in the desired values into our symbolic solution.

Experiences and Further Reading While we illustrated family-based prediction with the PPU, we also experimented with larger product lines with up to 430 features [KST14, Kow+15]. Especially for larger product lines, the family-based strategy significantly outperforms the separate analysis of every variant [KST14]. The above-mentioned approach has two major limitation, which we addressed by follow-up work [Kow+15]. First, service times are assumed to follow exponential distribution. Second, all computations are assumed to be performed without parallelism. For coxian-distributed multi-server stations, we measured similar performance gains of the family-based strategy [Kow+15].

8.2 Analysis Strategies for Software Versions

Section 8.1 covered performance analysis strategies for software variants, focusing on the problem of how to efficiently analyse large configuration spaces. Orthogonally, throughout the development and operation stages of a software system's life cycle, numerous software versions are created and evolved over time. With these versions, also the corresponding software artefacts (and their types) change and evolve based on the respective life cycle stages. Example types of artefacts are requirements and architectural models in the design stage, code artefacts that are available from the implementation stage, and descriptive models obtained from measurement data in the operations and maintenance stages. Connected with the changing versions and their related artefacts is the need for continuous quality assurance, for example with respect to performance as it is in the scope of this chapter.

This section covers three complementary approaches for supporting performance analyses of versions incorporating different types of software artefacts (models and code), analysis techniques (measurement-based and model-based), and suitability for the respective development stage and use case (e.g. online or offline evaluation). In Sect. 8.2.1, we present a declarative approach targeted to enable non-performance experts to select, configure, and execute performance evaluation with changing and evolving versions throughout the software life cycle. The approach presented in Sect. 8.2.2 helps to align the evolution and runtime adaptation of software versions employing models and measurements. Section 8.2.3 focuses on the co-evolution of architectural and analytical performance models.

CoCoME as a Motivating Example Figure 8.9 illustrates subparts of a performance model for the CoCoME case study, as introduced in Chap. 4. Relating to Fig. 8.1, it depicts concepts commonly found in architectural performance models, such as Palladio [Reu+16] or DML [Hub+17]. These formalisms follow common concepts known from architecture description languages (ADLs), such as config-

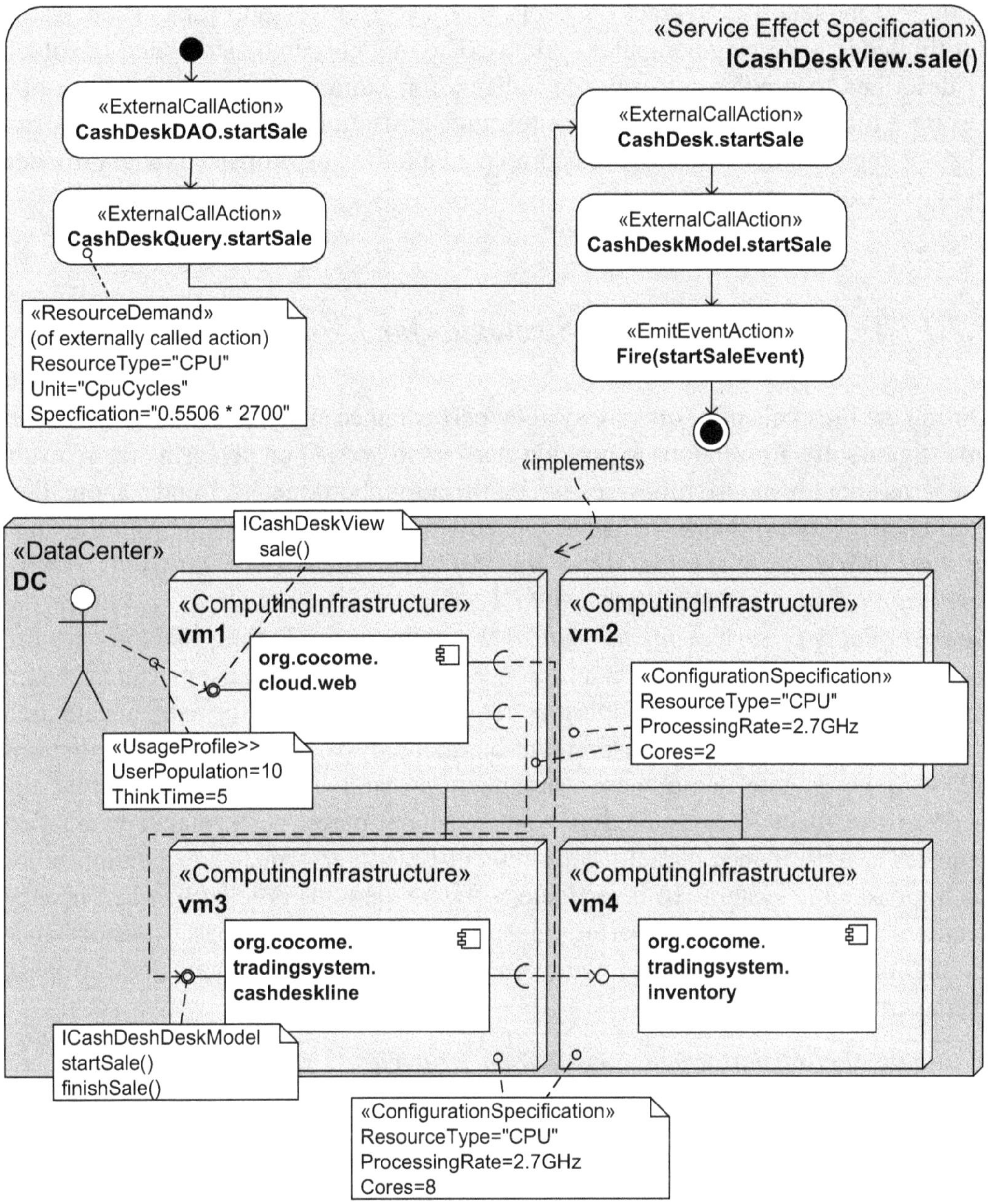

Fig. 8.9 Subparts of the CoCoME performance model in a UML-like notation

urations of components, interfaces, and connectors—presented in different views (e.g. component/connector and deployment). The example shows three CoCoME components being deployed to a networked computing infrastructure comprised of four (virtual) machines. The computing infrastructure is annotated by performance properties, such as information about the CPUs. The behaviour of the components' operations is modelled using a formalism similar to activity diagrams, including two types of actions: demands to local resources and calls to other operations. While architectural models provide a representation very close to software design models, analytical models use abstract concepts such as resources and jobs. Their use is not limited to analysing computer systems. The models can be simulated or solved as described to predict performance indices, for example statistics about method response times, system throughput, or resource utilisation. For illustration purposes, Fig. 8.9 depicts only a subset of the complete Palladio performance model provided by the CoCoME case study.

8.2.1 Declarative Analysis Strategies for Evolving Software

During the life cycle of a software system, performance analysts repetitively need to investigate software versions to provide answers to and act on performance-relevant concerns about response times, resource utilisation, bottlenecks, trends, anomalies, etc. Their everyday work includes concerns such as *What is the response time of the CoCoME sale service? Does the CoCoME sale service satisfy its service level agreements (SLAs)? What would be the required resources to ensure the desired quality of service for the CoCoME sale service?* During the software life cycle, the evaluation of performance concerns for software versions can be based on different evaluation methodologies requiring specific performance evaluation artefacts. Supplementing measurement-based analysis, model-based predictions allow to investigate deployments, architectures, and configurations without the need to test them in a production system. Model-based performance evaluation requires a performance model. Measurement-based performance evaluation relies on a measurable system. To investigate software versions efficiently when needed requires to switch between various measurement and model-based performance evaluation approaches. Hereby, two main challenges for a continuous performance management arise:

1. *Application of performance evaluation strategies:* Holistic performance engineering applies manifold performance evaluation strategies. Each strategy is connected to particular parametrisation options and challenges, which makes them employable only with extensive knowledge and experience [Wal+16a].
2. *Selection of performance evaluation techniques:* The situation-aware choice of a performance evaluation approach is challenging. It has to consider aspects like user concerns and system characteristics to asses applicability and analysis costs.

At system design, predicting the response time of CoCoME's sale service involves complex decisions such as the selection of a suitable modelling formalism, the choice of modelling granularity, solvers and solution techniques (e.g. Markovian analytical solvers, product-form solution, or simulation-based solvers), and the derivation of model parameters.

At the system testing and deployment stages, there is the opportunity to evaluate the sales service's response time by conducting performance measurements. However, complex decisions about the measurement configuration have to be made. Decision include sufficient experiment run length, the configuration of ramp-up time, and the choice of an appropriate instrumentation granularity allowing to obtain the required measurement data.

During system operations, it is about predicting the effects of possible system reconfigurations or the impact of an increased or changing workload mix. This enables proactive resource management but requires modelling techniques that support predicting future system states. At this time, the analysis approach and parametrisation have to be tuned for a fast response.

The concerns remain the same throughout the stages for the evolving software versions and artefacts. However, evaluation methodologies change. Selection and application affect the accuracy, as well as the speed and overhead of the analysis, and require a lot of expert knowledge.

Declarative Performance Engineering Analysing the performance of versions during the software life cycle is connected to significant efforts and complexity. Declarative performance engineering aims to provide a simplified and unified interface to investigate performance concerns for software versions abstracting from the underlying artefact and performance evaluation strategy [Wal+16a]. The idea is to use a declarative language allowing to specify performance concerns independent of the various approaches that can be applied in the context of the considered system to obtain the required information. The processing of a performance concern can be automated and optimised while hiding complexity from the user. The objective is to support system developers and administrators in performance-relevant decision-making. The declarative approach aims to reduce the huge abstraction gap between the level on which performance-relevant concerns are formulated and the level on which performance engineering techniques are typically applied. It decouples the specification of user concerns from their automated deduction. Performance concerns can be defined independent of the development stage, respective type of artefact, and evaluation method. Subsequently, suitable performance evaluation methods and techniques can be automatically selected and executed to answer the concern [Wal+18].

Expressing Performance Concerns Each version can be investigated based on different performance concerns. Figure 8.10 shows example performance concerns for CoCoME expressed using a declarative performance engineering language. Figure 8.10a shows querying of a performance metric. The processing has been constraint as `fast`, which can be interpreted by the framework to select a

```


SELECT sale.respTime
FOR SERVICE
"processSale" AS sale
CONSTRAINED AS fast
USING dml@'cocome';
```

(a)

```
EVALUATE AGREEMENTS
sla CONTAINS slo1
GOALS
slo1:processSale.respTime<1.3 ms
VARYING 'arrival rate workload'
AS rps <700 .. 3000 BY 500>
USING dml@'cocome';
```

(b)

```

MIN 'processing units cpu'
SATISFYING AGREEMENTS
sla CONTAINS slo1
GOALS
slo1:processSale.respTime<1.3 ms
USING dml@'cocome';
```

(c)

Fig. 8.10 Exemplary formulation of performance concerns using the declarative language. (**a**) Metric and constraint. (**b**) Contract evaluation and arrival variation. (**c**) System optimisation

fast solution strategy and configure the evaluation methodology accordingly, for example by a low required precision and a low maximum experiment run length. Figure 8.10b is about the evaluation of conformance to an SLA for different arrival rates. The concern in Fig. 8.10c proposes a resource efficient configuration that ensures conformance to SLAs. The declarative language supports further sophisticated performance analyses. It covers a wide range of performance concerns from the analysis of performance indices, aggregation, language-based system variation, determination of upper and lower bounds, SLA evaluation, threshold generation, system optimisation based on SLAs, etc.

Processing of Performance Concerns The processing of a performance concern means to automatically derive its answer. The answering process of a performance concern for a software version depends on available evaluation artefacts and situational requirements. The proposed language processing exploits a high degree of automation through a corresponding interpretation and execution infrastructure, which builds on established low-level performance evaluation methods, techniques, and tools. The architecture presented in Fig. 8.11 enables automated processing. The `Language & Editor` component provides the interface to users. The `Concern Execution Engine` provides the main execution logic. Here, all tasks independent of a specific performance evaluation technique take place. Implementations of the `Connector` interface provide functionality that is dependent on a specific performance evaluation technique. To integrate different performance evaluation approaches into the framework, multiple connectors can be subscribed at the central registry. A lean connector interface, limited to provided metrics, degrees of freedom [GBK14], and adaptations [Hub+14], allows for an easy technical connection of performance evaluation tooling to the declarative language processing framework. We provide exemplary connectors to measurement-based [Blo+16] and model-based [GBK14] analysis tooling. Besides specification of derivable indices, adaptation operations and degrees of freedom can be defined enabling additional kinds of analyses. Several analyses build upon basic performance indices. Such analyses depict reusable software parts that should be located within the `Concern`

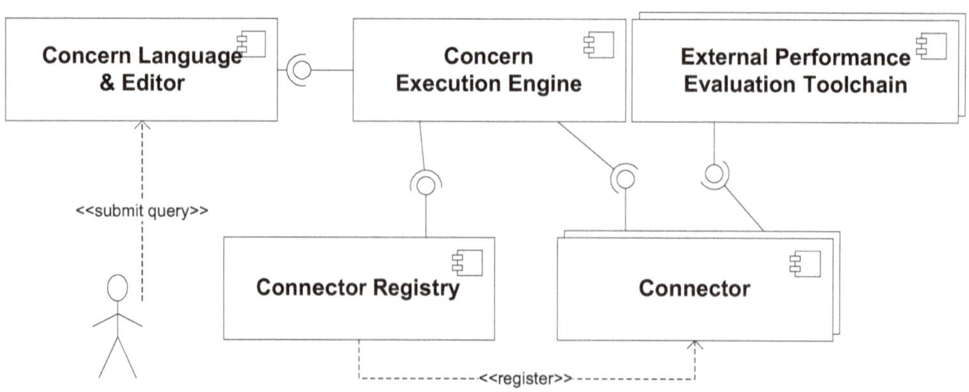

Fig. 8.11 Architecture of the DPE framework

`Execution Engine`. Indices can be forwarded to reusable algorithms, like the evaluation of SLAs [WOK17], sensitivity analysis, system optimisation [Rag+17a], etc. Also, the visualisation of analysis results can be reused independently of how values have been derived [Wal+16b].

We do not specify how to derive performance models. However, performance models are cumbersome to create manually. Therefore, automated model extraction from APM data [Heg+17], as discussed in [Wal+17a, Wal+17b], is essential to enable interchangeability of measurement and model-based performance evaluation.

Selection of Solution Strategies A solution strategy automates the answering of performance concerns by wrapping a performance evaluation method with bridging code, result filtering, and model-to-model transformations. For example, as depicted in Fig. 8.1, architectural performance models can be solved using simulation and analytical models. Existing performance engineering solution strategies come with different strengths and limitations concerning, for example, accuracy, time to result, or system overhead. While evaluation approaches allow for interchangeability, the choice of an appropriate approach and tooling to solve a given performance concern commonly relies on expert knowledge. Hence, it is a challenge to select a suitable solution strategy.

The declarative performance engineering approach allows for the automated selection of software performance engineering (SPE) approaches tailored to user concerns [Wal+16a]. To propose a solution strategy, the decision engine receives a performance concern and a description of the analysed system as input (which can be extracted from the concern definition). We provide a generic decision engine where solution strategy capability models can be registered. Instances of the capability meta-model represent analysis approaches like measurement, simulation, or analytical solvers. Compared to static decision trees, the separation of the decision engine logic and capability models allows to easily modify the description of characteristics on the evolution of performance evaluation strategies. It also facilitates the appending of additional solution strategies and rating criteria. To define capability models, we model three major aspects:

Functional Capabilities Performance evaluation approaches investigate different elements (e.g. services, processors, hard drives), metrics (e.g. response time, utilisation), and statistics (e.g. mean, sample, maximum, quantiles). The evaluable element specification integrates the named aspects and thereby defines functional capabilities of a solution approach.

Limitations The applicability of solution strategies can be limited by several constraints. Exemplary constraints for model-based analysis are on applicable input models (e.g. for product form solutions) [Bol+06] or limitations of model transformations [Bro+15]. While concepts can be transferred, measurement tools are limited to certain supported languages and technologies.

Costs Solution strategies differ in several cost types. The relevance of cost types depends on the specific application scenario. While for model-based analysis time to result is the dominating cost type, for measurement-based approaches

Table 8.4 Excerpt of capabilities for model-based analysis strategies

Analysis	Statistics	Time-to-result	Limitations
SimuCOM	Sample	High	–
LQNS	Mean	Very low	No loops, no fork-join, no parametric dependencies, no blocking-behavior
SimQPN	Sample	Medium	No loops, no fork-join, no parametric dependencies
SimQPN MVA	mean	high	No loops, no fork-join, no parametric dependencies

license costs or system overhead are the more common. Costs can either be static (e.g. fixed license costs) or dependent on the system characteristics and analysis configuration. The latter can be specified by arithmetic expressions capturing expert knowledge or various estimation techniques, for example using neural networks, machine learning, or regression approaches.

To illustrate, Table 8.4 depicts an excerpt of capabilities for analysis strategies of architectural performance models presented in [WHK17]. Supported solution strategies for the Palladio component model include SimuCOM, LQNS, SimQPN, and SimQPN MVA. SimuCOM transforms a Palladio instance to a process-based discrete-event simulation. A transformation to layered queueing networks allows triggering the analytical LQNS solver. A transformation to queueing Petri nets enables a simulation and a mean value analysis (MVA) using the SimQPN tool. Additional solution strategies for Palladio model instances, such as using SimuLizar and EventSim, can be included accordingly.

Summary During the software life cycle, multiple versions (also hypothetical ones not implemented) can be investigated for manifold performance concerns based on different evaluation artefacts. Declarative performance engineering simplifies respective analyses by automating the choice and execution of performance evaluation approaches based on a declarative specification of concerns. Other researchers have adopted the idea of declarative performance engineering also to load testing [FP18], which has not been the scope of this chapter.

8.2.2 Align Development-Level Evolution and Operation-Level Adaptation

Cloud-based software systems are subject to a wide range of changes during the operations stage [Hei16]. The usage intensity and the user behaviour that a system has to handle may change over time, which affects the system's performance. The deployment of (parts of) the software system may change, for example to address performance issues by migration and replication of components, which, however, may cause violations to privacy constraints. Execution contexts, for example virtual machines and containers, may become available (allocation) or disappear (de-allocation), which increases or decreases the design space for system adaptation. Consequently, operating a Cloud-based software system requires to continuously observe the system and to plan for adaptation to react on changes during the operation stage that mostly cannot be foreseen during development.

This section describes how to align development-level evolution and operation-level adaptation for analysis and adaptation planning in Cloud-based software systems. In extension to Sect. 8.2.1, this section is concerned with keeping architecture and performance models for software version up-to-date while facing repeated adaptations during operations stage. Operators and developers profit from utilizing the same kind of performance models as they can communicate and exchange of knowledge based on the same abstraction. This is especially useful in fast-changing Cloud-based software systems that rely on performance analysis for their adaptation planning.

In the following, the sale service of CoCoME and the platform migration scenario are applied as a demonstrative example. In the platform migration scenario, increased usage intensity of the sale service causes an upcoming performance bottleneck due to limited capacities in the given service offering of the Cloud provider currently hosting the database. A simplified overview of the platform migration scenario is given in Fig. 8.12. For the sake of simplicity, we assume that each Cloud provider owns exactly one data centre. Different data centres are available for deploying the database service of CoCoME. We discuss how the performance bottleneck can be identified by observing the running system and be solved by planning for adaptation.

Development-Level Evolution vs. Operation-Level Adaptation Development-level evolution and operation-level adaptation can be considered as two mutual, interwoven processes that influence each other. Figure 8.13 illustrates how both processes are interconnected for Cloud-based software systems.

In addition to the several versions of the software system created throughout the development and operations stage, as introduced in the previous section, variants play a central role in Cloud-based software systems when planning for adaptations. Adaptations rely on the evaluation of alternative variants of the software's deployment and configuration to identify a new version that allows to sustain the required quality properties.

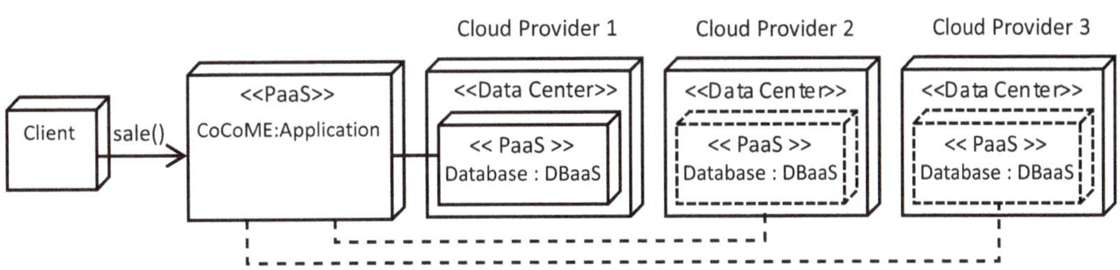

Fig. 8.12 Actual (solid line) and conceivable (dashed line) deployment in the platform migration scenario

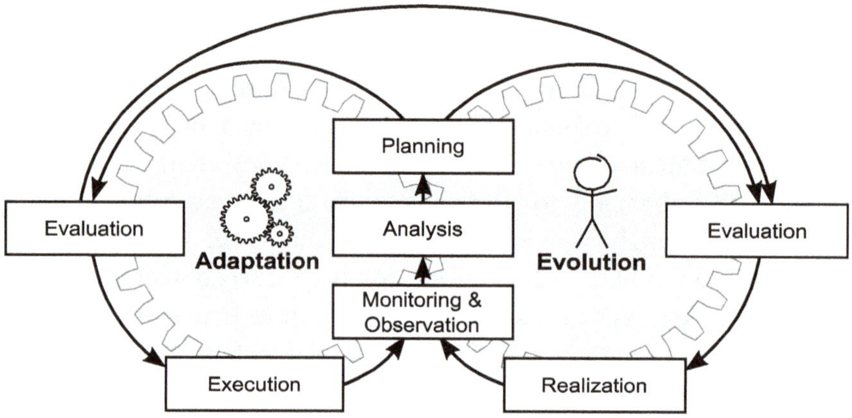

Fig. 8.13 Overview of development-level evolution and operation-level adaptation as mutual interwoven processes

Models are useful to reflect the software system and conduct analysis to identify quality flaws. A performance model of the sales services in a UML-like notation is depicted in parts in Fig. 8.9. During operations, software systems often drift away from their development models. In contrast, runtime models are kept in sync with the underlying system. Typical runtime models are close to the implementation level of abstraction. They are constructed based on observations related to source-code artefacts (e.g. service calls or class signatures) [Ben+14]. For example, observing the sales service of CoCoME results in monitoring records for the service itself and all invoked internal services. In addition, the class signature is monitored and recorded per service. While monitoring the software system, no information about its architecture is provided. Thus, it is hard to reproduce development component models from monitoring data as knowledge about the initial component structure and component boundaries is missing. This knowledge is important for system comprehension and reverse engineering. Consequently, we argue for runtime models that reflect extensive knowledge on the underlying architecture, its variability, deployment, and interaction with external services.

The iObserve Approach The iObserve approach [Has+13, Hei+14, Hei+17b] developed during the SPP 1593 addresses the aforementioned challenges by following the established MAPE-K (Monitor, Analyse, Plan, Execute, Knowledge) control loop model. MAPE-K is a feedback cycle for managing system adaptation [KC03]. iObserve extends the MAPE-K control loop with models shared between development and operations. These shared models carry architectural knowledge to ease the transition between development-level evolution and operation-level adaptation. The evolution activities are performed by human developers, while the adaption activities are executed automatically by predefined procedures, where possible, without human intervention.

The executed software system is observed to update architectural knowledge during operations. The model that reflects the architectural knowledge during operations is named architectural runtime model. As the architectural runtime model is constructed by enriching and updating development models with operational observations, it is comprehensible for developers and operators and can be fed back into software evolution without the need of conversion and the risk of loss of knowledge. Each update leads to a new version of the architectural runtime model. Based on the up-to-date model, the current system configuration is analysed to reveal anomalies (e.g. increased usage intensity) and predict quality impact (e.g. upcoming performance bottlenecks). The architectural runtime model is then applied as input either for adaptation or evolution activities, depending on the outcome of a planning step. In the adaptation process, an adaptation plan is selected and evaluated to handle the anomalies. For adaptation planning, various design variants are created and evaluated on model level. Finally, the plan is executed to update the software system and its configuration. In the evolution process, changes are designed, evaluated and implemented by human developers.

The iObserve approach applies a mega-model to bridge the divergent levels of abstraction in architectural models used during development and operations. Mega-models describe the relationships of models, meta-models, and transformations [Fav04]. The iObserve mega-model depicted in Fig. 8.14 serves as an umbrella to integrate development models, code generation, monitoring, runtime model updates, as well as adaptation candidate generation and execution. Rectangles depict models and meta-models, respectively. Solid lines represent transformations between models, while diamonds indicate multiple input or output models of a transformation. Dots are used to indicate multiple input or output models of a transformation. Dashed lines reflect the conformance of a model to a meta-model and, in case of implementation artefacts, the instance of relationship between data and data types, for example the monitoring data and their corresponding event types in the instrumentation aspects, as depicted in Fig. 8.14.

The iObserve mega-model exhibits four sections defined by two dimensions: one for development vs. operations and one for model vs. implementation level. We discuss these four sections based on the CoCoME case study and the migration scenario.

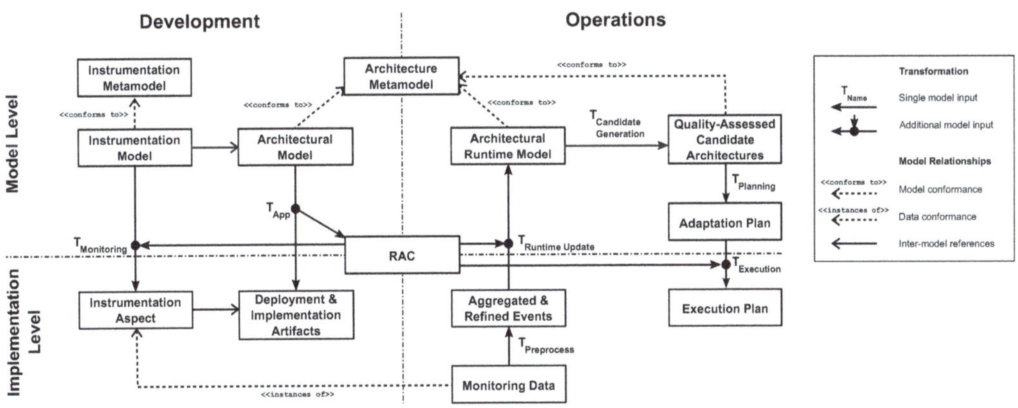

Fig. 8.14 Overview of the iObserve mega-model

For the interaction of the transformations in iObserve, we rely on the GECO approach [JHH16]. GECO defines patterns and methods to work with views and aspects on model and implementation level and describes how relationships between models and code can be shared between different transformations. These relationships are essential to map runtime observations to their corresponding runtime model elements, like classes and services, and design-time models to code artefacts. In iObserve, these relationships are created at design time with code generation or may be specified by hand in scenarios where the code is implemented by a developer. Subsequently, they are stored in the Runtime Architecture Correspondence Model (RAC). The RAC is the central element of the mega-model and is crucial for the use of an architectural model at development and operation time. At design time, they are used when generating and configuring the monitoring probes to map model-level pointcuts to implementation-level join points, select the correct probe technology, and probe introduction methods. At runtime, the same relationships are used in reverse to map runtime monitoring events, like an operation call, to their corresponding class and service instances.

Development Side On the development side at model level, the mega-model depicts the combination of an architectural model with our model-driven monitoring approach. We model the software architecture and deployment in a component-oriented fashion and generate the artefacts that are deployed and executed during operations. Therefore, iObserve relies on the Palladio Component Model [Reu+16] as an architecture description language defined through meta-models. The Palladio Component Model consists of several partial meta-models reflecting different architectural views on a software system. The monitoring part is specified using the instrumentation meta-model from our model-driven monitoring approach, consisting of two domain-specific languages used to describe monitoring events, for example operation calls, and the monitoring aspect [JHS13, JW16]. The aspect language allows to specify monitoring probes and their placements within the software system. For planning, we use probes to observe allocations/de-allocations, deployments/un-deployments, and user behaviour to learn the present system configuration and utilisation. The architectural and instrumentation models are then used to generate corresponding source code artefacts with the transformations T_{App}, for the software application, and the $T_{Monitoring}$, for the instrumentation [JW16].

At implementation level, the mega-model depicts development artefacts, including event types, instrumentation probes, and technology specific artefacts that implement the software system. For the CoCoME example, the software system is implemented by Enterprise Java Beans, and the monitoring uses Enterprise Java Beans interceptors to collect monitoring data.

Operations Side On the operation side at model level, monitoring data that adheres to source code artefacts is associated with the elements of the architectural runtime model. Consequently, the iObserve mega-model enables the reuse of development models during the operations stage by updating them based on operational observations. Moreover, the operation side shows the generation of adaptation candidate models and the adaptation plan construction. On implementation level, a continuous stream of events is gathered by the monitoring probes. iObserve filters and aggregates the monitoring data ($T_{Preprocess}$), relates the monitoring data to architectural model elements, and finally uses the aggregated information to update the architectural runtime model ($T_{Runtime\ Update}$). Following the CoCoME example, increased usage intensity of the sale service triggers changes in the workload specification. $T_{Preprocess}$ filters out single-entry and -exit events of the sales service and aggregates them to sequences of events. Based on the sequences, the new usage intensity is calculated, which is then transformed to the architectural runtime model by $T_{Runtime\ Update}$. Therefore, the architectural runtime model connects the development and operation stages. It allows for stage-spanning consideration of software architecture. Furthermore, it enables quality analyses based on the architecture specification and is the basis for adaptation planning.

If a performance or privacy issue has been recognised, adaptation candidates are generated by transformation $T_{Candidate\ Generation}$ in the form of candidate architectural runtime models. These candidate models are generated based on a degree of freedom model that specifies variation points in the software architecture, which have been specified at design time. Once an adaptation candidate has been selected, the model is operationalised by deriving concrete tasks of a plan for adaptation execution. The tasks are derived by transformation $T_{Planning}$ while comparing a candidate model to the original model. The adaptation plan is transferred to an execution plan at implementation level by $T_{Execution}$.

For example in our CoCoME scenario, increasing utilisation of the sales service results in increasing response time. Performance forecasts indicate that the average response time of the service may exceed the performance SLA. Therefore, the deployment must be altered. Thus, various candidate models of the CoCoME architecture model are generated by $T_{Candidate\ Generation}$ each differing in deployment of the database service to data centres. The candidate models are analysed for quality. Once an appropriate candidate is found, the system is adapted based on the candidate model using $T_{Execution}$. Subsequently, the monitoring observes events that cover the deployment changes and updates the runtime model.

In case that no specific model among the candidates can be selected fully automatically, for example when there are trade-offs between quality aspects, or if an adaptation plan cannot be derived fully automatically, the human operator chooses among the presented adaptation alternatives. Also when no candidate model can be generated, for example due to lack of information or criticality of decision, the operator will be involved.

Summary In conclusion, this section describes how design-time architecture models can be used at runtime for performance forecasts and to generate candidate architectures used to steer the adaptation. These candidate models are, in essence, different versions of the running system with variations that are assessed for performance during candidate selection. As iObserve utilises the same model type for runtime and design time, the updated runtime models can be used during evolution and adaptation to assist performance forecasts and predictions, receptively. Thus, it keeps evolution and adaptation models aligned.

8.2.3 Co-evolution of Architecture and Analysis Models

As introduced previously, model-based performance evaluation is conducted using architectural and analytical performance models, as well as transformations among these models. In our work, we refer to both architectural and analytical performance models as quality models. When being constructed at design time, quality models are constructed from a system model, and it is assumed that the quality models reflect the system. However, architectural models can evolve in the life cycle of software, and this new version can lead to unexpected results if the quality model does not represent the system anymore. An example problem is the addition of a new software component without a corresponding addition of the state in the respective Markov chain. This inconsistency can lead to wrong performance analysis results. Hence, any version has to be realised as a co-evolution of all related design and quality models.

Handling this (co-)evolution is not a straightforward task [Get+18] because the quality evaluation model cannot be completely generated out of the system models, and most relations between the different models are not one to one.

We developed a framework called CoWolf [Get+15a] that is capable of incremental transformations. Therefore, it isolates changes that were done to a model to selectively propagate only these changes to the other models. In detail, the contribution of the CoWolf tool comprises mainly two aspects:

1. *The co-evolution of an associated model on the basis of model versions.* As described, models may have to be updated if other models changed. Often, those updates can be described canonically. CoWolf features the definition of rules that define the relation between model types. Using these rules, co-evolutions can be done (semi)-automatically for all associated models.
2. *Deliver utilities for model development and analysis.* For consistent development of the models, CoWolf provides a common environment with graphical and textual editors. Furthermore, it implements interfaces to external tools to analyse models.

Such tool is proposed to help system and performance viewpoint versions consistent during the evolution. First, the outcome of the performance analysis remains to present more accurate results. Second, different versions of the performance models are provided from the system model versions to be used for a possible incremental performance analysis.

In the remainder of this section, we are presenting the incremental transformations and co-evolution between sequence diagrams and Layered Queueing Networks (LQNs), as well as state charts and Markov chains. We show the relations between architectural models and various performance models for incremental changes. Accordingly, we discuss how a co-evolution on the performance models helps for performance analysis. A detailed and generic description of the CoWolf framework is provided by Getir et al. [Get+15a].

Sequence Diagram to Layered Queueing Network

We implemented the transformation of sequence diagrams to LQNs based on the description of Cortellessa et al. [CMI11]. They suggest a transformation from three source models as activity diagrams, component diagrams, and sequence diagrams to one target LQN model. The CoWolf co-evolution framework currently supports one-to-one transformations and aims to help the developer in the co-evolution of LQNs and Markov chains.

Since sequence diagrams do not include hardware information, the initial assumption is that multiple associated tasks are performed on one CPU. In the first step of every sequence diagram to LQN transformation, CoWolf checks if a CPU is part of the model and creates a new processor if it is missing. The user can increase the number of processors and change their properties, for example type and name, in the graphical editor. Each lifeline from the sequence diagram is transformed to a new task and a new entry type in the target LQN. We demonstrate the mapping elements, namely a new task and a new entry in Fig. 8.15. The new task is associated with the default processor created in the initial step.

All synchronous messages directed from a lifeline l_1 to a lifeline l_2 in a sequence diagram are mapped to exactly one synchronous call in the LQN. The source task of the call is the task mapped from lifeline l_1. The target task of the synchronous call is the task corresponding to lifeline l_2.

All asynchronous messages directed from a lifeline l_1 to a lifeline l_2 in a sequence diagram are mapped to exactly one asynchronous call in the LQN (see Fig. 8.16). The source task of the call is the task mapped from lifeline l_1. The target task of the asynchronous call is the task corresponding to lifeline l_2.

State Charts to Continuous Time Markov Chains

The transformations between state charts and Continuous Time Markov Chains (CTMCs) can be achieved via two-step transformations, namely state charts to Discrete Time Markov Chains (DTMCs) and DTMC to CTMC. These transformations

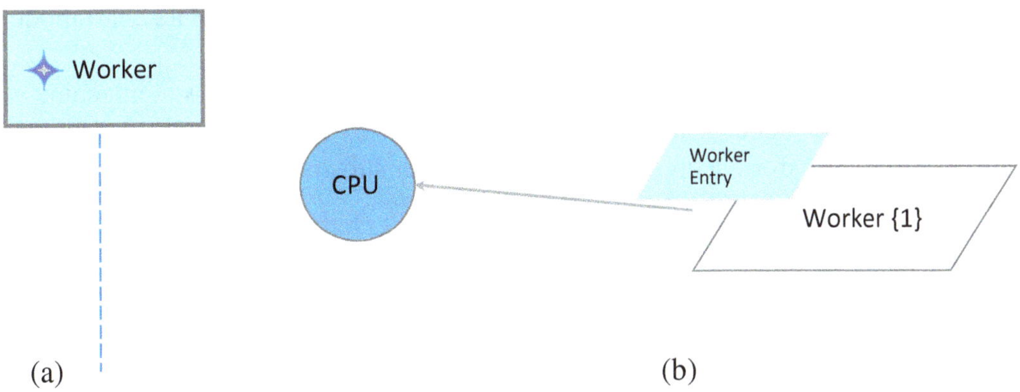

Fig. 8.15 Each lifeline will be transformed to a task. (**a**) Sequence diagram. (**b**) LQN

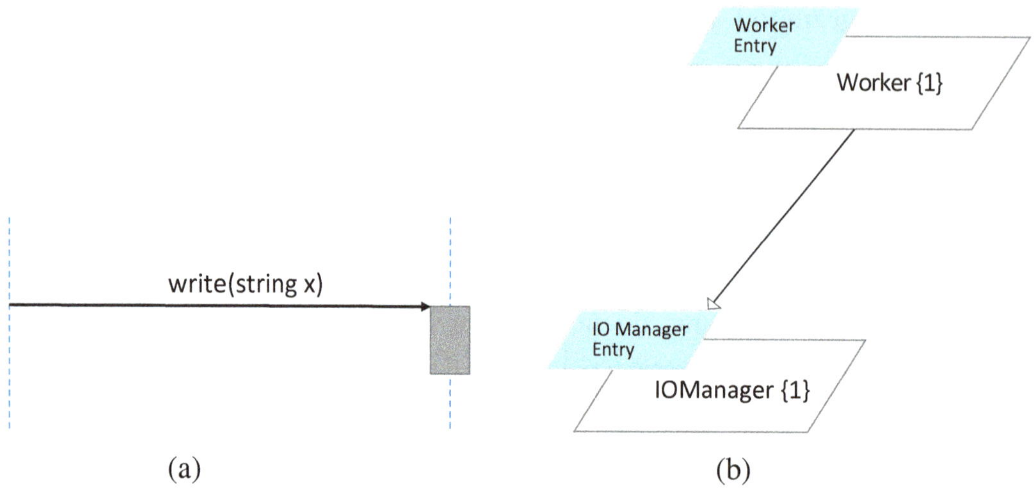

Fig. 8.16 All asynchronous messages between two lifelines (on direction) will be transformed to one asynchronous call in an LQN model. (**a**) Sequence diagram. (**b**) LQN

are implemented in a bidirectional way such that any change and any version can be reflected in both directions. The rules that are needed for the transformation between both model types are in all cases a simple bidirectional one-to-one mapping, where traces between elements of different diagram types could easily be created.

A CTMC is a common mathematical model to analyse software performance metrics like utility, throughput, etc. CTMC is a very similar but simpler model than PAAD, described in Sect. 8.1.3. However, this model is including more architectural information since it is an annotated form of an activity diagram.

The transformation is implemented only for the topmost states and transitions of a state chart model. States and transitions that are part of a composite state are not considered in the transformation. This does not match for `Action` elements (`Do`, `Entry`, `Exit`), which can call another sub-statemachine. For these actions, it is needed to find the first parent state that got transformed to DTMC and connect it by a transition to the initial state of the called sub-statemachine.

The transformation from DTMC to state chart has applied essentially the same transformation mappings. Additionally, some restrictions apply here:

- Created transitions in a DTMC always create a transition in the state chart model to avoid null name in the transformed model.
- Created states in DTMC always map to a state in the main sub-statemachine in the state chart model if there is no existing trace to a state elsewhere. It is not possible to transform a created state into another sub-statemachine.

After obtaining a DTMC from state charts, the user has to provide the probability distribution in the model. This looks a time-consuming task. However, assuming adding small information after many but small changes in the model, incremental transformations can be useful for the structural mapping and recommendations for the co-evolution step. Unlike in a state chart model, transitions cannot be named in a DTMC model.

DTMC and CTMC are very similar models—especially structurally. Every CTMC state equates to a DTMC state, every CTMC transition equates to a DTMC transition, and every CTMC label equates to a DTMC label. The only difference is that CTMC states have an exit rate. The exit rate is calculated automatically from all outgoing transitions of a state. Furthermore, each transition t, outgoing from a state s, in a CTMC contains a rate. This rate is calculated as a fixed point by:

$$t.rate = t.prob * s.exitRate \tag{8.1}$$

Both models have the same elements. Changes can be directly applied from source to target models in both directions (CTMC to DTMC and DTMC to CTMC). The difference mapping is executed by a graph transformation rule.

Analysis of LQN and CTMC Models with Model Solvers

The analysis of an LQN model is performed by the LQN Solver [Car18]. In order to solve an LQN model with the LQN Solver, it is necessary to transform the model into a *.lqn* file.

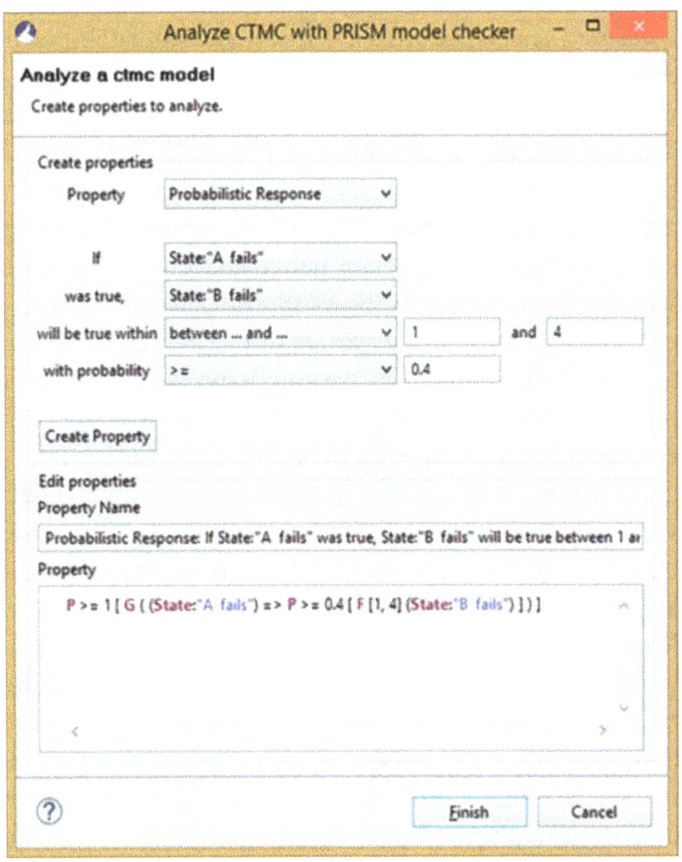

Fig. 8.17 CTMC properties wizard

DTMC and CTMC models are analysed using the PRISM model checker [KNP11]. CTMC models are used for performance and reliability analyses. Reliability can be validated using the reachability of critical states, for example error states. Performance can be validated in multiple ways. CoWolf provides a wizard (see Fig. 8.17) that helps to create default properties, which are "Steady State Probability", "Probabilistic Response", "Probabilistic Until", and "Probabilistic Existence". "Steady State Probability" calculates the probability that condition A will eventually become true. "Probabilistic Response" calculates the probability that condition B will always become true in a time frame after condition A was true. "Probabilistic Until" checks if condition A is always true before condition B becomes true. "Probabilistic Existence" checks if a condition becomes true in a time frame. As there are many more possibilities to evaluate CTMC models, additional properties can be created and edited in a text editor.

8.3 Conclusion and Road Map

Variants and versions of software challenge the measurement and prediction of performance. We illustrated selected strategies by means of two running examples, namely the PPU automation system and the service-oriented application CoCoME. The PPU comes with numerous variants, for which it does not scale to analyse each variant separately. We discussed solutions that reduce the variants that have to be measured and reduce the effort in assessing the performance for each variant by exploiting commonalities. CoCoME is an application that frequently evolves and requires to incorporate versions and different types of artefacts during performance analysis throughout the software life cycle. We discussed complementary solutions for performance analysis of software versions by making analysis techniques accessible and continuous by combining models and measurements.

In our experience, performance analysis of software does often not incorporate variants or versions at all. While all authors worked on improving the situation by explicitly supporting variants or versions, there is a research gap with respect to their combination. On the one hand, software being available in variants does indeed evolve over time, such that each variant exists in numerous versions. On the other hand, frequently evolving software is often also available in variants to tailor software to certain customers. However, techniques being used to address variants are often agnostic to versions, and techniques devoted to versions ignore the necessity to support variants. We envision that techniques for variants and versions are better integrated in the future but also that researchers focusing on variants can learn from research on versions and vice versa.

Performance analysis for variants can learn from research on versions. We and others have actively worked on sampling techniques to select a subset of variants that is sufficient to analyse. However, there is not a single sampling technique that incorporates the evolution of a product line. Furthermore, it is unclear to which extent currently available sampling techniques are stable (i.e. produce a largely similar sample after evolution). Stability is especially important when assessing the performance evolution of variants, as different variants are likely to have different performance. Similarly, family-based techniques exploiting the commonality of a product line during performance analysis are typically oblivious to evolution. The encoding of the commonality of variants, however, may also be applied to encode the commonality of versions. This could lead to more efficient analyses for evolving product lines but may also be applied to versions of a software that does not come in several variants.

Performance analysis for versions can learn from research on variants. For versions, we have focused on the challenges associated with evolving and changing types of artefacts throughout the software life cycle. Possible areas in which the approaches from variants could be promising for versions is the efficient evaluation of design space and runtime reconfiguration alternatives—which essentially comprise variants of possible next versions. Another possible point of interaction emerges from modern software engineering paradigms such as DevOps and Continuous Software Engineering (CSE). In this context, new versions are created with an increasing velocity, multiple variants of a version are developed in parallel branches, and fast feedback about the quality is expected as part of the continuous delivery infrastructure and processes. This requires novel approaches for selecting and prioritizing performance analysis tasks, such as performance predictions or load tests. The sampling-based and family-based approaches for variants will be promising sources of knowledge.

Chapter 9
Maintaining Security in Software Evolution

Jan Jürjens, Kurt Schneider, Jens Bürger, Fabien Patrick Viertel, Daniel Strüber, Michael Goedicke, Ralf Reussner, Robert Heinrich, Emre Taşpolatoğlu, Marco Konersmann, Alexander Fay, Winfried Lamersdorf, Jan Ladiges, and Christopher Haubeck

J. Jürjens (✉) · J. Bürger · D. Strüber
Institute for Computer Science, University of Koblenz-Landau, Koblenz, Germany
e-mail: juerjens@uni-koblenz.de; buerger@uni-koblenz.de; strueber@uni-koblenz.de

K. Schneider · F. P. Viertel
Institute of Software Engineering, Leibniz Universität Hannover, Hannover, Germany
e-mail: kurt.schneider@inf.uni-hannover.de; fabien.viertel@inf.uni-hannover.de

M. Goedicke
paluno – The Ruhr Institute for Software Technology, Specification of Software Systems, Universität Duisburg-Essen, Essen, Germany
e-mail: michael.goedicke@s3.uni-due.de

R. Reussner · R. Heinrich
Institute for Program Structures and Data Organization, Karlsruhe Institute of Technology (KIT), Karlsruhe, Germany
e-mail: reussner@kit.edu; robert.heinrich@kit.edu

E. Taşpolatoğlu
Department of Software Engineering, FZI Forschungszentrum Informatik, Karlsruhe, Germany
e-mail: taspolat@fzi.de

M. Konersmann
Institute for Software Technology, Research Group Software Engineering, Universität Koblenz-Landau, Koblenz, Germany
e-mail: konersmann@uni-koblenz.de

A. Fay · J. Ladiges
Institute of Automation Technology, Helmut Schmidt University, Hamburg, Germany
e-mail: alexander.fay@hsu-hh.de; jan.ladiges@hsu-hh.de

W. Lamersdorf · C. Haubeck
MIN-Faculty, Department of Informatics, Distributed Systems, Universität Hamburg, Hamburg, Germany
e-mail: lamersd@informatik.uni-hamburg.de; haubeck@informatik.uni-hamburg.de

R. Reussner et al. (eds.), *Managed Software Evolution*,
https://doi.org/10.1007/978-3-030-13499-0_9

The engineering of security-critical software systems faces special challenges regarding evolution. Even if a substantial effort went into ensuring security during the system's initial development, it is uncertain if the system remains secure when changes to the software, the execution platform, or the system environment occur. Relevant changes that might endanger security include new or evolving system requirements, changing laws, or updated knowledge regarding attacks and mitigations. Failure to keep up with such changes can lead to substantial breaches and losses, highlighting the need to actively maintain an established level of security [And08].

For preserving security in long-living systems, ongoing and systematic support for the evolution of knowledge and software is required. Reflecting the guiding theme *Methods and processes for evolution* of the priority program, there is a need for techniques, tools, and processes to support the evolution of systems in order to ensure *lifelong* compliance with security requirements. These techniques, tools, and processes need to address two main challenges, as outlined in the chapter "Challenges" of this book:

1. *How can security knowledge, available via diverse non-formal sources, be incorporated and utilised for long-living system design?* Establishing security depends on given *security knowledge*, which may only be available in a non- or semi-formal textual form. Whenever the security knowledge changes, earlier assumptions about the security of the system may no longer hold true; the system needs to be re-evaluated and adapted with regard to the security requirements.
2. *How can developers and security experts be supported to react to context evolution that may compromise the system's security design or compromise the system at run time?* New available security knowledge, as well as suspicious behaviour in the running system, may rely on a human developer for diagnosis and hardening. These human stakeholders can be assisted by providing them with appropriate information, for example about a relevant security pattern or behaviour violation.

To address these challenges, we present a suite of approaches that contribute to a three-layered framework (Fig. 9.1). On the bottom layer, developer, system, and environment activity is *monitored*. Usually, this activity is monitored in a non-invasive manner, for example by logging executed methods using a framework such as Kieker [VWH12] or in case of a production system by monitoring input and output signals [Hau+14a]. At this level, results from model-based security testing can be exploited (such as [JW01]). Additional aspects of human behaviour might be considered as well. On the middle layer, collected monitoring data are *analysed* in various ways: It is important to identify deviations of monitored behaviour from expected behaviour. Since there are different sources and types of expectations, the details of each analysis may differ. Assumptions associated with design patterns will be investigated in a different way than expectations held about user interaction. At this level, approaches such as model-based security analysis can

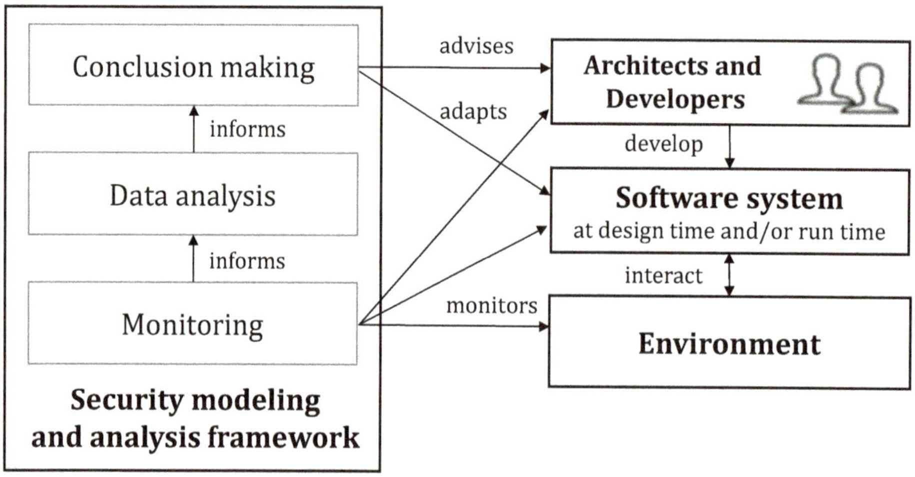

Fig. 9.1 Overview of a three-layered framework for maintaining security in software evolution at design time and run time

be used (such as [Jür01]). On the top layer, *conclusions* are derived. Warnings, hints, or technical adaptations are generated and released in order to preserve security, using approaches such as the SecReq approach to security requirement engineering [Sch+12].

In this chapter, we present a suite of five approaches that employ the above-mentioned framework. In combination, the approaches address all identified challenges for security maintenance at design time and run time. The first two approaches focus on the design time. The first approach (presented in Sect. 9.2) uses knowledge extracted from natural-language documents to identify potential steps for co-evolving the system design. The second one (Sect. 9.3) is on integrating architecture model information with program code. It creates a bidirectional mapping between model elements and code structures to automatically structure program code so that it contains model-based security properties and therefore survives code evolution. The third approach (Sect. 9.4) bridges design time and run time to support architects as the software evolves. It formally documents contextual information gathered from run time in architectural models at design time. Architects use model-based catalogues containing several security-related elements like attack types or security patterns, which are exploited as a lightweight metric for an architectural security analysis. The two remaining approaches focus on run-time security maintenance. The fourth one (Sect. 9.5) monitors run-time information in order to detect suspicious behaviour, which is reacted to automatically by adapting the system with mitigation measures. The fifth one (Sect. 9.6) focuses on interdisciplinary changes in automation software. It compares actual observed behaviour with intended behaviour expressed in signal-based models to find behaviour anomalies during run time.

Having presented these five approaches in detail, the chapter concludes with a discussion of how each approach contributes to addressing the challenges (Sect. 9.7).

9.1 Foundations

Modelling, Meta Modelling, and Model-Driven Software Development A model can be seen as an abstraction of a subject. An example for models can be mathematical formulas that describe the reality while ignoring factors that are irrelevant for the use case. Models of software are often represented as interconnected elements, for example structural models or behavioural models of the Unified Modeling Language (UML). Modelling is the activity to create models.

Meta models define a language for modelling. This means the elements where models are built from and how they can be connected. Thus, meta models define the abstract syntax of models that comply with the meta model. A model that complies with a meta model is called an *instance* of the meta model. Classically, the key concepts behind meta modelling are the relationship between a model element (often called *object* or *instance* in this context) and its meta-model element (*classifier* or *class*) and the ability to navigate from an object to its classifier. Multiple levels of instance-of relationships are possible, where the classifier of an object is itself the instance of a "higher level" classifier. Two *meta levels* mean that one level of objects and one level of classifiers exist. An arbitrary number of meta levels is possible, although typically two to four levels are used [Obj16, Section 7.3]. Instance-of relations in meta modelling build directed acyclic graphs, which build a hierarchy. In this context, we do not explore further the generalisations made by deep modelling [AG12].

Meta modelling is the activity to create meta models. This can follow a top-down or a bottom-up approach. Top-down meta modelling means to define a meta model for a subject to model and to create models afterwards. Bottom-up means to derive a meta model out of a modelled subject to classify the already modelled elements.

Model-driven software development (MDSD) [SVC06] uses models as central artefacts for software development activities. In MDSD, parts of the software are described using models that comply to domain-specific meta models [Mar10]. These domain models are refined with detailed technical models that are relevant not to the domain but to the platform that will run the software. Such models are the basis for automated code generation. The generated code has to be enriched with implementation details.

9.2 Design Time: Leveraging Knowledge from Natural Language for Design-Time System Adaptation

In this section, we present an approach to leverage knowledge from natural language for design-time system adaptation. This approach was developed in the SecVolution project within the priority program. To address the challenges overviewed in the introduction, the key idea is to maintain a *knowledge base* that collects knowledge about security concepts and instantiations within the given software system. Using this knowledge base, we can react to vulnerabilities occurring during evolution, such as changes in requirements, knowledge, or other environmental aspects. The knowledge base contains information on how to deal with a triggering change in order to preserve security. A semi-automated mechanism uses the knowledge base to update the system models.

The SecVolution approach harnesses formal design artefacts available in the regular development process, such as UML-based system models. However, many of the monitored sources of change and evolution are informal. In particular, we need to deal with artefacts on the requirements side, which include natural-language documents like the system's requirement specification or laws. To this end, we developed socio-technical methods for supporting elicitation of relevant changes in the environment. Like in our previous works (confer [Sch06, Sch09, Pha+13, AKK14]), the relevant knowledge is captured during regular development tasks with as little extra burden for the security expert as possible. Steps for restoring security are integrated into existing tasks as well and aimed to be as unintrusive as possible. By avoiding additional tasks and assignments and by keeping extra-effort low, acceptance by developers and security experts is increased and chances rise for effectively applying the SecVolution approach.

The approach can be applied to existing (*long-living*) software systems for which this information can be provided.

9.2.1 Overview

The overall design-time approach developed in SecVolution is shown in Fig. 9.3. It uses the FLOW notation [SSK08] (summarised in Fig. 9.2) to visualise the information flow within, and to highlight important aspects of, the SecVolution approach. FLOW is used in Figs. 9.3 and 9.19. Relevant aspects of a FLOW model

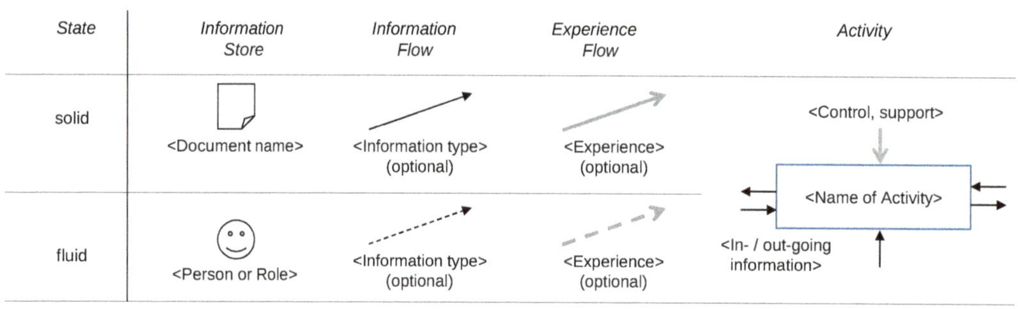

Fig. 9.2 FLOW notation symbols according to Schneider et al. [SSK08]

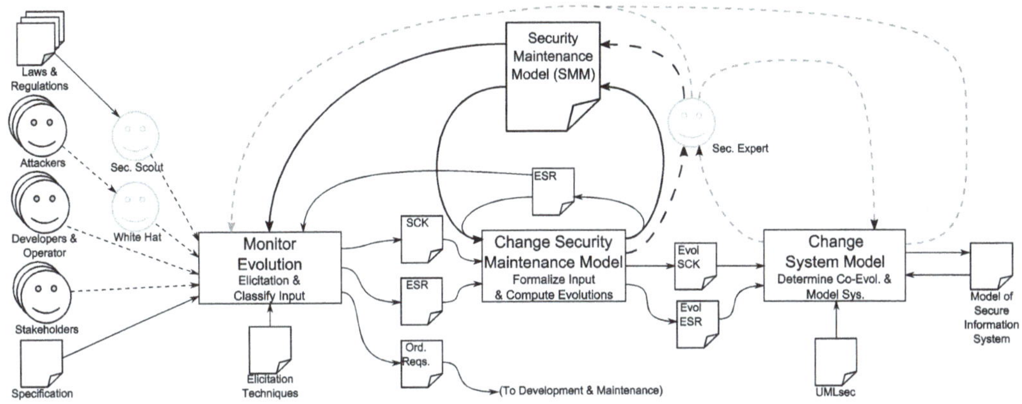

Fig. 9.3 Overview of the SecVolution design-time approach using the information flow syntax described in Fig. 9.2

include the fluid/solid state of information, the route of information, and the role of experience as a cross-cutting type of information:

- Document symbols and solid arrows represent documented project information or knowledge. That knowledge can be retrieved at any time without the need to involve the author.
- Faces and dashed arrows symbolise direct communication, for example in meetings, conversations, phone calls, or emails. This type of information representation is called *fluid* in FLOW [SSK08], as opposed to the *solid* information in documents and artefacts
- Rectangles represent activities with certain incoming and other outgoing information flows. As a black box, the internals of an activity are hidden. They may be detailed by another FLOW diagram.
- Project-specific information (in black) is attached to the left and right of an activity, whereas control and support enter from top and bottom of the activity rectangles.
- Grey colour indicates knowledge and experience. They are more generic than project-specific information and, thus, can be reused in other parts of the system.

In the following, we present the main process of SecVolution based on Fig. 9.3. The left part of Fig. 9.3 shows various sources of relevant knowledge. These are monitored for changes relevant to the approach. For deciding which information is relevant, Natural Language Processing methods are used to retrieve information from natural-language sources (Sect. 9.2.2). The monitored data is then split into three types:

- Ordinary requirements, which do not have any security relevance. These can be forwarded to the ordinary development process.
- New or evolved *Essential Security Requirements*. These are requirements that define basic security-relevant requirements for the system like "*Use secure encryption algorithms*".

- Information relevant for the security knowledge base, the *Security Context Knowledge*. This context knowledge is necessary to annotate the system model with concrete security requirements, for example a concrete encryption algorithm and appropriate key length.

The security knowledge base constituted by the *Security Context Knowledge (SCK)* requires a suitable representation, which we provide by using ontologies (Sect. 9.2.3). Security Context Knowledge and Essential Security Requirements both are managed within the *Security Maintenance Model*. Updating the Security Maintenance Model can make design decisions necessary, for example introduce a new cipher family because attacks have become known.

Security Maintenance Rules (SMR, Sect. 9.2.4) are the final part of the Security Maintenance Model. They decide if an evolution of the knowledge given by Security Context Knowledge and Essential Security Requirements makes co-evolution necessary. Figure 9.4 describes the overall idea and relationship between evolution and co-evolution. The development of a system model is accompanied by Security Context Knowledge. At its initial design, the system model was compliant with regard to the security knowledge that was current then. Over time, the Security Context Knowledge evolves. The system model now has to be co-evolved so that the then evolved system model is compliant with regard to the updated security knowledge.

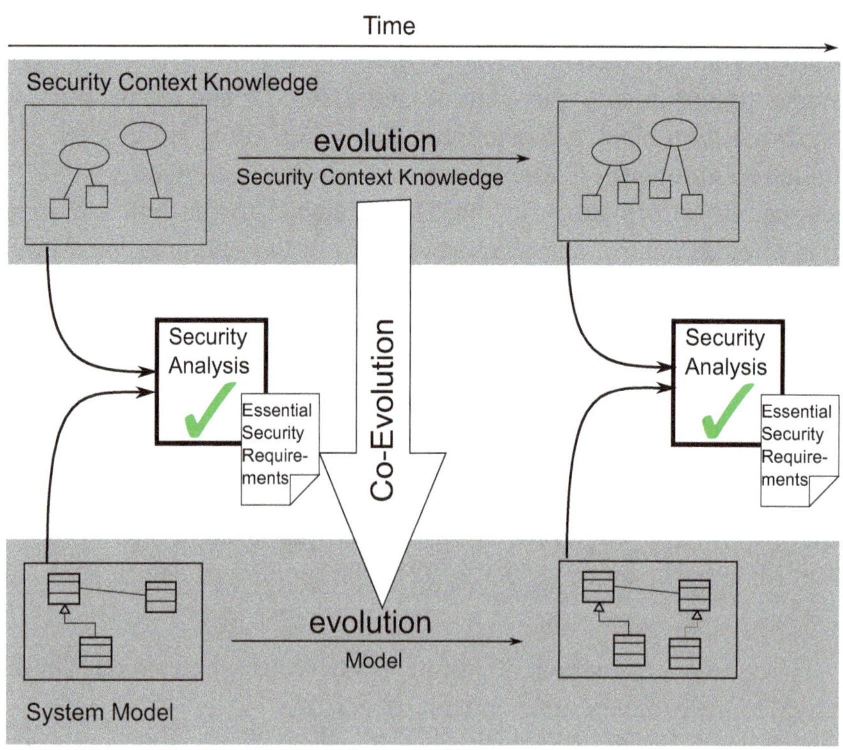

Fig. 9.4 Basic idea behind the design-time adaption, shown by the relationship of evolution to co-evolution

When required, co-evolution is carried out by using generic security knowledge and specific impact information derived from Security Maintenance Model by means of heuristic techniques. To express security requirements in the system design, the UMLsec approach [Jür05] is used. UMLsec provides a profile for UML that allows annotating UML models with security requirements, assumptions, and potential attackers. It also provides checks that determine if certain security requirements are satisfied by a given system model.

9.2.2 Capturing Security Requirements Using Natural-Language Processing

Requirements (e.g. in a specification) can be relevant for security. For example, requirements referring to *buying* something *on the Internet* may be more security-related than *buying* something in *cash in a local store*. Usually requirements are written in natural language so that everybody involved in a project is able to understand and review them. This refers to requirement engineers, developers, customers, and possibly managers. It is highly unlikely that they would learn a special language to understand requirements and check them for security relevance. The voluminous specifications of long-living software systems cannot be effectively screened manually by experts. Our approach provides an automated identification of requirements that are most likely security relevant. This identification starts from requirements in natural language, which can be ambiguous and imprecise. It makes use of the knowledge on security from several sources, including human experts and documented guidelines (Fig. 9.3). Heuristic automated support can reduce the load on human experts substantially. The final goal is to focus their attention and valuable time to the most security-relevant requirements.

To cope with problems of natural language and to semi-automate this process, we perform a linguistic approach to identify the semantic similarity of words. Two words have a high semantic similarity if they have the same meaning with simultaneous syntactical difference [Sch94a]. A numeric value identifies the level of semantic similarity of words. For the security assessment of requirements, we use a heuristic reasoning technique, which is based on Natural Language Processing. The heuristics and the calculation of the similarity value are described in more detail in Sect. 5.3. In this chapter, the security knowledge itself is seen as tacit knowledge of developers. In some cases, they also have a feeling of the security relevance of requirements, but sometimes they cannot explain the reason of the decision that a requirement is security related or not.

If the value of similarity is above a predefined threshold, the term is considered security related. In general, this method uses Security Context Knowledge of the knowledge base to determine about the security relevance of a requirement. The knowledge base is a hierarchical-structured ontology containing security-relevant words, which is introduced in Sect. 9.2.3. Security knowledge changes over time, such that it is necessary to keep it up-to-date by domain and security experts.

The security relevance of words is domain specific. In some domains, a word can be classified as non-security related; in another domain, it is highly security dependent. For example, on the one hand if we speak about a park in general, a *bank* is a place to sit down for multiple people. In this context, it is not a security-related word. On the other hand, in the context of Common Component Modeling Example (CoCoME) as online shopping platform, the word *bank* with the same syntax has a different semantic meaning. It refers to a company where customers can store their money and transfer it to another owner. The bank details of customers are highly security dependent. To handle this type of context ambiguity, our knowledge base must be enriched by domain-specific knowledge. If a term, which is into the knowledge base and in a requirement, has a linguistic dependency to another term, the requirement engineer is questioned whether the two terms mean the same. By similar meaning of the terms, the knowledge base will be enriched by the new security-relevant term. For example, in the requirement "The user enters an identification number and a PIN", *PIN* is a security-related term. Through the linguistic dependency between *PIN* and *identification number*, the requirement engineer is questioned whether the two terms mean the same. We interleaved the semi-automated acquisition of knowledge enrichment into the security assessment of requirements. The knowledge acquisition and the heuristics are described in detail in Sect. 5.4.3. In Fig. 9.5, the enrichment of the knowledge base through a requirement engineer or a security expert, for example in the context of linguistic dependencies, is visualised. The requirement engineer has to make a decision about the security relevance of words with linguistic dependencies. The approach takes advantage of the collected knowledge described in Sect. 9.2.

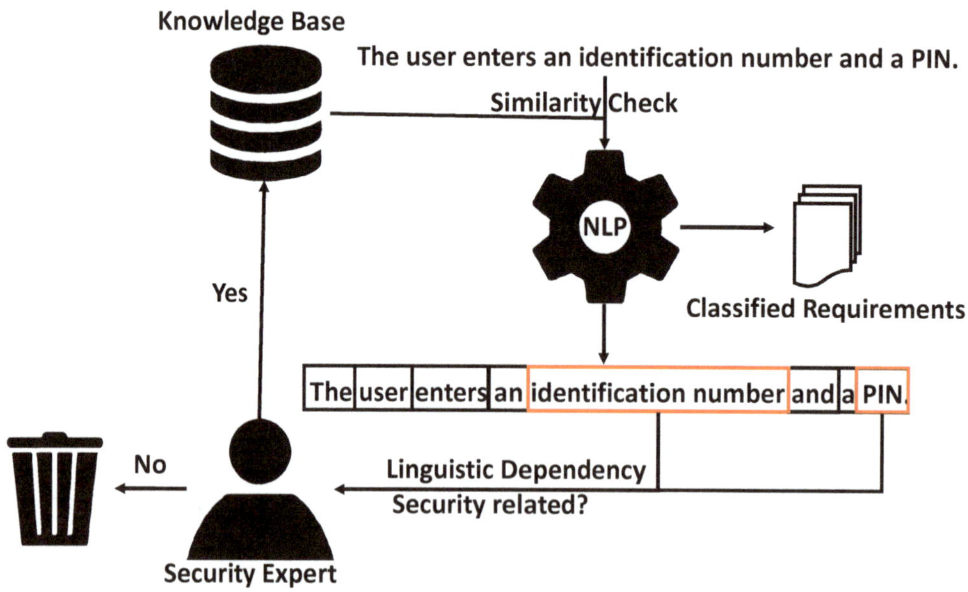

Fig. 9.5 Natural language processing approach—enrichment of security knowledge

9.2.3 Representing Security Knowledge Using Ontologies

The security context knowledge mined from the various information sources needs a suitable representation that is storable, updatable, and flexible enough to support different levels of abstraction and uncertainty. Specifically, security issues cannot be foreseen at system design time and are considered *unknown unknowns* [MH05]. Thus, a suitable knowledge representation that can be adapted to entirely new fields of knowledge is required. To this end, we use the knowledge representation concept of *ontologies* [Gru93]. An ontology contains the key concepts of a domain and the relationships between them. Our technical realisation of ontologies is based on Web Ontology Language (OWL), a standard ontology representation format [OWL09].

Software systems tend to get complex. Consequently, the knowledge necessary to ensure security during its life span grows accordingly. To support the handling of complexity and the sharing of knowledge between different projects within the same domain, the ontologies in our approach have three layers. We work with *nested ontologies* that include, for example, an upper ontology of general security concepts; a domain ontology of system-independent, domain-specific knowledge; and a system ontology of system-specific knowledge.

- We provide a generic *upper ontology* that is independent of a particular software domain or application. It represents the most general software security concepts, such as "encryption algorithm" and "attack". To identify these concepts, we performed a basic literature study [S G+14], followed by a more detailed systematic literature review (SLR, [Gär16, Bür+18]). SLR is an empirical method used to aggregate, summarise, and critically assess all available knowledge on a specific topic [KC07]. Figure 9.6 shows the resulting upper ontology, providing a taxonomy to define a system, its usage, and the surrounding security knowledge.
- *Domain ontologies* allow domain knowledge, as well as concrete security issues and measures, to be captured' for example, the encryption algorithm "DES" is subject to a specific attack called "Davies' attack". Domain ontologies (illustrated below) have to be created for each domain anew and can be shared by different systems in the same domain.
- *System ontologies* express security-relevant knowledge about a concrete system, for example that a specific banking system uses "DES" as its encryption algorithm. These system ontologies can be produced from existing artefacts, such as a UML-based system model.

Figure 9.7 illustrates an evolution step of the domain and system layers of a nested ontology. Class `data` are considered an asset of a system; thus, data are a subclass of class `Asset`. The domain level initially provides the information that data are to be further distinguished into anonymous data and personal data. Furthermore, the salary of an employee has to be considered personal data. Personal data is split into two further categories, and the individual `faith` is added. The evolution step is inspired by a refinement regarding privacy, in accordance with the German federal data protection law (Bundesdatenschutzgesetz, BDSG). Between

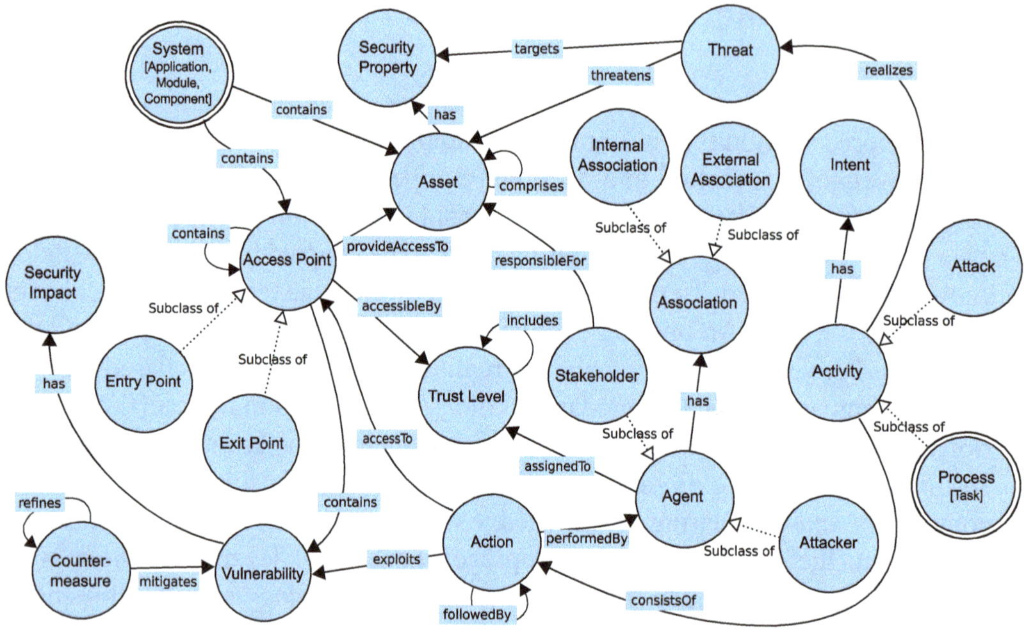

Fig. 9.6 Upper ontology for security

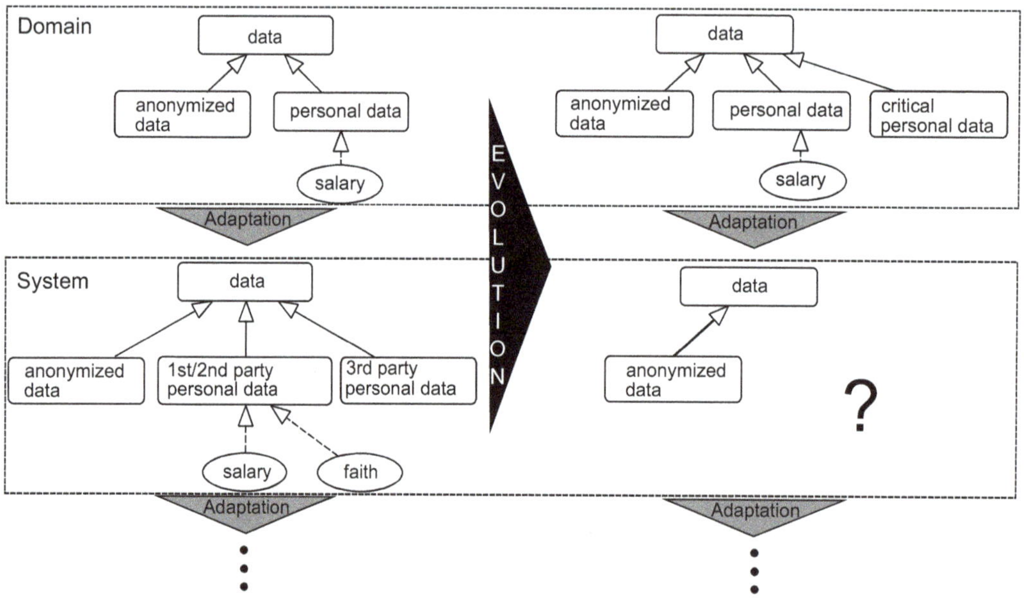

Fig. 9.7 Example of ontology layering and evolution

the 1990 and 2001 revision of the law [J B+15, Ruh+14a, Bür+18], an additional notion of *critical personal data* has been added, which leads to a change of the involved domain layer. Immediately, the question arises how we can adapt the system layer to be consistent with the domain layer again. This question leads us to model co-evolution, as discussed in the next section.

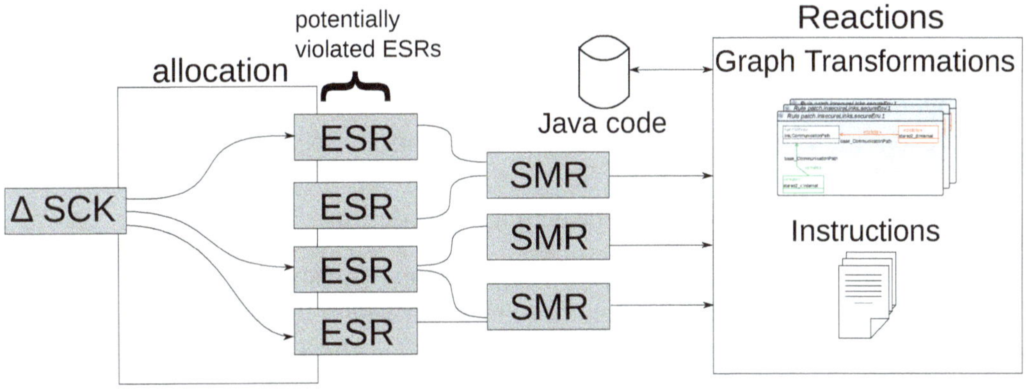

Fig. 9.8 Overview of SecVolution's co-evolution methodology

9.2.4 Rule-Based Model Co-evolution

Whenever the environment changes, the monitoring component may produce a corresponding change of the Security Context Knowledge, written as ΔSCK. Each change is analysed and, when necessary, used to produce reactions based on the process shown in Fig. 9.8.

First, in a step called *allocation*, we determine which Essential Security Requirements (ESRs) are potentially violated. This allocation is given by a mapping and can be supported, for example, by detailed information, where the ΔSCK occurs, that is relationship to specific elements of the upper ontology like *encryption*. To check if the system indeed is impacted by one or more flaws, the system model is investigated using model queries as given by the Security Maintenance Rules (SMRs). To express the model queries, we use model transformation technology, building on the model transformation language and framework Henshin [Are+10]. A system model can be interpreted as a graph. For instance, a class can be interpreted as node and the reference to another class can be interpreted as an edge. Thus, graph transformation techniques can be used to investigate and manipulate system models [JJS15]. A single graph transformation typically consists of two graphs, one called the left-hand side (LHS) and the other called the right-hand side (RHS). Whenever the LHS is matched to a given model, the matched parts are transformed according to the RHS. Elements can be added, removed, or preserved. LHS and RHS are connected through a mapping. Typically, a set of graph transformation rules is called a graph grammar. In Henshin, a number of graph transformation rules are encapsulated by a transformation model.

We implement model queries as rules in which the LHS equals the RHS. Thus, no changes to the model are made, but we can make use of the underlying matching algorithm. We use Henshin since it is built on EMF [Ecl], a standard platform to model software, and it allows us to specify change actions, as required for the next step.

To carry out the co-evolution, Security Maintenance Rules is used. To support this step appropriately, a Security Maintenance Rule consists of three parts:

- A link to ΔSCK
- A *precondition* that the model needs to fulfil for the Security Maintenance Rule to be applied
- A series of *reactions* to realise the actual co-evolution

The reactions itself can be of three different types, as shown in Fig. 9.8. The most formal way is using model transformations to directly alter the system model. Where model transformation approaches like Henshin fall short, for example complex clone operations or path-based analyses, reaction steps can be supported by Java code. Finally, showing the security expert (textual) instructions is meant as basic support for vulnerabilities, which additionally require reactions regarding a system's data or implementation (e.g. user passwords).

Using the *partial match* feature of Henshin, the application of co-evolution steps can be simplified [JJS15, J B+15]. For example, model queries or evaluation of preconditions provide links to concrete model elements of the system model for the transformation rule, that is EMF node instances. These instance links are used to populate the transformation rules, which in turn alter the system model. Using this technique and by additionally utilising the flexibility of Henshin transformation rule EMF objects, our rules actually need fewer elements and can be used in a flexible way. This helps to keep the set of transformation rules low and their understandability high. The co-evolution steps are applied semi-automatically. The security expert can be asked to make design decisions, that is choose an encryption algorithm to replace the now insecure one. Additionally, instructions can be given to the expert, for example "All users have to pick a new password".

9.2.5 Related Work

Natural Language Processing of Security Requirements Compagna et al. [Com+08] integrate legal patterns into a requirement engineering methodology for the development of security and privacy patterns using neuro-linguistic programming (NLP). The pattern design and validation process requires legal experts to describe patterns in natural language. This description is parsed by a natural language processor on the basis of a semantic template. Gegick and Williams [GW07] developed a methodology for the early identification of system vulnerabilities for existing threats. While in our approach we use suspicious sequences to encode hypotheses of possible attack patterns, they use Regular Expressions to encode attack patterns extracted from different web-based security vulnerability databases. A catalogue of such patterns is supplied to map the threat types to elements in the system model. By using a linguistic approach, the requirement engineer can concentrate on the domain-specific problem rather than modelling it formally. Thus, natural language provides a more flexible notation, and changes can be managed more efficiently.

Haley et al. [Hal+08] present a framework not only for security requirements elicitation but also for security analysis. Their method is based on constructing a context for the regarded system. Describing this context with a problem-oriented notation makes it possible to validate the system against the security requirements. The approach is powerful but needs a lot of security expertise to build the context and understand the results of the analysis. Evolution of the context is not supported.

9.2.6 Leveraging Security Knowledge to Infer Adequate Reaction to Context Changes

Tsoumas and Gritzalis [TG06] provide a security-ontology-based framework for enterprises linking high-level policy statements and deployable security controls. Security ontology is built by extending the Distributed Management Task Force (DMTF) Common Information Model standard. In contrast to our approach, it is focused on organisational controls like how to secure server hardware, recommendations for configuration of intrusion detection systems, and so on.

Ernst et al. [EBM11] use a formal description language to relate requirements to their implementation. Changes identified in the requirement specification are then used to trigger software evolution. The approach is rather formal and aims at providing a graph-based guidance for implementation rationale. Co-evolution is not considered so far, as well as an interface to system design level.

The *Water wave phenomenon* inspired Li et al. [Li+13] to develop an impact assessment approach based on call graphs. First, they analyse the core, which consists of the direct affected software artefacts. After that, the call graph is analysed, taking the interference of different changes into account. Their approach is focused on predicting how big (in terms of number of methods to change) the impact of changing a number of methods in a given source code project will be. Contrary to this, our approach aims at analysing impact regarding security properties.

9.2.7 Summary

In this section, we presented three contributions. First of all, we introduced systematic and experience-based elicitation and management of multiple, heterogeneous knowledge sources throughout the life cycle of a long-living system. This is considered a fundamental step in the process of overcoming the multitude of information sources for the sake of leveraging it do manage long-living systems. As soon as the knowledge has been elicited and structured, it needs to be investigated to assess the effects on a system's security. Thus, as a second contribution, we introduced a systematic analysis and optimisation of deciding how new knowledge affects the security of long-living software systems. After all, knowledge and reasoning made about the system's security is an additional challenge so that we showed, as a third contribution, how to maintain a consistent database of security requirements and security-relevant environment knowledge during evolution of a long-living information system.

The three core challenges tackled by the SecVolution design-time approach are related to the first challenge, as introduced in the chapter's preface (*How can security knowledge, available via diverse non-formal sources, be incorporated and utilised for a long-living system design?*). A process for elicitation of various knowledge sources is provided, which is able to deal with ever-changing knowledge that long-living systems are confronted with. Maintaining a database of security knowledge during evolution contributes to the second challenge (*How can developers and security experts be supported to react to context evolution, which may compromise the system's security design or compromise the system at run time?*). Developers are provided a consistent knowledge base that can be kept up to date when facing context evolution. The SecVolution design-time approach is focused on typical design-time development artefacts like UML models.

The SecVolution design-time approach has made the following contributions in detail. We developed a security assessment technique for supporting the maintenance of long-living information systems independent of the process model, domain, or technology in use [S G+14]. We created a core ontology usable for different security areas (e.g. privacy, information flow, attacker model) [Bür+18], as well as techniques for reusing and structuring the knowledge-modelling process [Ruh+14a]. We used UML profiles to define extension points in the models that are connected to the knowledge. For the case of an initially secure system, we developed a model-based security verification strategy [S W+14] that can efficiently determine whether a particular co-evolution restores security requirements that were satisfied before the evolution [Bür+18]. The strategy is supported by an extensible tool platform, CARiSMA, [Ahm+17] that reads the annotations of UML 2 models and computes a delta model containing all possible evolution paths of the given model. We presented an approach [JJS15, J B+15, Bür+18] in which changing security knowledge is analysed and possible reactions are derived. It also covers newly occurring knowledge about security issues or attacks.

9.3 Integrating Model-Based Security Constraints with Program Code

The reliability of security analyses is crucial for effective security strategies in long-living software systems. Figure 9.2 uses Unified Modeling Language (UML) profiles to define security information in models. One kind of model to which security information can be attached is architecture models, which usually describe components and their interconnection. This information can be used for architecture-based security evaluations. These evaluations are only reliable as long as the architecture implementation is consistent with the architecture models. This consistency can be invalidated via multiple influence factors during the life cycle of a long-living software system: (1) The program code evolves, so that it is no longer consistent with the security models. (2) Security models may be based on architecture models. When the underlying architecture models evolve, the architecture-based security model is inconsistent with the actual architecture. In both cases, the analysis models must be changed accordingly and the security analysis must be repeated or adapted, or the results of the security analysis might be invalid.

In this section, we present an approach to create a continuous consistency between architecture model information, architecture-based security information, and the program code. The approach has been developed as a part of the ADVERT project within the priority program. It addresses the challenge to document security information so that it is strongly related to the program code, to support the analysis and monitoring of security aspects.

9.3.1 *Codeling: Integrating Architecture Model Information with Program Code*

A set of abstract concerns commonly agreed upon seems to exist for defining software architectures, as manifested by the standard ISO/IEC 42010 [ISO11b]. These include the general structure of a system, usually expressed in components, interfaces, and their interconnection. They are often accompanied by abstract behaviour descriptions or quality aspects. During the development of software, the architecture is realised in the software artefacts, including the program code, configuration, and the use of existing platforms. The goal of the implementation is an executable system. The implementation of software architecture is driven by industry standards and platforms that define standard elements such as components and interfaces. Languages for architecture specification and for architecture implementation have common concerns (see, e.g., [MBG10]), typically at least the definition of components, interfaces, and their interconnections. However, they have different foci and include different types of architectural design and different details added to the architectural description.

The tool *Codeling* [Kon18, Kon16] creates a systematic mapping between architecture specification model elements, relations, and attributes and their implementation based on standardised or project-specific architecture implementation languages. These mappings specifically define places where arbitrary other code can be added. This kind of mapping allows to extract architecture specification models from program code and to propagate changes in these models back to the code.

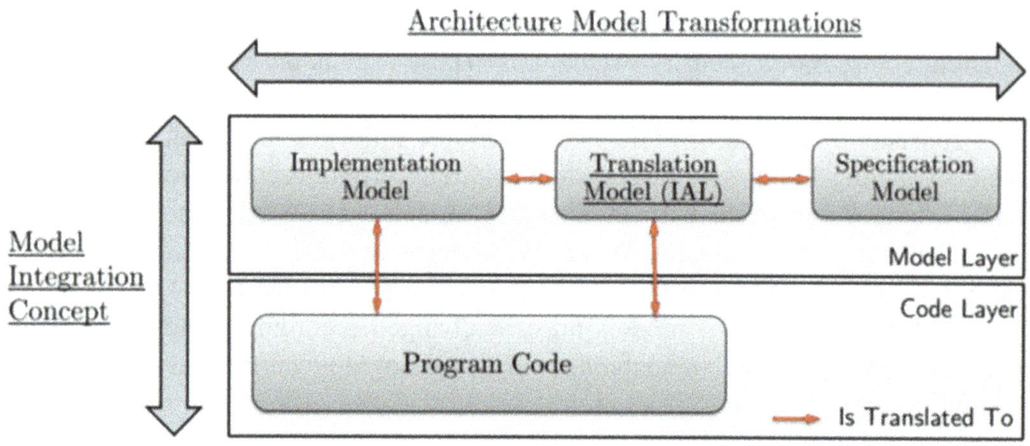

Fig. 9.9 The parts of Codeling for integrating architecture model information with code

Codeling comprises three parts. Figure 9.9 sketches an overview of these parts and their relations. The figure describes artefacts of the approach with rounded boxes and translations between these artefacts with arrows. The parts are used to bidirectionally translate between program code and a specification model expressed in an architecture specification language. The parts are underlined in Fig. 9.9. (1) An *Intermediate Architecture Language (IAL)* mediates between architecture implementation models and architecture specification models. The IAL has a small core with the common elements of architecture languages. The core is extended with a variety of stereotypes to represent, for example, different kinds of interfaces, component hierarchies, or quality attributes. Models expressed in the IAL are called *translation models*. (2) The *Model Integration Concept (MIC)* describes an approach for bidirectional formal mappings between program code structures and an implementation model expressed in a meta model of an architecture implementation language. As an example, a Java-type declaration that implements a specific marker interface might represent a component, and static final fields within this type declaration represent attributes of this component. In Codeling, the program code also contains information that is not part of an architecture implementation language but is only subject to a specification language. For example, many architecture implementation languages do not describe hierarchical architectures. The hierarchy information can be annotated in the program code. The translation model is enhanced with this information from the code using the Model Integration Concept. (3) Bidirectional architecture model transformations translate between implementation models, translation models, and specification models.

With the tool *Codeling*, architecture model specifications are integrated with program code. The models can be embedded into and reliably extracted from the code, leaving only the program code as single underlying model.

9.3.2 Application: Security Evolution Scenario

The running example within this section is CoCoME (see Sect. 4.2), a common case study for software architecture approaches. Figure 9.10 shows a subset of the CoCoME architecture expressed in the UML. In the running examples, three user roles interact with the system. *Cashiers* scan items at a cash desk and execute the sales process. *Store Managers* manage the store's inventory. They buy inventory and may see reports about their store's sales and inventory. *Enterprise Mangers* support the store managers. Therefore, they can see reports of sales, see the inventory of multiple stores, and trigger the exchange of inventory items between stores.

The excerpt shows two components: *ReportingServer* and *StoreServer*, both subcomponents of the component *Application*. These two components are user interfaces to the system and should provide their services only to authenticated users. The component *StoreServer* provides the interface *IStoreInventoryManager*, which should be accessible to store managers and enterprise managers. The component *ReportingServer* provides the interface *IReporting*, which should be accessible only to enterprise managers. For security reasons, customers are not allowed to use any of these interfaces.

The UML diagram in Fig. 9.10 is enhanced with Secure Information Flow (SIF) [RJ12] information. SIF annotations in UML diagrams define authorisation rules for structural elements in an architecture, which decide about the access of a partially ordered set of roles. In the running example, the following authorisation constraints are defined:

1. The component *StoreServer* provides the interface *IStoreInventoryManager*, which should be accessible to store managers and enterprise managers.
2. The component *ReportingServer* provides the interface *IReporting*, which should be accessible only to enterprise managers.

For security reasons, customers are not allowed to use any of these interfaces.

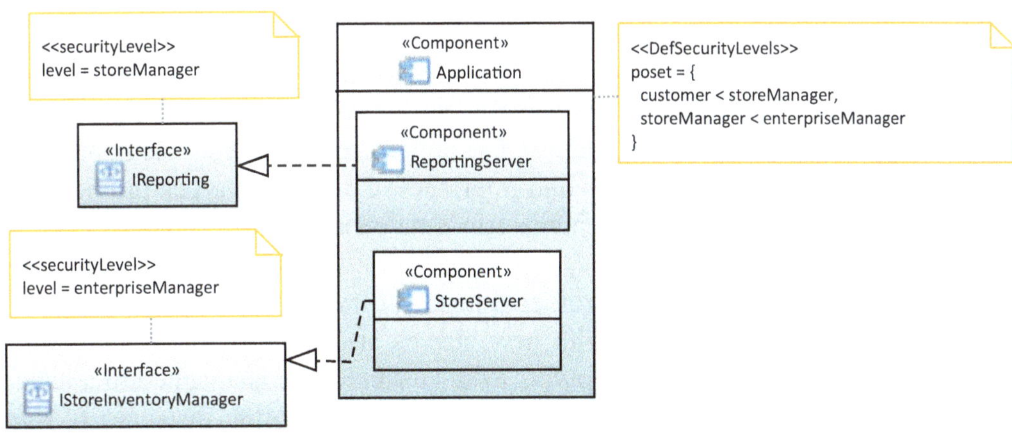

Fig. 9.10 Excerpt of the CoCoME architecture extended with SIF annotations in UML

Table 9.1 Overview of the mapping between UML meta-model elements, CoCoME meta-model elements, and program code structures

UML meta model element	CoCoME meta model element	Program code structures
Component with name "Server"	"Server" component	Type declaration with name "Server"
Composite component	Component with children	Package declaration with package or type declarations as subcomponents
Operation provided role	Provided interface	Implemented interface
Operation required role	Required interface	Interface instance given to type via constructor

In the context of the running example, Codeling is used to create a UML view upon the CoCoME architecture. A formal mapping between interconnected UML components and CoCoME program code already exists in Codeling. Table 9.1 gives an overview of the mapping between the CoCoME code, the corresponding architecture implementation language, and UML meta-model elements. The table only contains the mappings that are relevant for adding SIF information to the running example. To integrate SIF information on UML components, interfaces, and operations with Codeling (a), the IAL must be able to handle this information. Also mappings must be created (b) between the IAL and the CoCoME code and (c) between UML stereotypes for SIF and the IAL. In the following, these translations are described.

9.3.3 Security Aspects in the Intermediate Architecture Language

A translation model in Codeling is implemented using the IAL. Figure 9.11 shows the core of the IAL. Within Codeling, the IAL core is used to describe architectures with component types, which provide and require interfaces. Component instances represent single instances of placeholders for component instances that are dynamically created at run time. This core contains all relevant meta-model elements to describe the elements shown in Table 9.1. The architecture is the root element of the IAL. It comprises component types and interfaces. Component types provide and require interfaces. The IAL also contains run-time elements for component types, their provisions, and requirements.

The IAL core is extended with profiles [Lan+12] for describing SIF information. A profile extends a meta model with new classes and stereotypes. A stereotype application is an instance of a stereotype. When a stereotype is attached to a meta-modelled class, a stereotype application can be attached to the instances of that class. Such extended class instance can then use the attributes and references of the stereotype.

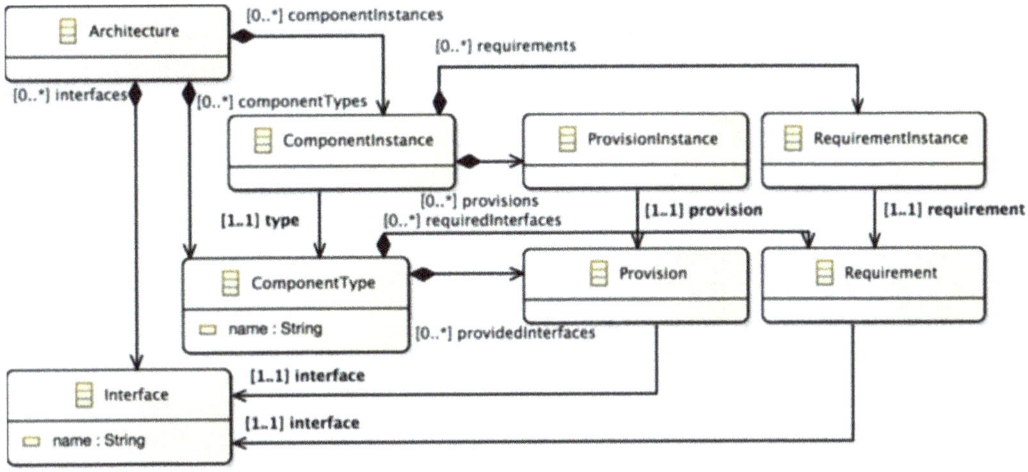

Fig. 9.11 The core of the IAL

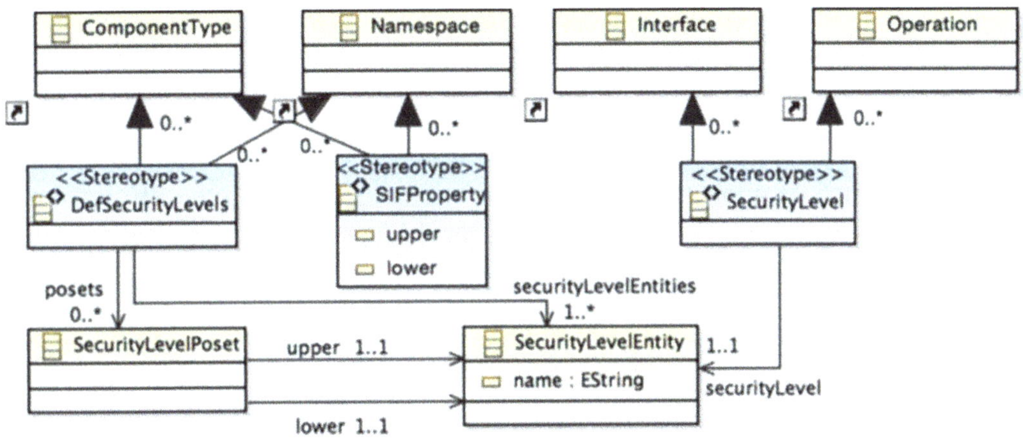

Fig. 9.12 SIF profile for the IAL

Figure 9.12 shows the profile for SIF information. This implementation is based on the definition of SIF from Ruhroth and Jürjens [RJ12]. The classes in the upper row of the figure are references to classes of the core or other profiles. The SIF profile defines three stereotypes. The stereotype *DefSecurityLevels* is applicable to component types or namespaces from the *namespaces* profile (not shown). With this stereotype applied, components or namespaces can declare partially ordered sets of *SecurityLevelEntities*, the *SecurityLevelPosets*. The entities correspond to roles in the system. The stereotype *SIFProperty* is also applicable to component types and namespaces. SIF properties describe the basic security predicates (BSPs). Each property takes two sets of names of BSPs as arguments the upper and lower BSPs [RJ12]. The stereotype *SecurityLevel* is applied to interfaces of the IAL core or operations of the profile for operation-type interfaces (not shown). With this stereotype, the minimum role necessary to use the interface or single operations of an interface is declared.

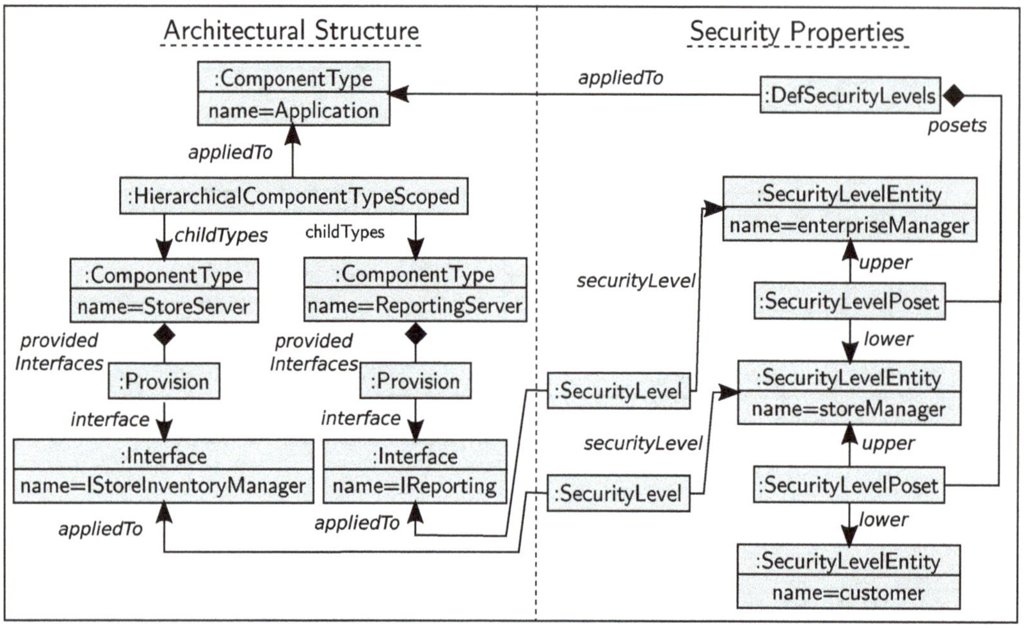

Fig. 9.13 Excerpt of the CoCoME architecture extended with SIF annotations in the IAL

In the running example, the CoCoME architecture, including the SIF information, is translated into an IAL model with the SIF profile applied. Bidirectional model transformations are used to create a formal mapping between the model types. Figure 9.13 shows an excerpt of the CoCoME architecture with the SIF information defined in Sect. 9.3.2. The left-hand side shows an excerpt of the CoCoME architecture expressed with the IAL. A composite component *Application* contains two subcomponents: *StoreServer* and *ReportingServer*. Each provides an interface. The right-hand side shows the SIF information attached to this architectural core. The composite component declares three security levels: *enterpriseManager*, *storeManager*, and *customer*. Their partial order is given with $enterpriseManager > storeManager$ and $storeManager > customer$. For using the interface *IReporting* of the component type *ReportingServer*, the user has to be an enterprise manager. For using the interface *IStoreInventoryManager* of the component type *StoreServer*, the user has to be a store manager or an enterprise manager. Customers are not allowed to access any of these interfaces.

9.3.4 *Integrating Security-Architectures with Code Using the Model Integration Concept*

Next, a mapping between SIF profile elements in the IAL and program code structures is necessary. These program code structures must work with the program code structures used for the translation of CoCoME architecture elements, briefly described in Table 9.1.

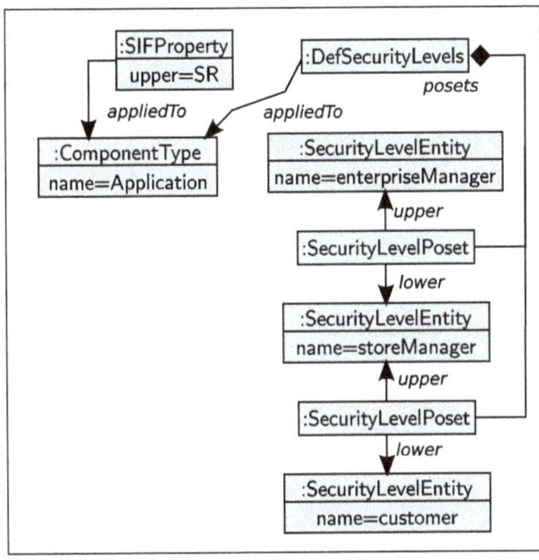


```
@SIFProperty(upper="SR")
@DefSecurityLevels(
  entities= {
        EnterpriseManager.class,
        StoreManager.class,
        Customer.class},
  posets = {
    @SecurityLevelPoset(
      upper=EnterpriseManager.class,
      lower=StoreManager.class),
    @SecurityLevelPoset(
      lower=StoreManager.class,
      upper=Customer.class)
  })
package org.cocome.tradingsystem.inventory.application;
```

Fig. 9.14 Mapping between the *DefSecurityLevel* and the *SIFProperty* stereotypes and program code structures in CoCoME

The stereotypes *DefSecurityLevels* and *SIFProperty* are applicable to components and namespaces. In the context of this example, a definition of security levels and SIF properties should be applied to the composite component *application*. In the CoCoME program code, this composite component is represented by a Java package with the name `org.cocome.tradingsystem.inventory.application`. A feasible code structure for the given SIF information is annotations on the package. Therefore, a file `package-info.java` is created in the corresponding folder, applying a respective annotation to the package declaration. The corresponding annotation declaration is part of an external, reusable library that is generated for this purpose. Figure 9.14 shows this mapping. The SIF property annotation owns two members of the type String: `upper` and `lower`, corresponding to the respective stereotype attributes. In the example in Fig. 9.14, the value "SR" for the member `upper` denotes *Strict Removal*. This means that all confidential events are independent of events that are visible or "neither-nor" [Man03, RJ12]. The annotation for the definition of security levels and their partial order `DefSecurityLevels` is also attached to the package declaration. Its reference `entities` takes an array of types as parameter, which extend a specific marker interface. This marker interface denotes that the implementing type represents a security entity. This mechanism is used to use the type-safety features of the Java compiler to validate the member values at compile time. In addition, typical IDEs propose known security entities via their code completion features. The same mechanism is used for `SecurityLevelPosets`, where a lower and an upper entity are given as values.

In the example, only enterprise managers are allowed to access the interface `IReporting`. In the CoCoME program code, this interface is represented by a Java interface with the same name. A feasible code structure for the security level is an annotation on the interface declaration. Figure 9.15 shows the mapping as an

Fig. 9.15 Mapping between the *SecurityLevel* stereotype and program code structures in CoCoME

example. The default annotation member is a reference to a type that represents a security entity, that is it implements the corresponding marker interface.

9.3.5 Related Work

The relationship between models and code is subject to related work. The field of model-code co-evolution describes how models and code can evolve together. Works in this area usually focus on one specific type of model. For example, Langhammer [Lan17] describes an approach for the co-evolution of Palladio architecture models and Java program code. Langhammer describes rules that preserve a consistency relationship between the architecture model and the program code during changes in either side. Ruhroth et al. [Ruh+14b] present an approach for managing the consistency between certain security models and code. Their approach synchronises atomic change operations on models and corresponding operations on code. Our approach instead explicitly integrates arbitrary model information with program code.

Approaches for the co-evolution of models and code often do not consider the evolution of the underlying languages. Rocco et al. [Roc+14] explicitly describe language evolution as aspect of model-code co-evolution. When a system is modelled using meta models and corresponding code is generated, a challenge arises when the meta model is subject to evolution. Such changes can break the code generators. This is a case of model-code co-evolution: the meta model can be regarded as model, and the code generator can be regarded as code in the context of model-code co-evolution. The authors propose a co-evolution approach where model changes are propagated via well-defined transformations, which operate on the code and take the model difference as input. This approach can be used to handle architecture language evolution regarding model editors but not regarding the code that implements a system's architecture.

The synchronisation between models and between models and code is subject to the area of (in)consistency management [Fel+15]. These approaches assume that two views upon a shared body of information overlap. When one view is changed in the overlapping part, these changes should be propagated to the other view. Consistency management deals with methods and tools to re-establish synchronisation. Existing consistency management approaches focus on coarse-grained program code structures, such as code files or classes, and relate them to model elements. Konersmann [Kon18] argues that a more fine-grained abstraction level is necessary and implements such consistency relationships in Codeling. Vitruv [KBL13] is a more general approach to keep different views consistent. It bases on coupling EMOF-specified meta models. For coupling the Palladio meta model for architectural specification with Java, see the PhD thesis of Langhammer [Lan17].

Already in 1995, Murphy et al. [MNS95] presented an approach for bridging the gap between program code elements and higher-level software models. In their approach, a mapping is created between higher-level model elements and program code elements. The approach of Murphy et al. is limited to mappings between model elements and program code files, neglecting the structures within the code files. Approaches need to address structures within the code files to add decision knowledge to specific architecture elements in the code.

9.3.6 Summary

This section presented the application of Codeling on security information. It is used to create a formal bidirectional mapping between security model information attached to architecture specification models and the program code that implements the security architecture. Therefore, the presented application addresses the first challenge of *diverse non- or semi-formal sources of security knowledge*. We have shown in this section that Codeling can be used to integrate model-based security information with program code, using a formal bidirectional mapping. The implementation allows to specify the security annotations in a model-based environment and in the program code. The program code takes the role of a single underlying model.

The program code structures that are used to represent the model information are also accessible at run time via introspection. Therefore, it is possible—and supported by Codeling—to create or extend a run-time environment so that the security constraints defined in the program code can automatically be verified. The approach can therefore be used not only for documentation and for relating security information to architecture model elements but also for monitoring the application security. This addresses the second challenge, because with this monitoring, developers and security experts are supported to react to context evolution, which may compromise the system's security design or compromise the system at run time.

9.4 Contextual Security Patterns

For the evolution of large and long-living software systems, it is essential to understand not just the existing parts of the software, like requirements, design/architecture, or code, but also how these elements could change over time and especially how the corresponding components (inter-) act or applied in run time. In particular, for maintaining the security of software-intensive systems, one has to consider not only changes to requirements, which result in adaptive, corrective, or perfective evolution steps in the system directly, but also changes to the context of this system. This context comprises the various parts of the execution platform, but also changes in attacker capabilities; changes to user role models, including defined use and misuse cases; new access policies; protocols; or run-time configurations.

An important factor for a successful architectural approach is the understanding that even with well-defined interfaces between components and subsystems, their inner behaviour (i.e. implementations) or usage profiles can change. This does not necessarily mean that the interfaces are accordingly modified, which can result in security problems, where especially the black-box-modelling is favoured. These factors need to be handled thoroughly and explicitly in design time, so the architects can foresee the possible outcomes of evolutionary changes and run-time differences before it is too late or any eventual costly and complex interferences are necessary. To address this issue, we provide a lightweight architectural documentation and analysis approach using security patterns enriched with explicit decision assumptions and prerequisites. In this section we introduce our approach.

9.4.1 Security Challenges in Software Evolution

Software security is a cross-cutting consideration with respect to various software life cycles (from requirements elicitation to maintenance) and with respect to other quality attributes (e.g. performance, reliability, etc.). Regarding the evolution software systems based on their security properties, there are several identified key challenges [Sei+16]. For our approach, the following issues are of great importance, which we categorise into two groups. System evolution is still an important factor as it is permanent and phase spanning. Changes within the known system boundaries can still be fuzzy, which need to be monitored thoroughly. However, context evolution results in more challenging issues, as the effects are not explicitly known or cannot be identified without further data in design time. We, again, list three main issues within the evolution of context of software-intensive systems as follows:

Threat Evolution Attackers' capabilities evolve very fast, and they are unpredictable. Therefore, continuous execution of security analysis are needed at run time to identify new vulnerabilities, which becomes a very costly process.

Deployment and Infrastructure There are a lot of factors regarding the resource environment and the allocation of the components that affect the correct application of security solutions and patterns. Furthermore, fuzzy system boundaries worsen the situation due to uncertainty during design phase about the deployment and application of the system.

Application and Run-Time Configurations Configurations of a software system at run time and for its possible applications have strong influence on the system security. Early extraction is especially difficult, and there are no general approaches for multiple configurations with respect to security.

Hence, the effects of evolution can have severe results on the security as well, making irrelevant attacks relevant or making security decisions invalid. Preserving security during software evolution can be promoted by understanding and reasoning the architecture and made design decisions of the software system. However, security vulnerabilities are most often code related; still architectural misconceptions will create security vulnerabilities. Hence, an architectural security analysis can yield such risks and vulnerabilities in prior phases of a project and support its evolution. However, it is not comprehensive as code-related vulnerabilities need additional analyses. But architectural design decisions, such as using specific security design patterns, suit very well, and as the software architectures are a specific abstraction of the whole system, security needs to be addressed on the same abstraction level. Well-structured security patterns, to be decided and modelled at design time, suit very well to address and mitigate such vulnerabilities and risks. On the other hand, abstracting security properties often result in loss of rational knowledge and makes it complex to validate design decisions regarding security, as changes to software or its environment happen. Security, as well as other non-functional requirements such as performance, must therefore be addressed explicitly by the architects because these properties are determined not just by individual architecture components but also by their interaction, coordination, and usage at run time. We call these factors, on which the correct functioning of security patterns rely, the *context* of the software system. If decision-making process does not involve this explicit context information, security is doomed to degrade. In this section, we describe our approach addressing this problem by handling context information regarding the security properties explicitly on software architectures.

9.4.2 Contextual Security

Software security is a quality attribute that depends on many factors based on the contextual nature of the software. Most of these factors are usually unknown to software architects at design time, like the attacker behaviour or run-time configuration. Architects need to assume such aspects, if they ever do it in the first place, regarding their security decisions. Furthermore, like in any software architecture, where an abstraction is necessary to focus on only relevant aspects of the system, a lot of information becomes implicit, including assumptions about the possible security threats and applied patterns. This type of unpersisted information gets usually neglected, especially as the software evolves and existing design decisions change, which would result in unnoticed security issues. Furthermore, due to the missing *security-related* information at design time, architects cannot foresee the probable security vulnerabilities that may arise first at run time, even if any related decision was made at design time. Hence, solutions addressing such security issues on architectural level need to consider the corresponding abstraction and has to be handled with limited amount of information, which still describes the *context* of the system in order to provide proper security for the data and function. Furthermore, in case the problems are repetitive, that is they happen to be recurring from time to time, even with contextual and application-specific differences, design patterns can be helpful in providing a generic solution, which needs to be made concrete later for the specific situation. One way to systematically deal with contextual security is the documented use of security patterns. Therefore, we extend descriptions of security patterns in their pattern catalogue with information on contextual security. This means we document which security-related assumptions a pattern needs to make on the context. This information is then used as structural logical constraints between the security patterns and threats, for whose mitigation they are designed to.

9.4.3 From Design Patterns to Security Patterns

Design patterns have their roots in civil engineering, where it is about the architecture of buildings and structures and not the software. According to Alexander [Ale77], "each pattern describes a problem which occurs over and over again in [...] environment, and then describes the core of the solution to that problem, in such a way that [...] can use this solution a million times over, without ever doing it the same way twice". Although this stands for a very different domain, the definition fits for software design patterns as well. In any case, patterns describe "a solution to a problem in a context" [Gam+95]. Furthermore, according to Schumacher et al. [Sch+05], a security pattern "[...] describes a particular recurring security problem that arises in specific contexts, and presents a well-proven generic solution to it. The solution consists of a set of interacting roles that can be arranged into multiple concrete design structures, as well as a process to create one particular such structure." This definition again underlines the importance of the context in which the problem and its solution resides, meaning the software and its context, including the run-time environment, user behaviour, etc.

It is important to mention, by analogy with design patterns of Gang of Four [Gam+95], that they are not invented on behalf but rather discovered/identified as a possible reusable security solution. Security patterns are specified using specific templates, like the design patterns. There is no standardised template, but in general they consist of at least a name, context, a problem statement, a solution, known uses, and consequences. A few simple examples for security patterns in real-life applications would be the **role-based access control** or **application firewall** [Fer13].

9.4.4 Security Patterns as a Means for Contextual Software Security

By using security patterns and patterns in general, no reinvention of the wheel is necessary, which grants time and resources, and also a concise unambiguous documentation is established. This documentation based on security concerns (incl. threats and security patterns), structurally applied on the architectural level, can encompass the necessary contextual information crucial to the validity of the security solutions chosen by the software architects. By using security patterns as a means of mitigation against the modelled attacks or for resolving security issues in software architectures, architects also support different aspects of design decision-making process. It plays a crucial role at the design time, which reduces the further complexity and unnecessary complexity at run time. Furthermore, integrating such solutions into software architectures as rational knowledge base allows them to use this structured documentation as first-class software entity if they are working with model-driven software engineering methods [Völ+13]. Hence, the security patterns can be treated equally to the code within the entire life cycle of the system, become a primary element in implementation, and support architects or developers with automatic code generation, maintaining the system as it evolves or analysing/monitoring the run-time security state of the system. However, within our approach, as described in previous sections, security patterns are extended by explicitly using formally structured context prerequisites. It allows us to exploit this architectural documentation to check the correct application of security patterns in case of evolutionary changes and trace the impact on concrete architectural components responsible for the security solutions.

These ideas led to an architecture-based approach [TH16a] as an extension to architectural description languages (ADL) with security patterns, context prerequisites, as well as other security artefacts (e.g. modelled threats). Within this, the necessary profiles and stereotypes are provided for the integration of the models and catalogues into a specific ADL, the Palladio Component Model [Reu+16]. An overview of this approach can be seen in Fig. 9.16.

The abstract workflow of using security patterns enriched with contextual information can be summarised in a few points:

- The security expert creates the initial reusable, model-based security catalogue and documents the security patterns in combination with the possible threat mitigations. In it, the main security elements, that is attacks and security patterns, are logically combined via prerequisites, as can be seen in Fig. 9.17. No direct relation otherwise exists between them. Prerequisites, the architectural

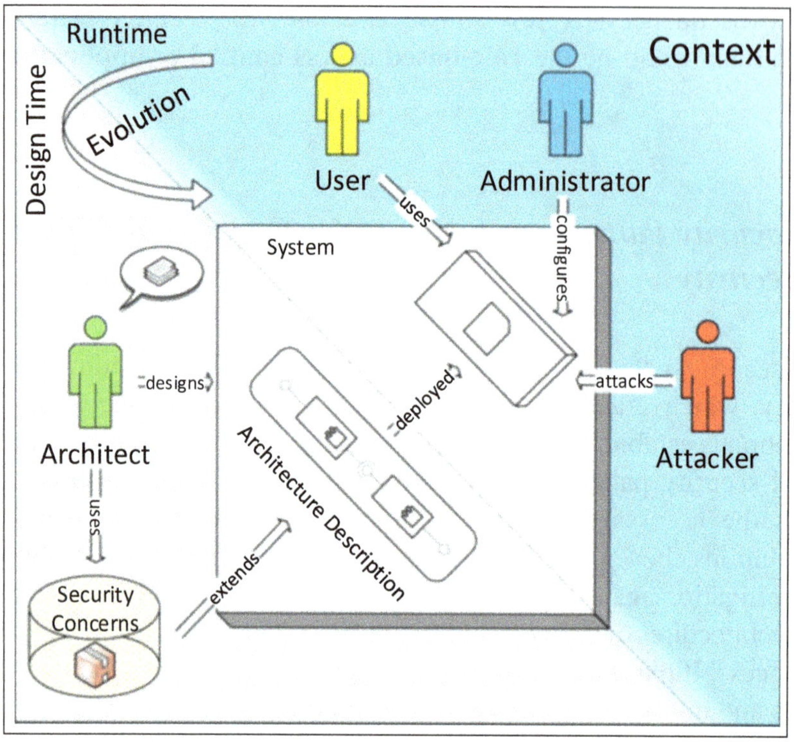

Fig. 9.16 Overview of the security pattern approach exploiting the contextual and run-time information on software architectures [TH16a]

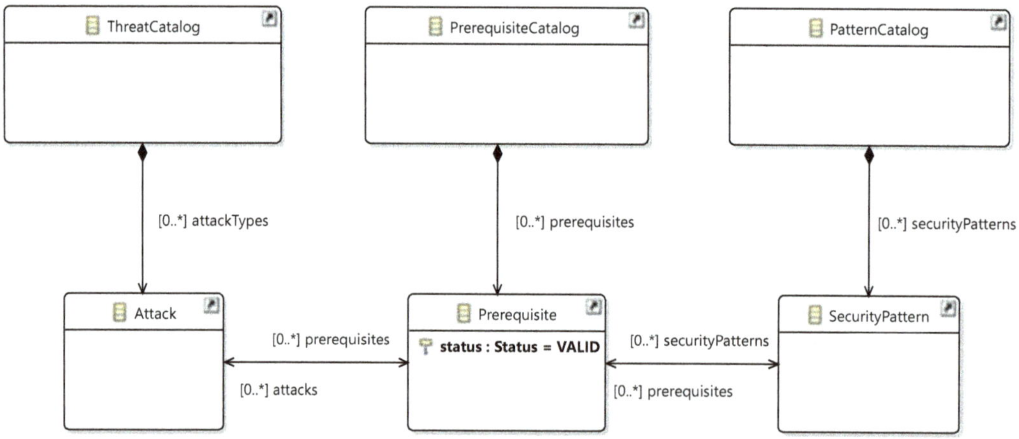

Fig. 9.17 Overview of catalogues containing the main security elements

representations of contextual assumptions, serve as success parameter for security patterns and are necessary for the correct and continuous application of the patterns.

- The software architect designs the software system and describes it using any architecture description language (ADL). The necessary knowledge of the systems context (spanning from usage profiles to possible configurations by the administrators or from deployment environment to even attacker behaviour) can then be derived from the security catalogue. The integration of the security catalogue with the corresponding architecture description language happens with the well-known profiling and stereotyping. For this, the structural roles of the security patterns are mapped by the architect to the software components, which are again extended by the relevant prerequisites from the same catalogue based on the made security decisions.

- As the system evolves or any changes are necessary to make security design decisions, the architect can check the state of the explicit prerequisites to analyse whether a security pattern is still functional and efficient against any threat or whether an attacker is again capable of exploiting a vulnerability despite the existence of a mitigation security pattern.

The described roles and the relation between the elements of our approach are depicted in Fig. 9.18. An initial application of our approach is already conducted within the CoCoME case study, and its more detailed description can be found in Sect. 12.1.3.

As for validating the systems' security in case of any changes that reflect themselves in the made prerequisites about the security decisions, an analysis method, which is based on the propositional logic, is introduced [TH16a]. Further improvements have been made since then, and the method is consisted of two parts: (1) security pattern analysis and (2) trace impact analysis.

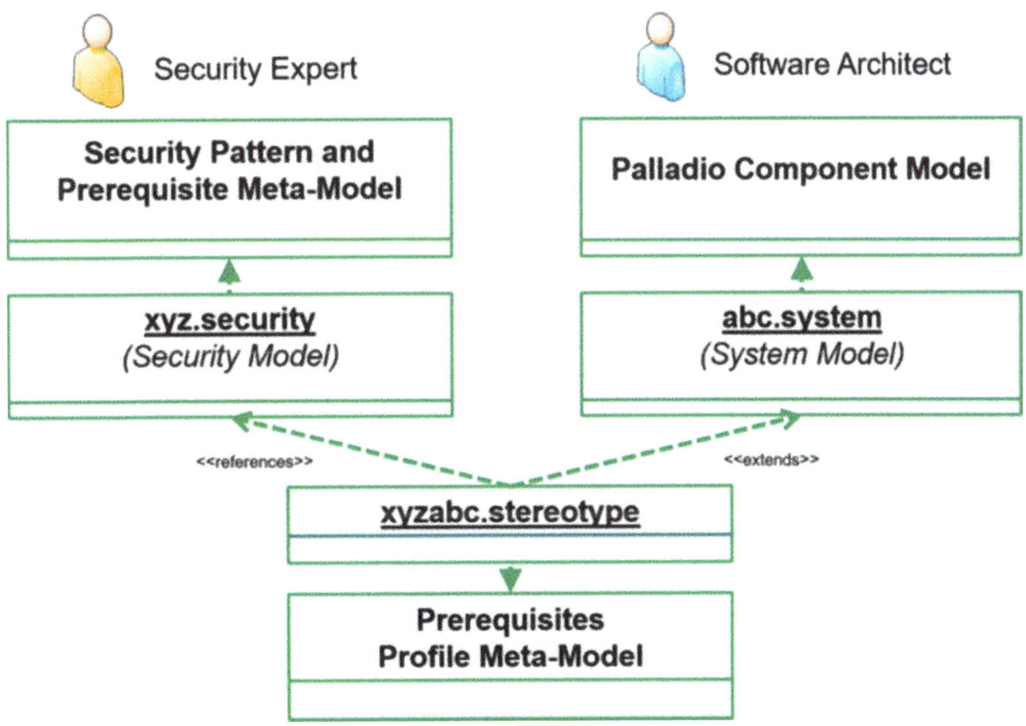

Fig. 9.18 Depiction of the roles and architecture elements for our approach

1. Security Pattern Analysis first checks whether all the necessary structural roles of security patterns are correctly applied on the architectural level. If a necessary role is missing in the first place, a security pattern cannot generally function correctly, and the vulnerabilities it should cover will be present. If all the necessary roles of a security pattern are present in the system's architecture, then contextual analysis is conducted. For this, it is checked whether any of the prerequisites of any possible attack on the system is covered by the security pattern. An attack can be successful and issue a risk if and only if all of its prerequisites are valid. Logic of the analysis anticipates to at least cover one of the required prerequisites for a possible mitigation of the corresponding attack. So if a security pattern is able to cover a required contextual prerequisite for an attack, it can be deemed to function correctly.
2. Trace Impact Analysis is conducted in case of any evolutionary changes, which result in changes to the secure state of the system. If an attack happens to be issuing a risk after the change happens and it is shown in security pattern analysis, the architect follows the roles of the security pattern in question over it stereotypes and changed prerequisites to trace to the architectural elements.

This analysis allows architects to react on possible evolutionary changes and different run-time scenarios with respect to security in early design phases, which becomes a complementary security measure to methods like code-based security analysis or penetration testing, where the code and concrete run-time environment have to be present.

9.4.5 Related Work

General-purpose (e.g. UML) or more specific (e.g. PCM) ADLs have often no direct support for security modelling. Nevertheless, there are several approaches and extensions addressing this gap, some of which also provide further support like analysis or simulations. Schneier [Sch11] introduced attack trees based on feature modelling to model threats, which are described based on the attackers capabilities. A tree-based structure is used to represent all possible attacks, with the main goal of an attacker placed in the root element and the different ways to achieve that goal exploited in the child nodes, which can be semantically enriched with values like probabilities or costs for validation purposes. However, this approach focuses only on the threat side and not on the architecture itself, including security patterns, or on its context, and due to neglected security patterns, it is not possible to easily handle security-related software evolution or any analysis thereof. An industrial approach to security modelling is "Security Development Lifecyle" (SDL) [Sho14], a practical process that is developed to accompany security-related decision-making. It is consisted of two catalogues: (1) STRIDE to model threats based on fix categories (e.g. tampering, denial of service, etc.) and (2) DREAD to evaluate the modelled threats based on possible impacts and a numeric scale. However, considering only the attack side of the security leads eventually to inconsistencies between threat possibilities and applied security solutions.

An extension to UML is SecureUML [LBD02], which focuses solely on the system access. It specifies constraints for authorisation to define role-based access control and analyse discrepancies. Another extension is UMLSec [Jür05], [Ahm+17]. It introduces predefined profiles containing security-related stereotypes to cover security properties on architectural level, which are used to represent the component roles and the threat abilities that can exploit these roles. SecVolution [J B+15], on the other hand, builds upon it to support evolution. It provides a process model (consisted of a system and maintenance model) for security requirement elicitation, which combines the experiences gathered during development and possible evolution scenarios, which can support co-evolution. These extensions therefore focus on single principles of security (access control and information flow respectively) in an information system, and the analysis and evolution supports are either non-existent or can be limited in representing generic security information. This is why we see the need for a more expressive and adaptable model based solely on using security patterns and their analysis.

9.4.6 Summary

Software security is a very fragile quality attribute that is dependent on a lot of factors existing from run time, which are mainly unknown, to software architects during design time. So architects can only assume and document these assumptions if at all. After a brief introduction regarding the security patterns is given, this section presents in this matter the contextual security patterns approach, which mainly incorporates two sides of security (threats/attacks and solutions/mitigations) into an extension for ADLs and combine them via explicitly documented and accordingly formalised context assumptions called prerequisites. This extension handles security concerns on architectural level, in which the context-related information of security patterns and attacks are explicitly gathered and structurally documented. These prerequisites are used as a metric for model-based security analysis, which checks the validity of applied security patterns based on the software system state or run-time information. That way, software architects can further use analysis results to foresee the impact of evolutionary changes and trace them on system models and accordingly during software evolution, which could ease the process of maintaining the secure state of the underlying system.

9.5 Self-adaptive Security Maintenance at Run Time by Identifying Suspicious Behaviour

An observation made is that evolution in the system environment may lead to vulnerabilities or ineffective security mechanisms at run time. For example, a new attack pattern may be invented or a regulation might call for a more rigid privacy policy. The information system remains insecure or must be shut down until the security violation has been fixed. Finding and implementing a solution takes time. In cases where the system needs to be shut down, this is costly or may even be impossible for large and long-living systems. To get a security fix right, by considering all involved artefacts such as requirements, UML models, or code units, and respecting the system design to avoid architecture decay, this even more calls for careful acting. The design-time approaches, as discussed so far, focus on design-time artefacts and thus fall short on analysing vulnerabilities coming from the source code or the execution context. Moreover, there are security requirements that are hard to check statically, for instance when mechanisms like Java reflection are used [EL02, Mur+98, CM04]. Apart from that, systems that are requested to be available via the Internet and without downtime are more likely to be affected by an attack previously undocumented. In this cases, to avoid downtime or to narrow the attack surface, it is desirable to also detect new attacks, for example based on suspicious behaviour. This section presents work towards monitoring and adapting a long-living system at run time.

9.5.1 Overview

Maintaining a critical system needs expertise in the field of security. Although more and more violations can be prevented by technical means, the experience and expertise of security experts to deal with new attacks remain irreplaceable because many processes and approaches cannot be fully automated.

According to the 2017 Global Information Security Workforce Study, commissioned by the Information System Security Certification Consortium $(ISC)^2$, Europe will face a gap of 350,000 cyber-security professionals by the year 2022 [Int17]. For example, even organisations like the European Telecommunications Standards Institute (ETSI) only employ external security experts for a limited time [Hou+10]. Thus, security experts are few in number, and it is reasonable to support them to become as efficient as possible. Technical mechanisms for preserving security must be complemented by procedures and cognitive support for human experts who are willing to share their knowledge; they must be empowered to do so at the least effort possible.

Challenges include eliciting and modelling adaption requirements. A static view on the system's security is not sufficient. Therefore, multifaceted run-time information of the software system needs to be continuously monitored and analysed

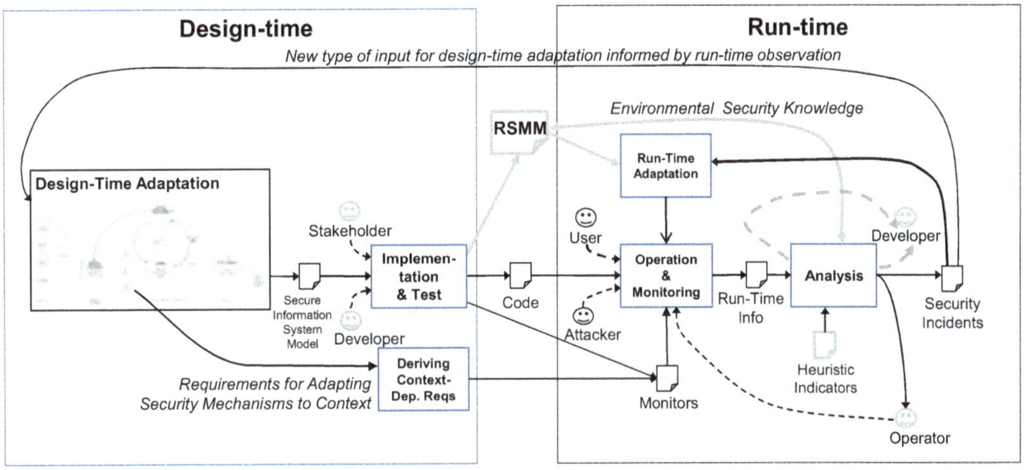

Fig. 9.19 Overview of the SecVolution run-time approach using the information flow syntax described in Fig. 9.2

with respect to given security requirements. Current infrastructure, configurations, and deployment information must be monitored, as well as relevant aspects of user behaviour. When an incident or a suspicious behaviour occurs, the adaption mechanism must make a decision as quickly as possible. After a system has been designed, it is implemented and gets deployed. To react to security breaches during run time, a specific security mechanism must be selected and put into operation and may be adapted to a certain extent.

Figure 9.19 presents the overview on the run-time security adaption approach. The rectangle captioned *Design-Time Adaption* captures the design-time process, as presented in Fig. 9.3. The outcome of this process is a model of the secure information system model. After the implementation and testing phase, executable code exists that is run and operated by the user. In contrast to the system design phase, an additional attack vector occurs from attackers challenging the system at run time. To bridge the gap between design time and run time, an extension of the security maintenance model, called *Run-Time Security Maintenance Model* (RSMM), is proposed. During the operation phase, the system is monitored. Monitoring data are continuously recorded and analysed. Supported by heuristic indicators, incoming monitor findings are assessed, with the assistance of the developer and operator. When a security incident is ascertained, it is decided if there needs to be a run-time or design-time adaption. Run-time adaptions are accomplished by adapting the running system. Moreover, security incidents discovered during run time can also trigger design-time changes.

In Sect. 5.4, an approach is presented to externalise tacit knowledge during run time. The focus is to gain insight of how users interact with the system to learn about which system requirements should be adapted, removed, or added. The focus of the run-time approach presented in this section is to assume a mostly static set of security requirements and check the system's compliance to this requirements, in conjunction with evolving security knowledge. While tacit knowledge in Sect. 5.4 is used for the way a user interacts with a system and which features he uses in which way, in this section it can be seen as attack sequences an attacker can carry out.

Application: Running Example

As this motivating example, we consider an extension of CoCoME as introduced in Sect. 4.2. For our motivating example, we consider an extension of CoCoME with mobile shopping applications for a CoCoME online store. Mobile shopping applications for a CoCoME online store need to prevent attackers from exploiting entry points like personal data of the other customers, as well as internal business data. Thus, various security mechanisms are used, like cryptographic hashes, to secure authentication procedures (login).

Assume a mobile application (App) for the CoCoME online store that uses the SHA-1 hash-algorithm for the login protocol. This algorithm was considered secure until the year 2005, when a method was published to break the security mechanism [WYY05]. Since the security of the authentication depends directly on the security of the hash algorithm, the developers of the application can react to this change in the security knowledge by replacing the algorithm with another from the SHA-2 family (*design-time mitigation*). The SHA-2 family consists of six similar hash algorithms, each providing a different security level. After the replacement, the application can now choose an appropriate algorithm for a requested connection. More secure algorithms need more computation power and reduce the speed of feedback to the user. Thus, usability and acceptance of the mobile application are at stake, and the client will have to make a compromise between security and usability.

When it was decided to replace the hash function by SHA-2, the developers realised that this would take some time. Since the mobile application generates significant revenues for the company, the mobile application should not be deactivated while performing this update. Therefore, it was decided to take a calculated risk: The company did not want to lose too much business and was willing to accept a certain, limited risk of loss. Since regular user monitoring showed that most customers buy for less than 100 € per month, this limit seemed to be a reasonable compromise: The application was quickly modified to limit the maximal monthly turnover to 100 € per customer. As a result, a few customers might be prevented from spending more money. Most customers, however, would not notice the limit since they spend less money anyway. The company's business is not obstructed, and the turnover is only endangered to a small extent during the time of patching the authentication algorithm. When the new algorithm was in place, the limit could be removed. This strategy ensured that a sufficient degree of security was preserved at all times and with an optimal trade-off to limit negative impact on business.

As computing devices get more powerful, breaking hashes comes within the reach of attackers. Therefore, the weaker variants of the SHA-2 family will also be considered breakable at some future point in time. The system stays the same, but the increasing ability and knowledge of attackers compromise security. Given that the whole family of algorithms is available for implementation now, the system can easily be adapted to prohibit the use of the insecure variants by an automated run-time adaption of the application.

9.5.2 Capturing Context for Security Adaption

As we briefly introduced in Sect. 9.5.1, a detailed view on the system's context is inevitable. Not only the code itself but also the execution context and information that can be gathered during run time, for example using monitoring, needs to be considered. They all belong to environmental aspects that can cause an adaption. Regarding the running example, if an access routine is executed, the corresponding assets may be at risk. Run-time monitoring can issue a warning at the conceptual level, and it can trigger heuristic reasoning. The new run-time extension of the security maintenance model, called *run-time Security Maintenance Model* (RSMM), constitutes as a formalisation of security-related knowledge at run time. When a concept is implemented, several components may be affected. For example, the asset of a password list can be stored in a database. It uses a granularity appropriate for design-time concepts (e.g. threats or assets). However, it is not sufficient to protect the database; instead, related access mechanisms, user interfaces, and supporting components need to be considered as potential entry points, too. Run-time monitoring [AJY11] and process mining [Aal11] can help spot executed parts of the implementation.

9.5.3 Leveraging Run-Time Information to Support Design-Time Security Adaption

A system during run time produces various kinds of data that may be relevant for assessing the system's security. Regarding the running example, monitoring CoCoME system generates various monitoring data: Not only internal server operations may be relevant for the system's security, but also the interaction that every customer with the system has is recorded. Not only call traces but also database transactions and application server messages can be put into an anomaly analysis.

Natural language analysis can play a role here. A family of heuristics can treat identifiers in source code as "expressions in natural language" (making use of results from work such as [DMJ08]). Through this assumption, certain identifiers are treated like words and can be mapped to security concepts such as *entry point* or *asset*. In an isolated environment, normal behaviour can be recorded. During run time, the monitored behaviour can be compared with the recorded one, also taking heuristic indicators into account to distinguish compliant behaviour from an ongoing security requirement violation. A procedure of selecting appropriate mechanisms to monitor the desired security requirements is annotated in the model. For example, systems can be proactively monitored to predict potential violations [Zha+11]. The source code corresponding to the model is then instrumented accordingly.

9.5.4 Heuristics-Based Run-Time Assessment to Detect Security Requirement Violations

Run-time information consists of fine-grained representations of what happened during the execution of code and models. For example, log files or code can be monitored to trace the execution of software. A large amount of monitoring data must be managed for complex information systems.

A heuristic indicator associates a defined input (e.g. sequence of monitored data) with a conclusion. For example, a heuristic indicator may conclude from a sequence of repeated online orders that there is a case of misuse underway, trying to bypass the 100 € limit regarding the running example. This could be a violation of a corresponding requirement. Heuristics use shortcuts and unproven conclusions, but they are fast and can be used earlier than an algorithm with a supposedly higher recall and precision [TF97].

9.5.5 Adaption During Run Time

As we argued in Sect. 9.5.1 and illustrated as part of the running example, adaption during run time is a necessary kind of reaction when a security issue is detected that can be reacted upon with a restricted risk. The system model can additionally be annotated to support run-time adaptions in order to reflect implementation details into the model level. This information is used to decide which of the security requirements can be mitigated at design time and which one can only be treated at run time. Furthermore, this can be used to cope with code that is initially generated but then manually altered. The challenge here is to have tracing of security requirements beyond the design time, for which preliminary work exists [L M+10, AJY11].

If a violation of security requirements is detected, appropriate mitigation actions must be taken. Violations such as loss of privacy, information leaks, or attacks on specific assets may be mitigated through different actions. For example, the system can be reconfigured, for example to use alternative encryption mechanisms, or an adaption can limit the access for certain roles. For example, roles that have access over the Internet can only access the system via a virtual private network if data are at risk and transmission over insecure connections should be reduced. Mitigation actions may be inferred from measured behaviour and additional information [EAS14]. The definition of fail-safe components can support an immediate reaction with minimal reduction of features. Detected security violations are reported to an expert system that retrieves priority and reaction knowledge from the modelled security knowledge. This escalation will use techniques for design-time mitigation.

9.5.6 Related Work

Regarding the question of when a system should be adapted to preserve security, [SDB14] presents how attacks on cyber-physical systems can be observed during run-time.

[ES10] introduces an approach to realise security adaptation at run-time using an ontology that takes context into account. This approach falls short of handling the automatic monitoring of the running system. Our results show that it is feasible to combine monitoring techniques with security adaptation techniques.

[Sal+12] gives an approach for modelling assets that can be used to model the requirements and (security) goals of a system. However, there is currently no security knowledge support. Our approach provides a seamless way of accompanying the development and maintenance process with context knowledge.

[Nhl+15] supports monitoring assumptions about security requirements at run time. However, this approach focuses on security of entities and does not address software development.

[Omo+12, Omo+13] focuses on privacy and the requirements-level within greenfield development of systems, while our goal is to cover security properties, to support also long-living systems (including legacy systems), to cover knowledge evolution, and to also cover system execution.

9.5.7 Summary

The SecVolution run-time approach has identified the following challenges:

- An evolution of the system environment may affect the system's security at run time.
- There are security properties that cannot be checked solely by regarding the system design. Security properties can depend on data that are stored in databases or can generally vary during run time, like access control configurations.
- Mitigating security incidents that arise during run time need to be acted upon also during run time. Investigating and adapting the system design to recover its security is not timely enough if the system needs to stay in service meanwhile.

The SecVolution run-time approach tackles these challenges. The run-time Security Maintenance Model (RSMM) bridges the gap between the design time and run-time development phases of a system. It connects artefacts like code that is based on the system design, as well as run-time relevant data like application server configuration. Run-time monitors are proposed depending on the security properties required by the system design. Using techniques like process mining and heuristic indicators, raw monitoring data can be used to map running code to parts of the system design. By comparing anticipated and actual system behaviour, supported by heuristics, suspicious behaviour can be detected. By making a system run-time adaptable, ad hoc reactions to security incidents can be realised. By providing alternative components or fail-safe states, for example, controlled precautions can be already part of the system design to deactivate critical system parts or minimise the risk when a security incident occurs during run time.

9.6 Anomaly Detection for Evolving Software Controlled Production Systems at Run Time

9.6.1 Overview

Another area for maintaining security during software evolution is Cyber-Physical Systems. Cyber-Physical Systems are software systems that interact with their physical environment (e.g. embedded systems, automated production systems) and are connected to the Internet. This section focuses on Cyber-Physical Systems in the area of production systems that consist of physical and cyber components that are getting into connection with each other in situation-dependent ways [Mon14]. At the same time, production systems collect information of the state of the production process, and based on these information their process is controlled and analysed. These functionalities are business and safety critical and should be designed, developed, and certified with care [IEC05]. Because various components of the system depend on each other, a secure design implies that every part of the process automation equipment is required to operate within the boundaries of its specifications [ÅAGB11]. Therefore, production system operated in a cyber-physical environment must carefully detect violations of their specification during the whole evolution process, which includes, as Monostri et al. stated, a "special emphasis on security aspects" as a major challenge. One of the most relevant behaviour of production systems is the interdisciplinary behaviour resulting from the interaction of the software with its environment [Vog+15c, Lad+13a]. Therefore, unknown, unwanted, and undocumented changes in the interdisciplinary behaviour have to be detected in the system in order to continuously operate under the specification and to ensure a secured system.

The here presented anomaly detection approach of the FYPA^{2}C project within the priority program tries to find behaviour changes as potential indicators for newly arising risks to the security during run time. In this way, the interdisciplinary behaviour is directly considered as an information source for knowledge that can affect security. The behaviour is expressed in models of the machine state of every subcomponent of a production system. These models are learned during a phase in which the system is assumed to show a well-specified and secured behaviour. To identify anomalies, actual behaviour observed in control signals of the current system operation is compared to previously learned behaviour specifications. These anomalies may increase the vulnerability of a system because they express unknown and undocumented behaviour changes that should be checked regarding the current security requirements. The anomalies can be intended or not intended during the evolution, which means that the change resulting in the anomaly might be reverted when it is not intended or transferred to the operator for adaptation. The adaptation is left in the hand of an experienced operator, but the operator is supported by given reasonable information about anomalies.

9.6.2 Detection Model: Machine State Petri Net

The model for anomaly detection used here describes the behaviour of a machine in terms of its state changes. The state of a discrete production system is described by a set of binary sensor and actor signals. Therefore, the behaviour of the system is described by the sequence of states that are observed in the production system. One state is characterised by a set of attribute-value pairs. One attribute describes one specific signal of the state, and the value of the signal is its elemental state. Consequently, the global state of a production system is expressed by the complete set of all elemental states. These set is, in case of the targeted discrete manufacturing systems like the Pick-and-Place Unit, deterministic and locally iteratively observable. The change between one elemental state to another is defined by an event. Therefore, the production system acts like an event-based system, whose events can be observed during the operation by monitoring its event bus, that is the digital sensor and actor signals.

The analysis of production processes is generally based on an analysis of models that reflect the behaviour of the production system [LFL16]. These models are systematically used as primary development artefacts, which are often iteratively developed and evolve during the production system's life cycle [Vog+15a]. The models serve as a formal specification of the dynamic interaction within the production system, for example to describe the signal behaviour. They can be learned by using learning techniques based on the observation of states (see Chap. 6 for details about learning methods). Different model types exist to express the behaviour of a production system. One of them is Petri Nets, which are a bipartite graph. This graph expresses the system states as places and the state changes as transitions. Places and transitions form the graph's nodes, which are linked with the arcs (edges).

Since the detection models used for detecting anomalies are based on the state changes, they are henceforth called *Machine State Petri Net (MSPN)*. A MSPN is a Petri Net $\langle P, T, F, M \rangle$, where P is the set of places, T is the set of transitions, and $F \subseteq (P \times T) \cup (T \times P)$ is the set of directed arcs between places and transitions. Furthermore, M is the set of tokens allocated to the places and describing the state of the MSPN. Each transition $t \in T$ is annotated with one or several events $e_i\ (t)$. Every event describes a specific binary signal change and can be observed at the system bus. All events annotated on a single transition occur nearly at the same time. The maximum time difference between these events is described by a threshold time T_{thresh}. The set of all events annotated on transition t is referred to as $\tilde{e}(t)$. Each transition has exactly one preplace and one postplace. Accordingly, an MSPN has the same properties as that of a state graph Petri Net (see, e.g., [DA10]). One property is that the number of tokens in the Petri Net remains constant. To describe the timing of an MSPN, each transition in T is annotated with a double $\langle d_{min}, d_{max} \rangle$. The included elements are:

- d_{min}: Minimum activation duration
- d_{max}: Maximum activation duration

A transition is called activated if and only if its preplaces are marked with a token. Furthermore, a transition t can fire if and only if:

1. It is activated.
2. The activation duration of t is between its annotated d_{min} and d_{max}.
3. All annotated events $\tilde{e}\,(t)$ occurred within a timing threshold T_{thresh}.

Such signal-based models can be, for example, learned during a phase in which the system is well specified and secured (cf. learning algorithms of Chap. 6).

9.6.3 Anomaly Detection Mechanism

For anomaly detection, the behaviour of the system is compared with the behaviour of its previously modelled MSPN. To do so, each event occurring in the real system is passed to the MSPN. The occurrence time t_{occ} of the kth event is henceforth referred to as $t_{occ}\,(e_k)$. If the events contradict a valid behaviour of the MSPN, an anomaly is detected. If not, the marking of the MSPN is updated according to the incoming events. The following events are defined for MSPN:

1. There is no activated transition that has the occurred e_k event annotated:
$$\nexists t : t\ activated \wedge e_k \subseteq \tilde{e}\,(t) \tag{9.1}$$
This anomaly detects changes in terms of new introduced signals, that is when a new sensor is implemented in the system.
2. There is an activated transition t, and the occurring event is annotated on it. But the time difference between the current event and the last occurred event that is not part of $\tilde{e}\,(t)$ (i.e. the last event that triggered a firing) is smaller than the annotated minimum activation duration $d_{min}\,(t)$:
$$\exists e_{k-n} \notin \tilde{e}\,(t)\,, e_k \in \tilde{e}\,(t) : (t_{occ}\,(e_k) - t_{occ}\,(e_{k-n})) > d_{min}\,(t) \tag{9.2}$$
If this anomaly occurs, it gives a hint that some behaviour of the observed system is carried out faster as given by the model.

3. The time difference between the actual time t_{now} and the last occurred event e_k is bigger than the annotated d_{max} of all activated transitions:

$$t_{now} - t_{occ}(e_k) > d_{max}(t), \forall t : activated \tag{9.3}$$

In contrast to the previous one, this anomaly indicates that some behaviour is slowed down.

4. An event occurred that is part of $\tilde{e}(t)$ of an activated transition t, but not all other events of $\tilde{e}(t)$ occurred within the given time threshold:

$$\exists e_k \in \tilde{e}(t) : (t_{now} - t_{occ}(e_k)) > T_{thresh} \tag{9.4}$$

If this anomaly occurs, events that should occur (nearly) at the same time do not show this behaviour any more.

9.6.4 Example: Using the PPU Case Study

The presented anomaly detection method has been applied on the PPU case study plant and tested on the PPU during various runs. To apply the approach, I/O events of the PLC controlling the PPU have been observed. All sensor events (PLC inputs, e.g. triggers of light barriers detecting a workpiece), as well as all actuator setpoint events (PLC outputs, e.g. command motor on or off), have been passed to the corresponding MSPN. Technically, the events have been compared with a state automata transformed from the MSPN. Figure 9.20 shows an example of an MSPN

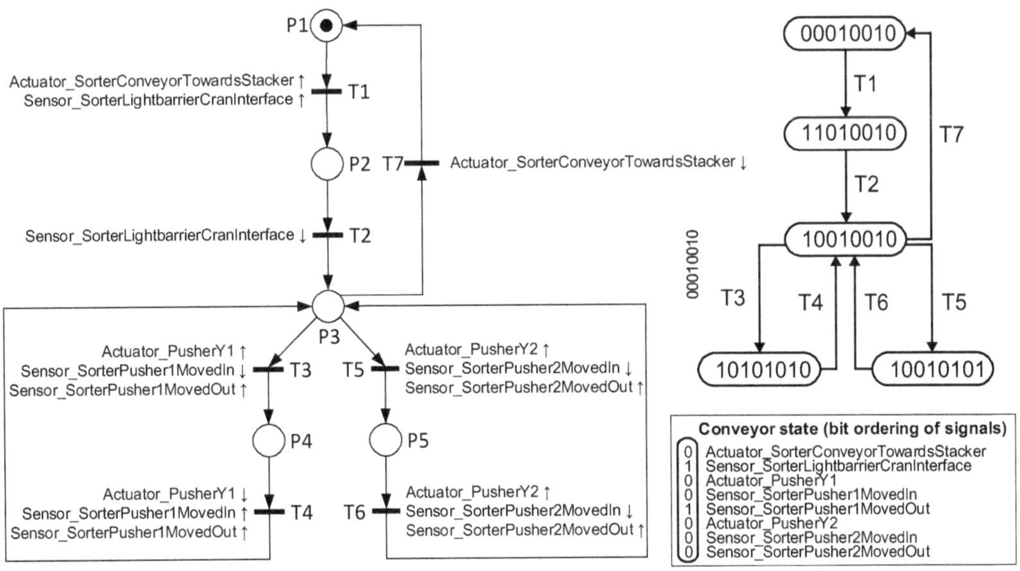

Fig. 9.20 MSPN of the PPU conveyor in Sc10 and corresponding state graph

describing the behaviour of the conveyor of the PPU in Scenario Sc10 (for scenario description, see [Vog+14b]). On the right side of Fig. 9.20, the constructed state graph is shown. For simplicity, the annotated timings are not shown here.

The evolution scenarios of the PPU have been executed consecutively from Sc1 to Sc12. MSPNs describing a specific scenario have been used for anomaly detection of the corresponding following scenario. For example, the shown MSPN from Sc10 has been used for anomaly detection in Sc11. Each evolution scenario could be detected with the anomalies defined above, as long as the evolution scenario resulted in a change of behaviour observable on the PLC I/Os. The change from Sc1 to Sc2, for example, could not be detected because it only includes an increase in the capacity of the output ramp. There is no change in the timing or order of any sensor or actuator events. Therefore, this change could not be detected. Most of the evolution scenarios of the PPU include the introduction of new sensors or actuators and could accordingly be detected by anomaly detection. In addition, further abnormal behaviour has been generated to test the anomaly detection mechanism. This includes arbitrary sensor triggering (e.g. manually triggering a light barrier), as well as stopping or slowing down workpiece transportation by removing or holding a workpiece. The anomaly detection mechanism was able to detect these anomalies during run time.

For further information regarding the application of the anomaly detection method for supporting evolution, see [LFL16, Lad+14b, Lad+15b].

9.6.5 Related Work: Finding Behaviour Anomalies

Methods for recognising behaviour changes are needed to support the evolution of systems that may change unintentionally or without model adaptation and analysis. One method includes observing the system behaviour on the software interface and comparing it with a model representing the last known behaviour. Such a method is called *anomaly detection*. The anomaly detection method described in this section is mainly oriented on fault detection known from fault diagnosis, for example [Ise06, HKW03, AA13, NF15, RLL10, AT12, LL11]. But, in contrast to fault detection, it is not assumed that a detected anomaly is faulty behaviour. A semi-automated process supporting to decide if a detected anomaly is intended or at least acceptable can be found in [Lad+14a]. It is assumed that the behaviour of the interdisciplinary system is fully discrete on its control interface, that is it can be observed in terms of input/output events of the software. This assumption holds, for example for discrete manufacturing systems [Chr06]. However, further methods also deal with continuous systems [Ise06] or hybrid systems [NF15]. The models to compare with are assumed to be time-based models having the corresponding events annotated on their transitions. The method introduced here describes a subset of the method introduced in [Lad+15a], where also a learning algorithm for automatic model generation is presented.

9.6.6 Summary

The here presented approach implements parts of the three-layered framework (Fig. 9.1) for production systems at run time. On the bottom layer, the interdisciplinary process of a production system is monitored in a non-invasive manner based on input/output signals of the production system. On the middle layer, this monitoring data are analysed regarding behaviour anomalies. Therefore, an anomaly detection method for Cyber-Physical Systems was presented that compares actual system behaviour at run-time with intended system behaviour expressed in signal-based models. If the observed behaviour contradicts the behaviour of the models, an anomaly as a potential risk is reported on a high-level model description to the top layer of the general framework. At this level, the conclusion regarding the potential risk and impact on the overall security and a suitable reaction to the anomaly can be made. The approach was evaluated on different scenarios of the PPU case study. Future work regarding anomaly detection includes to detect failures of the system based on an interdisciplinary a priori system model and finding anomalies of one production system by comparing its behaviour with the cyber-physical context of a distributed knowledge carrying network.

9.7 Conclusion

Preserving security in evolving software systems is challenging due to four main issues: First, security-relevant knowledge may only be available in a non- or semi-formal manner. Second, the impact of available knowledge to the security of the system at hand needs to be assessed. Third, as soon as the system is deemed insecure, a proper reaction to re-establishing security must be derived. Fourth, reactions may need to be performed automatically in a running software system.

In this chapter, we addressed these four challenges:

Diverse non- or semi-formal sources of security knowledge. The approach shown in Sect. 9.2 harnesses natural language processing to identify security requirements in given requirement descriptions, thus allowing to select a small portion of the overall requirements that deserve specific attention from experts. Security requirements can be captured systematically using a concept of nested ontologies that represent global and system-specific security knowledge. The approach in Sect. 9.3 can then be used to create a formal bidirectional mapping between security model information attached to architecture specification models and the program code that implements the security architecture. The approach in Sect. 9.4 extends the security knowledge by formalising and documenting contextual information from—if only—implicitly made assumptions about the security-related design decisions and from the system run time. These explicitly captured context prerequisites provide a formal relation between threats or vulnerabilities and security patterns on architectural level.

Assessing the impact of new security knowledge. The approach in Sect. 9.2 includes a concept of co-evolution rules that are triggered by specific changes to the security knowledge. The rules are designed in such a way that security weaknesses resulting from the changed knowledge can be detected and repaired. The approach in Sect. 9.3 relates security information to architecture model elements, which is also used for monitoring the application security. The approach in Sect. 9.4 uses the captured security prerequisites to assess the architectural validity of the security elements. In case of evolutionary changes to the software itself or in its context, prerequisites are used as a parameter for the architectural security analysis to check whether an attack type can then exploit a vulnerability or whether a security pattern still mitigates a specific threat. The approach in Sect. 9.5 proposes the use of run-time monitors for security properties required by the system design. Using techniques like process mining and heuristic indicators, raw monitoring data can be used to map running code to parts of the system design. The approach also proposes to compare anticipated and actual system behaviour to detect suspicious behaviour; however, it leaves open how this comparison is realised. A solution for the domain of production automation system is offered by the approach in Sect. 9.6, which expresses behaviour in learned models as a system specification, which is compared to actual system behaviour to find relevant violation at run time. These anomalies are provided to a human operator as high-level descriptions of suspicious behaviour.

Guiding architects and developers to (re)establish security. The approach in Sect. 9.2 proposes co-evolution steps to the human developer. A model-based security verification strategy is used to efficiently determine whether a particular co-evolution restores security requirements that were satisfied before the evolution step. The approach in Sect. 9.4 persists the extended knowledge in reusable extensible model-based catalogues. They are integrated into software architectures using tailored profiles and support architects in decision-making processes in case evolutionary changes impact the secure state of the system. The approach in Sect. 9.6 provides identified anomalies to a human operator as high-level descriptions of suspicious behaviour. By establishing an anomaly detection mechanism at run time, the approach guides human operators to find potential vulnerability in a complex, interdisciplinary environment in order to allow him to (re-)establish security by adapting the CPS or its environment.

Adapting the system to ensure and restore security. The approach in Sect. 9.5 makes a system run-time adaptable to realise ad hoc reactions to security incidents. By providing adequate precautions at design time, such as alternative components or fail-safe states, the system can be adapted at run time by switching between the available components or deactivating critical system parts. This way, the risk when a security incident occurs during run time is reduced.

In concert, these contributions allow to systematically capture, evaluate, and react to the evolving security knowledge. Based on these contributions, architects and developers are guided in addressing possible changes to the security knowledge and the resulting security loopholes in advance. Rather than in the ad hoc security engineering style of "fixing loopholes", security is managed in a systematic and by-design manner, thus allowing to better protect valuable assets in the face of a constantly changing environment.

9.8 Further Reading

Capturing and Leveraging Context Knowledge to Preserve Security Requirements During Design and Run Time At the time of writing, there is ongoing work on improving this part of the approach, especially focusing on the run-time phase and coupling design time and run time. Initial publications already exist [Bür+18, VKK17]. Moreover, research results are brought into the CARiSMA platform [Ahm+17].[1] Relevant results also have been produced by taking part in the ViSion project [AJ16].[2] The project is focused on privacy, which can be considered highly related to security. The contribution focuses on model-based privacy analyses of socio-technical systems.

Integrating Security Models with Program Code The integration of architecture models with code is subject to the work of Konersmann [Kon18]. It is based on the idea of embedded models by Balz [Bal11]. The tools for creating and executing translations between architecture-related program code and models are available on https://codeling.de. Konersmann et al. describe variants of this approach, for example for integrating deployment model information [KH16] or behaviour models [KG15] with program code and the use of integrated model information for locating and understanding errors [Kon14].

Anomaly Detection in Production Systems at Run Time Modelling the state of production system in signal-based Petri Nets has been presented by Ladiges et al. in [Lad+15a]. Further, anomaly detection is also defined for the material flow of a production system in [Lad+15c]. Malicious anomalies and their relation to production system is classified by Reichert et al. [Rei+17]. How to handle such anomalies within an ongoing evolution process is shown in [Lad+14a], and a fitting semi-automated decision process with a human in the loop targeting

[1] https://rgse.uni-koblenz.de/carisma/.

[2] https://cordis.europa.eu/project/rcn/194888_en.html.

anomalies of production system is presented in [Lad+14b]. Finally, Haubeck et al. [Hau+14a, HLF18] lay out how changes and their resulting anomalies can be managed within a knowledge carrying software.

Chapter 10
Learning from Evolution for Evolution

Stefan Kögel, Matthias Tichy, Abhishek Chakraborty, Alexander Fay, Birgit Vogel-Heuser, Christopher Haubeck, Gabriele Taentzer, Timo Kehrer, Jan Ladiges, Lars Grunske, Mattias Ulbrich, Safa Bougouffa, Sinem Getir, Suhyun Cha, Udo Kelter, Winfried Lamersdorf, Kiana Busch, Robert Heinrich, and Sandro Koch

S. Kögel · M. Tichy (✉)
Institut für Softwaretechnik und Programmiersprachen, Universität Ulm, Ulm, Germany
e-mail: stefan.koegel@uni-ulm.de; matthias.tichy@uni-ulm.de

A. Chakraborty · A. Fay · J. Ladiges
Helmut-Schmidt-Universität, Fakultät für Maschinenbau, Professur für Automatisierungstechnik, Hamburg, Germany
e-mail: chakraba@hsu-hh.de; alexander.fay@hsu-hh.de; jan.ladiges@hsu-hh.de

B. Vogel-Heuser · S. Bougouffa · S. Cha
Technische Universität München, Lehrstuhl für Automatisierung und Informationssysteme, Garching, Germany
e-mail: vogel-heuser@tum.de; safa.bougouffa@tum.de; suhyun.cha@tum.de

C. Haubeck · W. Lamersdorf
Universität Hamburg, MIN-Fakultät, Fachbereich Informatik, Hamburg, Germany
e-mail: haubeck@informatik.uni-hamburg.de; lamersd@informatik.uni-hamburg.de

G. Taentzer
Philipps-Universität Marburg, Fachbereich Mathematik und Informatik, Marburg, Germany
e-mail: taentzer@informatik.uni-marburg.de

T. Kehrer
Institut für Informatik, Humboldt-Universität zu Berlin, Berlin, Germany
e-mail: timo.kehrer@informatik.hu-berlin.de

L. Grunske · S. Getir
Institut für Informatik, Humboldt-Universität zu Berlin, Johann-von-Neumann-Haus, Berlin, Germany
e-mail: grunske@informatik.hu-berlin.de; getir@informatik.hu-berlin.de

M. Ulbrich
Institute of Theoretical Informatics, Karlsruhe Institute of Technology (KIT), Karlsruhe, Germany
e-mail: ulbrich@kit.edu

U. Kelter
Praktische Informatik/Softwaretechnik, Fachbereich Elektrotechnik und Informatik, Universität - GH - Siegen, Siegen, Germany
e-mail: kelter@informatik.uni-siegen.de

R. Reussner et al. (eds.), *Managed Software Evolution*,
https://doi.org/10.1007/978-3-030-13499-0_10

Missing knowledge about the system is often one of the root causes of failed software evolution in practice. For example, the well-known failed maiden launch of the Ariane 5 rocket [Dow97] can be attributed partly to missing knowledge about the behaviour of a software system reused from the Ariane 4 rocket. The old software was integrated into the Ariane 5 rocket, which, however, had a different flight trajectory compared to the Ariane 4 rocket. That integration problem led to a value conversion error eventually causing the self-destruction of the rocket.

This very costly error serves as an illustrative example of the effects of missing knowledge during the evolution of systems. One of the focus areas of the priority program aims at providing "Knowledge Carrying Software", that is avoiding missing knowledge in the first place. The other focus areas, "Methods and Processes" and "Platforms and Environments for Evolution", enable knowledge-carrying software.

For successful evolution, knowledge not only about a piece of software but also about its environment, hardware, network, other software, libraries, and ecosystem is needed. Furthermore, users are an important part of the environment, and thus knowledge about the number of users, their different roles as stakeholders in the software, and their behaviour is equally important. For the software itself, knowledge about its structure, that is architecture and design, and its behaviour, is required.

Based on the joint automation case study, the Pick and Place Unit (PPU) (see Chap. 4), several projects in the priority program address the process of acquiring such missing knowledge, that is they support the learning of missing knowledge as a prerequisite for successful software evolution.

Those projects provide different approaches to learning. One group of approaches takes a look at *past* evolutions of the software. This enables, for example, the identification of typical evolution steps or the understanding of how the evolution of one part of the software triggers changes in another software part.

Another group of approaches addresses the *present* state of the software and the impact of software evolution. Particularly, those approaches enable understanding and assessing how a planned software evolution affects the satisfaction of requirements. A complementary aspect is to learn about the behaviour of the system, including its environment, to ensure that non-functional requirements are satisfied.

The final group of approaches addresses *future* evolutions. For example, future evolutions can be semi-automatically predicted based on the learned knowledge, for example, about past evolutions done by engineers on the same system or similar systems.

In summary, the approaches support engineers to understand the *past* evolution of a system, assess *present* evolution scenarios, as well as recommend *future* evolution scenarios. Hence, they enable *learning from evolutions for evolutions*.

K. Busch · R. Heinrich · S. Koch
Institute for Program Structures and Data Organization, Karlsruhe Institute of Technology (KIT), Karlsruhe, Germany
e-mail: kiana.busch@kit.edu; robert.heinrich@kit.edu; sandro.koch@kit.edu

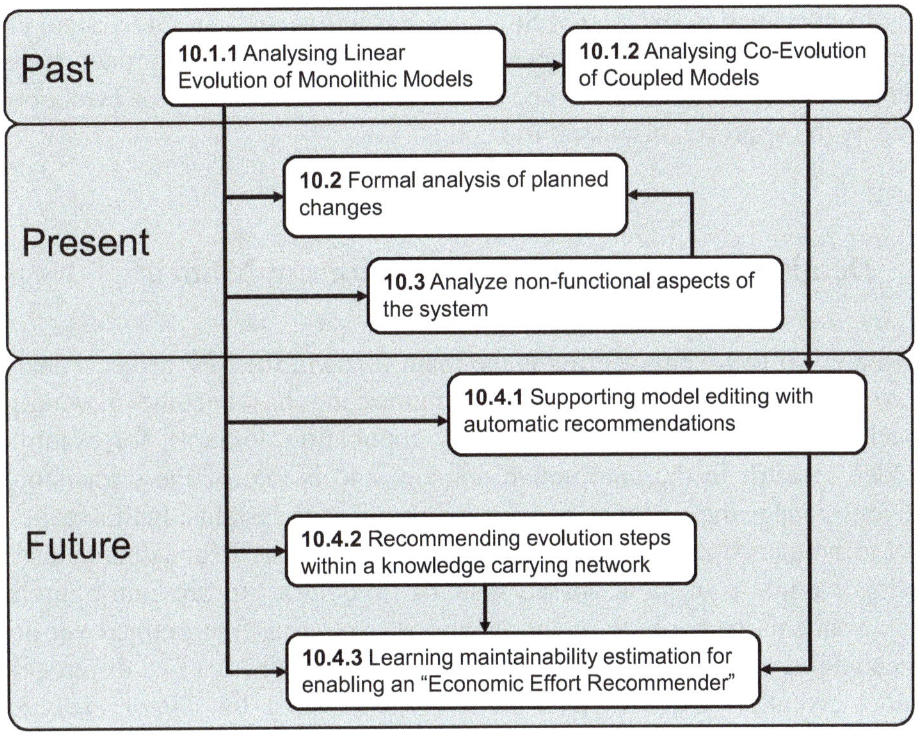

Fig. 10.1 Relations between the subchapters

Figure 10.1 shows these approaches and their relations. Section 10.1 covers the approaches analysing *past evolutions*, Sects. 10.2 and 10.3 cover *present evolutions*, and Sect. 10.4 covers *future evolutions*.

Past The foundation of the other presented approaches is the detailed analysis of historical changes. The approach of Sect. 10.1.1 analyses two versions of models to derive partially ordered sets of detailed changes reflecting the editing semantics of a particular modelling domain. The approach presented in Sect. 10.1.2 draws on this work to analyse the co-evolution of multiple models. Particularly, it supports the computation of co-evolution metrics, which show how much changes in one model result in changes in other models.

Present Two categories of approaches support the evolution of the current system. In Sect. 10.2, functional properties of the current system for small changes are verified using formal verification approaches. Section 10.3 contains two approaches to analyse the non-functional behaviour of systems. On the one hand, timed Petri Nets are learned from behavioural traces of the running system in order to analyse performance and flexibility. On the other hand, Markov chains are learned based on the running system under an evolving environment to continuously check the satisfaction of reliability requirements.

Future Finally, three approaches for assessing and recommending changes for future system evolutions are covered by Sect. 10.4. The first approach in Sect. 10.4.1 supports recommending model evolutions based on the approach for analysing past evolutions presented in Sect. 10.1. Similarly, evolution steps of one system can be applied in future evolutions to other similar systems using the approach presented in Sect. 10.4.2. Third, economic aspects in the recommendations of evolutions are covered by the approach discussed in Sect. 10.4.3.

10.1 Detailed Analysis of Past Evolutions of Models

Model-based software engineering is the main focus of the SPP projects analysing past evolutions. Model-based software engineering has become a widespread approach for developing software in many application domains, for example for embedded systems in the automotive domain, and is one of the cornerstones to effectively manage the evolution of long-living software systems. In this section, we present techniques that have been developed in the SPP as a fundamental basis for analysing evolutions of model-based systems. In contrast to previous approaches, our achievements particularly enable analyses exploiting fine-grained yet precise and meaningful information about model changes. We consider two different kinds of model evolution. First, in Sect. 10.1.1, we consider the *linear evolution of monolithic models*, that is the chronological evolution of models that are treated as self-contained development documents. As a second kind of evolution, we address the *co-evolution of coupled models* in Sect. 10.1.2, that is the parallel evolution of models, which represent different views or aspects of a system but that are logically and/or physically interrelated. Related work is considered in Sect. 10.1.3 before we conclude in Sect. 10.1.4, along with some pointers for further reading in Sect. 10.1.5.

10.1.1 Analysing Linear Evolution of Monolithic Models

Precise and meaningful descriptions of changes between revisions of models of long-living software systems are of utmost importance in understanding and analysing the evolution of a model-based system and can be considered as a basic form of knowledge about a software (see Chap. 1). However, during model evolution, model modifications are often conducted without proper documentation, for example by recording somehow the model changes that are applied. Even if so, the recorded changes are often of minor quality, or they get lost or unusable when models are exchanged across tool boundaries in a model-based development tool chain [Kü08, Ruh+14b, Keh15]. Moreover, revisions of a model may not be created by manual editing at all but, for example, by reverse engineering from other implementation artefacts [Keh+13a] or by observing and learning from the behaviour of an actual running system [Pie+18] (see also Sect. 10.3). Thus, descriptions of model changes often can only be reconstructed by comparing the different versions of a model with each other, that is by using model differencing techniques. Thus, the calculation of a *difference* (also referred to as *delta* in Chap. 2) between two models is one of the most basic operations for supporting

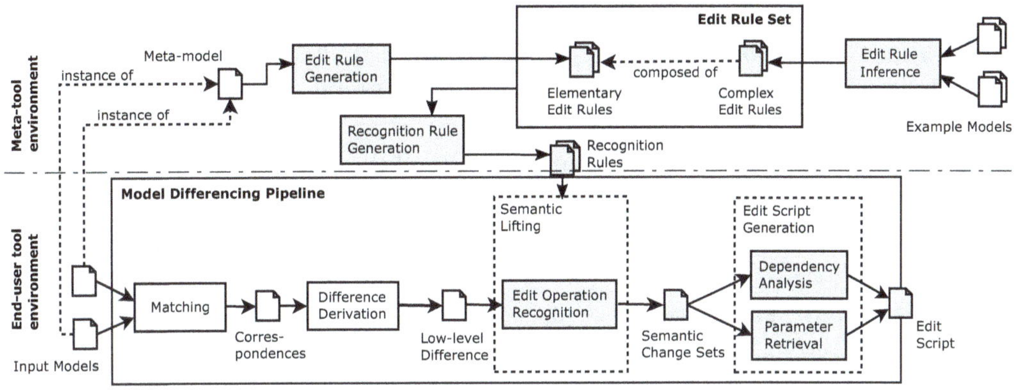

Fig. 10.2 Overview of the MOCA model differencing pipeline and related meta-tool chains

various kinds of model evolution analyses. In this section, we present the model differencing techniques that have been developed in the modular content archives (MOCA) project and that are implemented in the model differencing framework SiLift [Keh+12b], a set of Eclipse plug-ins realised on top of the widely used Eclipse Modeling Framework (EMF) and publicly available from the SiLift website.[1] In the remainder of this section, we first motivate our main technical research goals before we present an overview of our approach for achieving these goals. Finally, we give a selected set of example applications using these techniques for various kinds of evolution analyses and other development tasks in the context of model version and variant management.

Motivation and Goals

Traditional differencing techniques work on textual representations of documents and present document changes in terms of additions and deletions of lines of text. While this produces satisfactory results for source code and other kinds of textual documents, it is commonly agreed that comparing textual representations of models does not produce usable results [BE08, Ema12] and that models should be compared on the basis of graph-based representations. To that end, the internal structure of a model is typically considered as a typed, attributed, partly ordered graph, which is known as the *abstract syntax graph* (ASG) of this model. A meta-model such as, for example, the Unified Modeling Language (UML) meta-model, defines the allowed node and edge types, as well as additional well-formedness rules.

The usual processing pipeline employed by standard model differencing tools consists of the first two steps, depicted in the lower part of Fig. 10.2 (white coloured), referred to as matching and difference derivation: Initially, given two input models that are to be compared, a matching procedure [Kol+09] searches for pairs of corresponding ASG elements, which are considered the same in

[1]http://pi.informatik.uni-siegen.de/projects/SiLift.

both models. Subsequently, a difference is derived as follows: ASG elements not involved in a correspondence are considered to be deleted or created. However, describing model changes based on such primitive graph operations leads to *low-level differences*, which are hard to understand for tool users who are not familiar with the ASG-based representation of models and the related types of nodes and edges defined by a meta-model. Such "meta-model-based difference reports" are not intuitive, are confusing and Are of minor quality for many kinds of model evolution analyses [Alt+09, KKT12].

The main goal of the MOCA project is to lift model differencing techniques to the level of *edit operations* that tool users are familiar with and that capture the true nature of model changes. Elementary operations are the smallest edit operations from a user's point of view, that is they cannot be split into smaller operations, being applicable to a model in a meaningful way. In principle, one can construct arbitrarily many complex edit operations from elementary ones. An important criterion is that a complex edit operation is easier to understand than the single contained elementary edit operations. This includes complex edit operations such as model refactorings and other kinds of evolutionary edit operations that increase the understandability of model changes and that incorporate language-specific editing semantics. Concrete examples may be found later in this chapter in Sect. 10.4. Besides increasing the quality of model differences, the calculation of such high-level differences should scale up to real-world models comprising several thousands of model elements. Finally, since meaningful edit operations are highly specific for a given modelling language, the developed techniques shall be adaptable to domain-specific modelling languages with moderate effort.

Overview of the Approach

An overview of the model differencing approach and techniques developed in the MOCA project is illustrated in Fig. 10.2. As shown in the bottom part of the figure, the differencing of models takes place in several steps. The first two steps, referred to as *matching* and *difference derivation* (white-coloured boxes), constitute the usual model differencing pipeline, as described above. In brief, the matching step identifies the corresponding ASG elements in two models, while the difference derivation step derives a low-level difference in terms of creations and deletions of single ASG elements. The extended differencing pipeline, as developed in the MOCA project, comprises two further steps, which we refer to as *semantic lifting of low-level model differences* and the *generation of edit scripts*, respectively. To be adaptable to a given modelling language, both steps take the edit operations available for this language as configuration input. We use Henshin [Are+10, Str+17], a model transformation language and system based on graph transformation concepts [Ehr+06], in order to specify edit operations (a.k.a. *edit rules*) in a precise, declarative, and rule-based manner. Several meta-tools have been developed in the MOCA project in order to support the development of sets of both elementary and complex edit rules (upper part of Fig. 10.2).

Semantic Lifting of Low-Level Model Differences The goal of this step is to group a potentially large and unstructured set of low-level changes in such a way that model differences are explained in terms of edit operations. To that end, the low-level difference derived from a matching needs to be further processed by a semantic lifting component that identifies sets of low-level changes (called *semantic change sets*) that represent the effect of an edit operation.

In [KKT11], we present a technique for designing tool components that can semantically lift model differences. In our approach, difference information is structurally represented on the level of the ASG, and each edit operation leads to a characteristic change pattern in this difference representation. Thus, finding groups of related low-level changes is basically a pattern matching problem. We use the matching engine of the Henshin interpreter in order to solve this problem. The main task to adapt a semantic lifting component to a given modelling language is to provide a set of so-called *recognition rules*, which find groups of related low-level changes and which annotate these groups accordingly. We automatically derive these recognition rules from their corresponding edit rules.

The recognition rule application algorithm is efficient in the sense that it runs without backtracking. All recognition rules are applied in parallel, which is possible due to the parallel and sequential independence of recognition rules. Since this rule application strategy can lead to too many change sets, that is there can be several alternatives, of which one needs to be chosen eventually, the initial set of semantic change sets must be post-processed in order to obtain a partitioning of the overall set of semantic change sets. This is basically an optimisation problem with respect to some notion of quality of model differences, for example a minimal number of semantic change sets. In [KKT11], we present an efficient heuristic that aims at producing a partitioning comprising a minimal number of change sets. If the set of edit rules used as configuration input is complete in the sense that every possible model difference can be expressed without producing so-called transient effects, it is guaranteed that a partitioning can always be found. Practically, this means that there is an editing sequence in which the effect of every edit operation applied in that sequence is either removed completely by a later operation or is entirely preserved.

Experimental results obtained from different subjects show that the number of editing steps contained in a difference can be drastically compressed by semantic lifting. The compression rates vary depending on the model type and test series. For UML, compression factors of up to 18.0 were measured [KKT11]. Furthermore, results from stress testing our prototypical implementation of the semantic lifting engine show that the approach also scales for models of realistic size.

Generation of Edit Scripts Semantic lifting addresses the question on how to recognise the executions of edit operations in a given low-level difference. However, this technique identifies edit operation executions, also referred to as edit steps, only. This is useful for better understanding changes but not sufficient for some kinds of analyses or for replaying model differences in change propagation scenarios. Actually, two further details are required to generate executable differences, namely the actual *parameters* used as arguments of edit steps, as well as *dependencies* between edit steps. In [KKT13], we introduce an extended kind of model difference, which we refer to as *edit script*. Technically, an edit script is a complex data structure that contains (1) representations of the detected edit operations, including mappings of the parameters to objects in the low-level difference, and (2) representations of dependencies between these edit steps. Each dependency is annotated with information about its reason, for example one step produces model elements used by a later step. From a conceptual point of view, an edit script is a partially ordered set of edit steps.

Techniques for realising the *parameter retrieval* and *dependency analysis* steps in our differencing pipeline have been presented in [KKT13]. A particular challenge is to provide an efficient implementation of the dependency analysis. In general, two edit steps depend on one another if they can be executed in one order and not in the other order or lead to a different effect if executed in the reverse order, that is they do not commute. Obviously, testing this condition for every pair of edit steps is infeasible if model differences get large. To reduce the set of candidates for dependencies that have to be checked, all pairs of edit rules are statically analysed for potential dependencies using *critical pairs* [Ehr+06], which demonstrate a potential dependency between edit rules in a minimal context. Roughly speaking, a potential dependency between a critical pair of rules is an actual one between the applications of these rules if the minimal rule application of a critical pair can be embedded into the actual model changes [KKT13].

Adaptability of the Tool Environment The adaptability of the tool environment to specific (domain-specific) modelling languages has been addressed by various *meta-tools*, as indicated in the upper part of Fig. 10.2. Although being an exchangeable component in our differencing pipeline, our own model matching engine, which is known as the SiDiff model matcher, is adaptable by a dedicated *language for specifying matching strategies* and algorithms [Keh+12a] (not shown in Fig. 10.2. The configuration of the lifting algorithms is supported by an *edit rule generator*, which generates, for a given meta-model, a complete set of elementary edit operations as Henshin rules [Keh+13b, Keh+16] (see upper part of Fig. 10.2). Following the principle of model transformation by example [Kap+12], more complex edit rules may be deduced from example models using the inference techniques presented in [KAH17]. Finally, Henshin has been extended by an optimised static analysis of potential conflicts and dependencies between transformation rules [Bor+17]. New theoretical results on the critical pair analysis for amalgamated graph transformations [TG15] pave the ground for the analysis of complex edit operations.

Example Applications

The concepts and tools developed in the MOCA project have been applied and evaluated in several collaborations with other research projects. In all these collaborations, configurations of our generic components for specific modelling languages and other kinds of structural documents have been developed. The results of applying our tools were used for a variety of purposes, notably to solve concrete problems that occurred in other projects of the priority program. In the remainder of this section, we give a selected set of example applications.

In a research collaboration between the projects IMoTEP and MOCA, an approach and supporting tool for reasoning about software product-line evolution using differences on feature models has been developed [Bür+16]. A specific contribution of this collaboration is complex edit operations, whose semantic impact on the set of valid feature configurations can be classified semantically as refactoring, generalisation or specialisation of a feature model. We applied this differencing approach to the evolution of a feature model of the PPU and showed that it is possible to semantically classify feature model differences by using a structural model comparison approach instead of a solver-based solution. More details and further results of this research collaboration can be found in Chap. 7.

In a cooperation between the projects SecVolution and MOCA, a specific component for lifting low-level differences between ontologies has been developed. The general goal was the same as in the cooperation with IMoTEP, namely to get a more abstract, meaningful view on ontology changes by using complex edit operations. This more abstract view enables more adequate planning for changes in other dependent models, such as the security maintenance model [Ruh+14b].

The differencing techniques developed in the MOCA project are used to capture model changes in terms of edit operations within the methodological framework for statistically modelling the evolution of models presented in [Yaz+16]. A main motivation for, and application of, the resulting statistical models is to control the generation of realistic model histories that are intended to be used for evaluating model versioning tools [Yaz+14]. Further usages of the statistical models include various forecasting and simulation tasks. The suitability of the framework is shown by applying it to a large set of design models reverse engineered from real-world Java systems [Keh+13a].

We also evaluated the applicability of the techniques developed in the MOCA project using one of the main case studies of the SPP; the "Pick and Place Unit" (PPU) (see Chap. 4). As a contribution to this case study, we analysed the evolution of the SysML models of the 14 evolution scenarios that have been developed in the first funding period of the SPP. In this study, the developed difference calculation techniques were an effective tool to detect several inconsistencies in the SysML models. Such inconsistencies could be spotted, for example, due to low-level differences between successive evolution scenarios, which could not be entirely lifted to the abstraction level of edit operations. Based on the analysis results, all inconsistencies could be resolved in a collaboration between the projects MoDEMAS and MOCA.

Finally, high-level descriptions of model differences can also assist developers in better understanding the formal specifications of the behavioural differences between two software revisions, for example in the context of the regression verification approach presented in Sect. 10.2.

10.1.2 Analysing Co-evolution of Coupled Models

The development of complex software systems is typically supported by a set of interrelated (a.k.a. coupled) models specifying the system from different viewpoints. In sum, all of these views must reflect a consistent description of the system. Since it is natural that each of these models may change autonomously over time, model-based software evolution is also concerned with model co-evolution. Developers are faced with the problem of consistently co-evolving the different views of the system; that is, the different views must yield a consistent overall description of the system. A basic prerequisite to support developers in achieving such a consistent co-evolution is to understand the co-evolution of coupled models in a particular domain. Getting such an understanding of typical model co-evolutions is the main motivation for analysing the historical co-evolution of coupled models. To that end, an adaptable co-evolution analysis framework has been developed in a joined work by the projects ENSURE and MOCA. The framework draws on the techniques presented in Sect. 10.1.1 and enables statistical analyses of co-evolving models on top of the calculated changes. We present an overview of the analysis capabilities and summarise our results of applying the analysis framework to co-evolving software architecture and quality of service models of the PPU to get a deeper understanding of the nature of consistent co-evolution steps of these kinds of models.

A Generic Framework for Analysing Model Co-evolution

Our co-evolution analysis framework takes a version history of interrelated models, referred to as M_{src} and M_{tgt} in Fig. 10.3a, as input. A pair of successive model versions $i \rightarrow i+1$ from the given history is referred to as evolution step $ev_{i \rightarrow i+1}$, and we assume that the co-evolution history is comprised of consistent evolution steps. We first calculate the model differences $diff(M_i, M_{i+1})$ between successive model versions M_i and M_{i+1} of each evolution step. Thereupon, two kinds of quantitative analyses are supported by our co-evolution analysis framework [GRK14].

For the first analysis, we compute a *correlation* between the kinds of changes of the interrelated models, where the kinds of changes are formally captured by the sets of available edit operations for the source and target model type, respectively. Basically, we count the applied changes for each evolution step in both the source and the target model and compute the Pearson correlation coefficient [LL89] for all combinations of the different kinds of changes to assess the dependencies between the respective edit operations.

The correlation analysis has the advantage of only requiring the source and target models and the respective model changes as input. Thus, this approach can also be applied to study the co-evolution history in cases where no explicit trace links between the observed source and target model exist. However, a correlation between the observable changes does not imply causality.

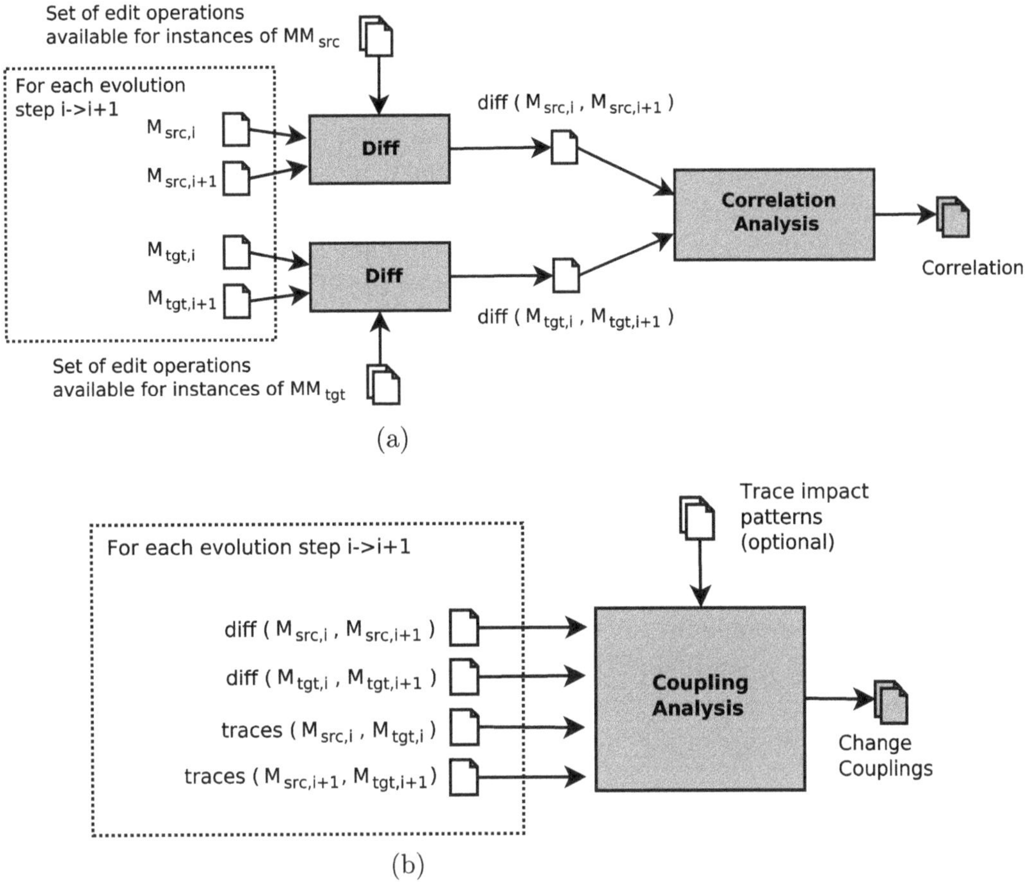

Fig. 10.3 Analysing co-evolutions. (**a**) Correlation analysis. (**b**) Coupling analysis

Hence, we provide a second analysis function referred to as *coupling* analysis, which allows us to identify so-called coupled changes. A coupled change is actually a pair of changes that happened in the same evolution step and where the affected model elements in the interrelated models are connected either directly or indirectly via trace links. In other words, the elements were not just coincidentally changed in the same evolution step. Connectivity of model elements may be formally specified by a graph pattern that relates the model elements of the source and target model, which are connected by trace links. We refer to these graph patterns as trace impact patterns. They are provided as additional domain-specific input parameters to guide the coupling analysis (see Fig. 10.4b).

Case Study on Architecture and Fault Tree Co-evolution

In a first exploratory step of our research on model co-evolution, we worked on understanding the co-evolution between architectural models and quality evaluation models (which we informally define here as models exposing a well-defined semantics amenable to various kinds of reasoning techniques). For that, we manually developed architectural and fault tree models [Ves+81] of the PPU for every safety-relevant evolution scenario. Based on these models, we first performed a qualitative analysis of the co-evolution that showed that the relation between change operations (e.g. addition/deletion of a component or an event) between fault trees and architectural models is not straightforward and that user interactions are needed for some cases [Get+13].

Figure 10.4a and b show the results of the quantitative analyses on the architectural and fault tree models for the evolution steps of the PPU using our co-evolution analysis framework. For example, there exists a high linear correlation (0.96) for additions of component types and additions of error types. However, looking at the results of the coupling analysis in Fig. 10.3b, we can trace only 17% of the addition of component types to additions of an error type. Instead, in 39% of the cases, the added component type is traced to an existing error type, that is one that was created in a previous scenario.

Without going into the details of the analysis results presented in Fig. 10.4a and b, the most important result is that both the correlation and the coupling analysis confirm our qualitative results [Get+13] for this case study that no simple and straightforward co-evolution of fault tree and architectural models exists that could be automated. However, the analysis results could be exploited in a co-evolution framework supporting model co-evolution as a recommender system (see Sect. 10.1.5).

10.1.3 Related Work

Valuable information can be uncovered by analysing the evolution of software systems and generalising the analysis results, as actively pursued by the Mining Software Repositories research community (see, e.g., [DAm+08]) with the ultimate goal of improving software engineering techniques, methods, and processes. Traditional approaches to software evolution analysis focus on classical code-centric software development where source code files are used as the primary development artefacts [KCM07]. However, software and system models are another kind of primary development artefact that are an integral part of a model-based system. Models typically have several characteristics that are substantially different from those of traditional source code documents, which demands for new methods and techniques in the context of software evolution analysis [BE08, Emal2, Alt+09].

Since the advent of model-driven engineering, model differencing has been addressed by a large number of publications; surveys can be found in [FW07, Sel07]. One class of approaches is based on logging [HK10]; that is, editing processes are logged at the level of user commands or lower levels. Thus, the problem addressed by our model differencing approach disappears. However, logging-based approaches require closed environments and do not work with independently created models; thus, they are not a general solution of the problem. Most state-based approaches have a similar processing structure like the basic differencing pipeline

System Architecture	Σ	#Scn.	Failure Model: +ErrorType	-ErrorType	+ErrorInstance	-ErrorInstance	+FailureType	+FailureInstance	Fault Tree1& 2: +BasicEvent	-BasicEvent	+Gate	-Gate	+IntermEvent
Σ			7	0	53	11	7	11	52	13	17	1	11
		#Scn.	3	0	11	3	4	6	11	3	7	1	6
+CpType	19	9	0,96	-	0,27	-0,25	0,80	0,84	0,22	-0,25	0,43	-0,09	0,84
-CpType	1	1	-0,13	-	-0,32	0,01	-0,18	-0,23	-0,31	-0,01	-0,27	-0,09	-0,23
+CpInstance	5	3	0,92	-	0,35	-0,24	0,92	0,85	0,28	-0,24	0,48	-0,15	0,85
-CpInstance	1	1	0,09	-	-0,13	-0,15	0,45	0,28	-0,12	-0,15	0,11	-0,09	0,28
+SCpInstance	49	12	0,75	-	0,70	-0,17	0,69	0,77	0,64	-0,16	0,61	-0,25	0,77
-SCpInstance	11	3	-0,21	-	-0,24	1,00	-0,30	-0,38	-0,16	1,00	-0,44	0,67	-0,38

(a)

System Architecture	Σ	#Scn.	Error Model: +ErrorType	-ErrorType	=ErrorType	+Error instance	-Error instance	=ErrorInstance	+Failure type	=FailureType	+FailureInstance	Fault Tree1& 2: +BasicEvent	-BasicEvent	=BasicEvent	+IntermEvent
Σ			7	0	-	53	11	-	7	-	11	52	13	-	11
		#Scn.	3	0	-	11	3	-	4	-	6	11	3	-	6
+CpType	19	9	0,17	-	0,39	0,06	-	0,00	0,07	0,11	0,18	0,56	0,00	-	0,18
-CpType	1	1	-	0,00	1,00	-	1,00	0,00	-	0,00	-		1,00	0,00	-
+CpInstance	5	3	0,11	-	0,00	0,11	-	0,00	0,33	0,00	0,33	0,11	0,00	-	0,33
-CpInstance	1	1	-	0,00	1,00	-	0,00	1,00	-	0,00	-	-	0,00	1,00	-
+SCpInstance	49	12	0,11	-	0,68	0,75	-	0,03	0,01	0,03	0,03	0,71	0,03	-	0,03
-SCpInstance	11	3	-	0,00	1,00	-	1,00	0,00	-	0,00	-	-	1,00	0,00	-

(b)

Fig. 10.4 Analyses results for the PPU case study. (**a**) Correlation between change elements of fault trees and architectural models. (**b**) Coupling analysis between change elements of fault trees and architectural models

shown in Fig. 10.2. They concentrate on the matching step of the differencing calculation [Kol+09], while they have in common the fact that they deliver only low-level model differences. The semantic lifting of model differences, as pursued by the MOCA approach, has been addressed by only a few approaches, however with different goals and assumptions compared to ours. Among them, the one presented by Langer et al. [Lan+13] is the most similar to ours. They use a custom format of edit operation specifications for detecting complex operations in differences that are obtained from EMF Compare. This approach does not intend to produce executable edit scripts that are being used as patches. Consequently, the identification of arguments, dependencies between operation invocations, etc. are not directly addressed.

10.1.4 Conclusion

The specification and calculation of model changes is a cross-cutting concern for supporting the evolution of long-living model-based systems and a fundamental basis for various kinds of evolution analyses. In Sect. 10.1.1, we presented the differencing techniques that have been developed in the MOCA project, along with a summary of selected applications for analysing the linear evolution of monolithic models. Most of the applications have been developed in cooperation with other research projects of the priority program. The presented case studies show that the information that may be extracted from high-level differences generated by our approach are much richer than for conventional model differencing or text-based difference tools. Thus, significant improvements could be achieved for many kinds of model evolution analyses.

In addition to the analysis of the linear evolution of monolithic models, we presented quantitative techniques for the analysis of model co-evolution, that is how changes in one model affect changes in the other model, in Sect. 10.1.2. The analysis techniques have been integrated into a general co-evolution analysis framework, which has been implemented on top of the differencing techniques presented in Sect. 10.1.1. The overall goal of the framework is to assist domain engineers in finding proper co-evolution rules, which can be finally used to support developers in the co-evolution process. The analysis framework has been instantiated to perform a thorough quantitative analysis of co-evolving architectural models and fault trees of the PPU. We show that the models do not co-evolve in a systematic, automatable way, and instead the expertise of the developer is required to achieve consistent co-evolution, confirming the findings of previous research in this context. Nonetheless, the results could be finally exploited to develop a set of model transformation rules supporting model co-evolution through a recommender system for model co-evolution (see Sect. 10.1.5).

10.1.5 Further Reading

In addition to the evolution analyses discussed in Sect. 10.1.1, exact and meaningful specifications of model changes, as provided by the MOCA approach, are an indispensable basis for many further software evolution activities (see Sect. 2.1). In particular, our model differencing approach has been used as a fundamental basis for many techniques supporting model configuration management, an inevitable discipline to manage the evolution of long-living software systems (see Sect. 2.3). Tools and tool functions that have been developed in the MOCA project include, for example, tools for updating local workspace copies [KKR14] and for propagating changes between variants in a product family [KKT14] and a complete environment for developing delta-oriented model-based software product lines [Pie+15, Pie+17].

Recently, we have started to apply our evolution analysis techniques to the field of automated model repair, inspired by the manual inconsistency resolutions as performed in the context of the PPU case study (see example applications in Sect. 10.1.1) The basic assumption is that inconsistencies are introduced by incomplete editing processes, and the idea is to automatically propose the necessary complementing edits to resolve an inconsistency [Tae+17, Ohr+18]. However, further research is needed to localise the origin of an inconsistency in the development history of a model, to develop strategies of how to deal with other conflicting edits that have been performed in the meantime, and to also offer (partial) undo operations as another repair alternative. Another promising line of research is to mine existing model histories for typical model repairs that have been actually performed by developers. The idea of history-based model repair recommendations can be generalised to develop a much broader set of *recommender systems* supporting developers in a variety of model evolution tasks. We will present more general notion of a recommender system for model-driven development later in this chapter in Sect. 10.4.1. The ultimate goal is to speed up modelling by automating repetitive tasks and to warn developers when they make atypical changes to a model. As we will see in Sect. 10.4.1, the methods and techniques developed within the SPP are a suitable basis for further research into this direction.

Concerning the co-evolution of models, understanding the nature of co-evolution in a particular domain is only the first step to reach the overall goal of supporting developers in achieving consistent model co-evolution. This is particularly challenging when co-evolution is not straightforward, as in the case of architectural and quality evaluation models. To that end, we developed the CoWolf tool suite [Get+15b], a generic yet adaptable framework that implements the idea of using a recommender system in order to support model co-evolution, focusing on the co-evolution of architectural and quality evaluation models. CoWolf currently supports seven different types of models: state charts, component diagrams, and sequence diagrams as architectural models, and discrete time Markov chains (DTMC), continuous time Markov chains (CTMC), fault trees, and layered queuing networks (LQN) as quality evaluation models. In fact, the results of a co-evolution analysis may be exploited by CoWolf to propose the most suitable co-evolutions when one of the interrelated models undergoes structural changes; that is, the co-evolution analysis serves as a machine learning approach to improve the effectiveness of the recommendations. Based on our analysis results presented, we tailored a CoWolf instantiation towards architectural models and fault trees, and research results obtained from an experiment based on the PPU case study show that the approach indeed has the potential to significantly reduce the manual effort for consistently evolving the respective kinds of models [Get+18].

10.2 Formal Analysis of Planned Changes

Automated Production Systems are long-living multi-disciplinary systems that are often operated for several decades. Therefore, automated Production Systems (aPS) often faces change requests due to various reasons, for example to fix bugs, to implement additional functionality, or to come up with some technology trends. For this *present* evolution, as introduced in the introduction of this chapter, see Fig. 10.1; analysis of the implementation and evaluation of the evolved system regarding functional and non-functional aspects confirms the outcome of the change. In principle, there are two categories of solutions for ensuring software correctness: testing and formal verification. Testing is widely used for fault detection because of its usability. However, the guarantees that it can provide is naturally limited to the specified test cases, which in most cases cannot cover the entire system behaviour. On the other hand, formal verification can provide proof that a system conforms to its specification in all possible situations. In spite of this nice coverage property, formal methods are not commonly used for quality assurance since they require a high level of expertise to be able to come up with suitable models and specifications.

Within the two SPP1593 projects, MoDEMMiCAS (Model-Driven Evolution Management for Microscopic Changes in Automation Systems) and Improve APS (Regression Verification in a User-Centered Software Development Process for Evolving Automated Production Systems), we want to enable the engineer to incorporate formal techniques into their development process. We will achieve this via two different directions: one is the model-based verification of interdisciplinary aPS combined with the incremental verification of their evolution, and the other is user-centred regression verification for the software.

The development of aPS is a complex task as it brings together at least three different disciplines in one system: mechanical, electrical, and software engineering. To date, each of the involved engineers works independently on a solution, and only then that the results of the engineering of each are finally integrated into one system. However, high-quality designs can be achieved by considering all the disciplines simultaneously [BFB14], and furthermore, shorter development cycle is required for a shortened time for marketing in order to handle ever-changing customer needs [KVD01]. Consequently, the challenges of integrating multi-discipline artefacts and ensuring the correctness of the system arise.

The other characteristic of the aPS is that the software often changes and the scale of the change is usually small. In other words, under the assumption that the previous version of the system confirms previous specification, Regression Verification [Bec+15] overcomes the need for function specification by letting the old version of the software serve as a partial specification of the new revisions where the preserved behaviour is expected. The developer profits from both versions in that they gain additional knowledge about the system.

As a possible situation, a developer from one of the disciplines wants to change the model. Through the development process, the application engineer is informed about how the implemented change on a specific domain model affects the overall system in view of the quality of the system. Another situation we can regard is that the application engineer revises the code of the automated system. During this code revision, the developer can execute the verification of the preserved and changed functionality and correct the code by using the information from the verification tool chain. Both approaches are based on the characteristic of aPS that changes are usually small variations, and this characteristic facilitates the inclusion of formal verification within the development process. In Sect. 10.2.1, we consider a model-driven evolution management, and Sect. 10.2.2 considers a user-centred software development using regression verification (see Chap. 11 for the detailed techniques of the formal verification used in the approaches)

10.2.1 Using Model-Based Verification of Interdisciplinary Models

In almost every engineering discipline, models are used to cope with system complexity. In addition, they are used as reusable and analysable artefacts to bridge the conceptual gap between requirements and target system implementations. A variety of sophisticated approaches exists for visually representing interdisciplinary models [SW10, Bas+11, Thr13]. However, our focus is on a formal model-based approach to manage the evolution of aPS, which integrates suitable means for quality assessment and automatic verification assuring model correctness in an interdisciplinary way.

In the MoDEMMiCAS project, we model the aPS based on the FOCUS theory [BS10], which is based on a (formal) foundation and provides well-elaborated notions of the system components and their interfaces, composition, and refinement. By that, formally verifying the functional conformance of the aPS' behaviour based on the composition of components, that is the system's architecture, is possible. Furthermore, the approach is fundamentally viewpoint based, providing three different viewpoints onto the aPS, which refer to different engineering concerns: requirement, process, and system. The system viewpoint consists of three scopes (see Fig. 10.5):

- **Context Scope** mainly contains information about the geometry of mechanical components.
- **Platform Scope** comprises everything from the sensor/actuator interface with the context scope to the programmable controller's variables available interfacing the software scope.
- **Software Scope** contains a model of the software architecture, including its components and their behaviour.

In order to ensure system correctness regarding the availability requirement as a part of the quality assurance of the aPS, the system behaviour model is extended with deviation models, which represent fault occurrences and effects of

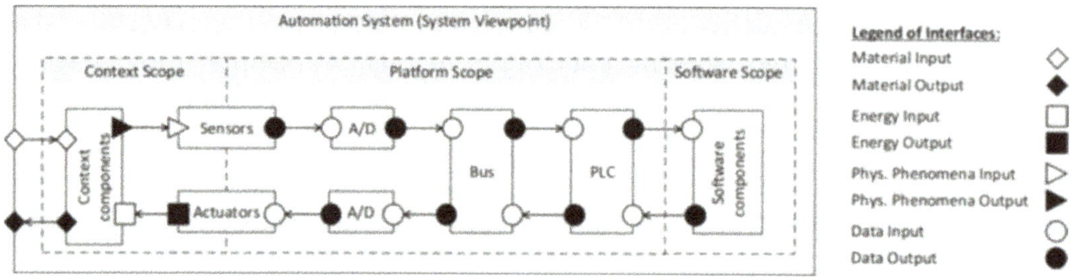

Fig. 10.5 Schematic overview of system control loop

the system components [Mun+17]. Within the presented approach, our focus was on the availability as a degree of correctness rather than binary distinction (i.e. correct or incorrect). Based on the extended specifications (i.e. deviation models), the actual behaviour of the plant is verified by means of failure definition and aggregation models and finally compared to requirements based on models of availability metrics. This is realised by translating the model for the probabilistic model-checker PRISM. The deviation model consists of three components, namely an input and output filter to model the altered behaviour of the component under consideration and an activation function (act) that represents the (de-)activation of those filters. In an aPS, faults may occur in the system's software, platform, or mechanical context. The exemplary case using extended Pick and Place Unit (xPPU) and the detailed verification procedure of this approach is described in Chap. 11.

Towards incremental model change verification, we consider the integration of verification technique (i.e. model checking) into a continuous integration (CI) environment. Maintaining high quality is the most important piece of delivery in a CI environment. Most development frameworks improve software efficiency by implementing automated processes, as well as imposing checks on the model. CI takes it a step further by finding any model integration issues by compiling the model as soon as the developer checks it in and running unit tests. Build status and unit test catch the initial errors in the model during compiling. However, those tests are insufficient to catch the deployment- and integration-related errors. Furthermore, continuous build and test systems today are used as part of the development activities to control and improve the process of software creation in software engineering domain [DMG07] and for the software of the aPS [Vog15]. However, adapting CI for other disciplines of aPS is challenging [Vog15].

Within the CI environment, incremental changes are applied on a regular basis to the aPS model and are integrated continuously. To ensure a conformance level of the overall system quality, continuous verification techniques that provide support for incremental and compositional verification are required [Vog+15c]. In other words, instead of checking the entire system model each time a change is applied, incremental and compositional verification is limited to the changed parts and the affected parts of the system model, as well as the environment model. Within CI, verification is organised along an increasing verification scope, starting with verifying the software in isolation (Fig. 10.6). In case the additional efforts for

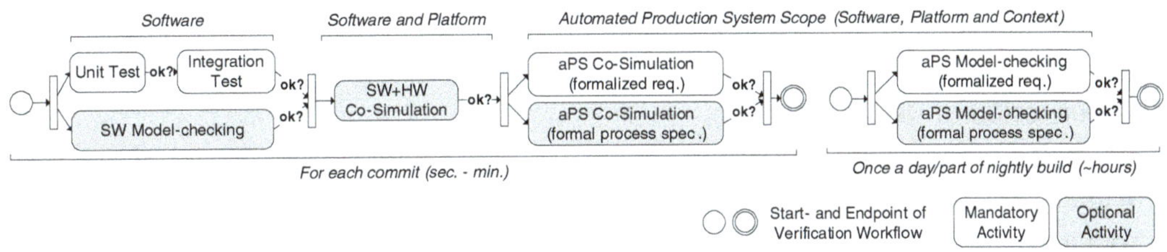

Fig. 10.6 Verification workflow as part of a CI approach [Mun+18]

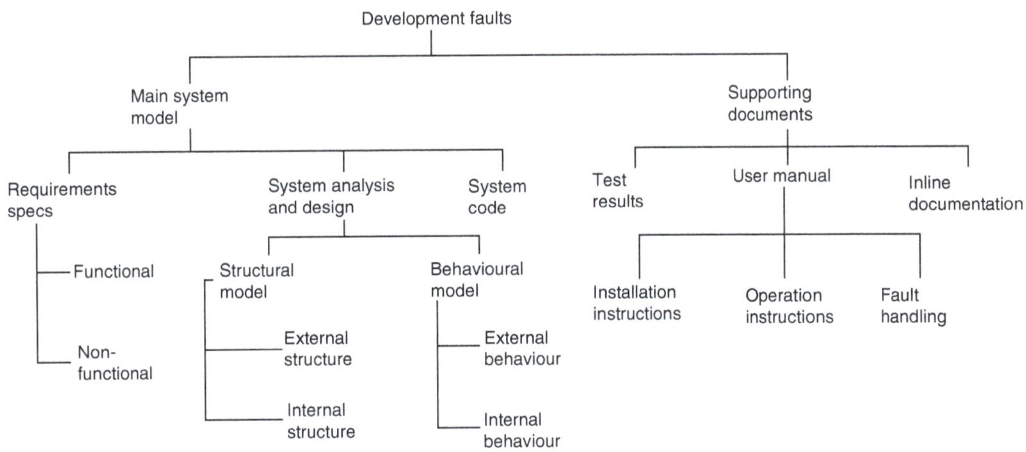

Fig. 10.7 Taxonomy of faults arising from incremental changes [BV18]

specifying logical constraints at the software level are acceptable, exhaustive model checking of the control software can be done in parallel to testing. After the software system is verified at the software scope, we use co-simulation to verify if it also has the desired effects on the automation hardware and, ultimately, achieves the desired plant behaviour. Finally, the continuous verification procedure suggests performing a co-simulation against formalised requirements, a formal specification of the technical process, or both. In case an automated hardware setup exists, this step can also be replaced by hardware in loop verification.

Based on an analysis of the incremental changes throughout the entire aPS life cycle, we develop a fault taxonomy [BV18]. This taxonomy builds on [Lau99], where faults are classified based on their cause into either physical faults due to changes in the underlying technical process or human faults associated with changes before and after commissioning. The taxonomy presented here is for analysing the effect of incremental changes associated with CI and hence focuses only on human faults occurring before commissioning. As illustrated in Fig. 10.7, development faults resulting from incremental changes to aPS span the different activities of the development life cycle. Due to the differences in their influencing effects on the overall aPS quality, development activities contributing to generating artefacts modelling the system are distinguished from those resulting in supporting documentation. Where faults in the former category may have an impact on the entire set of quality criteria, faults in the latter basically affect criteria such as usability, maintainability, and portability. For example, a change in the user manual in the section regarding the operational instructions may harm operability, which is a sub-criterion of usability.

A fault in the system model may occur during requirements specifications, system analysis and design, or system coding. A change in the system's requirements is associated with faults either in the functional or in the non-functional requirements. With the help of data associated with the changed artefact, a more precise prediction of the impacted quality criteria can be derived. For instance, a change of a non-functional requirement that indicates that the system's uptime shall be 99% is deemed to influence the availability criterion of the system.

Artefacts generated during analysis and design are decomposed according to their purpose into artefacts constituting the structural model and those forming the behavioural model. Each of these models is further decomposed out of the adopted point of view into external and internal. A fault in the external models basically affects the interrelationship between the aPS and the external actors, including the system user, as well as any interacting legacy systems. Accordingly, faults in the external categories are related to quality sub-criteria such as operability, interoperability, and coexistence. On the other hand, faults belonging to the internal structural and behavioural models need further investigation based on more specific data about the associated context to derive their expected impact on the quality criteria.

10.2.2 Using Regression Verification for Small Evolution Steps in PLC-Code

Formal verification proves the implementation correctness mathematically and exhaustively with respect to the formal specification. In spite of the full coverage, formal verification is not commonly used in aPS engineering for the functional implementation of the system. One of the barriers is achieving formal specification to use the formal verification. In our approach, we apply regression verification methods that do not require full functional specifications and minimise the complexity of the verification problem.

Verifying of the PLC program with respect to temporal specifications, for example especially safety and liveness, has been the subject of research in the automation field [Bec+15]. Formalisation of the PLC program [YF03a] and its validation [Lam+99a] have already been discussed, and various approaches to verify the behaviours of industrial machines using formal methods are suggested, for example [Wit+06]. Also, various transformation methods from IEC61131-3 languages into model checking available languages are suggested, for example from Sequential Function Chart (SFC) into Process Meta Language (PROMELA) for SPIN model checker [BM00] or into timed Computational Tree Logic (tCTL) for UPPAAL [Bau+04b] and from all IEC61131-3 languages into symbolic model

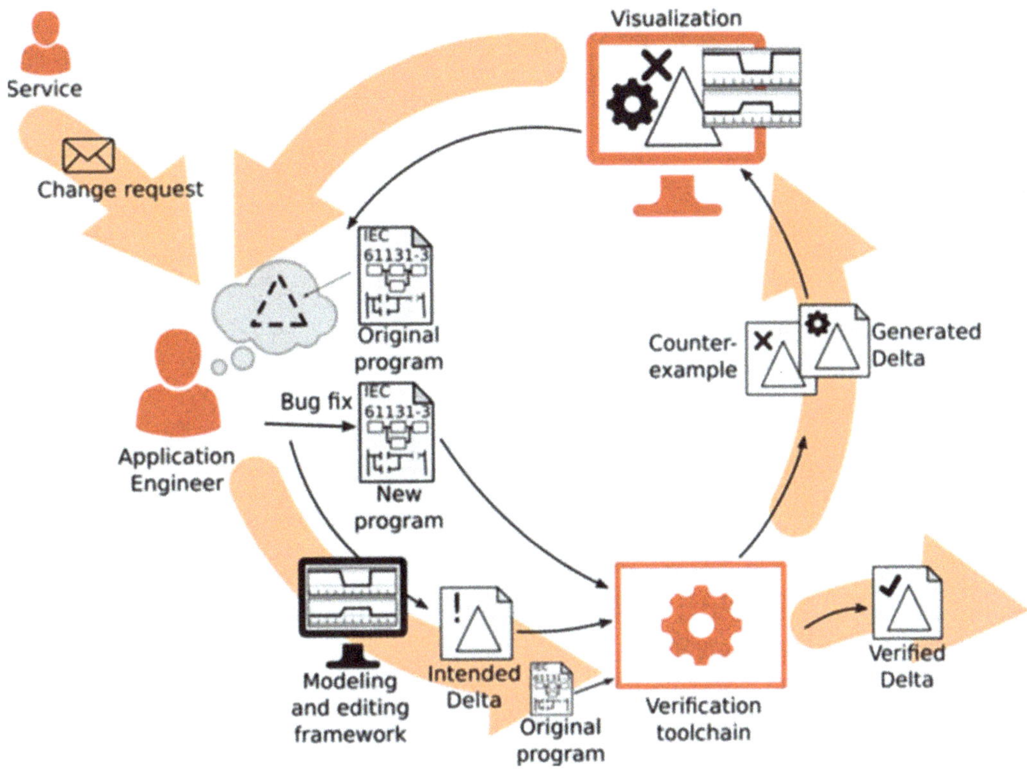

Fig. 10.8 Overview of user-centred regression verification process

for Cadence-Symbolic Model Verifier (SMV) [De +00]. However, for applying verification, the complete formal specification is still the bottleneck even though the system model can be obtained using the transformation methods.

In the Improve APS project, we deal with regression verification in a user-centred software development process for evolving aPS [Bec+15] (Fig. 10.8) by including the user into the process loop with more human-understandable notations and visualisations. A major prerequisite of this project is that the requested change is implemented on an already-implemented and being-operated system after the acceptance test or at least after the system is approved by customers. Change requests happen due to either the necessity of the different functionality or faults in the system. Once a change request is issued to the application engineer, the new change is implemented based on the existing code version to fulfil the change request. When the modification is done, the engineer verifies the regression of the code behaviour according to the original program and its deviation (i.e. intended delta). If it is verified that the new program satisfies the change request, the code block can be launched to the system. However, if it is not, the verification tool generates a counterexample and also actual differences between original and new, that is generated delta. (Follow the loopback path in Fig. 10.8.) This counterexample is provided to the engineer together with the delta information.

This overall process is suggested as a verification-supported evolution tool chain for automation software application engineers [Ule+16] with three phases. First,

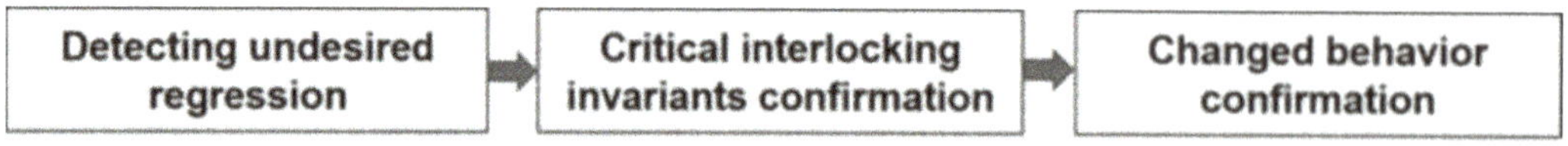

Fig. 10.9 Overview of aPS verification process

#	Input			Output			Dur.
	A	B	C	X	Y	Z	
0	1	1	2	0	0	5	1
1	0	3	3	6	6	5	7
2	1	4	2	2	8	5	2

(a)

#	Input			Output			Dur.
	A	B	C	X	Y	Z	
0	1	1	2	0	0	-	1
1	-	p	p	$2 * p$	X	$Z[-1]$	> 5
2	-	$p + 1$	-	$[0, p]$	$> Y[-1]$	$2 * Z > Y$	*

(b)

Fig. 10.10 An example of a concrete test table and a generalised test table from [Wei+17]

regression verification checks whether the retained behaviours in the new program is equivalent to the old version for all cases where no change in behaviour is intended. Second, the critical properties which need to hold also in the new software system against the interlocking invariant properties, for example safety properties. Third, the new behaviours are verified against how the program is expected to behave differently based on the properties describing the new situation (Fig. 10.9).

The precise verification technique in this project is explained in Chap. 11. However, even after setting aside the verification techniques, there arise user interaction issues. To verify a program, the application engineer should provide the verifier (model checker) a piece of software or its model and the property that needs to be verified in the target program. Also, the engineer is required to be able to understand the verification results, which consist of a success/fail verdict and a counterexample in the event of a failed case. Since formal notations are one of the barriers for using formal verification [Pak+16] and the counterexample of the verifier is usually a simple series of the values for a trace, this interacting information, which is provided by and provided to the user, needs to be represented in an easier way for the users than existing formal expressions.

As one possible user-friendly specification, we have extended the concept of test tables, which the software application engineers use for reactive system testing [UV15]. In [Wei+17] and [Bec+17a], we suggested an approach to support quality assurance by generalising the test tables such that they can be used for formal verification purposes in addition to testing.

An example of test table is shown in Fig. 10.10. A test table consists of three parts of expected input, its corresponding output, and allowed duration of the appearance of input-output pair with fixed values (Fig. 10.10a). Rows of the table describe the execution progress of the system under test. The example represents three input variables (A, B, and C) and three output variables (X, Y, and Z) during the duration of 10 s. The generalised test table represents all possible test table cases of the sort by generalising the cells with constraint expressions, while the test table just represents one specific or concrete test sequence. In the generalised test tables (GTTs), three generalisation concepts are used, such as below (Fig. 10.10b):

- Abstraction using constraint expressions, for example mathematical formulas (as in cell $(1, X)$), interval expressions (as in cell $(2, X)$, which means "a value in the interval from 0 to p", and $(2, Z)$, which means "the value which satisfies $2 * Z > Y$"), or *don't care* (as seen as "-")
- Relating cells using existing input/output variable names, together with relative cycle index (as in cell $(1, Y)$ for current value of the other cell and $(1, Z)$ for a value one cycle ago) or new variable symbols (as in cell $(1, B)$ and $(2, B)$)
- Various duration using interval expressions (as in the second row, which means "the row must be repeated more than 5 s") or *don't care*, which is equivalent to $>= 0$ (as seen as "$*$")

Using this GTTs, the developers can describe the specification of the function more easily and effectively since it is an already accepted form. And this specification is used by the verifier to prove the function behaviour. Together with these concepts, a graphical interface, that is Structured Text Verification Studio (STVS), is implemented for hands-down automation software proof against the GTTs, which is developed in IEC 61131-3 Structure Text (ST) (Fig. 10.11). Once the ST code and the GTT are typed in, the model checker called from STVS (nuXmv) verifies the program against the specification in GTTs. If not, counterexample in the form of concrete test table is displayed that violates the specification, that is GTT.

We also presented a monitoring block generation method based on the GTTs [Cha+17]. Since GTTs describe allowed behaviour sequences, a violation of this table means either a violation of the expected output for the given input or a violation of the expected input. The code of the monitoring block can be generated by converting the GTT systematically (see [Cha+17]). This block checks the input-output pair sequentially according to the defined description in GTT. This monitoring block can interact with the user by raising appropriate signals depending on its decision results: (1) in the case of *warning*, which means the output violation for the given input, the function block needs to be adjusted in order to execute as the specification defines and (2) in the case of *unknown*, which means the input violation for the specific sequence, the specification needs to be adjusted, that is revised or added, to cover the situation that occurred. This monitoring is applied during the machine execution. User interaction using the monitoring block decision results can be implemented in various ways, such as logging, displaying on human machine interface (HMI) system, and so on.

10.2.3 Conclusion and Outlook

In this section, we explored quality assurance approaches for aPS. Formal verification is applied to the incremental changes of aPS, and by introducing formal methods into the aPS engineering process, we can achieve higher quality aPS by

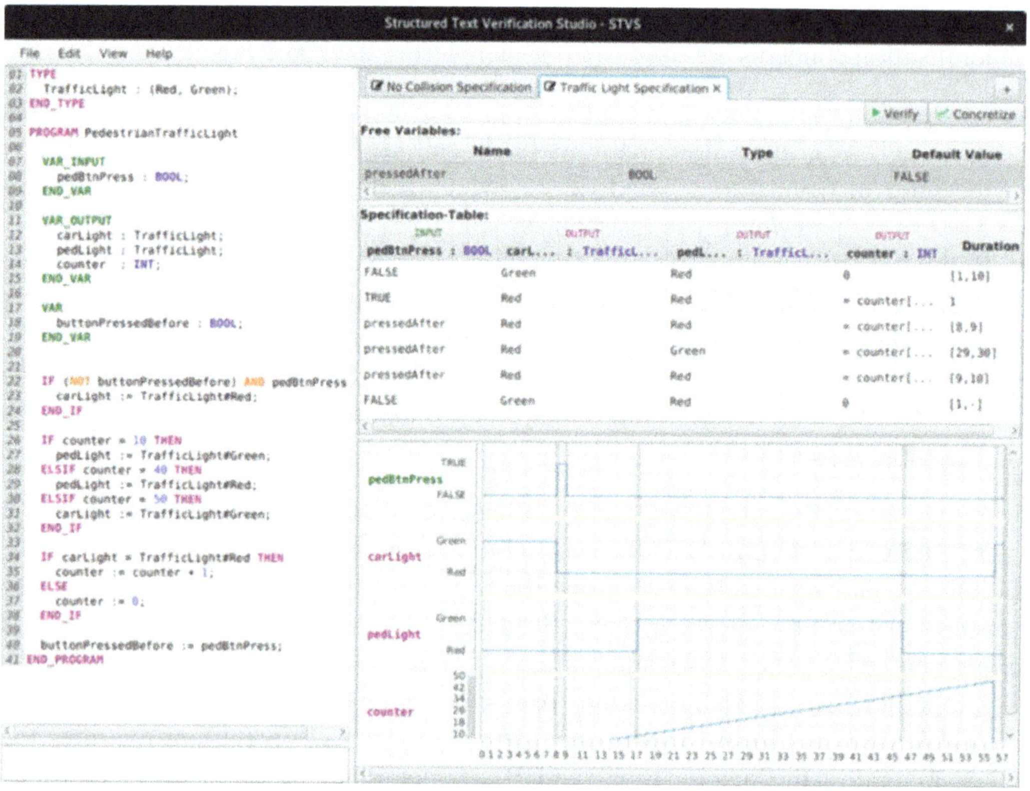

Fig. 10.11 Structured Test Verification Studio (STVS)

verifying them exhaustively in the model level, as well as in the code level. For model verification, we suggest a quality assurance (QA) model to verify the system in the CI approach capturing incremental changes. For code verification, regression verification is applied to verify system behaviour according to specification, as well as the new specification method suggested.

As a future work, we intend to enrich fault taxonomy model by analysing industrial practical cases to make it more generalised. Moreover, the applicability of the prototypical tool chains on the real machines needs to be measured, for example CI framework, by bonding the solutions with suggested bridges between them, or STVS plug-ins for IEC 61131-3 development environments, such as CODESYS and TwinCAT.

10.3 Analyse Non-functional Aspects of the System

Complementary to approaches which target a formal analysis of the functional aspects of software quality, the methods presented in this section consider non-functional quality aspects such as performance and robustness. Non-functional quality aspects are very crucial to ensure the quality of complex systems [II11]. However, due to tight time and cost restrictions in practice, evolution is often performed without pre- or post-evaluation of its influence on non-functional quality aspects [LFL16]. Reasons for that mainly include lack of good requirement engineering practice, cf. [MMW98, PR11]. One method to overcome this lack of quality based evolution evaluation is an automated analysis of the actual behaviour which is constantly performed during the evolution [Vog+15a]. To do so, models reflecting the current system behaviour and capturing the non-functional properties are needed. However, building such models manually is complex, tedious, and error prone, which contradicts aforementioned tight time and cost restrictions in practice [CM09]. One way to overcome this drawback is to enhance the models with runtime information like observed signal events [Epi+09] or even to completely generate models out of runtime data gathered from current system behaviour. To support evolution, it is shown in the following how different types of models capturing a variety of non-functional properties can be developed and learned from observation to analyse the system quality during the evolution of the system. Examples of the models and their automated generation are shown on the (x)PPU case study plant.

Firstly, Petri Nets are automatically derived for software-controlled manufacturing systems by the observation of input/output events [Lad+15a, Lad+15c]. The models are suitable for the performance and flexibility analysis of the interdisciplinary system. The Petri Nets are defined in a way that they reflect those non-functional properties. In production systems, these are typically metrics defined for each manufacturing plant, such as the throughput rate, the allocation ratio, or the utilisation efficiency [Lad+13b]. Secondly, Markov chains are used to analyse the system's reliability. A novel approach [FGL15] is presented that learns the Markov chains from the running system. The Markov chains can then later be used for probabilistic model checking [KNP04].

10.3.1 Learning and Analysing the Machine States and Material Flow of Evolving Manufacturing Systems

production automation systems have a strong focus on non-functional properties of the underlying production process. This production process is defined in the production plant's specification and inherently implemented in the plant's structure and behaviour. But when considering evolution, a systematic re-engineering for adapting production plants is often omitted and changes are directly implemented based on the informal requirements [FL00, Vog+15a, BS10]. Accordingly, this results in a gap between the actual production process and its specification [Hau+13]. Therefore, no (formal) up-to-date models of the plant are present, and especially evolution, including small and unanticipated changes, usually lacks appropriate documentation and evaluation [Vog+15a].

As a result, non-functional properties may be unsatisfied and unnecessary weaknesses are even not recognised by the staff. One approach to overcome these deficiencies is using automated model learning for creating formal behaviour models of the plant's production process, which is suitable for both automatic recognition of changes and their analysis regarding non-functional properties of the process. Contrary to the reliability approach for learning Markow chains, this learning approach concentrates on the structure of a production process and the order in which signal events occur in the plant. Therefore, this approach deals with generating Petri Nets from observations gathered at discrete inputs and outputs of *Programmable Logic Controllers (PLCs)* controlling production systems.

Three-Phase Evolution Support Process

In the following, an approach is presented that aims at automatically generating models from externally observable events of production systems. Figure 10.12 shows the process of the approach in three phases. In the first, phase knowledge about the underlying production process is gathered by observing input and output signals of the production system. In the second phase, an evolution cycle is established by learning observed behaviour in models at runtime and using them to detect changes that must be relearned. In a third phase, the evolution is assessed by deriving non-functional properties out of the learned models. Each phase is further described in more detail.

The first phase is data *acquisition*, in which data in terms of event traces are recorded. In order to lift the data to knowledge in terms of non-functional property values, the data have to be made semantically interpretable. Therefore, further meaning is added to the events by information modelling. An information model is intended to provide semantics of the event generating signals in order to be able to generate meaningful behaviour models. However, manual effort for creating an information model has to be kept to a minimum to meet the requirements regarding tight time and cost restrictions. Therefore, in contrast to a complete manual modelling of release and consumption of events in the plant, the semantics provided by the information model only contain the assignment of signals to the plant topology and the types of recorded signals [LFL16]. Types of signals are, for example, workpiece detection (e.g. stemming from a light barrier), workpiece

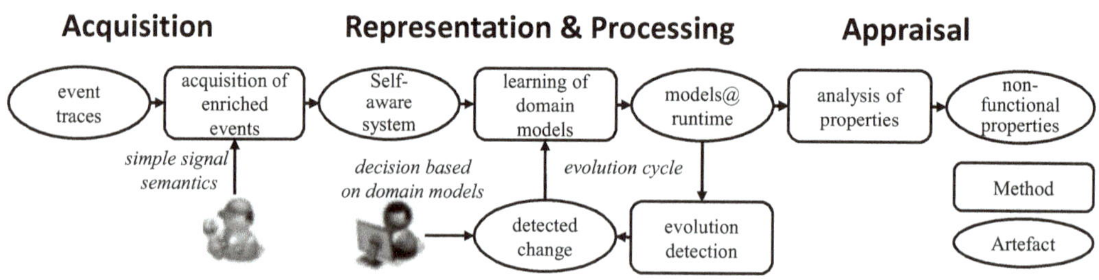

Fig. 10.12 Acquisition, representation and processing and appraisal to determine non-functional properties

modification (e.g. actuator turning on a drilling machine), or state detection signals (e.g. motor on/off). As a result, semantically enriched event traces are generated.

The second phase is called *representation and processing*. In this phase, the behaviour of the plant is represented in models that can be used and changed at runtime. Two different model types have been developed to apply the approach on manufacturing systems: Machine State Petri Nets (MSPN) and Material Flow Petri Nets. MSPNs represent the full behaviour of every single technical resource in the plant, and MFPNs capture the routing of workpieces of the whole plant. The models on one hand are used to detect evolutionary changes by using anomaly detection mechanisms (see Sect. 9.6) and on the other hand are used for analysing them regarding non-functional properties, as shown in this section. An overview of the model types, their automatic generation, as well as their analysis, is given in the following sections. More details can be found for MSPNs in [Lad+15a] and for MFPNs in [Lad+15c].

Both models are based on the state of the system, which is given by a vector of input/output binary sensor and actuator signals. The models are based on the recorded event traces with the semantics of the acquisition phase. One advantage of using the added signal semantics is the possibility of dividing the input/output vector of the plant into subvectors that reflect specific parts or specific aspects of the plant. For example, the event trace can be filtered by signals assigned to just one considered resource or reflect a specific action in the system.

Formally, both models are represented with Place/Transition (P/T) Petri Nets $\langle P, T, F \rangle$ in which transitions are annotated with signal names. T is the set of transitions, and $F \subseteq (P \times T) \cup (T \times P)$ is the set of directed arcs between places and transitions.

First, for each technical resource in the plant, one MSPN is generated from data observations reflecting the resource's behaviour by representing its full language in terms of all input/output events, as well as their timing dependencies. To do so, a preprocessing step combines events in a defined time interval to avoid an increase of model complexity due to imprecise and scattered timestamps. The actual learning is based on the causality specification of Lefebvre and Leclercq [LL11]. It uses an event propagation matrix that contains all direct successors of events. This matrix is used to calculate an incidence matrix, which replicates each successor relation with its firing sequences. In a last step, this matrix is reduced in complexity and its initial marking that represents the current state of the system is calculated. The permittivity of the MSPN is further reduced by exploiting the fact that binary signals can just toggle between their two states. Furthermore, timings are annotated as meta-information that is used to find timing anomalies and to derive performance properties.

In MFPN, the material flow is modelled, whereby tokens represent workpieces. In an MFPN, transitions represent events when one sensor or a combination of sensors detects a workpiece. Further, a place represents a region in which the workpiece is not detected by a sensor. As an example, consider a running conveyor belt that transports workpieces and a light barrier that detects workpieces on this belt. When a workpiece passes the light barrier, the binary sensor of the light barrier indicates the position of the workpiece, which in the MFPN is represented by the firing of a corresponding transition. When the light barrier is passed, the workpiece is in a region between two sensors, and therefore in the MFPN the token is situated in the place after the fired transition. To learn the MFPN first, the trace is separated according to the events' affiliation to the equipment in the information model, and all non-relevant events are filtered out. The actual learning is done by analysing the time stability between events in order to determine which events are triggered by the same workpieces during transportation through the plant. Subsequently, in a first step, the events are assigned to workpiece instances. If the same events are triggered several times within a stable time difference, they are assigned to the same workpiece instance. By using all instances for each workpiece type, a place-transition chain is generated. These chains are combined in such a way that the number of places and transitions is minimised and the net still fulfils the definition given above. As a last step, similar to MSPNs, timings, as well as identifications for workpiece types, are annotated.

The models are suitable for analysis regarding non-functional properties to evaluate changed behaviour of the underlying production process. Such an analysis takes place in the third phase of the process of Fig. 10.12, which is called knowledge *assessment*. The properties of interest here are mainly *Key Performance Indicators (KPIs)*, as defined for production systems in the ISO 22400-2 [DIS12]. These properties have to be operationalised in order to be measured directly at the production machine. An extensive literature research of such properties was done in [Lad+13b]. As an illustration, the throughput rate of a manufacturing plant describes the number of produced goods per unit time [DIS12]. Accordingly, it can be calculated by determining the number of produced goods during a specific production time. To determine the production duration, the time difference between the first event and the last event in the event trace is calculated. By summing up all mean transportation durations of each workpiece type in the MFPN, the mean production duration for one product of each type can be calculated.

Application on xPPU Case Study

For evaluation, an implementation of the knowledge-carrying software has been built based on a service-component architecture [Hau+14a]. It uses event source endpoints in a 1-to-1 mapping according to the available entry points of the production process. Each part of the physical plant hierarchy is mapped to self-contained representation components, which are in charge of implementing a consistent system state. The models are implemented as runtime artefacts that are decoupled from the real-time plant by using event statements that are learned and evaluated at runtime [Hau+17]. The software cannot decide if a performed change and its influences on its non-functional properties are intended (or at least acceptable); therefore, Fig. 10.12 includes a cycle with a "user in the loop" to decide whether an intended evolution has taken place (in which case the model has to be re-learned) or an undesired change in the production system occurred (which should

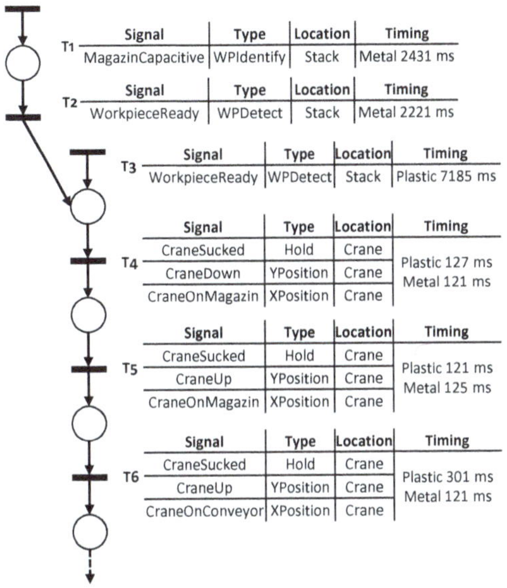

	Sc 1	Sc 3	Sc 5	Sc 10	Sc 11	Sc 12
MFPN (T)	5	12	12	18	17	15
MFPN (P)	5	11	11	16	16	14
$MSPN_{Stack}$ (T)	11	13	19	28	22	22
$MSPN_{Stack}$ (P)	8	9	11	15	13	12
$MSPN_{Crane}$ (T)	34	30	37	45	41	54
$MSPN_{Crane}$ (P)	34	30	37	45	41	54
$MSPN_{Stamp}$ (T)	-	13	16	18	18	16
$MSPN_{Stamp}$ (P)	-	12	13	13	14	13
$MSPN_{Conveyor}$ (T)	-	-	-	15	24	32
$MSPN_{Conveyor}$ (P)	-	-	-	11	19	23
$Utilisation_{Stack}$	49%	73%	80%	92%	92%	94%
$Utilisation_{Crane}$	100%	69%	87%	85%	82%	93%
$Utilisation_{Stamp}$	-	10%	37%	40%	18%	24%
$Utilisation_{Conveyor}$	-	-	-	38%	38%	35%
$Makespan_{White}$	-	-	-	20s	20s	28s
$Makespan_{Black}$	7s	10s	12s	11s	11s	10s
$Makespan_{Metal}$	-	15s	22s	26s	21s	23s

Fig. 10.13 (Left) Part of the resulting MFPN with semantics of signals. (Right) Utilisation and Make Span properties of some PPU scenarios

be fixed by an operator). This process is implemented by a goal-based management component that is based on the Belief-Desire-Intention architecture [Pok+14].

The MFPN learning algorithm has been evaluated on the Pick and Place Unit (in the state as described in [Vog+14b]). Figure 10.13 shows on the left side a part of the learned MFPN of Scenario 3. It shows the part where the workpieces are introduced into the PPU by the stack and picked up by the crane. The MFPN has two starting points, because the plastic workpieces are first detected by the *WorkpieceReady* sensor, which is a switch at the stack slide, and metallic workpieces are first detected by the *MagazinCapacitive* Sensor, which is mounted at the slide. Plastic workpieces do not show the *MagazinCapacitive* event since the sensor remains in its 0 state. Nonetheless, both workpieces are transported by the crane. Also, the semantic information is shown for the signals. For example, the crane has a combined signal for transition *T4*. This signal contains the *CraneSucked* signal, which indicates that a workpiece is in the crane, and two position signals of the crane (*CraneDown* and *CraneOnMagazin*). Also, the timing, distinguished by their type, for the combined signal is given.

Further on the right side of Fig. 10.13, an overview of the learned models is given in a table. It is indicated how complex the models are in terms of learned places and transitions. As a summary regarding the PPU case study, it can be stated that the PPU is steadily extended, which results in more complex models. Further, the crane is the most complex resource.

The resulting MFPN allows calculating relevant process-related non-functional properties, as described in the assessment phase. As examples, we show the makespan and utilisation on the right side of Fig. 10.13. The utilisation is measured on individual resources of the PPU, and the makespan is defined for workpieces.

Utilisation describes the amount of time a resource has operated on a given workpiece within the frame of the total time that the entire plant has taken to produce the given workpiece from beginning till the end. Hence, the value of utilisation of a particular given production module can have the maximum value of 100% if it has been in operation the entire time. One other property that we explored is the makespan for an individual module. Makespan is defined as the time that elapses from the beginning till the end of an operation performed on a given workpiece. For example, a workpiece is being shifted from point A to point B with the aid of a crane. In this case, the makespan of the crane would be the time taken for the crane to move the workpiece from point A to point B.

One exemplary finding out of these non-functional properties is that the optimisation of the crane behaviour of Scenario 5 indeed increases the utilisation of the crane (69% $\rightarrow$ 87%) but that the makespans of the products are not improved by the optimisation as intended (10 s $\rightarrow$ 12 s and 15 s $\rightarrow$ 22 s). This results from the long time the crane needs to turn between the stamp and the stack. Therefore, the "optimisation" of Scenario 5 is not advisable as an evolutionary change.

10.3.2 Learning and Analysing DTMCs for Reliability Evaluation

The learned Petri Nets from the previous approach are mainly used for performance evaluation. For reliability and safety, based on the results of the joined MOCA and ENSURE research on model-driven co-evolution (Sect. 10.1), we know how to co-evolve architectural models and probabilistic quality evaluation models, such as fault trees and Markov models or queuing networks@runtime. Markov models like Discrete-Time Markov Chains (DTMCs) are mainly used for reliability evaluation.

Since the behaviour of a system may change at runtime, for example user request rates for web systems, we also require a time-efficient, robust, and accurate learning algorithms to keep the parameters, for example transition probabilities, of a probabilistic model continuously updated. Most of the available approaches [CJR11, Cal+14, Epi+09, EGT10, ZWL08] achieve only one of different goals (time efficiency, robustness, and accuracy) at the price of the other.

Before we can go into the details of learning transition probabilities for DTMCs, we first need to define what a DTMC is. A DTMC is a state-transition system where the choices among successor states are governed by probability distribution. Formally, a DTMC is a tuple (S, s_0, P, L, AP) [BK08], where S is a (finite) set of states, $s_0 \in S$ is the initial state, $P : S \times S \rightarrow [0, 1]$ is a stochastic matrix, AP is a set of atomic propositions, and $L : S \rightarrow 2^{AP}$ is a labelling function that associates to each state the set of atomic propositions that are true in that state. An element p_{ij} of the Matrix P represents the transition probability from state s_i to state s_j, that is the probability of going from state s_i to state s_j in exactly one step.

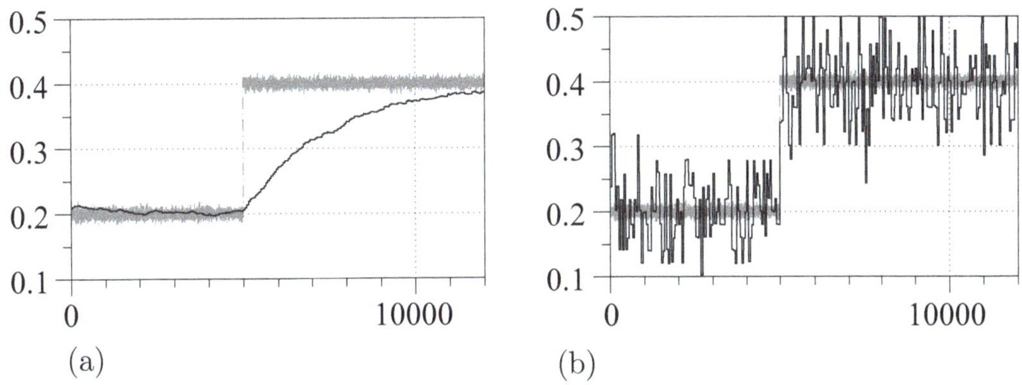

Fig. 10.14 Examples for behaviour with different a parameter values. (**a**) Noise filtering ($a = 0.98$). (**b**) Fast change tracking ($a = 0.02$)

The probability of moving from s_i to s_j in exactly two steps can be computed as $\sum_{s_x \in S} p_{ix} \cdot p_{xj}$, that is the sum of the probabilities of all the paths originating in s_i, ending in s_j, and having exactly one intermediate state. The previous sum is, by definition, the entry (i, j) of the power matrix P^2. Similarly, the probability of reaching s_j from s_i in exactly k steps is the entry (i, j) of matrix P^k. As a natural generalisation, the matrix $P^0 \equiv I$ represents the probability of moving from state s_i to state s_j in zero steps, that is 1 if $s_i = s_j$, 0 otherwise.

As time-efficient and accurate learning probabilities for DTMCs, the following lightweight adaptive filter (LAF) has been developed in the ENSURE project:

$$\begin{cases} e(k) = |p^m(k) - \widehat{p}(k-1)| \\ a(k) = a_0 + \Delta a \cdot f_a(e(k) - e_{thr}) \\ \widehat{p}(k) = a(k) \cdot \widehat{p}(k-1) + (1 - a(k)) \cdot p^m(k-1) \end{cases} \tag{10.1}$$

This filter, as shown in Eq. (10.1), is an extended version of a unity-gain, first-order discrete-time filter [Lev10]: $\widehat{p}(k) = a \cdot \widehat{p}(k-1) + (1-a) \cdot p^m(k-1)$, where a is a tuning parameter $0 < a < 1$. A value of a close to 1 provides a really good noise filtering, as can be seen in Fig. 10.14a, whereas a value of a close to 0 allows the filter to track changes really fast. To have a good performance, we have extended the filter (see Eq. (10.1)) to dynamically adapt the parameter a based on the characteristics of the data p^m we measure. This is done with the two functions $a(k)$ and $e(k)$. For details, we refer to the paper [FGL15]. The filter can be used to learn individual transition probabilities p_{ij} from observed system traces. However, the obtained estimates for each row of P would most likely not constitute correct categorical distributions (sum of the probabilities of the outgoing transitions of each state s_i is not 1). Consequently, [FGL15] presents a procedure to use these learned probabilities to update the provability matrix P of the discrete-time Markov chain (DTMC) via a convenient "correction" procedure. Furthermore, all existing procedure [CJR11, Cal+14, Epi+09, EGT10, ZWL08], including LAF [FGL15], estimate the probabilities based on the observed data; for further studies,

Table 10.1 MARE results for the six patterns

	LAF (%)	Kalman (%)	Cove (%)
Noisy	4.41	4.54	11.70
Step	4.19	8.51	8.65
Ramp	4.28	7.04	8.27
Square	6.54	21.47	8.50
Triangle	7.79	12.84	8.16
Outlier	3.68	3.78	8.56

it would be also interesting to apply forecasting procedures [AGC12, ACG12] to estimate the future development of the individual transition probabilities p_{ij}.

In the original paper [FGL15], two experiments have been performed to evaluate the quality of LAF. The first experiment evaluates the accuracy via the Mean Average Relative Error (MARE) and data that are generated to follow six common patterns: Noisy, Step, Ramp, Square, Triangle, Outlier. The results, as shown in Table 10.1, indicate that the developed algorithm (LAF) outperforms in terms of accuracy (MARE) the state-of-the-art approaches Cove [Cal+14] and Kalman filtering [ZWL08].

For the second experiment, [FGL15] uses a realistic and large-scale dataset of the users' browsing behaviour for the WorldCup98 website [WCL]. The logs of the browsing behaviour spread over a period of 3 months, and the website is composed of a total of over 32,000 pages. As a result, we show that LAF is able to scale to problems of a realistic size and complexity.

As mentioned before, in Sect. 10.1, we could obtain the structure of DTMC models. Together with LAF approach, learned models can be synthesised and verified using model checking techniques (e.g. Prism) specified with probabilistic computational tree logic (PCTL). Hence, we can reason about the reliability of large-scale systems by using probabilistic model checking.

Related Work

Many approaches using automated model generation from the observation of production systems stem from the domain of fault detection and isolation (FDI). Generated models are continuous models [Ise06, AA13], discrete event models [HKW03, LL11, RLL10], or hybrid models [Vod+11]. Approaches for continuous systems use machine learning techniques to, for example, parametrise differential equations, train neural networks, estimate initial states for observers, or estimate parameters for fuzzy models; cf. [Ise06, AA13]. Some approaches learn hybrid models of systems composed of both discrete and continuous dynamics; cf. [NF15]. Such approaches are suitable for process plants, that is plants dealing with continuous product flows (e.g. liquids, gases, or granules). The state of such plants is given by both continuous measurements (such as temperatures, pressures, or flow rates) and discrete measurements (such as open/close states of valves or on/off states of pumps).

The states of discrete manufacturing systems (i.e. production systems producing piecewise goods) are usually described by purely discrete state variables. These states are consisted of binary measurements (such as "workpiece present/not present" or "conveyor running/not running"). For discrete event systems, learning algorithms mostly generate automata (cf. [RLL10]) or Petri Nets (cf. [LL11]). However, manufacturing processes are usually highly concurrent, resulting in a huge amount of possible states. The cyclic control and difficult real-time conditions render it problematic to weave code for monitoring into the controlling software. Therefore, only the event traces, observed by monitoring the sensor and actuator signal changes, are available as a data source for monitoring approaches. Unfortunately, models generated from signal traces tend to be highly complex and are on a low level of abstraction compared to non-functional properties. The algorithm presented in [RLL10] reduces model complexity by automatically dividing the gathered data into subsets and creating partial automata. However, without any semantics of the data, an interpretation on non-functional property level is still rarely possible. Other approaches, for example, [AT12, HA05, Hus+06] use static a priori information. This includes modelling manually, which event consumes or releases resources for these processes. This allows an interpretation of generated models on a higher level of abstraction. But an automated analysis is not in the focus of those approaches, and therefore these approaches are, like most presented models for production systems, by design not suitable for automatically deriving non-functional properties during evolution.

Further Reading

A more detailed overview of possible non-functional requirements that can be derived is given in Ladiges [Lad+13b] and shown for the PPU, besides a more detailed description of the overall approach in Lagides [LFL16]. Anomaly detection to identify evolution changes is given in Chap. 5. How the models are handled within a knowledge-carrying software is shown in Haubeck [Hau+14a] and Haubeck [HLF18]. Further, Sect. 10.4.2 builds this knowledge-carrying software and the learned models by identifying evolution steps that can be exchanged in order to recommend changes by comparing slightly different but similar systems.

10.3.3 Conclusion and Outlook

This section has shown two approaches using learning algorithms for automatic model generation or model parametrisation. The resulting models are suitable for analysing current system behaviour regarding non-functional properties. The first approach aims at generating models of the machine state [Lad+15a] and material flow [Lad+15c] reflecting the behaviour of manufacturing systems. The approach contains different levels of knowledge. The lowest level is raw data. By adding the information model, that is the signal semantics, the data are made interpretable. Therefore, the considered events are first filtered and separated along the signal semantics, and then the models are learned out of traces. The presented models of the machine state and material flow, as well as the properties resulting from their analysis, are the top levels of contained knowledge and allow conclusions regarding evolution.

The second approach aims to efficiently learn the transition probabilities of a Discrete Time Markov Chain based on the observed traces from the actual running system [FGL15], and based on this model quantitative verification techniques can be applied. These quantitative verification techniques check whether the model satisfies quantitative properties, for example in PCTL (Probabilistic Computation Tree Logic) [HJ94], that can be defined via a specification pattern system [Gru08] and a controlled natural language [Aut+15].

The models of the presented approaches can be used to derive differences, as shown in Sect. 10.1.1. This allows identifying differences that result in changes of non-functional quality aspects, which were derived by the two approaches presented here. Further, runtime monitoring of non-functional quality aspects has synergies with model-driven development that deals with requirements in an interdisciplinary model (see Sect. 10.2.1), because monitoring allows the detection and evaluation of changes in the running system that can be transferred back to the model-driven models to use the advantages of both approaches (see [Hau+14b] for details).

10.4 Recommend and Assess Future Changes Based on Past Changes

The previous sections have proposed approaches for a wide range of evolution problems considering changing systems. One thing that is common in these approaches is that they provide valuable knowledge about past changes, which can be utilised to support future evolution processes. Therefore, this section presents three approaches on how the current state and past changes can be used to recommend and evaluate future changes. (1) The first approach concentrates on finding recurring changes on different model versions and meta-models. By using heuristics, atomic changes on the user level are combined to complex, recurring changes cutting across different models. (2) The second approach focuses on managing knowledge by establishing a knowledge-carrying network. This network exchanges experiences of past changes between similar systems characterised by their behaviour and context. (3) The third approach derives maintenance tasks from a certain change request and for a given architecture. These maintenance tasks can be used to identify the effort for changing the system architecture, realising an "Economic Recommender".

10.4.1 *Supporting Model Editing with Automatic Recommendations*

Models are key artefacts in model-driven software engineering, and software engineers typically spend much time creating and evolving models. Software engineers may even define new domain-specific models. Hence, good tool support is needed to efficiently work with models.

IDEs for source code offer many tools that make recommendations for working with text-based programming languages, for example auto completions, quick fixes, refactorings, and code templates. All major text-based programming languages can be defined via context-free grammars (e.g. EBNF), which simplifies the implementation of these source code recommenders. Also, there are few widespread text-based programming languages, which makes it feasible to develop or extend these recommenders manually.

Our goal is to improve the modelling speed and quality of model changes by recommending model changes to the engineer based on current changes and historical changes. Figure 10.15a shows an example recommendation for an Ecore meta-model. The original version of the model contains two classes with duplicated attributes. When a user adds a common superclass (green), the recommender systems notice that this change fits the pattern of the common *Pull-up-Attribute* (see Fig. 10.15b) refactoring and recommends the remaining steps, that is moving one attribute up (yellow) and deleting the other one (red). Accepting the recommendation automates several manual modelling steps.

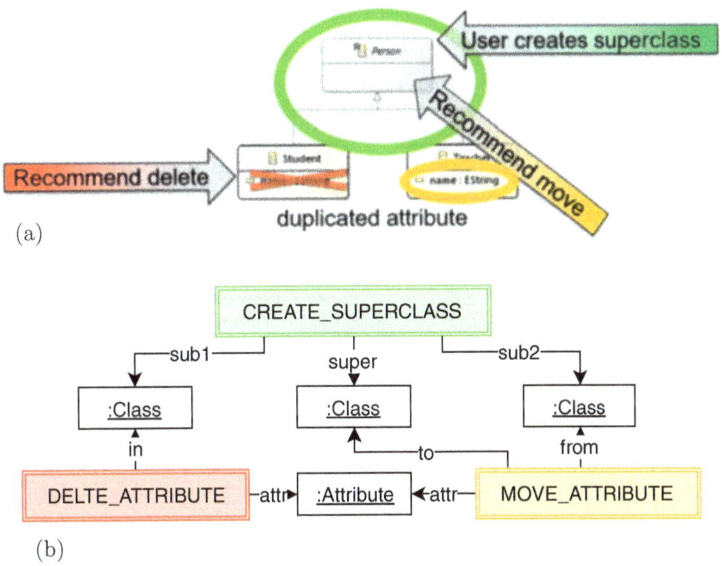

Fig. 10.15 Example of *Pull-up-Attribute* recommendation and blueprint. (**a**) Example *Pull-up-Attribute* recommendation (red and yellow) after a user creates a superclass (green). (**b**) Example blueprint for recommendation in **a**

The main challenge with this approach is that for most types of models, there is no list of common refactorings or frequent changes that could be used as a basis for a recommendation. This is especially true for proprietary domain-specific models. For example, Eclipse Projects hosts over 300 projects related to the Eclipse Modeling Framework. These Projects contain over 30,000 models; most of these are Ecore meta-models and UML models for which common refactorings are known. But there are also 260 types of models with only 10 to 100 instances. It is not realistic to expect that there is any documentation about common refactorings on these less common types of models.

Foundation

Our approach is based on the SiLift-Tool [Keh+12b, KKT13] from the MOCA project, which is also described in Sect. 10.1.1. This tool computes the differences between versions of meta- and instance models. We represent differences as sets of partially ordered model transformation invocations, where an invocation consists of model transformations and their parameter bindings. Model transformations are represented by Henshin rules [Are+10] that can take multiple parameters.

Figure 10.16a shows a simple Henshin rule with two parameters: *Selected* and *New*. The Henshin rule matches the *EModelElement* (grey) to the *Selected* parameter. If this match is successful, the rule creates a new *EAnnotation* (green) and matches it to the *New* parameter. A parameter binding can be, for example, the *id* of an element in a concrete model. The Henshin rules can be generated for every type of model for which an Ecore meta-model is available, using the SiLift tool Sect. 10.1.1.

Figure 10.16b is a screenshot of a difference computed by SiLift. It contains five Henshin rule invocations. One invocation with two parameter bindings (*selectedEObject* and *New*) is expanded. The corresponding Henshin rule is shown in Fig. 10.16a. This rule matches an *EModelElement* called *getAllChildContainers* and creates a new *EAnnotation* for it.

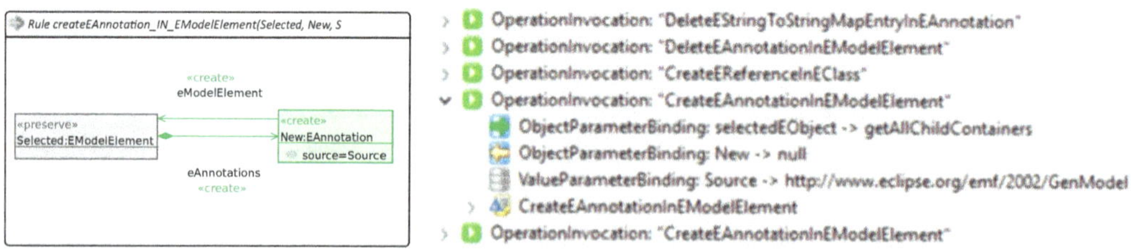

(a) (b)

Fig. 10.16 Example model difference. (**a**) Henshin rule for creating an *EAnnotation*. (**b**) Example model difference computed by SiLift

Analysis of Change Histories

The ENSURE 2 approach is to automatically infer the information that is required for making useful recommendations from the change histories of models. This information can be thought of as blueprints for recommendations that represent common refactorings or frequent changes to a type of model.

Figure 10.15b shows an example blueprint for the *Pull-up-Attribute* refactoring. Blueprints consist of model transformations (depicted as boxes with two borders) and parameters that may be shared between these transformations (depicted as boxes with single borders). The transformation boxes with two borders contain the name of the Henshin rule, and their outgoing edges are labelled with the names of their parameters. The parameter boxes with single borders contain the type of parameter. If a parameter is shared between transformations, it is only shown once.

The blueprint in Fig. 10.15b describes the creation of a new superclass with two subclasses, where the subclasses contain an attribute with the same name. The blueprint further describes that for one of the subclasses, the attributes have to be moved to the superclass, while it has to be deleted in the other subclass.

This approach has several advantages: No expert knowledge is required, recommendations can be specific to a model type and developer or development team, and this technique can be applied to private code bases without publishing the results. Note that it is still possible to integrate expert knowledge into the approach by manually creating additional blueprints and adding them to the automatically generated blueprints. Also note that we cannot automatically infer descriptive names for the blueprints.

Inferring recommendations from a model history allows the recommendations to be tailored to the model. This has the added benefit that users can influence future recommendations automatically with their current actions. A further benefit is that users don't have to do additional work to get recommendations, as long as a history of previous versions is available.

Inferring Blueprints

The history of model changes is very noisy. A commit can contain many changes that may not be related at all. Before we can automatically infer blueprints, we have to define metrics to identify good blueprints.

In a first step, we identified the following metrics for determining the quality of a blueprint:

Occurrences This metric counts how often a blueprint appears in the change history. *Occurrences* is a simple metric that prefers small blueprints, that is blueprints consisting of few Henshin rules, because these occur more often in the history. A higher number of *occurrences* is better because it means that the blueprint was applied more often in the history of the model.

Shared Parameters Henshin rules inside of a blueprint can have *shared parameters*. Thus, a blueprint can have fewer parameters than the sum of the parameters of its Henshin rules. The number of *shared parameters* is a measure of the blueprint's cohesion; thus, a high number of *shared parameters* is better. As the number of *shared parameters* goes up, the number of *occurrences* may decrease (but not increase).

Diversity We represent *diversity* as a partial order between blueprints. If a blueprint A contains a subset of the rules in a blueprint B, then A is less diverse than B. This metric prefers bigger blueprints, as opposed to the *Occurrences* metric. More *diverse* blueprints are better because they encode more complex refactorings.

We generate blueprints by evolving a population of blueprints using a genetic algorithm. Since we have three different metrics, we must solve a multi-objective optimisation problem. Thus, we use a Pareto front of our three metrics to choose the member of our population that is taken into the next generation.

We defined two mutation operators that evolve our blueprints: *extension* and *specialisation*.

Extension tries to add a new Henshin rule to a blueprint in such a way that the new rule shares one parameter with one of the existing rules. *Specialisation* tries to share two previously unshared parameters within the blueprint. Note that both mutation can never increase the *occurrences* of a blueprint, while *extension* will increase *shared parameters* and *diversity*. Note also that the graph of Henshin rules connected via shared parameters will stay connected after the application of a mutation.

For our initial population, we create all feasible blueprints that contain a single Henshin rule.

Evaluation

Figure 10.17 depicts a blueprint learned by our genetic algorithm from the PPU Fault Tree data set [Get+13]. The blueprint has an *occurrence* of 8 and 5 *shared parameters* (we do not count the shared *Root* element). Our algorithm did not find any more *diverse* blueprints in this data set.

In [KGT16] we performed an evaluation of a prototype recommender as a proof of concept that did not yet use blueprints. This early prototype created recommendations based on a single user change in version V_x and all changes from earlier versions $V_{x-1}..V_0$. If all recommended changes based on the history up to V_{x-1} were present in version V_x, then we counted this as a true positive, else it was a false positive. Changes in version V_x that were never recommended were counted as false negatives.

For the evaluation, we used the GMF data set from Herrmannsdoerfer et al. [HRW09] because it contained models with many versions, and it was also used by other researchers. The data set consists of three models with 10–110

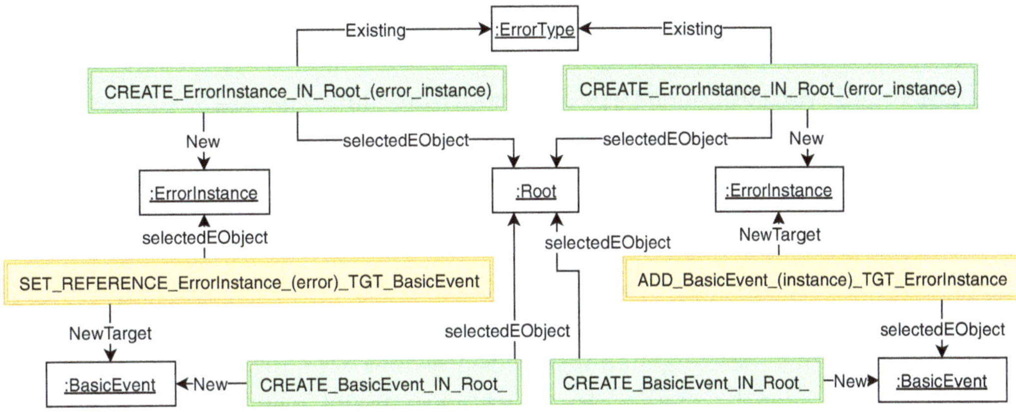

Fig. 10.17 Blueprint learned by our genetic algorithm from the PPU fault tree data set

Table 10.2 Recommendation results for different models

Name	TP	FP	Precision
gmfgen	554	217	0.72
gmfgraph	25	33	0.43
Mappings	36	8	0.82
Total	615	258	–
Average	205	86	–

Table 10.3 Recommendation results for PPU fault trees

Name	True positives	False positives	Precision
faulttree1	95	115	0.45
faulttree2	71	36	0.66

versions, and our prototype achieved a precision between 43% and 82%. This shows that it is possible to generate recommendations from model histories. The results are depicted in Table 10.2.

We also performed an evaluation on two fault trees created from the PPU evolution scenarios. These results are depicted in Table 10.3. We will also perform a further evaluation on the Petri Nets learned in Sect. 10.4.2.

Related Work

There already exist recommender systems for model-driven software development that are capable of performing the refactoring from Fig. 10.15a. Kuschke et al. [KMR13] translate common refactorings on models into constraint systems and use these to identify partially applied refactorings. They use a constraint solver to generate a recommendation based on a partial refactoring. Another approach from Taentzer et al. [Tae+17] focuses on model repair. They search for partially applied refactorings in models and recommend the remaining parts of the refactoring. This approach also works for inter-model refactorings.

Both of these approaches require expert knowledge about how common refactorings for certain types of models look like. But this knowledge is not generally available for all types of domain-specific modelling languages.

Note that our work is also related to model transformation by example (e.g. [Var06]). But this approach also requires an expert to generate clear examples of transformations for every type of model (i.e. pairs of models before and after the transformation).

Another approach by Sen et al. [SBV10] uses meta-models as graph grammars, these grammars are then used to compute possible additions to instances of these meta-models, so that the computed instances are valid w.r.t. the meta-models.

This approach can be applied to an instance model when its meta-model is available and its results are similar auto completions for text-based programming languages. Our approach, in contrast, aims to recommend refactorings that are more complex than auto completions.

Other related works are source code recommender systems [MKM13, BMM09, Muş+12]; these make use of different techniques for generating and prioritising recommendations based on previous changes to source code. All major text-based programming languages can be defined via context-free grammars (e.g. EBNF), which simplifies the implementation of these source code recommenders. Also, there are only few very widespread text-based programming languages, which makes it feasible to develop or extend these recommenders manually. Thus, this work is related, but the techniques cannot be directly applied to the more diverse and complex realm of domain-specific models.

Conclusion

Existing recommenders for model-driven software development are mostly model-type specific and require expert knowledge. Our vision was to automatically generate recommendations based on model change histories. For this we inferred blueprints of recommendations from model change histories. This work has also been presented in [Kög17].

Our blueprints and our methods to generate these blueprints will be useful for developing model agnostic recommender systems.

10.4.2 Recommending Evolution Steps Within a Knowledge Carrying Network

Contrary to the previous approach of recommending changes of one model, the following method targets horizontally integrated systems. Cyber Physical Production Systems (CPPS) are characterised by the interconnection of software and hardware components that are horizontally and vertically integrated. These CPPS cause the need to document their evolution systematically to support their maintainability over time [Vog+15a]. To handle this task, a collective memory for identifying and perceiving historical artefacts is needed to allow collaborative work in which not only the machine's behaviour arising from the dynamics of its hardware and software components is considered but also the evolution of the whole CPPS is considered holistically [GG08]. Here, the horizontal integration of machines provides new potentials to support evolution [Hau+17] because it allows for a comparison of one individual machine status among other machines by pushing information about their status in the networked cyber level of a CPPS [LBK14]. These statuses can be seen as steps of the evolution performed during their semi-automated operation. The recommendation of evolution has a strong focus on these steps, which goes along with the core idea of evolution that focuses the process of changes rather than how a machine looks like after the change. Therefore, in the following section, model-based evolution steps are showcased as first-class entities that form an evolution process in a peer-to-peer network. Recommendations are given to engineers on the basis of this evolution process by providing evolution steps of other similar systems that were already extracted during the evolution process. In this way, the vision of a marketplace for evolution steps is followed that allows exchange of already performed evolution steps [Hau+18c].

Express Evolution Steps of a System

To describe evolution within a horizontally integrated network, evolution should be fully expressed by the sequential execution of evolution steps. For the description, a step-based approach similar to the delta-modelling of software product lines is used. The idea of steps is to adapt to evolution by representing an evolution in a core step, which is the initial development, and apply evolution steps over time. Evolution steps represent changes that are following Buckley et al. [Buc+05] characterised in the form of questions. Evolution steps are described as answers to the six questions what, why, who, when, where, and how.

To understand the learned behaviour as evolution steps, it must be specified *what* is changed. In order to capture historical behaviour, runtime models are learned according to the signal behaviour of a machine, as presented in Sect. 10.3.1. The following approach is therefore explained and demonstrated on material flow models of production systems. These models are Petri Nets, which have signals as transitions. What is changed is expressed in accordance with these signals in lifted (edit) operations. To utilise the differencing pipeline of lifted (edit) operations, as explained in Sect. 10.1.1, a matching strategy of transitions and therefore signals is needed. The used matching strategy measures the similarity of signals by exploiting their additional context information. This is done in order to identify similar or even the same production sections, which are reflected in similar patterns of the signals and their context information (timing, type, and topology). As a similarity metric, the algorithm uses a Null Hypothesis for the timing according to a specified confidence and a relation matrix for the type and topology context. To find the matching, strongly related signals are identified by aligning different sequences of signals to each other. The best alignment is identified by an extended Needleman-Wunsch Algorithm, and the signals are matched following this alignment. Further details about the matching can be found in [Cha+18].

To identify the lifted edit operations, a template for the material flow production system is used. It determines how the structure of the signals evolves in the material flow. For structure changes, two (edit) operations apply when an additional signal occurs before or after a specific signal sequence and a third if two separated signal sequences in the model merge or split. Besides structural changes, changes in the meaning of signals are captured by operations for timing changes, as well as signal type and topology changes. For example, these changes in timing occur when the latency of the signal is changed, for example due to wear and tear. Based on these operations, edit scripts are derived (see Sect. 10.1.1) that represent what is changed in an evolution step. More details are given in [Pie+18].

Further, it is questioned in an evolution step *where* the evolution takes places. This describes the condition under which the evolution happened and therefore where the operations of signals are applied. Since in the practical implementation these conditions are sensitive parameters, three *privacy policies* are introduced: First, just the edit script with no additional information besides the changed signals is provided in the step. Second, neighbour information of signals directly related to the changed signals of the edit script are included in the evolution step, and, last, the entire structure of the material flow model from which the edit script stems is included.

Why a system evolves is evaluated in terms of non-functional properties such as performance or flexibility since it enables the operator to recognise weaknesses and to ensure the quality of complex systems [LFL16]. This part relies on the non-functional properties derived directly out of the material flow models as the reason for evolution. Properties express the change in properties that was observed when the step was introduced. The extraction of these properties was introduced in Sect. 10.3.1.

The temporal properties (*when*) build up an evolution process by linking to each other, which creates a partial order in the form of a directed tree. Vertexes of this tree represent steps, and edges represent the directions in which the evolution proceeded with respect to versions and variants. Versions describe an evolution step in the same system and variants a step derived by applying a step on another system. The leaves of the tree are the currently operated versions, which can be reconstructed using involved steps retrospectively starting from the tree's root. In this way, an evolution process of the whole network of systems is built.

One interesting question, when seeing evolution in exchangeable evolution steps of a network of systems, is *who* has evolved. This ownership is reflected in an evolution step by using a digital signature of the evolved system. For evolution steps, a valid digital signature gives assurance that a step really was provided by the signing system. In addition, this allows tracing back steps for evolution support.

How evolution is supported is considered in the environment of the network. From a technical point of view, the overall evolution process is a distributed ledger of evolution steps that is stored within a distributed network. Therefore, to support

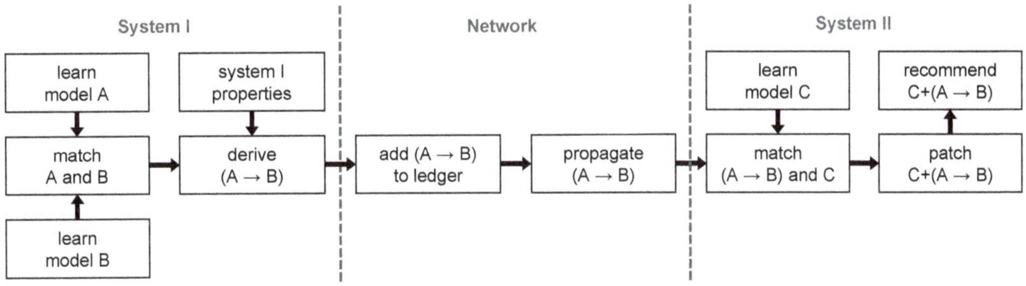

Fig. 10.18 Process of the extraction of an evolution step and its comparison to a model of another system

evolution, the steps must be propagated through the network. Figure 10.18 shows the evolution support process that provides recommendations to the engineer. The process assumes two different systems that observe and analyse models, as well as detect anomalies of the production system to extract different versions of models. This is performed by the knowledge-carrying software of the underlying learning approach that uses a model-based CPS architecture (see [Hau+18b] for details of the architecture). Whenever a change is detected, the previous model (model A) is matched with the model after the change (model B) to derive the evolution step ($A \rightarrow B$). To share the step, the network adds the step to the ledger and then propagates the step to all other nodes. Propagated evolution steps are used to recommend changes to the engineer. The shared step is matched and then patched to their own model (model C) with the help of model patching (see Sect. 10.1.1). The patched model is provided as a recommendation to the engineer to propose a behaviour change that was already positively experienced on other production systems.

To sum up, this section suggested evolution steps that use a model-based edit script (what) under a specific context condition (where) to achieve the desired effect (why). Then the evolution steps are structured by linking predecessor and inheritance as a process (when) that considers its originators (who) in a propagating network that gives recommendation to the engineer (how supported).

Application on xPPU Case Study

To evaluate the concept, a marketplace for evolution steps is envisioned (see [Hau+17]). This distributed marketplace should allow a platform to provide and request evolution steps in order to share experiences about evolution in the form of performed changes. The evolution steps were learned for Scenarios 1, 1b,[2] 2, 3, 5, and 10 of the xPPU case study. The distributed ledger of evolution steps is

[2] 1b is a modified version of the Pick-and-Place Unit (PPU) Scenario 1, which only uses metallic workpieces.

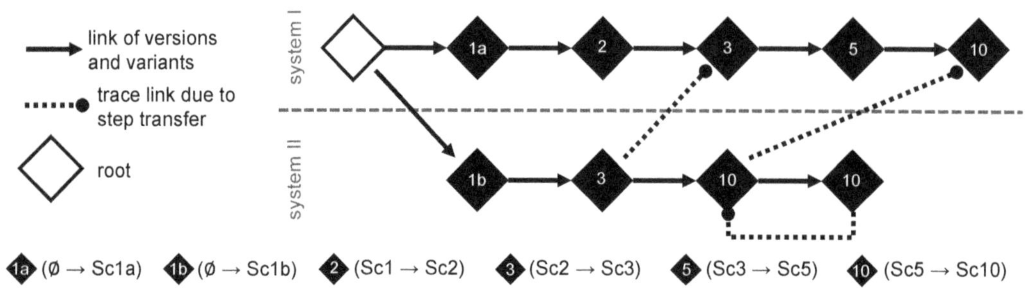

Fig. 10.19 Evolution process of performed steps over CPPS network

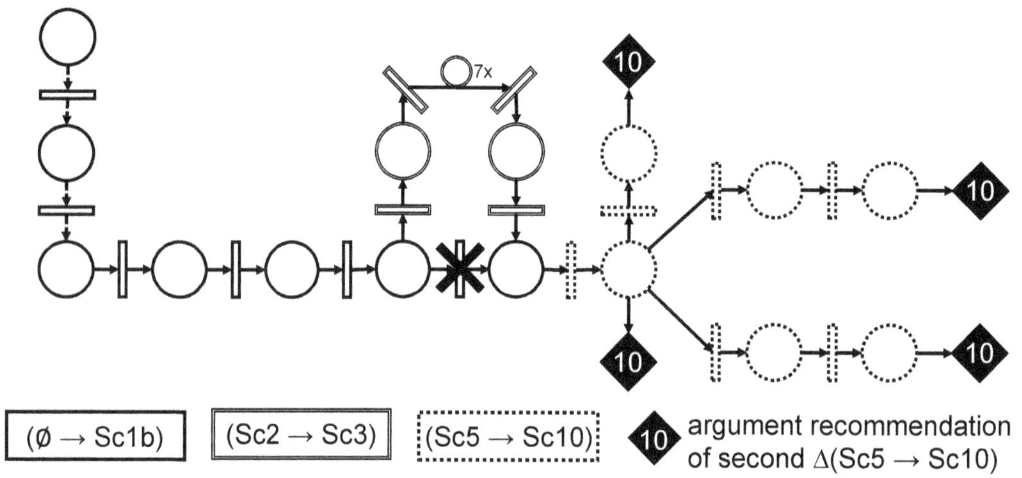

Fig. 10.20 Summary recommendation of the resulting material flows (refer: [Hau+18a])

implemented in a knowledge-carrying software managing material flow models at runtime, which includes a peer-to-peer network with blockchain functionalities to implement a distributed marketplace. The platform provides a common and secure ledger while eliminating the central authority with its peer-to-peer nature. This is done by a global consensus protocol that ensures a full copy of the blockchain available for each participant that contains every step of the build-up evolution process. The tested peer-to-peer network had one KCS for each evolution scenario of the case study and consisted of 6 (simulated) production systems.

Exemplary, Fig. 10.19 shows the resulting evolution process of two systems. It shows system I, which already underwent all scenarios from 1 to 10 with all possible evolution steps, and system II, which started as Scenario 1b with only metallic workpieces. As the figure illustrates, system II evolved through recommendation in three cases by applying the stamp ($Sc2 \rightarrow Sc3$) and two conveyors ($Sc5 \rightarrow Sc10$) without additional workpieces of Scenario 2 or the crane optimisation of Scenario 5. Furthermore, Fig. 10.20 shows a summary of the resulting recommendations given to the engineer before the last addition of a conveyor. The left-hand side of the model represents the root model with the initial step implemented on it ($\phi \rightarrow Sc1b$). It transports plastic workpieces to a ramp. The further steps are explained in details in [Hau+18a]. It can be seen that recommendations on the model layer can have errors. The recommendation contains a transition that will never be observed in the implemented system because it indicates that a workpiece is directly transferred from the stack to the ramp. This will not be observed in the implemented system because no plastic workpieces exist in the evolved system II and therefore no direct transport is done in system II. But the patched model still provides a good recommendation, and the mentioned transition is not included in the model after the operator implemented the signal behaviour. The last patching is not reflected in Fig. 10.20. Instead, it shows alternatives identified by the matching algorithm. An additional conveyor could be added instead of one of the output ramps served by the pushers (two alternatives at the right) or instead of the ramp at the end of the existing conveyor (alternative at the top), as well as in parallel to the existing conveyor (alternative at the bottom). Each option is valid (which is not necessarily the case). This example shows the variety of recommendations that might be provided by this approach.

Related Work

In cloud and agile manufacturing, similar approaches exist but aim at virtualisation of manufacturing capabilities and resource sharing [VH13]. As an example, the approach by Lee et al. [LBK14] suggested to send information to a centralised hub for special analytics. The presented evolution support approach can be seen as an instantiation of CPPS with cloud connection for the specific functionality of a cooperative evolution support but aims for decentralised capturing and sharing of model differences. Cooperative knowledge exchange about specific topics has already proven its benefits in other application domains like distributed data race detection [KZC12]. Therefore, the approach is also related to experience management in which approaches exist for capturing the users' or developers' field experiences of software systems [He13] or systems driven by user experiences [SVS14]. Here the approach follows the view of knowledge-sharing networks that combine the idea of (a) an advanced preparation of an individual itself and (b) an evolution steps by considering the knowledge of other individuals who already made these experiences.

Direct sharing of runtime evolution steps of machines is not the focus of the research so far, but, for example, Würsch et al. [WGG13] present a query network for software evolution data in a software development tool, which shows that sharing and exchanging can answer evolution questions. In software development, past changes are often captured in software variant and versioning tools. Such a repository provides data to find changes and is in this approach transferred to CPPS in the operational phase with evolution based on generated models. Furthermore, Kolovos et al. [KPP06] have laid out different ways of implementing model transformation tools of Eclipse Modelling Framework and Graphical Modelling Framework to optimise results in order to make them beneficial in terms of productivity and maintainability. Abdallah et al. [ATW08] already have demonstrated the applicability of model transformation aspects through different case studies. Brun and Pierantonio [BP08] have demonstrated how maintaining a database and tracking of design-level changes have made it possible to understand structural evolution processes. They have illustrated how to find differences and how to track them. They give reasons on how important it is to record differences between instances consisting of calculation and identification of such differential steps. In this section, we targeted a similar automated history of (quality) indicators on a model level in the operational phase for recommending behaviour changes.

Further Reading

More information about the model learning approach can be found in Sect. 10.3.1. Additional information about the matching used here has been published in [Cha+18] and the overall idea of a cooperative support in [Hau+17]. In [Pie+18], the use of the differencing approach for learned behaviour models of production systems is shown in more detail, and in [Hau+18c], the idea of a marketplace for evolution experience is described.

10.4.3 Learning Maintainability Estimation for Enabling an "Economical Effort Recommender"

In contrast to previously presented model learning approaches to automated identification of changes, this section deals with the automated analysis of change propagation in system models. For this purpose, we extend a change impact analysis approach in Information Systems (IS) to aPS, as IS and aPS face very similar challenges with respect to evolution. One target of the analysis of an IS or aPS with respect to its maintainability is giving an impression of the change effort initiated by a change request. Rather than identifying which changes were performed from a system alternative to another one, maintenance tasks are derived from a certain change request and for a given architecture. These maintenance tasks can be used to identify the effort for changing the system architecture, realising an "Economical Effort Recommender". In order to realise a change impact estimation approach for both IS and aPS, an architecture description in terms of meta-modelling and an architecture-based change impact identification for automating this procedure are necessary.

Challenges for Maintainability Estimation: Information Systems vs. Automated Production Systems

Both IS and aPS operate over time, often over decades, after deployment. During the runtime, they often face change requests that lead to the modifications on the system for most of the cases, and these modifications may include corrections, improvements, or adaptations of the system environment changes [Hei+18a, Vog+17a]. Therefore, maintainability, which is defined as the ease with which a system or a component can be retained in a state where it can perform its required functions [IEE90], is an important quality aspect of the system, especially for long-living systems.

However, maintainability estimation is already a difficult task for IS [Leh80] and even harder for aPS since they are comprised of multi-discipline artefacts from mechanical, electric/electronic, and software engineering. Moreover, aPS is implemented in modularised architectures that are in their own way different from pure software systems [Vog+17b]. In the following, we discuss the state of the art for the change impact analysis in IS and aPS.

State of the Art for Change Impact Identification in Information Systems In the domain of IS, there are several approaches to change impact identification [Ros+15]. Task-based project planning focuses on building a hierarchical decomposition of tasks into sub-tasks (e.g. [KA03] or [Car+83]). However, these approaches do not use the software's architecture. Further, the scale of the estimation is coarse grained. Architecture-based project planning approaches (e.g. [PB01] or [Car12]) are based on Conway's law [Con68] stating that the communication structure of organisations plays an important role in software design. However, the approaches in this category do not estimate the change effort or do not support an automated change impact analysis. A further category is architecture-based software evolution, for example as done in [Gar+09] and [Naa12]. They consider software architecture as the main artefact during the change process. However, the works are not extended to the change effort estimation. In scenario-based architecture analysis, supplementary information is taken into account, such as maintenance scenarios [BB99] or informal software architecture description [Cle+02]. Still management tasks are missing in the aforementioned approaches.

State of the Art for Change Impact Identification in Automated Production Systems Effort estimation in automation has been purely realised by counting the results of input and output signals multiplied by the hourly effort per signal for decades [Vog14]. However, this method provides just simple results, not all the necessary tasks in detail and corresponding costs. Recently, Prähofer et al. proposed a multi-purpose feature-modelling approach by mapping feature into modules [Pra+17], and this enables the impact measurement of a change, but this is not embracing the various type of features, that is all the features from different disciplines. This approach is based on the aPS meta-models. Meta-modelling is an important topic for this project since an aPS meta-model and its properties, which lie over the disciplines, are required ultimately. For the multi-disciplinary property of aPS, domain-specific models from each domain may be maintained separately [Bro+10]. The problem is synchronising all models [Fel+15], especially when a change happens in one domain. Especially, some works (e.g. [KV13] and [FKV14]) suggest discipline-encompassing modelling methods based on SysML to check compatibilities on changes in the interface level and functionality level.

Further, representing all the necessary information within one meta-model has also been researched by [BFS05]. This approach suggests a method to combine software structure, together with physical aspects in one common model. The approach of Berardinelli et al. [Ber+16] maps AutomationML into SysML. Recently, an integrated plant modelling using AutomationML is introduced in [Win+17]. However, models or meta-models focus on specific problems respectively, and there is no existing meta-model that encompasses all different disciplines, especially with the purpose of estimating change effort by examining change propagation.

Karlsruhe Architectural Maintainability Prediction for Automated Production Systems: An Architecture-Based Change Impact Analysis Method for aPS

In the DoMain project, we proposed a systematic and automated approach for effort estimation considering all disciplines within aPS instead of manual estimation, depending on the engineers' knowledge. As IS and aPS are very similar regarding evolution, we used an existing change propagation approach from IS—Karlsruhe Architectural Maintainability Prediction (Karlsruhe Architectural Maintainability Prediction (KAMP)) [Ros+15]. KAMP aims to analyse the change propagation in the model of the software architecture for a set of change requests. For this purpose KAMP uses change propagation rules based on domain knowledge. Based on the KAMP [Ros+15] and KAMP framework [HBK18a], we developed Karlsruhe Architectural Maintainability Prediction for automated Production Systems (KAMP4aPS) [Hei+18a, Vog+17a, Koc17]. KAMP4aPS allows automated change propagation analysis starting from an initial change in the system. To solve the issues discussed in the beginning of this subsection and to allow a more realistic change effort estimation, our approach considers technical and organisational tasks during the change process as well. To support change propagation in the system's structure, as well as in the technical and organisational tasks, we provide two meta-models, which serve as input for KAMP4aPS. Using the first meta-model, the system's structure can be described. The second meta-model describes the non-structural elements in the system for the structural elements. Examples of non-structural elements are documentation and test cases, as well as technical and organisational information. Thus, non-structural meta classes reference the corresponding structural meta classes. In other words, the input of KAMP4aPS is the descriptive model of the system structure and the description of non-structural elements for the structural elements. Based on the input and the initial change in the descriptive model, KAMP4aPS automatically generates a task list containing all tasks that should be potentially carried out to implement the change. These tasks refer to changing elements in the descriptive model of the system structure and of the non-structural elements. As effort estimation may differ according to different elements (e.g. the cost of changing a specific component, module, or program), there is a need for domain knowledge to accurately estimate the effort. Thus, effort estimation has to be done manually based on the generated task list.

Further, due to the diversity of artefacts in aPS domain due to electrical and mechanical parts, as well as software systems, some artefacts may be neglected when estimating the effort of a change implementation manually. As KAMP4aPS considers these artefacts during evolution (i.e. using the system structure model and the model of the non-structural elements), the cost of a change can be estimated more realistically. Another benefit is the way in which a change scenario can be implemented, as there are usually different ways to implement a change scenario. Using KAMP4aPS, different ways of implementation at model level can be simulated and compared with each other without implementing them in the real system [Hei+18a, Vog+17a, Koc17, Ros+15]. Thus, KAMP4aPS serves as an economical effort recommender as it allows selecting the most efficient and cost-effective implementation variant for a change scenario and estimating the change effort before implementing the change.

Overview of KAMP4aPS Approach Figure 10.21 gives an overview of KAMP4aPS. It is composed of two phases. In the first phase, the input has to be prepared. As illustrated in Fig. 10.21 and described previously, the first phase comprises (i) constructing structural models of the domain; (ii) annotating these models with further information regarding the non-structural elements, as well as the technical and organisational elements; and (iii) identifying the initial changes in the model based on a change scenario. In the second phase, KAMP4aPS automatically calculates the change propagation using a set of predefined change propagation rules. Change propagation rules are defined by the domain expert and describe from which meta class to which meta class of the system structure meta-model the change can propagate (e.g. change propagation from the sensor to its fixation). Based on the initial change, KAMP4aPS iteratively applies the change propagation rules on the system structure meta-model and identifies the affected model elements by the change. In other words, KAMP4aPS applies the change propagation rules to the model elements identified as affected in the previous iteration. In each iteration, KAMP4aPS adds the newly affected model elements of the system structure meta-

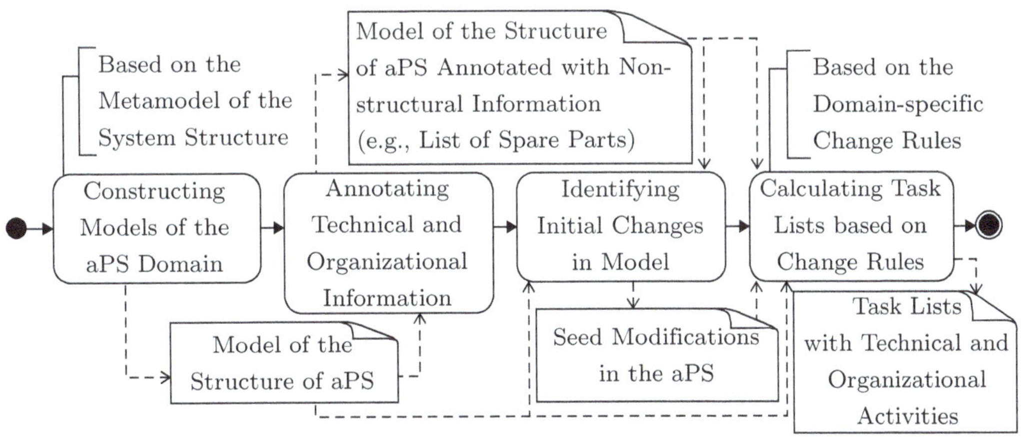

Fig. 10.21 Overview of KAMP4aPS task list derivation procedure [Hei+18a, Vog+17a]

model to a set containing all affected artefacts. The set of all affected artefacts does not contain any duplicates. Thus, KAMP4aPS terminates if no new model elements are added to the set of all affected artefacts in the last iteration. For each affected model elements of the system structure meta-model, KAMP4aPS identifies all affected model elements of the non-structural meta-model. For example, if there are test cases (i.e. model elements of the non-structural meta-model) for a component (i.e. model element of the structural meta-model) and the component is affected by a change, the test cases have also to be marked as changed. KAMP4aPS adds the affected model elements of the system structure meta-model and non-structural meta-model to a task list. The task list is the output of our approach. Each task in the task list refers to the affected elements of the system structure meta-model (e.g. changing a component), as well as technical (e.g. changing the corresponding test cases) and organisational activities (e.g. updating the list of spare parts) [Hei+18a, Ros+15, Vog+17a, Koc17].

Motivation Example: xPPU As an example, a certain component of the aPS might need to be replaced (e.g. the replacement of the microswitches within the crane module of xPPU, as in Scenario 13 [Vog+14b]). The crane module has used three microswitches to indicate the direction of the arm at stack, at stamp, and at conveyor, respectively (see the structure in Fig. 10.22a). With some reasons, for example contamination or defect of the microswitch, the accuracy is degraded and needs to be improved. For example, the crane is at the ramp position, as depicted in

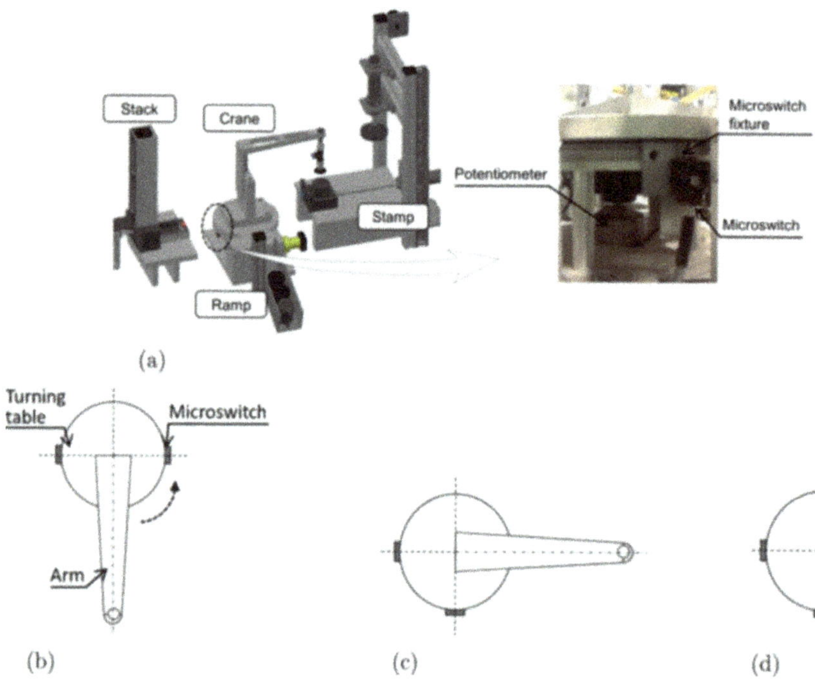

Fig. 10.22 Crane structure description and defective crane positioning. (**a**) Graphical representation and actual image of crane structure. (**b**) Crane at the ramp. (**c**) At the stamp (intent). (**d**) At the stamp (actuality) [Hei+18a]

Fig. 10.22b, and is supposed to turn to the stamp position, as depicted in Fig. 10.22c. However, the crane passes by the exact stamp position and stops at a wrong position, as illustrated in Fig. 10.22d. This performance issue leads the replacement of the microswitches with rotary potentiometer. In other words, to achieve a more accurate motion of the crane arm rotation, the engineer decides to replace all these three microswitches with one potentiometer, which provides more precise information about the rotation angle. Even with this simple example, through counting I/O, which is the conventional and common approach, this change effort can just be counted as removing three digital inputs and adding one analogue input. However, more detailed tasks (i.e. not just about the number of input/output port changes but rather about specific tasks on the relevant components) need to be done for this implementation from purchasing needed elements (i.e. potentiometer itself and additional fixture parts) to updating corresponding documents (e.g. operation instructions and stock lists) in addition to replacing the elements [Vog+14b].

As discussed previously, a change in a system propagates not only to the elements in the system structure but also to the non-structural elements (Fig. 10.23). Figure 10.24 shows an exemplary task list following the change for Scenario 13 [Vog+14b]. Tasks include not only the change activities for implementing the change but also the related activities, for example maintaining the artefacts, as seen in Fig. 10.24. Additionally, each type of the task is mapped into the specific

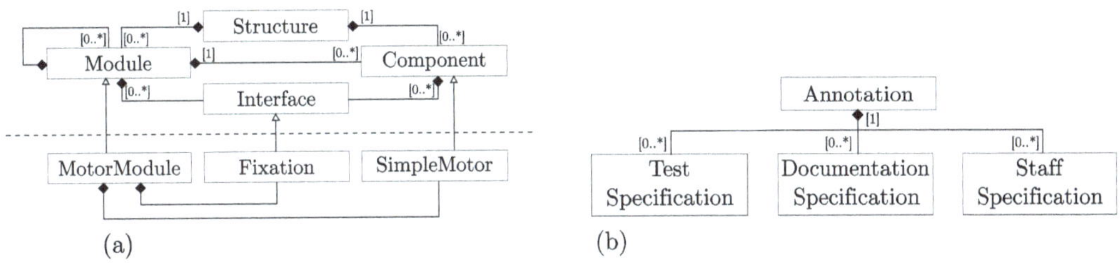

Fig. 10.23 aPS meta-models. (**a**) Structural aPS meta-model. (**b**) Non-structural aPS annotation meta-model [Hei+18a]

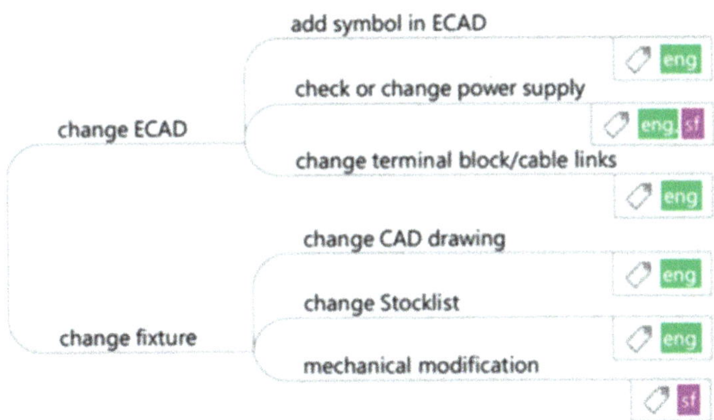

Fig. 10.24 Depiction of the task list on Scenario 13

personnel or department (as described using eng for engineering staff, m&p for material and procurement, and sf for shop-floor). Thus, the cost of the tasks can be calculated, for example, based on person-hour cost. Further, we can observe that the change causes tasks in other disciplines: removal of microswitch (i.e. an electrical component) causes mechanical modification. These mutual dependencies between disciplines are handled by a discipline-integrated meta-model. This meta-model specifies structural element descriptions of the system. The non-structural elements can be presented using a further meta-model. Each meta-class of this meta-model refers to the corresponding meta-classes of the structural elements. Figure 10.23 shows an excerpt from the structural (a) and the non-structural (b) meta-model [Hei+18a].

Application of KAMP4aPS to xPPU In order to use KAMP4aPS, the structural model of the plant has to be provided by the domain expert. A further model contains the non-structural elements of the plant, such as test cases, documentation, or ECAD. In this scenario, the seed modification is changing the three microswitches. Starting from seed modification, KAMP4aPS iteratively calculates other changing elements based on the change propagation rules. The change propagation rules highly depend on the underlying meta-model of structural elements. The domain expert can define the change propagation rules at a high abstraction level for a general plant (e.g. a change can propagate from an affected component to other components) or at a low abstraction level for a concrete plant (e.g. a change can propagate from an affected sensor to its fixture). For KAMP4aPS, we defined a set of generic change propagation rules, as well as a set of specific change propagation rules. The general change propagation rules can be extended to more concrete rules for a specific plant. If a change propagation rule specifies the change propagation from microswitch to its fixture, KAMP4aPS marks the corresponding fixture as modified. Further, it derives required task lists considering non-structural information based on predefined change propagation rules. In this way, the change propagates through the elements of the plant. Figure 10.25 describes the results of the KAMP4aPS tool regarding the change scenario introduced previously. Simplified version of the xPPU model is inserted, and the seed modification is defined as modification of microswitches. Ultimately, these tasks can be manually converted into cost. Based on this cost estimation information, better implementation, which means less costly solution, can be recommended [Hei+18a].

10.4.4 Conclusion and Outlook

This section has explored possibilities of how past changes can be used to recommend and assess future changes. Therefore, three possibilities are presented that allow a more guided evolution of software-intense systems. First, it was shown how information that is required for making useful recommendations can be inferred from the change histories of models. This information was used to

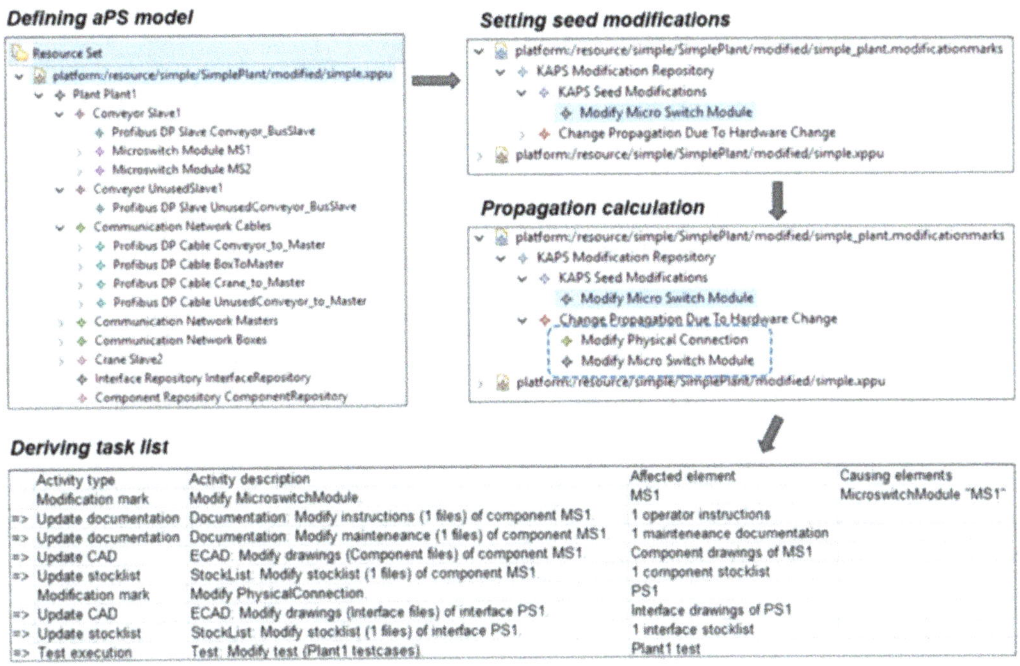

Fig. 10.25 Prototypical KAMP4aPS running results on microswitch replacement in xPPU

provide blueprints for recommendations that represent common refactoring or frequent changes to a type of model. A second approach considers how change information that is generated out of past changes can be used to establish a knowledge-carrying network for evolution experiences by providing changes as evolution steps in a service-component architecture. These evolution steps are used in similar production systems to identify potential improvements of the system and provide recommendation in the form of high-level model description of the change and its impact. The last approach focuses on presenting tasks to the operator of a production system. Therefore, a systematic and automatic change impact analysis approach and an interdisciplinary meta-model for production systems were shown. The approach allows achieving the task list based on the architectural model considering the multiple disciplines. The task list can be used for manual effort estimation by mapping the tasks to the costs instead of coarse-grained manual estimation depending on the engineers' knowledge.

As future work, it is intended to integrate the three presented approaches. High-level changes of the monitored signal models in the knowledge-carrying network should be learned with the automatic recommendation approach for model editing. Further, the integration of both case studies establishes the economical effort recommender in a supply chain of Common Component Modeling Example (CoCoME) and xPPU so that possible tasks based on KAMP4aPS using the interdisciplinary model and exchanged evolution steps containing the learned high-level changes can be provided.

10.5 Conclusion

Software is ever changing. Hence, software evolution is a continuous process that requires knowledge about the software. The existence and quality of this knowledge have a high impact on the success of software evolutions. We presented in this chapter several approaches to learn from past software evolutions and, thus, guide future evolutions. Several approaches have been developed around the joint Pick-and-Place case study.

Analysing and understanding past evolutions is a foundation for the evolution of a software. The approaches in Sect. 10.1 support systematically analysing how single models have evolved in the past and multiple ones have co-evolved.

The approaches in Sects. 10.2 and 10.3 address functional and non-functional requirements during software evolution. Whereas the former approaches focus on functional correctness of the evolved software, the latter approaches provide learning of models from running systems in order to analyse non-functional requirements.

Finally, the approaches in Sect. 10.4 support software engineering during a software evolution by recommending future evolutions from previous software evolutions either of the same system or from other similar systems.

While all those approaches solve their respective challenges and particularly the analysis of past evolutions is used in multiple approaches, future work includes a tighter integration to holistically address software evolution.

Chapter 11
Formal Verification of Evolutionary Changes

Bernhard Beckert, Jakob Mund, Mattias Ulbrich, and Alexander Weigl

In this chapter, we elaborate how formal verification techniques can be used to ensure safety properties of automated production systems during their evolution. First we discuss the opportunities that formal methods offer, particularly when dealing with the evolution of automated production systems, but also which special needs this particular domain requires from the formal methods to be applied. We argue that evolution allows the seamless combination of experiential knowledge with formally founded reasoning.

We exemplarily present three approaches that successfully incorporate a formal verification technique for analysis, modelling, or reasoning, into the system evolution process, namely, *regression verification*, *generalised test tables*, and *model checking* of holistic (multidomain) models.

All three approaches contribute to the guiding theme *Methods and Processes for Evolution* of the priority programme.

While formal verification methods have the potential of being used in several application fields, we concentrate on the aspect of ensuring **correctness** (in the form of maintaining safety properties or **consistency** with earlier versions). We focus on techniques that operate on the actual implementation (the code executed on a plant) rather than on more abstract behavioural descriptions. Here, we describe the logical foundations and technical aspects of the applied formal verification techniques and their applications; their benefits for the user, as far as system and model comprehensibility are concerned; and the embedding into development processes are discussed in Sect. 10.

B. Beckert · M. Ulbrich (✉) · A. Weigl
Institute of Theoretical Informatics, Karlsruhe Institute of Technology (KIT), Karlsruhe, Germany
e-mail: beckert@kit.edu; ulbrich@kit.edu; weigl@kit.edu

J. Mund
Institute of Informatics L4, Technical University of Munich, Garching, Germany
e-mail: mund@in.tum.de

R. Reussner et al. (eds.), *Managed Software Evolution*,
https://doi.org/10.1007/978-3-030-13499-0_11

11.1 Verifying Production Systems: Assessment of Opportunities

System analyses based on formal methods are powerful techniques to ensure that a system has desired properties. Formal methods provide a versatile toolbox that can be used for many reliability- or safety-enhancing tasks like formal verification, advanced testing, modelling, formal specification and design, etc. Formal methods are known for being very thorough analysis techniques since they import mathematical rigour into the analysis process.

As in the case for many very general notions, the question of when a technique is to be called formal has no definite answer. Moreover, different people from different communities are likely to give very different answers. Within this chapter, by "formal verification method", we denote a formal technique that mathematically proves that a system or component satisfies its specified requirements [IEE90]. Such a formal technique usually comprises a formal description of the system (i.e. a model of the system expressed using a formal notation), a formal specification of the requirements, and rigorous (formal) rules that allow one to reason that the system satisfies the requirements. In addition, we focus on techniques that allow automated verification, where the actual verification step is conducted by a computer program requiring as little guidance to user input as possible.

11.1.1 Peculiarities of Automated Production Systems

For the remainder of this chapter, instead of discussing the application of formal verification in general, we will focus on the application of a particular kind of systems, namely, automated production systems. Distinctive characteristics of such a system are as follows:

1. They are *long running*. Oftentimes, the plants that a software drives are designed to run for several decades, which makes a thorough design-time analysis worthwhile that takes potential evolutionary developments into consideration.
2. They are often mission or safety *critical*. Due to immense forces and speeds that can build up in a plant, a malfunctioning automated production system may cause considerable damage to products or production systems and may even bring people to harm. Damaged systems may cause immense costs if plants stand still.
3. They are *multidisciplinary* in the sense that their design spans several engineering disciplines that must work together to achieve the desired system behaviour and *heterogeneous* in the sense that they comprise analogue as well as digital components. For instance, a software engineer may be responsible for developing the software that controls a conveyor belt installed by a mechanical engineer. The controller actions are based on sensor information obtained from a bus system designed by an electrical/electronical engineer.

4. While automated production systems remain in service for a long time, their requirements often are not cast in stone, but *change over time*: New types of products are to be manufactured, systems are upgraded to increase throughput or to keep up with technological development, etc. Moreover, flaws in the controlling software or the hardware design may have to be fixed. Production systems therefore frequently *evolve* during their lifetime. Thus, methods and means that accompany the transition induced by evolution must be put into action. One has to ensure that a revision does not break existing intended behaviour while achieving the intended change effect.

Based on these peculiarities, we subsequently identify and describe both the general intricacies and the opportunities for formal verification in the domain of automated production systems on an abstract level and come back to these points in the sections on the individual approaches.

11.1.2 Intricacies of the Application of Formal Verification

Formal methods have been the subject of scientific investigation for decades. However, the industry is very reluctant to incorporate them into their development processes. Only in recent years have formal methods gained reputation, for instance, by being added as acceptable verification techniques for avionics [GP12] or for the automotive industry [ISO11a]. Based on our experience in the priority programme, we see the following intricacies (or challenges) for formal verification of evolutionary changes in automated production systems:

Specification efforts One of the main reasons for reluctance to adopt formal methods in industrial contexts is that many of their use cases have in common that they require a formal description of the properties to be established (a "formal specification"). Obtaining for formal specifications or models is hard [Pak+16], as this requires training in the formal system and due to the additional workload it puts on industrial-sized projects. During evolution, specifications have to be consistently co-evolved alongside the code, which increases the required overhead even more.

Cyber-physical systems Automated production systems have an interdisciplinary nature which combines discrete software-driven controllers with continuous physical dimensions. Hence, hybrid systems that combine models for both types of behaviours are a natural fit to represent automated production systems. For instance, the geo-spatial translation of workpieces may be modelled in terms of a function from continuous time to a continuous variable, i.e. the position, by means of differential equations. Continuous behaviour inherently induces that the system state space becomes infinite. Checking correctness thus becomes a more difficult problem and inaccessible for explorative techniques like many model-checking approaches. Hence, finding suitable (finite) abstractions that model physical phenomena both correctly and sufficiently precisely becomes a key challenge for verification.

Large state space As a reactive system running for long periods of time, automation software must always be validated by analysing traces of system responses; it does not suffice to analyse individual cycles of the software individually. The state space that needs to be considered during verification grows exponentially in the number of steps that are analysed. Moreover, the output of the software also depends on the behaviour of the hardware on which it operates. The (often nondeterministic) hardware models which are often used in the validation make the state space grow even larger.

Specific languages/tools Control software for automated production system is typically written in languages fairly different from commonplace programming languages used for other embedded systems, e.g. C/C++. The IEC61131 [Com02] standard defines five different textual and graphical languages to program automated production systems. As a consequence, the use of existing approaches and tools requires adaptation.

11.1.3 Opportunities for the Application of Formal Verification

Based on our experiences from our research on formal methods within the priority programme, we also see potential for the application of formal methods in the practice of automated production system development and evolution.

Existing older system versions Due to the evolutionary aspect, we can assume the existence of older revisions of the system (the plant and the software). Such existing system versions can be leveraged for formal verification in several ways. For instance, the analysis can be restricted to investigating the *difference* (structural or behavioural difference) of the new revision w.r.t. the old revision. Furthermore, old revisions allow obtaining precise models of the system efficiently using observations and model learning techniques.

Limited structural complexity Typically, due to the cyclic behaviour of the programmable logic controller and the imposed timing restrictions, the structural complexity of the software of an individual controller is rather limited compared to other software programs such as database management systems. For instance, program loops with complex exit conditions and algorithmic traversal of complex data structures are rarely found in control software of automated production systems.

Economically justifiable efforts Due to the longevity of automated production systems, initial efforts put into formalisation have a longer period to break even. Hence, higher efforts typically associated with formal verification are more likely to be economically justified for automated production systems.

Infeasibility of alternatives Common alternatives to verification, first and foremost testing, are often economically or technically infeasible since neither the actual testing environment nor the system under test can be used, since that would require to either hold production at the customer site or install a prototypical machine for testing purposes. Hence, the value of testing, i.e. the ability to find bugs in an efficient way, is diminished. In turn, formal verification operates solely on the controller software code and, thus, does not suffer from these drawbacks and may therefore be a suitable addition or alternative (especially in early stages of the development process) to verification by testing of automated production systems.

In conclusion, while the applicability of formal verification depends on the specific system and engineering context, the above opportunities suggest that it is particularly well suited for engineering automated production system, compared to engineering software systems in general.

11.1.4 Addressed Software Evolution Challenges

To illustrate the applicability and benefits of formal verification, this chapter reports on three formal approaches that each verifies a distinct aspect of the correctness of automated production systems. They address two complementary questions from the collection of general challenges regarding software evolution in Chap. 3.

How to model, specify, and verify that a system retains desired behaviour during system evolution? In Sect. 11.2, we present an approach to verify that defined aspects of the behaviour of the system software are preserved during system evolution.

The approach takes the code of two versions of the system software as input and a formal condition under which the two should behave equivalently and a formal definition of when two behaviours are considered equal. Using a state-of-the-art model checker, the verification approach then asserts that for all admissible input sequences, the two revisions satisfy the required equivalence condition.

This kind of equivalence checking is called *regression verification* and particularly helpful since it reduces the need for specification: The old software versions serve as (partial) specification for the new version. The verification transfers the trust in the correctness of the old software revision onto the new one. Regression verification does not require formally specified system properties: The old revision defines the functional property to be verified for the new revision.

How to model, specify, and verify intentionally changed behaviour during system evolution? In Sect. 11.3, a novel temporal specification language is introduced which allows a comprehensible specification of reactive systems like the software of automated production systems. For those parts of the software behaviour which are intended to change, this temporal specification language can be used to describe the new behaviour.

Sometimes, a specification of the software changes alone does not suffice. To answer the question for cases in which not only the software but entire systems evolve, we present in Sect. 11.4 an approach to verify that the integrated plant behaviour, i.e. the composition of software, automation platform, and mechanical components, satisfies the system requirements. Specifically, the approach is based on creating multidomain models of automated production systems in a coherent model that represents the results of several involved engineering disciplines by using a common (formal) modelling language. By translating those models into formal representations, model-checking tools give us qualitative or quantitative results that can be used to decide whether the system meets the specified requirements.

11.2 Regression Verification

One of the main bottlenecks for using formal methods in practice is coming up with suitable system and requirement specifications. This problem is particularly severe in the domain of automated production systems as formal specifications are even less common in this domain than in other software disciplines. In the following, we give a brief introduction to the concept of regression verification which exploits existing software revisions as specifications of new releases of the system—thus severely reducing the need to formulate specifications. In this section, we explain our application of regression verification to PLC software (more details are given in [Bec+15]). The embedding into the software development process is outlined in Sect. 10.2.2. The idea of regression verification is to formally prove that a version of code driving a plant after an evolution step shows the same reactive input/output behaviour as the code version before evolution. Only desired deviations that are explicitly stated are allowed. Thus, the original code serves as a formal specification for the new implementation, and formal verification techniques like model checking or deductive theorem proving can be applied to prove that the behavioural effect of the code remains the same. Regression verification covers all parts of system behaviour that are intended to remain untouched during an evolution step.

In this and the following sections, we consider PLCs to be reactive systems with a periodic cyclic data processing behaviour, repeating the same control procedure indefinitely. A PLC cycle consists of the following steps: (1) read input values (input space I), (2) execute task(s), (3) write output values (output space O), and (4) wait till next cycle starts. This leads to the following formal definition using infinite sequences over inputs and outputs (I^ω and O^ω):

Definition 11.2.1 The semantics of a PLC program P is a causal-deterministic function $b(P) : I^\omega \to O^\omega$. That is, $i_1{\downarrow_n} = i_2{\downarrow_n}$ implies $b(P)(i_1){\downarrow_n} = b(P)(i_2){\downarrow_n}$ for all $n \in \mathbb{N}$, where $x{\downarrow_n}$ denotes the finite initial subsequence of x of length n.

PLCs are modelled as causal-deterministic systems as we assume they are stateful, deterministic programs whose output is a function of the inputs received since system start—but that cannot depend on the input which is still to come.

The aim of regression verification is to formally prove that the existing (good) behaviour of PLC code is retained during system evolution—which is (as a verification goal) different to proving that PLC code satisfies a functional specification and different to showing that the whole production system works correctly. We assume that the old software revision has proved its value during its lifespan and has thus gained "trust by experience". Regression verification formally transfers this trust to the new revision. The main advantage of regression verification is that no functional/behavioural specification is required for the part of the behaviour to be retained (besides the old code version). The application area of software in automated production systems is particularly well suited for a treatment with regression verification for the following reason: During the lifespan of a plant, its software usually needs to adapt to changing requirements. As a rule, the requirements for the machine behaviour do not change entirely but only in certain well-defined aspects while most parts are to be retained in an evolution step.

In an ideal verification scenario, regression verification and regression testing should go side by side as both approaches have their particular advantages. Regression verification provides a formal equivalence proof for all considered input sequences and not only for the (usually restricted) set of selected test cases. Also, while regression testing of PLC software requires either a hardware test bed or an executable hardware model, this is not needed for regression verification. It suffices to provide a formal relational description of how the hardware has changed during the evolution step (if it has changed at all). Testing, on the other hand, is not limited to an analysis of the software alone but allows comprising the physical entities of the machine.

We define a notion of reactive conditional and reactive relational equivalence together with a proof methodology, also in the presence of environment models. Our method concentrates on the PLC software that runs on the controller and for now disregards all effects outside the software (in particular the context and the platform). Some additional measures for incorporating models of effects outside the software into the verification are discussed below.

A core element of our verification method is a translation of PLC code into the input language for model checkers. Using this translation on both the old and the new software revision, we can specify the retained behaviour. Our technology targets PLC code written in Structured Text (ST) and Sequential Function Chart (SFC), two languages of the IEC 61131 standard [Com02]; an adaptation to other languages is easily possible. A further core element is the use of a model checker supporting invariant generation. It is an important insight that this allows the automatic generation of *coupling invariants*, which in many cases make regression verification more efficient than symbolic or explicit state model checking. Accordingly, we have adapted the concept of coupling invariants to the world of reactive systems. We have implemented our approach in a tool chain using the model checker nuXmv [Cav+14]. It supports techniques for predicate abstraction and invariant generation by interpolant inspection [Bra11, McM03].

The first notion of equivalence we define is that of perfect, bit-wise equivalence of two PLC programs in which both systems always answer with the same response to sensor stimuli:

Definition 11.2.2 (Trace Equivalent PLC Programs) Two PLC programs P, Q whose variable declarations contain the same input/output variables are called *perfectly equivalent* if they produce the same output sequence when presented with the same input sequence, i.e. $b(P)(\bar{i}) = b(Q)(\bar{i})$ for all $\bar{i} \in I^\omega$.

When considering the semantics of programs to be sets of traces, this definition is equivalent to requiring that $b(P) = b(Q)$.

This first definition of trace equivalence is too strong a condition in most cases since software re-factorisation is the answer to changed requirements and the software is indeed intended to behave differently. Hence, we introduce a second notion of equivalence: conditional equivalence:

Definition 11.2.3 (Conditionally Equivalent PLC Programs) Two PLC programs P and Q are called *conditionally equivalent* modulo the condition $\varphi : I^\omega \rightarrow$ *bool* if they produce the same result for all input sequences that satisfy condition φ, i.e. if $\varphi(\bar{i})$ then $b(P)(\bar{i}) = b(Q)(\bar{i})$ for all $\bar{i} \in I^\omega$.

During evolution, the behaviour of the system's sensors and actors may be changed in addition to software changes. Then, the notion of *conditional* equivalence may still be too strong and needs to be further relaxed. This leads to the notion of *relational* equivalence:

Definition 11.2.4 (Relationally Equivalent PLC Programs) Two PLC programs P, Q are called *relationally equivalent* modulo relations $\sim_{in} \subseteq I_P^\omega \times I_Q^\omega$ and $\sim_{out}$: $O_P^\omega \times O_Q^\omega$ if they produce related output sequences when presented with related input sequences, i.e.

$$\text{if } \bar{i} \sim_{in} \bar{i}' \text{ then } b(P)(\bar{i}) \sim_{out} b(Q)(\bar{i}') \text{ for all } \bar{i} \in I_P^\omega, \bar{i}' \in I_Q^\omega.$$

With these notions we have established the different proof obligations for regression verification. Figure 11.1 shows how the approach is realised. After processing the program code of the two revisions to be compared into formal models ("SMV"), these two models are combined into one product automaton, which is then—together with the properties to be checked—encoded into a combined model that is sent to a model checker tool. The program code is translated into an automaton by first normalising the code to a restricted programming language ST_0 with limited feature set and then symbolically executing it. The model checker either proves the equivalence property (✓), finds a counterexample that exposes that the two versions are not equivalent (✗), or times out (🕒).

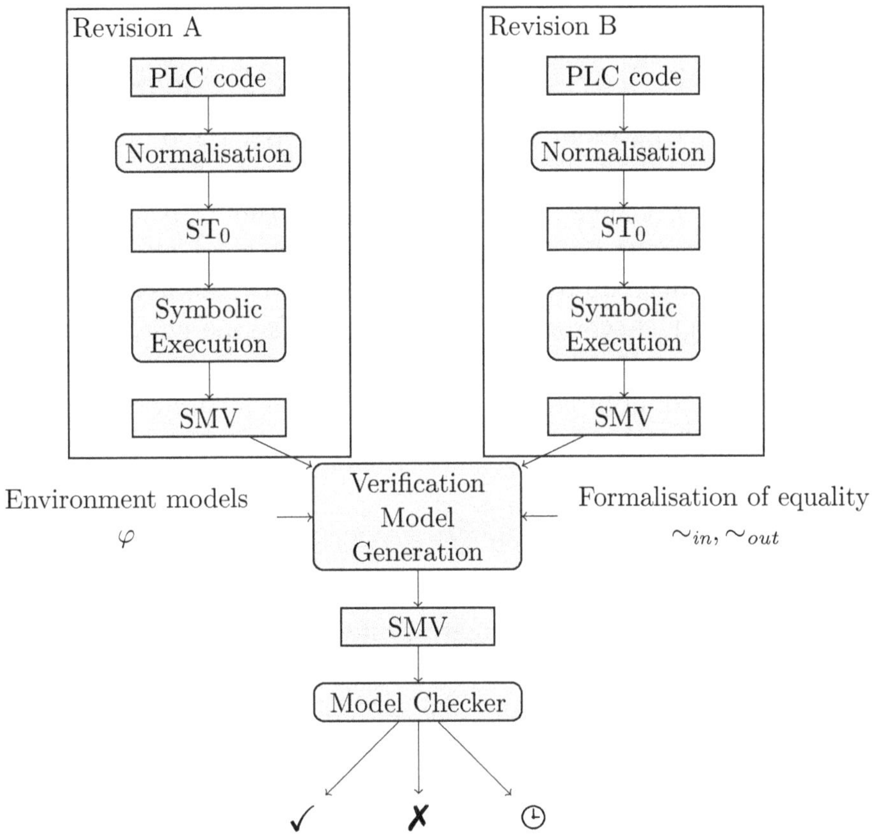

Fig. 11.1 Overview of the regression verification method

11.2.1 Environment Models

There are realistic software evolution steps which would, in general, change the behaviour of an automated Production Systems (aPS), but which do not change the behaviour of a particular plant since not every sequence of input signals is possible. For instance, two software versions may behave differently, if two signals `movingLeft` and `movingRight` are simultaneously set. Since this will never be the case in reality (at least in normal operation), the software revisions can still be called equivalent if they behave equivalently in all other cases.

To make the approach more precise by allowing such verification cases, we include a mechanism to incorporate models of the plant environment into the verification chain. By definition, equivalence needs to hold for all conceivable sequences of input values, which is a very strong requirement. However, it suffices that the systems behave equivalently for all input sequences that can occur in practice. It is therefore sensible to add knowledge on the possible sensor inputs as assumptions to the process and perform a conditional regression verification, where the condition not only excludes inputs for which the systems are intended to behave differently but also inputs that cannot occur in practice. Our methodology allows incorporating environment models either as LTL formulas or as automata. In both cases, the models are added as assumptions.

For example, the crane of the Pick-and-Place Unit (PPU) (Sect. 4.3) can never be in more than one of the positions Magazine (M), Stamp (S), and Conveyor Belt (C) at the same time. Assuming correctly working sensors, at most one of the Boolean input variables M, S, C can be true at the same time. Thus, it is irrelevant whether the two program revisions react differently in case, e.g. M and S are signalled simultaneously, but still are equivalent for all other inputs. This assumption adds the implicit precondition that sensors never fail. If they fail, no guarantees are made. The regression verification approach is flexible in the sense that it allows one either to add such assumptions or to show equivalence also for failure cases.

11.2.2 Case Study: PPU

For evaluation, we have applied our regression verification tool chain to the PPU case study introduced in Sect. 4.3 in this book. The case study covers different aspects of evolution, containing pure software changes as well as changes that incorporate adaptations to the mechanics and automation hardware in their 16 different variants. In the largest of the original scenarios, the PPU has 22 digital input, 13 digital output, and 3 analogue output signals and defines a number of simple discrete event automation tasks.

We discovered some unintentional regressions in the PPU using our approach. In four cases, a regression by delaying the system answer one cycle for each workpiece has been caused by newly added code blocks. Due to the short cycle time of the PPU (4 ms), the discrepancy between the programs was not revealed during testing. Moreover, regression verification discovered that a fix for a safety violation had not been ported to an earlier version in the PPU evolution sequence. It is possible that the crane tries to grab a workpiece while it is still in motion which might under very unfortunate circumstances cause damages.

In the following, we discuss two evolution scenarios from the PPU and show how they can be subject to regression verification. More details can be found in [Wei15]; see Table 11.1[1] for the time required for verification. Not all evolution scenarios include a software modification or have an intentional behaviour difference. The scenarios for which the equivalence verification is trivial have been omitted from the table.

In the evolution scenario Ev3, the new stamping hardware for metallic products brings with it a new emergency stop button E_2 (triggering the same emergency logic as the existing button E_1) and a new start switch S_3 (complementing S_1 and S_2 already present). Only after *all* three start switches have been pressed does the plant

[1]Verification with nuXmv in version 1.0.1 on an Intel Dual-Core with 2.7 GHz and 4 GB RAM running OpenSUSE 12.2; see [Wei15, Bec+15] for detail information.

Table 11.1 Results of the experiments

Scenario	In	State	Min	Max	Scenario	In	State	Min	Max
Ev1	10	140	4 s	8 s	Ev6+EM	11	299	2 min	21 min
Ev1+EM	12	146	7 s	12 s	Ev8	20	289	13.7 min	20.9 min
Ev2	11	141	4 s	8 s	Ev9	20	305	50.5 min	1.3 h
Ev3	19	246	9 s	17 s	Ev10	23	365	13 s	24 s
Ev6+A	19	284	15.1 min	155.4 h	Ev11	28	576	3.5 h	6.3 h
Ev6+A_m	19	284	8.9 min	9.1 h	Ev12	34	860	22.2 h	56.4 h
Ev6+A_{nm}	19	284	18.1 min	13 h	Ev13	34	1225	21.9 h	21.9 h
Ev6+AEM	11	299	25.7 min	104.1 h	Ev14	47	1663	22.1 h	22.1 h

"Scenario" is the name of the evolution scenario in [Vog+14b], "In" is the size of the sensor input space in bits, "State" is the size of the state space in bits, and "Min/Max" show the minimum and maximum time needed for verification using nuXmv in seconds (s), minutes (min), or hours (h). +EM indicates that an environment model has been used

start processing workpieces. Trace equivalence between the two revisions of this evolution step can only be shown for traces where these new components do not influence the flow of signals already present in the old software. This is the case if (1) no metallic workpiece is ever detected in the plant, (2) button E_2 is only pressed if simultaneously E_1 is also pressed, and (3) S_3 is not activated after the other switches S_1 and S_2 have been pressed. Under these assumptions, conditional equivalence can indeed be proved by our tool chain.

In evolution scenario Ev14, the three position sensors at Crane A, Magazine B, and Stamp C are replaced by a single angle transmitter that reports the angular position of the crane (in degrees). Now, the PLC programs take their input from two different value domains such that we need to express the relationship between these input spaces by a predicate $\sim_{in}$ which relates each Boolean position switch (A, B, and C) to a 5° interval in the angular input space represented by the continuous value α:

$$
\begin{aligned}
(A, B, C) \sim_{in} \alpha = {} & (A \leftrightarrow 0 \leq \alpha \leq 5) \land (B \leftrightarrow 90 \leq \alpha \leq 95) \\
& \land (C \leftrightarrow 180 \leq \alpha \leq 185) \ .
\end{aligned}
$$

11.3 Generalised Test Tables

In the last section, an approach is presented which permits one to prove that a software revision behaves (partially) equivalently to an earlier revision. But when a system evolves, regression verification presented in the last section can cover validation for inputs where system behaviour does not change. But how to deal with the part of the behaviour which is *intended to change*? For those inputs where different behaviour is expected, we cannot simply specify by reference to the old version. A formal specification is needed to fill this unspecified gap.

We fall back to assurance of functional correctness, with the same application issues as mentioned in Sect. 11.1.2, especially the specification efforts. A specification language and methodology are needed which are accessible and applicable to engineers. To address the challenge of lacking languages and tools for formal specification of automated production systems, we introduced *generalised test tables*, a practical specification methodology with which PLC systems can be conveniently formally specified and verified. We present syntax and semantics of the specification technique and show how they can be used to model check reactive system behaviour.

Test cases are commonly written in the form of *test tables*, in which each row contains the input stimuli for one cycle and the expected response of the reactive system. Thus, the whole table captures the intended behaviour of the system (the sequence of actuator signals) for one particular sequence of input signals. Generalised test tables extend the concept of test tables, which are already frequently used in quality management of aPS. The main idea is to allow more general table entries, thus enabling a table to capture not just a single test case but a family of similar behavioural cases.

In Sect. 10.2.2, the shape of generalised test tables and their generalisation concepts have already been introduced. Here, we describe the formal foundations of generalised test tables and reports about their principal suitability for formal specification and automatic verification.

11.3.1 Formal Syntax

Formally, a generalised test table is a finite sequence of rows. Each row consists of three constraining formulas: *symIn* for the inputs, *symOut* for the outputs, and *symDur* for the duration (the number of repetitions) of that row. The constraints are formulated in a generalisation of the expression language of Structured Text (see Sect. 10.2.2 for details).

Definition 11.3.1 (Generalised Test Table) Let T be a generalised test table with m rows; let $\mathscr{I}_T$ and $\mathscr{O}_T$ be the set of input variables resp. the set of output variables of T; and let $\mathscr{G}_T$ be the set of global variables occurring in T. Then T is identified with the sequence

$$(symIn_1, symOut_1, symDur_1) \cdots (symIn_m, symOut_m, symDur_m) ,$$

where $symIn_i$ is the conjunction of all constraints contained in cells in row i that correspond to *input* variables, $symOut_i$ is the conjunction of all constraints contained in cells in row i that correspond to *output* variables, and $symDur_i$ is the interval contained in the duration column at row i.

The constraint $symIn_i$ on the input values is the precondition of the ith row, and analogously $symOut_i$ is its post-condition. The duration constraint $symDur_i$ describes how often the ith row is allowed to be repeated successively.

11.3.2 Semantics

The semantics of generalised test tables is discussed in detail in [Bec+17a]; here, we give a summary. The definition of the semantics is based on a two-party game—between a challenger and the system—for which a generalised test table describes the allowed moves. The challenger tries to force the system to violate the generalised test table, whereas the system tries to conform to the generalised test table.

Like any two-party game, this game is played alternately. At each turn, the challenger provides a set of input values, and the system replies with output values. If the challenger has played an invalid input value not allowed by the generalised test table, then the system wins. Analogously, the challenger wins if the system provides an output that is in conflict with the generalised test table. In addition, the system wins if the generalised test table has been played to the end, such that there are no more valid input values available.

We define the conformance of a system to a generalised test table based on the outcome of the plays against any possible challenger.

Definition 11.3.2 (Conformance) The reactive system P *strictly conforms* to the generalised test table T if it wins against every possible challenger for all instantiations of the global variables in T. The reactive system P *weakly conforms* to T if its strategy never loses.

11.3.3 Model-Checking Generalised Test Tables

The first step towards formally verifying the conformance of a reactive system to a generalised test table T is the normalisation of T such that the normalised version T' represents the same family of concrete test tables, but the duration column in T' only contains the constraints $[0, 1]$ (at most one cycle), $[1, 1]$ (exactly one cycle), and $[0, -]$ (arbitrary number of cycles).

The second step then is to generate input for a model checker that represents the game to be played w.r.t. T'. The system is, in particular, modelled using the set $\tilde{R}$ of rows of T' to which a given system state can correspond To keep track of $\tilde{R}$, in every move of the game, the constraint pairs $(symIn_i, symOut_i)$ for $i \in \tilde{R}$ need to be considered in the current state of the game. After each move of the challenger or the system, the row set $\tilde{R}$ is adapted. Rows that violate the pre- or post-condition are removed. Rows that can be reached by the system in this move are added. If $\tilde{R}$ becomes empty, the last party to have moved has violated the generalised test table and loses the game.

Technically, we use the state-of-the-art model checker nuXmv [Cav+14] to verify that $\tilde{R}$ becomes empty only through the violation of the input constraint. For this we encode both, the software and the generalised test table automaton, into the SMV format. On the concept level, a product automaton is built. For *strictly conformance* we assert via an LTL that the software reaches the end of the table, represented by the sentinel, under assumption of a fair challenger. The checking of *weak conformance* is more efficient, as it can be asserted with an invariant.

11.3.4 Application Example

As an example, we consider a function block `MinMaxWarning` that is commonly used in safety-critical applications (more details may be found in [Bec+17a]). The purpose of this function block is to watch over the input values and to raise a warning if they repeatedly, for a certain number of cycles, exceed a range of allowed values that is fixed during an initial learning phase.

More precisely, the system under test is a function block `MinMaxWarning`, written in ST, with input variables `mode`, `learn`, *and* `I` and output variables `Q` *and* `W`. It operates in two modes, `Active` and `Learn`, as selected by the caller via input `mode`. During the learning phase, it learns the minimum and the maximum of the input `I` that occur while the `learn` flag is activated. When switched into the active phase, the function block checks that the input `I` stays within the previously learned interval. The output `Q` is equal to `I` if `I` is within the learned interval; otherwise, the nearest value from the interval is returned. If the input value keeps being out of range for a specified number of cycles, then the function block raises an alarm via the variable `W`. The alarm is reset after a certain cooldown time if the input value falls back into the learned interval. An unlearned function block always signals a warning. The expected behaviour of `MinMaxWarning` is partially described in Fig. 11.2.

	Input			Output		⏲
#	`mode`	`learn`	`I`	`Q`	`W`	
1	`Active`	–	–	0	`TRUE`	–
2	`Learn`	`TRUE`	q	0	`FALSE`	1
3	`Learn`	`TRUE`	p	0	`FALSE`	1
4	`Active`	–	$[p, q]$	$[p, q]$	`FALSE`	*
5	`Active`	–	$>q$	q	`FALSE`	5
6	`Active`	–	$<p$	p	`FALSE`	5

	Input			Output		⏲
#	`mode`	`learn`	`I`	`Q`	`W`	
1	`Learn`	`TRUE`	q	0	`TRUE`	1
2	`Learn`	`TRUE`	p	0	`TRUE`	1
3	`Active`	–	$>q$	q	`FALSE`	10
4	`Active`	–	$>q$	q	`TRUE`	≥ 1
5	`Active`	–	$[p, q]$	$[p, q]$	`TRUE`	5
6	`Active`	–	$[p, q]$	$[p, q]$	`FALSE`	≥ 1

Fig. 11.2 Two generalised test tables for the specification of the function block `MinMax-Warning`

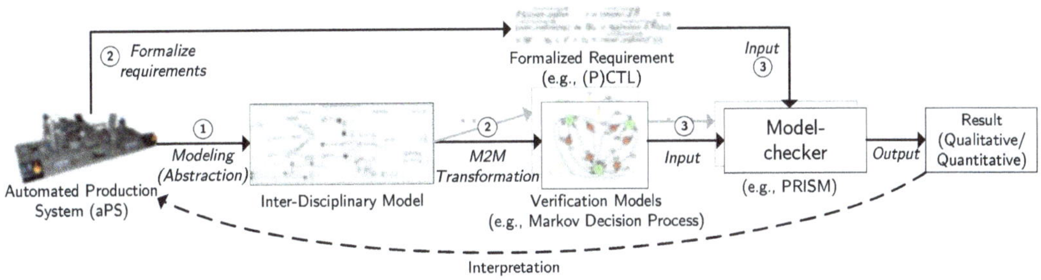

Fig. 11.3 MoDEMMiCAS approach for model-checking interdisciplinary systems (simplified)

Using the implementation of our approach, we were able to prove that a given implementation of `MinMaxWarning` conforms to the tables shown in Fig. 11.2. The `MinMaxWarning` function block consists of 61 lines of source, translated into a space of 131 bits (state and input variables) in the model checker. The verification needs 0.53 CPU seconds for proving weak conformance of the first generalised test table and 0.63 CPU seconds for the second one (median, $n = 6$). With the same setup, the verification of strict conformance takes 1.35 resp. 1.39 CPU seconds. Proving strict conformance requires an additional fairness condition to avoid infinite stuttering on the nondeterministic input variables.[2]

11.4 Model-Checking Changes in Multidisciplinary Systems

aPS are cyber-physical systems which can be best formally analysed by not only considering there software. In this section, we present an overview of techniques to verify such interdisciplinary systems by means of model checking. The general idea behind those approaches is illustrated in Fig. 11.3. First, we model the aPS by means of a formal modelling language and leveraging model abstractions (step 1). Second, for a property of interest, we select an alternative model and specification language and apply a model-to-model transformation (step 2). Finally, we run the model checker on the resulting model and for the property under consideration and obtain a quantitative or qualitative verification result (step 3).

In the remainder of this section, we present the modelling approach in more detail and exemplarily illustrate its use for verifying the system's availability based on the probabilistic model checker PRISM [KNP11] for the PPU case study [LFV13].

[2]The experiments were run on a 3.20 GHz system with Intel Core i5-6500 and 16 GB RAM with version 1.1.1 of the model-checker nuXmv. The files are available the companion website: https://formal.iti.kit.edu/ifm2017.

11.4.1 Modelling Interdisciplinary Systems

Formal System Model

The fundamental system model used in our approach is based on the FOCUS theory [BS01] to provide a strict formal semantics. Central to the FOCUS system model is the notion of components and their interfaces. Firstly, a component's *static interface*, i.e. its *typed* input and output ports, defines what signals the component may receive and send. The interfaces can be used to ensure structural compatibility between composed components. Secondly, the behaviour observable at a component's interface regarding those ports is called *semantic interface*. It is defined in terms of *behavioural functions* that map input streams to output streams. Intuitively, a stream is a sequence of messages sent or received over time on an input and output port, respectively.

Originally, the FOCUS theory was primarily conceived for modelling distributed embedded systems based on a discrete time execution. Modelling automation systems holistically by considering software and mechanical aspects originate the need of a common language for the description of physical processes and phenomena. For this reason, the FOCUS theory was extended to support continuous time elaboration and data types [Cam13, Bro12]. The behaviour of hybrid components is defined by a modified version of the hybrid automaton, called I/O hybrid state machine [Cam13]. Components that have discrete as well as continuous interfaces are referred to as hybrid components.

Formally, given a set of (typed) input ports I and output ports O with $I \cap O = \emptyset$ and types $T_{i \in I \cup o \in O}$, a continuous stream $\overrightarrow{c} \in \overrightarrow{I}$ is a function $\overrightarrow{c} : \mathbb{R}_+ \rightarrow T_i \cup \{\Box\}$ that maps logical time instants to messages of type T_i. The symbol $\Box \notin T_i$ denotes that no message occurred. In contrast, discrete streams are represented as partial functions $\mathbb{R}_+ \cdot\!\!\rightarrow T_i \cup \{\Box\}$. The interface behaviour is then defined as a function $F : \overrightarrow{I} \rightarrow \overrightarrow{O}$, and we denote the set of all behaviour functions with input ports I and output ports O as $[I \triangleright O]$. Input/output state machines (e.g. Mealy machines) are one particular means to specify behavioural functions which is commonly regarded as suitable for describing the system's behaviour [De +09].

Furthermore, as presented in more detail in [Mun+17], we use the probabilistic extensions developed in [Neu12] to model faulty behaviour of individual components. To this end, we generalise behaviour functions to $F : \overrightarrow{I} \rightarrow \wp(\mathbf{Pr}(\overrightarrow{O}))$, where $\mathbf{Pr}(\overrightarrow{O})$ denotes probabilistic spaces of output streams. Intuitively, it refers to a set of possible outputs and their associated probability. As input streams are mapped to sets of probabilistic spaces, generalised behaviour functions enable both nondeterministic (due to the superset) and probabilistic (due to the probabilistic spaces) behaviour specifications. To specify those behaviour functions, we extend the state machine transitions with probability values.

Finally, individual components are connected by input and output ports via *channels*. The respective interface types must be compatible, i.e. $T_i = T_o$ for input interfaces $i \in I$ and output interfaces $o \in O$. The well-defined *composition* operator

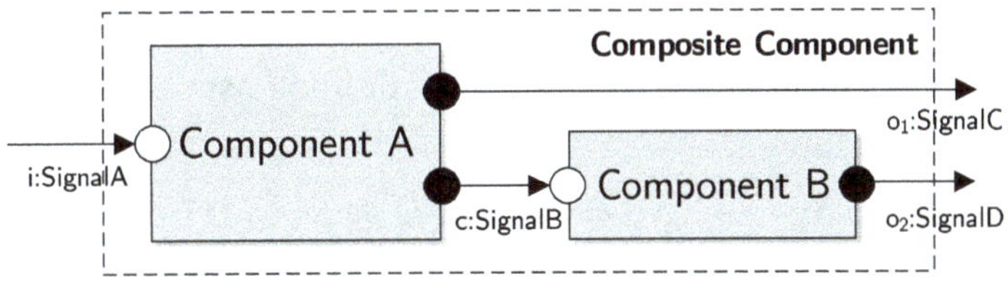

Fig. 11.4 FOCUS in a nutshell: two components connected via channel c forming a composite with semantic interface $F : \overrightarrow{\{i\}} \rightarrow \overrightarrow{\{o_1, o_2\}}$

$\otimes$ ensures that a set of interfaces and channels form a composite component, where the composite component's interface is derived from the member components and their channels, thus enabling hierarchical specifications (see Fig. 11.4).

To avoid the anomalies described in [Kel77], for any set of mutually recursive components, we demand at least one component to be strongly history-deterministic,[3] i.e. require its output at time $t + 1$ to be solely determined by inputs up to time t for any $t \geq 0$.

This formal modelling extends from the one in Definition 11.2.1. In the former definition input, sequences are infinite sequences of signal values I^{ω}, with one value for each PLC cycle. In this section, to model physical effects more adequately, the inputs are not given as discrete traces but as continuous streams $\overrightarrow{I}$ in which every point in time may provide a value.

Model Abstractions

We apply the above formalism to model interdisciplinary systems such as automated production systems as outlined in Sect. 5.3.3. However, to cope with the inherent complexity of (continuous) physical processes, we require model abstractions which are suitable to find design errors, on the one hand, but are also amenable to automated verification on the other hand.

To this end, we model the (mechanical) context and the automation platform (e.g. bus systems, programmable logic controllers (PLCs)) using discrete abstractions obtained by combining two techniques. First, discrete time and variables behaviour can be obtained by prior simulation (see [Vog+15b]) and the use of non-uniform sampling techniques (see [Cam13]). Second, given a specific component that can be precisely specified by a function S_2, we may rely on a (more abstract) function S_1, if S_2 is a behaviour refinement of S_1. This is denoted as $S_1 \rightsquigarrow S_2$ and formally defined as:

$$S_1 \rightsquigarrow S_2 \Leftrightarrow \forall \overrightarrow{i} \in \overrightarrow{I} \,.\, S_2(\overrightarrow{i}) \subseteq S_1(\overrightarrow{i}) \ .$$

[3] See Definition 11.2.1, also called *causal*.

In addition, our model may also incorporate more abstract input and/or output ports (data types) by means of interface abstractions, defined as:

$$S_1 \overset{(D,U)}{\rightsquigarrow} S_3 \Leftrightarrow S_1 \rightsquigarrow (D \otimes S_3 \otimes U)$$

with $S_1, S_2 \in [I \rhd O]$ and $S_3 \in [I' \rhd O']$, $D \in [I \rhd I']$, $U \in [O' \rhd O]$. For more details on those refinement relations, see [BS01].

While those techniques can be used to obtain a model of various size (and accuracy), the level of detail of the resulting model we relied on can be seen in, e.g. [Leg+14].

11.4.2 Verifying Availability Requirements Using Probabilistic Model Checking

Based on the modelling approach described in the previous section, we now outline how model-to-model transformations can be applied to automated verification in terms of an example. In this example, we translate the interdisciplinary model to Markov Decision Processes (MDP), as supported by the probabilistic model checker PRISM [KNP11], to verify the specified system satisfies its availability constraints.

Translation to PRISM

A specification of an MDP consists of a set of global variables and modules. Each module defines a set of variables and a set of commands consisting of guards and probabilistic actions, i.e. updates on variables associated with a probability distribution. The standard composition of modules in PRISM is composition by interleaving; from the set of commands, at most one action is executed in each step. However, synchronous composition can be achieved by attaching a common label to commands that should always synchronise. In addition, PRISM supports to associate a number, called reward, with transitions and states (specified by logical formulas over the model's variables). Rewards can be used to quantitatively query the model.

We automatically translate our system model (extended with availability models; see also [Mun+17]) into an MDP as follows: We translate each software, platform, and context component into a PRISM module. For the syntactic interface, we introduce variables for input and output ports. For the behaviour, we encode state machines in PRISM using internal variables and commands to represent their current state and state transitions, respectively. The same translation is applied to the components of the availability models of our approach, with the sole exception of availability metrics, for which the output is mapped to rewards instead of variables. For instance, the uptime metric associates a failure-free state with a reward of 1 and a failure with 0. Finally, to achieve synchronisation among all modules, we introduce a common action label.

Verification of Availability Constraints

Based on this translation, we can use the `Rmin=?[C<=t]` query in PRISM to compute the cumulative reward up until t steps of the system have been executed. This corresponds to the system's uptime, i.e. the expected time the system is operating without failure in the time interval $[0; t[$.

11.4.3 Application to PPU Case Study

We now illustrate the approach on a concrete example of the PPU case study. For a more comprehensive presentation of this case study, the reader is referred to its publication [Mun+17].

Model As an example for the microswitch sensors used for crane positioning, we describe the particular sensor that observes whether a workpiece is pushed out of the stack and is ready for pickup by the crane. Therefore, the sensor has an input port that specifies whether a workpiece is indeed located there (as a consequence of the mechanical processes of the context model) and a single output port that outputs an electrical voltage. If a workpiece is present, the sensor outputs 24 V. Otherwise, it outputs 0 V. Consequently, in this mode, the sensor is perfectly reliable and available all the time.

To account for availability issues, we extend this with a deviation model that models two failures, namely, temporal unavailability (e.g. due to pollution) and permanent unavailability (e.g. permanent damage due to wear out). This deviation model is illustrated in Fig. 11.5. Therein, we introduce an activation function (`Micro-switch Failure Activation`), an input filter (`IF: Identity`), and an output filter (`OF: Missing WP`). The activation function signals whether the microswitch failed to the input and output filter by means of a probabilistic state machine illustrated at the bottom of the figure. Initially, it is in the "Available" state. The output filter outputs 0V in case of a failure or behaves as specified above otherwise. Therefore, the failure activation causes the sensor to potentially miss workpieces located at the stack. In contrast, the physical phenomenon of the workpiece position is not altered by the deviation model. The input filter is modelled as an identity function for the sake of illustration which merely forwards the workpiece position.

Verification To analyse the availability of the crane's transportation function, the model can be translated to the PRISM model checker. Essentially, we provide a component that represents an uptime metric which associates rewards of 1 and 0 with a timeliness or (potentially infinitely) delayed transportation, respectively. Then, we can verify that the required availability is achieved by querying

```
Rmin=?[C<=36000],
```

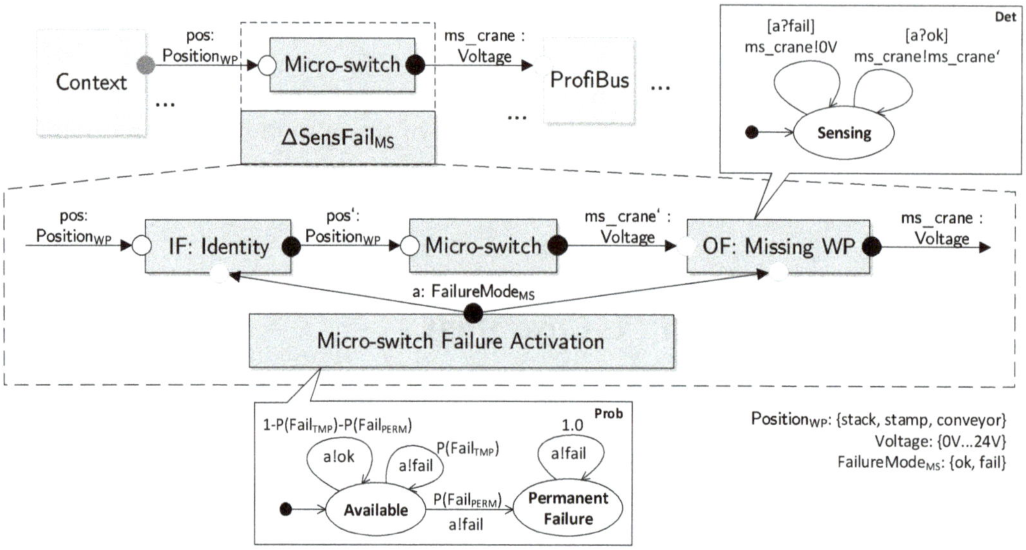

Fig. 11.5 The extended system model of the microswitch sensing whether a workpiece is available for pickup by the crane at the stack position using a probabilistic state machine for activation

where `Rmin` refers to the cumulative rewards associated with the uptime metric within 1 h (i.e. 36,000 ticks with a 100 ms cycle time), and comparing the resulting value to the availability requirement, e.g. 0.9965 if an 99.65% availability of the transportation function is required.

11.5 Related Work

The verification of PLC programs w.r.t. temporal logic specifications (for safety, liveness, and time properties) has been subject of a number of publications already. The paper [YF03a] gives an overview of the field, and the survey [Lam+99b] discusses transformation processes for program languages to verifiable models. Various translations from IEC 6113-3 languages into the input languages of model checkers have been presented: Brinksma et al. [BMF02] present a translation of SFCs into Promela input for the SPIN model checker [Hol97]; De Smet et al. [Sme+00] translate all languages within IEC 61131-3 into input for the symbolic model checker Cadence-SMV [Bur+92]; and Bauer et al. [Bau+04b] translate SFCs into timed automata to be used with UPPAAL [Beh+01]. This model checker is also used to verify properties of continuous function charts (CFC) in [WFV09]. In [Bau+04a, BHL00] a unifying semantics for SFC is given where the ambiguities of the standard are addressed in a formal fashion.

Süflow and Drechsler [SD08] present a framework to verify that the *same* program behaves equivalently on *different* PLC platforms, a scenario closely related to ours. The authors employ a SAT solver to verify the arising proof conditions.

Strichman and Godlin [GS13] coined the term *regression verification* and presented a verification methodology based on replacing function calls by uninterpreted function symbols within a bounded software model-checking framework for C programs. In [GS08] they define "reactive equivalence", which is closely related to our notion of perfect trace equivalence. In earlier work [Fel+14], we presented an automated approach to regression verification based on invariant generation using Horn clauses. Many other approaches [Ver+10, VJB12, Haw+13, BCK11, WP12] exist on regression verification for imperative programming languages.

Equivalence checking is an established issue for the verification of hardware circuits. In *sequential equivalence checking*, the perfect trace equivalence between clocked circuits is analysed; see [HC98] or [KE02] for an overview. Lu and Cheng [LC09] present an approach based on inferred invariants, in which conditional or relational equivalence is not considered.

Table-based languages for visualisation of mathematical are common. For example, *Parnas tables* are a tabular representation of relations. Lorge et al. [PMI94] use them in addition to first-order logic for the specification of procedure contracts.

Also, *Software Cost Reduction* approach (SCR) [Hei+05] claims to be understandable and comprehensible by exploiting table-based syntax. SCR is a method for managing formal requirements, which was successful applied in practice, e. g. mission-critical systems from the NASA [HJ07]. It bases synchronous state machines to describe the behaviour of a system. The state machine is specified by tables, similar to the Parnas tables, to define the transition relation and the output relation. SCR benefits from a various tools that are built upon the formal semantics: the simulation and validation of specifications, the generation of system invariants and source code, and the formal verification of application properties. A commonality between an SCR specification and generalised test table is that both describe an automaton. For generalised test tables, this automaton is given by the transformation rules and is therefore restricted. Otherwise, generalised test tables are optimised for specification of sequential stimulus and responses. They allow the direct access to past values via back references or global variables; SCR requires an encoding of these values into the state.

CocoSpec [Cha+16] is a specification language for reactive programs that are written in the *Lustre* programming language. *CocoSpec* follows *assume-guarantee* paradigm using Boolean expression for specifying assumptions and assertion on the current in every time step. Like SCR, *CocoSpec* exploits a state machine to make these assertions and assumptions time-dependent. The state machine is written in *Lustre*. In contrast, the assumptions (input) and assertions (output) of a generalised test table are always time-dependent, i.e. they depend on the table rows.

Moszkowski [Mos85] follows with his Interval Temporal Logic (ITL), a different approach to the classical temporal specification languages CTL and LTL. ITL bases regular expression and therefore it is ω-regular. For concatenation, ITL introduces the chop operator $(r_1; r_2)$ which – similar to our concept of rows – divides a given trace into a suffix and prefix, where r_1 has to be valid on the suffix, resp. r_2 on the suffix. An unbounded repeated application concatenation is denoted by star operator r^*, identical to our "–" in the duration column. A generalised test table can be expressed as an ITL formula, under the costs of an exponential blow-up [Bec+17a].

The idea of using regular expression can be combined with Linear Temporal Logic (LTL) as *ForSpec Temporal Logic* (FTL) proves. FTL was developed by

Intel [Arm+02]. In addition to LTL operators (until, always, eventually), it supports the corresponding past operators, *regular events* and *time windows*. A regular event is a finite regular language in a similar fashion as ITL or generalised test tables. Time windows are helpful to specify that certain events need to occur with a defined time window (bounded LTL operators). Additionally, FTL allows the composition with temporal connectives (a composition of generalised test tables is possible on the automata level). In [Lju+10], Ljungkrantz et al. propose ST-LTL, which enriches LTL with the arithmetical operators of Structured Text, syntactical abbreviations for specifying the rising or falling edges of variables, and access to previous variable value.

Becker et al. [Bec+12] present the MechatronicUML language for modelling and analysing component-based software for mechatronic systems, which supports links between engineering disciplines. SysML4Mechatronics [KV13] is a language for interdisciplinary modelling, which addresses mechanical, electrical/electronic, and software aspects explicitly. A formal semantics for automatic verification of structural compatibility has been proposed [FKV14], but verifying functional conformance is not considered yet. Shah et al. [Sha+10] present a multi-discipline modelling framework based on SysML.

Various lines of research are meant to analyse the reliability and availability of technical systems. Several established modelling techniques, such as Reliability Block Diagrams (RBD) [Bir10, DP09] and Fault Trees [DBB92], are based on combinatorial models. In both cases, the diagrams model which elementary faults lead to a failure of the whole system or a system function. A problem with these kinds of models is that only rather simple scenarios can be captured [Bir10]. Besides those combinatorial approaches, several approaches for an architecture-based availability prediction have been proposed (see, e.g.[Kub89, Lap84, Lit79]). More recently, availability analysis also gained widespread attention for the domain of aPS. In [Lai+02], a general model is built based on the Markov model to predict the availability of distributed software and hardware systems. The authors use the Kolmogorov differential equations to calculate the probability that a system process is in a certain state and then derive the availability function for the respective system.

11.6 Conclusion

In this chapter, we have presented the opportunities and challenges for the application of formal verification during system evolution of automated production systems that we identified from our experiences in the projects MoDEMMiCAS and IMPROVE APS within the priority programme.

In addition, we have presented three approaches for formal verification of evolutionary steps that exploit the opportunities that automated production systems provide and address the challenges that arise:

Regression verification uses an older revision of the PLC software as specification for a newer release and allows one to prove that desired aspects of the system behaviour are retained by the evolution step. It thus leverages evolution by using the old code revision as specification. Model checking is feasible due to the limited structural complexity.

Generalised test tables allow specifying desired system behaviour as tables. They thus address the challenge of reducing the specification efforts by providing a user-friendly specification technology.

Model-checking interdisciplinary models translates multidomain models of automated production system, composed of software, automation hardware, and mechanical components into representations amenable to model checking. To verify that the software achieves the intended behaviour at the system level, we rely on a common formal modelling approach for all system components, which may also include continuous behaviour and make extensive use of model abstractions. We claim that the initial modelling effort may be justified by the longevity of such systems and the lack of effective alternatives, while the software's limited structural complexity benefits model checking despite the potentially large space state.

All techniques perform a full verification of the properties they claim to be true by using modern model-checking tools. Automated production systems have a limited state space by design and are thus suitable targets for such formal verification systems.

One cross-cutting challenge for all three presented techniques is that they need to make assumptions about the behaviour of the physical plant on which the software is deployed. The interdisciplinary approach relies on an explicit model for the environment as part of the verification input. Generalised test tables have columns for input signals such that signal sequences can be restricted to those occurring in practice. Thus, a plant model is specified implicitly. Regression verification often works without environment models, but not always. There are cases where parts of the plant behaviour need to be added as an explicit.

The presented approaches exemplarily demonstrate the ability of formal verification to provide valuable support and feedback in engineering long-living systems, especially automated production systems, thus suggesting a promising field of application for future research and motivating transfer into engineering practice.

11.7 Further Reading

The interested reader is invited to find more and more detailed information about the presented verification approaches in the following scientific publications:

The idea of regression verification for PLC programs developed in the project IMPROVE APS within the priority programme has originally been presented by Beckert et al. [Bec+15]. Ulewicz et al. [Ule+15] have shown how the presented regression verification approach can be extended to comparing different variants of PLC software in order to reduce unneeded variant diversity. Moreover, we show in [Ule+16] how the regression verification approach for PLC code can be embedded into the development process for aPS software.

Regression verification can not only be applied to PLC software, but a similar approach has been presented by Kiefer et al. [Fel+14, KKU16] for the automatic regression verification of C programs. The tool LLRÊVE compares two C routines for various types of equivalence. It can be applied to programs with certain heap data structures [KRU17] and combines static and dynamic analyses to extend the reach of the regression verification approach [KKU17]. LLRÊVE can be accessed as a publicly available web application: https://formal.iti.kit.edu/projects/improve/reve/. The tool *semantic slicer* [Bec+17b] employs LLRÊVE to produce very precise slices that a syntactical analysis cannot find. In [BKU15] Beckert et al. reduce Java regression verification problems to equivalent secure information flow problems on the JML* specification language and the KeY prover [Ahr+16].

Generalised test tables were first introduced by Weigl et al. [Wei+17], and their formal semantics was defined by Beckert et al. [Bec+17a]. The automatic verification tool GETETA that proves that a PLC program behaves as specified in a generalised test table is an open source project hosted at github. Current releases and more information can be found on the companion webpage https://formal.iti.kit.edu/geteta/.

The *ST Verification Studio* (STVS) is a tool that provides a user-friendly frontend for the specification and verification of PLC software using generalised test tables. It is presented in Fig. 10.11, and details can be found on the companion webpage https://formal.iti.kit.edu/stvs/.

The multidisciplinary modelling approach of our verification is based on a model-based development for cyber-physical systems [Bro97, Hub+98, Sch+02, Bro+10], which is extended to automated production systems by [Leg+14]. Essentially, it extends the FOCUS theory described in [Bro86, BS01] with notions of discrete and dense time [Bro12], spatio-temporal systems [Hum09, Bot+09], and using dynamic sampling [Cam13]. Finally, those concepts were implemented in the AutoFOCUS 3 tool, which is described in more detail in [Hub+96, SHT12, Ara+15]

Part III
Results and Spin-Offs

Chapter 12
Case Studies for the Community

Safa Bougouffa, Kiana Busch, Robert Heinrich, André van Hoorn, Marco Konersmann, Stephan Seifermann, Emre Taşpolatoğlu, Felix Ocker, Cyntia Vargas, Mina Fahimipirehgalin, Ralf Reussner, and Birgit Vogel-Heuser

This chapter describes the benefits and deliverables of the case studies in SPP1593 for the outside community. Section 12.1 sums up the benefits of the Common Component Modeling Example (CoCoME) case study together with the deliverables for the community. Section 12.2 describes the benefits of the Pick-and-Place Unit (PPU) and its extension (xPPU) as well as the deliverables for the outside community. Section 12.3 describes the benefits and deliverables of the industry 4.0 case study that integrates CoCoME and xPPU.

S. Bougouffa (✉) · F. Ocker · C. Vargas · M. Fahimipirehgalin · B. Vogel-Heuser
Technische Universität München, Lehrstuhl für Automatisierung und Informationssysteme, Garching, Germany
e-mail: safa.bougouffa@tum.de; felix.ocker@tum.de; mina.fahimi@tum.de; vogel-heuser@tum.de

K. Busch · R. Heinrich (✉) · S. Seifermann · R. Reussner
Institute for Program Structures and Data Organization, Karlsruhe Institute of Technology (KIT), Karlsruhe, Germany
e-mail: kiana.busch@kit.edu; robert.heinrich@kit.edu; stephan.seifermann@kit.edu; reussner@kit.edu

A. van Hoorn
Institute of Software Technology, University of Stuttgart, Stuttgart, Germany
e-mail: van.hoorn@informatik.uni-stuttgart.de

M. Konersmann
paluno – The Ruhr Institute for Software Technology, Spezifikation von Softwaresystemen, Universität Duisburg-Essen, Essen, Germany
e-mail: marco.konersmann@paluno.uni-due.de

E. Taşpolatoğlu
Software Engineering, FZI Forschungszentrum Informatik, Karlsruhe, Germany
e-mail: taspolat@fzi.de

R. Reussner et al. (eds.), *Managed Software Evolution*,
https://doi.org/10.1007/978-3-030-13499-0_12

12.1 Benefits and Deliverables of CoCoME for the Outside Community

CoCoME has been designed as a demonstrator for software systems to satisfy research requirements on architecture modelling and evolution of the SPP1593 community. CoCoME is open to the research community. As a community case study, CoCoME aims at providing several benefits to researchers of SPP1593 and the outside community:

- By building upon existing specifications and implemented source code and settings, less effort in scenario definition, study setup, and execution is required by researchers.
- A common case study increases comparability of evaluation results to those of other researchers and leads to increased evaluation confidence.
- A common case study also increases community acceptance by interaction with other researchers.

CoCoME is limited in size and complexity; however, it shows all characteristics of an information system used in industrial practice. Therefore, CoCoME provides a trade-off between modelling complexity and evaluation effort. CoCoME represents a comprehensive knowledge base for the evaluation process that can be exploited and extended by researchers with different backgrounds and research interests. It provides assistance on diverse characteristics important for software evolution, like artefacts in different revisions, comprehensive evolution scenarios, and coverage of different life-cycle phases. The distinct evolution scenarios specified for CoCoME in the course of SPP1593 cover a wide range of adaptive and perfective changes to the system and result in various deliverables to the outside research community.

The several evolution scenarios of CoCoME address a variety of changes to the software architecture and infrastructure. For each scenario detailed description, requirements specification, and design documentation in the form of technical reports [HRR16, HKR18] are publicly available. The implemented source code in Java is available on github[1] for each evolution scenario of CoCoME in SPP1593. Furthermore, models to represent the structure (i.e. architecture) and behaviour of the different variants of CoCoME in the form of PCM are deliverables of the priority programme. These models can be applied for analysing and simulating CoCoME with respect to different quality properties like performance, maintainability, and security. In the following, we give a detailed description of models delivered to the community by SPP1593 to represent the architecture, deployment, and behaviour of CoCoME. Furthermore, we describe how the community applied CoCoME and the models delivered by SPP1593 beyond the scope of the priority programme.

[1]https://github.com/cocome-community-case-study.

12.1.1 *Structural, Deployment, and Behavioural Models of CoCoME*

The architecture of a software system represents the design decisions during its development and evolution [TMD+09]. Therefore, the architecture of a software system can be considered as one of the main influence factors on its quality properties such as performance, maintainability, or security [TMD+09]. The implementation of design decisions without knowing their effects can be a costly and risky task. Thus, modelling the architecture of a software system and simulating the model of the software architecture enable software architects to understand the effects of different design decisions on software quality properties before implementation. The software architect has to consider the following aspects while modelling the architecture of a software system: its structure, its deployment, and its control and data flow. The model of the software architecture can serve as the input of a simulator [Reu+16, Ros+15].

Palladio is an approach for modelling and simulating the architecture of the component-based software systems [Reu+16]. Palladio can predict the quality properties of the software architecture such as performance, maintainability, or security at design time. Palladio is based on Palladio Component Model (PCM). PCM is the architectural modelling language for component-based software systems. It was initially developed to model and predict the performance properties of a software system. In order to model the architecture of a software system, PCM provides the following view types: (1) repository, (2) system, (3) resource environment, (4) allocation, and (5) usage model [Reu+16].

To support model-driven approaches to predicting quality properties, we provide PCM of the CoCoME architecture. These models were created for the hybrid cloud-based variant of CoCoME describing its structure, deployment, and behaviour.

Modelling the Structure of CoCoME

CoCoME represents a component-based software system. A component-based software system can be modelled by its interfaces and components and their composition (also referred to as composite components) [Reu+16]. The hybrid cloud-based variant of CoCoME consists of the following composite components:

- `org.cocome.cloud.web`
- `org.cocome.tradingsystem.inventory`
- `org.cocome.cloud.webservice.inventory`
- `org.cocome.tradingsystem.cashdeskline`
- `org.cocome.cloud.logic.webservice.cashdeskline.cashdeskservice`

These components are composed of further composite components or individual components. The current architecture model of the hybrid cloud-based variant of CoCoME contains more than 40 components. The architecture of CoCoME was modelled using the system-independent structural elements of the PCM, namely, components, interfaces, events, and data types. Additionally, the PCM allows assembling the components and composite components to further composite components. Thus, the current model of CoCoME can easily be extended to future implementation (e.g. adding or removing components, interfaces, or data types). Further, the PCM allows modelling the control flows in components at a high abstraction level. Thus, the effect of different control flows (i.e. implementations on a high abstraction level) on the quality properties of CoCoME can be analysed. The repository view type of the PCM allows modelling the previously described model elements.

After the software architect modelled the individual model elements, such as components and interfaces, the architecture of CoCoME can be modelled by assembling these model elements. Further, modelling individual elements allows assembling other variants of CoCoME by different composition of existing model elements, exchanging the model elements by other model elements, or adding new model elements. Thus, the resulting architecture variant of CoCoME and its effect on the quality properties can be determined at design time. The system view type of the PCM allows assembling the software system using the individual model elements defined in the repository view type [Reu+16]. Figure 12.1 shows different components with their provided and required interfaces. The required and provided interfaces are connected to each other using connectors.

The system model of CoCoME is composed of the previously described composite components at the highest level of abstraction. CoCoME provides various services as method invocation of its interfaces. The interfaces of the CoCoME system are defined as follows:

- `ICashDeskView`: This interface mainly provides support for the selling products and managing the express checkout.
- `IShowReportView`: This interface provides services for creating stock reports.
- `IReceiveOrderView`: This interface allows handling ordered products, which have been arrived, such as viewing received orders.
- `IStockOrderView`: This interface can be used to manage purchase orders in the stock.
- `IShowStockView`: This interface provides services for managing stock orders, such as the creation of a new stock order.

Modelling the Deployment of CoCoME

Using the PCM, the resource environment, such as resource containers or linking resources, can be modelled. Further, the resource containers can be annotated with values of different quality metrics, such as mean time to failure (MTTF) for the hard disk or resource demands for central processing units (CPUs) [Reu+16, BKR09].

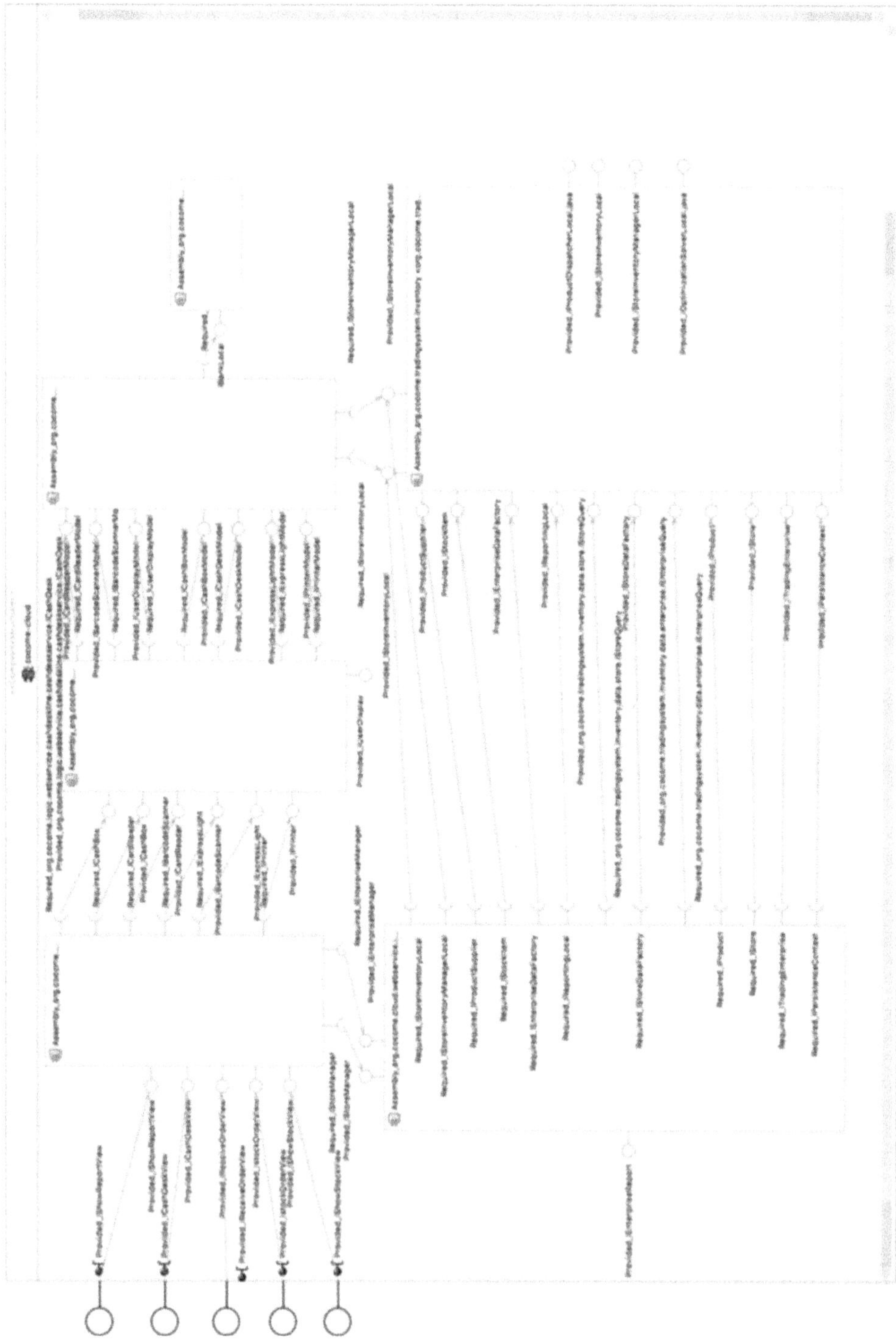

Fig. 12.1 The system model of CoCoME

The resource environment view type of the PCM allows modelling the resource environment. Examples of resource containers for CoCoME are enterprise server, store server, and web node.

After modelling the resource containers, the software architect has to determine which components of CoCoME should be deployed on which resource containers. The system-specific deployment is specified by the allocation view type. For example, the composite component `org.cocome.cloud.webservice.inventory` can be deployed on the resource container enterprise server. It is conceivable that different allocations between components of CoCoME and resource containers are possible. Thus, simulation allows analysing the effects of different allocations on the system's quality properties.

Modelling the Behaviour of CoCoME

The usage model of CoCoME can be specified by the PCM behaviour view type [Reu+16]. Modelling the behaviour allows specifying the interaction of users with CoCoME. For example, different user interactions with CoCoME can affect the performance of the software system. To enable the business process designers to model the usage models, we provided a business process meta-model within SPP1593. This meta-model extends the PCM usage model by actor steps and the resource usage. The business process models allow analysing the effects of changes in CoCoME on the interaction of its users [Ros+17]. This is especially important when we analyse the maintainability of CoCoME regarding different usage scenarios. The business processes can also to be used to analyse the performance of the software system and its business processes [Hei+17a].

To model the business process, the PCM usage model is extended by the specific elements of business process (hereafter referred to as business process usage model). Business process can be considered as a set of connected activities. At the lowest abstraction level, activities can be actor steps, system steps, or steps regarding the resource device usage. The main difference between the actor steps and the system steps is that the actor steps are completely performed by human actors, whereas system steps are executed automatically by the software system. Further, human actors can use the resource devices to perform their activities. Therefore, they can acquire the resource devices before using or release the device resources after using [Hei+17a].

The processes of CoCoME can be modelled using the business process usage model. The previously described services of CoCoME are part of processes (e.g. sale process), which CoCoME provides (cf. [Her+08a]). In the following we describe different processes of CoCoME:

- *ProcessSale* deals with selling products. It can be considered as the main process of CoCoME (cf. process 1 in [Her+08a]).
- *ManageExpressCheckoutProcess* describes the fast sale process for purchasing only few products (cf. process 2 in [Her+08a]).

- *OrderProducts* describes how new products can be ordered (cf. process 3 in [Her+08a]).
- *RecieveOrderedProducts* defines how to manage the arrived ordered products (cf. process 4 in [Her+08a]).
- *ShowStockReports* describes the process of the creating the stock reports (cf. process 5 in [Her+08a]).
- *ShowDeliveryReports* deals with creating the delivery reports (cf. process 6 in [Her+08a]).
- *ChangePrice* defines how the prices of products can be changed (cf. process 7 in [Her+08a]).

In the following section, we describe how the models of CoCoME can be applied to analyse different quality properties.

12.1.2 Analysing Maintainability for CoCoME

The maintainability of a system can be considered as the ease of implementing changes in that system [ISO10]. In other words, the maintainability of a system in the case of a change request correlates with the set of system elements that have to be changed [HBK18a]. As a community case study, several development artefacts of CoCoME are available. Examples of such artefacts are code, requirement descriptions, and aforementioned models. Thus, CoCoME is well suited for comparing different maintainability estimation approaches. The application of an approach to CoCoME allows comparing it with other approaches that have been applied to CoCoME. For example, if we have different maintainability estimation approaches, which estimate a set of changed elements for a change request, we can compare these sets with each other for given change requests. Thus, the application of maintainability estimation approaches to CoCoME allows improving them with regard to the change propagation analysis. Additionally, having a common community case with its development artefacts allows analysing how the change requests affect different artefacts [Ros+17].

The CoCoME models described in the previous section can serve as the input of model-driven approaches to maintainability analysis in software systems. In this context, the models describing the structure of CoCoME are especially important, as the structure of a software system affects the change propagation in that system [HBK18a]. Modelling CoCoME by components and interfaces in a fine-grained manner improves the change impact analysis in the software architecture.

Software systems can be used to support business processes of organisations. Therefore, there are mutual dependencies between the software systems and the corresponding business processes [Ros+17]. Thus, we have to consider both software systems and the corresponding business processes while analysing the change impact. In addition to the structural models of CoCoME, the maintainability estimation approaches regarding software systems and business processes can also use its usage models describing the behaviour of CoCoME. As described in the previous section, the processes of CoCoME are modelled as a set of connected actor steps and system steps. This allows analysing the effects of changes based on the mutual dependencies between the software system and the corresponding business processes [Ros+17].

In the model of software systems, the structural model elements such as interfaces and components can be used to analyse the propagation of change [Ros+15]. In the model of business processes, the activities such as system steps and actor steps can be used to calculate the change propagation [Ros+17]. Further, the data flow plays an important role in change propagation [HBK18a]. The change can propagate based on the data flow between a software system and its corresponding business processes [HBK18a, Ros+17]. To model the data flow in CoCoME, we modelled different data types in its software model and different data objects in its business process model. As a data object can correspond to a data type and vice versa, the models of CoCoME allow analysing the change propagation based on the data flow [Ros+17].

To model the change request and to analyse the change propagation in terms of affected model elements, we also provided a further meta-model—the modification marks meta-model [Sta15, HBK18a]. Modification marks meta-model allows software architects and business process designers of CoCoME to mark the initially affected model elements (hereafter referred to as seed modification). Based on the seed modifications, the task list can be generated automatically. The generated task list contains a set of maintainability tasks, where each task refers to a model element that is potentially affected by the change. The maintainability tasks are grouped in different change propagation steps based on the cause of the change propagation [HBK18a]. Figure 12.2 illustrates a generated task list for the change request modifying the interface IBarcodeScanner. Thus, the interface IBarcodeScanner is the seed modification. Each task in the task list corresponds to a model element of CoCoME. Further, Fig. 12.2 shows several change propagation steps. For example,

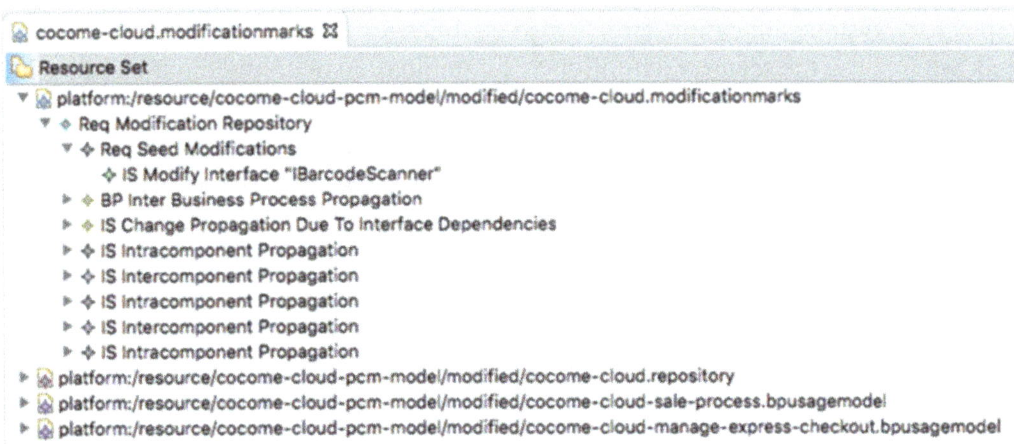

Fig. 12.2 Analysing the change propagation in CoCoME using the modification marks meta-model

business process (BP) inter-business process propagation indicates that the change propagates only in the business process. This change propagation step contains only business process model elements. As described previously the data flow may cause the change propagation [HBK18a]. Information system (IS) change propagation due to data dependencies in Fig. 12.2 refers to structural model elements of CoCoME software system that is affected by the change due to the data flow. The change can also propagate between the provided roles of a component and the required role of other components (i.e. IS intracomponent propagation in Fig. 12.2) and between the required role of a component and its provided role (i.e. IS intercomponent propagation in Fig. 12.2).

12.1.3 Modelling Security Patterns and Attacks for CoCoME

Security plays a crucial role in systems with important assets like critical tasks or such that includes personal information. Long-living systems going through software evolution face security problems similar to any other quality requirements which are open to degradation. It is very important to preserve the secure state of a system, as itself or its environment, usage, configuration, etc. change, which can affect directly or indirectly the correct functioning of security mechanisms. In such cases, made design decisions for mitigating threats and addressing possible security vulnerabilities can lose their validity. Furthermore, it would be worse if there are no signs for such invalidations, so that the problem based on any change can be first discovered after an attack occurs or a vulnerability is exploited. Hence, the software engineers confront the degrading security, and addressing it becomes a more challenging job, if any corresponding documentation of the security decisions made and their assumptions do not persist over time.

As previously described, Palladio architecture models are historically developed for performance simulations and analyses. However, being a model-based documentation of complex software systems and providing several abstract views (i.e. repository, system, allocation, etc.), it also qualifies for investigating security. To this end, we first use the security definition as a combination of confidentiality, integrity, and availability [CH13], which can be interpreted on architecture models.

The approach **PreReqSec** [TH16a] supports software engineers and architects to consider security as early as possible in the design time, which considers runtime, configuration, or usage information. Further support is provided during the software evolution, as the possible changes can be reflected upon the architecture, where less complex but still powerful security analyses are possible. To this end, security-related information is modelled as first-class entities on architectural level in so-called security catalogues, which at the time are being developed for the case study CoCoME. The hybrid cloud-based variant of CoCoME provides several evolution scenarios, in which different aspects and entities of the system change (see Sect. 4.2). The corresponding architecture models are well suited for demonstrating the application of PreReqSec. In the following, we discuss two evolution scenarios from a security perspective.

- `Platform Migration:` This evolution scenario migrates several local resources (i.e. enterprise server and database) of the system to cloud for reducing operating costs and providing flexibility in adaptation and reconfiguration. However, it also introduces new challenges such as the privacy concerns or third-party trust that might affect the confidentiality and availability. Furthermore, providing such flexibility can make design time decisions obsolete. For example, before cloud integration, the system had to handle all private data in local servers, where no remote calls to data stored in cloud were necessary, which was no subject for, e.g. man-in-the-middle threats.
- `Adding a Pick-Up Shop:` As the customer landscape and competition between other providers grow, this evolution scenario provides new business models such as online shopping and new use cases like online payment. A completely new system interface is introduced. Hence, the attack surface expands and new attack vectors become possible. These changes affect both confidentiality and integrity as well as availability. As the very fundamental requirements and therefore the system itself change, it becomes necessary to validate the already-made security decisions as well as consider new ones.

Security catalogues within the PreReqSec approach can be used globally due to their reusable nature, or they can also be project- or application-specific. A small snippet from the security catalogue for CoCoME can be seen in Fig. 12.3. The catalogue is open for further development and also can be used in other web- and cloud-based software applications.

Mainly, the catalogues consist of three parts corresponding to two different pillars of security. These are the attacks and security patterns, which are combined by so-called prerequisites. Prerequisites in the PreReqSec approach are structural and logical information corresponding to assumptions or requirements that define in which cases a threat can succeed or a security measure can mitigate a given attack.

Threat models provide information about vulnerabilities and possible attacks, which are analogous to the usage profiles of the Palladio Component Model. They are in the PreReqSec approach, a simplified version of usage models, which are modelled as basic interface calls for maliciously getting into the software system. Based on black-box modelling, we do not provide any further information once the interfaces are passed, which is to be interpreted as the risk of any malicious penetration through system boundaries. However, if necessary an attack vector can be modelled with the help of profiling/stereotyping for representing more complex attacks like advanced persistent threats (APT attacks). Based on the evolution scenarios, a security expert provides the information regarding possible threats.

The security catalogue includes the following attacks: `HTTP-Flooding`, `SYN-Flooding`, `Persistent-Cross-Site-Scripting`, or `Cross-Site-Request-Forgery`.

On the other hand, security patterns (analogous to the well-known design patterns) provide the necessary information for a structural solution to recurring

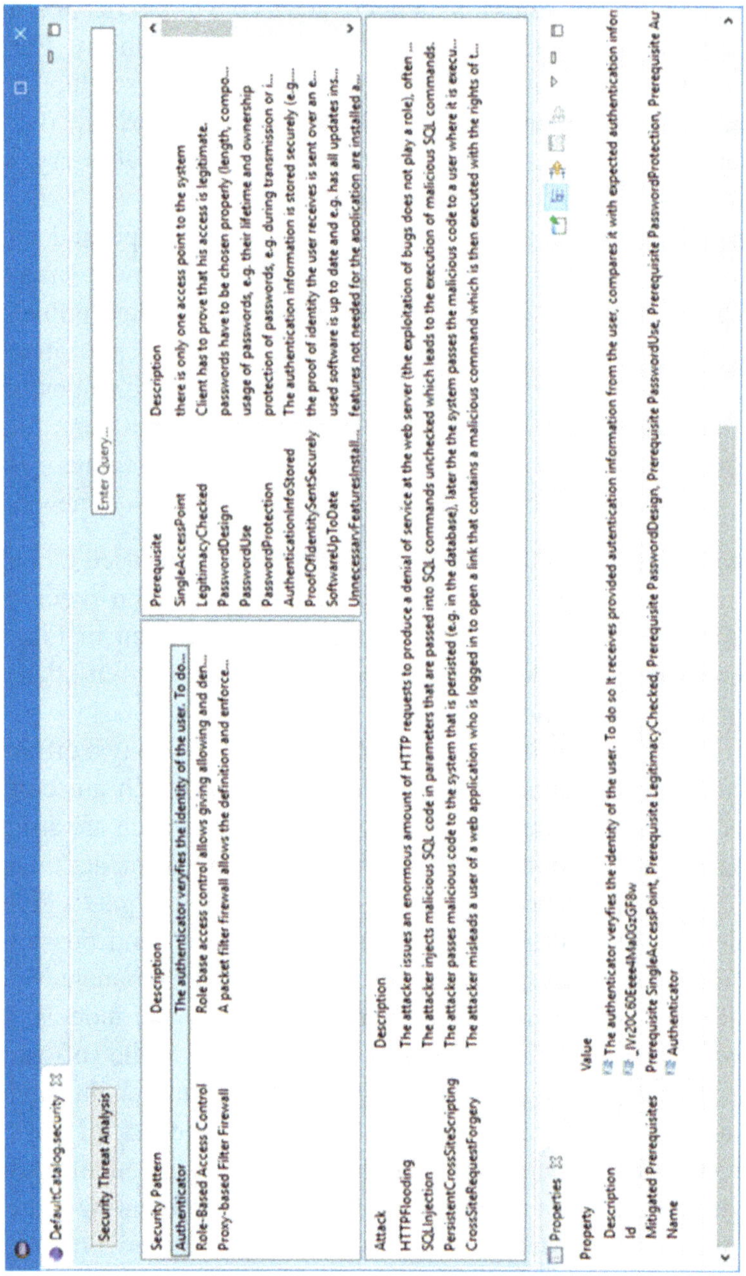

Fig. 12.3 A snippet from the security catalogue—shown in the column-based editor integrated with Eclipse properties view

security problems from the threat catalogue. Every security pattern consists of structural roles. A role corresponds always to one or more software (or in some cases hardware) components. It basically states that (in case) the related component fulfils a specific task within the entire security pattern. To provide reusability and to be able to use the security catalogues with any given architecture description language, security patterns are separated from the system models and used profiling/stereotyping to connect the elements of security pattern (i.e. roles) with the corresponding architectural elements (e.g. composite components, system interfaces). Due to these separation of security patterns as well as attacks, the PreReqSec approach provides a new security view.

After defining possible threats, security expert and software architect can first check which of the already-made security decisions may become obsolete, since they cannot mitigate the new threats. This is mainly a task within the security analysis, which is at the time an ongoing development within the PreReqSec approach. However, extending the documentation (i.e. security catalogues) is now possible with the security expert and software architect. Based on their expertise, state of the art, and security best practices, they make new decisions about possible security patterns, which are able to mitigate the newly introduced or changed attacks. Following security patterns are for the time being defined and modelled in the catalogues for CoCoME, for which several extensions are planned directly in CoCoME system models, such as:

- `Role-based Access Control` is a security pattern to provide secure access control for different users to different assets. The pattern is structured within several different elements from CoCoME like `org.cocome.cloud.webservice.LoginManager`, `org.cocome.tradingsystem.inventory.data.UserManager` or `org.cocome.tradingsystem.inventory.application.UserManager`.
- `Proxy-based Firewall` is a well-known firewall pattern for web applications. `org.cocome.cloud.proxybasedfirewall` is the main component for firewall security pattern. It is deployed on web node and traffics the communication of `org.cocome.cloud.web` composite component.

After instantiating the attacks and security patterns, it comes to how to combine them structurally. The combining elements between the attacks and security patterns are the logical prerequisites, as previously described, which are used as parameters for the analysis to validate the made security design decisions with respect to possible changes or to design time unknown information. However, besides the development of automated architecture-based security analysis, extending the security patterns and threats with modelled prerequisites is an ongoing part within this research. Due to highly considerable manual effort which involves many views and roles, it makes a very steady foundation for considering security within software architectures and allows analysing this very important quality attribute without having to code, deploy, or penetration test the software system under consideration.

12.1.4 Modelling and Analysing Data Flow for CoCoME

Software architects can analyse many quality properties of software architectures by means of activities executed in the way a control flow defines. However, there are quality properties such as compliance with data privacy constraints that are naturally defined in terms of data and data flows. Ongoing research in the field of architectural data flow analyses [Sei16] tries to leverage definitions data and its processing as well as concise privacy constraint descriptions to determine compliance of architectures with privacy constraints. CoCoME serves as a case study for evaluating architectural data flow analyses.

The pick-up shop evolution scenario implies many privacy constraints because it introduces user-related data. In a first step, a subset of CoCoME about the creation of reports has been chosen. Depending on the realisation of the use case, the store manager might get access to data that (s)he does not actually need but are worth protecting. This includes personal information about users. An access control policy defines which roles have access to which data, which serves as an input for an analysis. The second step is making exchanged data explicit and specifying the data processing. As a third step, we create several realisations of the use case that imply privacy violations and analyse them for violations.

Even if extending CoCoME by data and data processing requires considerable effort, it is a good foundation for case studies in the field of data privacy. It processes sensitive and non-sensitive data in various ways defined by the use cases. Therefore, it defines a reasonable network of data processing operations and data exchanges. However, the case study is not artificial but realistic, which allows to draw conclusions about applicability.

12.1.5 Diagnosis of Privacy and Performance Problems for the CoCoME Mobile App Client

Users of mobile apps expect fast response times and high throughput. However, there are a lot of different mobile devices with different specifications, which makes it hard to show adequate performance on each of them. Another important quality property of mobile apps is privacy as lot of sensitive data is stored at mobile devices and transferred over a bunch of different networks. Thus, observing and analysing mobile apps for performance and privacy issues are crucial. The monitoring and analysis approach proposed in [MHH18] is capable of identifying both privacy and performance problems of mobile apps.

The approach has been evaluated based on the mobile app client evolution scenario of the CoCoME case study. In the mobile app client, the use cases AuthenicateAppUser and ProcessAppSale have been executed. Monitoring data for the use cases have been recorded and analysed for performance and privacy problems in order to evaluate the accuracy of the analysis and overhead of the mobile monitoring approach [MHH18].

12.1.6 Functional Decomposition for Identifying Microservices in CoCoME

A big challenge in designing microservice architectures is to find an appropriate partition of the system into microservices. Microservices are usually designed intuitively, based on the experience of the designers. A systematic approach to identify microservices in early design phase is described in [Tys+18]. The approach is based on the specification of the system's functional requirements and uses functional decomposition to identify microservices.

CoCoME has been used as a case study for evaluating this approach. Starting with the use case specification of CoCoME, system operations and state variables have been extracted and clustered for identifying microservices. The clusters identified by the proposed approach have been compared to microservices identified by human developers based on the CoCoME source code and design documentation (the component diagrams and sequence diagrams given in [HRR16]). For this purpose, CoCoME has been applied as a case study at the Centre for Research and Innovation in Software Engineering at Southwest University in Chongqing, China, and the Karlsruhe Institute of Technology, Germany. The outcome of the functional decomposition of CoCoME is analogous to the evolution scenario microservice architecture.

12.1.7 Distributed Quality Property Optimisation for CoCoME

Software products must satisfy a considerable number of non-functional quality properties, e.g. regarding performance and modifiability. It is known that quality properties may conflict with each other. The reason is that software changes aimed to improve one quality properties can and usually do have a negative impact on another property. Hence, trade-offs between quality properties need to be managed to achieve an overall accepted level of quality for the software product. Architecture-based optimisation aims for evaluating such trade-offs in early design stages [Ale+13].

CoCoME is being used as a case study for a novel distributed approach for optimising quality properties of software architectures, in an approach called

SQuAT [Rag+17a]. While the approach is property-agnostic, the evaluation focused on the quality properties performance and modifiability. SQuAT builds on the idea of scenario-based architecture evaluation [BCK12], which proposes to evaluate architectures based on their ability to support quality scenarios. In the SQuAT framework, so-called bots evaluate and try to optimise "their" respective quality scenario. In multiple iterations, a moderator aims to support the mediation and negotiation between the bots, by sharing solutions that can be further improved by the bots to find a joint solution. SQuAT employs model-based quality prediction, currently focusing on the Palladio Component Model (PCM). It currently, support two types of bots—one for performance and one for modifiability [Rag+17a].

CoCoME is used for a large-scale evaluation of the SQuAT approach, whose basic effectiveness has been evaluated in a smaller study before [Rag+17a]. The existing PCM are used with slight modifications. In total, eight scenarios are defined—four for modifiability and four for performance. Accordingly, eight bots execute to find an architectural CoCoME candidate by incrementally improving architectural candidates, using modifiability and performance tactics.

While the case study is still in progress, it has already greatly helped to reveal and resolve challenging situations related to the model size and topology in the SQuAT framework.

12.1.8 Extracting Architecture Models of CoCoME

Software architecture models in different modelling languages were automatically generated from the source code of the plain-Java variant of CoCoME in [Kon18]. These models and their generation serve as a showcase of architecture model extraction using *Codeling*.[2] In this context, two types of architecture models have been extracted—PCM and UML composite structure diagrams. The generated PCM and UML models are available for the community.[3] Codeling is a tool that can extract architecture models from the source code and maintain traces between the model and the code. That is, when the model is changed, the source code is changed accordingly. The source code that is not represented by the model is not lost during this operation. For example, when a component is renamed, the corresponding source code will still contain its operations and their implementation.

Code that follows the specification of a component framework—such as the Java Enterprise Edition (JEE) [Ora17]—is forced to be structured in specific ways for representing architectural elements such as components and their interconnection. For example, any type of "bean" in JEE can be considered a component. Beans in the JEE are Java class declarations with specific Java annotations. That means that a class declaration in the program code, which has that specific Java annotation, can

---

[2] https://www.codeling.de.

[3] https://github.com/cocome-community-case-study/models/tree/master/Codeling/.

be identified as a component. Codeling uses such predescribed code structures to generate a translation model that complies to an intermediate architecture language developed for Codeling. This translation model can be translated into multiple architecture description languages. Two architecture models of the CoCoME program code were extracted. The plain-Java variant of the CoCoME program code was used for this purpose. That variant actually does not follow any standardised component framework but established a custom notion of components and other architecture-related concepts. This project-specific component framework needed to be analysed first, to find out which structures were used to implement architectural elements. In the following sections, we present the models and briefly describe how they were extracted from the program code with Codeling.

PCM Extracted from the CoCoME Source Code

In the first case study, PCM were generated, which allow for performance simulations of the architecture. The PCM defines multiple view types for modelling an architecture. In this case study, we extracted the repository model, the system model, and the instance models of CoCoME's composite components from the code. Neither the resource environment and allocation nor usage models for performance simulations are encoded in the program code. These have to be added manually for the purpose performance simulations. The originally planned architecture model of the plain-Java CoCoME system is shown in Fig. 4.5 on page 43. Figures 12.4 and 12.5 show the PCM repository and system, which were extracted from the plain-Java CoCoME program code using Codeling. The repository contains all identified components and composite components, alongside with their required and provided interfaces and operations. For each composite component, the model declares an instance of each subcomponent, correctly interconnected as defined in the program code. These diagrams are not shown in the figures at hand. The system diagram declares one instance of each of the top-most components in the repository and interconnects them as declared by the program code. Provided interfaces are propagated to the system's context.

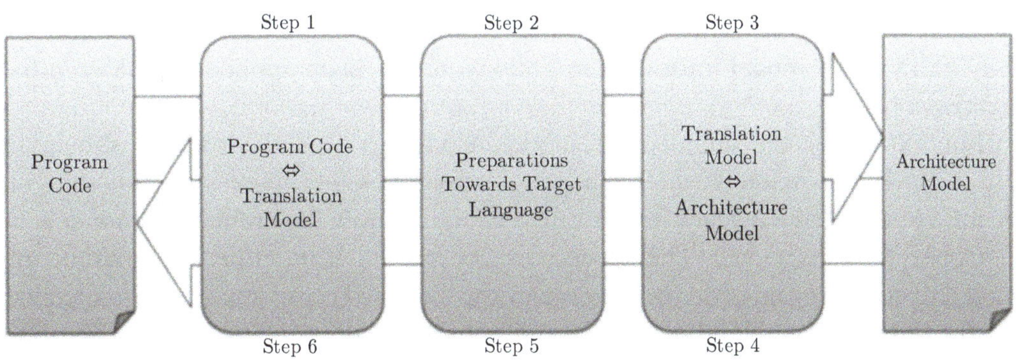

Fig. 12.4 The CoCoME architecture in an PCM repository diagram, as extracted with Codeling

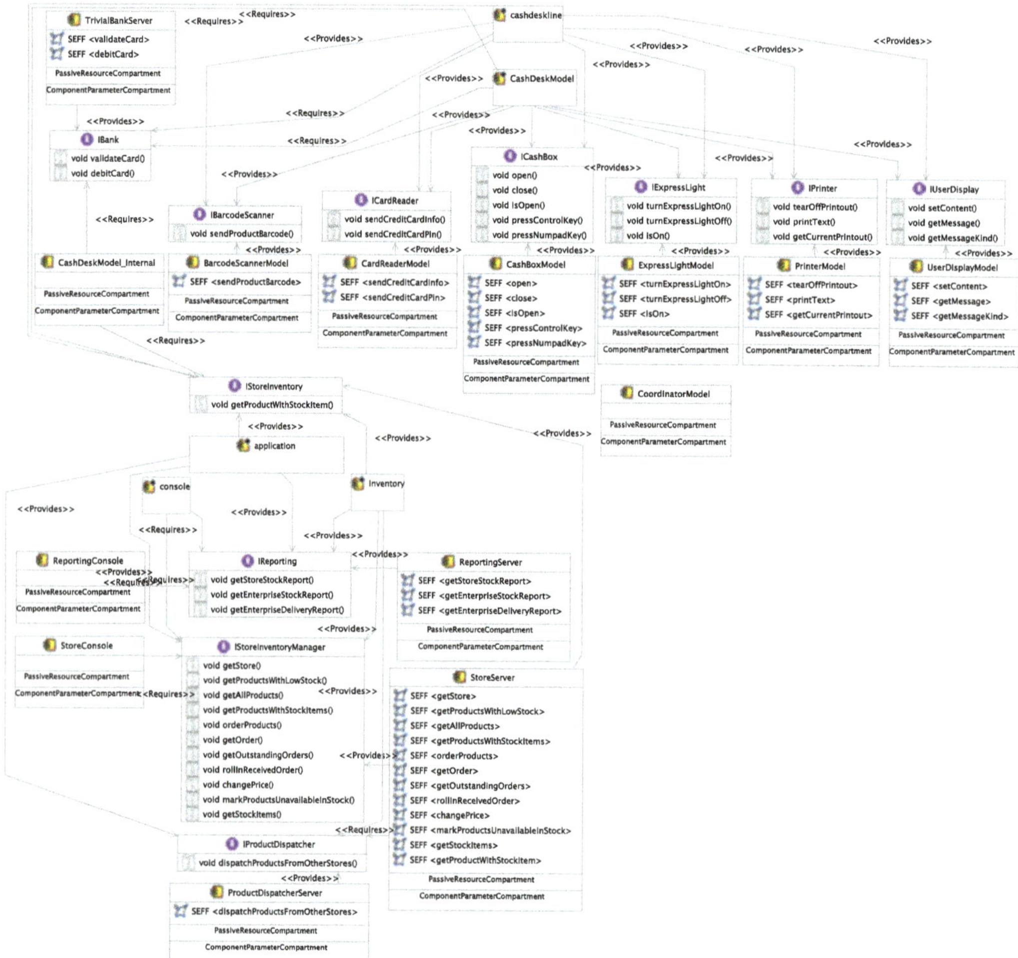

Fig. 12.5 The CoCoME architecture in an PCM system diagram, as extracted with Codeling

The translation between the CoCoME source code and the intermediate language is not complete in the sense that the event mechanism has not been translated. Therefore, the component *JMSEventBus* is missing in this model as well as event-based interfaces. Also, the data access components have not been translated in this case study. The missing pieces could also be extracted, if the corresponding code structures would be added to the Codeling. It should also be noted that Codeling only extracts the model information. The layout has been applied manually in the figures at hand.

For extracting the architecture model, Codeling uses the process shown in Fig. 12.6. Konersmann [Kon18, Chapter 8] describes the process and all steps in detail. Here we give an overview for understanding how the architecture models of CoCoME were extracted. The process can be started from either the architecture model or the program code. In the case of the CoCoME case study, an architecture model was extracted from code. Therefore, here the process was started from the program code.

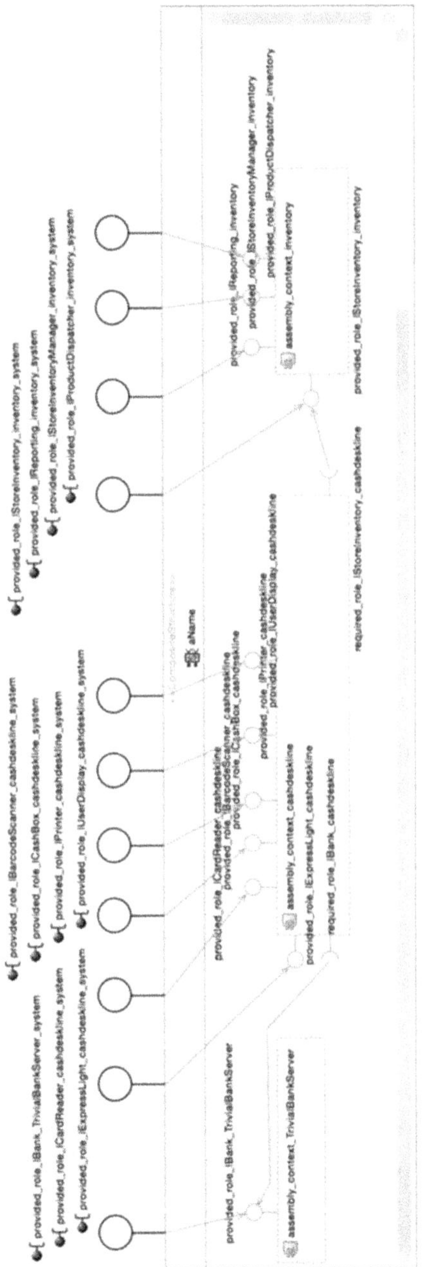

Fig. 12.6 Overview of the process to extract architecture models form program code with Codeling and the propagation of changes in the model to the code

The process defines three main steps for each direction. For extracting an architecture model, the following steps are executed:

Step 1 extraction of a translation model from the program code via an implementation model

Step 2 preparation of the translation model to the necessities of the target language

Step 3 translation of the translation model into the targeted architecture modelling language

In the step *Program Code to Translation Model*, a translation model is created based on the source code. The step comprises substeps: First, an implementation model of the source code is extracted. This model describes the implementation with the terms of the component framework in use. As described above, the CoCoME implementation uses a project-specific component framework. This framework needed to be analysed first, to find out which structures were used to implement architectural elements. Second, this model is then translated into a translation model, which complies to Codeling's intermediate architecture language.

In the step *Preparations Towards Target Language*, the translation model is prepared for the targeted architecture modelling language. This is used to compensate differences between component frameworks and architecture modelling languages. For example, imagine a component framework, which requires deployment information to be valid. In this step, minimal deployment information would be added in the intermediate language to enable the translation. In the step *Translation Model to Architecture Model*, the translation model is translated into the targeted architecture modelling language, in this case study into a PCM representation.

When the architecture model is available, it can be viewed, analysed, and changed with its original tools. For propagating the changes to the code, reverse steps (**steps 4 to 6**) are executed, while following the traces collected during the translation from the code to the model.

UML Models Extracted from the CoCoME Source Code

In the second case study, a UML composite structure diagram was generated from the same translation model, effectively reusing the transformations between the program code and the intermediate language. Parts of the transformation between the intermediate language and the UML were reused from another case study. The UML model extracted with Codeling is shown in Fig. 12.7. The arrows without a keyword are *ComponentRealization* relations in UML.

The extraction of the UML model is based on the same translation model as the extraction of the PCM. Therefore, the translation between the CoCoME source code and the implementation model and the transformation between the implementation model and the intermediate architecture language of Codeling can be reused from the PCM extraction case study presented above. As these translations do not include event-based communications and data management, these are also not included

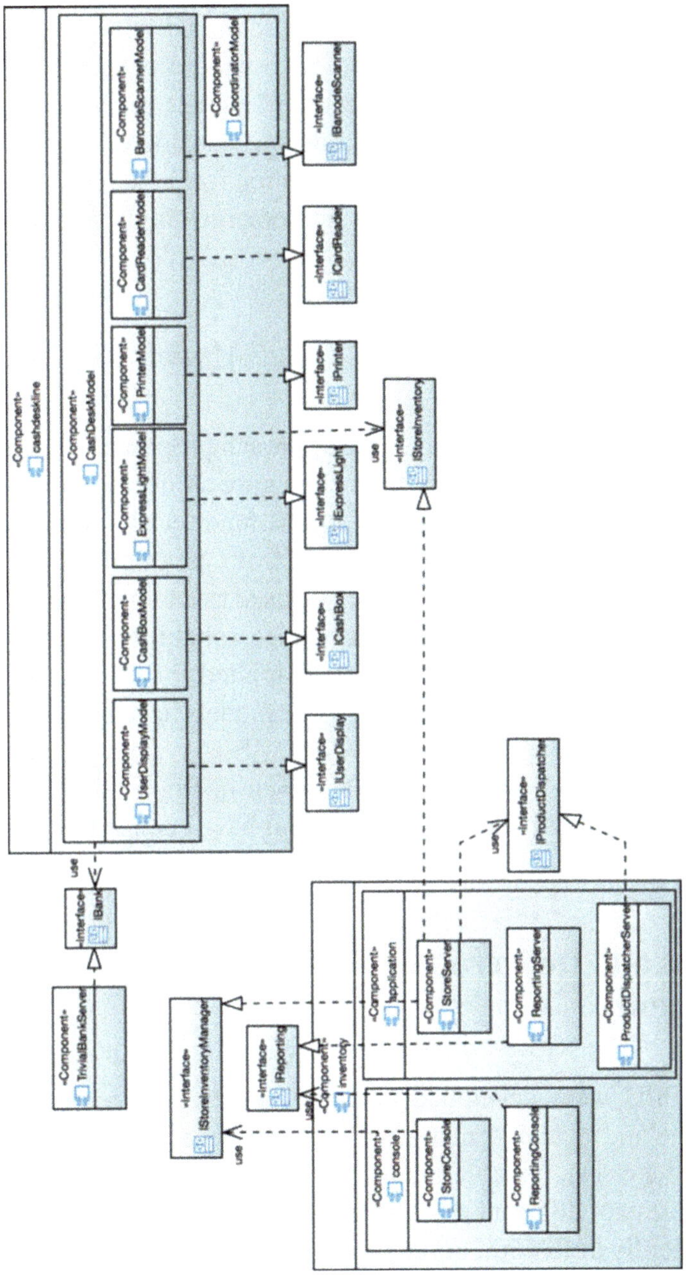

Fig. 12.7 The CoCoME architecture in an UML composite structure diagram, as extracted with Codeling

in the UML diagram. Translations between the intermediate language and UML already exist from another case study, which translates between JEE program code and a UML representation [Kon18, Section 10.1]. The UML is flexible to use, and the use of the UML can vary in different contexts. The existing translations between the intermediate language and the UML are project-specific in their handling of composite components. Therefore, we derived a new, more general translation between the intermediate architecture language and the UML.

The goal of the case studies presented above was to extract PCM and UML models, respectively. The propagation of model changes to the CoCoME source code was not intended, because the source code was considered legacy code, which is not maintained anymore. Therefore, the translation from the model representation to CoCoME source code structures was not implemented in these case studies.

12.1.9 Extracting Behaviour and Usage Models of CoCoME

Similar to the approach by Konersmann, the approach proposed by Langhammer et al. in [Lan+16] and [Lan17] extracts static architecture models of CoCoME from the source code. The automated approach by Langhammer et al. additionally extracts behaviour and usage models in the form of PCM from very limited information like source code and test cases. The PCM can then be used as an input to existing analysis techniques like the aforementioned for performance, reliability, and maintainability.

The plain-Java variant of CoCoME has been applied for validating the accuracy of the usage model extraction in [Lan+16]. Usage models have been extracted based on existing unit tests for the use cases of CoCoME. An example of an extracted usage model for the *ProcessSale* use case is given in Fig. 12.8. Further PCM for specifying the system's architecture and behaviour have been extracted in [Lan17].

12.2 Benefits and Deliverables of xPPU for the Outside Community

The PPU and xPPU were developed to meet the research requirements on the evolution in plant and machine manufacturing of the SPP1593 community. The xPPU is open to the researcher community providing some promising opportunities such as comparability of different approaches and facilitating the tackling of aspects that are less frequently dealt with. Furthermore, an eased exchange of research ideas and a simplified coordination are given.

The xPPU is limited in size and complexity but nevertheless provides a trade-off between problem complexity and evaluation effort. To support different research directions, the xPPU evolution scenarios were extended regarding more sophisticated requirement modelling, as well as fault handling functionality. Evolution in

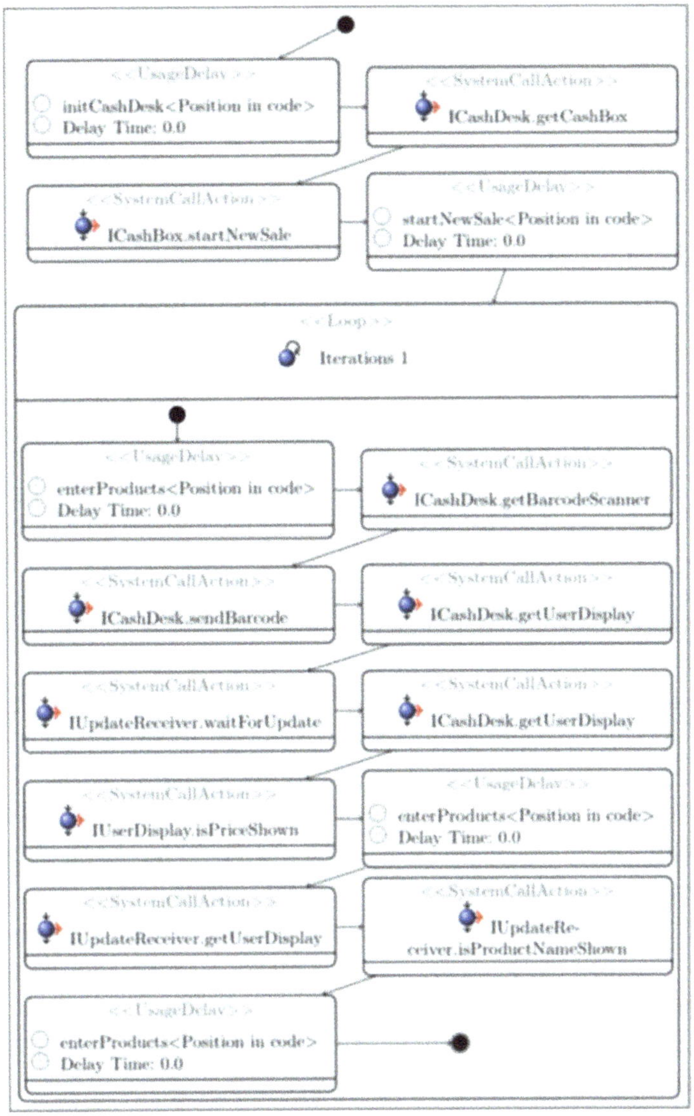

Fig. 12.8 Usage Model of the *ProcessSale* use case extracted from unit tests [Lan+16]

xPPU not solely includes sequential development but also parallel and asynchronous evolution; see Fig. 12.9. Due to the demand for higher throughput of workpieces (WPs), Scenario 12a with a faster sorting of WPs is developed. A drive with increased dynamics is installed to realise faster WP movement, which entails that faster pushers are required for extruding WPs. In parallel, a customer demands an adjusted variant of xPPU's Scenario 12, which is able to handle larger and heavier WPs. Furthermore, depending on the country, a machine or plant should be located in, different supply and control voltage must be supported by field devices. Whereas the existing xPPU is engineered to be located in Germany, a customer requests an xPPU which can be operated with different supply and control voltage (as used, e.g. in the USA). Accordingly, all field bus components, which are not capable to handle the desired control voltage, have to be replaced. This results in another

Triggering requirement	Scenario	Transportation belt			Remarks
		M	AH	S	
Higher throughput of workpieces	12a	×	0	×	Increased dynamics of pneumatics for pushing WPs into slide resulting in different time constraints for monitoring
Increase in workpiece size and weight	12b	×	0	×	Larger slide and increased pneumatic force and dynamics
Different control voltage	12c	×	×	0	Different I/O modules required
Different platform supplier, e.g. Siemens, Rockwell, Beckhoff or Microcontroller	12d	0	×	(×)	Difference in automation components, i.e. drives, fieldbus and I/O modules or HMI may be required
Other than IEC 61131-3 environment requested by customer	12e	0	×	×	Different PLC and software required, e.g. IEC 61499 or C++
Additional functionality selfhealing machine and diagnosis	12f	×	0	×	Additional sensors and software required, automatic mode enlarged
Remote service required	12g	0	×	×	Data logging and analysis, remote access necessary

Fig. 12.9 Parallel evolution influencing mechanics (M), automation hardware (AH), and software (S) [Vog+14a]

variant of the xPPU referred to as Scenario 12c. In addition, a typical variation point driven by automation hardware is the requirement of a specific vendor platform, e.g. Siemens or Rockwell. This aspect is reflected in Scenario 12d, which is a version controlled by a vendor other than CODESYS platform. Besides the platform, another typical variation driven by automation technology is the implementation environment, i.e. whether the PLC software is, e.g. implemented according to IEC 61131-3 or IEC 61499. In Scenario 12e of the xPPU, an implementation framework other than the currently applied IEC 61131-3 environment is used. In parallel to these variants, Scenario 12f is more reliable due to the realisation of self-healing functionality. To extend the business cases of plant and machine suppliers, a variant supporting remote services is provided with Scenario 12g. To realise remote service functionality, data logging and analysis techniques are required as well as the possibility to remotely access operational data.

The different evolution scenarios of the xPPU targeting a variety of sequential changes in system architecture and behaviour are publicly available. These scenarios are documented with structural and behavioural models, PLC implementations in classical IEC 61131-3 as well as implementations based on state charts in plcUML (i.e. an alternative way to implement PLC software), Matlab/Simulink simulation projects, mechanical CAD files, and describing products, processes, and resources of the xPPU is available in Automation Markup Language (AML). Furthermore, a technical report of the scenarios is available to allow the understanding of the different evolutions capturing models as well as detailed description of changes in each scenario [Vog+14b].

12.2.1 Structural and Behavioural Design Models of the xPPU

The language profile SysML was developed to support the physical systems' design [Esp+09]. SysML covers the modelling of functional requirements and corresponding software applications as well as the modelling of non-functional requirements [Fra+11]. SysML models consisting of class, state machine, and block definition diagrams of the xPPU's evolution scenarios are provided.

The SysML models of the xPPU are based on the ANSI/ISA S-88 standard of batch process control [Com+95], published by the International Society of Automation, and the OMAC State Machine, part of the Packaging Modelling Language (Pack ML) standard [Are+06]. The ISA88 standard processes a recipe of hierarchical management of batch control and frameworks to segment batch manufacturing processes. The separation of product and process by the hierarchical structure enables flexibility and reuse of equipment, as well as easier integration of new equipment or alteration of the production flow. ISA88 separates batch management into Procedural Control Model and Physical Model; see Fig. 12.10.

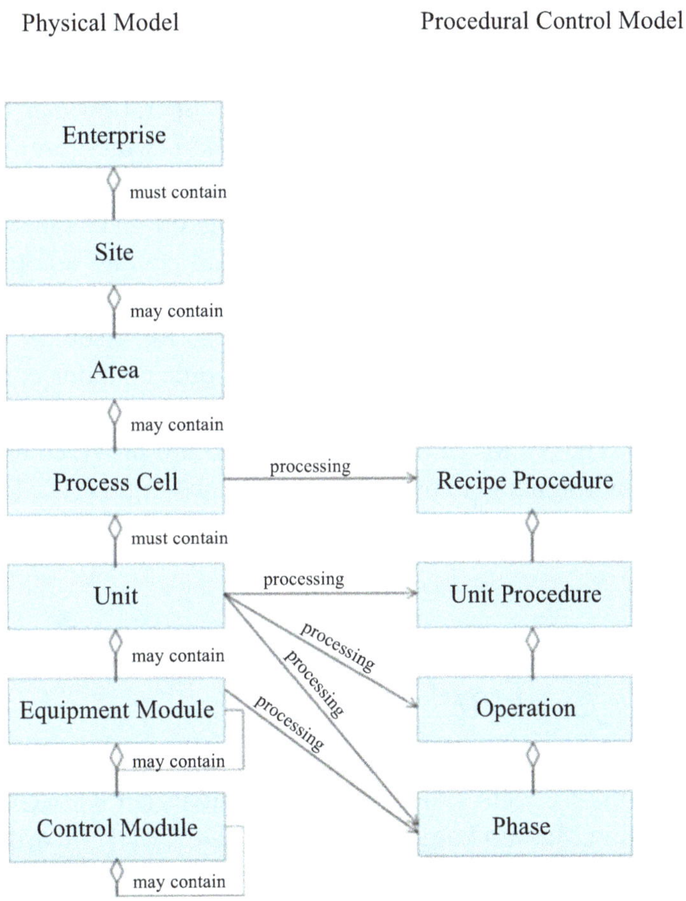

Fig. 12.10 Overview on the ISA88 structure [Com+95]

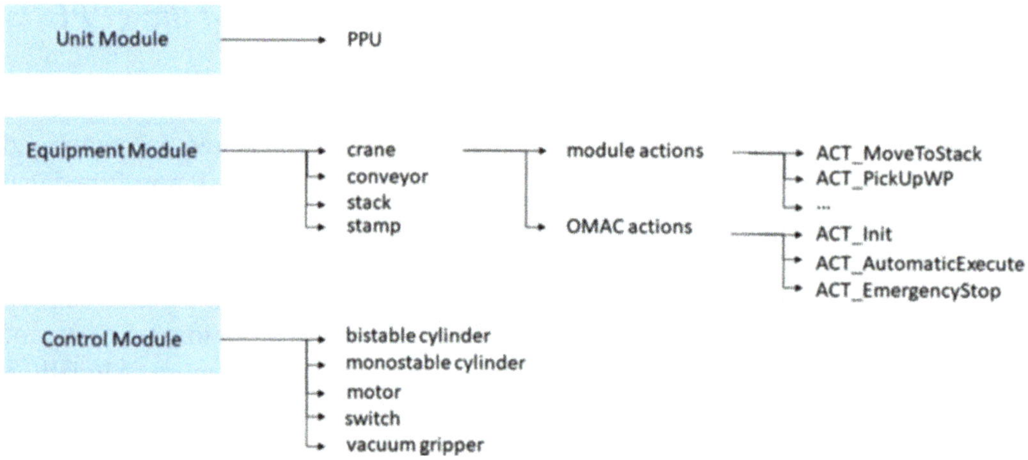

Fig. 12.11 Overview on the module structure of the PPU

The Procedural Control Model describes the production flow of the current batch as it is linked to the physical equipment. This model consists of recipe procedure, unit procedure, operations, and phases. The production flow of a single unit is controlled by the unit procedure. Each unit has an exclusive operating unit procedure, which is bound to this single unit. However, a single unit is allowed to contain more than one operation, but only one operation can be active at a time. An operation consists of a set of phases (tasks), which are allowed to run simultaneously. The xPPU as a unit is part of a process cell. A unit is an independent set of equipment, running a recipe and operating on a batch simultaneously. Units must contain equipment modules, which could contain equipment modules themselves. As a functional group of equipment, it fulfils a finite number of tasks, only one activity at a time. Equipment modules are, for instance, the crane, the conveyor, the stack, or the stamp. An equipment module contains control modules, and these are the most basic elements of an equipment, such as motors, cylinders, or valves (Fig. 12.11). The SysML models of the xPPU are provided as editable files in the modelling environment "Papyrus" [Lan+09]; see Fig. 12.12. The models are available for the community.[4]

12.2.2 Products, Processes, and Resources as Industry 4.0 Enabler for xPPU

The three viewpoints, products, processes, and resources (PPR), were initially supported by Automation Markup Language (AML) [SD09, SL15]. AML is extensible in a way that it can be enriched with other data formats to increase acceptance

[4] https://github.com/x-PPU/Models.

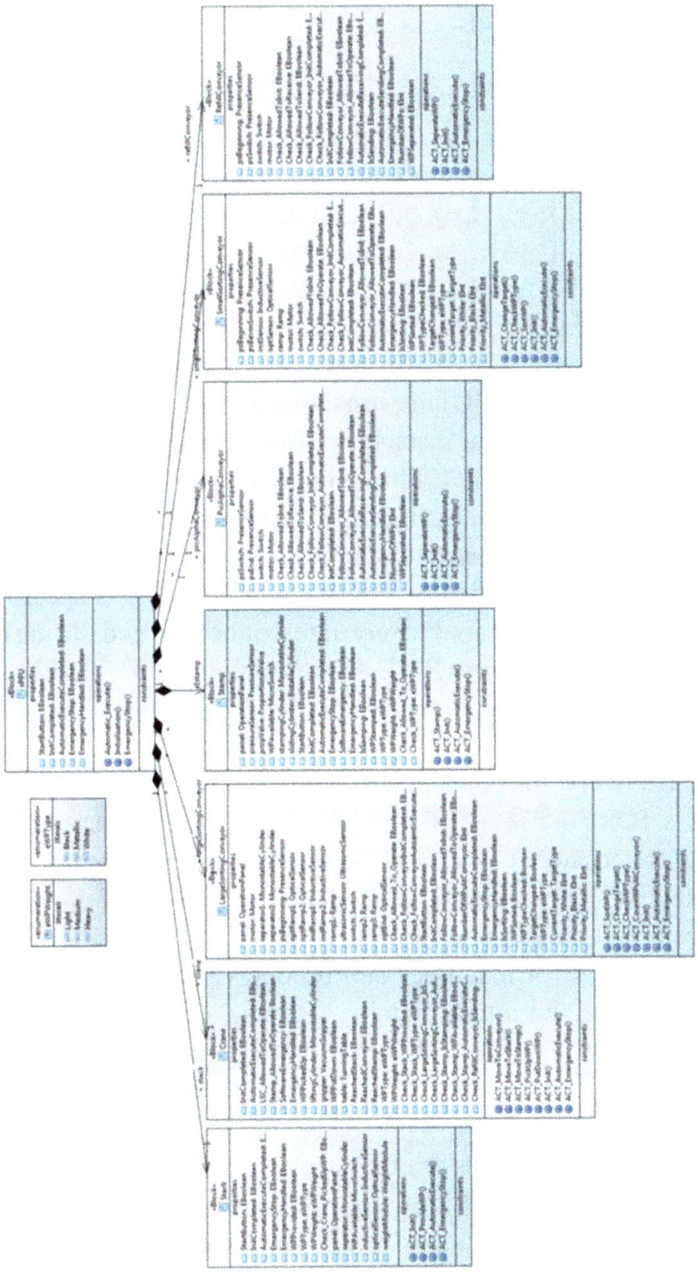

Fig. 12.12 Overview of the xPPU's class diagram of Scenario 15

[Dra+08]. The topology of the production system and the included relations are represented by the use of CAEX, while CAD information is represented in COLLADA and control related logic data is expressed in PLCopenXML [SL15]. AML and the corresponding engineering process intertwine the different domains more closely, increase flexibility, and reduce engineering costs [Lüd+10, SL15]. Schmidt et al. [Sch+14] also ascertained that an integrated approach like AML is more promising, concerning a reduction in engineering costs, than further optimisations of individual tools.

Schmidt et al. [Sch+14] also identified the main requirements towards a cross-disciplinary exchange format in the same expert survey. Firstly, industry needs a consistent, lossless exchange of data among heterogeneous engineering tools, which is enabled by AML itself. Secondly, version management is necessary. This is partially realised within AML but should be further supported by additional tools [MB15, Ber+16]. And thirdly, the involved disciplines need means to ensure consistency. This is not part of AML itself, but external reasoning tools are being developed [Bif+14, Sab+16]. The AML architecture is structured into four parts [SL15]. These are the role class (RC) library, the system unit class (SUC) library, the interface class (IC) library, and the instance hierarchy (IH). The RC library defines the general object semantics, the SUC library includes reusable components, and the IC library defines relevant interfaces. Interfaces can thereby be either internal, i.e. among different instances, or external, in which they reference external data such as COLLADA files. Within the IH, finally, the actual project data is specified.

These three viewpoints PPR are closely interconnected and strongly influence each other. At the example of the xPPU, the resource stamp executes the process stamping on a product (i.e. workpiece). Within AML, engineers can express these three viewpoints as separate hierarchies derived from the roles, product, process, and resource, respectively. To connect these three hierarchies, engineers can use the interface class PPRConnector [SD09]. If necessary, more specific subclasses can be specified. Trentesaux et al. [Tre+13] propose to describe products via jobs, i.e. processes, executed by machines, i.e. resources. This way of thinking conforms to the PPR concept and results in appropriate role classes and four SUC libraries in AML. The role classes for machines and products provide templates including typical attributes such as the article number or weight for products. The process role class library already provides different sorts of generic machine operations. These range from logistics, exemplarily (un)loading, to manufacturing, exemplarily stamping; see Fig. 12.13.

The three relevant SUC libraries are the product model, the process model, and the resource model (Fig. 12.14). Within the product model, engineers specify the products throughout all relevant stages in the production process. In case of the xPPU, this includes, e.g. a "black plastic workpiece" but also the resulting "product 3".

The process model defines jobs that can be executed by machines to realise products. Jobs are defined as "sub-assemblies" by [Tre+13] and include production steps. Jobs are included in the SUC library, because they may apply to different products and can then simply be instantiated multiple times. Additionally, the

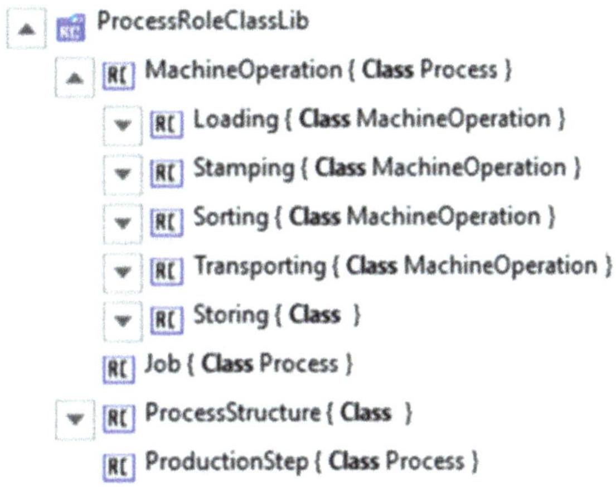

Fig. 12.13 An excerpt of process role class library

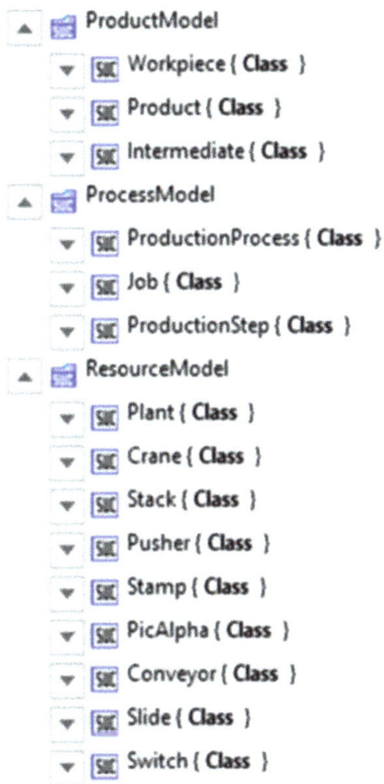

Fig. 12.14 PPR of SUC library

process model includes an SUC production process that is used as a superordinate element in the instance hierarchy to group the jobs. The resource model finally includes all available sorts of machines, namely, the crane, the stack, the pusher, the stamp, the PicAlpha module, and the conveyor. Additionally, the machine model includes the class plant for grouping the machines within the instance hierarchy.

To combine the three different points of view of the PPR concept, three interfaces are derived from PPRConnector within the InterfaceClassLib. Connector Device-Operation associates machines with production steps; Connector WPOperation represents the connection between processes and their workpieces, i.e. their inputs;

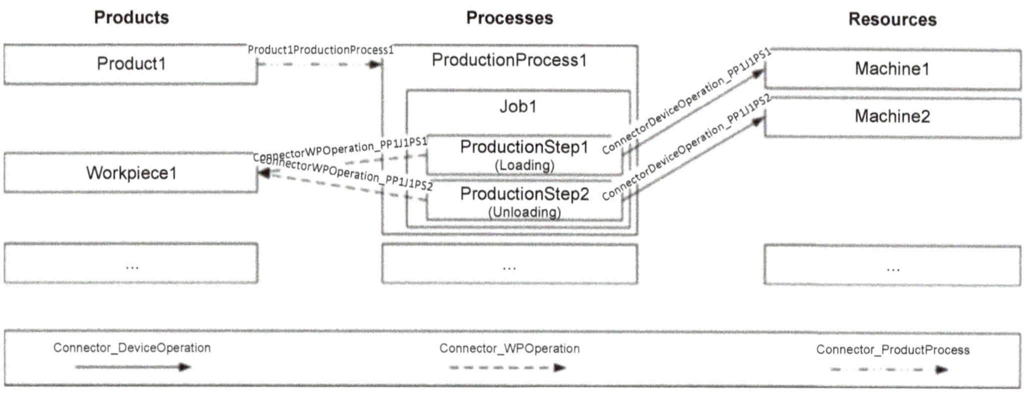

Fig. 12.15 Schema for PPR connections

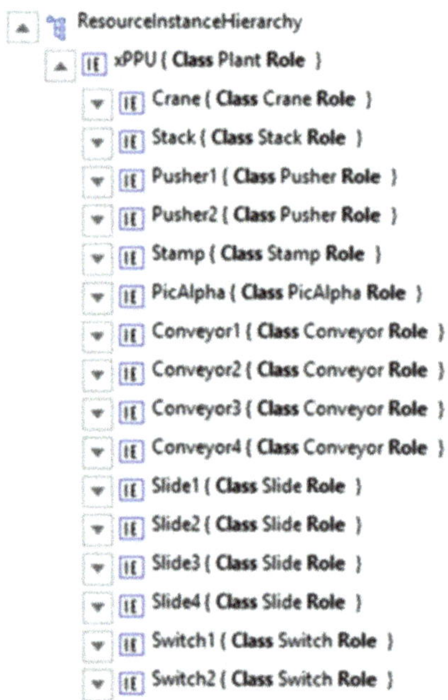

Fig. 12.16 Representation of xPPU's topology on instance level

and Connector ProductProcess is used to connect products to their respective production processes (Fig. 12.15).

The three different SUC libraries have corresponding instance hierarchies, in which SUC classes are instantiated to represent reality. The resource SUCs are used within the instance hierarchy to represent the actual plant in the form of a topology. This topology, which includes the crane, the stack, the pushers, the stamp, the PicAlpha module, and the conveyors, is depicted in Fig. 12.16. A bird view of the layout of the xPPU with its resources is presented in Fig. 12.17. The bird view also depicts the paths of the various products.

The process instance hierarchy includes the production processes for the different products. Each production process consists of at least one job, which, in turn,

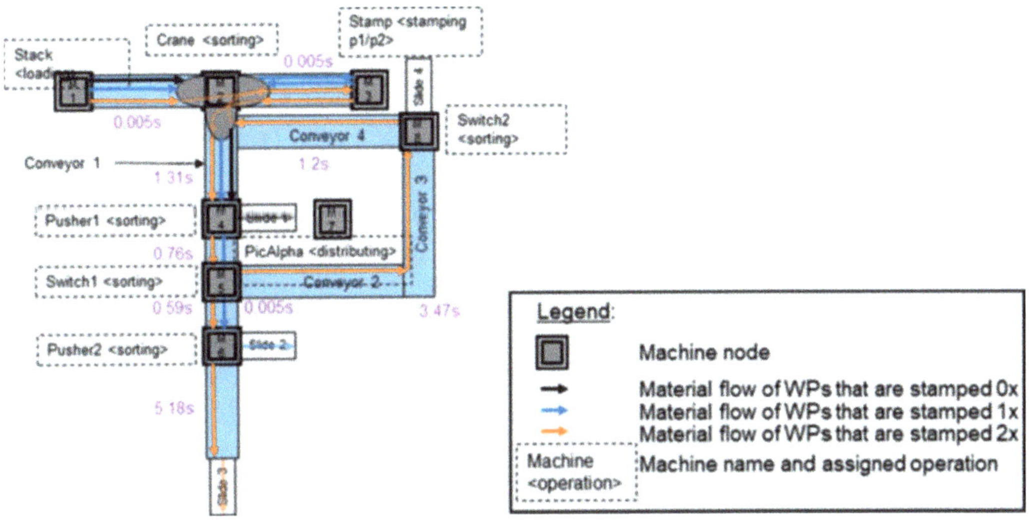

Fig. 12.17 Bird view of the xPPU

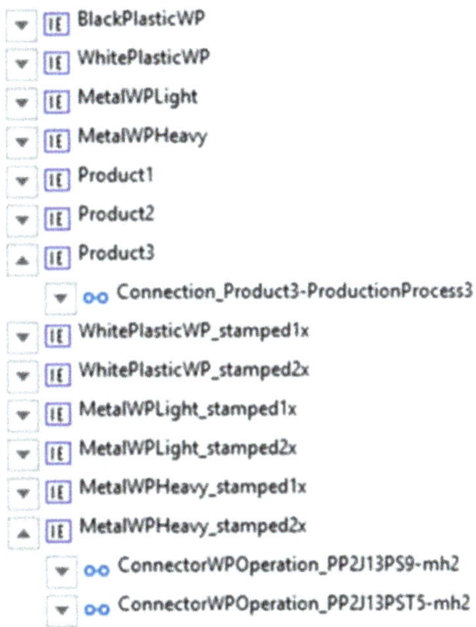

Fig. 12.18 An excerpt of internal links of PPR of the xPPU

consists of at least one production step. Since attributes of the jobs, such as the processing time, may differ depending on the product, the jobs are associated with production processes and thus with products. The IH also include the links among the PPRConnectors, which tie the different views together. Figure 12.18 gives an overview of the links realised to represent the manufacturing of products 1, 2, and 3. These internal links also include all TransportConnections, which are used in two ways. First, they are used to link resources, which can transfer products. That is, all possible ways a product can take through a plant are represented. Second, every sorting or transporting production step is connected to the resource that provides

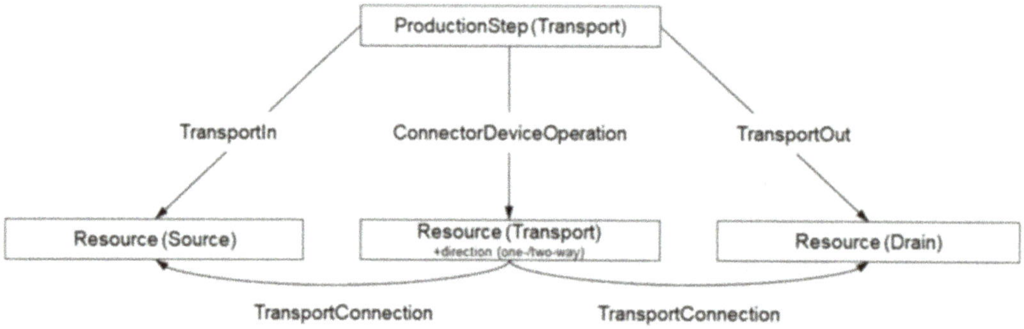

Fig. 12.19 Connections among resources and between processes and resources

the product (source) and to the resource the product is transferred to (drain); see Fig. 12.19.

Changes in any of the three views may lead to changes in the other views, too. For example, if Conveyor2 is not working anymore, it can be substituted by the PicAlpha module. This is because the PicAlpha module can not only change the order of products, but it can also fulfil a transport task from Switch1 to Conveyor3. Thus, a redundancy concerning this specific task is created, and the alternative production process may be chosen. Changes to a product may also propagate to the other domains. Mainly, it will influence the associated production process, which possibly influences the linked machines. Through the interconnectedness of the different views, the propagation of changes can be easily traced.

12.2.3 Simulation Models for Testing

For each evolutionary stage, a simulation model was created in Matlab/Simulink including an own 3D visualisation, which represents the behaviour of the real demonstration system. The Matlab/Simulink models are available to the community via an OPC interface (object linking and embedding for process control) with known time constraints. An OPC interface is also available for the demonstration system itself, in order to keep the cost of the conversion during the evaluation on the real laboratory installation low. Alternatively, it is possible to create the control code directly in IEC 61131-3 or the state chart diagram (CODESYS) and to evaluate this simulation or the real system coupled to the OPC. Due to the properties of the PPU, the OPC interface is sufficiently for most project approaches. In addition, a PLC-based controller is available in the TUM laboratory for direct connection to automation technology.

12.2.4 Generating PLC Code Using UML Models

In the work of [Wit13], the authors provided a methodology to generate PLC software based on UML diagrams. Therefore, the PLC software of the xPPU's evolution scenarios from Sc0 to Sc13 was generated based on UML diagrams. The UML diagrams consist of UML class diagram for the implementation of a PLC-project structure as well as state chart diagrams and activity diagrams for the implementation of the behaviour of the elements of the UML-PLC (e.g. classes, methods). This approach was implemented using the development environment CODESYS. Moreover, the PLC code of the xPPU scenarios was developed according to the international standard IEC 61131-3 [JT10], which is widely used for programming PLCs in the domain of aPS, comprising five programming languages: two are textual (the assembler-like Instruction List (IL) and the Pascal-like Structured Text (ST)) and three are graphical (Ladder Diagram (LD) in the style of circuit diagrams, Function Block Diagram (FBD), and Sequential Function Chart (SFC)). The PLC code of the evolution scenarios of the xPPU is available for the community.[5]

12.2.5 Detecting Anomaly Behaviour by Analysing Signal Data of the xPPU

The available data set includes the values of the different variables in xPPU in each time stamp, while it is working based on different scenarios (time stamp, variable, value). The recorded variables are most of the time logical variables, which take only zero or one values. However, there are a few variables like analogue sensors, which have analogue values (e.g. analogue pressure). Since the most variables in the data set are logical variables, it can be considered that the data set includes the activation and deactivation information of the variables in each time stamp while xPPU is running. This data set can be used for different purposes. One example of the usage of this data is to recognise the cycle of activation (deactivation) of different variables. Then it would be possible to check that during the activation (deactivation) period of one variable, which other variables are activated (deactivated). It can be helpful to recognise the dependencies between variables and detect what is the consequent effect of activation (deactivation) of some variables on the other variables. In addition, the hierarchical dependencies among variables can be useful to get some information concerning the hierarchical structural of the plant using the data-driven methods. For example, it can be found which part of a plant (including special variables) is a subset of a larger part of the plant (with more variables and longer activation period). By using both the dependencies between variables and the

[5] https://github.com/x-PPU/PLC_TwinCAT_Projects.

Fig. 12.20 Example of sequence of activation and deactivation of different variables

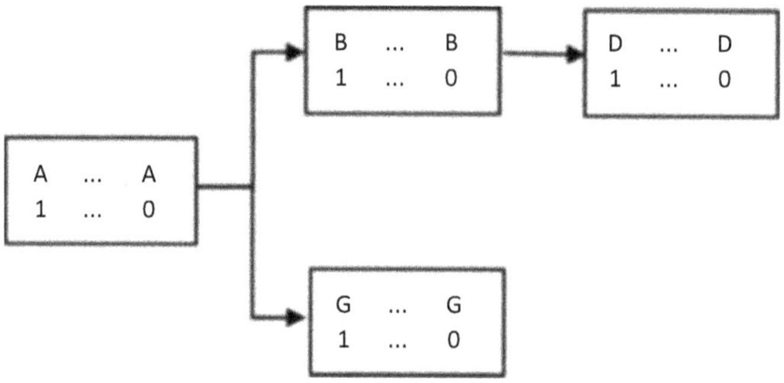

Fig. 12.21 Hierarchical structure using the activation period of different variables

hierarchical structure of the plant, it will be possible to detect the source of some anomaly behaviours of the plant using the data-driven methods. In this case, we can analyse that after the activation (deactivation) of some variables at the top of the hierarchy, we expect to see the activation (deactivation) of which variables at the bottom of the hierarchy. Then, this information can be used to predict the behaviour of the plant, and if the behaviour of the plant is not based on our expectation, we can see which variable (or variables) does not have a proper value, which leads to abnormal behaviour.

The first approach, which is used to achieve this goal, is to derive a tree structure from the data based on the activation (deactivation) period of the variables. In this case, the variables are sorted from the longest activation (deactivation) period to the shortest period. Then, we try to detect which variables with shorter period can be seen during the period of the variables with longer activation (deactivation) period. This hierarchy can lead to the shortest activation duration of one variable (activated and deactivated immediately) at the lowest level of hierarchy. The Deep First Search (DFS) algorithm is used to construct the tree structure based on the activation (deactivation) period of variables. In this tree, the children of each node can be considered as the set of variables, which are dependent to the variables in this node, and they are activated (deactivated) after the variable in the parent node. Here, there is an example to illustrate the method (Fig. 12.20). Based on the activation period of the variables and DFS algorithm, the tree structure in Fig. 12.21 can be constructed.

The first result of this analysis on xPPU data is provided and discussed with the expert. Based on expert knowledge, most of the hierarchical relationships between variables in the tree structure are meaningful. The next step of this analysis will be to detect the anomaly behaviour of the plant based on the expected values and dependencies between variables. It is worth mentioning that the proposed approach can also be useful in analysing PLC software. In this case, the structure of the code, e.g. function blocks, can be considered as an input into the DFS algorithm. Therefore, DFS tree can be constructed based on the function calls in each function block. Parent nodes include the functions in high level of hierarchy which call some other functions, and the called functions can be considered as the children nodes. The benefit of this analysis is that it is possible to follow the code based on the structure of the constructed DFS tree. In this case, we expect that a function call, which is a child node, has to be done completely to make sure that the higher-level function in the parent node can also be done consequently. This approach can be useful to detect which function blocks in children nodes do not perform properly which leads to the propagation of the abnormality to a higher level of hierarchy of function blocks.

12.2.6 Maintaining Security of the xPPU

The middleware application that allows to remotely access and interact with the xPPU demonstrator increases the opportunities for malicious users to compromise the information and correct behaviour of the xPPU and its interacting parties (e.g. CoCoME). Hence, it is necessary to improve the security of the middleware application, as well as its environment in order to reduce the vulnerabilities that might be exploited for malicious purposes. Within the context of the xPPU demonstrator and CoCoME, an exemplary goal of this kind of malicious purposes may be to provide erroneous information to both the xPPU and CoCoME which may result in unnecessary production being carried out (e.g. a wrong number of product orders being placed) that may increase costs, incorrect warehouse information provided to the supply chain that may affect sales and generate disgruntled and unsatisfied customers, and manipulation of the cyber-physical system that may compromise the safety of personnel, among others.

The main focus of security from the point of view of an information system developer or service provider is to protect against targeted attacks towards the system. However, from the point of view of system integrators and asset owners, the main focus is to correctly implement the security mechanisms provided by the product vendors and integrate any changes that may be required based on system- and domain-specific characteristics and requirements. Within the context of the ongoing work of the xPPU demonstrator, these two points of view are considered on the middleware application and the automation environment, respectively.

Many methodologies to elicit system requirements exist [Poh10, NE00]. The two methodologies most widely used to elicit security requirements are to carry out risk assessments and derive them from well-defined documentation such as guidelines, regulations, laws, or standards.

Risk assessments are commonly performed at later stages of the development life cycle (e.g. after design) or after a system has already been deployed, as previous knowledge of the target system and its assets is required. It also requires participation from multiple stakeholders and knowledge regarding the threat landscape that such assets may be susceptible to and their likelihood and impact. The goal of a risk assessment is to identify appropriate countermeasures that allow to decrease both security risks and unnecessary security costs.

On the other hand, security elicitation from well-defined documentation is more straightforward. In this type of elicitation, the requirements are abstracted by analysing such documentation and verifying its applicability to the target system based on its characteristics, target environment, or specific security assets. The goal of this type of elicitation is to prove compliance with well-known regulations. This compliance may be important for accountability and/or product or system certification.

As both the middleware application and the xPPU exist within the context of a demonstrator and are located at a facility within a wider educational infrastructure, it is assumed that the likelihood for any type of risk is unknown, as this may depend on the infrastructure itself. Therefore, in order to identify their security requirements, these are abstracted from well-defined documentation rather than from a risk assessment.

The documentation considered to elicit these security requirements is the ISA/IEC 62443 standards of Security for Industrial Automation and Control Systems. This set of standards was selected as they are the de facto standards in the industrial field. They are divided into multiple parts, two of which address the two points of view previously mentioned.

The IEC 62443-3 parts target system integrators; hence, they are relevant to abstract security requirements that can be applied system-wide (i.e. environment). On the other hand, IEC 62443-4 parts target component developers or manufacturer; hence, they are relevant to abstract component-specific requirements such as the middleware application. These requirements are found in parts IEC 62443-3-3 and 62443-4-2, respectively.

IEC 62443-3-3 provides a set of security requirements that must be fulfilled for specific systems based on their desired security level. On the other hand, IEC 62443-4-2 provides a set of security requirements that must be fulfilled by components of the system.

From these standards, a set of ten security requirements have been abstracted. These requirements can be summarised in three classifications: security requirements to ensure secure communication among the interacting parties (i.e. PLC—middleware—client), security requirements that ensure user authentication, managed access control and accountability, and security requirements to ensure secure and reliable session management.

The validation of these security requirements has been carried out implementing the Secure Tropos methodology [MGM05]. This methodology allows to analyse the interaction among actors, tasks, goals, resources, and their dependencies in order to better understand the system and possibly identify missing security requirements or constraints that were not considered previously during requirement elicitation; see Fig. 12.22.

Fig. 12.22 Secure Tropos diagram [Tsc18]

The aforementioned security requirements involve modifications to the middleware application. These modifications ensure the protection of the application against targeted attacks.

However, as it is well known from security incidents and other reports provided by multiple research and analysis authorities [CS17, Cor17], the most common approach to compromise a system is to exploit vulnerabilities. These vulnerabilities may or may not be found on the targeted components. This occurs as security attacks commonly exploit these vulnerabilities in unsuspecting or vulnerable parties (e.g. system components or personnel) that provide means to reach the attack target.

In order to decrease system vulnerabilities, the requirements presented in IEC 62443-3-3 are relevant. From these requirements, a set of appropriate open-source security solutions have been identified. These security solutions are being integrated into the xPPU demonstrator in order to provide protection to key system components and locations. One of these solutions is a vulnerability scanner (i.e. OpenVAS) that allows, among other things, to scan system components in order to identify possible vulnerabilities in them.

The usage of pre-existing security solutions provides seamless integration with automation systems. Depending on the case, it may be possible to install them and manage them without affecting the automation system itself during runtime. This is especially important, as one of the many fears of security in industrial systems is that they may negatively influence the performance or behaviour of the automation system.

As the technological and threat landscape keeps changing, so must these security considerations. Security, just as information systems, must evolve. The lifetime of the hardware components of an automation system may last years, and the lifetime of its software components may last months or years; however, the lifetime of security is extremely unpredictable. Hence, it is necessary to continuously monitor any new requirements that may arise in order to maintain the same security level throughout the whole system's lifetime.

12.3 Benefits and Deliverables of Industry 4.0 Demonstrator for the Outside Community

Recent trends in industrial digitalisation, i.e. Industry 4.0, require the systems to be connected with each other. In particular, boundaries between the information systems and the production systems are blurred in this era. The Industry 4.0 demonstrator (Chap. 4) implements the common use cases of the information system, which is represented by CoCoME, and the automated production system, which is represented by xPPU. With the integrated case study, it can be demonstrated that production system information is more visible and controllable from the information system side and end user needs are more visible from the production side. Therefore, Industry 4.0 demonstrator enables researches on the integrated environments such as ordering a customisable product, creating a production plan for a customisable product on multiple abstraction layers, and observing the progress of batch size on productions. The CoCoME was extended to allow integration with an aPS plant. An example of a plant is the interface offered by xPPU. Further, CoCoME enables the domain experts to use a mock-up of a plant without actually connecting a physical plant. This allows simulating the integration using an arbitrary plant [Bic+18]. Furthermore, the xPPU was extended with the interface to be connected to the remote users (including external systems). This interface allows the users to connect to the xPPU over the web service either to run it or to gather some data about the plant from the remote site without any effort to travel to the plant (see Fig. 12.23). Also, uses can take the advantage of the model-based dynamic reconfiguration

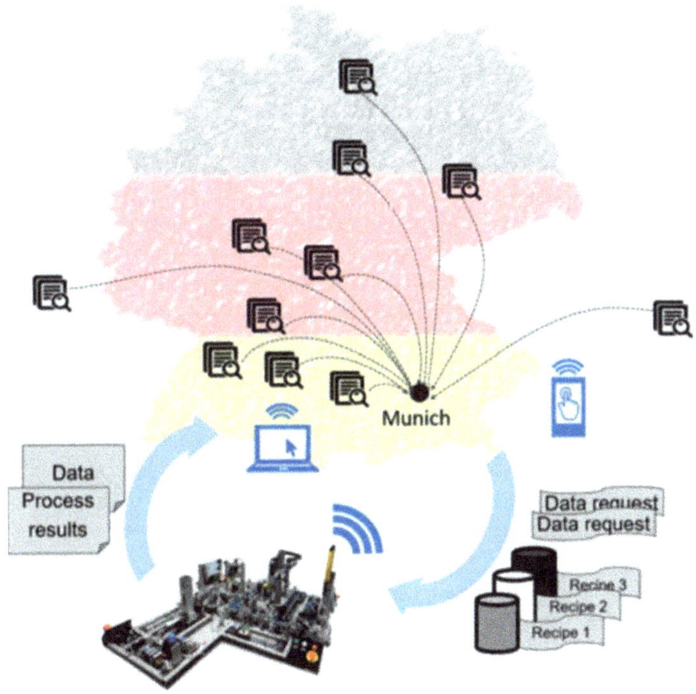

Fig. 12.23 Remote connection of the xPPU Industry 4.0 interface

implementation from this case study. In addition, security issues which might happen on these interfaces are also envisioned and accessible (see Sect. 12.2.6).

The Industry 4.0 demonstrator shows the prototypical implementation of cyber-physical production systems (CPPS) by containing the following characteristics [VBF12]:

Architecture models: by using ISA88 architecture model for the plant that provides hierarchical structure and process-based model for batches and coupling modules and processes.

Data analysis: by allowing synchronising values over plants or systems as well as gathering and transferring operation-related values (online and offline).

Flexible production unit: combining the generated services from the systems in different ways support various recipes which allows flexible production.

Digital networks and interfaces for communication: by enabling both OPC-UA connection to the PLC side and RESTful web service to the user side, the middleware enables to connect the remote user to the plant (Fig. 12.24). The middleware places between the xPPU side and the remote user side. Using this connection, users can either execute the desiring operations (e.g. transporting or sorting materials) or get information about xPPU (e.g. execution history or archived variable values). Android mobile application[6] as well as a web page is also available to ease the user connection (see Fig. 12.25).

[6]https://github.com/x-PPU/I4.0_Interface.

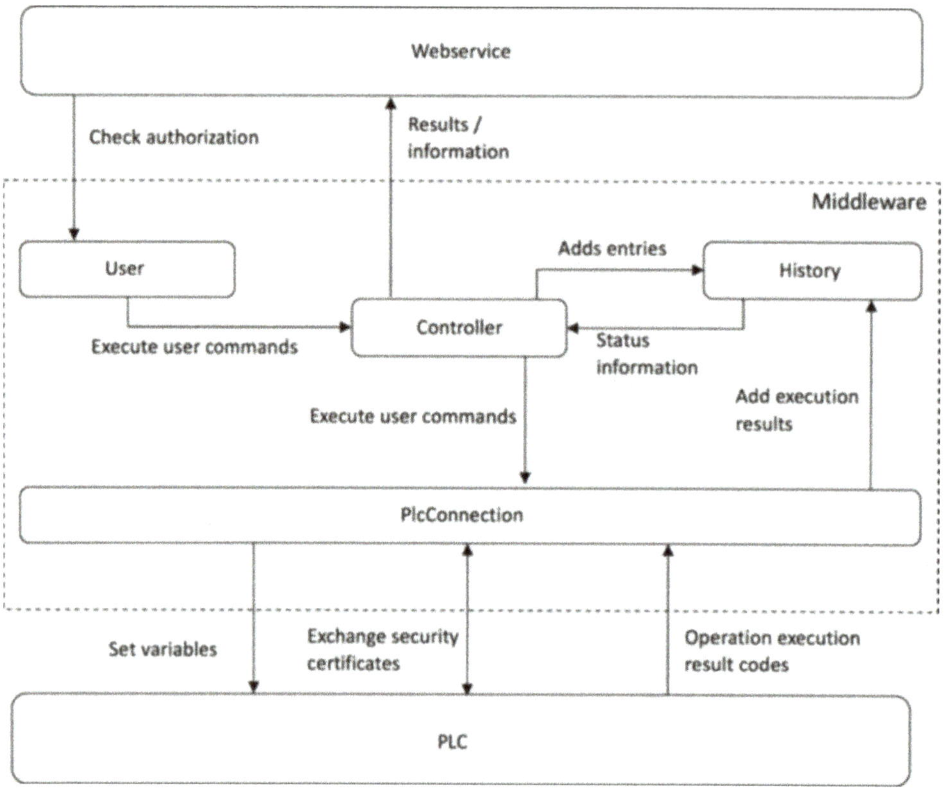

Fig. 12.24 Middleware architecture of the xPPU Industry 4.0 interface

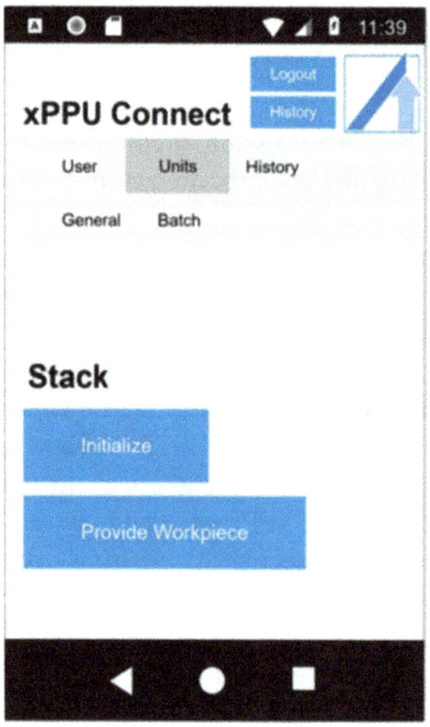

Fig. 12.25 Mobile application of the xPPU Industry 4.0 interface

Worldwide distribution of data, high availability, and access protection: on both sides of the systems' connection, security is implemented by setting standard authentications.

Chapter 4 describes the architecture of the Industry 4.0 case study (i.e. the integration of CoCoME and xPPU). This architecture can be used for applying approaches to domain-spanning change impact analysis. An example of a change can be the modification of the interface provided by the xPPU. This change can propagate to CoCoME, which uses this interface. Further, the case study allows analysing other quality attributes such as security or performance by the approaches in Industry 4.0 context [Hei+18a].

Chapter 13
Lessons Learned

Ralf Reussner, Michael Goedicke, Wilhelm Hasselbring, Birgit Vogel-Heuser, Jan Keim, and Lukas Märtin

The lessons learned while investigating new methods and techniques for knowledge-carrying software in SPP 1593 are summarised below. Some lessons indicate promising areas for future work, which will be discussed in Chap. 14.

Extracting tacit usage knowledge during runtime raises various challenges; see Chap. 5. Potentially *wrong* usage behaviour might transition into a pattern that is of interest and relevant for a new feature or functionality of an application. This learning phase needs to be a core element in the detection of usage behaviour, making it an important reference that points to tacit knowledge. Likewise, it is important to distinguish tacit knowledge from any kind of *noise* effects. We learned that only a limited set of new features can be detected, while the quality

R. Reussner · J. Keim
Institute for Program Structures and Data Organization, Karlsruhe Institute of Technology (KIT), Karlsruhe, Germany
e-mail: reussner@kit.edu; jan.keim@kit.edu

M. Goedicke
paluno – The Ruhr Institute for Software Technology, Spezifikation von Softwaresystemen, Universität Duisburg-Essen, Essen, Germany
e-mail: michael.goedicke@s3.uni-due.de

W. Hasselbring (✉)
Software Engineering Group, Department of Computer Science, Kiel University, Kiel, Germany
e-mail: hasselbring@email.uni-kiel.de

B. Vogel-Heuser
Technische Universität München, Lehrstuhl für Automatisierung und Informationssysteme, Garching, Germany
e-mail: vogel-heuser@tum.de

L. Märtin
Institute for Programming and Reactive Systems, Technische Universität at Braunschweig, Braunschweig, Germany
e-mail: l.maertin@tu-braunschweig.de

R. Reussner et al. (eds.), *Managed Software Evolution*,
https://doi.org/10.1007/978-3-030-13499-0_13

of insights highly depends on the application in question. We acknowledge that requirements which lead to new features might be relevant for security. Identifying tacit knowledge in the form of security knowledge is a difficult task for which a good understanding of security and the domain of the software is necessary. Natural language processing can support the requirement engineer during this task.

Software product lines require continuous evolution over time, as discussed in Chap. 7. In particular, a software product line comprises numerous diverse yet inter-related and thus co-evolving artefacts (e.g. a feature model, implementation artefacts and test cases), where the evolution of one software product line artefact may also result in changes to other software product line artefacts, resulting in successive versions of an the entire software product line. While conceptually coping with respective software product line co-evolution scenarios, we observed that existing strategies for handling variant-rich software systems may also be adopted for handling version-rich software, as well as combinations of both dimensions of variability. In particular, efficient family-based analysis techniques based on explicitly available variant knowledge attached to software product line artefacts, so-called presence conditions, can be adapted to handle both variant- and version-rich software systems, as well as arbitrary combinations thereof. However, we encountered three main differences in handling versions as compared to variants:

- All variants of a product line coexist "in space," while different versions emerge successively "over time".
- Variant information is usually available already during requirement engineering, thus being traceable throughout all subsequent engineering phases and respective artefacts down to the code level, whereas new versions are often introduced ad hoc, thus being only barely documented. Hence, handling, analysing, and integrating new versions of an SPL usually requires additional up-front effort (e.g. model differencing, model merging) to fully understand the impact of SPL artefact evolution.
- For encoding variant information, it is usually sufficient to use Boolean variables and respective operators, whereas version information additionally requires some ordinal data types (e.g. Integers) to express (partial) ordering among versions. The latter may complicate automated tool support for automated reasoning.

Model-based round-trip engineering in embedded systems has to tackle the problem of on-site changes in mechanics, electrics, and software code. During the operation of such embedded systems, changes are induced by faulty devices, faulty code, or even spare parts no longer available. Such changes are often not documented or not known by the embedded system supplier. To enable a proper round-trip engineering, such changes need to be evaluated and included into the model. Merge mechanisms are required to merge different bug fixes that were conducted concurrently, even on different sites. Employing meta-models for coupling models of multiple disciplines is a promising idea. However, achieving consensus for constructing and evolving these meta-models remains a great challenge.

Strategies on how to efficiently address performance for variants and versions have been developed throughout the last years, and we have presented selected and complementary approaches based on the two SPP 1593 cases studies in Chap. 8:

- Regarding performance analysis of variants, we presented three strategies that tackled the challenge of combinatorial explosion of variants. We experienced that reducing the number of variants to be analysed and exploiting commonalities lead to promising results. Additional case studies were used to evaluate the approaches.
- Regarding the performance analysis of versions, we presented three strategies that focused on the management of versions, which evolve as different types of artefacts throughout the software's life cycle. We experienced that the amount and diversity of existing types of artefacts, modelling formalisms, evaluation techniques, and tool challenges impose a challenge for the widespread adoption of the strategies in practice. Moreover, the non-availability of suitable case studies and data sets involving all aspects to evaluate the research is a challenge.

We have observed a research gap with respect to the combination of strategies for variants and versions. First, the developed strategies seem to focus on either the analysis of versions or on the analysis of variants. Second, both types of strategies would benefit from an exchange of techniques used.

An approach to combine informal and formal techniques into an integrated approach is presented in Chap. 9. Informal requirements in natural language are used as the starting point for analysing security relatedness. At a clearly defined interface of security knowledge, the formal part takes over and applies existing and new techniques to the formal analysis and co-evolution. It was demonstrated how a socio-technical system, such as a large and long-lasting software product, can be monitored in full and be improved. Persons and their natural ways of communication were analysed. They met with adapted formal techniques at a novel interface: a layered ontology with a generic security part was extended evolutionarily towards a project-specific representation of knowledge. This way, feasible approaches to keep knowledge alive—and the software useful—are introduced.

As discussed in Chap. 10, embedded software in cyber-physical systems may evolve implicitly when its context—the surrounding physical world—changes. Even when the functional requirements remain stable, it may happen that the surrounding physical world changes, which may drive the software's evolution. This context consists not only of electronics and mechanics but also of human users and legal entities, all of which may drive the software's evolution. For cyber-physical systems, it is not sufficient to restrict knowledge to software:

- In general, it is useful to regard existing development artefacts (program code, hardware descriptions, design models and decisions, test cases, requirements, etc.) as valuable assets and to transfer these artefacts into knowledge-carrying software. This holds for any type of software in cyber-physical systems—embedded software and information systems—to allow for long-lasting maintenance of this knowledge and the software.

- Observing the dynamic behaviour of software at its interfaces and generating models from these observations is a successful approach to generate new knowledge about the software. Observation of dynamic behaviour may also achieve consistent co-evolution of running systems and its specification (models @ runtime). However, the applicability is restricted to recurring observable behaviour—ideally cyclic, repetitive behaviour. Causality cannot be addressed via observation, but regressions in quality characteristics may be identified among evolving software versions.
- Runtime observation via monitoring may be combined with other methods for knowledge-carrying software such as model-based and model-driven engineering. Model-based variant and version management offers techniques for mastering the evolution of knowledge at design and runtime of systems, both in sequential and parallel development processes. Multi-disciplinary variant and version management in multi-SPL settings remains a great challenge.
- Continuous integration is still a challenge for embedded systems: the application of continuous integration in the software part of embedded systems linked to mechanic and electric changes is possible but is mainly focused on testing. The design principles and the production of the mechanic and electrical parts of an embedded system differ from software, and therefore smaller changes are hard to integrate continuously, besides on the simulation level. One reason is the required manufacturing process of mechanics and electrics, compared to software.

Formal verification is not commonly applied in the industrial practice of software development for the automation domain. One of the main reasons is that, in practice, sufficiently accurate specifications or models of the intended behaviour are not available. Coming up with adequate specifications often requires an effort that companies are not willing to invest at present; it would not be economically beneficial. Moreover, when software (or some other component of a system) evolves, formal specifications must co-evolve—which increases the required overhead for formal specification even further. Formally verifying the behaviour of cyber-physical systems is, thus, often infeasible due to the absence of formal requirement specifications. However, the research on formal methods within the priority program focused on the application of formal modelling, specification, and verification to evolving software, in particular in the automation domain. The identified idiosyncrasies of this application scenario are explicated in Chap. 11:

- Formal methods can benefit from the fact that during evolution, a history of software artefacts is available. For *regression verification*, an old revision serves as formal specification for the new one. The verification essentially checks (behavioural) equivalence between the two programs. Experience from our experiments shows that regression verification (using a state-of-the-art model checker with invariant generation) can be successfully applied to software systems with a considerable state space. We have experienced that, in some cases, the two software revisions do not suffice as input for regression verification. In general, environment models are needed to define those parts of the plant behaviour relevant to establish equivalence. These models are generally difficult to obtain and validate. While modern automatic model checkers employ a number of optimisations and scale way better than earlier tools, applying the approach to systems with larger state spaces is sometimes possible, but not always, depending on how similar states in related runs of the two programs are. Since the new version is usually intended to behave differently in some situations and equivalently in others, there must be means to define the notion of equivalence. For conditional and relational equivalences, some form of temporal specification is required, formulated in a relational behavioural specification language. The design principles of usable and expressive languages is still an active research topic. Regression verification against some previous executable system version—considered as an executable specification—is a promising approach, which requires further improvements with respect to scalability.

- Generalised test tables are a formal specification language building on the well-known and accepted paradigm of test tables (used in industry to specify test cases). We have seen that they are expressive enough to specify interesting properties of realistic systems and have applied them for the (partial) behavioural specification of production plant systems on the signal level. Specifying relevant properties of the entire system on this low level was shown to be possible yet rather technical and unintuitive. On the other hand, generalised test tables are very well suited for the specification and verification of individual general-purpose function blocks, for example within a software library for the automation domain. We have adapted this easy-to-comprehend specification technique to be also usable as specification language for the temporal relational specifications in regression verification.
- The software of automated production systems can often not be analysed in isolation, separated from its application context (the physical entities of the plant, manufacturing management system, etc.). It is important to model different viewpoints (requirements, process, and system) simultaneously for precise and successful model checking of multi-disciplinary systems. A challenge for this verification is to model the continuous processes of a cyber-physical system faithfully, sufficiently, and precisely and to validate these models. The experiments show that probabilistic modelling and subsequent probabilistic model checking are a feasible way to deal with the arising problems.

As an overarching lesson, we can report that shared case studies—see Chaps. 4 and 12—are an invaluable means in collaborative research programs such as SPP 1593 for communication and evaluation of research results. However, implementing and maintaining such shared case studies require significant effort and resources.

Chapter 14
Future Research

Ralf Reussner, Michael Goedicke, Wilhelm Hasselbring, Birgit Vogel-Heuser, Jan Keim, and Lukas Märtin

The overall result of the priority program, as discussed in the previous chapter, shows that the SPP 1593 projects covered a wide range of aspects regarding evolution. However, the entire field is still much broader than the usual set of projects that an SPP can cover in a 6-year period. Deep results have been achieved, and various central ideas have been put forward, as discussed in the previous chapters. In many cases, these results are related to "the system" or "family of systems" and various additional artefacts, including a special sort of meta information: the specification(s) of the system. Such specifications define the functions and qualities of the system like performance and security but also internal qualities like maintainability and evolvability.

R. Reussner · J. Keim
Institute for Program Structures and Data Organization, Karlsruhe Institute of Technology (KIT), Karlsruhe, Germany
e-mail: reussner@kit.edu; jan.keim@kit.edu

M. Goedicke (✉)
paluno – The Ruhr Institute for Software Technology, Specification of Software Systems, Universität Duisburg-Essen, Essen, Germany
e-mail: michael.goedicke@s3.uni-due.de

W. Hasselbring
Software Engineering Group, Department of Computer Science, Kiel University, Kiel, Germany
e-mail: hasselbring@email.uni-kiel.de

B. Vogel-Heuser
Technische Universität München, Institute of Automation and Information Systems, Garching, Germany
e-mail: vogel-heuser@tum.de

L. Märtin
Institute for Programming and Reactive Systems, Technische Universität at Braunschweig, Braunschweig, Germany
e-mail: l.maertin@tu-braunschweig.de

R. Reussner et al. (eds.), *Managed Software Evolution*,
https://doi.org/10.1007/978-3-030-13499-0_14

14.1 General Aspects: Interaction of Multiple Qualities

As has been put forward, one needs to consider—ideally all—software qualities during the entire lifetime of a software system in an integrated way to prevent their degradation during the software system's evolution. In addition, a new dimension has been used: the deployment and operation of the system. Thus, in principle, better informed design and implementation decisions during the development can be done using configuration and runtime information. In order to propose a grand view, the SPP's specific notion of *knowledge-carrying software* has been put forward. Still this notion of *knowledge-carrying code* is worthwhile to consider in future research and development methods. The basic idea was to create a lasting relationship between the code of the system and its specifications and other related documentation. This will be the basic mechanism to build a tightly coupled network of the code and specifications, which need to be maintained by the development actions during evolution.

The challenge here is to define and manage the various qualities and their mutual interdependencies. For example, performance and security interact in many cases in a negative way—which, of course, is not the desired outcome. This means that a naïve implementation of secure communication in distributed system entails complex mathematical operations to encode and decode the messages between the components of the distributed system. Usually, by performing these frequently, the related operations will significantly "steal" execution cycles and as a consequence degrade the performance for other functions of the system. Thus, by introducing security, additional computing power is needed to run the entire system. This is especially an issue in embedded systems that normally use SoCs (System on a Chip) with limited computing power for economic reasons. Even in such cases, a clever software architecture or cheap encoding/decoding coprocessor can be instrumental to help out in such a dilemma. In case of performance and reliability, the use of redundancy can provide a suitable solution to enhance both qualities in many situations.

This is one aspect. In addition and more important in the context here, the evolution of a system will change the (source)code of the system. Having security and performance as quality goals, the complexity of the system grows. For example, the system has a cache for storing and retrieving intermediate results for faster access. Such cache structures pose challenges for security, for example Meltdown [Lip+18] and Spectre [Koc+19], which is of course not directly related to this area but should be taken as an indicator for the increase of complexity when auxiliary structures like caches are introduced. A change in functionality will possibly impact the system's structure in more than one place since the cache (not only the change in the function) has to be taken into consideration as well. This can easily be done in a non-strict and insufficient way, which can degrade one or both of the two qualities.

This is only a simple example and should be taken as a hint that the interdependencies between qualities, when viewed from the evolution perspective, will pose challenges. This is probably even more relevant if one wants to formulate general rules applicable at the whole range of software qualities and sorts of software systems. Thus, a main issue here is not only to address these interdependencies but also to consider the possible influences of the change introduced in the evolution steps. The range of qualities and aspects as a whole needs more attention. This is certainly easier to say than to pursue actually. Managing a specific individual pair or subsets of qualities and their related multilateral interaction, especially in view of evolution, is a challenge in itself. In addition, the overall management of all relevant qualities in software development is beyond the range of the usual single DFG research project.

14.2 Specific Areas

In addition to this large area of further and future research, a number of topics have been hinted at in the previous section on lessons learned, which need further elaboration.

14.2.1 The Use and Extension of NLP Techniques

One specific topic is the use of natural language processing/understanding in the software development process in order to support the detection of issues in the documentation and communication between stakeholders, including developers. The problem of understanding real-world utterances and generating useful hints from those natural language fragments is still an unsolved problem at the general level. However, the area we address here has a number of characteristics, which might improve the situation in a way that allows for better results in understanding natural language comments and statements contained in the code, specifications, documentation, and dedicated communication between stakeholders. For example, integrated development environments and dedicated social media, like Slack,[1] provide such communication channels, which help the stakeholders to keep track. The additional gain as compared to the general problem is due to the at least semi-structured documentation in specifications and code, which reduces the ambiguity in natural language. Given the known model world of the software system in question, it helps to disambiguate natural language statements more easily, and the missing explicit knowledge (tacit knowledge) might be inferred in an easier way than in the general case. In summary, the combination of natural language understanding in the context of models and code (knowledge carrying code) is one area to explore.

It should be noted that this kind of analysis causes concerns in the area of the involved persons' privacy. This dimension is seen differently in the various

[1] https://slack.com/.

geographic and political areas of our planet but in any case introduces a possible bias in communication, which might influence the communication negatively concerning the degree of interesting findings related to the software systems' properties and, of course, not related to the involved persons representing the various stakeholders' views. In the same way, sentiment analysis of the spoken words can be helpful or also be detrimental.

14.2.2 The Organization of the Whole Range of Software Qualities

This area sketched above can be seen as a special case of the situation wherein a software development code, specifications, models, and natural language descriptions have to be integrated. When assessing the integrity of the various specifications/presentations, it is useful to derive information which helps to pursue further development steps. This is especially the case when inconsistencies between those presentations/specifications can be spotted. As has been discussed in the previous chapter, it is desirable to have more than one representation of the system at different levels of abstraction and detail. Given this is done in a structured and systematic way, better insight and consequently better informed development decisions can be made. Such an approach is often referred to as view-based software engineering and is addressed in the previous chapter to coordinate these views at the meta level; that is, the general level about type of actions, type of changes, etc. is still quite difficult.

There are numerous works available regarding views in Software Engineering [MG10]. The systematic development of structures supporting evolution at the meta/type level needs to be addressed in an actual useful way for stakeholders and specifically developers. This not only is a technical discussion but also entails empirical work. This has been addressed in the SPP, and some findings are available. More work needs to be done to obtain valid data, how useful such structures—including at the meta level—should be created to foster better understanding and design actions/design decisions.

This is also problematic since the usual independent multi-factor studies using test persons of the necessary skill levels and the size of studies in terms of entire projects and the involved software system itself is actually impossible in practice. A new approach needs to be developed to provide insight on how empirical results can be obtained here in the situation of large projects.

A part of this aspect is a specific *diversity* aspect of software development: *variants* and *versions*. It is obvious that in many cases, not the *single-purpose* software system is developed, but various variants, for example depending on context and/or configuration, are developed and deployed in a given operating environment. In software product line development, these variants are usually created by specifying a *family of software systems*, and a given instance is created based on a set of particular choices.

In addition, over time evolution of a software system or a family of software systems not only removes errors and inconsistencies but also adds new functionality and features. These additions usually create *new versions* of the software system/family of systems. The research (c.f. previous chapter) revealed that it is still conceptually not very well defined how these various strands of development can be related to each other and as a consequence also how the management of these variants and version can be improved as well.

It could be the case that a proper organization of the views mentioned above will possibly yield a better understanding. Hence, this means that structuring the development work entails a better understanding of the purposes of variants, product lines and versions. When done at the meta level, useful general insight can be generated, which extends the Software Engineering knowledge in a very important area.

14.2.3 Agility in Software Development

In industrial practice, evolution appears to be the norm, *and* the speed of a given development cycle from perceiving a specific need/inconsistency between expectation and actual behaviour has increased in a dramatic way during the last 10 years. The agile development agenda has addressed the inevitable learning curve during a specific software development endeavour in a way that sometimes some qualities of a given software system are not addressed explicitly any more. One could view, for example, the use of AB testing as an implicit elicitation of requirements: various parts of the user community get different versions of the software system or service to use, and the actual usage and resulting use effects (e.g. user satisfaction but also generated traffic, monetary value, etc.) determine which of the versions will be the base for the next evolutionary development steps.

This implies a frequent generation and deployment of a new version or time frames of the system. It is not uncommon that any new deployment of a system is done in time frame in the order of magnitude of 10 s while a given to be tested new feature takes from inception to deployment a time frame of about 1 or 2 weeks. Given such circumstances, the careful elicitation, documentation, and analysis of requirements; the design of solution elements in the form of a changed software architecture; and the subsequent high-performance implementation and deployment are not done explicitly in every aspect any more.

This specific way of working and also the related infrastructure of tools are referred to as *continuous delivery/continuous integration*. In general, the approach to automate the process to integrate all artefacts, automate the acceptance test, and deploy the solution—if passing all tests—is good for all software development processes. Of course, these are badly needed for continuous delivery. However, not all software development endeavours are of this kind. Embedded systems in high-integrity application areas, for example health care, pharmaceuticals, transportation, critical infrastructures often require certification and approval processes, which have to be signed off by human experts in the end.

Much of the research presented here and in other documentation and publications of the SPP's projects rely on explicitly documented qualities, design, design decisions, etc. Thus, one can see in continuous delivery development profiles a mismatch between requirements from practice and the assumptions of research in Software Engineering. How can developers in such situations and beyond produce good quality solutions in terms of robust and correct software systems/families of software systems?

The answer to this question is to scale up the involved persons' productivity by using automated tools. In many cases, an initial investment into (non-executable) specifications/description of software properties and related qualities seems to be a good one. The problem comes when the system evolves and grows substantially. Many of the more advanced (formal) methods and tools are not really scalable in the sense that truly incremental approaches are available. Usually formally verifying a software system of realistic industrial size is not performed within 10 s and—if feasible at all—will last days if not weeks. An incremental approach which starts small and grows with system's growth only in small steps according to changes/additions is still not a solved task. The main problem here is that a small change to a software system is not—in a mathematical sense—continuous and has only a small effect. Advancements in *incremental verification/regression verification* would also be beneficial for other fields in computer science as well.

As a slightly smaller version of the incremental verification procedures sketched above, better, automated *detection of inconsistencies* might be also helpful. Not so much the ubiquitous stack trace or lengthy/indigestible logfiles or memory dumps but specific identification of erroneous behaviour and related potential causes will be helpful. This has to be incremental and also related to the many software qualities. For example, a security analysis could detect whether the change in the software introduces the potential of a new attack vector which wasn't there before the change was applied.

For both areas, verification and inconsistency management of modular approaches would be beneficial for increasing their respective scalability in order to tackle real-sized problems in the industry.

The application of the approaches to the case studies in this SPP shows the applicability of the various approaches in somewhat realistic settings. This means that for the two application domains, the various attempts and approaches showed their usefulness in these settings. However, this also showed that there is more need for connecting models in the respective application domain and the related code in, for example, microcontrollers and PLCs (xPPU) in such a way that the changes in the environment, general context, and the application domain area can easily be traced/connected to the implementation.

This seems also to be a prolific research area to join forces in other areas like business management (CoCoMe) and mechanical engineering (production automation PPU). It is easy to imagine the additional benefit when the actual problem grows in size and complexity well beyond the two case studies of this SPP.

14.2.4 Summary

The priority program investigated several facets of the notion of knowledge-carrying software. In particular, the relationship between requirements, architecture, code, and runtime data was investigated in several projects. Design decisions leading from requirements to architecture and to code were seen to make the transition between requirements, architecture, and code easier. Also, the decisions' relationship to reusable artefacts such as design patterns was investigated. In summary, at the end of the funding period of the priority program, we see that the idea of knowledge-carrying software is quite broad and carries further. It has a good chance to act as a conceptual frame to also include data which drive software functionality increasingly.

This leads also to an emerging area of research which addresses the question on how a software system and all the related artefacts in additional documentation of the system and the design process can be of help when it comes to the question on how and why the result of applying a software product yields a specific result. This ability to derive such an explanation of a result becomes more difficult in the context one might call Data-Driven Software Engineering.

This term addresses software products which use additional sources of information, for example streams of data to compute their results. Examples are systems using artificial neural nets to process data, categorize and assess it, and produce some output which might affect already our purchase decisions or other similar important aspects of our life.

Such systems existed for a long time, but at the start of the SPP they had not much practical use. After the start of the SPP, we saw a rise in the production and use of such systems in the area of data-driven software. Data determine the functionality of the system in a similar way as the implemented code does. For example, machine learning can improve the quality of the functions, or in the case of multi-tenant systems, customer-specific data help create customer-specific services based on the same service implementation.

For evolution, this poses new challenges. Firstly, it needs to be ensured that data privacy is preserved during evolution. This means that analyses on the accessibility of data need to be applied during evolutionary development—ideally in an incremental way. It also includes that one can provide evolving configuration files related to data access rights for such analyses. Secondly, the use of machine learning to drive software functionality leads to an increase need of means to make the resulting decisions and operations of a software system understandable. In such cases, looking into the code of the software system does not help explain why a certain function performed in the way it did. This creates an urgent need to assess the influence of evolving data sets on the software system and its services and functions.

Bibliography

[AA13] C. Aldrich and Lidia Auret. *Unsupervised process monitoring and fault diagnosis with machine learning methods*. Advances in computer vision and pattern recognition. London, New York: Springer, 2013. ISBN: 1447151852.

[Aal11] W.M.P van der Aalst. *Process Mining*. Springer, 2011.

[AB12] Areej AlHogail and Jawad Berri. "Enhancing IT security in organizations through knowledge management". In: *Proceedings of the International Conference on Information Technology and e-Services (ICITeS)*. IEEE. 2012, pp. 1–6.

[ACG12] Ayman Amin, A Colman, and Lars Grunske. "An Approach to Forecasting QoS Attributes of Web Services Based on ARIMA and GARCH Models". In: *Proceedings of the IEEE 19th International Conference on Web Services (ICWS 2012)*. IEEE, June 2012, pp. 74–81. https://doi.org/10.1109/ICWS.2012.37.

[AG12] Colin Atkinson and Ralph Gerbig. "Melanie: Multi-level Modeling and Ontology Engineering Environment". In: *Proceedings of the 2Nd International Master Class on Model-Driven Engineering: Modeling Wizards*. MW '12. Innsbruck, Austria: ACM, 2012, 7:1–7:2. ISBN: 978-1-4503-1853-2. URL: http://doi.acm.org/10.1145/2448076.2448083.

[ÅAGB11] Johan ÅAkerberg, Mikael Gidlund, and Mats Björkman. "Future research challenges in wireless sensor and actuator networks targeting industrial automation". In: *Industrial Informatics (INDIN), 2011 9th IEEE International Conference on*. IEEE. 2011, pp. 410–415.

[AGC12] A. Amin, L. Grunske, and A. Colman. "An automated approach to forecasting QoS attributes based on linear and non-linear time series modeling". In: *Proceedings of the 27th IEEE/ACM International Conference on Automated Software Engineering (ASE 2012)* IEEE, Sept. 2012, pp. 130–139. https://doi.org/10.1145/2351676.2351695.

[Ahm+17] Amir Shayan Ahmadian et al. "Model-based privacy and security analysis with CARiSMA". In: *Proceedings of the 2017 11th Joint Meeting on Foundations of Software Engineering, ESEC/FSE 2017, Paderborn, Germany September 4–8, 2017*. 2017, pp. 989–993. URL: http://doi.acm.org/10.1145/3106237.3122823.

[Ahr+16] Wolfgang Ahrendt et al., eds. *Deductive Software Verification - The KeY Book: From Theory to Practice*. Vol. 10001. Lecture Notes in Computer Science Springer, Dec. 2016. https://doi.org/10.1007/978-3-319-49812-6.

[AJ16] A. S. Ahmadian and J. Jürjens. "Supporting Model-Based Privacy Analysis by Exploiting Privacy Level Agreements". In: *2016 IEEE International Conference on Cloud Computing Technology and Science (CloudCom)*. Dec. 2016, pp. 360–365. https://doi.org/10.1109/CloudCom.2016.0063.

R. Reussner et al. (eds.), *Managed Software Evolution*,
https://doi.org/10.1007/978-3-030-13499-0

[AJY11] A. Bauer, J. Jürjens, and Y. Yu. “Run-Time Security Traceability for Evolving Systems”. In: *The Computer Journal* 54.1 (2011), pp. 58–87. http://dx.doi.org/10.1093/comjnl/bxq042.

[AKK14] A. Averbakh, K. Niklas, and K. Schneider. “Knowledge from Document Annotations as By-Product in Distributed Software Engineering”. In: *The 26th Int. Conf. on Software Eng. and Knowledge Engineering* (2014).

[Ale+13] A. Aleti et al. “Software Architecture Optimization Methods: A Systematic Literature Review”. In: *IEEE Transactions on Software Engineering* 39.5 (2013).

[Ale+17] Mounifah Alenazi et al. “Traceability for Evolving Automated Production Systems”. In: *The Grand Challenges of Traceability 2017: 10 Years Later*. Slade Natural Bridge State Resort Park, USA, Mar. 2017.

[Ale77] Christopher Alexander. *A Pattern Language: towns, buildings, construction*. Center for Environmental Structure series 2. 85 A 1588: Oxford University Press, New York, 1977.

[AlH+16a] Mustafa Al-Hajjaji et al. “IncLing: Efficient Product-line Testing Using Incremental Pairwise Sampling”. In: *Proceedings of the 2016 ACM SIGPLAN International Conference on Generative Programming: Concepts and Experiences*. GPCE 2016. Amsterdam, Netherlands: ACM, 2016, pp. 144–155. ISBN: 978-1-4503-4446-3. URL: http://doi.acm.org/10.1145/2993236.2993253.

[AlH+16b] Mustafa Al-Hajjaji et al. “Tool Demo: Testing Configurable Systems with FeatureIDE”. In: *Proceedings of the 2016 ACM SIGPLAN International Conference on Generative Programming: Concepts and Experiences*. GPCE 2016. Amsterdam, Netherlands: ACM, 2016, pp. 173–177. ISBN: 978-1-4503-4446-3. URL: http://doi.acm.org/10.1145/2993236.2993254.

[Alk+17a] Rana Alkadhi et al. “Rationale in Development Chat Messages: An Exploratory Study”. In: *Proceedings of the 14th International Conference on Mining Software Repositories* MSR ’17. Buenos Aires, Argentina: IEEE Press, 2017, pp. 436–446. ISBN: 978-1-5386-1544-7. https://doi.org/10.1109/msr.2017.43.

[Alk+17b] Rana Alkadhi et al. “REACT: An Approach for Capturing Rationale in Chat Messages”. In: *11th ACM/IEEE International Symposium on Empirical Software Engineering and Measurement (ESEM’17)*. Toronto, Ontario, Canada: IEEE, 2017. https://doi.org/10.1109/esem.2017.26.

[Alk+18] Rana Alkadhi et al. “How do developers discuss rationale?” In: *2018 IEEE 25th International Conference on Software Analysis, Evolution and Reengineering (SANER)*. Campobasso, Italy: IEEE, Mar. 2018, pp. 357–369. https://doi.org/10.1109/saner.2018.8330223.

[Alm+15] Diogo Almeida et al. “Towards a Catalog of Usability Smells”. In: *Proceedings of the 30th Annual ACM Symposium on Applied Computing*. SAC ’15. Salamanca, Spain: ACM, 2015, pp. 175–181. ISBN: 978-1-4503-3196-8. https://doi.org/10.1145/2695664.2695670.

[Alt+09] Kerstin Altmanninger et al. “Why model versioning research is needed!? an experience report”. In: *Proceedings of the MoDSE-MCCM 2009 Workshop@ MoDELS* Vol. 9. 2009.

[Alv+08] Vander Alves et al. “FLiP: Managing Software Product Line Extraction and Reaction with Aspects”. In: *Software Product Lines, 12th International Conference, SPLC 2008, Limerick, Ireland, September 8–12, 2008, Proceedings*. 2008, p. 354. URL: https://doi.org/10.1109/SPLC.2008.51.

[And08] Ross J. Anderson. *Security engineering - a guide to building dependable distributed systems (2. ed.)* Wiley, 2008, pp. I–XL, 1–1040. ISBN: 978-0-470-06852-6.

[ÁP03] Gonzalo Álvarez and Slobodan Petrovic. “A new taxonomy of Web attacks suitable for efficient encoding”. In: *Computers & Security* 22.5 (2003), pp. 435–449.

[Ape+13] Sven Apel et al. *Feature-Oriented Software Product Lines: Concepts and Implementation* Springer Publishing Company Incorporated, 2013. ISBN: 9783642375200.

[APM16] Zoya Alexeeva, Diego Perez-Palacin, and Raffaela Mirandola. "Design Decision Documentation: A Literature Overview". In: *Software Architecture* Ed. by Bedir Tekinerdogan. Vol. 5292. Lecture Notes in Computer Science. Berlin, Heidelberg: Springer Berlin Heidelberg, 2016, pp. 84–101. ISBN: 978-3-540-88029-5. DOI: https://doi.org/10.1007/978-3-319-48992-6_6.

[Ara+15] Vincent Aravantinos et al. "AutoFOCUS 3: Tooling Concepts for Seamless, Model-based Development of Embedded Systems". In: *Joint Proceedings of the 8th International Workshop on Model-based Architecting of Cyber-physical and Embedded Systems and 1st International Workshop on UML Consistency Rules (ACES-MB 2015 & WUCOR 2015) co-located with ACM/IEEE 18th International Conference on Model Driven Engineering Languages and Systems (MoDELS 2015), Ottawa, Canada, September 28, 2015.* Ed. by Iulia Dragomir et al. Vol. 1508. CEUR Workshop Proceedings. CEUR-WS.org, 2015, pp. 19–26. URL: http://ceur-ws.org/Vol-1508/paper4.pdf.

[Are+06] David Arens et al. "Packaging Machine Language V3. Mode & States Definition Document". In: *OMAC Motion for Packaging Working Group* (2006).

[Are+10] Thorsten Arendt et al. "Henshin: Advanced Concepts and Tools for In-Place EMF Model Transformations". In: *MoDELS 2010.* 2010, pp. 121–135. https://doi.org/10.1007/978-3-642-16145-2_9.

[Arm+02] Roy Armoni et al. "The ForSpec Temporal Logic: A New Temporal Property-Specification Language". In: *Tools and Algorithms for the Construction and Analysis of Systems.* Ed. by Joost-Pieter Katoen and Perdita Stevens. Berlin, Heidelberg: Springer Berlin Heidelberg, 2002, pp. 296–311.

[ASW09] K. Altmanninger, M. Seidl, and M. Wimmer. "A survey on model versioning approaches". In: *International Journal of Web Information Systems* 5.3 (2009), pp. 271–304.

[AT12] L. V. Allen and D. M. Tilbury. "Anomaly Detection Using Model Generation for Event-Based Systems Without a Preexisting Formal Model". In: *Systems, Man and Cybernetics, Part A: Systems and Humans, IEEE Transactions on* 42.3 (2012), pp. 654–668. ISSN: 1083–4427. https://doi.org/10.1109/TSMCA.2011.2170418.

[ATW08] Firas Abdallah, Claudine Troffolon, and Bruno Warin. "Models transformation to implement a Project-Based Collaborative Learning (PBCL) scenario: Moodle case study In Advanced Learning Technologies". In: *ICALT'08. Eighth IEEE International Conference.* 2008.

[Aut+15] M. Autili et al. "Aligning Qualitative, Real-Time, and Probabilistic Property Specification Patterns Using a Structured English Grammar". In: *Software Engineering, IEEE Transactions on* PP.99 (2015), pp. 1–1. ISSN: 0098–5589. https://doi.org/10.1109/TSE.2015.2398877.

[Avi+04] Algirdas Avizienis et al. "Basic Concepts and Taxonomy of Dependable and Secure Computing". In: *IEEE Trans. Dependable Secur. Comput.* 1.1 (Jan. 2004), pp. 11–33. ISSN: 1545–5971. URL: http://dx.doi.org/10.1109/TDSC.2004.2.

[Bal11] Moritz Balz. "Embedding Model Specifications in Object-Oriented Program Code: A Bottom-up Approach for Model-based Software Development". PhD thesis. Universität Duisburg-Essen, May 2011.

[Bas+11] Luca Bassi et al. "A SysML-based methodology for manufacturing machinery modeling and design". In: *IEEE/ASME transactions on mechatronics* 16.6 (2011), pp. 1049–1062.

[Bau+04a] Nanette Bauer et al. "A Unifying Semantics for Sequential Function Charts". English. In: *Integration of Software Specification Techniques for Applications in Engineering.* LNCS 3147. Springer, 2004. ISBN: 978-3-540-23135-6. URL: http://dx.doi.org/10.1007/978-3-540-27863-4_22.

[Bau+04b] Nanette Bauer et al. "Verification of PLC Programs Given as Sequential Function Charts". English. In: *Integration of Software Specification Techniques for Applications in Engineering.* Ed. by Hartmut Ehrig et al. Vol. 3147. Lecture Notes in

Computer Science. Springer Berlin Heidelberg, 2004, pp. 517–540. ISBN: 978-3-540-23135-6. URL: http://dx.doi.org/10.1007/978-3-540-27863-4_28.

[BB08] Janet E. Burge and David C. Brown. "Software Engineering Using RATionale". In: *Journal of Systems and Software* 81.3 (Mar. 2008), pp. 395–413. ISSN: 01641212. https://doi.org/10.1016/j.jss.2007.05.004.

[BB99] PerOlof Bengtsson and Jan Bosch. "Architecture Level Prediction of Software Maintenance". In: *Proc. of 3rd CSMR* 1999, pp. 139–147.

[BCK11] Gilles Barthe, Juan Manuel Crespo, and César Kunz. "Relational Verification Using Product Programs". In: *Proceedings, 17th International Symposium on Formal Methods (FM)*. Ed. by Michael Butler and Wolfram Schulte. Vol. 6664. Lecture Notes in Computer Science. Springer, 2011, pp. 200–214.

[BCK12] L. Bass, P. Clements, and R. Kazman. *Software Architecture in Practice*. 3rd. Addison-Wesley Professional, 2012. ISBN: 9780321815736.

[BE08] Lars Bendix and Pär Emanuelsson. "Diff and merge support for model based development". In: *Proceedings of the 2008 international workshop on Comparison and versioning of software models*. ACM. 2008, pp. 31–34.

[Bec+12] Steffen Becker et al. *The MechatronicUML Method – Process, Syntax, and Semantics*. Tech. rep. tr-ri-12-318. Software Engineering Group, Heinz Nixdorf Institute University of Paderborn, Feb. 2012.

[Bec+15] Bernhard Beckert et al. "Regression Verification for Programmable Logic Controller Software". In: *17th International Conference on Formal Engineering Methods (ICFEM 2015)*. Vol. 9407. LNCS. Springer, 2015, pp. 234–251. ISBN: 9783642209246. https://doi.org/10.1007/978-3-319-25423-4_15.

[Bec+17a] Bernhard Beckert et al. "Generalised Test Tables: A Practical Specification Language for Reactive Systems". In: *Integrated Formal Methods 13th International Conference, IFM 2017, Turin, Italy, September 20–22, 2017, Proceedings* Ed. by Nadia Polikarpova and Steve Schneider. Vol. 10510. Lecture Notes in Computer Science. Springer, 2017, pp. 129–144. ISBN: 978-3-319-66844-4. URL: https://doi.org/10.1007/978-3-319-66845-1_9.

[Bec+17b] Bernhard Beckert et al. "SemSlice: Exploiting Relational Verification for Automatic Program Slicing". In: *13th International Conference on integrated Formal Methods (iFM 2017)* Vol. 10510. Lecture Notes in Computer Science. Springer, Sept. 2017, pp. 312–319. https://doi.org/10.1007/978-3-319-66845-1_20.

[Bec99] Kent L. Beck. "Embracing Change with Extreme Programming". In: *IEEE Computer* 32.10 (1999), pp. 70–77. URL: https://doi.org/10.1109/2.796139.

[Beh+01] G. Behrmann et al. "UPPAAL - present and future". In: *Proceedings of the 40th IEEE Conference on Decision and Control (Cat. No.01CH37228)*. Vol. 3. 2001, 2881–2886. https://doi.org/10.1109/.2001.980713.

[Ben+14] N. Bencomo et al. *Models@run.time: Foundations, Applications, and Roadmaps*. Lecture Notes in Computer Science. Springer International Publishing, 2014.

[Ber+13] Thorsten Berger et al. "A Study of Variability Models and Languages in the Systems Software Domain". In: *IEEE Trans. Softw. Eng.* 39.12 (Dec. 2013), pp. 1611–1640. ISSN: 0098–5589. URL: http://dx.doi.org/10.1109/TSE.2013.34.

[Ber+16] Luca Berardinelli et al. "Cross-disciplinary engineering with AutomationML and SysML". In: *at-Automatisierungstechnik* 64.4 (2016), pp. 253–269. https://doi.org/10.1515/auto-2015-0076.

[Bey+04] D. Beyer et al. "Generating tests from counterexamples". In: *Proceedings. 26th International Conference on Software Engineering*. 2004, pp. 326–335.

[BFB14] Giacomo Barbieri, Cesare Fantuzzi, and Roberto Borsari. "A model-based design methodology for the development of mechatronic systems". In: *Mechatronics* 24.7 (2014). 1. Model-Based Mechatronic System Design 2. Model Based Engineering, pp. 833–843. ISSN: 0957–4158. http://dx.doi.org/10.1016/j.mechatronics.2013.12.004. URL: http://www.sciencedirect.com/science/article/pii/S0957415813002389.

[BFS05] M. Bonfe, C. Fantuzzi, and C. Secchi. "Object-oriented modeling of multi-domain systems". In: *IEEE International Conference on Automation Science and Engi- neering, 2005.* Aug. 2005, pp. 363–368. https://doi.org/10.1109/COASE.2005.1506796.

[Bha+17] Manoj Bhat et al. "Automatic Extraction of Design Decisions from Issue Management Systems: A Machine Learning Based Approach". In: *11th European Conference on Software Architecture (ECSA'17)* Ed. by Antónia Lopes and Rogério de Lemos. Cham, Switzerland: Springer, 2017, pp. 138–154. ISBN: 978-3-319-65830-8. https://doi.org/10.1007/978-3-319-65831-5_10.

[BHL00] Sébastien Bornot, Ralf Huuck, and Ben Lukoschus. "Verification of Sequential Function Charts Using SMV". In: *PDPTA* Ed. by Hamid R. Arabnia. CSREA Press, 2000.

[Bic+18] Rudolf Biczok et al. *An Industry 4.0 Case Study: The Integration of CoCoME and xPPU.* Tech. rep. 2018-08; Karlsruhe Reports in Informatics. Karlsruhe Institute of Technology (KIT), 2018.

[Bif+14] Stefan Biffl et al. "Semantic mapping support in AutomationML". In: *Emerging Technology and Factory Automation (ETFA), 2014 IEEE.* IEEE. 2014, pp. 1–4.

[Bir10] Alessandro Birolini. "Basic Concepts, Quality and Reliability Assurance of Complex Equipment and Systems". In: *Reliability Engineering: Theory and Practice* Berlin, Heidelberg: Springer Berlin Heidelberg, 2010, pp. 1–24. ISBN: 978-3-642-14952-8. URL: https://doi.org/10.1007/978-3-642-14952-8_1.

[BK08] C. Baier and J.-P. Katoen. *Principles of Model Checking* MIT Press, 2008. ISBN: 9780262026499.

[BKK05] Petros Belsis, Spyros Kokolakis, and Evangelos Kiountouzis. "Information systems security from a knowledge management perspective". In: *Information Management & Computer Security* 13.3 (2005), pp. 189–202. ISSN: 0968-5227. https://doi.org/10.1108/09685220510602013.

[BKR09] Steffen Becker, Heiko Koziolek, and Ralf Reussner. "The Palladio component model for model-driven performance prediction". In: *Journal of Systems and Software* 82.1 (Jan. 2009), pp. 3–22. https://doi.org/10.1016/j.jss.2008.03.066.

[BKU15] Bernhard Beckert, Vladimir Klebanov, and Mattias Ulbrich. "Regression verification for Java using a secure information flow calculus". In: *Proceedings of the 17th Workshop on Formal Techniques for Java-like Programs, FTfJP 2015, Prague, Czech Republic, July 7, 2015* Ed. by Rosemary Monahan. ACM, 2015, 6:1–6:6. ISBN: 978-1-4503-3656-7. URL: http://doi.acm.org/10.1145/2786536.2786544.

[Blo+16] Matthias Blohm et al. "Kieker4DQL: Declarative Performance Measurement". In: *Proceedings of the 2016 Symposium on Software Performance (SSP)* 2016.

[BM00] Ed Brinksma and Angelika Mader. "Verification and optimization of a PLC control schedule". In: *SPIN* Vol. 1885. Springer. 2000, pp. 73–92.

[BMF02] Ed Brinksma, Angelika Mader, and Ansgar Fehnker. "Verification and Optimization of a PLC Control Schedule". English. In: *STTT* 4.1 (2002). ISSN: 1433-2779. URL: http://dx.doi.org/10.1007/s10009-002-0079-0.

[BMM09] Marcel Bruch, Martin Monperrus, and Mira Mezini. "Learning from examples to improve code completion systems". In: *Proceedings of the the 7th joint meeting of the European software engineering conference and the ACM SIGSOFT symposium on The foundations of software engineering.* ACM. 2009, pp. 213–222.

[Bol+06] Gunter Bolch et al. *Queueing networks and Markov chains: modeling and performance evaluation with computer science applications.* John Wiley & Sons, 2006.

[Bor+17] Kristopher Born et al. "Granularity of Conflicts and Dependencies in Graph Transformation Systems". In: *International Conference on Graph Transformation.* Springer. 2017, pp. 125–141.

[Bos14] Jan Bosch. *Continuous Software Engineering: An Introduction.* Springer, 2014, pp. 3–13. ISBN: 978-3-319-11282-4. https://doi.org/10.1007/978-3-319-11283-1.

[Bot+09] Jewgenij Botaschanjan et al. "Integrated Behavior Models for Factory Automation Systems". In: *Proceedings of 12th IEEE International Conference on Emerging*

Technologies and Factory Automation, ETFA 2009, September 22-25, 2008, Palma de Mallorca, Spain. IEEE, 2009, pp. 1–8. ISBN: 978-1-4244-2727-7. URL: https://doi.org/10.1109/ETFA.2009.5347021.

[Bou+17a] Safa Bougouffa et al. "Industry 4.0 Interface for Dynamic Reconfiguration of an Open Lab Size Automated Production System to Allow Remote Community Experiments". In: *IEEE International Conference on Industrial Engineering and Engineering Management (IEEM)*. Singapur, Singapur, Dec. 2017.

[Bou+17b] Safa Bougouffa et al. "Scalable Cloud Based Semantic Code Analysis to Support Continuous Integration of Industrial PLC Code". In: *15th IEEE International Conference on Industrial Informatics (INDIN)*. Emden, Germany July 2017. https://doi.org/10.1109/INDIN.2017.8104843.

[BP08] Céderic Brun and Alfonso Pierantonio. "Model differences in the Eclipse Modeling Framework". In: *UPGRADE, The European Journal for the Informatics Professional*. 2008.

[BR00] Keith H. Bennett and Václav T. Rajlich "Software Maintenance and Evolution: A Roadmap". In: *Proceedings of the Conference on The Future of Software Engineering*. ICSE '00. Limerick, Ireland: ACM, 2000, pp. 73–87. ISBN: 1-58113-253-0. URL: http://doi.acm.org/10.1145/336512.336534.

[Bra11] Aaron R. Bradley. "SAT-Based Model Checking without Unrolling". In: *Verification, Model Checking, and Abstract Interpretation 12th International Conference, VMCAI 2011, Austin, TX, USA, January 23-25, 2011. Proceedings*. Ed. by Ran jit Jhala and David A. Schmidt. Vol. 6538. Lecture Notes in Computer Science. Springer, 2011, pp. 70–87. ISBN: 978-3-642-18274-7. URL: https://doi.org/10.1007/978-3-642-18275-4_7.

[Bro+10] Manfred Broy et al. "Seamless Model-Based Development: From Isolated Tools to Integrated Model Engineering Environments". In: *Proceedings of the IEEE* 98.4 (2010), pp. 526–545. URL: https://doi.org/10.1109/JPROC.2009.2037771.

[Bro+15] Fabian Brosig et al. "Quantitative Evaluation of Model-Driven Performance Analysis and Simulation of Component-based Architectures". In: *Transactions on Software Engineering (TSE)* 41.2 (Feb. 2015), pp. 157–175. https://doi.org/10.1109/TSE2014.2362755.

[Bro+98] William J. Brown et al. *AntiPatterns: Refactoring Software, Architectures, and Projects in Crisis*. 1998.

[Bro12] Manfred Broy. "System behaviour models with discrete and dense time". In: *Advances in Real-Time Systems*. Springer, 2012, pp. 3–25.

[Bro86] Manfred Broy. "A Theory for Nondeterminism, Parallelism, Communication, and Concurrency". In: *Theor. Comput. Sci.* 45.1 (1986), pp. 1–61. URL: https://doi.org/10.1016/0304-3975(86)90040-X.

[Bro97] Manfred Broy. "Compositional refinement of interactive systems". In: *J. ACM* 44.6 (1997), pp. 850–891. URL: http://doi.acm.org/10.1145/268999.269004.

[Bru+14] João Brunet et al. "Do developers discuss design?" In: *Proceedings of the 11th Working Conference on Mining Software Repositories MSR 2014*. Hyderabad, India: ACM Press, 2014, pp. 340–343. ISBN: 9781450328630. https://doi.org/10.1145/2597073.2597115.

[Bru+15] Andreas Brunnert et al. *Performance-oriented DevOps: A Research Agenda*. Tech. rep. SPEC-RG-2015-01. SPEC Research Group — DevOps Performance Working Group, Standard Performance Evaluation Corporation (SPEC), Aug. 2015. URL: http://arxiv.org/abs/1508.04752.

[BS01] Manfred Broy and Ketil Stølen. *Specification and development of interactive systems: focus on streams, interfaces, and refinement*. Springer Science & Business Media, 2001. ISBN: 0-387-95073-7.

[BS07] Sean Barnum and Amit Sethi. "Attack Patterns as a Knowledge Resource for Building Secure Software". In: *OMG Software Assurance Workshop: Cigital*. 2007.

[BS10] Monica Bellgran and Kristina Säfsten. *Production development: Design and operation of production systems*. London: Springer, 2010. ISBN: 9781848824959.

[Buc+05] Jim Buckley et al. "Towards a taxonomy of software change". In: *Journal of Software Maintenance* 17.5 (2005), pp. 309–332. URL: https://doi.org/10.1002/smr.319

[Bür+15a] Johannes Bürdek et al. "Facilitating Reuse in Multi-goal Test-Suite Generation for Software Product Lines". In: *Fundamental Approaches to Software Engineering 18th International Conference, FASE 2015, Held as Part of the European Joint Conferences on Theory and Practice of Software, ETAPS 2015, London, UK, April 11-18, 2015. Proceedings*. 2015, pp. 84–99.

[Bür+15b] Johannes Bürdek et al. "Reasoning about Product-Line Evolution using Complex Feature Model Differences". In: *Automated Software Engineering Special Issue on Long Term Evolution of Software Systems Response* (2015).

[Bür+16] Johannes Bürdek et al. "Reasoning about product-line evolution using complex feature model differences". In: *Automated Software Engineering* 23.4 (2016), pp. 687–733.

[Bür+18] Jens Bürger et al. "A framework for semi-automated co-evolution of security knowledge and system models". In: *Journal of Systems and Software* 139 (2018), pp. 142–160. ISSN: 0164-1212. https://doi.org/10.1016/j.jss.2018.02.003.

[Bur+92] J.R. Burch et al. "Symbolic model checking: 10^{20} States and beyond". In: *Information and Computation* 98.2 (1992), pp. 142–170. ISSN: 0890-5401. http://dx.doi.org/10.1016/0890-5401(92)90017-A. URL: http://www.sciencedirect.com/science/article/pii/089054019290017A.

[Bus+96] Frank Buschmann et al. *A System of Patterns: Pattern-Oriented Software Architecture* 1st ed. Wiley Publishing, 1996. ISBN: 9780471958697.

[BV18] I Badr and B Vogel-Heuser. "A taxonomy of faults influencing the quality of automated production systems". In: *Proceedings of the 2018 3rd IFAC Conference on Embedded Systems, Computational Intelligence and Telematics in Control (to be appeared)*. 2018.

[Cal+14] Radu Calinescu et al. "Adaptive model learning for continual verification of non-functional properties". In: *ACM/SPEC Int. Conference on Performance Engineering*. ACM, 2014, pp. 87–98. https://doi.org/10.1145/2568088.2568094.

[Cam13] Alarico Campetelli. "Dynamic Sampling for FOCUS Hybrid Components". In: *International Journal of Modeling and Optimization* 3.5 (2013), p. 402.

[Cap+16] Rafael Capilla et al. "10 years of software architecture knowledge management: Practice and future". In: *Journal of Systems and Software* 116 (2016), pp. 191–205. ISSN: 01641212. https://doi.org/10.1016/j.jss.2015.08.054.

[Car+83] Stuart K. Card et al. *The Psychology of Human-Computer Interaction*. L. Erlbaum Associates Inc., 1983. ISBN: 0898592437.

[Car12] Ralf Carbon. "Architecture-centric software producibility analysis". PhD thesis. 2012.

[Car18] Carleton University, Real Time and Distributed Systems Group. *Layered Queueing Network Solver and Simulator Website*. URL: http://www.sce.carleton.ca/rads/lqns/. 2018.

[Cav+14] Roberto Cavada et al. "The nuXmv Symbolic Model Checker". In: *CAV* Ed. by Armin Biere and Roderick Bloem. Vol. 8559. Lecture Notes in Computer Science. Springer, 2014, pp. 334–342. ISBN: 978-3-319-08866-2.

[CE00] Krzysztof Czarnecki and Ulrich W. Eisenecker. *Generative Programming: Methods, Tools, and Applications*. New York, NY, USA: ACM Press/Addison-Wesley Publishing Co., 2000. ISBN: 0-201-30977-7.

[CH13] Y. Cherdantseva and J. Hilton. "A Reference Model of Information Assurance amp; Security". In: *2013 International Conference on Availability, Reliability and Security*. Sept. 2013. https://doi.org/10.1109/ARES.2013.72.

[Cha+01] Ned Chapin et al. "Types of Software Evolution and Software Maintenance". In: *Journal of Software Maintenance* 13.1 (Jan. 2001), pp. 3–30. ISSN: 1040-550X. URL: http://dl.acm.org/citation.cfm?id=371697.371701.

[Cha+16] Adrien Champion et al. "CoCoSpec: A Mode-Aware Contract Language for Reactive Systems". In: *Software Engineering and Formal Methods* Ed. by Rocco De Nicola and Eva Kühn. Cham: Springer International Publishing, 2016, pp. 347–366. ISBN: 978-3-319-41591-8.

[Cha+17] Suhyun Cha et al. "Generation of Monitoring Functions in Production Automation Using Test Specifications". In: *IEEE 15th International Conference on Industrial Informatics*. 2017.

[Cha+18] Abhishek Chakraborty et al. "Signal-based Context Comparative Analysis for Identification of Similar Manufacturing Modules". In: *16th IFAC Symposium on Information Control Problems in Manufacturing* 2018.

[Chr06] George Chryssolouris. *Manufacturing Systems: Theory and Practice*. New York: Springer Science+Business Media Inc, 2006. ISBN: 9780387256832. URL: http://dx.doi.org/10.1007/0-387-28431-1.

[CJR11] Radu Calinescu, Kenneth Johnson, and Yasmin Rafiq. "Using observation ageing to improve markovian model learning in QoS engineering". In: *Second WOSP/SIPEW Int. Conference on Performance Engineering*. ACM, 2011, pp. 505–510. https://doi.org/10.1145/1958746.1958823.

[Cle+02] P Clements et al. *Evaluating Software Architectures: Methods and Case Studies*. AW, 2002.

[Cle+13] Jane Cleland-Huang et al. "Decision-Centric Traceability of architectural concerns".In: *2013 7th International Workshop on Traceability in Emerging Forms of Software Engineering (TEFSE)*. San Francisco, CA, USA: IEEE, 2013, pp. 5–11. ISBN: 978-1-4799-0495-2. https://doi.org/10.1109/TEFSE.2013.6620147.

[CM04] Brian Chess and Gary McGraw. "Static Analysis for Security". In: *IEEE Security & Privacy* 2.6 (2004), pp. 76–79.

[CM09] Josá Creissac Campos and J. Machado. "Pattern-based Analysis of Automated Production Systems". In: *13th IFAC Symposium on Information Control Problems in Manufacturing (INCOM)*. Ed. by Natalia Bakhtadze and Alexandre Dolgui. Moscow: Elsevier, 2009, pp. 972–977.

[CMI11] Vittorio Cortellessa, Antinisca Di Marco, and Paola Inverardi. "Model-Based Software Performance Analysis". In: (2011). https://doi.org/10.1007/978-3-642-13621-4.

[CMT16] Maria Carla Calzarossa, Luisa Massari, and Daniele Tessera. "Workload Characterization: A Survey Revisited". In: *ACM Comput. Surv.* 48.3 (Feb. 2016), 48:1–48:43. ISSN: 0360–0300.

[CN01] P. Clements and L. Northrop. *Software Product Lines: Practices and Patterns*. Addison-Wesley Longman Publishing Co., Inc., 2001.

[CN02] P. Clements and L. Northrop. *Software Product Lines: Practices and Patterns*. SEI series in software engineering. Addison-Wesley, 2002. ISBN: 9780201703320. URL: https://books.google.de/books?id=tHGFQgAACAAJ.

[Cod+15] Mihai Codoban et al. "Software history under the lens: A study on why and how developers examine it". In: *2015 IEEE International Conference on Software Maintenance and Evolution (ICSME)* Bremen, Germany: IEEE, 2015, pp. 1–10. ISBN: 978-1-4673-7532-0. https://doi.org/10.1109/ICSM.2015.7332446.

[Col02] Robert E. Cole. "From continuous improvement to continuous innovation". In: *Total Quality Management* 13.8 (2002), pp. 1051–1056. URL: https://doi.org/10.1080/09544120200000001.

[Com+08] Luca Compagna et al. "How to integrate legal requirements into a requirements engineering methodology for the development of security and privacy patterns". In: *Artificial Intelligence and Law* 17.1 (Nov. 2008), pp. 1–30.

[Com+95] SP88 Committee et al. "Batch Control Part 1: Models and Terminology". In: *ISA—The Instrumentation, Systems, and Automation Society, North Carolina* (1995).

[Com02] International Electrotechnical Commission. *IEC 61131: Programmable Controllers— Part 3: Programming languages*. Tech. rep. International Electrotechnical Commission, Feb. 2002.

[Con68] Melvin Conway. "How do Committees Invent?" In: *Datamation* 14 (1968), pp. 28–31.

[Con94] Sue A. Conger. *The New Software Engineering*. 1st. International Thomson Publishing, 1994. ISBN: 0534171435.

[Coo99] Alan Cooper. *The Inmates Are Running the Asylum*. Indianapolis, IN, USA: Macmillan Publishing Co., Inc., 1999. ISBN: 0672316498.

[Cor+14] Luis Fernando Cortés-Coy et al. "On Automatically Generating Commit Messages via Summarization of Source Code Changes". In: *14th International Working Conference on Source Code Analysis and Manipulation*. Victoria, BC, Canada: IEEE, 2014, pp. 275–284. ISBN: 978-1-4799-6148-1. https://doi.org/10.1109/SCAM.2014.14.

[Cor17] Symantec Corporation. *Internet security threat report* Apr. 2017. URL: https://www.symantec.com/content/dam/symantec/docs/reports/istr-22-2017-en.pdf.

[CS14] Scott Chacon and Ben Straub. *Pro Git: Everything you need to know about Git*. Ed. by Louise Corrigan. 2nd ed. New York, USA: Apress, 2014, p. 441. ISBN: 978-1-4842-0077-3. https://doi.org/10.1007/978-1-4842-0076-6.

[CS17] William A Carter and Daniel G Sofio. "CYBERSECURITY LEGISLATION AND CRITICAL INFRASTRUCTURE VULNERABILITIES". In: *Foundations of Homeland Security: Law and Policy* (2017), pp. 233–249.

[D B+13] D. Beyer et al. "Information Reuse for Multi-goal Reachability Analyses". In: *Proc. ESOP*. LNCS 7792. Springer, 2013, pp. 472–491.

[DA10] René David and H. Alla. *Discrete, continuous, and hybrid Petri Nets*. 2nd ed. Berlin and London: Springer, 2010. ISBN: 3642106692.

[DAm+08] Marco D'Ambros et al. "Analysing software repositories to understand software evolution". In: *Software evolution*. Springer, 2008, pp. 37–67.

[Dam+17] Kostadin Damevski et al. "Mining Sequences of Developer Interactions in Visual Studio for Usage Smells". In: *IEEE Transactions on Software Engineering* 43.4 (Apr. 2017), pp. 359–371. ISSN: 0098-5589. https://doi.org/10.1109/TSE.2016.2592905.

[Dav93] Alan M. Davis. *Software Requirements: Objects, Functions, and States*. Prentice-Hall, Inc., 1993. ISBN: 0-13-805763-X.

[DBB92] Joanne Bechta Dugan, Salvatore J Bavuso, and Mark A Boyd. "Dynamic fault-tree models for fault-tolerant computer systems". In: *IEEE Transactions on Reliability* 41.3 (1992), pp. 363–377.

[De +00] O De Smet et al. "Safe programming of PLC using formal verification methods".In: *Computer Science* 7 (2000), p. 8.

[De +09] B De Schutter et al. "Survey of modeling, analysis, and control of hybrid systems". In: *Handbook of Hybrid Systems Control–Theory, Tools, Applications* (2009), pp. 31–55.

[De +13] Rogério De Lemos et al. "Software Engineering for Self-Adaptive Systems: A Second Research Roadmap". In: *Software Engineering for Self-Adaptive Systems*. Ed. by Rogério De Lemos et al. Vol. 7475. Dagstuhl Seminar Proceedings. Springer, 2013, pp. 1–26. https://doi.org/10.1007/978-3-642-35813-5_1. URL: https://hal.inria.fr/inria00638157.

[DIS12] DIS/ISO. *Automation systems and integration - Key performance indicators for manufacturing operations management- Part 2: Definitions and descriptions*.2012.

[DMG07] Paul M Duvall, Steve Matyas, and Andrew Glover. *Continuous integration: improving software quality and reducing risk* Pearson Education, 2007.

[DMJ08] D. Ratiu, M. Feilkas, and J. Jürjens. "Extracting Domain Ontologies from Domain Specific APIs". In: *12th European Conference on Software Maintenance and*

Reengineering (CSMR 08). IEEE. 2008, pp. 203–212. http://dx.doi.org/10.1109/CSMR.2008.4493315.

[Dow97] Mark Dowson. "The Ariane 5 software failure". In: *ACM SIGSOFT Software Engineering Notes* 22.2 (1997), p.84.

[DP09] Salvatore Distefano and Antonio Puliafito. "Dependability Evaluation with Dynamic Reliability Block Diagrams and Dynamic Fault Trees". In: *IEEE Trans. Dependable Secur. Comput.* 6.1 (Jan. 2009), pp. 4–17. ISSN: 1545-5971. URL: http://dx.doi.org/10.1109/TDSC.2007.70242.

[DR13] Zoya Durdik and Ralf Reussner. "On the appropriate rationale for using design patterns and pattern documentation". In: *9th International ACM SIGSOFT Conference on the Quality of Software Architectures (QoSA'13)* Vancouver, BC,Canada: ACM, 2013, pp. 107–116. ISBN: 9781450321266. https://doi.org/10.1145/2465478.2465491.

[Dra+08] Rainer Drath et al. "AutomationML-the glue for seamless automation engineering".In: *Emerging Technologies and Factory Automation, 2008. ETFA 2008. IEEE International Conference on*. IEEE. 2008, pp. 616–623.

[Dur14] Zoya Durdik. "Architectural Design Decision Documentation with Reuse of Design Patterns". PhD thesis. Karlsruhe, Germany: Karlsruher Institut für Technologie (KIT), 2014. ISBN: 9783731502920. https://doi.org/10.5445/KSP/1000043807.

[Dut+06] Allen H. Dutoit et al. *Rationale Management in Software Engineering: Concepts and Techniques*. Springer, 2006.

[EAS14] A. Evesti, H. Abie, and R. Savola. "Security Measuring for Self-adaptive Security". In: *Proc. of the 2014 European Conf. on Software Architecture Workshops*. ECSAW '14. Vienna, Austria: ACM, 2014, 5:1–5:7. ISBN: 978-1-4503-2778-7. URL: http://doi.acm.org/10.1145/2642803.2642808.

[EBM11] Neil A Ernst, Alexander Borgida, and John Mylopoulos. "Requirements evolution drives software evolution". In: *International Workshop on Principles of Software Evolution and ERCIM Workshop on Software Evolution*. ACM. 2011, pp. 16–20.

[Ecl] Eclipse Foundation. *Eclipse Modeling Framework Project (EMF)*. URL: http://eclipse.org/modeling/emf/ (visited on 11/11/2018).

[Ecl18] Eclipse Foundation. Eclipse Modeling Framework (EMF). 2018. URL: http://www.eclipse.org/emf/.

[EGT10] Ilenia Epifani, Carlo Ghezzi, and Giordano Tamburrelli. "Change-point detection for black-box services". In: *Proceedings of the 18th ACM SIGSOFT Int. Symposium on Foundations of Software Engineering*. ACM, 2010, pp. 227–236.

[Ehr+06] H. Ehrig et al. *Fundamentals of Algebraic Graph Transformation (Monographs in Theoretical Computer Science. An EATCS Series)*. Secaucus, NJ, USA: Springer-Verlag New York, Inc., 2006. ISBN: 3540311874.

[Eic11] Jörn Eichler. "Lightweight Modeling and Analysis of Security Concepts". In: *Proc. of the Third Int. Conference on Engineering Secure Software and Systems. ESSoS*. Madrid, Spain: Springer, 2011, pp. 128–141. ISBN: 978-3-642-19124-4.

[EL02] David Evans and David Larochelle. "Improving Security using Extensible Lightweight Static Analysis". In: *IEEE Software* 19.1 (2002), pp. 42–51.

[Ema12] Pär Emanuelsson. "There is a strong need for diff/merge tools on models". In: *Softwaretechnik-Trends* 32.4 (2012), pp. 30–31.

[EN96] Steve Easterbrook and Bashar Nuseibeh. "Using ViewPoints for Inconsistency Management". In: *Software Eningeering Journal* 11.1 (1996), pp. 31–43.

[Epi+09] Ilenia Epifani et al. "Model Evolution by Run-time Parameter Adaptation". In: IEEE International Conference on Software Engineering. Washington, DC, USA: IEEE Computer Society, 2009, pp. 111–121. ISBN: 978-1-4244-3453-4. URL: http://dx.doi.org/10.1109/ICSE.2009.5070513.

[Erl00] Len Erlikh. "Leveraging legacy system dollars for e-business". In: *IT professional* 2.3 (2000), pp. 17–23.

[ES10] A. Evesti and S.P. Syväniemi. "Towards micro architecture for security adaptation". In: *4th European Conference on Software Architecture (ECSA 2010)*. Companion Volume. ACM, 2010, pp. 181–188.

[Esp+09] Huascar Espinoza et al. "Challenges in combining SysML and MARTE for modelbased design of embedded systems". In: *European Conference on Model Driven Architecture-Foundations and Applications*. Springer. 2009, pp. 98–113.

[EYZ09] Golnaz Elahi, Eric Yu, and Nicola Zannone. "A vulnerability-centric requirements engineering framework: analyzing security attacks, countermeasures, and requirements based on vulnerabilities". In: *Requirements Engineering* 15.1 (2009), pp. 41–62. https://doi.org/10.1007/s00766-009-0090-z.

[Fal+11] Davide Falessi et al. "Decision-Making Techniques for Software Architecture Design: A Comparative Survey". In: *ACM Computing Surveys* 43.4 (2011), pp. 1–28. ISSN: 03600300. https://doi.org/10.1145/1978802.1978812. URL: http://dl.acm.org/citation.cfm?doid=1978802.1978812.

[Fav04] Jean-Marie Favre. "Foundations of Model (Driven) (Reverse) Engineering – Episode I: Story of The Fidus Papyrus and the Solarus". In: *Dagstuhl post-proccedings*. 2004.

[FCÁ16] Felipe Febrero, Coral Calero, and M. Ángeles Moraga. "Software Reliability Modeling Based on ISO/IEC SQuaRE". In: *Inf. Softw. Technol.* 70.C (Feb. 2016), pp. 18–29. ISSN: 0950–5849. URL: https://doi.org/10.1016/j.infsof.2015.09.006.

[FE09] Stefan Fenz and Andreas Ekelhart. "Formalizing information security knowledge". In: *Proc. of the 4th Int. Symposium on Information, Computer, and Communications Security (ASIACCS)*. ACM, 2009, p. 183. ISBN: 9781605583945. https://doi.org/10.1145/1533057.1533084.

[Fel+14] Dennis Felsing et al. "Automating regression verification". In: *ACM/IEEE International Conference on Automated Software Engineering, ASE '14, Vasteras, Sweden - September 15 - 19, 2014*. Ed. by Ivica Crnkovic, Marsha Chechik, and Paul Grünbacher. ACM, 2014, pp. 349–360. ISBN: 978-1-4503-3013-8. URL: http://doi.acm.org/10.1145/2642937.2642987.

[Fel+15] Stefan Feldmann et al. "A Comparison of Inconsistency Management Approaches using a Mechatronic Manufacturing System Design Case Study". In: *IEEE International Conference on Automation Science and Engineering, CASE 2015, Gothenburg, Sweden, August 24–28, 2015*. IEEE, 2015, pp. 158–165. https://doi.org/10.1109/CoASE.2015.7294055.

[Fel+16] Stefan Feldmann et al. "A Comprehensive Approach for Managing Inter-Model Inconsistencies in Automated Production Systems Engineering". In: *12th IEEE International Conference on Automation Science and Engineering (CASE)*. Fort Worth, USA, Aug. 2016, pp. 1120–1127.

[Fel98] Christiane Fellbaum. *Word-Net: An Electronic Lexical Database*. MIT Press, 1998.

[Fer13] Eduardo Fernandez-Buglioni. *Security Patterns in Practice: Designing Secure Architectures Using Software Patterns*. 1st. Wiley Publishing, 2013. ISBN: 9781119998945.

[FGL15] A. Filieri, L. Grunske, and A. Leva. "Lightweight Adaptive Filtering for Efficient Learning and Updating of Probabilistic Models". In: *2015 IEEE/ACM 37th IEEE International Conference on Software Engineering*. Vol. 1. May 2015, pp. 200–211. https://doi.org/10.1109/ICSE.2015.41.

[FKV14] Stefan Feldmann, Konstantin Kernschmidt, and Birgit Vogel-Heuser. "Combining a SysML-based Modeling Approach and Semantic Technologies for Analyzing Change In uences in Manufacturing Plant Models". In: *47th CIRP Conference on Manufacturing Systems (CMS)*. Windsor, Canada, Apr. 2014, pp. 451–456. https://doi.org/10.1016/j.procir.2014.01.140.

[FL00] G. Frey and L. Litz. "Formal methods in PLC programming". In: *IEEE International Conference on Systems, Man, and Cybernetics*. 2000. https://doi.org/10.1109/ICSMC.2000.884356.

[FP18] Vincenzo Ferme and Cesare Pautasso. "A Declarative Approach for Performance Tests Execution in Continuous Software Development Environments". In: *Proceedings of the 2018 ACM/SPEC International Conference on Performance Engineering (ICPE '18)*. ACM, 2018, pp. 261–272.

[Fra+11] Timo Frank et al. "Dealing with non-functional requirements in distributed control systems engineering". In: *Emerging Technologies & Factory Automation (ETFA), 2011 IEEE 16th Conference on*. IEEE. 2011, pp. 1–4.

[Frö18] Michael Fröhlich. "User Classification based on Behavior Patterns in Mobile Applications". MA thesis. Technische Universität München, 2018.

[FS17] Brian Fitzgerald and Klaas-Jan Stol. "Continuous software engineering: A roadmap and agenda". In: *Journal of Systems and Software* 123 (2017), pp. 176–189. ISSN: 01641212. https://doi.org/10.1016/j.jss.2015.06.063.

[FW07] Sabrina Förtsch and Bernhard Westfechtel. "Differencing and merging of software diagrams state of the art and challenges". In: *Intl. Conf. Software and Data Technologies (ICSOFT)*. 2007.

[Gad+17] Daniele Gadler et al. "Mining Logs to Model the Use of a System". In: *2017 ACM/IEEE International Symposium on Empirical Software Engineering and Measurement (ESEM)*. 2017.

[Gam+95] Erich Gamma et al. *Design Patterns: Elements of Reusable Object-oriented Software*. Boston, MA, USA: Addison-Wesley Longman Publishing Co., Inc., 1995. ISBN: 0-201-63361-2.

[Gar+06] Hilke Garbe et al. "KARaCAs: Knowledge Acquisition with Repertory Grids and Formal Concept Analysis for Dialog System Construction". In: *Managing Knowledge in a World of Networks*. Ed. by Steffen Staab and Vojtěch Svátek. Berlin, Heidelberg: Springer Berlin Heidelberg, 2006, pp. 3–18. ISBN: 978-3-540-46365-8.

[Gar+09] D. Garlan et al. "Evolution styles: Foundations and tool support for software architecture evolution". In: *Software Architecture, WICSA/ECSA*. IEEE, 2009, pp. 131–140.

[Gär+14] Stefan Gärtner et al. "Maintaining requirements for long-living software systems by incorporating security knowledge". In: *2014 IEEE 22nd International Requirements Engineering Conference (RE)*. Aug. 2014, pp. 103–112. https://doi.org/10.1109/RE.2014.6912252.

[Gär16] Stefan Gärtner. "Heuristische und wissensbasierte Sicherheitsprüfung von Softwareentwicklungsartefakten basierend auf natürlichsprachlichen Informationen". PhD thesis. 2016.

[GBK14] Fabian Gorsler, Fabian Brosig, and Samuel Kounev. "Performance Queries for Architecture-Level Performance Models". In: *Proceedings of the 5th ACM/SPEC International Conference on Performance Engineering (ICPE 2014)*. ACM, Mar. 2014. https://doi.org/10.1145/2568088.2568100.

[Get+13] Sinem Getir et al. "Co-Evolution of Software Architecture and Fault Tree models: An Explorative Case Study on a Pick and Place Factory Automation System." In: *NiM-ALP @ MoDELS*. 2013, pp. 32–40.

[Get+15a] Sinem Getir et al. "CoWolf - A Generic Framework for Multi-view Co-evolution and Evaluation of Models". In: *Theory and Practice of Model Transformations - 8th International Conference, ICMT 2015, Held as Part of STAF 2015, L'Aquila, Italy, July 20–21, 2015. Proceedings*. 2015, pp. 34–40. URL: https://doi.org/10.1007/978-3-319-21155-8_3.

[Get+15b] Sinem Getir et al. "CoWolfA generic framework for multi-view co-evolution and evaluation of models". In: *International Conference on Theory and Practice of Model Transformations*. Springer. 2015, pp. 34–40.

[Get+18] Sinem Getir et al. "Supporting semi-automatic co-evolution of architecture and fault tree models". In: *Journal of Systems and Software* 142 (2018), pp. 115–135. ISSN: 0164–1212. https://doi.org/10.1016/j.jss.2018.04.001.

[GG08] Michael W Godfrey and Daniel M German. "The past, present, and future of software evolution". In: *Frontiers of Software Maintenance*, 2008. FoSM 2008. IEEE. 2008, pp. 129–138.

[Gig08] Gerd Gigerenzer. *Bauchentscheidungen: Die Intelligenz des Unbewussten und die Macht der Intuition*. Goldmann Verlag, 2008.

[Gla01] Robert L Glass. "Frequently forgotten fundamental facts about software engineering". In: *IEEE software* 3 (2001), pp. 112–110.

[Gol+15] Ursula Goltz et al. "Design for future: managed software evolution: The DFG priority programme for long-living software systems". In: Computer Science - Research and Development 30.3–4 (2015), pp. 321–331. ISSN: 18652042. URL: http://link.springer.com/article/10.1007/s00450-014-0273-9/fulltext.html.

[GP12] Gabriella Gigante and Domenico Pascarella. "Formal Methods in Avionic Software Certification: The DO-178C Perspective". In: *Proceedings of the 5th International Conference on Leveraging Applications of Formal Methods, Verification and Validation: Applications and Case Studies - Volume Part II*. ISoLA'12. Heraklion, Crete, Greece: Springer-Verlag, 2012, pp. 205–215. ISBN: 978-3-642-34031-4. URL: http://dx.doi.org/10.1007/978-3-642-34032-1_21.

[Gre+14] Alexander Grebhahn et al. "Experiments on Optimizing the Performance of Stencil Codes with SPL Conqueror". In: *Parallel Processing Letters* 24.3 (2014). URL: https://doi.org/10.1142/S0129626414410011.

[Gre+17] Alexander Grebhahn et al. "Performance-influence models of multigrid methods: A case study on triangular grids". In: *Concurrency and Computation: Practice and Experience* 29.17 (2017). URL: https://doi.org/10.1002/cpe.4057.

[GRK14] Sinem Getir, Michaela Rindt, and Timo Kehrer. "A Generic Framework for Analyzing Model Co-Evolution." In: *ME @ MoDELS*. 2014, pp. 12–21.

[Gro11] ARC Advisory Group. *PLC & PLC-based PAC Worldwide Outlook: Five year market analysis and technology forecast through 2016*. 2011.

[Gru08] Lars Grunske. "Specification patterns for probabilistic quality properties". In: *30th International Conference on Software Engineering (ICSE 2008)*. Ed. by Wilhelm Schäfer, Matthew B. Dwyer, and Volker Gruhn. ACM, 2008, pp. 31–40. https://doi.org/10.1145/1368088.1368094.

[Gru93] Thomas R Gruber. "A translation approach to portable ontology specifications". In: *Knowledge acquisition* 5.2 (1993), pp. 199–220.

[GS08] Benny Godlin and Ofer Strichman. "Inference Rules for Proving the Equivalence of Recursive Procedures". In: *Acta Inf.* 45.6 (2008), pp. 403–439.

[GS13] Benny Godlin and Ofer Strichman. "Regression Verification: Proving the Equivalence of similar Programs". In: *JSTVR 23.3* (2013). ISSN: 1099–1689. URL: http://dx.doi.org/10.1002/stvr.1472.

[Guo+13] Jianmei Guo et al. "Variability-aware Performance Prediction: A Statistical Learning Approach". In: *Proceedings of the 28th IEEE/ACM International Conference on Automated Software Engineering*. ASE'13. Silicon Valley, CA, USA: IEEE Press, 2013, pp. 301–311. ISBN: 978-1-4799-0215-6. URL: https://doi.org/10.1109/ASE.2013.6693089.

[GW07] Michael Gegick and Laurie Williams. "On the design of more secure softwareintensive systems by use of attack patterns". In: *Information and Software Technology* 49.4 (Apr. 2007), pp. 381–397.

[GW09] Minzhe Guo and Ju An Wang. "An Ontology-based Approach to Model Common Vulnerabilities and Exposures in Information Security". In: *ASEE Southest Section Conference*. 2009.

[HA05] J. Huselius and J. Andersson. "Model synthesis for real-time systems". In: *Ninth European Conference on Software Maintenance and Reengineering*. 2005, pp. 52–60.

[Hal+08] Charles B. Haley et al. "Security Requirements Engineering: A Framework for Representation and Analysis". In: *IEEE Trans. Software Eng.* 34.1 (2008), pp. 133–153.

[Has+13] Wilhelm Hasselbring et al. iObserve: *Integrated Observation and Modeling Techniques to Support Adaptation and Evolution of Software Systems*. Forschungsbericht. Kiel, Germany: Kiel University, Oct. 2013.

[Hau+13] Christopher Haubeck et al. "Keeping Pace with Changes - Towards Supporting Continuous Improvements and Extensive Updates in Production Automation Software". In: *Electronic Communications of the EASST* Volume 56 (2013).

[Hau+14a] C. Haubeck et al. "An active service-component architecture to enable self-awareness of evolving production systems". In: *IEEE International Conference on Emerging Technology and Factory Automation (ETFA)*. 2014. https://doi.org/10.1109/ETFA.2014.7005157.

[Hau+14b] Christopher Haubeck et al. "Interaction of Model-driven Engineering and Signal-based Online Monitoring of Production Systems". In: *IECON 2014 - 40th Annual Conference of the IEEE Industrial Electronics Society*. IEEE Industrial Electronics Society. IEEE Los Alamitos, Oct. 2014, pp. 2071–2077.

[Hau+17] Christopher Haubeck et al. "Evolution of Cyber-Physical Production Systems supported by community-enabled experiences". In: *IEEE 15th International Conference of Industrial Informatics INDIN 2017*. 2017.

[Hau+18a] C. Haubeck et al. "Step-based Evolution Support among Networked Production Automation Systems". In: *at-Automatisierungstechnik* (2018).

[Hau+18b] Christopher Haubeck et al. "A Knowledge Carrying Service-Component Architecture for Smart Cyber Physical Systems: An Example based on self-documenting production systems". In: *International Workshop on Engineering Service-Oriented Applications and Cloud Services, in conjunction with ICSOC*. 2018.

[Hau+18c] Christopher Haubeck et al. "Step-based Evolution Support among Networked Production Automation Systems". In: *AT - Automatisierungstechnik* (2018). In Press.

[Haw+13] Chris Hawblitzel et al. "Towards Modularly Comparing Programs Using Automated Theorem Provers". In: *Automated Deduction - CADE-24 - 24th International Conference on Automated Deduction, Lake Placid, NY, USA, June 9–14, 2013. Proceedings*. Ed. by Maria Paola Bonacina. Vol. 7898. Lecture Notes in Computer Science. Springer, 2013, pp. 282–299.

[HBK18a] Robert Heinrich, Kiana Busch, and Sandro Koch. "A Methodology for Domainspanning Change Impact Analysis". In: *Euromicro Conference on Software Engineering and Advanced Applications (SEAA)*. IEEE, 2018.

[HC98] Shi-Yu Huang and Kwant-Ting Cheng. *Formal Equivalence Checking and Design DeBugging*. Norwell, MA, USA: Kluwer Academic Publishers, 1998. ISBN: 079238184X.

[He13] Wu He. "A process-oriented framework for knowledge-centered support in field experience management". In: *7th International Conference on Knowledge Management in Organizations: Service and Cloud Computing*. Springer. 2013, pp. 59–67.

[Heg+17] Christoph Heger et al. "Application Performance Management: State of the Art and Challenges for the Future". In: *Proceedings of the 8th ACM/SPEC International Conference on Performance Engineering (ICPE '17)*. ACM, 2017, pp. 429–432.

[Hei+05] C. L. Heitmeyer et al. "Tools for constructing requirements specifications: The SCR toolset at the age of ten". In: *International Journal of Computer Systems Science and Engineering* 20.1 (2005), pp. 19–35.

[Hei+14] Robert Heinrich et al. "Integrating Run-Time Observations and Design Component Models for Cloud System Analysis". In: *Proceedings of the 9th Workshop on Models@run.time*. Vol. 1270. Workshop Proceedings. CEUR, Sept. 2014, pp. 41–46.

[Hei+15a] Robert Heinrich et al. "A Platform for Empirical Research on Information System Evolution". In: *27th International Conference on Software Engineering and Knowledge Engineering*. 2015, pp. 415–420.

[Hei+15b] Robert Heinrich et al. *The CoCoME Platform: A Research Note on Empirical Studies in Information System Evolution*. Tech. rep. 9–10. Karlsruhe Institute of Technology, 2015, pp. 1715–1720. URL: http://www.worldscientific.com/doi/10.1142/S0218194015710059.

[Hei+17a] Robert Heinrich et al. "Integrating business process simulation and information system simulation for performance prediction". In: *Software & Systems Modeling* 16.1 (2017), pp. 257–277. ISSN: 1619–1374. URL: https://doi.org/10.1007/s10270-015-0457-1.

[Hei+17b] Robert Heinrich et al. "Software Architecture for Big Data and the Cloud". In: Elsevier, 2017. Chap. An Architectural Model-Based Approach to Quality-aware DevOps in Cloud Applications, pp. 69–89.

[Hei+18a] Robert Heinrich et al. "Architecture-based change impact analysis in cross-disciplinary automated production systems". In: *Journal of Systems and Software* 146 (2018), pp. 167–185. ISSN: 0164–1212. DOI: https://doi.org/10.1016/j.jss.2018.08.058.

[Hei16] Robert Heinrich. "Architectural Run-time Models for Performance and Privacy Analysis in Dynamic Cloud Applications". In: *SIGMETRICS Perform. Eval. Rev.* 43.4 (Feb. 2016), pp. 13–22. ISSN: 0163–5999. URL: http://doi.acm.org/10.1145/2897356.2897359.

[Her+08a] Sebastian Herold et al. "The Common Component Modeling Example". In: Springer, 2008. Chap. CoCoME-The Common Component Modeling Example.

[Her+08b] Sebastian Herold et al. "CoCoME-the common component modeling example". In: *The Common Component Modeling Example*. Springer, 2008, pp. 16–53.

[Hes+14] Tom-Michael Hesse et al. "Semiautomatic security requirements engineering and evolution using decision documentation, heuristics, and user monitoring". In: *2014 IEEE 1st International Workshop on Evolving Security and Privacy Requirements Engineering (ESPRE)*. Karlskrona, Sweden: IEEE, Aug. 2014, pp. 1–6. https://doi.org/10.1109/espre.2014.6890520.

[Hes+15] Tom-Michael Hesse et al. "Documenting Implementation Decisions with Code Annotations". In: *27th International Conference on Software Engineering and Knowledge Engineering (SEKE'15)*. Pittsburgh, PA, USA, 2015, pp. 152–157. https://doi.org/10.18293/SEKE2015-084.

[Hes+16] Tom-Michael Hesse et al. "Documented decision-making strategies and decision knowledge in open source projects: An empirical study on Firefox issue reports". In: *Information and Software Technology* 79 (2016), pp. 36–51. ISSN: 09505849. https://doi.org/10.1016/j.infsof.2016.06.003.

[HJ07] L. Heitmeyer and R. D. Jeffords. "Applying a Formal Requirements Method to Three NASA Systems: Lessons Learned". In: *2007 IEEE Aerospace Conference*. Mar. 2007, pp. 1–10. https://doi.org/10.1109/AERO.2007.352764.

[HJ94] Hans Hansson and Bengt Jonsson. "A Logic for Reasoning about Time and Reliability". In: *Formal Aspects of Computing* 6.5 (1994), pp. 512–535.

[HK10] Markus Herrmannsdoerfer and Maximilian Koegel. "Towards a generic operation recorder for model evolution". In: *Proceedings of the 1st International Workshop on Model Comparison in Practice*. ACM. 2010, pp. 76–81.

[HKR16] Tom-Michael Hesse, Arthur Kuehlwein, and Tobias Roehm. "DecDoc: A Tool for Documenting Design Decisions Collaboratively and Incrementally". In: *1st International Workshop on Decision Making in Software ARCHitecture (MARCH 2016)*. Venice, Italy: IEEE, 2016, pp. 30–37. ISBN: 978-1-5090-2573-2. https://doi.org/10.1109/MARCH.2016.9.

[HKR18] Robert Heinrich, Sandro Koch, and Ralf Reussner. *The CoCoME Platform for Collaborative Empirical Research on Information System Evolution – Evolution scenario in the second founding period of SPP 1593*. Tech. rep. 2018,10; Karlsruhe Reports in Informatics. Karlsruhe Institute of Technology, 2018.

[HKW03] S. Hashtrudi Zad, R. H. Kwong, and W. M. Wonham. "Fault diagnosis in discreteevent systems: framework and model reduction". In: *IEEE Transactions on Automatic Control* 48.7 (2003), pp. 1199–1212. https://doi.org/10.1109/TAC.2003.814099.

[HL98] John D. Howard and Thomas A. Longstaff. *A common language for computer security incidents*. Tech. rep. Sandia National Laboratories, 1998.

[HLF18] Christopher Haubeck, Winfried Lamersdorf, and Alexander Fay. "A Knowledge Carrying Service-Component Architecture for Smart Cyber Physical Systems: An Example based on self-documenting production systems". In: *International Workshop on Engineering Service-Oriented Applications and Cloud Services, in conjunction with ICSOC*. 2018.

[Hol97] Gerard J Holzmann. "The model checker SPIN". In: *IEEE Transactions on software engineering* 23.5 (1997), pp. 279–295.

[Hou+10] Siv Hilde Houmb et al. "Eliciting security requirements and tracing them to design: an integration of Common Criteria, heuristics, and UMLsec". In: *Requirements Engineering* 15.1 (Mar. 2010), pp. 63–93. ISSN: 1432–010X. URL: https://doi.org/10.1007/s00766-009-0093-9.

[HP13] Tom-Michael Hesse and Barbara Paech. "Supporting the Collaborative Development of Requirements and Architecture Documentation". In: *3rd International Workshop on the Twin Peaks of Requirements and Architecture*. Rio de Janeiro, Brazil: IEEE, 2013, pp. 22–26. ISBN: 978-1-4799-0962-9. https://doi.org/10.1109/TwinPeaks-2.2013.6617355.

[HP16] Tom-Michael Hesse and Barbara Paech. "Documenting Relations Between Requirements and Design Decisions: A Case Study on Design Session Transcripts". In: *Requirements Engineering: Foundation for Software Quality: 22nd International Working Conference, REFSQ 2016*. Ed. by Maya Daneva and Oscar Pastor. Vol. LNCS 9619. Gothenburg, Sweden: Springer, 2016. Chap. Documentin, pp. 188–204. ISBN: 978-3-319-30282-9. https://doi.org/10.1007/978-3-319-30282-9_13.

[HR06] Wilhelm Hasselbring and Ralf Reussner. "Toward Trustworthy Software Systems". In: *Computer* 39 (Apr. 2006), pp. 91–92. ISSN: 0018–9162. URL: doi.ieeecomputersociety.org/10.1109/MC.2006.142.

[HR83] Theo Haerder and Andreas Reuter. "Principles of Transaction-oriented Database Recovery". In: *ACM Comput. Surv.* 15.4 (Dec. 1983), pp. 287–317. ISSN: 0360–0300. https://doi.org/10.1145/289.291.

[HRR16] Robert Heinrich, Kiana Rostami, and Ralf Reussner. *The CoCoME Platform for Collaborative Empirical Research on Information System Evolution*. Tech. rep. 2016,2; Karlsruhe Reports in Informatics. Karlsruhe Institute of Technology, Feb. 2016. URL: http://digbib.ubka.uni-karlsruhe.de/volltexte/1000052688.

[HRW09] Markus Herrmannsdoerfer, Daniel Ratiu, and Guido Wachsmuth. "Language evolution in practice: The history of GMF". In: *International Conference on Software Language Engineering*. Springer. 2009, pp. 3–22.

[HSD07] Almut Herzog, Nahid Shahmehri, and Claudiu Duma. "An Ontology of Information Security". In: *IJISP* 1.4 (2007), pp. 1–23.

[Hub+14] Nikolaus Huber et al. "Modeling run-time adaptation at the system architecture level in dynamic service-oriented environments". In: *Service Oriented Computing and Applications* 8.1 (2014), pp. 73–89.

[Hub+17] Nikolaus Huber et al. "Model-Based Self-Aware Performance and Resource Management Using the Descartes Modeling Language". In: *IEEE Trans. Software Eng.* 43.5 (2017), pp. 432–452.

[Hub+96] Franz Huber et al. "AutoFocus | A tool for distributed systems specification". In: *Formal Techniques in Real-Time and Fault-Tolerant Systems*. Ed. by Bengt Jonsson and Joachim Parrow. Berlin, Heidelberg: Springer Berlin Heidelberg, 1996, pp. 467–470. ISBN: 978-3-540-70653-3.

[Hub+98] Franz Huber et al. "Tool Supported Specification and Simulation of Distributed Systems". In: *International Symposium on Software Engineering for Parallel and Distributed Systems, PDSE 1998, Kyoto, Japan, April 20–21, 1998*. IEEE Computer Society, 1998, p. 155. ISBN: 0-8186-8467-4. URL: https://doi.org/10.1109/PDSE.1998.668174.

[Hum09] Benjamin Hummel. "A Semantic Model for Computer-Based Spatio-temporal Systems". In: *16th Annual IEEE International Conference and Workshop on the Engineering of Computer Based Systems, ECBS 2009, San Francisco, California, USA, 14-16 April 2009*. IEEE Computer Society, 2009, pp. 156–165. ISBN: 978-0-7695-3602-6. URL: https://doi.org/10.1109/ECBS.2009.19

[Hus+06] J. Huselius et al. "Automatic Generation and Validation of Models of Legacy Software". In: *IEEE International Conference on Embedded and Real-Time Computing Systems and Applications*. 2006. https://doi.org/10.1109/RTCSA.2006.19.

[IEC05] IEC. IEC61508: *Functional safety of electrical/electronic/programmable electronic safety-related systems*. Tech. rep. International Electrotechnical Commission, 2005.

[IEE90] IEEE Standard 610.12. *Standard Glossary of Software Engineering Terminology*. Institute of Electrical and Electronics Engineers, 1990. https://doi.org/10.1109/IEEESTD.1990.101064.

[II11] ISO and IEC. ISO/IEC 25010: *Systems and software engineering - Systems and software Quality Requirements and Evaluation (SQuaRE) - System and software quality models*. Norm. Mar. 2011.

[Int09] International Electrotechnical Commission. *Programmable Logic Controllers – Part 3: Programming Languages*. 2009.

[Int17] International Information System Security Certification Consortium ISC^2. *2017 Global Information Security Workforce Study*. 2017. URL: https://iamcybersafe.org/wp-content/uploads/2017/06/Europe-GISWS-Report.pdf.

[Int18] International Requirements Engineering Board. The CPRE Glossary. 2018. URL: https://www.ireb.org/en/cpre/cpre-glossary/.

[Ise06] Rolf Isermann. *Fault-Diagnosis Systems: An Introduction from Fault Detection to Fault Tolerance*. Berlin and Heidelberg: Springer-Verlag Berlin Heidelberg, 2006. ISBN: 3540241124. URL: http://dx.doi.org/10.1007/3-540-30368-5.

[ISO10] ISO/IEC. *25010 - Systems and software: Engineering, Quality Requirements and Evaluation, Quality Models*. Tech. rep. 2010.

[ISO11a] ISO. *Road vehicles – Functional safety*. Norm. 2011.

[ISO11b] IEC ISO. *Systems and software engineering — Architecture description*. Standard. International Organization for Standardization, 2011. URL: https://www.iso.org/standard/50508.html.

[J B+15] J. Bürger et al. "Restoring Security of Long-Living Systems by Co-Evolution". In: *39th Annual IEEE Computer Software and Applications Conf. (COMPSAC 2015)*. 6 pp. IEEE Computer Soc. 2015.

[Jac63] James R. Jackson. "Jobshop-like Queueing Systems". In: *Management Science* 10.1 (1963), pp. 131–142.

[Jäg+11] Tobias Jäger et al. "Mining technical dependencies throughout engineering process knowledge". In: *Emerging Technologies & Factory Automation (ETFA), 2011 IEEE 16th Conference on*. IEEE. 2011, pp. 1–7.

[JB05] Anton G J Jansen and Jan Bosch. "Software Architecture as a Set of Architectural Design Decisions". In: *5th Working IEEE/IFIP Conference on Software Architecture (WICSA'05)*. Pittsburgh, PA, USA: IEEE, 2005, pp. 109–120. ISBN: 0-7695-2548-2. https://doi.org/10.1109/WICSA.2005.61.

[JC97] Jay J. Jiang and David W. Conrath. "Semantic similarity based on corpus statistics and lexical taxonomy". In: *Proceedings of International Conference Research on Computational Linguistics (ROCLING)* (1997).

[Jen94] Angus Jenkinson. "Beyond segmentation". In: *Journal of targeting, measurement and analysis for marketing* 3.1 (1994), pp. 60–72.

[JG12] Natalia Juristo and Omar S. Gómez. "Empirical Software Engineering and Verification". In: ed. by Bertrand Meyer and Martin Nordio. Berlin, Heidelberg: Springer-Verlag, 2012. Chap. Replication of Software Engineering Experiments, pp. 60–88. ISBN: 978-3-642-25230-3. URL: http://dl.acm.org/citation.cfm?id=2184075.2184077.

[JHF12] Martin Fagereng Johansen, Oystein Haugen, and Franck Fleurey. "An Algorithm for Generating T-wise Covering Arrays from Large Feature Models". In: *Proceedings of the 16th International Software Product Line Conference - Volume 1*. SPLC '12. Salvador, Brazil: ACM, 2012, pp. 46–55. ISBN: 978-1-4503-1094-9. URL: http://doi.acm.org/10.1145/2362536.2362547.

[JHH16] Reiner Jung, Robert Heinrich, and Wilhelm Hasselbring. "GECO: A Generator Composition Approach for Aspect-Oriented DSLs". In: *Theory and Practice of Model Transformations*. Vol. 9765. Lecture Notes in Computer Science. Springer International Publishing, July 2016, pp. 141–156. https://doi.org/10.1007/978-3-319-42064-6_10.

[JHS13] Reiner Jung, Robert Heinrich, and Eric Schmieders. "Model-driven Instrumentation with Kieker and Palladio to forecast Dynamic Applications". In: *Proceedings Symposium on Software Performance: Joint Kieker/Palladio Days 2013 (KPDAYS 2013)*. Vol. 1083. CEUR Workshop Proceedings. CEUR, Nov. 2013, pp. 99–108. URL: http://eprints.uni-kiel.de/22655/.

[JHS99] Changduk Jung, Ingoo Han, and Bomil Suh. "Risk analysis for electronic commerce using case-based reasoning". In: *International Journal of Intelligent Systems in Accounting, Finance & Management* 8.1 (Mar. 1999), pp. 61–73. ISSN: 1055-615X. https://doi.org/10.1002/(SICI)1099-1174(199903)8:1<61::AID-ISAF156>3.0.CO;2-6.

[JJS15] J. Bürger, J. Jürjens, and S.Wenzel. "Restoring Security of Evolving Software Models using Graph-Transformation". In: *Int. Journal on Software Tools for Technology Transfer (STTT)* (2015). Springer Online First. https://doi.org/10.1007/s1000901403648.

[Joh+17a] Jan Ole Johanssen et al. "Towards a Systematic Approach to Integrate Usage and Decision Knowledge in Continuous Software Engineering". In: *Proceedings of the 2nd Workshop on Continuous Software Engineering co-located with Software Engineering (SE 2017)*. CSE 2017. Hannover, Germany, 2017, pp. 7–11.

[Joh+17b] Jan Ole Johanssen et al. "Towards the Visualization of Usage and Decision Knowledge in Continuous Software Engineering". In: *5th IEEE Working Conference on Software Visualization (VISSOFT 2017)*. Shanghai, China, 2017, pp. 104–108. https://doi.org/10.1109/VISSOFT.2017.18.

[Joh+18a] Jan Ole Johanssen, Anja Kleebaum, Bernd Bruegge, Barbara Paech. "Feature Crumbs: Adapting Usage Monitoring to Continuous Software Engineering". In: *Product-Focused Software Process Improvement*. Ed. by Marco Kuhrmann, Kurt Schneider, Dietmar Pfahl, Sousuke Amasaki, Marcus Ciolkowski, Regina Hebig, Paolo Tell, Jil Klünder, Steffen Küpper. Springer International Publishing, Cham, 2018, pp. 263–271. ISBN: 978-3-030-03673-7. https://doi.org/10.1007/978-3-030-03673-7_19.

[Joh+18b] Jan Ole Johanssen et al. "Practitioners' Eye on Continuous Software Engineering: An Interview Study". In: *Proceedings of the 2018 International Conference on Software and System Process*. ICSSP '18. Gothenburg, Sweden: ACM, 2018, pp. 41–50. ISBN: 978-1-4503-6459-1. https://doi.org/10.1145/3202710.3203150.

[Joh18] Jan Ole Johanssen. "Continuous User Understanding for the Evolution of Interactive Systems". In: *Proceedings of the ACM SIGCHI Symposium on Engineering Interactive Computing Systems*. EICS '18. Paris, France: ACM, 2018, 15:1–15:6. ISBN: 978-1-4503-5897-2. https://doi.org/10.1145/3220134.3220149.

[JT10] Karl Heinz John and Michael Tiegelkamp. IEC 61131-3: *programming industrial automation systems: concepts and programming languages, requirements for pro-*

gramming systems, decision-making aids. Springer Science & Business Media, 2010.

[Jür01] Jan Jürjens. "Modelling Audit Security for Smart-Cart Payment Schemes with UMLSEC". In: *Trusted Information: The New Decade Challenge, IFIP TC11 Sixteenth Annual Working Conference on Information Security (IFIP/Sec'01), June 11–13, 2001, Paris, France*. Ed. by Michel Dupuy and Pierre Paradinas. Vol. 193. IFIP Conference Proceedings. Kluwer, 2001, pp. 93–108. ISBN: 0-7923-7389-8. URL: https://doi.org/10.1007/0-306-46998-7_7.

[Jür05] J. Jürjens. *Secure Systems Development with UML*. Springer, 2005.

[JW01] Jan Jürjens and Guido Wimmel. "Formally Testing Fail-Safety of Electronic Purse Protocols". In: *16th IEEE International Conference on Automated Software Engineering (ASE 2001), 26-29 November 2001, Coronado Island, San Diego, CA, USA*. IEEE Computer Society, 2001, pp. 408–411. ISBN: 0-7695-1426-X. URL: https://doi.org/10.1109/ASE.2001.989840.

[JW16] Reiner Jung and ChristianWulf. "Advanced Typing for the Kieker Instrumentation Languages". In: *Symposium on Software Performance 2016*. Nov. 2016. URL: http://eprints.uni-kiel.de/34626/.

[KA03] B. Kirwan and L.K. Ainsworth. *A Guide To Task Analysis: The Task Analysis Working Group*. Taylor & Francis, 2003. ISBN: 9780203221457.

[KAH17] Timo Kehrer, Abdullah Alshanqiti, and Reiko Heckel. "Automatic Inference of Rule-Based Specifications of Complex In-place Model Transformations". In: *International Conference on Theory and Practice of Model Transformations*. Springer. 2017, pp. 92–107.

[Kan+90a] K. C. Kang et al. *Feature-Oriented Domain Analysis (FODA) Feasibility Study*. Tech. rep. Carnegie-Mellon Univ Pittsburgh Pa Software Engineering Inst, 1990.

[Kan+90b] Kyo Kang et al. *Feature-Oriented Domain Analysis (FODA) Feasibility Study*. Tech. rep. CMU/SEI-90-TR-021. Pittsburgh, PA: Software Engineering Institute, Carnegie Mellon University, 1990. URL: http://resources.sei.cmu.edu/library/asset-view.cfm?AssetID=11231.

[Kap+12] Gerti Kappel et al. "Model transformation by-example: a survey of the first wave". In: *Conceptual Modelling and Its Theoretical Foundations*. Springer, 2012, pp. 197–215.

[Kar+06] Maria Karyda et al. "An Ontology for Secure e-Government Applications". In: *Proceedings of the First International Conference on Availability, Reliability and Security*. IEEE, 2006, pp. 1033–1037. ISBN: 0-7695-2567-9. https://doi.org/10.1109/ARES.2006.28.

[Käas+11] C. Kästner et al. "Variability-aware Parsing in the Presence of Lexical Macros and Conditional Compilation". In: *Proceedings International Conference on Object Oriented Programming Systems Languages and Applications*. OOPSLA '11. 2011, pp. 805–824.

[KB17] Stephan Krusche and Bernd Bruegge. "CSEPM - A Continuous Software Engineering Process Metamodel". In: *2017 IEEE/ACM 3rd International Workshop on Rapid Continuous Software Engineering (RCoSE)*. Buenos Aires, Argentina: IEEE, May 2017, pp. 2–8. ISBN: 978-1-5386-0428-1. https://doi.org/10.1109/RCoSE.2017.6.

[KBL13] Max E. Kramer, Erik Burger, and Michael Langhammer. "View-Centric Engineering with Synchronized Heterogeneous Models". In: *Proceedings of the 1st Workshop on View-Based, Aspect-Oriented and Orthographic Software Modelling*. VAO '13. Montpellier, France: ACM, 2013, 5:1–5:6. ISBN: 978-1-4503-2070-2. https://doi.org/10.1145/2489861.2489864.

[KC03] J. O. Kephart and D. M. Chess. "The vision of autonomic computing". In: *Computer* 36.1 (Jan. 2003), pp. 41–50. ISSN: 0018–9162. https://doi.org/10.1109/MC.2003.1160055.

[KC07] Barbara Kitchenham and Stuart Charters. *Guidelines for performing systematic literature reviews in software engineering*. Tech. rep. Technical report, EBSE Technical Report EBSE-2007-01, 2007.

[KCD09] Philippe Kruchten, Rafael Capilla, and Juan Carlos Dueñas. "The Decision View's Role in Software Architecture Practice". In: *IEEE Software* 26.2 (2009), pp. 36–42. ISSN: 0740–7459. https://doi.org/10.1109/MS.2009.52.

[KCM07] Huzefa Kagdi, Michael L Collard, and Jonathan I Maletic. "A survey and taxonomy of approaches for mining software repositories in the context of software evolution". In: *Journal of software maintenance and evolution: Research and practice* 19.2 (2007), pp. 77–131.

[KE02] Andreas Kuehlmann and Cornelis A.J. van Eijk. "Combinational and Sequential Equivalence Checking". English. In: *Logic Synthesis and Verification*. Springer, 2002. ISBN: 978-1-4613-5253-2. URL: http://dx.doi.org/10.1007/978-1-4615-0817-5_13.

[Keh+12a] Timo Kehrer et al. "Adaptability of model comparison tools". In: *IEEE/ACM International Conference on Automated Software Engineering (ASE), Essen, Germany*. ACM, 2012, pp. 306–309.

[Keh+12b] Timo Kehrer et al. "Understanding model evolution through semantically lifting model diffierences with SiLift". In: *28th IEEE International Conference on Software Maintenance (ICSM), Trento, Italy*. IEEE. 2012, pp. 638–641.

[Keh+13a] Timo Kehrer et al. "Detection of High-Level Changes in Evolving Java Software". In: *Softwaretechnik-Trends* 33.2 (2013).

[Keh+13b] Timo Kehrer et al. "Generating Edit Operations for Profiled UML Models". In: *Proceedings of the Workshop on Models and Evolution (ME) co-located with ACM/IEEE 16th International Conference on Model Driven Engineering Languages and Systems (MoDELS), Miami, FL, USA*. Vol. 1090. CEURWorkshop Proceedings. 2013, pp. 30–39.

[Keh+16] Timo Kehrer et al. "Automatically deriving the specification of model editing operations from meta-models". In: *International Conference on Theory and Practice of Model Transformations*. Springer. 2016, pp. 173–188.

[Keh15] Timo Kehrer. "Calculation and propagation of model changes based on user-level edit operations". In: *A Foundation for Version and Variant Management in Modeldriven Engineering (Doctoral Dissertation, Universität Siegen). Siegen, Germany* (2015).

[Kel77] Robert M Keller. *Denotational models for parallel programs with indeterminate operators*. University of Utah, Department of Computer Science, 1977.

[KG15] Marco Konersmann and Michael Goedicke. "Integrating Protocol Contracts with Program Code – A Leightweight Approach for Applied Behaviour Models that Respect Their Execution Context". In: *Behavior Modeling – Foundations and Applications*. Ed. by Ella Roubtsova et al. Springer International Publishing, 2015, pp. 197–219. ISBN: 978-3-319-21912-7. https://doi.org/10.1007/978-3-319-21912-7_8.

[KGT16] Stefan Kögel, Raffaela Groner, and Matthias Tichy. "Automatic Change Recommendation of Models and Meta Models Based on Change Histories." In: *ME at MODELS*. 2016, pp. 14–19.

[KH16] Marco Konersmann and Jens Holschbach. "Automatic Synchronization of Allocation Models with Running Software". In: *Softwaretechnik-Trends* 36.4 (Nov. 2016), pp. 28–29. ISSN: 0720–8928. URL: http://pi.informatik.uni-siegen.de/stt/36_4/./01_Fachgruppenberichte/SSP2016/ssp-stt/24-Automatic_Synchronization_of_Allocation_Models_with_Running_Software.pdf.

[KKR14] Timo Kehrer, Udo Kelter, and Dennis Reuling. "Workspace updates of visual models". In: *Proceedings of the 29th ACM/IEEE International Conference on Automated Software Engineering, Vasteras, Sweden*. ASE '14. New York, NY, USA: ACM, 2014, pp. 827–830. ISBN: 978-1-4503-3013-8. https://doi.org/10.1145/2642937.2648623.

[KKT11] Timo Kehrer, Udo Kelter, and Gabriele Taentzer. "A rule-based approach to the semantic lifting of model differences in the context of model versioning". In: *26th IEEE/ACM International Conference on Automated Software Engineering (ASE),*

Lawrence, KS, USA. ASE '11. Washington, DC, USA: IEEE Computer Society, 2011, pp. 163–172. ISBN: 978-1-4577-1638-6. https://doi.org/10.1109/ASE.2011.6100050.

[KKT12] Timo Kehrer, Udo Kelter, and Gabriele Taentzer. "Integrating the Specification and Recognition of Changes in Models". In: *Softwaretechnik-Trends* 32.2 (2012), pp. 41–42.

[KKT13] Timo Kehrer, Udo Kelter, and Gabriele Taentzer. "Consistency-preserving edit scripts in model versioning". In: *2013 IEEE/ACM 28th International Conference on Automated Software Engineering (ASE)*. Nov. 2013, pp. 191–201. https://doi.org/10.1109/ASE.2013.6693079.

[KKT14] Timo Kehrer, Udo Kelter, and Gabriele Taentzer. "Propagation of Software Model Changes in the Context of Industrial Plant Automation". In: *Automatisierungstechnik* 62.11 (2014), pp. 803–814.

[KKU16] Moritz Kiefer, Vladimir Klebanov, and Mattias Ulbrich. "Relational Program Reasoning Using Compiler IR". In: *Verified Software. Theories, Tools, and Experiments - 8th International Conference, VSTTE 2016, Toronto, ON, Canada, July 17–18, 2016, Revised Selected Papers*. Ed. by Sandrine Blazy and Marsha Chechik. Vol. 9971. Lecture Notes in Computer Science. 2016, pp. 149–165. ISBN: 978-3-319-48868-4. URL: https://doi.org/10.1007/978-3-319-48869-1_12.

[KKU17] Moritz Kiefer, Vladimir Klebanov, and Mattias Ulbrich. "Relational Program Reasoning Using Compiler IR – Combining Static Verification and Dynamic Analysis". In: *Journal of Automated Reasoning* (2017). To appear.

[Kle+18a] Anja Kleebaum et al. "Decision knowledge triggers in continuous software engineering". In: *Proceedings of the 4th International Workshop on Rapid Continuous Software Engineering - RCoSE '18*. Gotheburg, Sweden: ACM Press, 2018, pp. 23–26. https://doi.org/10.1145/3194760.3194765.

[Kle+18b] Anja Kleebaum et al. "Tool Support for Decision and Usage Knowledge in Continuous Software Engineering". In: *3rd Workshop on Continuous Software Engineering*. 2018, pp. 74–77. https://doi.org/10.11588/heidok.00024186.

[KMR13] Tobias Kuschke, Patrick Mäder, and Patrick Rempel. "Recommending auto-completions for software modeling activities". In: *International Conference on Model Driven Engineering Languages and Systems*. Springer. 2013, pp. 170–186.

[KNP04] Marta Z. Kwiatkowska, Gethin Norman, and David Parker. "Probabilistic symbolic model checking with PRISM: a hybrid approach". In: *STTT* 6.2 (2004), pp. 128–142.

[KNP11] M. Kwiatkowska, G. Norman, and D. Parker. "PRISM 4.0: Verification of Probabilistic Real-time Systems". In: *Proc. 23rd International Conference on Computer Aided Verification (CAV'11)*. Ed. by G. Gopalakrishnan and S. Qadeer. Vol. 6806. LNCS. Springer, 2011, pp. 585–591.

[Koc+19] Paul Kocher et al. "Spectre Attacks: Exploiting Speculative Execution". In: *40th IEEE Symposium on Security and Privacy (S&P'19)*. 2019.

[Koc17] Sandro Koch. "Automatische Vorhersage von Änderungsausbreitungen am Beispiel von Automatisierungssystemen". MA thesis. Karlsruhe Institute of Technology (KIT), 2017.

[Kög17] Stefan Kögel. "Recommender system for model driven software development". In: *Proceedings of the 2017 11th Joint Meeting on Foundations of Software Engineering*. ACM. 2017, pp. 1026–1029.

[Kol+09] Dimitrios S Kolovos et al. "Different models for model matching: An analysis of approaches to support model differencing". In: *ICSE Workshop on Comparison and Versioning of Software Models (CVSM)*. IEEE. 2009, pp. 1–6.

[Kon+13] Marco Konersmann et al. "Towards Architecture-centric Evolution of Long-living Systems (the ADVERT Approach)". In: *9th International ACM Sigsoft Conference on Quality of Software Architectures*. 2013, pp. 163–168. ISBN: 978-1-4503-2126-6. https://doi.org/10.1145/2465478.2465496.

[Kon14] Marco Konersmann. "Rapidly Locating and Understanding Errors Using Runtime Monitoring of Architecture-carrying Code". In: *Proceedings of the 1st International*

Workshop on Rapid Continuous Software Engineering. RCoSE 2014. Hyderabad, India: ACM, 2014, pp. 20–25. ISBN: 978-1-4503-2856-2. https://doi.org/10.1145/2593812.2593814.

[Kon16] Marco Konersmann. "A Process for Explicitly Integrated Software Architecture". In: *Softwaretechnik-Trends* 36.2 (2016). ISSN: 0720–8928. URL: http://pi.informatik.uni-siegen.de/stt/36_2/01_Fachgruppenberichte/WSRE2016/WSRE2016_24_DFF_2016_paper_4.pdf.

[Kon18] Marco Konersmann. "Explicitly Integrated Architecture - An Approach for Integrating Software Architecture Model Information with Program Code". PhD thesis. University of Duisburg-Essen, Mar. 2018.

[Kow+15] Matthias Kowal et al. "Scaling Size and Parameter Spaces in Variability-Aware Software Performance Models (T)". In: *Proceedings of the 2015 30th IEEE/ACM International Conference on Automated Software Engineering (ASE)*. ASE '15. Washington, DC, USA: IEEE Computer Society, 2015, pp. 407–417. ISBN: 978-1-5090-0025-8. URL: https://doi.org/10.1109/ASE.2015.16.

[KPP06] Dimitrios Kolovos, Richard F Paige, and Fiona AC Polack. "Model comparison: a foundation for model composition and model transformation testing". In: *Proceedings of the 2006 international workshop on Global integrated model management. ACM*. 2006.

[KR07] Someswar Kesh and Pauline Ratnasingam. "A knowledge architecture for IT security". In: *Communications of the ACM* 50.7 (2007).

[Kru+14] Stephan Krusche et al. "Rugby: An Agile Process Model Based on Continuous Delivery". In: *Proceedings of the 1st International Workshop on Rapid Continuous Software Engineering (RCoSE 2014)* (2014), pp. 42–50. https://doi.org/10.1145/2593812.2593818.

[Kru03] Philippe Kruchten. The Rational Unified Process: *An Introduction*. 3rd ed. Boston, MA, USA: Addison-Wesley Longman Publishing Co., Inc., 2003. ISBN: 0321197704.

[KRU17] Vladimir Klebanov, Philipp Rümmer, and Mattias Ulbrich. "Automating Regression Verification of Pointer Programs by Predicate Abstraction". In: *Journal on Formal Methods in System Design* (Aug. 2017). https://doi.org/10.1007/s10703-017-0293-8.

[KST14] Matthias Kowal, Ina Schaefer, and Mirco Tribastone. "Family-Based Performance Analysis of Variant-Rich Software Systems". In: *International Conference on Fundamental Approaches to Software Engineering*. Vol. 8411. Lecture Notes in Computer Science. Springer Berlin Heidelberg, 2014.

[Kub89] Peter Kubat. "Assessing reliability of modular software". In: *Operations research letters* 8.1 (1989), pp. 35–41.

[Kü08] Jochen M Küster et al. "Detecting and resolving process model differences in the absence of a change log". In: *International Conference on Business Process Management*. Springer. 2008, pp. 244–260.

[KV13] Konstantin Kernschmidt and Birgit Vogel-Heuser. "An interdisciplinary SysML based modeling approach for analyzing change in uences in production plants to support the engineering". In: *2013 IEEE International Conference on Automation Science and Engineering, CASE 2013, Madison, WI, USA, August 17–20, 2013*. IEEE, 2013, pp. 1113–1118. URL: https://doi.org/10.1109/CoASE.2013.6654030.

[KVD01] Xenophon Koufteros, Mark Vonderembse, and William Doll. "Concurrent engineering and its consequences". In: *Journal of Operations Management* 19.1 (2001), pp. 97–115. ISSN: 0272–6963. http://dx.doi.org/10.1016/S0272-6963(00)00048-6. URL: http://www.sciencedirect.com/science/article/pii/S0272696300000486.

[KVF04] Uwe Katzke, Birgit Vogel-Heuser, and Katja Fischer. "Analysis and state of the art of modules in industrial automation". In: *Automatisierungstechnische Praxis (atp)* 46.1 (2004), pp. 23–31.

[KWC98] Rick Kazman, Steven G. Woods, and S. Jeromy Carrière. "Requirements for Integrating Software Architecture and Reengineering Models: CORUM II". In:

Proceedings of the Working Conference on Reverse Engineering (WCRE'98). WCRE '98. Washington, DC, USA: IEEE Computer Society, 1998, pp. 154–. ISBN: 0-8186-8967-6. URL: http://dl.acm.org/citation.cfm?id=832305.837030.

[KWN05] Udo Kelter, Jürgen Wehren, and Jörg Niere. "A Generic Difference Algorithm for UML Models." In: *Proc. Software Engineering*. LNI 64, GI. 2005, pp. 105–116.

[KZC12] Baris Can Cengiz Kasikci, Cristian Zamfir, and George Candea. "CoRD: A collaborative framework for distributed data race detection". In: *Hot Topics in System Dependability*. EPFL-CONF-181200. 2012.

[L M+10] L. Montrieux et al. "Tool Support for Code Generation from a UMLsec Property". In: *25th IEEE/ACM Int. Conf. on Automated Software Eng. (ASE'10)*. 2010. http://doi.acm.org/10.1145/1858996.1859074.

[Lad+13a] J. Ladiges et al. "Evolution of Production Facilities and its Impact on Non-Functional Requirements". In: *IEEE International Conference on Industrial Informatics (INDIN)*. 2013.

[Lad+13b] Jan Ladiges et al. "Operationalized Definitions of Non-Functional Requirements on Automated Production Facilities to Measure Evolution Effects with an Automation System". In: *IEEE International Conference on Emerging Technologies and Factory Automation (ETFA)*. 2013.

[Lad+14a] J. Ladiges et al. "Semi-automated decision making support for undocumented evolutionary changes". In: Workshop Software-Reengineering & Evolution (WSRE). 2014. URL: http://fg-sre.gi.de/fileadmin/gliederungen/fg-sre/wsre2014/wsre_dff_2014_proceedings.pdf.

[Lad+14b] Jan Ladiges et al. "Evolution Management of Production Facilities by Semi-Automated Requirement Verification". In: *at - Automatisierungstechnik*. Vol. 62. 11. Berlin, Oct. 2014, pp. 781–793.

[Lad+15a] J. Ladiges et al. "Learning Behaviour Models of Discrete Event Production Systems from Observing Input/Output Signals". In: *IFAC/IEEE/IFIP/IFORS Symposium on Information Control Problems in Manufacturing (INCOM)*. 2015.

[Lad+15b] J. Ladiges et al. "Supporting Commissioning of Production Plants by Model-Based Testing and Model Learning". In: *International Symposium on Industrial Electronics (ISIE)*. 2015.

[Lad+15c] Jan Ladiges et al. "Learning Material Flow Models for Manufacturing Plants from Data Traces". In: *IEEE International Conference on Industrial Informatics (INDIN)*. 2015.

[Lai+02] C.D. Lai et al. "A model for availability analysis of distributed software/hardware systems". In: *Information and Software Technology* 44.6 (2002), pp. 343–350. ISSN: 0950–5849. https://doi.org/10.1016/S0950-5849(02)00007-1.

[Lam+99a] S. Lampérière-Couffin et al. "Formal Validation of PLC programs: a survey". In: *European Control Conference 1999, ECC'99*. IEEE. Sept. 1999, pp. 2170–2175.

[Lam+99b] S. Lampérière-Couffin et al. "Formal Validation of PLC programs: a survey". In: *ECC*. 1999.

[Lan+09] Agnes Lanusse et al. "Papyrus UML: an open source toolset for MDA". In: *Proc. of the Fifth European Conference on Model-Driven Architecture Foundations and Applications (ECMDA-FA 2009)*. 2009, pp. 1–4.

[Lan+12] Philip Langer et al. "EMF Proles: A Lightweight Extension Approach for EMF Models." In: *Journal of Object Technology* 11.1 (2012), pp. 1–29.

[Lan+13] Philip Langer et al. "A posteriori operation detection in evolving software models". In: *Journal of Systems and Software* 86.2 (2013), pp. 551–566.

[Lan+16] Michael Langhammer et al. "Automated Extraction of Rich Software Models from Limited System Information". In: *2016 13th Working IEEE/IFIP Conference on Software Architecture (WICSA)*. Apr. 2016, pp. 99–108. https://doi.org/10.1109/WICSA.2016.35.

[Lan17] Michael Langhammer. "Automated Coevolution of Source Code and Software Architecture Models". PhD thesis. Karlsruhe, Germany: Karlsruhe Institute of Technology (KIT), 2017. 259 pp. https://doi.org/10.5445/IR/1000069366.

[Lap84] Jean-Claude Laprie. "Dependability evaluation of software systems in operation". In: *IEEE Transactions on Software Engineering* 6 (1984), pp. 701–714.

[Lau99] P Lauber. *Göhner: Prozessautomatisierung 1*. 1999.

[LBD02] Torsten Lodderstedt, David A. Basin, and Jürgen Doser. "SecureUML: A UMLBased Modeling Language for Model-Driven Security". In: *Proceedings of the 5th International Conference on The United Modeling Language*. UML '02. London, UK, UK: Springer-Verlag, 2002, pp. 426–441. ISBN: 3-540-44254-5. URL: http://dl.acm.org/citation.cfm?id=647246.719477.

[LBK14] Jay Lee, Behrad Bagheri, and Hung-An Kao. "Recent Advances and Trends of Cyber-Physical Systems and Big Data Analytics in Industrial Informatics". In: 2014.

[LC09] Feng Lu and Kwang-Ting Cheng. "SEChecker: A Sequential Equivalence Checking Framework Based on k-th Invariants". In: *IEEE Transactions on Very Large Scale Integration (VLSI) Systems* 7.6 (2009), pp. 733–746.

[Lee+06] Seok-Won Lee et al. "Building problem domain ontology from security requirements in regulatory documents". In: *Proceedings of the International workshop on Software engineering for secure systems (SESS)*. ACM, 2006, pp. 43–50. https://doi.org/10.1145/1137627.1137635.

[Lee91] Jintae Lee. "Extending the Potts and Bruns Model for Recording Design Rationale". In: *13th International Conference on Software Engineering (ICSE'91)*. Austin, TX, USA: IEEE, 1991, pp. 114–125. ISBN: 0-8186-2140-0. https://doi.org/10.1109/ICSE.1991.130629.

[Leg+14] Christoph Legat et al. "Interface behavior modeling for automatic verification of industrial automation systems' functional conformance". In: *at-Automatisierungstechnik* 62.11 (2014), pp. 815–825.

[Leh80] M. Lehman. "On understanding laws, evolution, and conservation in the largeprogram life cycle". In: *Journal of Systems and Software* 1 (1980), pp. 213–221. URL: http://dx.doi.org/10.1016/0164-1212(79)90022-0.

[Lev10] W.S. Levine. *The Control Handbook*. Electrical Engineering Handbook. Taylor &Francis, 2010. ISBN: 9781420073669.

[LFL16] Jan Ladiges, Alexander Fay, and Winfried Lamersdorf. "Automated Determining of Manufacturing Properties and Their Evolutionary Changes from Event Traces". In: *Intelligent Industrial Systems* 2.2 (2016), pp. 163–178. ISSN: 2199-854X. URL: http://dx.doi.org/10.1007/s40903-016-0048-7.

[LFV13] Christoph Legat, Jens Folmer, and Birgit Vogel-Heuser. "Evolution in industrial plant automation: A case study". In: *Industrial Electronics Society, IECON 2013 - 39th Annual Conference of the IEEE*. Nov. 2013, pp. 4386–4391. ISBN: 9781479902248. https://doi.org/10.1109/IECON.2013.6699841.

[LG99] Rudolf Lauber and Peter Göhner. *Prozessautomatisierung 1-Automatisierungssysteme und–strukturen, Computer und Bussysteme für die Anlagen und Prozessautomatisierung, Echtzeitprogrammierung und Echtzeitbetriebssysteme, Zuverlässigkeitsund Sicherheitstechnik*. 1999.

[Li+12] Fang Li et al. "Specification of the requirements to support information technologycycles in the machine and plant manufacturing industry". In: *IFAC Proceedings Volumes* 45.6 (2012), pp. 1077–1082. URL: https://doi.org/10.3182/20120523-3-RO-2023.00146.

[Li+13] Bixin Li et al. "Using water wave propagation phenomenon to study software change impact analysis". In: *Advances in Engineering Software* 58 (2013), pp. 45–53.

[Lip+18] Moritz Lipp et al. "Meltdown: Reading Kernel Memory from User Space". In: *27th USENIX Security Symposium (USENIX Security 18)*. 2018.

[Lit+15] Sascha Lity et al. "Re-Engineering Automation Systems as Dynamic Software Product Lines". In: *11th Dagstuhl-Workshop Model-Based Development of Embedded Systems, MBEES '15, March 22-25, 2015*. 2015.

[Lit+18] Sascha Lity et al. "175% Modeling for Product-Line Evolution of Domain Artifacts". In: *Proceedings of the 12th International Workshop on Variability Modelling of Software-Intensive Systems, VAMOS 2018, Madrid, Spain, February 7-9, 2018*. 2018, pp. 27–34. URL: http://doi.acm.org/10.1145/3168365.3168369.

[Lit79] Bev Littlewood. "Software reliability model for modular program structure". In: *IEEE Transactions on Reliability* 28.3 (1979), pp. 241–246.

[Lju+10] O. Ljungkrantz et al. "A formal specification language for PLC-based control logic". In: *2010 8th IEEE International Conference on Industrial Informatics*. July 2010, pp. 1067–1072. https://doi.org/10.1109/INDIN.2010.5549591.

[LL11] D. Lefebvre and E. Leclercq. "Stochastic Petri Net Identification for the Fault Detection and Isolation of Discrete Event Systems". In: *IEEE Transactions on Systems, Man and Cybernetics, Part A: Systems and Humans* 41.2 (2011), pp. 213–225. https://doi.org/10.1109/TSMCA.2010.2058102.

[LL89] I Lawrence and Kuei Lin. "A concordance correlation coefficient to evaluate reproducibility". In: *Biometrics* (1989), pp. 255–268.

[Loc+12] Malte Lochau et al. "Incremental Model-Based Testing of Delta-Oriented Software Product Lines". In: *Tests and Proofs - 6th International Conference, TAP 2012, Prague, Czech Republic, May 31 - June 1, 2012. Proceedings*. 2012, pp. 67–82. URL: https://doi.org/10.1007/978-3-642-30473-6_7.

[Loc+14] Malte Lochau et al. "Applying Model-based Software Product Line Testing Approaches to the Automation Engineering Domain". In: *Automatisierungstechnik* 62.11 (2014), pp. 771–780.

[LR03] Meir M. Lehman and Juan F. Ramil. "Software Evolution: Background, Theory, Practice". In: *Inf. Process. Lett.* 88.1–2 (Oct. 2003), pp. 33–44. ISSN: 0020–0190. URL: http://dx.doi.org/10.1016/S0020-0190(03)00382-X.

[LS00] Bev Littlewood and Lorenzo Strigini. "Software Reliability and Dependability: A Roadmap". In: *Proceedings of the Conference on The Future of Software Engineering*. ICSE '00. Limerick, Ireland: ACM, 2000, pp. 175–188. ISBN: 1-58113-253-0. URL: http://doi.acm.org/10.1145/336512.336551.

[LS80] Bennet P. Lientz and Burton E. Swanson. "*Software Maintenance Management: A Study of the Maintenance of Computer Application Software in 487 Data Processing Organizations*. Addison-Wesley, 1980, pp. 1–160.

[Lüd+10] Arndt Lüder et al. "Manufacturing system engineering with mechatronical units". In: *Emerging Technologies and Factory Automation (ETFA), 2010 IEEE Conference on*. IEEE. 2010, pp. 1–8.

[LVD06] Thomas D. LaToza, Gina Venolia, and Robert DeLine. "Maintaining Mental Models: A Study of Developer Work Habits". In: *Proceedings of the 28th International Conference on Software Engineering*. ICSE '06. Shanghai, China: ACM, 2006, pp. 492–501. ISBN: 1-59593-375-1. https://doi.org/10.1145/1134285.1134355.

[Mac+96] Allan MacLean et al. "Questions, Options and Criteria". In: *Design rationale, concepts, techniques and use*. Ed. by J M T. P. C. Moran. Mahwah, NJ. USA: Lawrence Erlbaum Associates, Inc., 1996, pp. 53–106.

[Man03] Heiko Mantel. "A Uniform Framework for the Formal Specification and Verification of Information Flow Security". In: (2003).

[Mar10] Rebecca Parsons Martin Fowler. *Domain-Specific Languages*. The Addison-Wesley Signature Series (Fowler). Addison-Wesley Professional, Sept. 2010. ISBN: 978-0-321-71294-3.

[MB15] Richard Mordinyi and Stefan Biffl. "Versioning in cyber-physical production system engineering: best-practice and research agenda". In: *Proceedings of the First International Workshop on Software Engineering for Smart Cyber-Physical Systems*. IEEE Press. 2015, pp. 44–47.

[MBB16] Mariem Mefteh, Nadia Bouassida, and Hanêne Ben-Abdallah. "Mining Feature Models from Functional Requirements". In: *Comput. J.* 59.12 (2016), pp. 1784–1804. URL: https://doi.org/10.1093/comjnl/bxw027.

[MBG10] Marco Müller, Moritz Balz, and Michael ' Goedicke. "Representing Formal Component Models in OSGi". In: *Software Engineering*. Ed. by Gregor Engels, Markus Luckey, andWilhelm Schäfer. Vol. 159. LNI. GI, 2010, pp. 45–56. ISBN: 978-3-88579-253-6. URL: http://subs.emis.de/LNI/Proceedings/Proceedings159/P-159.pdf.

[McG01] John McGregor. *Testing a Software Product Line*. Tech. rep. CMU/SEI-2001-TR-022. Pittsburgh, PA: Software Engineering Institute, Carnegie Mellon University, 2001. URL: http://resources.sei.cmu.edu/library/asset-view.cfm?AssetID=5715.

[McM03] K.L. McMillan. "Interpolation and SAT-Based Model Checking". English. In: *Computer Aided Verification*. Ed. by Jr. Hunt WarrenA. and Fabio Somenzi. Vol. 2725. Lecture Notes in Computer Science. Springer Berlin Heidelberg, 2003, pp. 1–13. ISBN: 978-3-540-40524-5. URL: http://dx.doi.org/10.1007/978-3-540-45069-6_1.

[MD08] Tom Mens and Serge Demeyer, eds. *Software Evolution*. Springer, 2008. ISBN: 978-3-540-76439-7. URL: https://doi.org/10.1007/978-3-540-76440-3.

[Med+16] Flávio Medeiros et al. "A Comparison of 10 Sampling Algorithms for Configurable Systems". In: *Proceedings of the 38th International Conference on Software Engineering*. ICSE '16. Austin, Texas: ACM, 2016, pp. 643–654. ISBN: 978-1-4503-3900-1. URL: http://doi.acm.org/10.1145/2884781.2884793.

[Mei+17] Jens Meinicke et al. *Mastering Software Variability with FeatureIDE*. BerlinHeidelberg: Springer, 2017. ISBN: 978-3-319-61442-7.

[Men02] T. Mens. "A state-of-the-art survey on software merging". In: Software Engineering, IEEE Transactions on 28.5 (2002), pp. 449–462.

[MG10] Anthony Finkelstein Mehrdad Sabetzadeh and Michael Goedicke. "Viewpoints". In: *Encyclopedia of Software Engineering*. Ed. by Phillip A Laplante. Vol. 1. Auerbach Publications, 2010, pp. 1318–1329.

[MGM03] Haralambos Mouratidis, Paolo Giorgini, and Gordon Manson. "An Ontology for Modelling Security: The Tropos Approach". In: *Knowledge-Based Intelligent Information and Engineering Systems*. Ed. by Vasile Palade, Robert J. Howlett, and Lakhmi Jain. Vol. 2773. LNCS. Springer, 2003, pp. 1387–1394. ISBN: 978-3-540-40803-1. https://doi.org/10.1007/978-3-540-45224-9_187.

[MGM05] Haralambos Mouratidis, Paolo Giorgini, and Gordon Manson. "When security meets software engineering: A case of modelling secure information systems". In: *Information Systems* 30.8 (2005), pp. 609–629. ISSN: 03064379.

[MH05] Hugh McManus and Daniel Hastings. "A Framework for Understanding Uncertainty and its Mitigation and Exploitation in Complex Systems". In: *INCOSE International Symposium*. Vol. 15. 1. Wiley Online Library. 2005, pp. 484–503.

[MHH18] David Monschein, Robert Heinrich, and Christoph Heger. "Diagnosis of Privacy and Performance Problems in the Context of Mobile Applications". In: Companion of the 2018 ACM/SPEC International Conference on Performance Engineering. ACM, 2018, pp. 167–172. ISBN: 978-1-4503-5629-9.

[MHR09] Walid Maalej, Hans-Jörg Happel, and Asarnusch Rashid. "When Users Become Collaborators: Towards Continuous and Context-aware User Input". In: *Proceedings of the 24th ACM SIGPLAN Conference Companion on Object Oriented Programming Systems Languages and Applications*. OOPSLA '09. Orlando, Florida, USA: ACM, 2009, pp. 981–990. ISBN: 978-1-60558-768-4. https://doi.org/10.1145/1639950.1640068.

[Mie+10] André Miede et al. "A Generic Metamodel for IT Security Attack Modeling for Distributed Systems". In: Int. Conference on Availability, Reliability and Security (ARES) (2010), pp. 430–437. https://doi.org/10.1109/ARES.2010.17.

[MKM13] Na Meng, Miryung Kim, and Kathryn S McKinley. "LASE: locating and applying systematic edits by learning from examples". In: Proceedings of the 2013 International Conference on Software Engineering. IEEE Press. 2013, pp. 502–511.

[MMW98] Philip Morris, Marcelo Masera, and Marc Wilikens. "Requirements engineering and industrial uptake". In: *Requirements Engineering* 3.2 (1998), pp. 79–83. ISSN: 1432-010X. URL: http://dx.doi.org/10.1007/BF02919966.

[MNS95] Gail C. Murphy, David Notkin, and Kevin Sullivan. "Software Reflexion Models: Bridging the Gap between Source and High-Level Models". In: *IEEE Transactions on Software Engineering*. 1995, pp. 18–28.

[Mon14] László Monostori. "Cyber-physical Production Systems: Roots, Expectations and R & D Challenges". In: *Procedia CIRP* 17.Supplement C (2014). Variety Management in Manufacturing, pp. 9–13.

[Mos85] B. Moszkowski. "A Temporal Logic for Multilevel Reasoning about Hardware". In: Computer 18.2 (Feb. 1985), pp. 10–19. ISSN: 0018-9162. https://doi.org/10.1109/MC.1985.1662795.

[Mun+17] Jakob Mund et al. "Model-based Availability Analysis for Automated Production Systems: A Case Study". In: *Proceedings of the 15th ACM-IEEE International Conference on Formal Methods and Models for System Design*. MEMOCODE '17. Vienna, Austria: ACM, 2017, pp. 46–55. ISBN: 978-1-4503-5093-8. URL: http://doi.acm.org/10.1145/3127041.3127051.

[Mun+18] J Mund et al. "Towards Continuous Verification in Model-Based Engineering of Automated Production Systems". In: *Contribution planned for Automatisierungstechnik* (2018).

[Mur+98] Gail C. Murphy et al. "An Empirical Study of Static Call Graph Extractors". In: *ACM Transactions on Software Engineering and Methodology (TOSEM)* 7.2 (1998), pp. 158–191.

[Muş+12] Kıvanç Muşlu et al. "Speculative analysis of integrated development environment recommendations". In: *ACM SIGPLAN Notices* 47.10 (2012), pp. 669–682.

[Naa12] Matthias Naab. "Enhancing architecture design methods for improved flexibility in long-living information systems". PhD thesis. Fraunhofer, 2012.

[Nai+17] Vivek Nair et al. "Using Bad Learners to Find Good Configurations". In: *Proceedings of the 2017 11th Joint Meeting on Foundations of Software Engineering*. ESEC/FSE 2017. Paderborn, Germany: ACM, 2017, pp. 257–267. ISBN: 978-1-4503-5105-8. URL: http://doi.acm.org/10.1145/3106237.3106238.

[ND86] Donald A. Norman and Stephen W. Draper. *User Centered System Design; New Perspectives on Human-Computer Interaction*. Hillsdale, NJ, USA: L. Erlbaum Associates Inc., 1986. ISBN: 0898597811.

[NE00] Bashar Nuseibeh and Steve Easterbrook. "Requirements engineering: a roadmap".In: *Proceedings of the Conference on The Future of Software Engineering* Ed. by Anthony Finkelstein. 2000, pp. 35–46.

[Neu12] Philipp Neubeck. "A Probabilitistic Theory of Interactive Systems". Dissertation. München: Technische Universität München, 2012.

[Nev+15] L. Neves et al. "Safe Evolution Templates for Software Product Lines". In: J. Syst. Softw. 106.C (Aug. 2015), pp. 42–58. ISSN: 0164-1212. URL: http://dx.doi.org/10.1016/j.jss.2015.04.024.

[NF15] Oliver Niggemann and Christian Frey. "Data-driven anomaly detection in cyber-physical production systems". In: *at - Automatisierungstechnik* 63.10 (2015). ISSN: 0178-2312. https://doi.org/10.1515/auto-2015-0060.

[NHJ16] Najam Nazar, Yan Hu, and He Jiang. "Summarizing Software Artifacts: A Literature Review". In: *Journal of Computer Science and Technology* 31.5 (Sept. 2016), pp. 883–909. ISSN: 1000-9000. https://doi.org/10.1007/s11390-016-1671-1.

[Nhl+15] A. Nhlabatsi et al. "Managing security control assumptions using causal traceability". In: *8th Int. Symp. on Software and Systems Traceability (SST)*. 2015.

[Nor13] Don Norman. *The design of everyday things: Revised and expanded edition* Basic Books (AZ), 2013.

[NT12] Ikujiro Nonaka and Hirotaka Takeuchi. *Die Organisation des Wissens: Wie japanische Unternehmen eine brachliegende Ressource nutzbar machen* Campus Verlag, 2012.

[NW70] Saul B. Needleman and Christian D. Wunsch. "A general method applicable to the search for similarities in the amino acid sequence of two proteins". In: *Journal of Molecular Biology* 48.3 (1970), pp. 443–453. ISSN: 0022–2836. http://dx.doi.org/10.1016/0022-2836(70)90057-4.

[Obj11] Object Management Group, Inc. UML Profile for MARTE: *Modeling and Analysis of Real-Time Embedded Systems*, Version 1.1. http://www.omg.org/spec/MARTE/1.1/. 2011.

[Obj16] Object Management Group. *OMG Meta Object Facility (MOF) Core Specification, Version 2.5.1.* Object Management Group (OMG), Nov. 2016. URL: http://www.omg.org/spec/MOF/2.5.1.

[Ohr+18] Manuel Ohrndorf et al. "ReVision: A Tool for History-based Model Repair Recommendations". In: *IEEE International Conference on Software Engineering*. ACM,2018.

[Omo+12] I. Omoronyia et al. "Caprice: a tool for engineering adaptive privacy". In: *Proc. of the 27th IEEE/ACM Int. Conf. on Automated Software Eng. - ASE 2012* (2012), p. 354. https://doi.org/10.1145/2351676.2351745. URL: http://dl.acm.org/citation.cfm?doid=2351676.2351745.

[Omo+13] I. Omoronyia et al. "Engineering adaptive privacy: On the role of privacy awareness requirements". In: *Proc. - Int. Conf. on Software Engineering* (2013), pp. 632–641. ISSN: 02705257. https://doi.org/10.1109/ICSE.2013.6606609.

[Ora17] Oracle America, Inc. *JavaTM Platform, Enterprise Edition (Java EE) Specification, v8*. https://jcp.org/en/jsr/detail?id=366. Oracle America, Inc., 2017.

[OWL09] W3C OWL Working Group. *OWL 2 Web Ontology Language: Document Overview*. Available at http://www.w3.org/TR/owl2-overview/. W3C Recommendation,Oct. 2009.

[PA98] Shari Lawrence Peeger and Joanne M Atlee. *Software engineering: theory and practice*. Pearson Education India, 1998.

[Pag13] Dennis Pagano. *PORTNEUF-A Framework for Continuous User Involvement*. Verlag Dr. Hut, 2013.

[Pak+16] Antti Pakonen et al. "User-friendly formal specification languages - conclusions drawn from industrial experience on model checking". In: *2016 IEEE 21st International Conference on Emerging Technologies and Factory Automation (ETFA)*. 2016, pp. 1–8. https://doi.org/10.1109/ETFA.2016.7733717.

[Par94] David Lorge Parnas. "Software aging". In: Software Engineering, 1994. Proceedings. *ICSE-16., 16th International Conference on*. IEEE. 1994, pp. 279–287.

[PB01] Daniel J. Paulish and Len Bass. *Architecture-Centric Software Project Management: A Practical Guide*. AW, 2001. ISBN: 0201734095.

[PBL05a] Klaus Pohl, Günter Böckle, and Frank J. van der Linden. *Software Product Line Engineering: Foundations, Principles and Techniques*. 1st ed. Springer, Aug. 3, 2005. 496 pp. ISBN: 978-3-540-24372-4. https://doi.org/10.1007/3-540-28901-1. URL: http://www.ebook.de/de/product/4437317/guenter_boeckle_klaus_pohl_frank_j_van_der_linden_software_product_line_engineering.html.

[PCW84] David Lorge Parnas, Paul C Clements, and David MWeiss. "The modular structure of complex systems". In: *Proceedings of the 7th international conference on Software engineering*. IEEE Press. 1984, pp. 408–417.

[PDH14] Barbara Paech, Alexander Delater, and Tom-Michael Hesse. "Supporting Project Management Through Integrated Management of System and Project Knowledge". In: *Software Project Management in a Changing World*. Ed. by Günther Ruhe and Claes Wohlin. Heidelberg, Germany: Springer, 2014. Chap. 7, pp. 157–192. ISBN: 978-3-642-55034-8. https://doi.org/10.1007/978-3-642-55035-5.

[Pha+13] R. Pham et al. "Tailoring video recording to support efficient GUI testing and debugging". In: *Software Quality Journal* (June 2013), pp. 1–20. URL: http://dx.doi.org/10.1007/s11219-013-9206-2.

[Pie+15] Christopher Pietsch et al. "SiPL–A Delta-Based Modeling Framework for Software Product Line Engineering". *In: Automated Software Engineering (ASE), 2015 30th IEEE/ACM International Conference on*. IEEE. 2015, pp. 852–857.

[Pie+17] Christopher Pietsch et al. "A tool environment for quality assurance of deltaoriented model-based SPLs". In: *Proceedings of the Eleventh International Workshop on Variability Modelling of Software-intensive Systems*. ACM. 2017, pp. 84–91.

[Pie+18] Christopher Pietsch et al. "Using Model Differencing to reason about Observable Behaviour Changes of Manufacturing Systems". In: *AT - Automatisierungstechnik* (2018). In Press.

[PM97] Lawrence H Putnam and Ware Myers. *Industrial Strength Software: Effective Management Using Measurement*. IEEE, 1997.

[PMI94] D. Lorge Parnas, J. Madey, and M. Iglewski. "Precise documentation of wellstructured programs". In: *IEEE Transactions on Software Engineering* 20.12 (Dec. 1994), pp. 948–976. ISSN: 0098-5589. https://doi.org/10.1109/32.368133.

[Poh10] Klaus Pohl. *Requirements engineering: Fundamentals, principles, and techniques*. Heidelberg: Springer, 2010.

[Pok+14] Alexander Pokahr et al. "Programming BDI Agents with Pure Java". In: *Proceedings of Tenth German conference on Multi-Agent System TEchnologieS (MATES-2014)*. Springer, 2014.

[PPM04] Ted Pedersen, Siddharth Patwardhan, and Jason Michelizzi. "WordNet::Similarity: Measuring the Relatedness of Concepts". In: *Demonstration Papers at HLT-NAACL 2004*. HLT-NAACL–Demonstrations '04. Boston, Massachusetts: Association for Computational Linguistics, 2004, pp. 38–41.

[PR11] Klaus Pohl and Chris Rupp. *Requirements Engineering Fundamentals - A Study Guide for the Certified Professional for Requirements Engineering Exam: Foundation Level - IREB compliant*. rockynook, 2011, pp. I–XVIII, 1–163. ISBN: 978-1-933952-81-9.

[Pra+17] Herbert Prahofer et al. "Feature-oriented development in industrial automation software ecosystems: Development scenarios and tool support". In: *IEEE International Conference on Industrial Informatics (INDIN)* (2017), pp. 1218–1223. ISSN: 19354576. https://doi.org/10.1109/INDIN.2016.7819353.

[PS09] Michael Polanyi and Amartya Sen. *The Tacit Dimension*. University of Chicago Press, 2009. ISBN: 9780226672984.

[Rag+17a] Alejandro Rago et al. "Distributed Quality-attribute Optimization of Software Architectures". In: *Proceedings of the 11th Brazilian Symposium on Software Components, Architectures, and Reuse (SBCARS '17)*. ACM, 2017, 7:1–7:10. ISBN: 978-1-4503-5325-0. https://doi.org/10.1145/3132498.3132509.

[Ras+01] Victor Raskin et al. "Ontology in information security: a useful theoretical foundation and methodological tool". In: *Proceedings of the Workshop on New security paradigms*. NSPW. Cloudcroft, New Mexico: ACM, 2001, pp. 53–59. ISBN: 1-58113-457-6. https://doi.org/10.1145/508171.508180.

[Raz+16] Maryam Razavian et al. "In Two Minds: How Reflections Influence Software Design Thinking (Towards a Thinking Model of Software Design Reasoning and Reflection)". In: 28.6 (2016), pp. 394–426. https://doi.org/10.1002/smr.1776.

[RC03] Mary Beth Rosson and John M. Carroll. "The Human-computer Interaction Handbook". In: ed. by Julie A. Jacko and Andrew Sears. Hillsdale, NJ, USA: L. Erlbaum Associates Inc., 2003. Chap. Scenario-based Design, pp. 1032–1050. ISBN: 0-8058-3838-4.

[RC13] J. Rubin and M. Chechik. "N-way Model Merging". In: *Proceedings of the 2013 Joint Meeting on Foundations of Software Engineering*. ESEC/FSE 2013. New York, NY, USA: ACM, 2013, pp. 301–311. ISBN: 978-1-4503-2237-9.

[Rei+17] Kim Reichert et al. "A Taxonomy of Anomalies in Distributed Cloud Systems: The CRI-Model". In: *Intelligent Distributed Computing XI. Ed.* by M. Ivanovic et al. Springer, 2017.

[Reu+16] Ralf H. Reussner et al. *Modeling and Simulating Software Architectures – The Palladio Approach*. Cambridge, MA: MIT Press, 2016. 408 pp. ISBN: 9780262034760. URL: http://mitpress.mit.edu/books/modeling-and-simulatingsoftware-architectures.

[RJ12] T. Ruhroth and J. Jürjens. "Supporting Security Assurance in the Context of Evolution: Modular Modeling and Analysis with UMLsec". In: IEEE: 14th Int. Symp. on High-Assurance Systems Eng. (HASE 2012). IEEE CS, Oct. 2012. https://doi.org/10.1109/HASE.2012.35.

[RLL10] M. Roth, J.-J Lesage, and L. Litz. "Black-box identification of discrete event systems with optimal partitioning of concurrent subsystems". In: *American Control Conference (ACC)*. 2010.

[RM13] Sarah Rastkar and Gail C. Murphy. "Why did this code change?" In: *35th International Conference on Software Engineering*. IEEE, 2013, pp. 1193–1196.

[Rob+17] Martin P Robillard et al. "On-Demand Developer Documentation". In: *International Conference on Software Maintenance and Evolution*. 2017, p. 5. ISBN: 9781538609927. https://doi.org/10.1109/ICSME.2017.17.

[Roc+14] Juri Di Rocco et al. "Dealing with the Coupled Evolution of Metamodels and Model-to-text Transformations". In: *Proceedings of the Workshop on Models and Evolution co-located with ACM/IEEE 17th International Conference on Model Driven Engineering Languages and Systems (MoDELS 2014), Valencia, Spain, Sept 28, 2014*. Ed. by Alfonso Pierantonio, Bernhard Schätz, and Dalila Tamzalit. Vol. 1331. CEUR Workshop Proceedings. 2014, pp. 22–31.

[Roe+12] Tobias Roehm et al. "How Do Professional Developers Comprehend Software?" In: *Proceedings of the 34th International Conference on Software Engineering*. ICSE '12. Zurich, Switzerland: IEEE Press, 2012, pp. 255–265. ISBN: 978-1-4673-1067-3. https://doi.org/10.1109/ICSE.2012.6227188.

[Roe+13a] Tobias Roehm et al. "Monitoring user interactions for supporting failure reproduction". In: *2013 21st International Conference on Program Comprehension (ICPC)*. May 2013, pp. 73–82. https://doi.org/10.1109/ICPC.2013.6613835.

[Roe+13b] Tobias Roehm et al. "Towards Identification of Software Improvements and Specification Updates by Comparing Monitored and Specified End-User Behavior". In: *2013 IEEE International Conference on Software Maintenance*. Sept. 2013, pp. 464–467. https://doi.org/10.1109/ICSM.2013.73.

[Roe15] Tobias Roehm. "The MALTASE Framework For Usage-Aware Software Evolution". Dissertation. München: Technische Universität München, 2015.

[Rog+14] Benjamin Rogers et al. "Using Text Mining Techniques to Extract Rationale from Existing Documentation". In: *6th Int. Conf. on Design Computing and Cognition*. Springer, 2014, pp. 457–474.

[Rös+14] S. Rösch et al. "Model-based Testing of PLC Software: Test of Plants' Reliability by using Fault Injection on Component Level". In: *19th IFAC World Congress*. accepted. 2014.

[Ros+15] Kiana Rostami et al. "Architecture-based Assessment and Planning of Change Requests". In: *11th International ACM SIGSOFT Conference on Quality of Software Architectures (QoSA '15)*. Montréal, QC, Canada: ACM, 2015, pp. 21–30. ISBN: 9781450334709. https://doi.org/10.1145/2737182.2737198. URL: http://dl.acm.org/citation.cfm?doid=2737182.2737198.

[Ros+17] Kiana Rostami et al. "Architecture-based Change Impact Analysis in Information Systems and Business Processes". In: *2017 IEEE International Conference on Software Architecture (ICSA2017)*. IEEE, 2017, pp. 179–188. ISBN: 978-1-5090-5729-0. URL: https://doi.org/10.1109/ICSA.2017.17.

[RTV15] Susanne Rösch, Sabine Teufl, and Birgit Vogel-Heuser. "Model-based quality assurance in machine and plant automation using sequence diagrams—A comparison of two research approaches". In: *Industrial Informatics (INDIN), 2015 IEEE 13th International Conference on*. IEEE. 2015, pp. 302–307.

[Ruh+14a] T. Ruhroth et al. "Towards Adaptation and Evolution of Domain-specific Knowledge for Maintaining Secure Systems". In: *15th Int. Conf. of Product Focused Software Development and Process Improvement (Profes'14)*. Vol. 8892. LNCS. Springer, 2014, pp. 239–253. https://doi.org/10.1007/978-3-319-13835-0_17.

[Ruh+14b] Thomas Ruhroth et al. "Versioning and Evolution Requirements for Model-Based System Development". In: *Softwaretechnik-Trends* 34.2 (2014). ISSN 0720–8928.

[S G+14] S. Gärtner et al. "Maintaining Requirements for Long-Living Software Systems by Incorporating Security Knowledge". In: *22nd IEEE Int. Requirements Eng. Conference*. IEEE. 2014.

[S W+14] S. Wenzel et al. "UMLchange – Specifying Model Changes to Support Security Verification of Potential Evolution". In: *Journal of Computer Standards & Interfaces* 36 (4 2014). Special Issue on Security in Information Systems., pp. 776–791. http://dx.doi.org/10.1016/j.csi.2013.12.011.

[Sab+16] Marta Sabou et al. "Supporting the engineering of cyber-physical production systems with the AutomationML analyzer". In: *Cyber-Physical Production Systems (CPPS), 2016 1st International Workshop on*. IEEE. 2016, pp. 1–8.

[Sai+17] Shinobu Saito et al. "How Much Undocumented Knowledge is there in Agile Software Development? Case Study on Industrial Project using Issue Tracking System and Version Control System". In: *2017 IEEE 25th International Requirements Engineering Conference*. Lisbon, Portugal: IEEE Computer Society, 2017, pp. 186–195.

[Sal+12] M. Salehie et al. "Requirements-driven adaptive security: Protecting variable assets at runtime". In: *2012 20th IEEE Int. Requirements Eng. Conf. (RE)* (Sept. 2012), pp. 111–120. https://doi.org/10.1109/RE.2012.6345794. URL: http://ieeexplore.ieee.org/lpdocs/epic03/wrapper.htm?arnumber=6345794.

[Sar+15] Atri Sarkar et al. "Cost-Efficient Sampling for Performance Prediction of Configurable Systems (T)". In: *Proceedings of the 2015 30th IEEE/ACM International Conference on Automated Software Engineering (ASE)*. ASE '15. Washington, DC, USA: IEEE Computer Society, 2015, pp. 342–352. ISBN: 978-1-5090-0025-8. URL: http://dx.doi.org/10.1109/ASE.2015.45.

[SAZ17] Mojtaba Shahin, Muhammad Ali Babar, and Liming Zhu. "Continuous Integration, Delivery and Deployment: A Systematic Review on Approaches, Tools, Challenges and Practices". In: *IEEE Access* 5.Ci (2017), pp. 3909–3943. ISSN: 2169-3536. https://doi.org/10.1109/ACCESS.2017.2685629.

[SBV10] Sagar Sen, Benoit Baudry, and Hans Vangheluwe. "Towards domain-specific model editors with automatic model completion". In: *Simulation* 86.2 (2010), pp. 109–126.

[Sch+02] Bernhard Schätz et al. "Model-Based Development of Embedded Systems". In: *Advances in Object-Oriented Information Systems, OOIS 2002 Workshops, Montpellier, France, September 2, 2002, Proceedings*. Ed. by Jean-Michel Bruel and Zohra Bellahsene. Vol. 2426. Lecture Notes in Computer Science. Springer, 2002, pp. 298–312. ISBN: 3-540-44088-7. URL: https://doi.org/10.1007/3-540-46105-1_34.

[Sch+05] Markus Schumacher et al. *Security Patterns: Integrating Security and Systems Engineering*. John Wiley & Sons, 2005. ISBN: 0470858842.

[Sch+12] Kurt Schneider et al. "Enhancing security requirements engineering by organizational learning". In: *Requir. Eng.* 17.1 (2012), pp. 35–56. URL: https://doi.org/10.1007/s00766-011-0141-0.

[Sch+14] Nicole Schmidt et al. "AutomationML for user requirements fulfilment related to engineering process efficiency". In: *Industrial Electronics Society, IECON 2014-40th Annual Conference of the IEEE*. IEEE. 2014, pp. 4902–4908.

[Sch06] Kurt Schneider. "Rationale as a By-Product". In: *Rationale Management in Software Engineering*. Ed. by Allen H. Dutoit et al. Springer-Verlag Berlin Heidelberg, 2006, pp. 91–109. ISBN: 978-3-540-30997-0. https://doi.org/10.1007/978-3-540-30998-7_4.

[Sch08] Guus Schreiber. "Knowledge Engineering". In: *Foundations of Artificial Intelligence* 3 (2008). Handbook of Knowledge Representation, pp. 929–946. ISSN: 1574-6526. http://dx.doi.org/10.1016/S1574-6526(07)03025-8.

[Sch09] Kurt Schneider. *Experience and Knowledge Management in Software Engineering*. Springer-Verlag, 2009.

[Sch11] Bruce Schneier. *Secrets and lies: digital security in a networked world*. John Wiley & Sons, 2011.

[Sch83] Donald A. Schön. *The reflective practitioner*. 1983.

[Sch94a] Helmut Schmid. "Probabilistic Part-of-Speech Tagging Using Decision Trees". In: *Proc. of the Int. Conference on New Methods in Language Processing*. 1994, pp. 44–49.

[Sch94b] Andy Schürr. "Specification of Graph Translators with Triple Graph Grammars". In: *Proceedings of the 20th International Workshop on Graph-Theoretic Concepts in Computer Science, WG '94*. Ed. by Ernst W. Mayr, Gunther Schmidt, and Gottfried Tinhofer. Vol. 903. Lecture Notes in Computer Science. Herrsching, Germany: Springer, June 1994, pp. 151–163. ISBN: 3-540-59071-4. https://doi.org/10.1007/3-540-59071-4_45.

[Sch96] Kurt Schneider. "Prototypes As Assets, Not Toys: Why and How to Extract Knowledge from Prototypes". In: *Proceedings of the 18th International Conference on Software Engineering*. ICSE '96. Washington, DC, USA: IEEE Computer Society, 1996, pp. 522–531. ISBN: 0-8186-7246-3.

[SD08] Andre Süflow and Rolf Drechsler. "Verification of PLC Programs using Formal Proof Techniques". In: *FORMS/FORMAT*. 2008.

[SD09] Miriam Schleipen and Rainer Drath. "Three-view-concept for modeling process or manufacturing plants with AutomationML". In: *Emerging Technologies & Factory Automation, 2009. ETFA 2009. IEEE Conference on*. IEEE. 2009, pp. 1–4.

[SDB14] V. Skormin, A. Dolgikh, and Z. Birnbaum. "The behavioral approach to diagnostics of cyber-physical systems". In: *AUTOTESTCON, 2014 IEEE*. Sept. 2014, pp. 26–30. https://doi.org/10.1109/AUTEST.2014.6935117.

[SDJ07] D. I. K. Sjoberg, T. Dyba, and M. Jorgensen. "The Future of Empirical Methods in Software Engineering Research". In: *Future of Software Engineering, 2007. FOSE '07*. May 2007, pp. 358–378. https://doi.org/10.1109/FOSE.2007.30.

[Sei+16] Stephan Seifermann et al. "Challenges in Secure Software Evolution - The Role of Software Architecture". In: *3rd Collaborative Workshop on Evolution and Maintenance of Long-Living Software Systems*. Softwaretechnik-Trends. 2016.

[Sei16] Stephan Seifermann. "Architectural Data Flow Analysis". In: *Proceedings of the 13th Working IEEE/IFIP Conference on Software Architecture*. WICSA'16. IEEE, 2016, pp. 270–271.

[Sel07] Petri Selonen. "A review of UML model comparison approaches". In: *Nordic Workshop on Model Driven Engineering*. Citeseer. 2007, p. 37.

[SFG99] Helen Sharp, Anthony Finkelstein, and Galal Galal. "Stakeholder identification in the requirements engineering process". In: *Proceedings. Tenth International Workshop on Database and Expert Systems Applications. DEXA 99*. 1999, pp. 387–391. https://doi.org/10.1109/DEXA.1999.795198.

[Sha+10] Aditya A. Shah et al. "Multi-view Modeling to Support Embedded Systems Engineering in SysML". In: *Graph Transformations and Model-Driven Engineering: Essays Dedicated to Manfred Nagl on the Occasion of his 65th Birthday*. Ed. by Gregor Engels et al. Berlin, Heidelberg: Springer Berlin Heidelberg, 2010, pp. 580–601. ISBN: 978-3-642-17322-6. URL: https://doi.org/10.1007/978-3-642-17322-6_25.

[Sho14] Adam Shostack. *Threat modeling: Designing for security*. John Wiley & Sons, 2014.

[SHT12] Maria Spichkova, Florian Hölzl, and David Trachtenherz. "Verified System Development with the AutoFocus Tool Chain". In: *Proceedings 2nd Workshop on Formal Methods in the Development of Software, WS-FMDS 2012, Paris, France, August 28, 2012*. Ed. by César Andrés and Luis Llana. Vol. 86. EPTCS. 2012, pp. 17–24. URL: https://doi.org/10.4204/EPTCS.86.3.

[Sie+12a] Norbert Siegmund et al. "Predicting Performance via Automated Feature-interaction Detection". In: *Proceedings of the 34th International Conference on Software Engineering*. ICSE '12. Zurich, Switzerland: IEEE Press, 2012, pp. 167–177. ISBN: 978-1-4673-1067-3. URL: http://dl.acm.org/citation.cfm?id=2337223.2337243.

[Sie+12b] Norbert Siegmund et al. "SPL Conqueror: Toward optimization of non-functional properties in software product lines". In: *Software Quality Journal* 20.3-4 (2012), pp. 487–517. URL: https://doi.org/10.1007/s11219-011-9152-9.

[Sie+13] Norbert Siegmund et al. "Scalable prediction of non-functional properties in software product lines: Footprint and memory consumption". In: *Information & Software Technology* 55.3 (2013), pp. 491–507. URL: https://doi.org/10.1016/j.infsof.2012.07.020.

[Sie+15] Norbert Siegmund et al. "Performance-influence Models for Highly Configurable Systems". In: *Proceedings of the 2015 10th Joint Meeting on Foundations of Software Engineering*. ESEC/FSE 2015. Bergamo, Italy: ACM, 2015, pp. 284–294. ISBN: 978-1-4503-3675-8. URL: http://doi.acm.org/10.1145/2786805.2786845.

[Sim+09] Chris Simmons et al. "AVOIDIT: A cyber attack taxonomy". In: *Proc. of 9th Annual Symposium On Information Assurance-ASIA*. Vol. 14. 2009.

[SL15] N Schmidt and A Lüder. "AutomationML in a Nutshell". In: *AutomationML eV* (2015).

[Sme+00] O. De Smet et al. "Safe programming of PLC using formal verification methods". In: *Int. PLCopen conference on Industrial Control Programming*. 2000.

[Som10] Ian Sommerville. *Software engineering*. New York: Addison-Wesley, 2010.

[SRG11] Klaus Schmid, Rick Rabiser, and Paul Grünbacher. "A comparison of decision modeling approaches in product lines". In: *Fifth International Workshop on Variability Modelling of Software-Intensive Systems, Namur, Belgium, January 27–29, 2011. Proceedings*. 2011, pp. 119–126. URL: http://doi.acm.org/10.1145/1944892.1944907.

[SS04] Frank Swiderski and Window Snyder. *Threat Modeling*. Microsoft Press Corp., 2004.

[SSA14] Christoph Seidl, Ina Schaefer, and Uwe Aßmann. "Capturing variability in space and time with hyper feature models". In: *The Eighth International Workshop on Variability Modelling of Software-intensive Systems, VaMoS '14, Sophia Antipolis, France, January 22–24, 2014*. 2014, 6:1–6:8. URL: http://doi.acm.org/10.1145/2556624.2556625.

[SSA17] Norbert Siegmund, Stefan Sobernig, and Sven Apel. "Attributed Variability Models: Outside the Comfort Zone". In: *Proceedings of the 2017 11th Joint Meeting on Foundations of Software Engineering*. ESEC/FSE 2017. Paderborn, Germany: ACM, 2017, pp. 268–278. ISBN: 978-1-4503-5105-8. URL: http://doi.acm.org/10.1145/3106237.3106251.

[SSK08] K. Schneider, K. Stapel, and E. Knauss. "Beyond Documents: Visualizing Informal Communication". In: *Proc. of Third Int. Works. on Requirements Eng. Visualization (REV '08)*. 2008.

[Stå+03] Tor Stålhane et al. "Post Mortem - An Assessment of Two Approaches". In: *Empirical Methods and Studies in Software Engineering, Experiences from ESERNET*. Vol. 2765. Lecture Notes in Computer Science. Springer, 2003, pp. 129–141. URL: https://doi.org/10.1007/978-3-540-45143-3_8.

[Sta14a] International Organization for Standardization. *ISO/IEC 14764*. 2014. URL: www.iso.org/standard/39064.html.

[Sta14b] International Organization for Standardization. *ISO/IEC 25000*. 2014. URL: www.iso.org/standard/64764.html.

[Sta15] Johannes Stammel. "Architekturbasierte Bewertung und Planung von Änderungsanfragen". PhD thesis. KIT, 2015.

[Ste+09] David Steinberg et al. *EMF: Eclipse Modeling Framework 2.0*. 2nd. Addison-Wesley Professional, 2009. ISBN: 0321331885.

[Ste09] William J. Stewart. *Probability, Markov Chains, Queues, and Simulation*. Princeton University Press, 2009.

[Str+17] Daniel Strüber et al. "Henshin: A Usability-Focused Framework for EMF Model Transformation Development". In: *Graph Transformation - 10th International Conference, ICGT 2017, Held as Part of STAF 2017, Marburg, Germany, July 18–19, 2017, Proceedings*. Vol. 10373. Lecture Notes in Computer Science. Springer, 2017, pp. 196–208.

[SVC06] Thomas Stahl, Markus Völter, and Krzysztof Czarnecki. *Model-Driven Software Development: Technology, Engineering, Management*. John Wiley & Sons, 2006. ISBN: 0470025700.

[SVS14] Janne Seppänen, Martín Varela, and Aggeliki Sgora. "An autonomous QoE-driven network management framework". In: *Journal of Visual Communication and Image Representation* 25.3 (2014), pp. 565–577.

[SW10] Wilhelm Schäfer and Heike Wehrheim. "Model-Driven Development with Mechatronic UML". In: *Graph Transformations and Model-Driven Engineering: Essays Dedicated to Manfred Nagl on the Occasion of his 65th Birthday*. Ed. by Gregor Engels et al. Berlin, Heidelberg: Springer Berlin Heidelberg, 2010, pp. 533–554. ISBN: 978-3-642-17322-6. URL: https://doi.org/10.1007/978-3-642-17322-6_23.

[Tae+17] Gabriele Taentzer et al. "Change-Preserving Model Repair". In: *International Conference on Fundamental Approaches to Software Engineering*. Springer. 2017, pp. 283–299.

[TBK09] T. Thüm, D. Batory, and C. Kästner. "Reasoning about edits to feature models". In: *ICSE*. ACM, 2009, pp. 254–264.

[TF97] T. Fawcett and F.J. Provost. "Adaptive Fraud Detection". In: *Data Min. Knowl. Discov.* 1.3 (1997), pp. 291–316.

[TG06] Bill Tsoumas and Dimitris Gritzalis. "Towards an Ontology-based Security Management". In: *20th International Conference on Advanced Information Networking and Applications (AINA)*. Vol. 1. IEEE, 2006, pp. 985–992. ISBN: 0-7695-2466-4. https://doi.org/10.1109/AINA.2006.329.

[TG15] Gabriele Taentzer and Ulrike Golas. "Towards Local Confluence Analysis for Amalgamated Graph Transformation". In: *Graph Transformation - 8th International Conference, ICGT 2015, Held as Part of STAF 2015, L'Aquila, Italy, July 21-23, 2015. Proceedings*. Ed. by Francesco Parisi-Presicce and Bernhard Westfechtel. Vol. 9151. Lecture Notes in Computer Science. Springer, 2015, pp. 69–86. URL: https://doi.org/10.1007/978-3-319-21145-9_5.

[TH15] Sabine Teufl and Georg Hackenberg. "Efficient impact analysis of changes in the requirements of manufacturing automation systems". In: *IFAC-PapersOnLine* 48.3 (2015), pp. 1482–1489.

[TH16a] Emre Taspolatoglu and Robert Heinrich. "Context-based Architectural Security Analysis". In: *Proceedings of the 13th Working IEEE/IFIP Conference on Software Architecture*. WICSA'16. Venice, Italy: IEEE, 2016, pp. 281–282.

[Thr13] Kleanthis Thramboulidis. "Overcoming mechatronic design challenges: the 3+ 1 SysML-view model". In: *Computing Science and Technology International Journal* 1.1 (2013), pp. 6–14.

[Thü+11] Thomas Thüm et al. "Abstract Features in Feature Modeling". In: *Proceedings of the 2011 15th International Software Product Line Conference*. SPLC'11. Washington, DC, USA: IEEE Computer Society, 2011, pp. 191–200. ISBN: 978-0-7695-4487-8. URL: http://dx.doi.org/10.1109/SPLC.2011.53.

[Thü+14a] T. Thüm et al. "A Classification and Survey of Analysis Strategies for Software Product Lines". In: *ACM Comput. Surv.* 47.1 (June 2014), 6:1–6:45. ISSN: 0360-0300. URL: http://doi.acm.org/10.1145/2580950.

[Thü+14b] Thomas Thüm et al. "FeatureIDE: An Extensible Framework for Feature-oriented Software Development". In: *Sci. Comput. Program.* 79 (Jan. 2014), pp. 70–85. ISSN: 0167-6423. URL: http://dx.doi.org/10.1016/j.scico.2012.06.002.

[TMD+09] Richard N Taylor, Nenad Medvidovic, and Eric Dashofy. *Software Architecture: Foundations, Theory, and Practice*. Wiley, 2009.

[Tre+13] Damien Trentesaux et al. "Benchmarking exible job-shop scheduling and control systems". In: *Control Engineering Practice* 21.9 (2013), pp. 1204–1225.

[Tsc18] André Tschapeller. "Semi-Automatic Security Requirements Elicitation and Evolution for Information Systems in an Industrial Environment". semesterthesis. Technische Universität München, June 2018.

[Tys+18] Shmuel Tyszberowicz et al. "Identifying Microservices Using Functional Decomposition". In: *Symposium on Dependable Software Engineering Theories, Tools and Applications*. Springer, 2018.

[UJP03] Jeffrey Undercoffer, Anupam Joshi, and John Pinkston. "Modeling Computer Attacks: An Ontology for Intrusion Detection". In: *6th International Symposium on Recent Advances in Intrusion Detection*. Springer, 2003, pp. 113–135.

[UL07] Mark Utting and Bruno Legeard. *Practical Model-Based Testing. A Tools Approach*. M. Kaufmann, 2007. ISBN: 978-0-12-372501-1. URL: http://www.elsevierdirect.com/product.jsp?isbn=9780123725011.

[Ule+15] Sebastian Ulewicz et al. "Proving Equivalence between Control Software Variants for Programmable Logic Controllers - Using Regression Verification to Reduce Unneeded Variant Diversity". In: *20th IEEE International Conference on Emerging Technologies and Factory Automation (ETFA 2015)*. Sept. 2015.

[Ule+16] Sebastian Ulewicz et al. "A verification-supported evolution approach to assist software application engineers in industrial factory automation". In: *2016 IEEE International Symposium on Assembly and Manufacturing (ISAM)* (2016), pp. 19–25. https://doi.org/10.1109/ISAM.2016.7750714. URL: http://ieeexplore.ieee.org/document/7750714/.

[UV15] Sebastian Ulewicz and Birgit Vogel-Heuser. "Automatisiertes Testen von Sondermaschinen - von der Modulbibliothek bis zur Anlage". In: *Tagungsband Automation Symposium*. Feb. 2015, pp. 53–65.

[Var+18] Mahsa Varshosaz et al. "A Classification of Product Sampling for Software Product Lines". In: *Proceedings of the 22nd International Systems and Software Product Line Conference - Volume 1*. SPLC '18. Gothenburg, Sweden: ACM, 2018, pp. 1–13. ISBN: 978-1-4503-6464-5. URL: http://doi.acm.org/10.1145/3233027.3233035.

[Var06] Dániel Varró. "Model transformation by example". In: *Model Driven Engineering Languages and Systems* (2006), pp. 410–424.

[VB02] Jilles Van Gurp and Jan Bosch. "Design erosion: problems and causes". In: *Journal of systems and software* 61.2 (2002), pp. 105–119.

[VBF12] Birgit Vogel-Heuser, Gülden Bayrak, and Ursula Frank. *Forschungsfragen in "Produktionsautomatisierung der Zukunft"*. acatech MATERIALIEN,München, Deutschland, Apr. 2012.

[Ver+10] Sven Verdoolaege et al. "Experience with Widening Based Equivalence Checking in Realistic Multimedia Systems". In: *J. Electronic Testing* 26.2 (2010), pp. 279–292.

[Ves+81] William E Vesely et al. *Fault tree handbook*. Tech. rep. Nuclear Regulatory Commission Washington DC, 1981.

[VH13] Omid Fatahi Valilai and Mahmoud Houshmand. "A collaborative and integrated platform to support distributed manufacturing system using a service-oriented approach based on cloud computing paradigm". In: *Robotics and Computer-Integrated Manufacturing* 29.1 (2013), pp. 110–127.

[VH16] B. Vogel-Heuser and D. Hess. "Guest Editorial Industry 4.0–Prerequisites and Visions". In: *IEEE Transactions on Automation Science and Engineering* 13.2 (Apr. 2016), pp. 411–413. ISSN: 1545-5955. https://doi.org/10.1109/TASE.2016.2523639.

[VJB12] Sven Verdoolaege, Gerda Janssens, and Maurice Bruynooghe. "Equivalence Checking of Static Affne Programs Using Widening to Handle Recurrences". In: *ACM Trans. Program. Lang. Syst.* 34.3 (2012), 11:1–11:35. https://doi.org/10.1145/2362389.2362390.

[VKK17] Fabien Patrick Viertel, Oiver Karras, and Schneider Kurt. "Vulnerability Recognition by Execution Trace Difierentiation". In: *2017 ACM/IEEE International Symposium on Software Performance (SSP), Karlsruhe*. Software Technik Trends, 2017.

[Vod+11] A. Vodencarevic et al. "Identifying Behavior Models for Process Plants". In: *IEEE International Conference on Emerging Technologies and Factory Automation (ETFA)*. 2011.

[Vog+09] Birgit Vogel-Heuser et al. "Global Information Architecture for Industrial Automation." In: *Automatisierungstechnische Praxis (atp)* 51.1 (Jan. 2009), pp. 108–115.

[Vog+14a] Birgit Vogel-Heuser et al. "Challenges of Parallel Evolution in Production Automation Focusing on Requirements Specification and Fault Handling". In: *Automatisierungstechnik (at)* 11.62 (Nov. 2014), pp. 758–770. https://doi.org/10.1515/auto-2014-1111.

[Vog+14b] Birgit Vogel-Heuser et al. *Researching evolution in industrial plant automation: Scenarios and documentation of the pick and place unit*. Tech. rep. TUM-AIS-TR-01-14-02. Institute of Automation and Information Systems, Technische Universität München, 2014. URL: https://mediatum.ub.tum.de/node?id=1208973.

[Vog+15a] Birgit Vogel-Heuser et al. "Selected challenges of software evolution for automated production systems". In: *Industrial Informatics (INDIN), 2015 IEEE 13th International Conference on*. IEEE. 2015, pp. 314–321.

[Vog+15b] Birgit Vogel-Heuser et al. "Coupling simulation and model checking to examine selected mechanical constraints of automated production systems". In: *Industrial Informatics (INDIN), 2015 IEEE 13th International Conference on*. IEEE. 2015, pp. 37–42.

[Vog+15c] Birgit Vogel-Heuser et al. "Evolution of software in automated production systems: Challenges and Research Directions". In: *Journal of Systems and Software* 110 (2015), pp. 54–84. ISSN: 0164-1212.

[Vog+17a] Birgit Vogel-Heuser et al. "Maintenance effort estimation with KAMP4aPS for cross-disciplinary automated Production Systems - a collaborative approach". In: *20th IFAC World Congress*. Toulouse, France, 2017.

[Vog+17b] Birgit Vogel-Heuser et al. "Modularity and Architecture of PLC-based Software for Automated Production Systems: An analysis in industrial companies". In: *Journal of Systems and Software (JSS)* 131.1 (May 2017), pp. 35–62. https://doi.org/10.1016/j.jss.2017.05.051.

[Vog14] Birgit Vogel-Heuser. "Usability experiments to evaluate UML/SysML-based Model driven Software Engineering Notations for logic control in Manufacturing Automation". In: *Journal of Software Engineering and Applications* 7.11 (Nov. 2014), pp. 943–973. https://doi.org/10.4236/jsea.2014.711084.

[Vog15] Birgit Vogel-Heuser. *Testen in der Automatisierungstechnik vom Gerät bis zur Anlage*. 2015.

[Völ+13] Markus Völter et al. *Model-driven software development: technology, engineering, management*. John Wiley & Sons, 2013.

[VPF17] Birgit Vogel-Heuser, Dorothea Pantförder, and Jens Folmer. "Strategien zur Systemvernetzung und den Einsatz von Industrie 4.0 und Cyberphysischen Produktionssystemen zur Schadesnfeststellung von Ventilen". In: 5. *VDI-Fachtagung Industrie 4.0*. Düsseldorf, Deutschland, Jan. 2017.

[VWH12] André Van Hoorn, Jan Waller, and Wilhelm Hasselbring. "Kieker: A framework for application performance monitoring and dynamic software analysis". In: *Proceed-*

ings of the 3rd ACM/SPEC International Conference on Performance Engineering. ACM. 2012, pp. 247–248.

[Wal+16a] Jürgen Walter et al. "Asking "What?", Automating the "How?": The Vision of Declarative Performance Engineering". In: *Proceedings of the 7th ACM/SPEC International Conference on Performance Engineering (ICPE 2016)*. ACM, Mar. 2016. ISBN: 978-1-4503-4080-9. http://dx.doi.org/10.1145/2851553.2858662.

[Wal+16b] Jürgen Walter et al. "PAVO: A Framework for the Visualization of Performance Analyses Results". In: *Proceedings of the 2016 Symposium on Software Performance (SSP)*. 2016.

[Wal+17a] Jürgen Walter et al. "An Expandable Extraction Framework for Architectural Performance Models". In: *Proceedings of the 3rd International Workshop on Quality-Aware DevOps (QUDOS'17)*. ACM, Apr. 2017.

[Wal+17b] Jürgen Walter et al. "Online Learning of Run-time Models for Performance and Resource Management in Data Centers". In: *Self-Aware Computing Systems*. Springer Verlag, 2017.

[Wal+18] Jürgen Walter et al. "Tools for Declarative Performance Engineering". In: *Companion of the 2018 ACM/SPEC International Conference on Performance Engineering*. ICPE '18. Berlin, Germany: ACM, 2018, pp. 53–56. ISBN: 978-1-4503-5629-9. URL: http://doi.acm.org/10.1145/3185768.3185777.

[WB10] Wei Wang and Janet E. Burge. "Using Rationale to Support Pattern-Based Architectural Design". In: *2010 ICSE Workshop on Sharing and Reusing Architectural Knowledge - SHARK '10*. Cape Town, South Africa: ACM Press, 2010, pp. 1–8. ISBN: 9781605589671. https://doi.org/10.1145/1833335.1833336.

[WCL] WCLog Hewlett-Packard Labs. *WorldCup98 web logs*. http://ita.ee.lbl.gov/html/contrib/WorldCup.html.

[Wei+17] Alexander Weigl et al. "Generalized Test Tables: A Powerful and Intuitive Specification Language for Reactive Systems". In: *IEEE 15th International Conference on Industrial Informatics*. IEEE, 2017.

[Wei08] D. M. Weiss. "The Product Line Hall of Fame". In: *SPLC 08*. IEEE, 2008, p. 395.

[Wei15] Alexander Sebastian Weigl. "Regression Verification for Programmable Logic Controller Software". MA thesis. Karlsruhe Institute of Technology, Jan. 2015.

[WFP07] Murray Woodside, Greg Franks, and Dorina C. Petriu. "The Future of Software Performance Engineering". In: *2007 Future of Software Engineering*. FOSE '07. Washington, DC, USA: IEEE Computer Society, 2007, pp. 171–187. ISBN: 0-7695-2829-5. URL: http://dx.doi.org/10.1109/FOSE.2007.32.

[WFV09] A. N. I.Wardana, J. Folmer, and B. Vogel-Heuser. "Automatic program verification of continuous function chart based on model checking". In: *35th Annu. Conf. IEEE Ind. Electron.* (2009), pp. 2422–2427.

[WGG13] Michael Würsch, Emanuel Giger, and Harald C Gall. "Evaluating a query framework for software evolution data". In: ACM Transactions on Software Engineering and Methodology (TOSEM) 22.4 (2013), p. 38.

[WHK17] Jürgen Walter, Andre van Hoorn, and Samuel Kounev. "Automated and Adaptable Decision Support for Software Performance Engineering". In: *Proceedings of the 11th EAI International Conference on Performance Evaluation Methodologies and Tools*. 2017.

[Win+17] Dietmar Winkler et al. "Towards Model Quality Assurance for Multi-Disciplinary Engineering". In: *Multi-Disciplinary Engineering for Cyber-Physical Production Systems: Data Models and Software Solutions for Handling Complex Engineering Projects*. Ed. by Stefan Biffl, Arndt Lüder, and Detlef Gerhard. Cham: Springer International Publishing, 2017, pp. 433–457. ISBN: 978-3-319-56345-9. URL: https://doi.org/10.1007/978-3-319-56345-9_16.

[Wit+06] Daniel Witsch et al. "Performance analysis of industrial Ethernet networks by means of timed model-checking". In: *IFAC Proceedings Volumes* 39.3 (2006), pp. 101–106.

[Wit13] Daniel Witsch. *Modellgetriebene Entwicklung von Steuerungssoftware auf Basis der UML unter Berücksichtigung der domänenspezifischen Anforderungen des Maschinenund Anlagenbaus*. Vol. 2. Sierke Verlag, 2013.

[WOK17] Jürgen Walter, Dusan Okanovic, and Samuel Kounev. "Mapping of Service Level Objectives to Performance Queries". In: *Proceedings of the 2017 Workshop on Challenges in Performance Methods for Software Development (WOSP-C'17) co-located with 8th ACM/SPEC International Conference on Performance Engineering (ICPE 2017)*. l'Aquila, Italy: ACM, Apr. 2017.

[WP12] Yannick Welsch and Arnd Poetzsch-Heffter. "Verifying Backwards Compatibility of Object-oriented Libraries Using Boogie". In: *Proceedings of the 14th Workshop on Formal Techniques for Java-like Programs*. FTfJP '12. ACM, 2012, pp. 35–41.

[WYY05] X. Wang, Y.L. Yin, and H. Yu. "Finding Collisions in the full SHA-1". In: *Advances in Cryptology–CRYPTO 2005*. Springer. 2005, pp. 17–36.

[Yaz+14] Hamed Shariat Yazdi et al. "Synthesizing Realistic Test Models". In: *Computer Science–Research and Development (CSRD)* (2014), pp. 1–23.

[Yaz+16] Hamed Shariat Yazdi et al. "A framework for capturing, statistically modeling and analyzing the evolution of software models". In: *Journal of Systems and Software* 118 (2016), pp. 176–207.

[YF03a] M Bani Younis and Georg Frey. "Formalization of existing PLC programs: A survey". In: *Proceedings of CESA*. 2003, pp. 0234–0239.

[ZBS16] Xiang Zhang, Hans-Frederick Brown, and Anil Shankar. "Data-driven Personas: Constructing Archetypal Users with Clickstreams and User Telemetry". In: *Proceedings of the 2016 CHI Conference on Human Factors in Computing Systems*. CHI '16. Santa Clara, California, USA: ACM, 2016, pp. 5350–5359. ISBN: 978-1-4503-3362-7. https://doi.org/10.1145/2858036.2858523.

[ZCM07] Carmen Zannier, Mike Chiasson, and Frank Maurer. "A model of design decision making based on empirical results of interviews with software designers". In: *Information and Software Technology* 49.6 (2007), pp. 637–653. ISSN: 09505849. https://doi.org/10.1016/j.infsof.2007.02.010.

[Zha+11] P. Zhang et al. "Run-time systems failure prediction via proactive monitoring". In: *Automated Software Eng. (ASE), 2011 26th IEEE/ACM Int. Conf. on*. Nov. 2011, pp. 484–487. https://doi.org/10.1109/ASE.2011.6100105.

[Zim+08] Olaf Zimmermann et al. "Combining Pattern Languages and Reusable Architectural Decision Models into a Comprehensive and Comprehensible Design Method". In: *Seventh Working IEEE/IFIP Conference on Software Architecture (WICSA 2008)*. Ed. by Philippe Kruchten, David Garlan, and Eoin Woods. Vancouver, BC, Canada: IEEE, Feb. 2008, pp. 157–166. ISBN: 978-0-7695-3092-5. https://doi.org/10.1109/WICSA.2008.19.

[Zim11] Olaf Zimmermann. "Architectural Decisions as Reusable Design Assets". In: *IEEE Software* 28.1 (Jan. 2011), pp. 64–69. ISSN: 0740-7459. https://doi.org/10.1109/MS.2011.3.

[Zou+18] Minjie Zou et al. "Design Parameter Optimization of Automated Production Systems". In: *14th IEEE International Conference on Automation Science and Engineering (CASE)*. Munich, Germany, Aug. 2018.

[ZWL08] Tao Zheng, C. Murray Woodside, and Marin Litoiu. "Performance Model Estimation and Tracking Using Optimal Filters". In: *IEEE Trans. Softw. Eng.* 34.3 (2008), pp. 391–406. https://doi.org/10.1109/TSE.2008.30.

www.ingramcontent.com/pod-product-compliance
Lightning Source LLC
LaVergne TN
LVHW082108200926
848484LV00008B/1930